An Introduction to Java Programming

Developing Applets Using Microsoft® Visual J++®

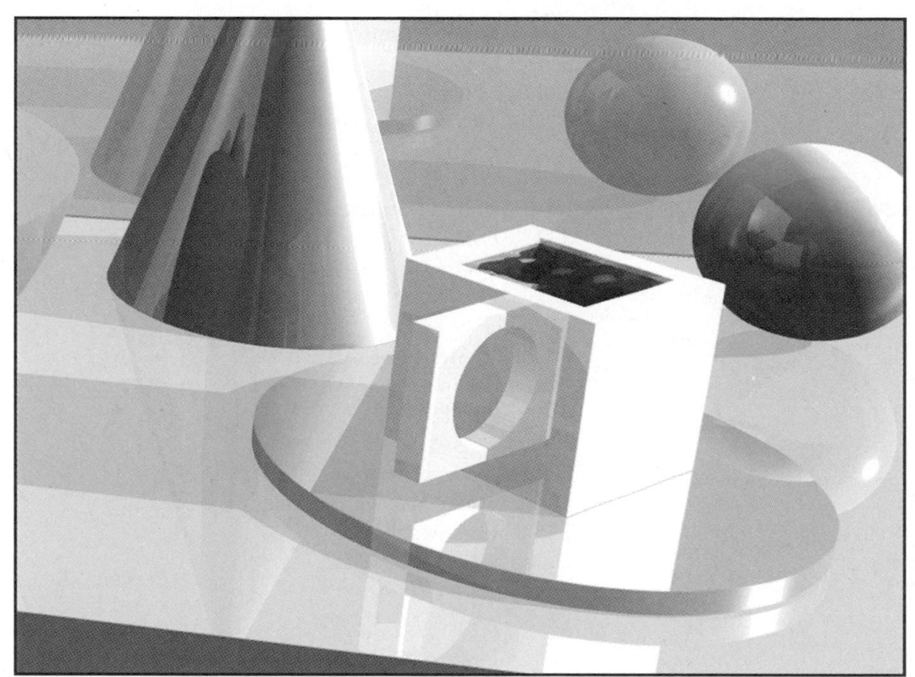

Carol Stoker and G. Thomas Plew
Azusa Pacific University

ONE MAIN STREET, CAMBRIDGE, MA 02142

an International Thomson Publishing company I(T)P®

Cambridge • Albany • Bonn • Boston • Cincinnati • London • Madrid • Melbourne • Mexico City
New York • Paris • San Francisco • Singapore • Tokyo • Toronto • Washington

An Introduction to Java Programming: Developing Applets Using Microsoft Visual J++ is published by Course Technology.

Managing Editor	Kristen Duerr
Product Manager	Cheryl Ouellette
Associate Product Manager	Ellina Tsirelson
Editorial Assistant	Margarita Donovan
Developmental Editor	Jessica Evans
Production Editor	Daphne E. Barbas
Text and Cover Designer	Douglas Goodman
Cover Illustrator	Douglas Goodman

For more information contact:

Course Technology, Inc.
One Main Street
Cambridge, MA 02142

International Thomson Editores
Seneca, 53
Colonia Polanco
11560 Mexico D.F. Mexico

ITP Europe
Berkshire House 168-173
High Holborn
London WCIV 7AA
England

ITP GmbH
Königswinterer Strasse 418
53227 Bonn
Germany

Nelson ITP, Australia
102 Dodds Street
South Melbourne, 3205
Victoria, Australia

ITP Asia
60 Albert Street, #15-01
Albert Complex
Singapore 189969

ITP Nelson Canada
1120 Birchmount Road
Scarborough, Ontario
Canada M1K 5G4

ITP Japan
Hirakawacho Kyowa Building, 3F
2-2-1 Hirakawacho
Chiyoda-ku, Tokyo 102
Japan

ISBN 0-7600-5043-0

Printed in the United States of America

1 2 3 4 5 6 7 8 9 B 02 01 00 99 98

Preface

An Introduction to Java Programming: Developing Applets Using Microsoft Visual J++ is designed for a second programming course or assumes students have a basic programming background. This book uses Visual J++ version 1.1 for Windows 95 to teach Java programming concepts. This book capitalizes on the energy and enthusiasm students naturally have for Windows-based applications and teaches students how to take full advantage of Java programming. Additionally, it assumes that students have mastered basic Windows skills and file management, and that they have experience with some other programming language and a basic understanding of World Wide Web concepts.

Organization and Coverage

An Introduction to Java Programming contains an Overview and seven tutorials that present hands-on instruction. In these tutorials students learn how to plan and program Java applets. This book presents important concepts in Lesson A, and then provides hands-on programming instructions in Lessons B and C to accomplish specific tasks. When students complete this book, they will know how to code class objects, if..else, switch, for, and while statements, and how to process data using arrays and files. Students also will learn how to program applets and use Visual J++ Wizards to create GUI elements on a Web page. This book emphasizes GUI design skills and object-oriented design and programming.

Approach

An Introduction to Java Programming distinguishes itself from other Java textbooks because of its unique two-pronged approach. First, it motivates students by demonstrating why they need to learn Java concepts and skills. This book teaches programming concepts using a task-driven, rather than a command-driven, approach. By working through the tutorials—which are each motivated by a realistic case—students learn how to use programming applications they are likely to need in the workplace. This is much more effective than memorizing a list of commands out of context. Second, the content, organization, and pedagogy of this book emphasize the Windows environment. The material presented in the tutorials capitalizes on the power of Visual J++ to perform complex programming tasks earlier and more easily than was possible under other operating systems.

Features

An Introduction to Java Programming is a superior textbook because it also includes the following features:

- **"Read This Before You Begin" Page** This page is consistent with Course Technology's unequaled commitment to helping instructors introduce technology into the classroom. Technical considerations and assumptions about hardware, software, and default settings are listed in one place to help instructors save time and eliminate unnecessary aggravation.
- **Tutorial Cases** Each tutorial begins with a programming-related problem that students could reasonably expect to encounter in business, followed by a demonstration of an application that could be used to solve the problem. Showing students the completed application before they learn how to create it is motivational and instructionally sound. By allowing the students to see the type of application they will be able to create after completing the tutorial, students will be more motivated to learn because they can see how the

programming concepts that they are about to learn can be used and, therefore, why the concepts are important.

- **Lessons** Each tutorial is divided into three lessons—A, B, and C. Lesson A introduces the programming concepts that will be used in the completed application. In Lessons B and C, the student creates the application required to solve the problem specified in the Tutorial Case.
- **Step-by-Step Methodology** The unique Course Technology methodology keeps students on track. They click buttons or press keys always within the context of solving the problem posed in the Tutorial Case. The text constantly guides students and lets them know where they are in the process of solving the problem. The numerous illustrations include labels that direct students' attention to what they should look at on the screen.
- **HELP?** paragraphs anticipate the problems students are likely to encounter and help them resolve these problems on their own. This feature facilitates independent learning and frees the instructor to focus on substantive issues rather than on common procedural errors.
- **Tips** provide additional information about a procedure—for example, an alternative method of performing the procedure.
- **Summaries** Following each lesson is a Summary that recaps the programming concepts and commands covered in the lesson.
- **Questions and Exercises** Each lesson concludes with meaningful, conceptual Questions that test students' understanding of what they learned in the lesson. Exercises that provide students with additional practice of the skills and concepts they learned in the lesson follow the Questions. The Exercises increase in difficulty and are designed to allow the student to explore the language and programming environment independently.
- **Applet Programming Cases** Instructions and exercises are centered around developing Java applets rather than stand-alone applications. This coverage gives the student current skills necessary for Internet programming.
- **Student Online Companion** The Online Companion is a special Course Technology Web site that is available specifically for students using this book. Having students use this Online Companion ensures that they will access live links and gives them a more successful Internet and Java experience. See the "Read This Before You Begin" page before the Overview and the Instructor's Manual for more information.

Microsoft Visual J++, Version 1.1

The Trial Edition of Visual J++ 1.1 is packaged with this book. The Trial Edition includes all of the necessary elements of the Professional Edition including the graphics and applet wizards. All of the examples and exercises in this book will work with the Trial or Professional Editions of Visual J++ Version 1.1. This will allow students to expand their exploration of the Java language by allowing them to work at home as well as in a computer laboratory. The code of the examples was developed using the constructs of the language as specified in the standard for Java 1.0. With minor changes in the compiler operating instructions, the examples and exercises in this book also will run with the Sun Microsystem's JDK and Symantec's Visual Cafe environments that conform to the 1.0 standard.

The Supplements

- The authors wrote the Instructor's Manual and it was quality assurance tested. It is available electronically on CD-ROM or through the Course Technology Faculty Online Companion on the World Wide Web. (Call your customer service representative for the URL and your password.) The Instructor's Manual contains the following items:
  - **Cases** that can be assigned as semester projects.
  - **Answers** to all of the questions and solutions to all of the exercises.
  - **Tutorial notes** that contain background information from the authors about the Tutorial Case and the instructional progression of the tutorial.

- **Technical notes** that include troubleshooting tips as well as information on how to customize the students' screens to match the figures in the book.
- **Course Test Manager** provides a powerful testing and assessment package that enables instructors to create and print custom tests from a test bank of questions designed specifically for this book. The questions can be selected individually or at random, and it can print scrambled versions of the same test. In addition, instructors with access to a networked computer lab (LAN) can administer, grade, and track tests on-line.
- **Solution files** are included for every file students are asked to create or modify in the tutorials and exercises.
- **Student files** containing all of the data that students will use for the tutorials and exercises are provided through Course Technology's Online Companion, as well as on disk. A Readme file includes technical tips for lab management. See the inside front cover of this book and the "Read This Before You Begin" page before the Overview for more information on Student Files.
- An **Online Companion** that is a special Web site is available specifically for this book at the Course Technology Web site. This Web page can be found at the following URL address: http://www.course.com. Once you are at the course.com site, click on Downloads, click Student Online Companions, and then type the ISBN for the book which is 0-7600-5043-0 to jump to your Online Companion for this book. This Web page is referred to throughout the tutorials as the Online Companion. Using this Online Companion ensures a more successful Internet and Java experience. See the "Read this Before You Begin" page before the Overview for more information on the Online Companion.

Acknowledgments

We would like to thank all of the people who helped make this book a reality, especially Jessica Evans, our Development Editor and Product Manager. You have provided great service with patience and humor. We could not have completed this task without your expert assistance. Thanks also to Kristen Duerr, Managing Editor; Ellina Tsirelson, Associate Product Manager; Daphne Barbas, Production Editor; and Brian McCooey, Seth Freeman, and John McCarthy, Quality Assurance testers. We are grateful to the many reviewers who provided helpful and insightful comments during the development of this book, including Cynthia B. Kirby, Onondaga Community College; Robert Saldarini, Bergen Community College; Tim Price, Indiana University Purdue University Indianapolis; and Don Rueter, Orange Coast College. Thanks also to our Java mentors, Bill McCarty and Steven Gilbert, who spent many hours helping us to debug our examples, correct our misunderstandings, and ignite our enthusiasm for the Java language.

I would like to personally thank my husband, Jim. Your love and support mean more than words can say. For my daughters, Sylvia and Rebecca, you put up with my spending more time in my office and on the at-home computer than any two angels should have to cope with. Special thanks to my mother-in-law, Carolyn Stoker, and my parents, Howard and Rhoda Backer, for both emotional support and baby-sitting assistance.

Carol Stoker

I would like to personally thank my patient and helpful wife, Sharon. You have endured many long hours and late evenings and I could not have completed the task without your input and help. I also thank my sister, Susie Wilcox, and her late husband, Bill, for their encouragement, support and belief in my ability to write this book. Finally, thanks to Gordon Coulter, my friend and colleague, who encouraged me to believe we can climb any mountain by taking one step at a time.

G. Thomas Plew

Contents

Read This Before You Begin

To the Student

Student Disks

To complete the tutorials and exercises in this book, you need Student Disks. Your instructor will provide you with Student Disks or ask you to make your own.

If you are asked to make your own Student Disks, you will need seven blank, formatted high-density disks. You will need to copy a set of folders from a file server or standalone computer onto your disks. Your instructor will tell you which computer, drive letter, and folders contain the files you need. The following table shows you which folders go on each of your disks, so that you will have enough disk space to complete all of the tutorials and exercises:

Student Disk	Write this on the disk label	Put these folders on the disk
1	Tutorial 1	*BeanJar, Exercises, Welcome*
2	Tutorial 2	*Ball, Koffee, Exercises*
3	Tutorial 3	*BeanJar3, Exercises, Tutorial3C*
4	Tutorial 4	*ABCOil, Exercises, Koffee*
5	Tutorial 5	*BeanJar5, BeanJar5a, Exercises, GraphGrade, Invest, Tut5C*
6	Tutorial 6	*Exercises, Invest, Order*
7	Tutorial 7 and Appendices	*Exercises, Interest, UserInterface, Appendix*

When you begin each tutorial, be sure you are using the correct Student Disk. See the inside front cover of this book for more information on Student Disk files, or ask your instructor or technical support person for assistance.

Using Your Own Computer

If you are going to work through this book using your own computer, you will need:

- **Computer System** Microsoft Visual J++ version 1.1 Trial Edition or Professional Edition must be installed on your computer. This book assumes a complete installation of the Trial Edition of Microsoft Visual J++ 1.1. The Trial Edition of Microsoft Visual J++ 1.1 is provided with each copy of this book. You also must have a full installation of Microsoft Internet Explorer 3.01 or higher, or another compatible Web browser. This book uses Internet Explorer 3.01 as the default Web browser because it is automatically installed with the Trial Edition of Visual J++. The following system requirements apply:
  - Personal computer with a 486 or higher processor (Pentium recommended)
  - Microsoft Windows 95 or Windows NT Workstation version 4.0 or later
  - 8 MB of memory (12 MB recommended) if running Windows 95
  - 12 MB of memory (20 MB recommended) if running Windows NT Workstation
  - 70 MB of hard drive disk space for a full installation; 43 MB for a minimum installation (an additional 22 MB is required during installation)
  - VGA or higher resolution monitor (SuperVGA recommended)
  - Microsoft mouse or compatible pointing device

The Trial Edition of Visual J++ has all the functionality of the Professional Edition of Visual J++, excluding:

- Database support for other database systems, such as dBase, Excel, FoxPro, Paradox, and Oracle. The Trial Edition supports only Access databases.
- The source code for the Java class libraries
- The toolkit for creating compressed, self-extracting Cabinet (.cab) files
- The toolkit for digitally signing files
- OLEView tool for registering ActiveX™ components
- Productivity tools such as Zoomin and WinDiff
- Books and documentation, such as printed class hierarchy chart, Microsoft Developer Network Library CD, and the book, *Learn Java Now*
- Microsoft technical support
- Free or discounted upgrades to later versions of Visual J++ Professional Edition

- **Student Disks** Ask your instructor or lab manager for details on how to get Student Disks. You will not be able to complete the tutorials or exercises in this book using your own computer until you have Student Disks. The student files may also be obtained electronically through the Internet. See the inside front cover of this book for more details.

Visit Our World Wide Web Site

Additional materials designed especially for you are available on the World Wide Web. Go to **www.course.com.**

Student Online Companion

The Student Online Companion includes links to Web sites that contain live Java programs. Go to **www.course.com.** Once you are at the course.com site, click on downloads, click on Student Online Companions, then type in the ISBN which is 0-7600-5043-0 to jump to the Online Companion for this book.

Setting Up Your Visual J++ 1.1 Environment

To set your Visual J++ 1.1 environment so your screens match the figures shown in the text, do the following:

1. Click **Tools** on the menu bar, and then click **Customize.** Click the **Toolbars** tab.
2. Make sure that only the Menu bar, Standard, and Build toolbars check boxes are selected.
3. Click the **Close** button.

To the Instructor

To complete the tutorials in this book, your students must use a set of student files. These files are included in the Instructor's Resource Kit. They may also be obtained electronically through the Internet. See the inside front cover of this book for more details. Follow the instructions in the Readme file to copy the student files to your server or standalone computer. You can view the Readme file using a text editor such as WordPad or Notepad.

Once the files are copied, you can make Student Disks for the students yourself, or tell students where to find the files so they can make their own Student Disks. Make sure the files get copied correctly onto the Student Disks by following the instructions in the Student Disks section, which will ensure that students have enough disk space to complete all of the tutorials and exercises in this book.

Course Technology Student Files

You are granted a license to copy the Student Files to any computer or computer network used by students who have purchased this book.

OVERVIEW

objectives

In this overview you will:

- Review the purpose of the Internet
- Describe a client/server system, and explore its significance for Java
- Learn how HTML and Java are used on the Internet
- Learn how to use the tutorials in this book effectively

An Overview of HTML and the Internet

A History of the Web and Java

A Brief Description of Java and this Book

Welcome to the exciting world of the Internet and the World Wide Web. You are about to embark on a journey that will allow you to explore Internet and intranet programming and processing. In this book you will broaden your expertise in general programming skills and learn the basics of Java programming. **Java** is a programming language that is becoming the standard for Internet applications. The power and versatility of the Java language provide interactive processing and increased use of graphics and animation on the Internet. You can use Java to make a ball bounce across the screen, play music by clicking a button, and design forms for business.

This book is written for students who have completed at least one programming course. Therefore, many programming concepts that are taught in an introductory programming course will not be repeated in this book so the Java language can be the primary focus of discussion.

The Internet and the World Wide Web

Imagine yourself in a very large room with thousands of other people. As you enter the room, you are escorted to a glass cubicle that is soundproof. Although many of the people in the room have stories and facts that you would like to hear, you cannot communicate with them. Suddenly you see a button on the right side of the cubicle. You press the button and a phone rises from the floor with an address book for all of the people in the room. Now you can talk to any person in the room that interests you. In addition, there is a special button on the phone that allows you to connect to several people at once. Your world has changed from dependency and isolation to a world that includes many different types of people and resources. These resources, cultural views, and knowledge are limited only by the amount of time you spend on the technology.

The **Internet** or **World Wide Web** (or **Web**) is a group of computers linked by network cables or a given operating system, but the Web is not used in that way. The Web is the people and resources that comprise an international database of knowledge and experiences. You can use the Web to communicate using electronic mail (e-mail), to browse for information, and to communicate with one or more people. The idea of the Web is to provide a forum with a logical collection of resources shared freely without constraints to any of its users.

The **ARPNET**, which was a resource for information exchange among governmental clients, was the beginnings of the network we know today as the Internet. Organizations and universities combined their expertise and resources to expand the original network. There are four basic services provided by the Internet: electronic mail, telnet or remote computer linkage, file transfers, and resource searching and sharing. These services exist by linking thousands of computers internationally through a network. Java has made many of these services more visual and interactive than was previously possible.

The Technology of the Internet

Physically, the Internet is a connection of thousands of computers around the world that are connected using network technology. A **network** is two or more computers that have the ability to communicate using hardware such as network cards, modems, and telephone services. (For the purposes of this book, consider a network to be a group of computers linked by some type of communication media.) The individual computers need the ability to service their own user's needs as well as to communicate with other computers that provide resources that are not available on the user's computer. A **local area network** (**LAN**) links individual computers with network cables and cards in a limited physical space, such as an office. Sometimes computers are connected to several LANs, or LANs are connected to other LANs using telecommunication technology to establish a **wide area network** (**WAN**). The Internet is a massive WAN of LANs that communicate using certain predefined protocols and methods. The logical arrangement of this type of information sharing is sometimes referred to as a client/server system.

A **client/server system** is a system with a server that processes data, and clients that communicate user needs to the server and display the results. For example, if your computer lab has a limited number of printers and many computers, the computers in the lab might be connected to the printers through a print server. When you want to print from your computer, which is the client, you tell your program to print and the information is sent to the server that processes and sends the job to the printer. Many programming languages and utilities make this task possible not only in a LAN but in the WAN known as the Internet. Two very important tools that support these functions are HTML (hypertext markup language) and the Java programming language.

HTML and Java

As the Internet continues to grow in size, it is no longer possible for remote computers to rely totally on a single mainframe computer to process all of the user requests. The client/server architecture was adopted by the Internet to solve this problem. The servers of the Internet became collection locations for resources and information but the clients do most of the processing. You probably are familiar with a **Web page**, which is a collection of files of information that an organization makes available to the general public or to a limited number of users. You view the information on a Web page one screen at a time. Sometimes, the Web page might provide links to related information on other Web pages. When a user clicks a **link**, the browser jumps to the Web page addressed in the link.

To reduce the amount of work involved in providing this service, files typically are transferred to your computer and then an Internet browser processes them. A **browser** is a program that reads the special files and codes retrieved from the Internet to format the text, to place and display graphics, and to provide links to other files on the page or to other pages. This processing requires a standard method of arranging files so that different browsers can interpret the pages in similar ways. The tool that was developed for this purpose is really a mini-language called HTML. **HTML** is a hypertext formatting language that informs the browser of how to display the page and the links that are available in a format that you can use.

In this context, **hypertext** is any tool that allows the logical movement around a large document through the use of links, while providing support for graphics, animation, sound, and other applications. An **HTML file** is a text file of the information that the user wants to display on a Web page with some additional code that gives instructions to the browser. As HTML became more familiar and accessible to organizations that design and maintain Web pages, the types of instructions available have broadened to include commands for placing graphics on Web pages, for linking to other pages, and for starting application programs designed for the Web. Most of the HTML commands are enclosed in angle brackets (< and >) and include a beginning and ending marker or **tag**. For example, an HTML document begins with the <HTML> tag, followed by a return, and ends with the </HTML> tag. You can consult Appendix A for more information about using HTML tags.

While HTML provides the linking and graphics capability that was necessary for Web page development, support for applications and animation was not included. Web software developers needed a language that would allow Web pages to run applications in a client/server environment so the client, instead of the Web page, could run the application program. Because the Internet consists of many different types of computers and operating systems such as Windows 95 and UNIX, a common language was needed to enable clients running under many different operating systems to be able to run Web programs. Sun Microsystems developed the Java language to address this need.

Java is a programming language that provides many of the functions of high-level languages as well as increased graphics, animation, and sound. Java was developed as a standardized language so a client machine with a Java compiler could run a Web program that was transferred from a server. When this process is completed using Web pages, these programs are called **applets**. An applet might be used to create an interactive survey for business, access information about your favorite sports team, or guide you through a lesson on careers. Do you want to make your Web page play your favorite music at the click of a button? Would you like to use animation on your personal home page? Java applets are designed to enable you to do all of these activities. This book focuses on the development of Java applets.

Using the Tutorials Effectively

The tutorials in this book will help you learn about Microsoft Visual J++ version 1.1 and Java. The tutorials are designed to be used at your computer. Begin by reading the text that explains the concepts. Then when you come to the numbered steps, follow the steps on your computer. Read each step carefully and completely before you try it.

As you work, compare your screen with the figures to verify your results. Don't worry if your screen display differs slightly from the figures. The important parts of the screen display are labeled in many figures. Just be sure you have these parts on your screen. The figures in the book show how your screen will look if you are using the Trial Edition of Microsoft Visual J++, version 1.1.

Don't worry about making mistakes; that's part of the learning process. Help? notes identify common problems and explain how to get back on track. You should complete the steps in the Help? box only if you are having the problem described. Appendices B and C also provide assistance for correcting common problems. Tip boxes provide additional information about a procedure—for example, an alternative method of performing the procedure.

Each tutorial is divided into three lessons. You might want to take a break between lessons. Following each lesson is a Summary section that lists the important elements of the lesson. After the Summary section are multiple-choice questions and exercises designed to review and reinforce that lesson's concepts. You should complete all of the end-of-lesson questions and exercises before going on to the next lesson. You can't learn Java without a lot of practice, and future tutorials assume that you have mastered the information found in the previous tutorials.

Before you begin the tutorials, you should know how to use Microsoft Windows 95. This book assumes that you have learned basic Windows-navigation and file-management skills from Course Technology's *New Perspectives on Microsoft Windows 95 Brief* or an equivalent book.

QUESTIONS

1. What are the four basic functions of the Internet?
2. A group of computers that is connected using local network technology is called a __________.
   a. WAN
   b. Web site
   c. LAN
   d. client
3. A(n) __________ system consists of computers that provide resources to local machines that use these resources for processing.
   a. client/server
   b. ARPNET
   c. local user
   d. remote user
4. A group of computers connected by a communication medium is known as a(n) __________.
   a. file transfer protocol
   b. e-mail
   c. network
   d. Web language
5. A markup language that provides hypertext capabilities on the Web is known as __________.
   a. LAN
   b. WAN
   c. Java
   d. HTML
6. __________ is a programming language that provides interactive capabilities for the Internet.
   a. LAN
   b. WAN
   c. Java
   d. HTML
7. A __________ is a program that displays HTML documents.
   a. network
   b. browser
   c. Java compiler
   d. hypertext controller
8. When you __________ several files, you are providing a means of connecting documents so that users can move back and forth between them.
   a. link
   b. animate
   c. connect
   d. compile

9. Which functions are provided by the Java language?
a. networking
b. animation
c. hypertext
d. security

10. A(n) __________ is a Java program that is designed to run on the Internet in a Web browser.
a. applet
b. LAN
c. WAN
d. HTML file

TUTORIAL 1

Getting Started with Microsoft Visual J++ and Java

Viewing the Applet for Koffee Koncoctions International

case ▶ You work at Koffee Koncoctions International, a large company that sells flavored coffees. Sales are made exclusively through the company's toll-free telephone number and mailings in major markets. Recently Koffee Koncoctions has experienced a decline in sales, and company management has determined that the company needs to expand its market base. Management decided to establish a Web site on the Internet that could be used to generate interest in the company and promote sales.

Maria Jinnez, Director of Marketing and Information Systems, wants to be able to add an online Web ordering system that customers can use to place orders using the Web page. You decide to insert a brochure into packages that are shipping to customers who have used the toll-free number to place orders. The brochure invites patrons to visit the Web site and enter the company's "grand opening" drawing to win a year's supply of free coffee. To make the Web page interesting, you decide to design a program that lets visitors calculate how many coffee beans can fit in a jar. Eventually you will develop a bean jar guessing program that allows users to guess how many beans are in a jar. In this book you will help Koffee Koncoctions develop these applets for its Web page.

LESSON A

objectives

In this lesson you will learn how to:

- Use a computer program to solve a problem
- Translate an algorithm into a computer program
- Describe the three kinds of programming errors
- Describe the differences between compilers and interpreters
- Understand how interactive development environments work

Programming Basics Review

Planning and Creating a Program

Writing a computer program to solve a problem is a complex task. There are many ways to write a program—different problem-solving methods have been studied over the years, and some methods have been adapted to the process of developing computer programs. After all, writing a computer program is just another way of solving a problem.

People have solved problems for many years. Now, however, computers are used to solve problems faster and more accurately than non-computer methods. To use a computer to solve a problem, you must develop a program that is written specifically to solve the stated problem. The problem-solving process includes five key steps: understand the problem, design a solution, write the computer program, test and debug the program, and implement the program. The problem-solving process is not dependent on the programming language that will be used, so this design process is similar for any programming language. The Java language, and its use, will be introduced in Lesson B. The problem-solving steps are explained next.

Understand the Problem

You must understand and define your problem clearly before you can solve it. For the Koffee Koncoctions Web page, what are the requirements of the coffee bean jar problem? You must write a program that determines how many coffee beans fit in the jar. Before you can write this program, you need to determine the volume of an average coffee bean and the dimensions (height and diameter) of each bean.

After determining these requirements, you need to consider the problem in terms of its computing requirements. Most programs run on an **IPO cycle**, which stands for input, processing, and output. **Output** is the result of the program; it is the solution to the problem. A program with no output is useless, so the output of the program is the driving force behind the development of the program. For example, the output of an invoice system is a completed invoice form. The **input** to the system is the raw data entered into the program, such as item numbers, pounds ordered, price per pound, and so on. Finally, the **processing** is what the computer does with the input to generate the output.

The coffee bean jar problem can be analyzed using the IPO method. To make the problem easier to understand, you will use only one input—the height of the jar. The processing includes calculating the volume of one coffee bean, calculating the volume of a jar that is four inches in diameter with the height in inches provided by the user, and calculating how many beans fit in a jar with the specified volume. The output is the number of beans that fit in the jar. Figure 1-1 shows the IPO program requirements to solve the problem.

IPO Requirement	Program Requirement
Input	Jar height in whole inches
Processing	Calculate volume of one coffee bean Calculate volume of jar Calculate number of beans
Output	Display the number of beans that fit in the jar

Figure 1-1: IPO program requirements

Design a Solution

After understanding your problem, you need to design a solution. A solution to a computer problem is called an algorithm. An **algorithm** is a step-by-step list of instructions that the computer uses to solve a problem. A recipe is a type of an algorithm used outside of computing. In an algorithm, the instructions list exactly what actions need to be taken in the exact order they are to be performed. Programmers use a special kind of language called **pseudocode** to write algorithms. Pseudocode is not a formal programming language so it does not follow all the strict vocabulary and punctuation requirements in programming. Because algorithms do not follow the rules for any programming language, you must translate an algorithm into a computer language before using it on the computer. Programmers use pseudocode as a planning tool because it is easier to use than a formal programming language. Pseudocode must make sense to programmers, but not necessarily to the computer.

Figure 1-2 shows examples of the pseudocode and the actual computer program that is used to accomplish the same thing. (You will learn more about the Java code in Tutorial 2.) Notice that pseudocode is simpler to read and use than the Java code used in the computer program. The computer program is a Java program that does exactly what the pseudocode requests—it displays the sentence "Koffee Koncoctions are the best!" on the screen. When you use pseudocode to write your program, the exact words and punctuation do not matter because the pseudocode is used to help you write the program. The computer does not use pseudocode to execute the program. You can use the words "display," "write," or "print" to indicate the same action because these words need to make sense only as a planning tool.

Pseudocode	Java code
Display "Koffee Koncoctions are the best!"	import java.applet.*;
	import java.awt.*;
	public class Advertising extends Applet
	{ Label Ad = new Label ("Koffee Koncoctions are the best!");
	public void init()
	{ add (Ad);
	}
	}

Figure 1-2: Pseudocode vs. computer program

One of the nice things about using the IPO design process is that the product of each step helps the programmer write the next step in the program. Each IPO requirement aids in the development of the algorithm. If possible, the simplest algorithm does all the input first, then the processing, and then produces the desired output. Figure 1-3 shows the algorithm to solve the coffee bean jar problem using the IPO requirements.

IPO Requirement	Algorithm
Input	Input JarHeight
Processing	Calculate BeanVolume
	Calculate JarVolume
	Calculate NumberBeans = (JarVolume / BeanVolume) * FudgeFactor
Output	Display "The jar will hold " NumberBeans "coffee beans"

Figure 1-3: Algorithm based on IPO requirements

Write the Computer Program

The next step in writing a program to solve the coffee bean jar problem is to transform the algorithm developed in the previous step into the computer program that solves the problem. In Figure 1-4, the program is written in the Java programming language because you are solving a problem on the Internet. Whatever the programming language, a well-designed algorithm paves the way to writing a good program. Figure 1-4 shows the transition from algorithm to Java program.

Algorithm	Java Program

	import java.applet.*;
	import java.awt.*;
	public class BeanJar extends Applet
	{
	TextField Height = new TextField(10);
	Button Calculate = new Button("Calculate");
	Label Title = new Label("How many coffee beans can fit in a jar?");
	Label Title2 = new Label("The jar has a 4-inch diameter");
	Label Prompt = new Label("Enter the jar height (whole inches)");
	TextArea Result = new TextArea(2,20);
	double NumberBeans = 0;
	double JarVolume;

Calculate BeanVolume BeanVolume = (3.1416 * (0.125 *0.125) * 0.15) + (0.25 * 0.25 * 0.15)	double bean = (3.1416 * (0.125 *0.125) * 0.15) + (0.25 * 0.25 * 0.15);

	public void init()
	{
	add(Title);
	add(Title2);
	add(Prompt);
	add(Height);
	add(Calculate);
	add(Result);
	}
	public boolean action(Event thisEvent, Object thisObject)

Input JarHeight	{ int JarHeight = Integer.parseInt(Height.getText());
Calculate JarVolume JarVolume =3.1416 * 4 * JarHeight	JarVolume = 3.1416 * 4 * JarHeight;
Calculate NumberBeans NumberBeans =(JarVolume / BeanVolume) * 0.6	NumberBeans = (JarVolume / bean) *0.6; long BeanInt = Math.round(NumberBeans);
Display Ouput Display "The jar will hold "NumberBeans" coffee beans"	Result.appendText("The jar will hold "+'\n'); Result.appendText(" "+BeanInt + " coffee beans");
	return true; } }

Figure 1-4: Transforming algorithms into a Java program

When you write an algorithm, you should not worry about how the details are handled, but when you write the program, there are some details that you have to add. In the Java program shown in Figure 1-4, there are many Java statements that do not match up with an algorithm statement. For now, just think of these statements as "overhead" that are included in any programming language. At the moment, the Java program might not be very understandable to you, but you will understand this program soon.

Test and Debug the Program

After writing the program, you need to test it to ensure that it works the way it was designed and produces the desired output. **Testing** the program involves translating the program into a language that the computer understands, which is discussed later in this tutorial. For a short program, like the coffee bean jar program, a programmer writes the complete program and then tests it. However, when programming larger projects, the project is divided into smaller modules or logical pieces that are developed and tested independently and then combined into the larger program and tested. Even the simplest program must be tested.

If you discover errors in your program, the process of fixing the errors is called **debugging**. There are only three types of programming errors: syntax errors, run-time errors, and logic errors. A **syntax error** is the easiest type of programming error to fix because it is an error that is grammatical in nature. Usually a syntax error indicates that there is a problem with punctuation, spelling, or word order within the program. Syntax errors also are the easiest programming errors to find because the error message will contain what type of syntax error occurred and then the error message also will try to report the location of the error. An example of a syntax error is typing the word "new" as "knew."

The next type of programming error is more difficult to find and fix. A **run-time error** is an error condition that occurs while the program is running. For example, a run-time error will occur if you try to divide a value by zero, which is an illegal operation. In this case, the program will stop running and report the error message.

The last type of programming error is the most difficult to find and fix. A **logic error** occurs when the program seems to run correctly, but it does not obtain the desired output. A logic error indicates an error in your plan for solving the problem. An example of a logic error in the coffee bean jar program occurs if the output indicates that only two beans fit in a jar that is 10 inches tall. Logic errors are difficult to correct because to the computer, no error has occurred so no error is reported. The computer executes the programmer's instructions perfectly and does not perform any illegal operation. When a logic error occurs, it is the programmer's responsibility to find and correct the error. Careful planning and implementing error avoidance strategies help to reduce the possibility of having logic errors in your program.

Implement the Program

After writing, testing, and correcting any errors in your program, it is provided to users for implementation. In many cases, after the program is released for use, many programmers will start working on the next version of the program, which will contain faster logic and more features.

Programming Languages

When implementing a program, how do you decide which programming language is the best one to use to solve your problem? The first step in this decision is to divide the different programming languages into two categories: low-level and high-level.

Low-Level Programming Languages

Low-level programming languages are called "low" because they resemble or are identical to the actual programming language that the computer understands. Program instructions are written in **machine language** that consists of sequences of zeros and ones to represent commands such as open, save, or print. Two problems are common when using machine language. The first problem is when the programmer transposes the code, which results in a logic error in the program output. Programmers must know the exact memory locations of the data they want to process, and must specify where processed data is to be stored. The other problem is that machine language is not common on all types of computers. If a program is written for a specific computer, then it will need to be rewritten to work on another type of computer.

Because of the inherent problems of machine language, a second type of low-level language known as assembly language was developed. **Assembly language** uses short abbreviations, called **mnemonics**, as instructions in the program. The advantages of using assembly language are that it is easier to remember and it uses mnemonics rather than the machine language, and instead of having to keep track of memory locations, the programmer can assign a name to stored values. After writing an assembly language program, the programmer uses a program called an **assembler** to translate the program into the machine language of zeros and ones. The main disadvantage of using assembly language is that it also is different on various computers. To develop a program that will run on more than one type of computer, it is necessary to rewrite the program in an entirely new form of assembly language. Another disadvantage is that it requires many assembly language instructions to process simple tasks.

With these disadvantages in mind, a new category of programming languages, called **high-level programming languages**, is available to address these problems. Figure 1-5 shows the machine language code, assembly language code, and high-level programming code to calculate a total. Notice how much simpler it is to read and understand the high-level programming code.

Machine	Assembly	High Level (Java)
10100001 00000000 00000010	MOV AX, TOTAL	Total = Total + Value;
00000011 00000110 00000010	ADD AX, VALUE	
00000010 1010011 00000000	MOV TOTAL, AX	
00000010		

Figure 1-5: Programming language comparisons

High-Level Programming Languages

As you can see in Figure 1-5, it is much easier to understand a high-level programming language than it is to interpret a low-level programming language. High-level programming code is written similarly to simple English sentences. High-level code is **portable**, so it can run on more than one kind of computer, and it uses **natural language** that is similar to spoken language. Although all high-level languages use words that are common to natural languages, there usually is only one way to invoke a desired outcome from the program.

Interpreters and Compilers

All high-level programming languages require a way to translate the program code into machine language so the computer can produce the desired output. There are two methods to translate natural language into machine language. The first method is to use an interpreted version of the language. An **interpreter** translates one line of program code at a time into machine language, just like an interpreter who translates a speaker's speech into another language. Because the computer does two things at once—translating code into machine language and following the program's instructions—interpreted languages run slower than languages translated by a compiler.

The second method of translating program code into machine language uses a compiler. A **compiler** translates the entire high-level program into machine language all at once, sort of like buying a book that was written originally in Russian but now has been translated into English. Compiled languages run faster than interpreted languages because the computer executes only the program's instructions, and does not translate them.

Click the first Tutorial 1 link of the Online Companion for this book (http://www.course.com) to see a live Java program that illustrates this topic.

Interactive Development Environments

In the 1970s, program input consisted of punchcards that included holes in a card to represent the zeros and ones of machine language. These punchcards were fed into the computer to obtain the desired output. When errors existed in the program code, it could take several hours for the system to report them. As technology changed, programmers worked at terminals connected to the main computer and used an **editor**, or a simple word processing program, to type and save their program. A compiler translated the program generated by the editor into machine language. Errors were reported immediately.

Programmers now use software based on an **integrated development environment**, or **IDE**, that combines the editor, compiler, and other useful tools in the same software package. Having the editor and the compiler in the same software package offers a great advantage. When a program with syntax errors is compiled, the programmer sees the error messages and the original program at the same time. IDEs make debugging much easier for the programmers because many IDEs include a program debugger. Visual J++ is an IDE program and is the compiler that is used in this book.

Now you can take a break or complete the end-of-lesson questions and exercises.

S U M M A R Y

- The five steps in the problem-solving process are: understand the problem, design a solution, write the computer program, test and debug the program, and implement the program.
- Understanding a problem requires you to consider the IPO (input, processing, and output) requirements of the problem.
- An algorithm is a step-by-step outline of a solution to a problem.
- Pseudocode does not follow the strict syntax rules of programming languages; it is used as a planning tool.
- The process of writing a computer program involves translating the algorithm into the correct programming language.
- Debugging is the process of removing errors from the computer program.
- There are three types of programming errors: a syntax error is caused by a grammatical, punctuation, or typing error; a run-time error occurs while the program is running; and a logic error occurs when there is an error in the planning of the program that causes the program to produce an incorrect result.
- Programming languages can be divided into low-level and high-level categories. High-level languages are translated into machine language by using an interpreter or a compiler.
- In an interactive development environment (IDE), the program editor, compiler, and debugger are integrated into one software package. Visual J++ is an IDE program.

Q U E S T I O N S

1. What are the steps in the problem-solving process? List the steps in the correct order.
2. The IPO method is used during which stage of the problem-solving process?
   a. writing the program
   b. understanding the problem
   c. implementing the program
   d. designing a solution
   e. testing and debugging the program
3. The algorithm is written in which stage of the problem-solving process?
   a. writing the program
   b. understanding the problem
   c. implementing the program
   d. designing a solution
   e. testing and debugging the program
4. Generally, an algorithm is written in which language?
   a. English
   b. Pseudocode
   c. Java
   d. Basic
5. The process of correcting mistakes in your program is called __________.
   a. testing
   b. error removal
   c. bug extermination
   d. debugging

6. A syntax error occurs when ________.
   a. the program has incorrect output
   b. the programmer omits a semicolon
   c. the user input causes the computer to divide by zero
7. A run-time error occurs when ________.
   a. the program has incorrect output
   b. the programmer omits a semicolon
   c. the user input causes the computer to divide by zero
8. A logic error occurs when ________.
   a. the program has incorrect output
   b. the programmer omits a semicolon
   c. the user input causes the computer to divide by zero
9. Which of the following items is a problem with low-level languages?
   a. speed of execution
   b. portability
   c. long variable names
   d. different languages for different computers
10. Which of the following items is an advantage for high-level languages?
   a. programs execute faster than low-level languages
   b. portability
   c. uses zeros and ones
   d. differences in computers

EXERCISES

1. In this exercise, you need a program to calculate discounted prices. You know the original price and the discount percent, and you need to calculate the price after subtracting the discount. Write an IPO chart and an algorithm for the solution to this problem.
2. In this exercise, you need to know how much interest you will earn if you deposit $10,000 in a savings account that pays different interest rates. The interest rate is input. Write an IPO chart and an algorithm for the solution to this problem.
3. In this exercise, you need to generate invoices for your childcare business. The rate per child is $45 a day. At the end of the month you bill the parents for the total number of days their child was in the program. Write an IPO chart and an algorithm for the solution to this problem.
4. In this exercise, you need to generate invoices for your telephone installation company. You are given the cost of the materials, the hours worked by each employee, and the per hour charge for each employee. You also include a five percent surcharge on the subtotal. Write an IPO chart and an algorithm for the solution to this problem.

LESSON B

objectives

In this lesson you will learn how to:

- Describe the features of the Java language
- Identify the different windows in the Visual J++ environment
- Use InfoViewer and Books Online to get Help in Visual J++
- Correct errors in a program
- Save, build, and execute a Java file

Understanding Java and the Visual J++ Environment

The Java Language

One of the hottest topics in the computing world is development of the Java language. Java's unique features and its relationship to another hot topic, the Internet, have sparked a lot of interest. To understand the excitement, it helps to understand the history of Java.

In 1990, a group of programmers at Sun Microsystems decided to branch out into the consumer electronics marketplace. The group developed a language called Oak that was similar to the powerful and popular C++ programming language, but was small enough to fit on chips that could be placed in palm-sized computing devices. Subsequent attempts to produce different types of small electronic devices failed. In 1994, the group focused on adapting Oak as a language that could be used to develop online Web multimedia. Sun renamed the Oak language to Java, and then decided that the best way to gain support for the new language was to give it away. Shortly thereafter, Netscape Communications Corporation started offering support for Java in its Netscape Navigator Web browser. Soon thereafter, Microsoft upgraded its Microsoft Internet Explorer Web browser to support Java.

Some of Java's most interesting features make it unique among high-level programming languages. Java is a programming language that runs over the Internet, runs on multiple platforms, includes security features, is easy to use, allows you to develop two types of programs, and is an object-oriented program.

Using Java on the Internet

tip

Click the second Tutorial 1 link of the Online Companion for this book (http://www.course.com) to see a live Java program that illustrates this topic.

You or your friends probably have used a CD-ROM or disk to install and play a game on a computer. What if you could use your Web browser, such as Netscape Navigator or Microsoft Internet Explorer, to play the same game on the same computer? Java allows you to do just that. Java programs can range from cute little enhancements to Web pages to full-blown Internet applications. One potential vision of the future allows consumers to use the Internet to obtain current releases of application software, including word processors, spreadsheets, and databases. The only language that can be used to accomplish this online delivery of application software is Java.

Using Java on Multiple Platforms

As you learned in Lesson A, one of the goals in the development of high-level programming languages was portability, or the ability to run programs on different types of computers. You probably have been frustrated when you find the software that you need, only to discover that it's available for another computer type, so it won't run on your computer. Java is a true **machine independent language**, which means that it can run on any computer platform that is equipped with a Web browser and an Internet connection.

Security Features of Java

You might have heard news stories about the federal government's concerns for security on the Internet. The government's concern is legitimate because the Internet was not developed with security issues in mind. Java, on the other hand, was designed with the specific intention of protecting Internet users from viruses and hackers. Programs written in Java, unlike those programs that contain a virus, cannot take over a user's system, access files on a user's system, or interfere with other system programs.

Ease of Use

The Java language has features that make it a simple, yet powerful programming tool. One of the elements that protects users of Java programs and makes the language easier to use is the elimination of the pointer data type. A **pointer data type** is a way of "pointing" or referencing a value in memory. A pointer data type is a security risk because it is possible to make the pointer reference (and therefore change) a memory location—which it should not change. The possibility exists for pointers to do things that the user might not like. Also, from the programmer's side, pointers are difficult to program and keep track of in a program.

The Java development team at Sun also gave the language another feature that makes it easy to use: Java is a strongly typed language. A **strongly typed language** does not allow you to convert a variable from one type to another automatically. In Java programming, a value can be stored in a memory location and referred to by a variable name. A value can be classified by its type: integer (45), floating point number (45.6), character (A), and so on. To set up a variable in Java, you need to give it a name and a type. You will get an error message from the compiler if you try to put the wrong type of value into the variable. This typing is helpful because the compiler error message will tell you not only that there is an error, but where the error is. If the compiler allows this mistake, your program would run, but the output might be incorrect. You will learn more about types in Tutorial 3.

Two Types of Programs

There are two types of programs that can be developed in Java: applets and applications. An **applet** is a small Java program that executes only as part of a Web page. Currently, applets are the most popular type of Java program and as such applets are the focus of this book. A Java **application**, on the other hand, is a stand-alone program that runs separately from a Web page, such as the computer game discussed previously. Because a Java application runs separately from a Web page and must be stored on the user's system in order to run, security restrictions for applications are less powerful than those for applets. An applet cannot modify files stored on a user's system, whereas an application can write to the drive. Another important distinguishing feature is that an application uses less internal (RAM) memory because it runs without a Web browser.

Object-Oriented Java

The final feature of Java is that it is designed around the object-oriented model. The **object-oriented model** is a way of integrating the data inside the program with the program code that manipulates the data. For instance, in the coffee bean jar program, there is a jar object that has certain characteristics—height, diameter, and volume—that are the data about the jar. The programmer also can attach program code that computes the volume from the height and diameter, and given the size of a coffee bean, computes how many coffee beans fit in the jar.

The Microsoft Visual J++ Environment

In Lesson A, you learned about the advantages of IDEs. Visual J++ is an integrated development environment that is part of the Microsoft Developer Studio. The Developer Studio is designed to aid programmers who work with more than one programming language by providing a consistent environment from which more than one language system may be accessed. The Visual J++ environment includes conventional IDE components such as a text editor, compiler, and an online debugger. Included in the Visual J++ environment are three **wizards**, which are special tools that help build program elements by asking questions of the programmer, and then using the answers to construct or modify program files. (You will learn more about wizards in Tutorial 7.) Other special elements are the resource editors that allow the programmer to edit special files, such as graphics files, and Books Online, which is a complete set of program documentation accessible within the Visual J++ environment.

Starting Visual J++

In order to maximize your knowledge of Visual J++ and Java, you must complete the steps in this book at the computer. The steps in this book are intended for use with the Trial Edition of Visual J++ 1.1 that came with your book.

To start Visual J++:

1. If necessary, start Windows 95 and place your Student Disk in the appropriate disk drive.
2. Click the **Start** button on the Windows 95 taskbar to display the Start menu.
3. Point to **Programs** on the Start menu to display the list of available programs on your system.
4. Click **Microsoft Visual J++ 1.1 Trial Edition**, and then click **Microsoft Developer Studio**, as shown in Figure 1-6 to start the program.

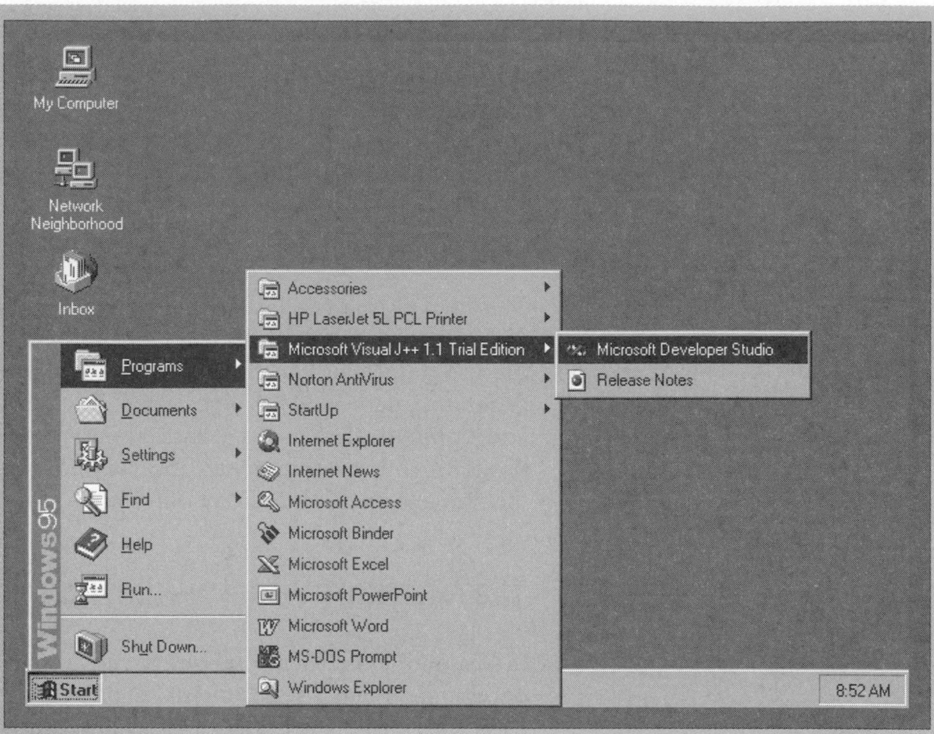

Figure 1-6: Starting Microsoft Visual J++

If you do not want the Tip of the Day dialog box to open every time you start the program, click the Show tips at startup check box to clear it.

5 After the Microsoft Developer Studio starts, you might see the Tip of the Day dialog box, as shown in Figure 1-7. Click the **Close** button to close the dialog box.

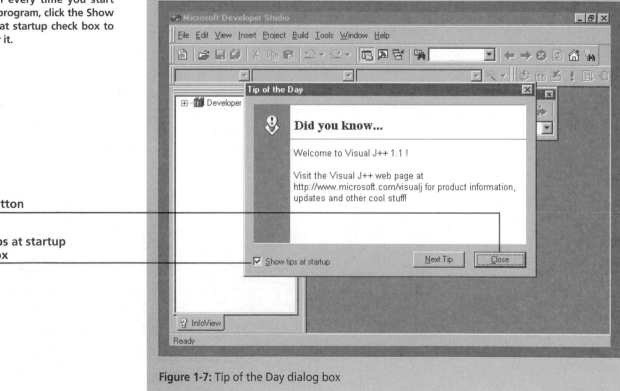

Close button

Show tips at startup check box

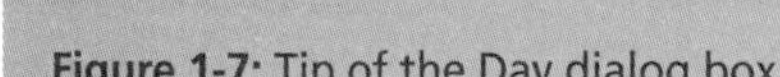

Figure 1-7: Tip of the Day dialog box

6 If necessary, maximize the Microsoft Developer Studio window by clicking the **Maximize** button on the program title bar.

HELP? The Windows 95 taskbar has been hidden in the figures in this book. To hide the Windows 95 taskbar, click the Start button, point to Settings, and then click Taskbar to display the Taskbar Properties dialog box. On the Taskbar Options tab, click the Auto hide check box. A check mark appears in the check box. Click the OK button to close the Taskbar Properties dialog box. The taskbar is now hidden from view; only a thin line appears in its place at the bottom of the screen. (Depending on how Windows 95 is configured, your taskbar could be at the top, right, left, or bottom edge of the screen.) To display the hidden taskbar temporarily, move the mouse pointer to a location below the thin line at the bottom of the screen. To hide the taskbar again, move the mouse pointer back to a location above the thin line at the bottom of the screen. To display the taskbar again permanently, clear the Auto hide check box in the Taskbar Properties dialog box.

Note: In the future, you will be instructed simply to "start Visual J++."

The Visual J++ Environment

A goal behind the Microsoft Developer Studio approach is that all the programming languages share a common interface. That is, if a programmer switches between languages such as Visual J++, Visual Basic, Visual C++, and other languages, the environments will be identical. When the Developer Studio opens for the first time, the InfoViewer toolbar, the Workspace window, and the Editor window open, as shown in Figure 1-8. The third major window—the Output window—might not open on startup.

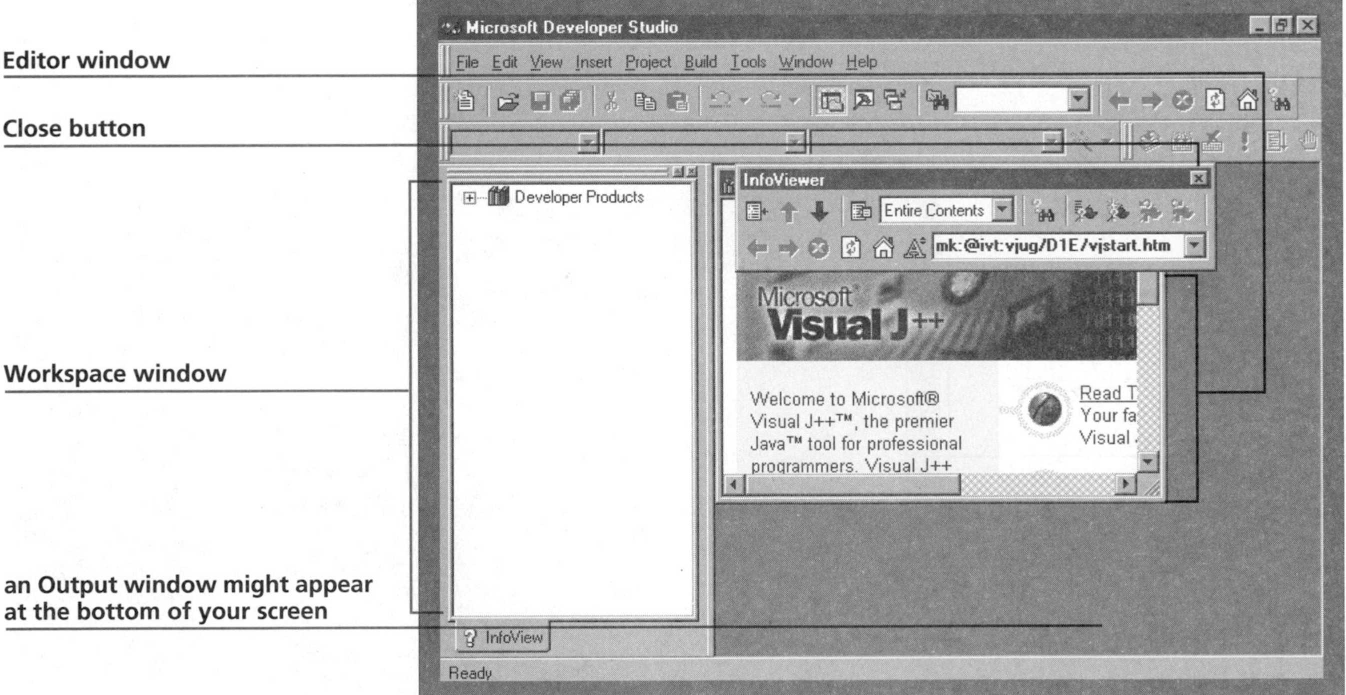

Figure 1-8: Visual J++ environment

HELP? If you are working in a computer lab, your screen might look different from the one shown in Figure 1-8. Once the InfoViewer toolbar is turned off, it has to be turned on to appear again. On startup, you might see the Workspace window and the Editor window (Figure 1-8), no windows (Figure 1-9), or only the Workspace window (Figure 1-10).

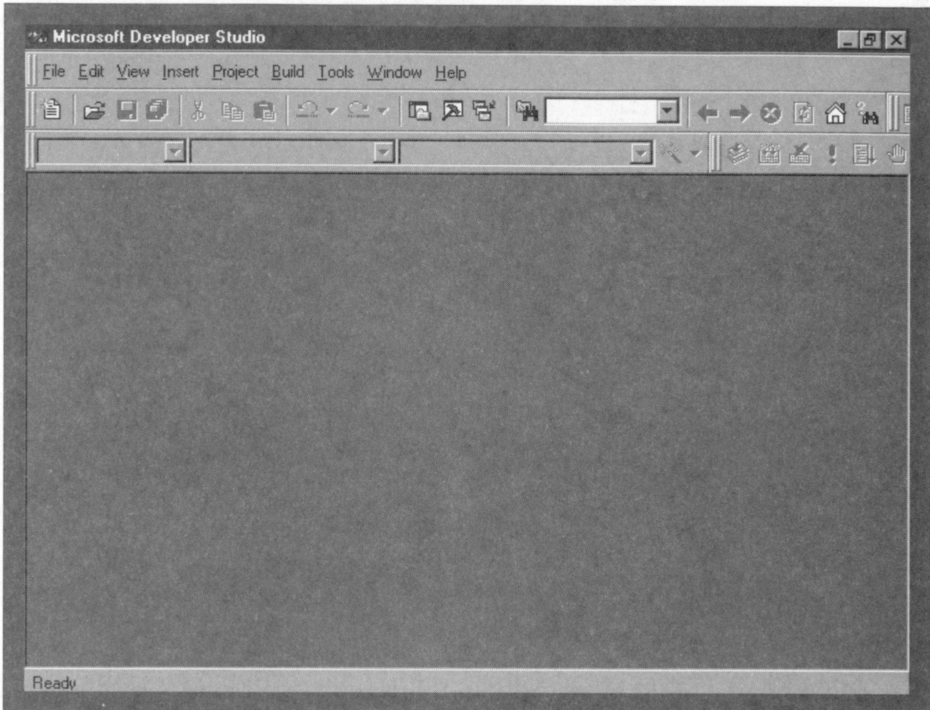

Figure 1-9: Microsoft Developer Studio with no windows open

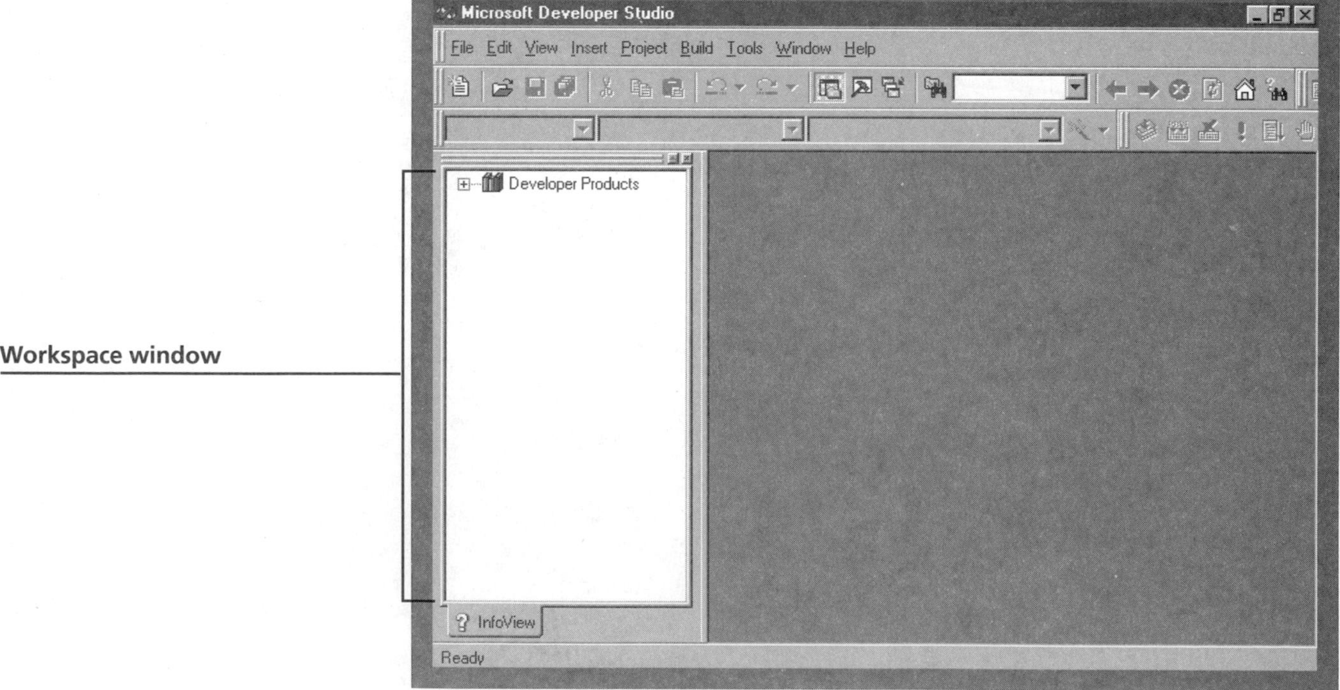

Figure 1-10: Microsoft Developer Studio with Workspace window open

You might need to change your screen to match what is shown in Figure 1-10. Visual J++ permits users to display and move different toolbars, and to customize the toolbar buttons. Your screens might look different from those shown in the text depending on which toolbars are configured to appear and where they appear on the screen. The contents of the Editor window should be the same, however, regardless of the toolbars.

To close the InfoViewer toolbar and Editor window:

1. If the InfoViewer toolbar is visible, click the **Close** button ☒ on the InfoViewer toolbar.
2. If the Output window is visible, right-click anywhere in the Output window, and then click **Hide** on the shortcut menu.
3. If your screen looks like Figure 1-9, open the Workspace window by clicking **View** on the menu bar, and then clicking **Workspace**. Your screen should look like Figure 1-10.

The Workspace Window

As shown in Figure 1-10, the Workspace window displays the books available in **Books Online**, which is the program's Help system. At the bottom of the window is a tab named InfoView. When you work on a project, three tabs appear at the bottom of the window: InfoView tab, ClassView tab, and FileView tab. The Workspace window helps the programmer to manage a Java project under construction or to navigate the information provided in Books Online.

The Editor Window

As shown in Figure 1-8, the Editor window might display information from Books Online, or it could be empty. The programmer uses the information in the Workspace to change the contents of the Editor window. In InfoView mode, the programmer can request documents from Books Online. In FileView mode, the programmer can request to view project files.

The Output Window

The Output window displays messages from the compiler when you either compile a program or build a project. It will display across the bottom of the screen when you are working on a program. The messages indicate any syntax errors that occur in the program.

Using InfoViewer and Books Online

The InfoViewer provides a way to access Books Online. This help information can be accessed using more than one method. One method is to use the book list, select a book, and then select documents or chapters from that book, as you will see next. Another method is to highlight information in the Editor window, and then press the F1 key, as you will see later in this lesson. You will use both methods to practice using Books Online.

Selecting and Viewing Books Online Documents

One of the documents provided with Books Online, "An Introduction to Visual J++," is a good document to review because it gives you a quick understanding of how to use Visual J++ to develop Java applets. Accessing a document using InfoViewer is just a matter of pointing and clicking. You can read documents using the InfoViewer and then print them when necessary.

To open a Books Online document:

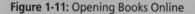

1 Click the **plus** box ⊞ in front of the bookshelf named Developer Products in the Workspace window. The plus box changes to a minus box after you click it. Developer Products might contain one or more bookshelves for different Developer Studio applications. Figure 1-11 only shows the books for Visual J++.

Figure 1-11: Opening Books Online

2 Click the **plus** box ⊞ in front of the Visual J++ bookshelf to open it. You will now see the list of 11 Visual J++ online books, as shown in Figure 1-12.

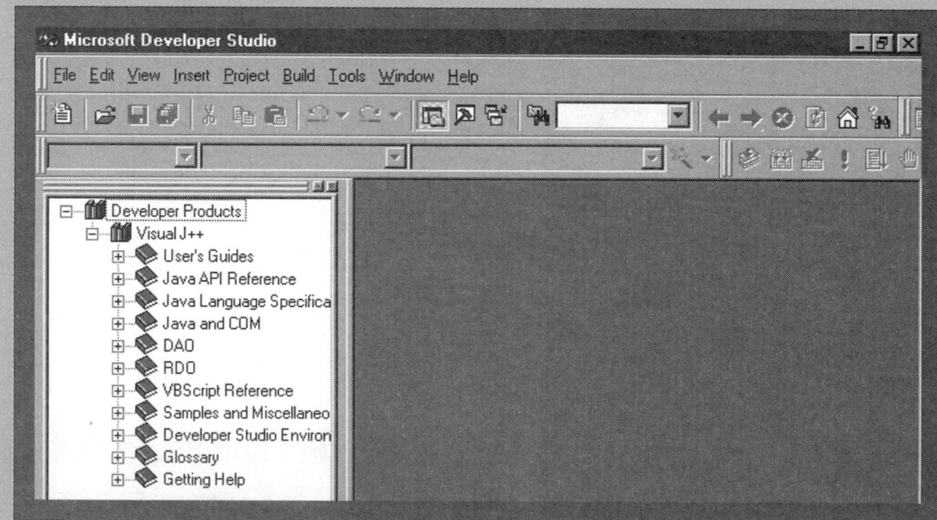

Figure 1-12: Displaying all the Visual J++ books

3 Click the **plus** box ⊞ in front of the User's Guides book to open it.

4 Click the **plus** box ⊞ in front of the Test Drive book to open it. See Figure 1-13.

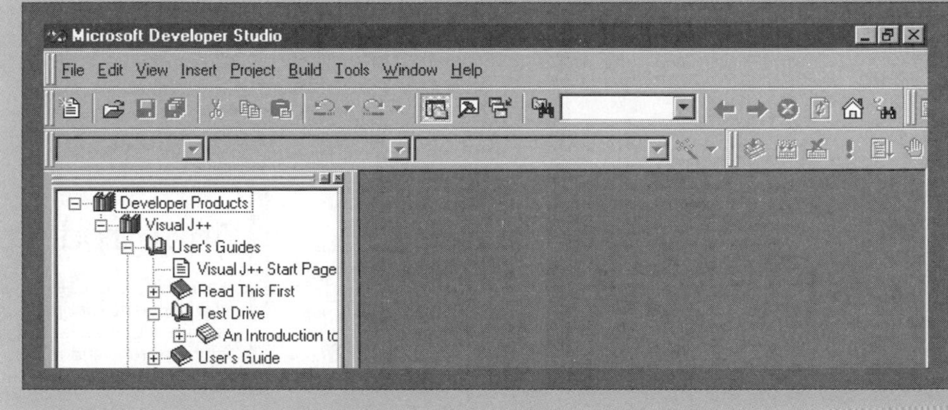

Figure 1-13: After Opening the Test Drive book

5 Double-click the **An Introduction to Visual J++** book to open it. The document appears in the Editor window. See Figure 1-14.

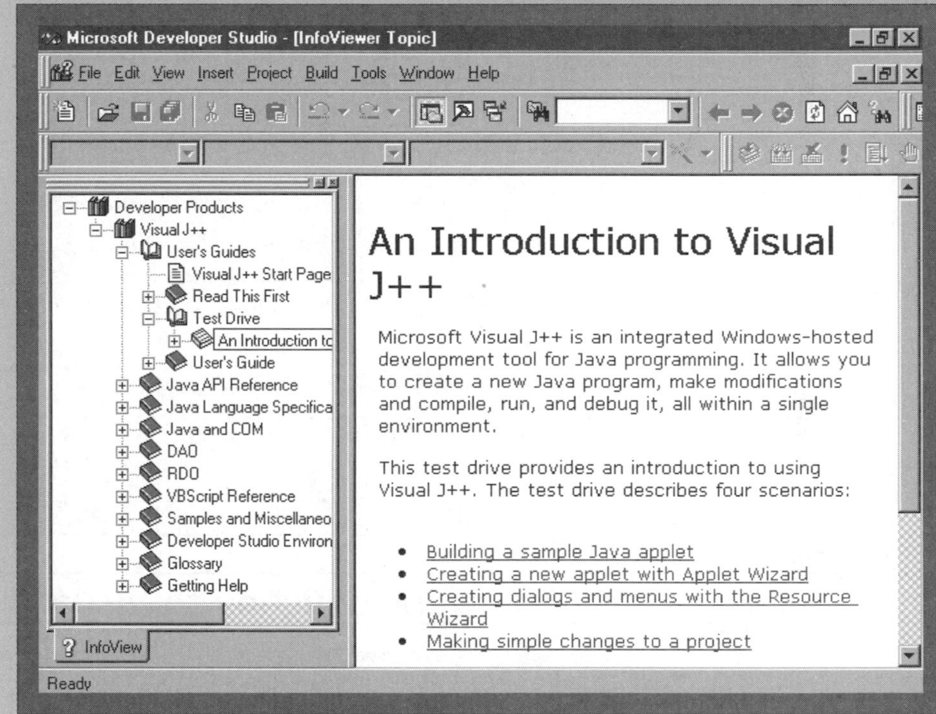

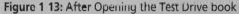

Figure 1-14: Viewing An Introduction to Visual J++ document

HELP? If a Connect To dialog box opens, click the Cancel button to close it.

6 To make the document easier to read on the screen, hide the Workspace window by right-clicking anywhere in the Workspace window, and then clicking **Hide** on the shortcut menu, as shown in Figure 1-15.

You might need to maximize the Editor window so your screen will match the figures in this book.

Microsoft Developer Studio - [InfoViewer Topic]
File Edit View Insert Project Build Tools Window Help
3.1416
Developer Products
Visual J++
User's Guides
Docking View
Hide
Properties
Java and COM
An Introduction to Visual J++
Microsoft Visual J++ is an integrated Windows-hosted development tool for Java programming. It allows you to create a new Java program, make modifications and compile, run, and debug it, all within a single environment.
This test drive provides an introduction to using Visual J++. The test drive describes four scenarios:

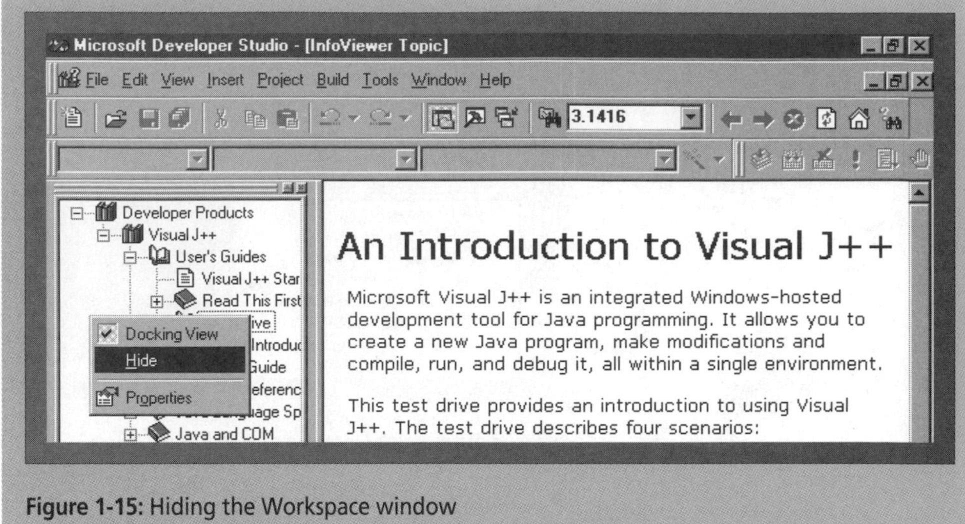

Figure 1-15: Hiding the Workspace window

tip

You can read the document online, or you can print it by clicking File on the menu bar, and then clicking Print.

You can navigate through the Books Online document by using the table of contents in the Workspace window or by using the navigation toolbar buttons. You will use the Go Back button and the Go Forward button to move around in the Books Online.

To navigate through the Books Online document:

1 Position the pointer on the **Building a sample Java applet** hypertext link. Hypertext links appear in a different color (such as blue), and the pointer changes to ☝ when it rests on a hypertext link. See Figure 1-16.

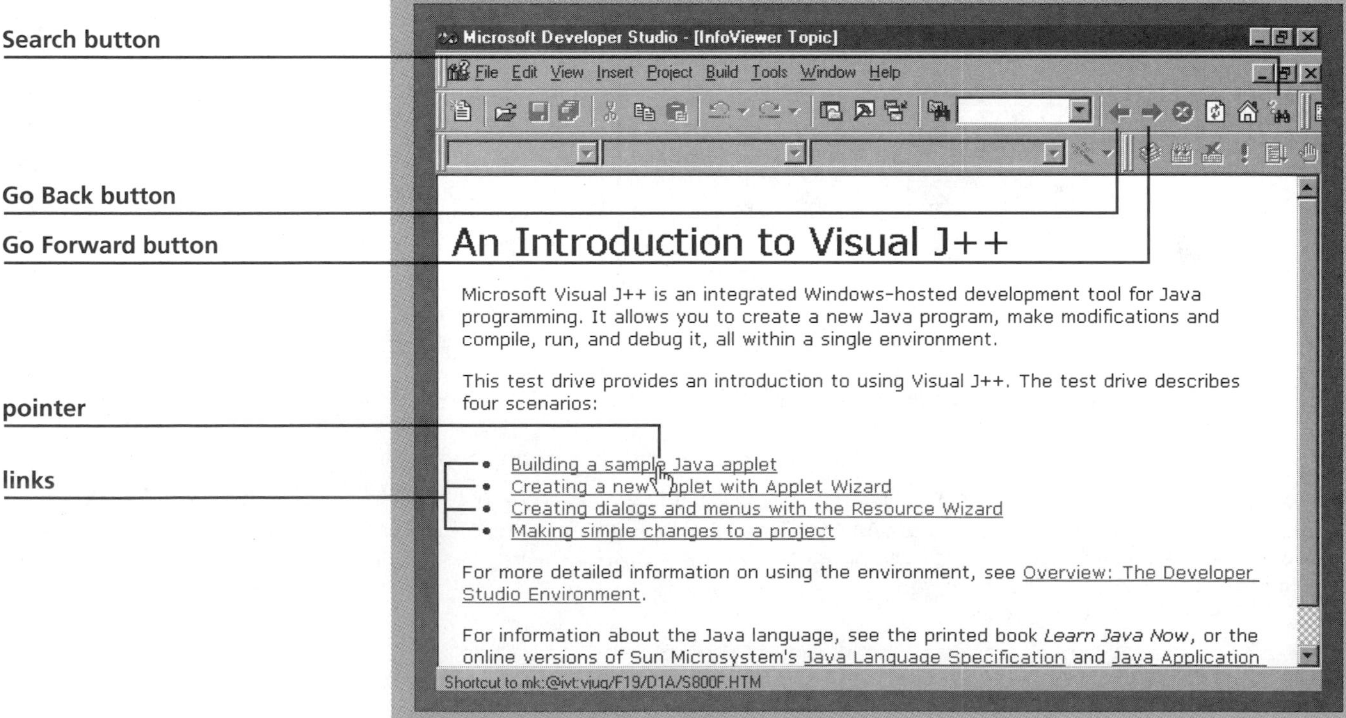

Search button
Go Back button
Go Forward button
pointer
links
Microsoft Developer Studio - [InfoViewer Topic]
File Edit View Insert Project Build Tools Window Help
An Introduction to Visual J++
Microsoft Visual J++ is an integrated Windows-hosted development tool for Java programming. It allows you to create a new Java program, make modifications and compile, run, and debug it, all within a single environment.
This test drive provides an introduction to using Visual J++. The test drive describes four scenarios:
Building a sample Java applet
Creating a new applet with Applet Wizard
Creating dialogs and menus with the Resource Wizard
Making simple changes to a project
For more detailed information on using the environment, see Overview: The Developer Studio Environment.
For information about the Java language, see the printed book Learn Java Now, or the online versions of Sun Microsystem's Java Language Specification and Java Application
Shortcut to mk:@ivt:vjug/F19/D1A/S800F.HTM

Figure 1-16: Using hypertext links

2 Click the **Building a sample Java applet** link to open the Building a Sample Java Applet document. This document contains hyperlinks to other Books Online documents and to other sources.

3 Click the **Go Back** button on the Standard toolbar to return to the "An Introduction to Visual J++" document.

4 Click the **Go Forward** button on the Standard toolbar to return to the "Building a Sample Java Applet" document.

When you need help while using Visual J++, you can use Books Online at any time to access the Help system. There are two more ways to use the online books. The first method requires you to wait until there is a Java program in the Editor window, but you can see the other method now. Many times, you will have a question about a specific topic. There is a way to search Books Online for a single topic. One feature of all Microsoft products is the use of shortcut keys. Next you will search Books Online for information on shortcut keys.

To use the Search button to access online Help information:

1 Click the **Search** button on the Standard toolbar to open the Search dialog box, as shown in Figure 1-17.

your keyword text box might look different

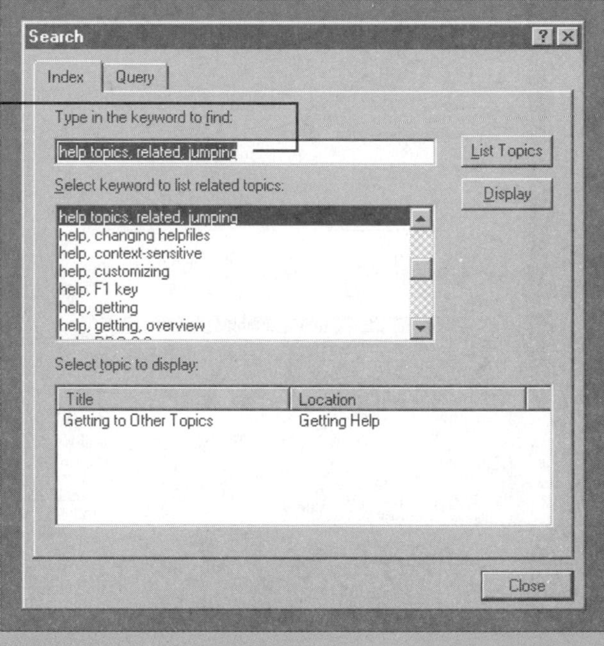

Figure 1-17: Search dialog box

HELP? The contents of the your Search dialog box will be different because the contents depend on what has happened previously in Visual J++.

2 Type **short** in the Type in the keyword to find text box. Notice that the list of topics changes as you type each letter. Click the **shortcut keys** topic, as shown in Figure 1-18.

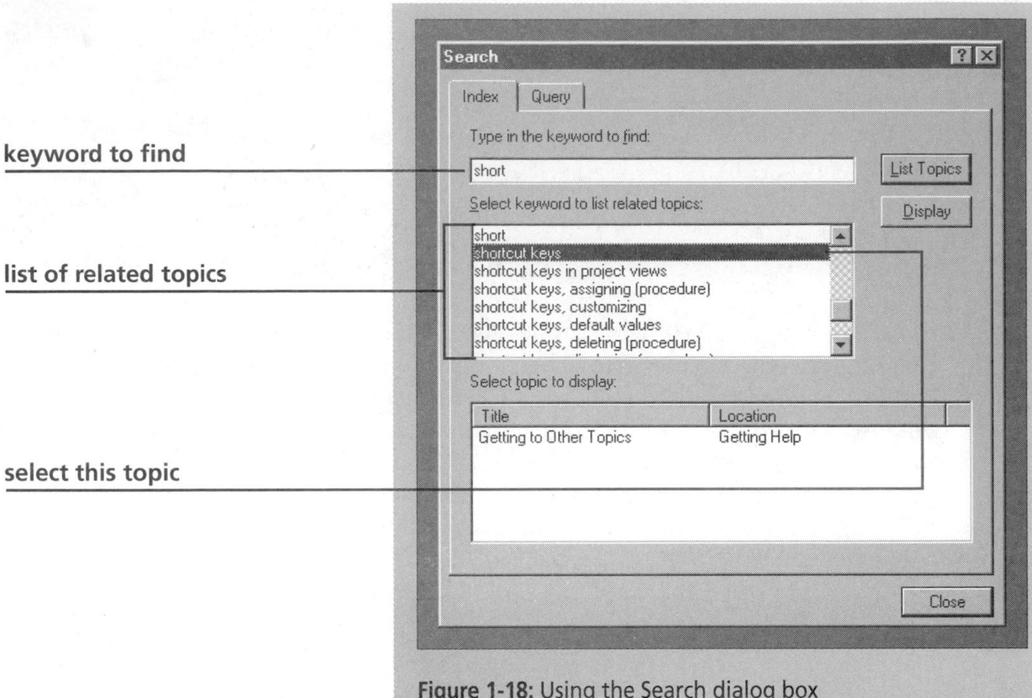

Figure 1-18: Using the Search dialog box

3 Click the **List Topics** button. Figure 1-19 shows the list of associated topics in the bottom list box.

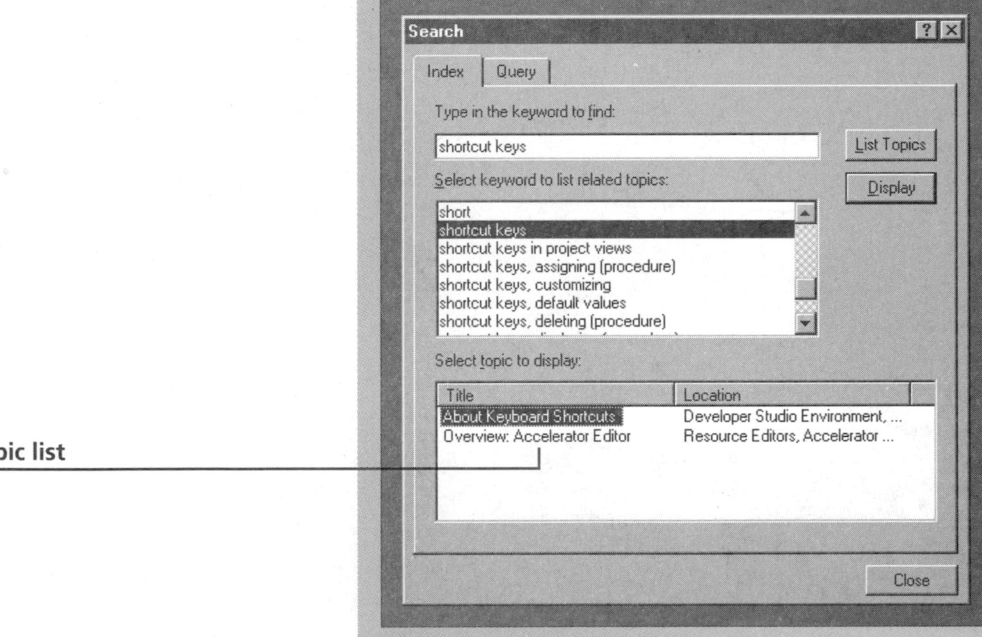

Figure 1-19: Displaying topics

4 Double-click the **About Keyboard Shortcuts** topic in the bottom list box to read about this topic.

Now that you know how to start Visual J++ and use Books Online, you are ready to open some files and learn how to use the Visual J++ environment. To use a previously constructed project, there are three steps: open the workspace file, build the project, and then execute the project.

Opening the Workspace File

The first graphics applet that you will view is saved on your Student Disk. Opening the files and using them to build and execute or to run a project is the first step in learning the Visual J++ environment.

To open a workspace file:

1 Click **File** on the menu bar, and then click **Open Workspace**. Click the **Look in** list arrow, and then click **3½ Floppy (A:)** (or whichever drive contains your Student Disk). Double-click the **Tutorial1** folder to open it. See Figure 1-20.

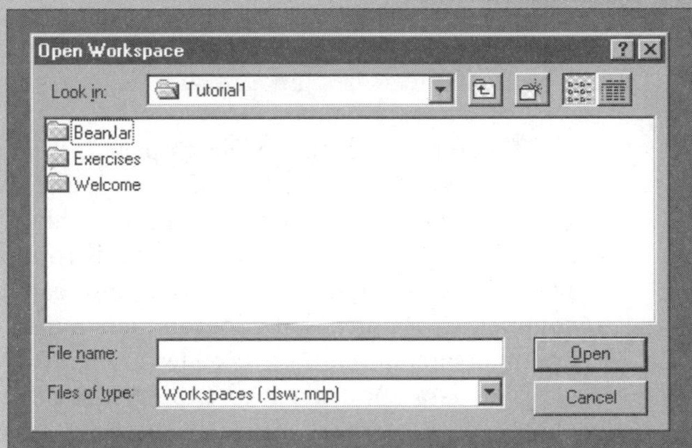

Figure 1-20: Open Workspace dialog box

2 Double-click the **Welcome** folder to open it. The only workspace file in the Welcome folder is named Welcome.dsw.

3 Double-click the **Welcome.dsw** file to open it. The contents of the file appear in the Editor window. See Figure 1-21.

HELP? If you see a warning message that the specified file cannot be opened as a workspace, click the OK button and then repeat Steps 1 through 3.

HELP? If you do not see the Java file shown in Figure 1-21, click the FileView tab on the Workspace window, double-click the Welcome classes folder to open it, and then double-click the Welcome.java file.

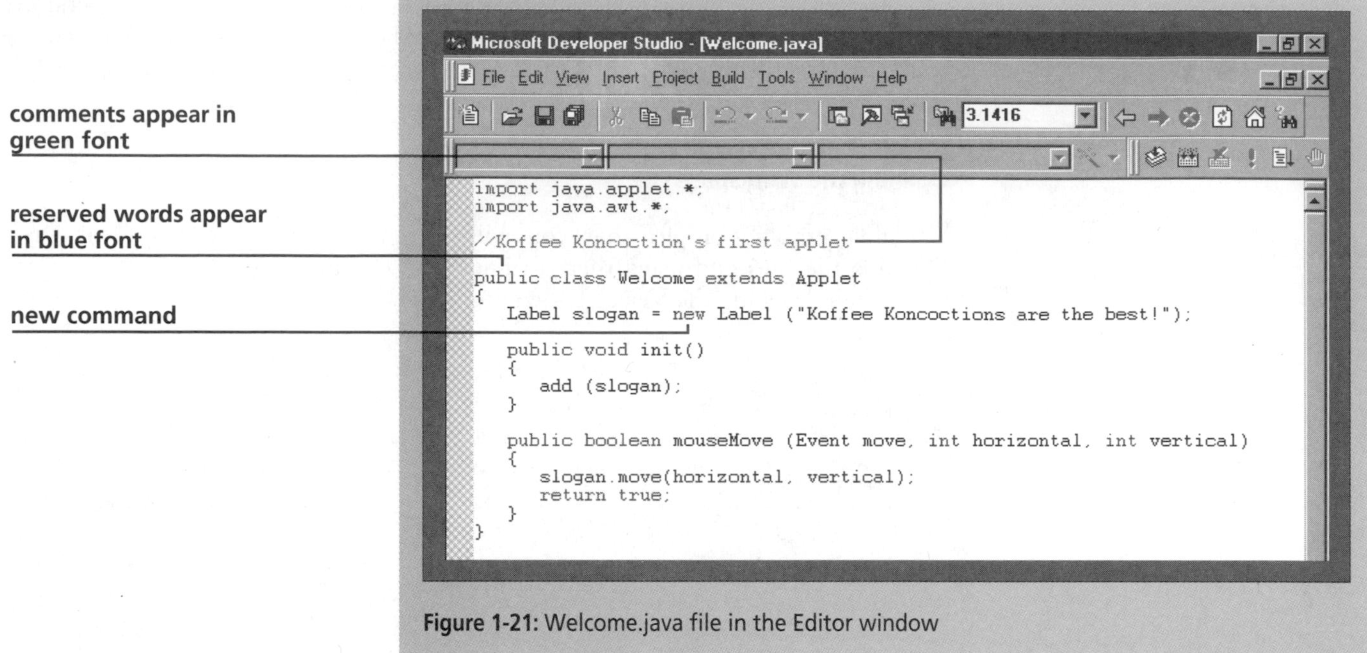

Figure 1-21: Welcome.java file in the Editor window

When the Welcome project opened, some files loaded into Visual J++. The file that appears in the Editor window is the Welcome.java file. Notice that some words in the Editor window display in different colors. In Visual J++, words that display in blue type are **reserved words** to indicate special command words in the Java language that are reserved and cannot be redefined. Green words are **comments**, or notes that programmers put in their programs to inform other programmers about features or codes in the program.

This is a good place to explore the other method for accessing online Help. When you need more information about anything typed in the program, you can select the word, and then press the F1 key to retrieve the Help information for that word.

To access online Help using the F1 key:

1. Click the word **new** in the fifth line of typing, and then press the **F1** key.

   The Class Instance Creation Expressions page appears in the Editor window, as shown in Figure 1-22. This document is from the Java Language Specification book in Books Online. This page explains that the word "new" in the program creates a new instance, or example, of an object and then describes how to use the new command. You will learn more about objects in Tutorial 2, but for now, an object in Java is like a collection of variables and the programming code that manipulates the variables.

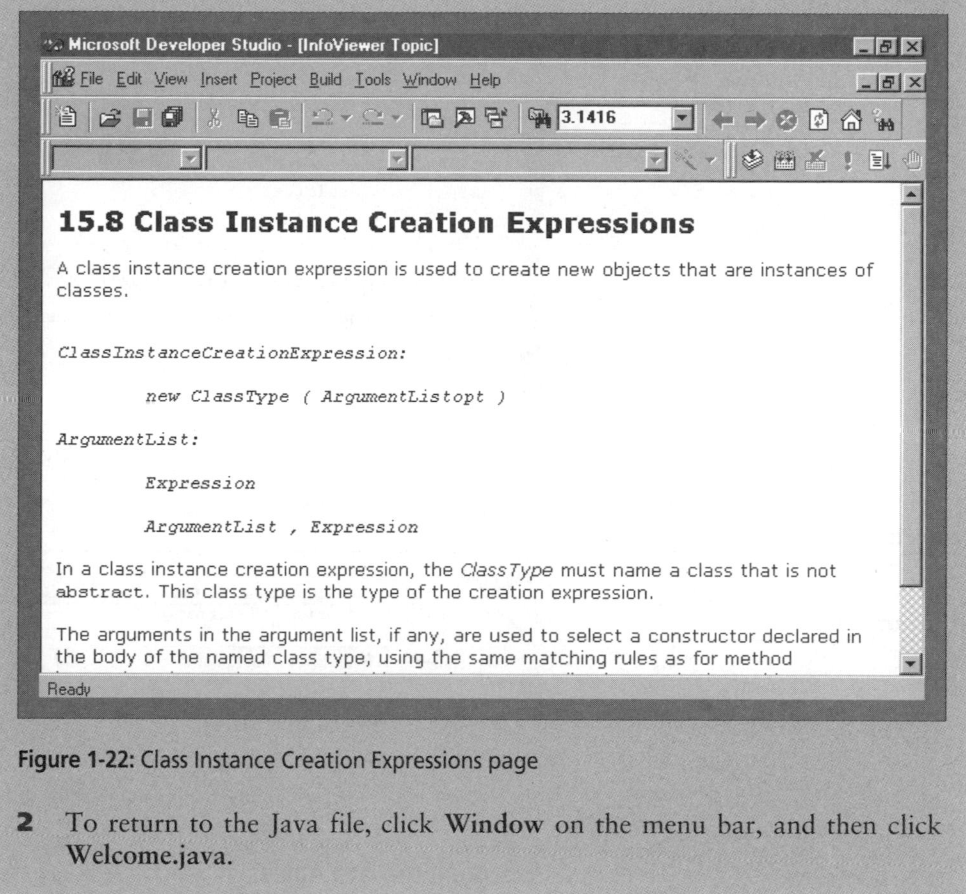

Figure 1-22: Class Instance Creation Expressions page

2 To return to the Java file, click **Window** on the menu bar, and then click **Welcome.java.**

Building a Java Applet

Building a Java applet is a way of compiling multiple files into one unified project. All the files in a project constitute the project workspace. Opening a workspace, as you did earlier, allows you access to all the related files in the workspace. In fact, any of the workspace files that were opened when you last accessed that workspace will open again when you reopen the workspace. In Lesson A, you learned about interpreted and compiled languages. Java is a compiled language—when the programmer finishes writing, testing, and debugging the program, all files in the program must be built, or translated into machine language, before it can run. There is an option to compile only one file, but compiling one file will not run the program, which is the current goal. You will build the project next.

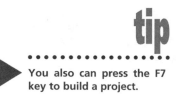

You also can press the F7 key to build a project.

To build a project:

1 Click the **Build** button on the Build toolbar. See Figure 1-23. The Output window at the bottom of the screen displays the message that indicates a successful build of the Welcome project. If your project contains any problems, an appropriate error message would display in the Output window.

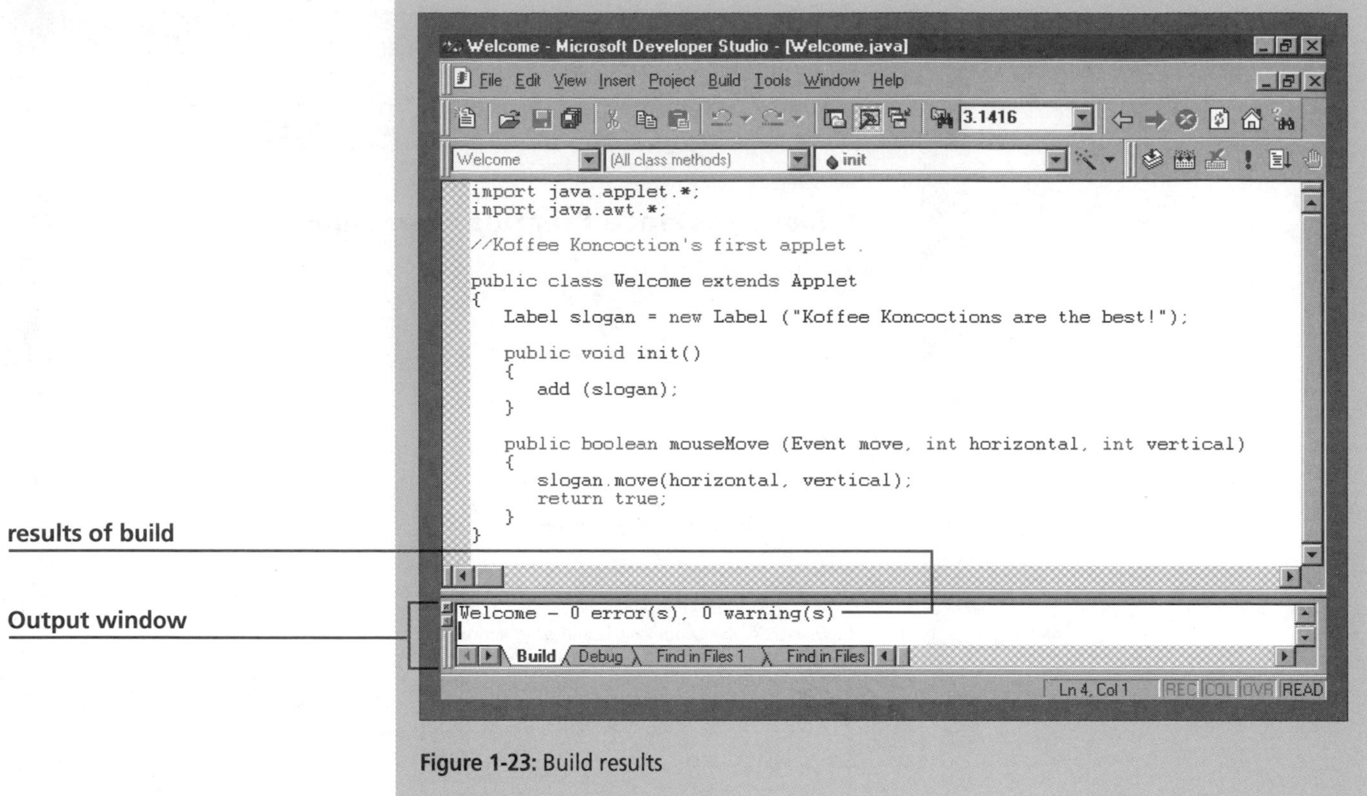

Figure 1-23: Build results

Executing the Java Applet

One useful feature of Visual J++ is that it will create an HTML file in which to execute or run your Java applet. Java applets, by definition, run only in the context of an HTML page. Although creating an HTML page is not difficult, it is nice to be able to run an applet without having to generate the HTML code prior to running it.

You also can press Ctrl + F5 to execute a program.

The Java language is case sensitive. A case-sensitive language is one in which a capital "W" and a lowercase "w" are *not* the same character. Typing the class name as "welcome," for example, represents a different class to the compiler.

To execute the Java applet:

1 Click the **Execute Program** button on the Build toolbar. Internet Explorer (or your default Web browser) opens and runs the applet (using an HTML file from your Student Disk).

2 To see what this applet does, move the pointer around the screen (between the two horizontal lines). It appears with the text "Koffee Koncoctions are the Best!". See Figure 1-24.

HELP? If an Information For Running Class dialog box opens, type "Welcome" in the Class file name text box, and then click the OK button. Internet Explorer will start and run the Java applet. The class filename is listed at the top of the program in the "public class *className* extends Applet" statement.

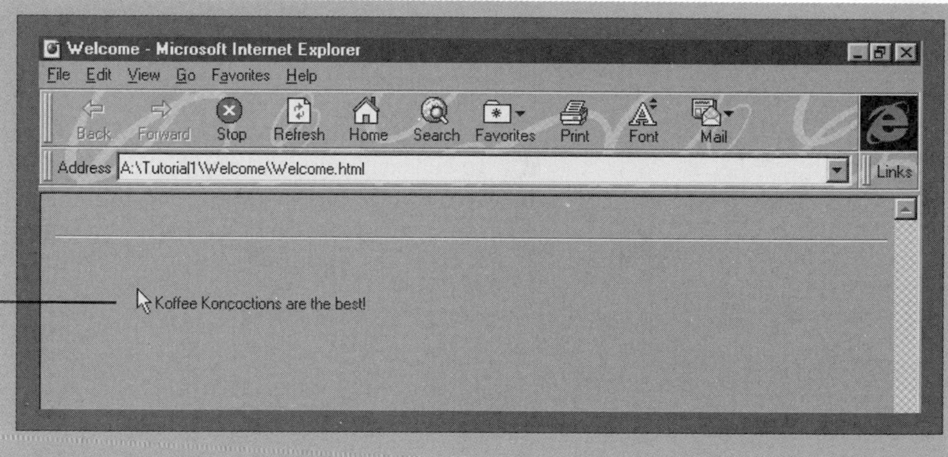

Figure 1-24: Welcome applet executing in Internet Explorer

tip

Click the third Tutorial 1 link of the Online Companion for this book (http://www.course.com) to see a live Java program that illustrates this topic.

3 Click the **Close** button ☒ on the Internet Explorer title bar to close the browser.

4 Click **File** on the menu bar, and then click **Close Workspace** to close your project. Click the **Yes** button to close all document windows.

5 Click ☒ to close Visual J++.

Now you know how to run a Java applet in Visual J++. In Lesson C, you will complete a project by entering commands in an incomplete Java file. You can either take a break or complete the end-of-lesson questions and exercises.

SUMMARY

- Some important Java features are that Java can be used for Web-based applets and stand-alone applications; it is machine independent; it has good security features; it is easy to use; and it is object-oriented.
- To start Visual J++:
  Click the Start button.
  Point to Programs.
  Click Microsoft Visual J++ 1.1 Trial Edition.
  Click Microsoft Developer Studio.
- To hide the Windows 95 taskbar:
  Click the Start button.
  Point to Settings.
  Click Taskbar.
  On the Taskbar Options tab, click the Auto hide check box.
  Click the OK button.
- To open books in the InfoView mode (or Workspace window), click the plus box ⊞ in front of the desired book.
- To close books in the InfoView mode (or Workspace window), click the minus box ⊟ in front of the book to be closed.
- You can search for terms in Books Online by clicking the Search button on the Standard toolbar, and then typing your search text and displaying the topics.

- To open a project workspace:
  Click File on the menu bar.
  Click Open Workspace.
  Select the drive and folder that contains the workspace file.
  Double-click the filename that you want to open.
- To build an applet, click the Build button on the Build toolbar.
- To run or execute an applet, click the Execute Program button on the Build toolbar. If you are asked for a class name, type the name as it appears on the line that reads "public class *className* extends Applet" in the file, and then click the OK button.

QUESTIONS

1. Originally, Java was named ________.
   a. Pine
   b. Maple
   c. Oak
   d. C++
2. The type of Java program that runs on a Web page is a(n) ________.
   a. application
   b. apple
   c. project
   d. applet
3. A Visual J++ wizard is a(n) ________.
   a. part of Books Online
   b. Visual J++ expert
   c. tool built into Visual J++
   d. offline documentation program
4. Which of the following items is not one of the three major windows in Visual J++?
   a. Editor window
   b. Workspace window
   c. Output window
   d. Input window
5. How do you open a book in Books Online?
   a. Click the plus box ⊞ in front of the book.
   b. Click the minus box ⊟ in front of the book.
   c. Click the book title, and then press the F1 key.
   d. Click the book title, and then press the F4 key.
6. The three steps for running an applet from Visual J++, in order, are ________.
   a. build, load, and execute
   b. load, build, and execute
   c. load, compile, and execute
   d. load, execute, and build
7. Reserved words in Java are ________.
   a. variable names
   b. filenames
   c. special command words
   d. notes to other programmers
8. Comments in Java are ________.
   a. variable names
   b. filenames

c. special command words
d. notes to other programmers

9. If you need information about a command or word in your Java program, click the command or word, and then press ________.
a. Alt + ?
b. the F1 key
c. the F4 key
d. Ctrl + Q

10. Before running a Java applet, you must __________.
a. open an HTML file
b. write an HTML file
c. build it
d. start your Web browser

E X E R C I S E S

1. In this exercise, use the Overview: Text Editor document in Books Online to answer the following questions. This document is located in the Text Editor section of the Developer Studio Environment Guide User's Guide.
a. What kind of source files can be created in the editor?
b. What happens if you click the right mouse button in the Editor window?
c. Explore the Editor Commands and Keystrokes link, and then find out how to get a complete list of commands.

2. In this exercise, use the Overview: The Developer Studio Environment document in Books Online to answer the following questions. This document is located in the Developer Studio Environment section of the Developer Studio Environment Guide User's Guide.
a. Under what operating systems does Developer Studio run?
b. What program features are included with Developer Studio products?
c. Explore the Viewing the World Wide Web from Developer Studio link, and then list the ways to use Developer Studio to access the Web if your computer has Web access.

3. In this exercise, use the Search button and find out about the graphics editor, and then answer the following questions:
a. What two graphic formats does Java understand?
b. How do you open the graphics editor?
c. Click the Create image files link to list the steps needed to create a new GIF or JPEG image file.

4. In this exercise, you will use an applet to take as input the number of seconds between lightning and the thunder during a storm to determine how far away a storm is located. Load the Lightning.dsw workspace from the Lightning folder in the Exercises folder on your Student Disk, and then build and execute the applet. (*Note:* If a dialog box opens with a "Not all windows in this workspace could be opened" error, click the OK button.) Use the applet to calculate the storm distance for 4 seconds and for 56 seconds. Close Internet Explorer and then close the workspace.

5. In this exercise, you will use an applet to calculate how much weight a person will lose by jogging. One hour of jogging burns 475 calories, and a person needs to burn 3500 calories to lose one pound. Load the Jogging.dsw workspace from the Jogging folder in the Exercises folder on your Student Disk, and then build and execute the applet. (*Note:* If you receive a message that not all of the workspaces could be opened, click the OK button.) Calculate the weight loss for one and four hours of jogging, close Internet Explorer, and then close the workspace and Visual J++.

LESSON C

objectives

In this lesson you will learn how to:

- Design an applet
- Revise a Java program
- Create Java objects
- Build and execute an applet
- Test and debug an applet

Programming with Visual J++ and Java

Designing an Applet

In Lesson B, you learned how to open, build, and execute a Java applet. In Lesson C, you will complete the Java coffee bean jar applet and then construct a project workspace. After completing the applet, you will run it using Internet Explorer (or your default Web browser).

Maria helped you plan the coffee bean jar applet, but there is another type of program documentation tool to cover. In Lesson A, you learned about the five-step problem-solving process. Java is not only an object-oriented programming language, but many Java elements also are elements of **graphical user interface**, or **GUI**, programming. All GUI programs have a similar look to them with common elements such as windows, menus, dialog boxes, and toolbars. You need to plan which GUI elements to use in your applet, and what each element will do.

Another planning tool that you can use is the TOE (task object event) chart. A **TOE chart** assigns the tasks that need to be accomplished in the program to the various objects in the program, and then lists what events will trigger the tasks. You decide that you need labels, a text field, a text area, and a button in the coffee bean jar applet. A **label** is an object that displays one line of text on the screen. Both the **text field** and the **text area** can be used for both input and output, but the text field is limited to just one line, and the text area can have multiple lines. A **button** is a GUI object that responds with a predefined action when you click it. Figure 1-25 shows your TOE chart for the program.

Task	Object	Event
Explain the applet purpose	Title label	Start
Ask for input	Prompt label	Start
Accept input	Text field	User types a number
Calculate beans	Button	Click button
Display result	Text area	Button click

Figure 1-25: BeanJar applet TOE chart

Revising the Program

Maria started the BeanJar.java file for you and has asked you to finish it. She added comments where programming statements need to be added. There are three places that need to be completed: the opening comment area, the object declaration or set-up area, and the applet initialization area.

The first step is to modify the opening comments. Remember that you add comments to write notes to other programmers. Comments in Java are marked by special symbols. One way to insert a comment in your program is to type two slashes (//), and then type the comment. Visual J++ (and all other Java compilers) ignore any characters from the double slashes to the end of the line. A more dangerous method for marking comments is to start with the symbols /*, type your comment, and then end with the symbols */. Text that appears between the symbols is treated as a comment. In Visual J++, because of the syntax coloring, it is easy to see where the comments are. In environments without syntax coloring, it is easy to make the dangerous mistake of placing an essential part of the programming code inside a comment.

To insert a comment in a Java file:

1. Start Visual J++. Close any open workspaces by clicking **File** on the menu bar, and then clicking **Close Workspace**. Click the **Yes** button to close all windows.

If the Close Workspace command on your File menu is dimmed, there is no open workspace.

2. Insert your Student Disk into the appropriate drive, and then click the **Open** button on the Standard toolbar. Double-click the **Tutorial1** folder, and then double-click the **BeanJar** folder to open it. If necessary, click the **Files of type** list arrow, and then click **Java Files (.java)** to show a list of files with the .java extension.

You also can press Ctrl + O to open a file.

3. Double-click the **BJ.java** file to open it. The BJ.java program opens in the Editor window. See Figure 1-26.

Earlier you opened a workspace, and now you are opening a file. Visual J++ can open files of many different types; you are not limited to opening only Java programs. When you open a Visual J++ workspace, you are opening an entire project. Opening a file just opens one file.

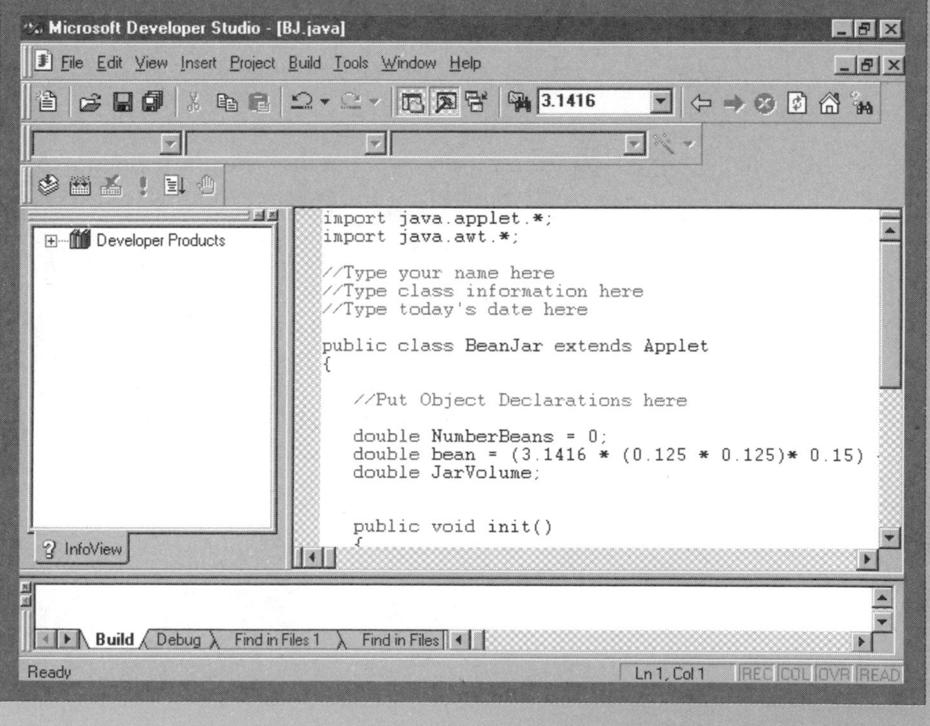

Figure 1-26: BJ.java file

Most of the time, when you are asked to select a placeholder comment, you will select and replace the comment markers (//) as well. The only exception to this rule is when you are inserting comments, such as when you type your name or any other information your instructor asks you to insert.

Make sure that you type filenames exactly as indicated in the text. Java recognizes files with different capitalization as different filenames. For example, the files BeanJar.java and beanjar.java are different files.

4 Hide the Workspace window by right-clicking anywhere in the Workspace window, and then clicking **Hide** on the shortcut menu.

For the rest of this book, the figures will show only the Editor window unless another window is open in the program window.

5 Use the mouse pointer to select the comment text that reads Type your name here, but do not select the slashes (//), and then type your name. Selected text is replaced automatically when you start typing. If the comment markers were deleted (//), just retype them.

For the remainder of this book, replace the "Enter your class information here" comment with any information requested by your instructor.

6 Use the same technique to type your class information and today's date where indicated.

7 Click **File** on the menu bar, and then click **Save As** to open the Save As dialog box. The default filename is selected in the File name text box. When you type a new filename, it replaces the default filename. Type **BeanJar.java** and then click the **Save** button.

Creating Objects

To use any of Java's predefined GUI components, your program must include statements to declare them. The BeanJar program is designed to use four of the predefined types: labels, text fields, text areas, and buttons. Declaring objects is a way of indicating which elements appear in the program, and then naming these elements and assigning values to them. Values can be assigned when you declare objects, like the objects that you will type now, or can be assigned later, like the JarVolume object that is already in the file.

In the English language, you must follow grammar rules when constructing sentences. In Java, the rules you must follow when constructing statements are called **syntax rules**. When your statements are not constructed properly, you will receive a syntax error, as you learned in Lesson A. The general rule for declaring GUI objects in Java is as follows:

ObjectType ObjectName **= new** *ObjectType***(***Arguments***);**

where the items in italics (*ObjectType, ObjectName, Arguments*) are placeholders that are replaced by the actual item. The bolded items (**=**, **new**, **(**, **)**, and **;**) are required items in the object; they are not placeholders. Figure 1-27 lists some examples of declarations for GUI objects.

GUI Object	Declaration	Purpose
Label	Label Welcome = new Label("Welcome to Java");	Declares a label with the given text
Label	Label Blank = new Label();	Declares a label with no text; can be assigned text later
TextField	TextField Phone = new TextField(13);	Declares a blank text field that holds 13 characters
TextField	TextField Message = new TextField("Wear seatbelts!");	Declares a text field to hold the message "Wear seatbelts!"
TextField	TextField Output = new TextField(10);	Declares a text field to hold 10 characters
Button	Button OK = new Button("OK");	Declares a button that displays "OK"
Button	Button Later = new Button();	Declares a blank button that displays text; can be assigned later

Figure 1-27: Legal object declarations

Case Sensitivity in Java

Java is a **case-sensitive** program; that is the letters "a" and "A" are considered to be different letters. For example, Java interprets the words "label" and "Label" as different words. Punctuation also is very important in your programs. Figure 1-27 shows a semicolon at the end of each statement, which is a required element in Java. Although line indenting is not important in how Java understands your program, keeping your program organized and making it easy to read is important, so you should follow the conventions in the examples used in this book. Next you will place the object declaration code in the BeanJar program.

To place an object declaration code in the BeanJar program:

1. Use the mouse pointer to select the comment that reads **//Put Object Declarations here**, and then type the text *exactly as it appears* in Figure 1-28. Remember to delete the comment markers (//) this time. After typing each line of text, press the **Enter** key to go to the next line.

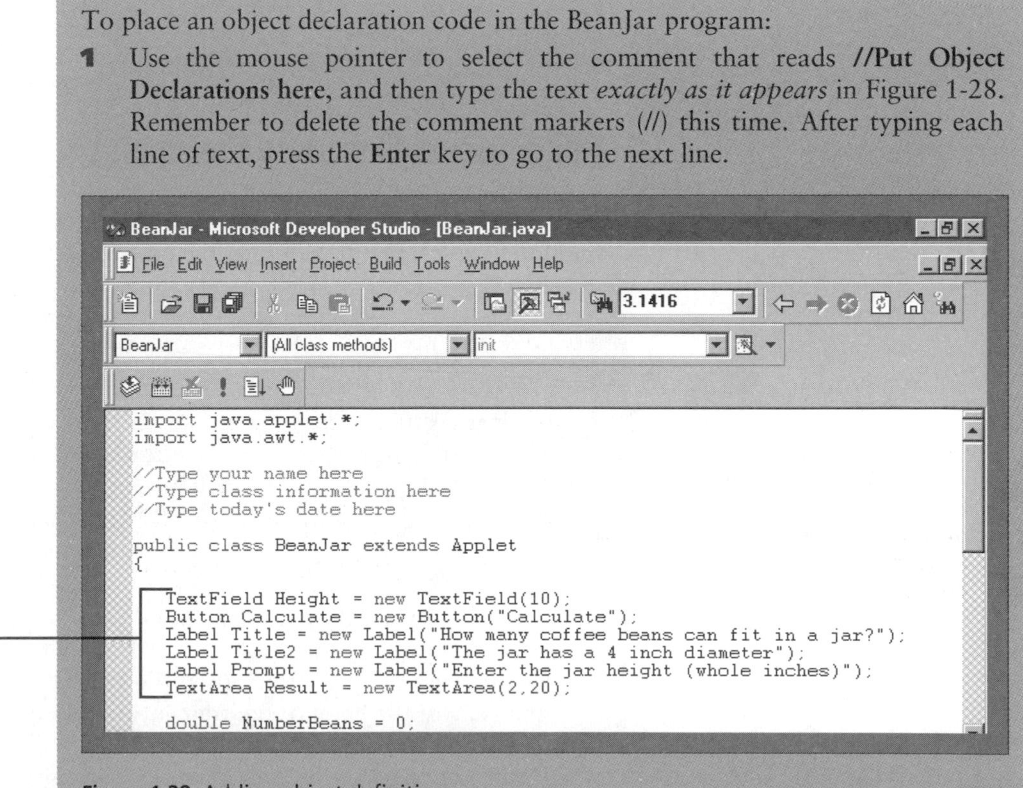

Figure 1-28: Adding object definitions

Placing the Objects in the Applet

The last code to place in the file actually "places" the object in the program. Declaring an object and using the object are two different things. A program can have many declared objects, but the objects are useless until they are included in an "action" part of the program.

To place objects in the applet:

1 Scroll down to the comment that reads **//Place the objects here**, and then select the comment and type the text *exactly as shown* in Figure 1-29. Press the **Enter** key after typing each line of text to go to the next line.

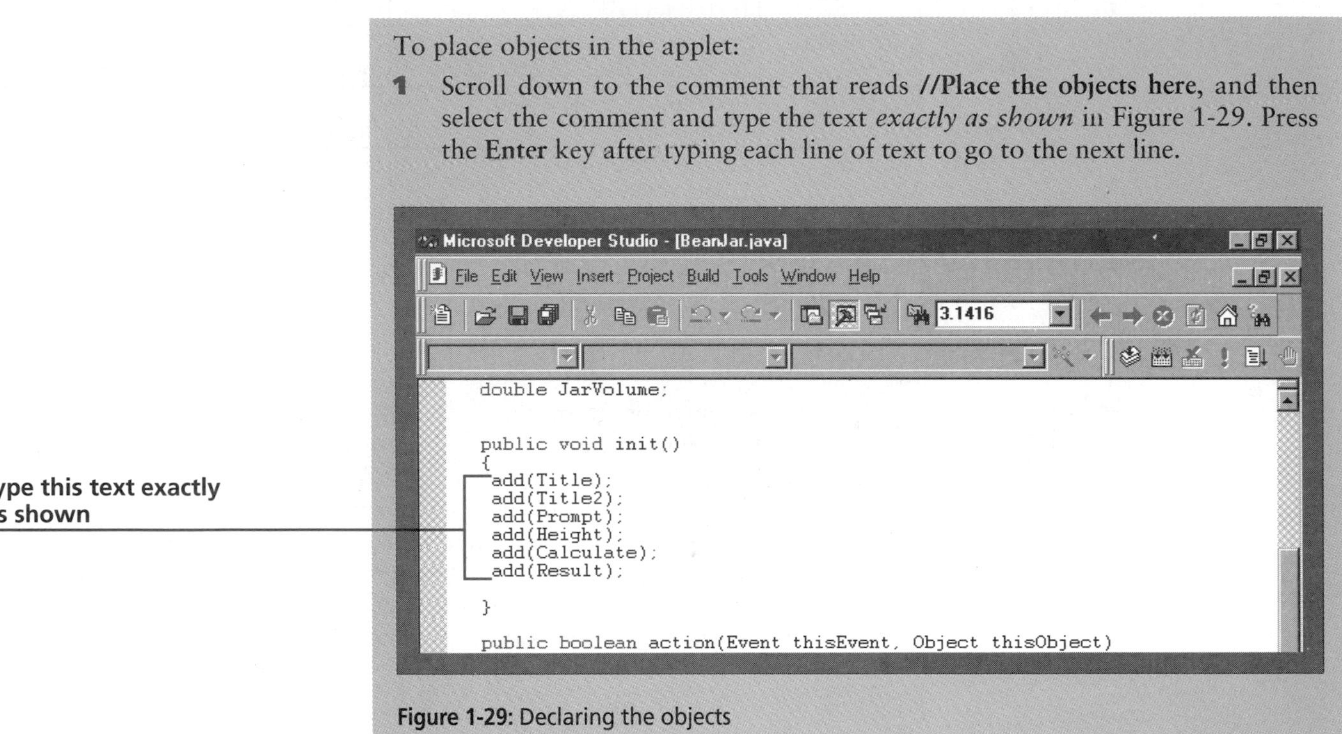

Figure 1-29: Declaring the objects

Building and Executing the Applet

Now that you have created and placed your objects in the program, it is time to build the applet. Before building, the new code must be checked for syntax errors.

tip

Always save your work before compiling, building, or executing a file. You also can save a file by pressing Ctrl + S.

To build the applet:

1 Click the **Save** button on the Standard toolbar to save your work.

2 Click the **Build** button  on the Build toolbar. A dialog box opens to tell you that this build command requires an active project workspace, and asks if you would like to create a default project workspace.

3 Click the **Yes** button to close the dialog box, create the workspace, and build the program.

HELP? If your Output window indicates that the program contains errors, check your typing against Figures 1-28 and 1-29 to make sure that you have not transposed any letters, used the wrong case, omitted the semicolons at the ends of the lines, or omitted any parentheses. Then save the file and click the Build button. If the Output window still indicates errors, contact your instructor or technical support person for assistance.

Now that you have built the program, you can execute the applet.

To execute the applet:

1 Click the **Execute Program** button on the Build toolbar. The Information For Running Class dialog box opens, in which you can type the class filename. See Figure 1-30.

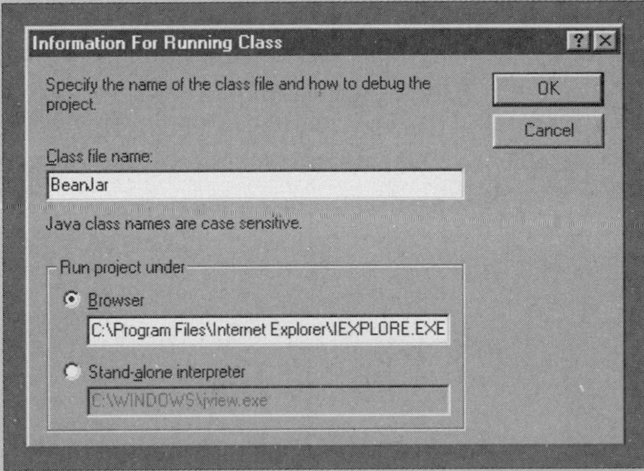

Figure 1-30: Information For Running Class dialog box

2 Type **BeanJar** in the Class file name text box, and then click the **OK** button. Internet Explorer starts and loads the BeanJar applet.

3 Click in the Enter the jar height text box, type 5, and then click the **Calculate** button. The applet calculates the number of beans that will fit in a jar with a 5-inch diameter, and then displays the results. See Figure 1-31.

Refresh button

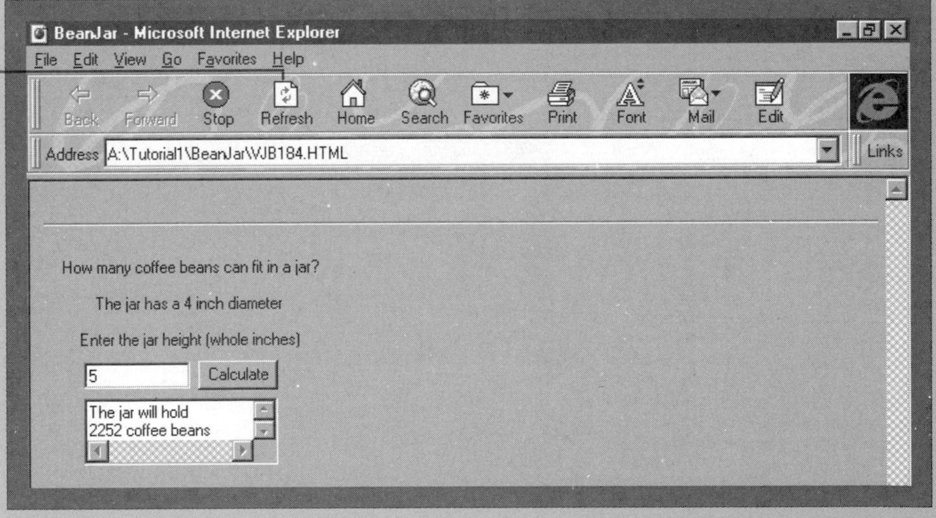

Figure 1-31: Executing the BeanJar applet

4 To run the applet again, click the **Refresh** button on the Internet Explorer toolbar. Now you can use the applet for a new calculation.

HELP? If the Internet Explorer toolbar does not display, click View on the menu bar, and then click Toolbar.

5 Close Internet Explorer and return to Visual J++.

Testing and Debugging an Applet

Now that you have executed your first program successfully, you need to know what to do when a program fails. Next you will see how to debug an applet. In Lesson A, you learned about three types of programming errors. To show how an IDE like Visual J++ makes debugging easier, you will change the BeanJar.java applet to create intentional syntax and logic errors.

To change the applet to make intentional errors:

1 Delete the semicolon from the end of the TextField Height line, as shown in Figure 1-32. This change will create a syntax error.

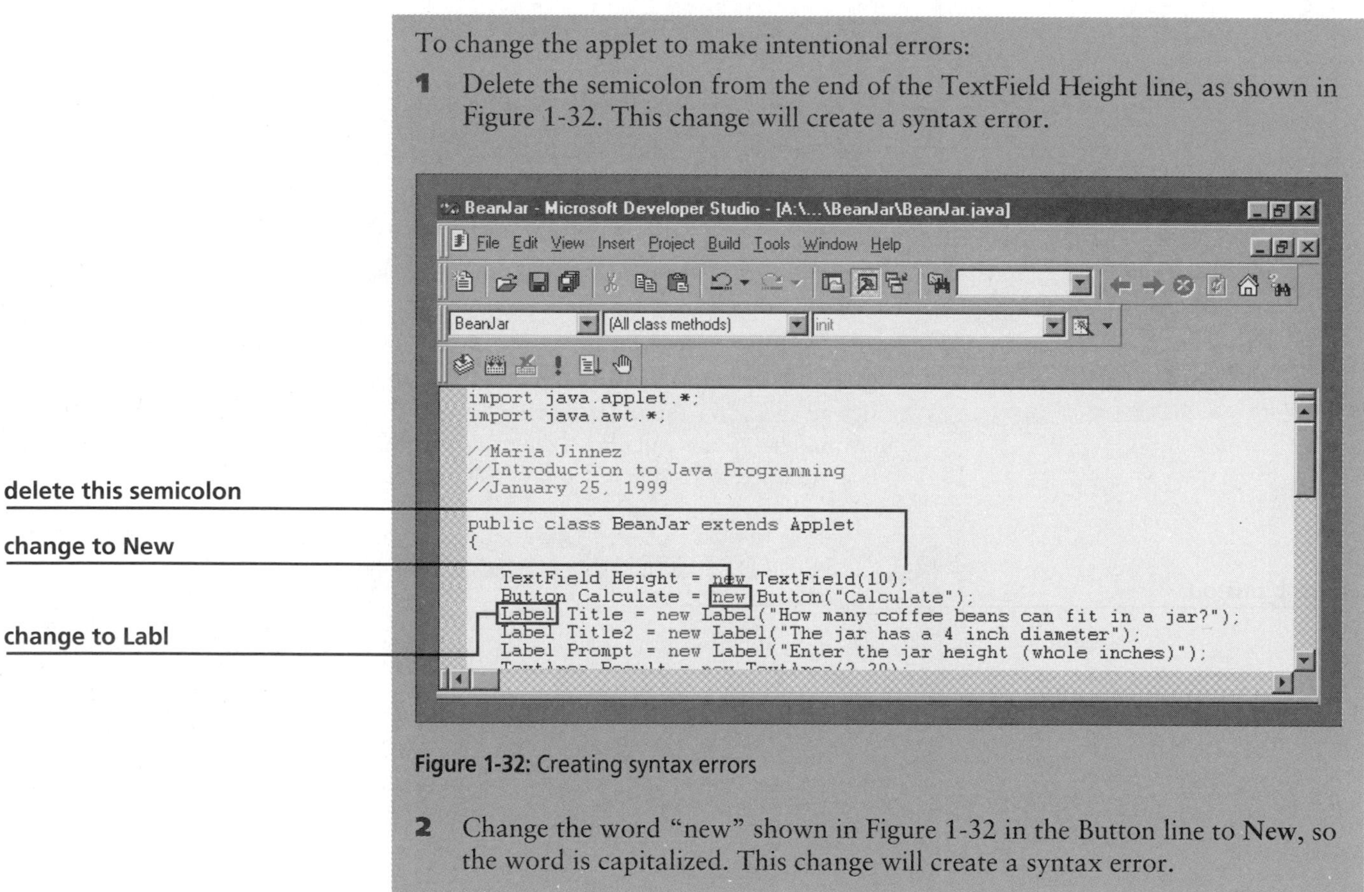

Figure 1-32: Creating syntax errors

2 Change the word "new" shown in Figure 1-32 in the Button line to New, so the word is capitalized. This change will create a syntax error.

3 Change the word "Label" shown in Figure 1-32 in the third line to **Labl** to create another syntax error. Make sure that your screen looks like the one shown in Figure 1-33.

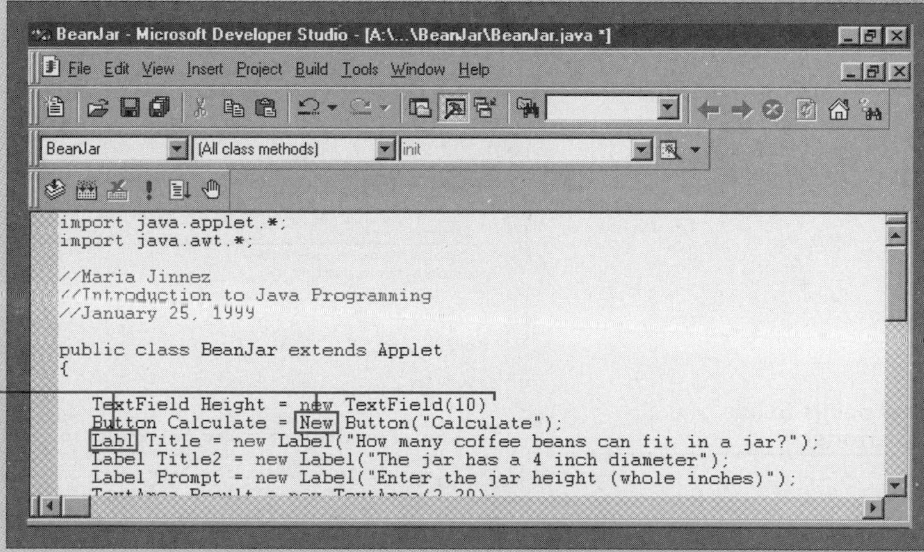

Figure 1-33: BeanJar file with intentional errors

4 Scroll down the window, and then change the 0.6 in the line that reads "NumberBeans = (JarVolume / bean) * 0.6;" to **60**. This change will create a logic error.

Before building the applet, you should save your work. Remember to save your work frequently, as you never know when a system problem might cause your work to be lost.

To save your changes and then build the applet:

1 Click the **Save** button on the Standard toolbar to save your work. Now you can build the program again to see what happens when errors are reported.

2 Click the **Build** button on the Build toolbar to build the program. The Output window reports four errors. You must debug the program to correct these errors.

3 Press the **F4** key to highlight the first error message, "Expected ';'". Notice the arrow in the Editor window that points to the line following the line that is missing the semicolon. See Figure 1-34. When a semicolon is missing, the arrow points to the next line, because this is when the error was detected.

arrow points to line with error(s)

error selected

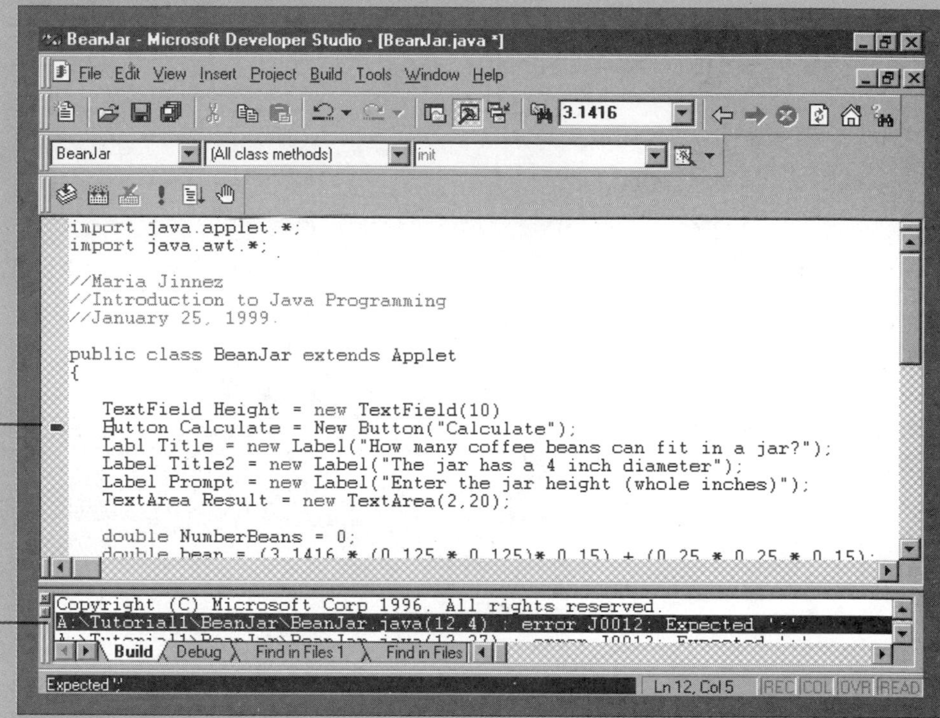

Figure 1-34: Location of first error message

4 Click the mouse pointer at the end of the TextField Height line, and then type ; at the end of the line to correct this omission.

5 Press the **F4** key again to see the next error. This error message appears at the bottom of the screen, as shown in Figure 1-35.

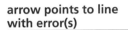

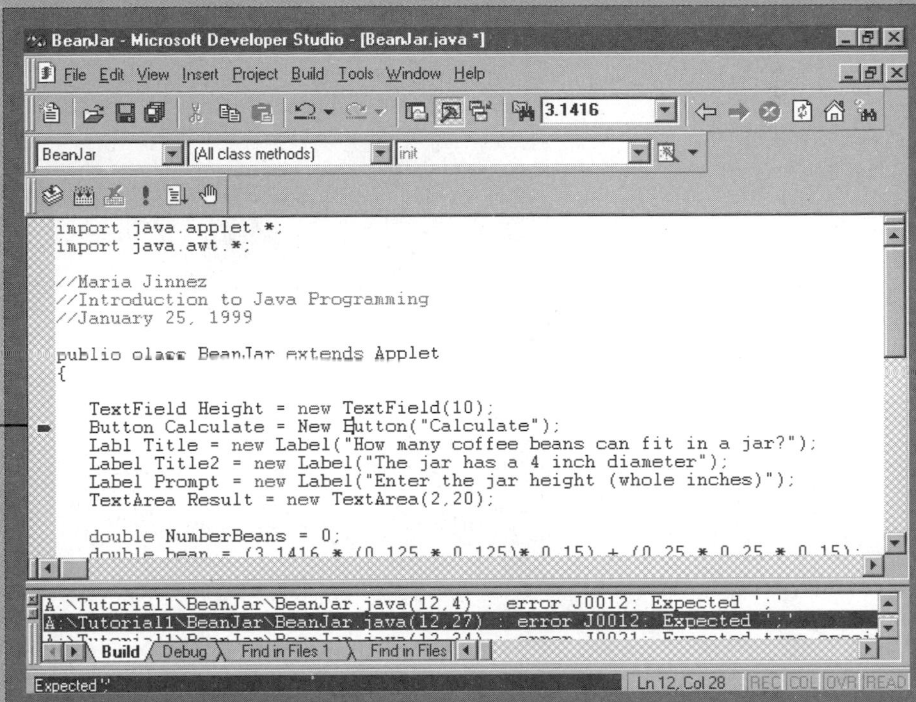

Figure 1-35: Location of second error message

6 Change the word "New" to **new** to correct the error, and then press the **F4** key to go to the next error. This error is from the same programming error that you just corrected. There are two reasons why you would know that this is a second error message from the same mistake. The first indication is that the location of the error is on the same line, only a few characters away. Because the error message states that there is a missing semicolon, the compiler expected a new line, so this message points to the fact that there was a major mistake earlier in the line. The other reason is that you found (and put) only one error on that line. Sometimes one mistake can generate more than one error message. Because you fixed this error, you can go to the next error message.

7 Press the **F4** key again to see the last error message. The arrow still points to the same line. There is a discrepancy between what the compiler is looking for and what is in the program, so the build process has stopped without finding the last error. To find the last error, click the **Build** button on the Build toolbar, and then press the **F4** key to see the error. Now you should see only one error message, as shown in Figure 1-36.

8 Change the word "Labl" to **Label** to correct the error.

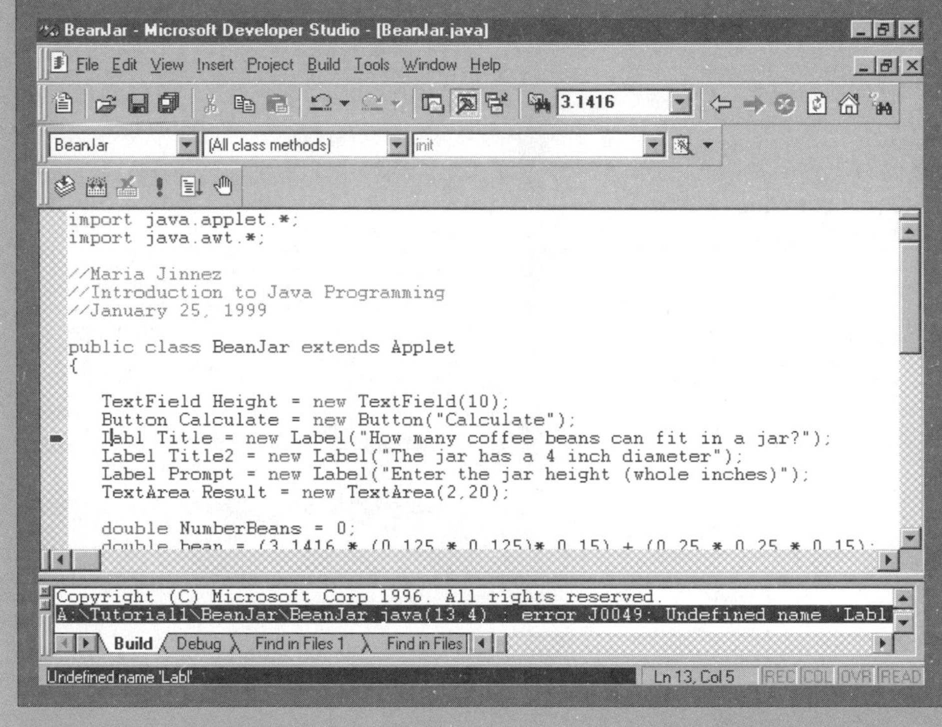

Figure 1-36: BeanJar file after second build

HELP? Your arrow might point to a different line, even though the same error message is displayed as shown in Figure 1-36.

You will find that as you become more proficient in Java you will be able to find and correct syntax errors quickly and easily. Now that you have corrected your programming errors, you can save the file, rebuild it, and run it again.

To save the file, rebuild it, and run it:

1 Click the **Save** button on the Standard toolbar to save your work.

2 Click the **Build** button on the Build toolbar. You should see zero errors in the Output window. If the Output window locates any errors, check your typing and make any necessary corrections.

3 Click the **Execute Program** button on the Build toolbar. The applet runs in Internet Explorer. You should test it to make sure it works correctly.

HELP? If a dialog box opens and asks to rebuild out of date or missing files, click the Yes button to rebuild them.

4 Type 5 in the Enter the jar height text box, and then click the **Calculate** button. See Figure 1-37. When you calculated the number of beans earlier, the result was 2252; now it is 225230! You need to correct this logic error from your program.

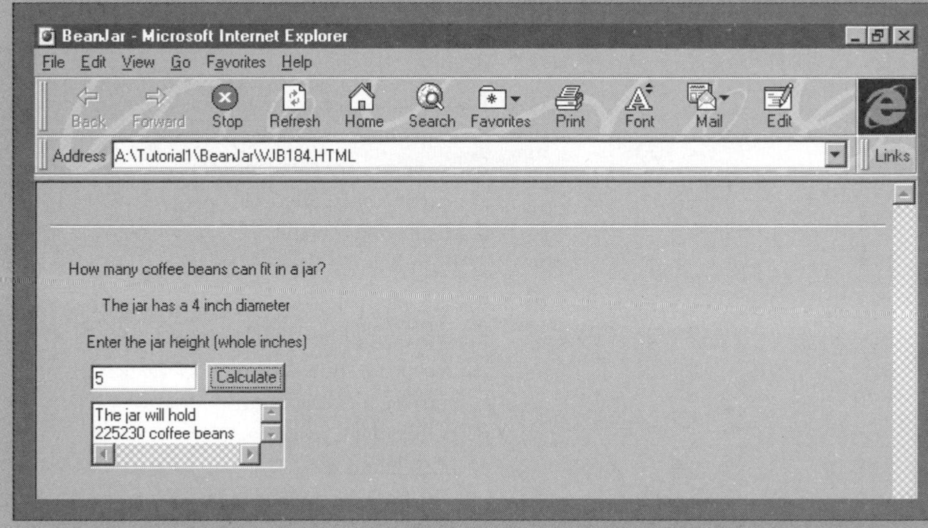

Figure 1-37: Logic error in applet

5 Close Internet Explorer, and then change the 60 to **0.6**, so this line reads "NumberBeans = (JarVolume / bean) * 0.6;".

6 Save your work, rebuild the program, and then execute the program. Make sure that the program works correctly, and then close Internet Explorer.

7 Close your workspace and all document windows, and then close Visual J++.

Now you can take a break or complete the end-of-lesson questions and exercises.

S U M M A R Y

- A TOE chart specifies the tasks, events, and objects of a program.
- To close a workspace:
  Click File on the menu bar.
  Click Close Workspace.
  Click the Yes button to close all windows.
- To open a single Java file in Visual J++:
  Click the Open button on the Standard toolbar.
  Change the Files of type to Java Files (*.java).
  Select the drive and folder that contains the file you want to open.
  Double-click the filename.
- The syntax used to declare an object is *ObjectType ObjectName* = new *ObjectType* (*arguments*);.
- To debug an applet, press the F4 key to locate the error in the file and to see the error message.

QUESTIONS

1. Common GUI elements in Java include __________.
   a. text boxes
   b. buttons
   c. dialog boxes
   d. all of the above
2. For which of the following tasks could you use a label?
   a. explaining the applet purpose
   b. accepting shoeSize input
   c. starting a calculation
   d. displaying a result
   e. both b and d
3. For which of the following tasks could you use a text field?
   a. explaining the applet purpose
   b. accepting shoeSize input
   c. starting a calculation
   d. displaying a result
   e. both b and d
4. For which of the following tasks could you use a button?
   a. explaining the applet purpose
   b. accepting shoeSize input
   c. starting a calculation
   d. displaying a result
   e. both b and d
5. Which item below shows an incorrect method of marking a comment?
   a. //a comment
   b. */a comment /*
   c. /*a comment*/
   d. //a comment//
6. Java is case sensitive for which of the following items?
   a. reserved words
   b. object names
   c. filenames
   d. all of the above
7. Which of the following statements is a correct declaration of a button object?
   a. Button OK("OK");
   b. Button OK = new Button("OK");
   c. button OK = New button("OK");
   d. button ok("OK") = new Button;
8. You can press the __________ key to identify errors that occur after building or compiling a file.
   a. F4
   b. F1
   c. Alt + ?
   d. F10
9. What occurs during the testing and debugging phase of program design?
10. If you have three errors in your program, is there any way to predict how many error messages the compiler will report? Why?

EXERCISES

1. In this exercise, open the TS.java file from the TripSeconds folder in the Exercises folder on your Student Disk, and then use the Save As command to save the file as TripSeconds.java.
   a. Add your name, class information, and date as comments.
   b. Replace the //place objects here comment with the following:

GUI ELEMENT	NAME	ARGUMENTS
Label	Title	"Trip time in seconds"
Label	lblHours	"How many hours"
Label	lblMinutes	"How many minutes"
Label	lblSeconds	"How many seconds"
TextField	Hours	5
TextField	Minutes	5
TextField	Seconds	5
Button	Calculate	"Calculate"
TextField	Result	20

   c. Replace the // add objects here line with the following code:

```
add(Title);
add(lblHours)
add(Hours);
add(lblMinutes);
add(Minutes);
add(lblSeconds);
add(Seconds);
add(Calculate);
add(Result);
```

   d. Save, build, and execute the applet. The class name is TripSeconds.
   e. Use the applet to calculate the trip time for 4 hours, 15 minutes, and 36 seconds in total seconds.
   f. Close the applet and then close the workspace.

2. In this exercise, open the ER.java file in the ExpenseReport folder in the Exercises folder on your Student Disk, and then use the Save As command to save the file as ExpenseReport.java.
   a. Add your name, class information, and date as comments.
   b. Replace the //place objects here comment with the following:

GUI ELEMENT	NAME	ARGUMENTS
Label	Title	"Expense Report"
Label	lblHotel	"Hotel Bill"
Label	lblTransport	"Transportation Cost"
Label	lblFood	"Food Expense"
TextField	Hotel	10
TextField	Transport	10
TextField	Food	10
Button	Calculate	"Calculate"
TextField	Total	20

c. Replace the // add objects here line with the following code:

```
add(Title);
add(lblHotel)
add(Hotel);
add(lblTransport);
add(Transport);
add(lblFood);
add(Food);
add(Calculate);
add(Total);
```

d. Save, build, and execute the applet. The class name is ExpenseReport.

e. Use the applet to calculate the total expenses for a $359 hotel bill, $59 in transportation costs, and $68 in food costs.

f. Close the applet and then close the workspace.

3. In this exercise, open the Lightning.java file from the Lightning folder in the Exercises folder on your Student Disk, and then use the Save As command to save the file as myLightning.java.

a. Change the line in the program that reads "public class Lightning extends Applet" to "public class myLightning extends Applet".

b. Print the file by clicking the File on the menu bar, and then clicking Print. Click the OK button. Make the following changes to the file, and then write down the error messages (or what happens) after making each change by building the file:

- Remove the import statements
- Remove "extends Applet"
- Change the 5 in the distance calculation to 10

c. Correct the mistakes by returning them to their original state.

d. Close the program without saving changes.

4. In this exercise, open the Jogging.java file from the Jogging folder in the Exercises folder on your Student Disk, and then use the Save As command to save the file as myJog.java.

a. Rename the class in the line that reads "public class Jogging extends Applet" to "public class myJog extends Applet".

b. Print the file by clicking the File on the menu bar, and then clicking Print. Click the OK button. Make the following changes to the file, and then write down the error messages (or what happens) after making each change by building the file. Record the error messages (or what happens) after each change.

- Change "init" to "Init"
- Delete the arguments from the "public boolean action (Event theEvent, Object theObject)"
- Change the 475 calories in the calculation to 47500 calories

c. Correct the mistakes back to the original.

d. Close the applet without saving changes.

TUTORIAL

2

Understanding and Using Objects

Creating Objects for an Online Order Entry Applet for Koffee Koncoctions International

case The BeanJar applet that you worked on in Tutorial 1 for Koffee Koncoctions International is coming along nicely. To help organize your work for this week, you decide to compile a list of things to accomplish. Your list includes:

1. Learn about objects and object-oriented programming
2. Talk with Maria about the order entry program you will create using Visual J++ and Java
3. Create the objects for the order entry program

In this tutorial you will learn about objects and object-oriented programming. You will put these concepts to work in Lessons B and C to develop objects for the order entry program for Koffee Koncoctions International.

LESSON A

objectives

In this lesson you will learn how to:

- Describe the difference between structured analysis and object-oriented design
- Define an object and its parts
- Describe the difference between an instance and a class of objects
- Design simple and super objects
- Describe inheritance in super objects

Understanding Objects

Using Object-Oriented Design Methods

There are two basic approaches to program design. Both approaches focus on taking a problem and breaking it into smaller problems or pieces, in a process known as **decomposition**. The first design method is structured analysis. **Structured analysis** is the process of designing a program based on the functions that the program will perform. For example, Figure 2-1 shows a task breakdown structure chart for a banking system that was designed using this method.

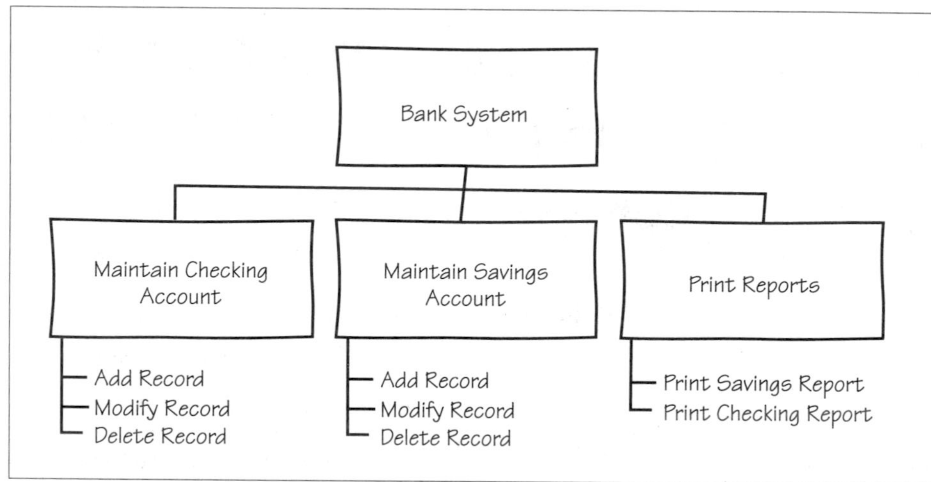

Figure 2-1: Task breakdown structure chart for a banking system

A **task breakdown structure chart** is a graphical way of representing the parts of a program to be developed. Figure 2-1 shows that the banking system consists of three major parts. The first part maintains checking account records, the second part maintains savings account records, and the third part prints reports. You might notice that the parts under the maintaining checking and savings account records are identical. Each process has three parts: add record, modify record, and delete record. The printing process is broken into the reports that the program produces.

The second method of program design is object-oriented design. **Object-oriented design** is the process of breaking apart a problem by looking at the data and activities to be performed on that data. In other words, you must consider the programs as data first and then as functions so you can develop code that can be used many times by many different programs. Object-oriented design also can be represented graphically using an **object structure chart**, such as the one shown in Figure 2-2 that shows the object structure chart for an account.

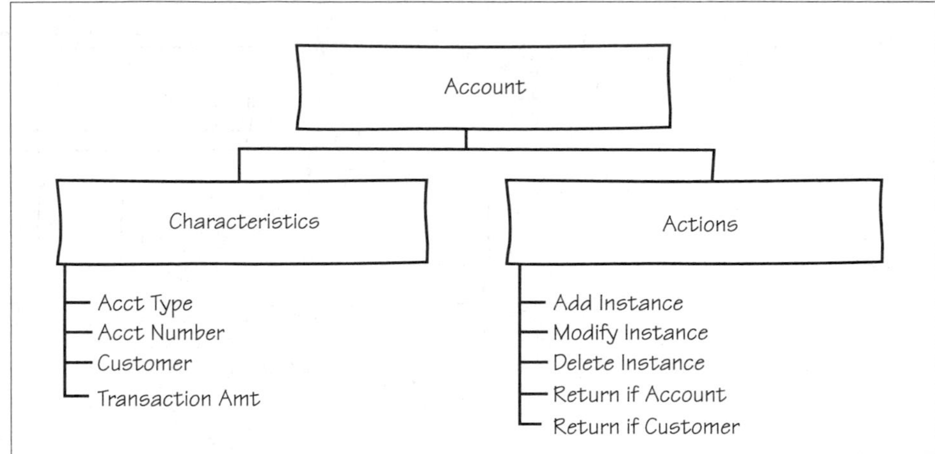

Figure 2-2: Object structure chart for the account object

The object structure chart shown in Figure 2-2 is headed by the name of the object that you want to define. The object name box in Figure 2-2 has two child boxes—one for characteristics and one for actions. The data items of the object appear under the characteristics box, and the functions that can be performed on the characteristics are listed under the actions box.

The first major breakdown of the program is based on the data that the program processes. This breakdown does not have duplicate functions for adding, modifying, or deleting records because the type of account record is kept in the data items. Eliminating duplicate functions decreases the size of the program because you do not have to create subprograms that are written using the same code, only for a different set of data.

Understanding Objects

An **object** is anything that can be described in terms of its characteristics and actions. Take something that you are familiar with—such as a baseball, football, tennis ball, or a basketball—if you can see these items, you should be able to describe them, and if you can describe them, then they must be objects. These items are all examples of a simple object called a ball. You can describe the ball's characteristics and the activities that can be performed with a ball in an object structure chart, as shown in Figure 2-3.

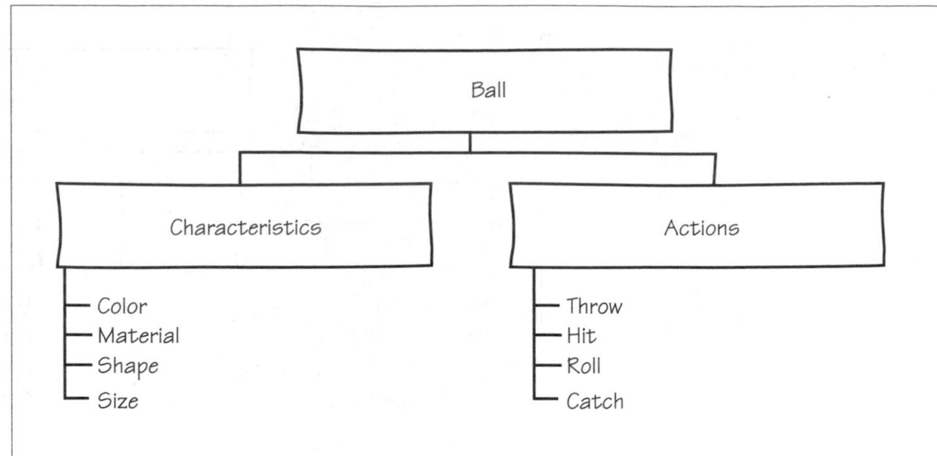

Figure 2-3: Ball object structure chart

This chart illustrates that a ball is made up of certain characteristics and actions that can be done with it. The characteristics are color, material, shape, and size. You can describe each ball using this list. For example, a baseball is white, made of leather, round, and small; a football is brown, made of pigskin, oval in shape, and medium in size. You can describe each ball with the same set of characteristics.

Next you must consider the list of actions that can be performed using each ball. Your object structure chart shows that a ball can be thrown, hit, rolled, and caught. Each type of ball can be used to perform these actions. The fact that objects have similar characteristics and actions is an important concept because it allows a programmer to name a large group of things that have similar characteristics and actions that are performed on them. Using objects allows a programmer to use the same code many different times for each of the different objects that are in a program. However, how can you use this method to show that a football is different than a baseball? After all, baseballs and footballs are different balls, even though they have similar characteristics and actions. These balls are just different instances of the ball object.

An **instance** of another object is an object with the characteristics of the specified object. An object is the general definition of the item (such as ball), while the instance is a specific occurrence of the item (such as baseball). Footballs and baseballs are both balls, but they represent different instances of the ball object. The concept of an object is easy to apply to other items, as well. For example, all ice cream objects share the same characteristics and actions, and the different flavors are instances of the ice cream object. A car object has different instances based on the different models. Abstract objects, on the other hand, are not as easy to describe. An **abstract object** is an object that you cannot touch or see but that you can describe. Computer programs use abstract objects, which are known as data objects.

Data objects are not different from physical objects—a data object has characteristics and actions that can be described, just as physical objects do. Data objects can be objects just like balls, ice cream, or cars. Data objects are abstract objects, and physical objects are concrete objects. For example, you cannot see your checking account, but it does exist in the form of transactions and balances. Another example is a retail catalog organization that maintains a mailing list of its customers. An object structure chart for one customer of the retail company is shown in Figure 2-4.

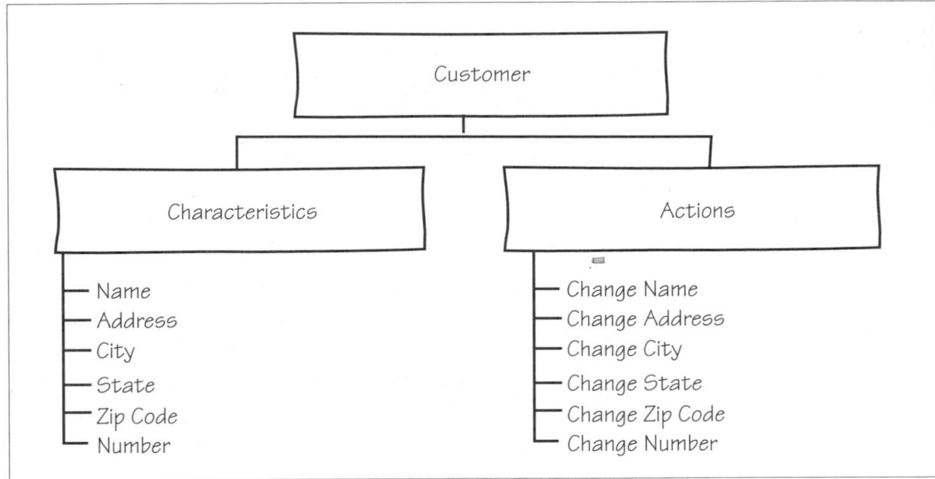

Figure 2-4: Object structure chart for the customer object

In this chart the customer object is made up of the characteristics of name, address, city, state, zip code, and customer number. The actions are change a name, change an address, change a city, change a state, change a zip code, and change a customer number. These actions can be performed on any instance of the customer object.

The parts of an object are characteristics and actions but in programming characteristics are called properties (or a property list) and actions are called **methods**. You can describe the physical objects around you based on their properties and methods. You also can express a programming problem using objects, but you must design the objects first.

Designing Simple Objects

You can use a four-step process to design an object: name the object, define the properties of the object, describe the methods of the object, and combine the object information in an object structure chart.

Step 1: Name the Object

Objects are described in terms of their properties and methods, but also by name. If you cannot name an object, then you might be considering something that is a collection of objects or something that is not an object at all. Consider the ball object again. You can name the object as a ball, so you pass the first test of defining an object.

Step 2: Define the Properties of the Object

The **properties** (or **property list**) of an object are the characteristics that allow you to describe specific instances of the object. You must be careful when defining the properties of an object to make sure that there are enough properties to ensure that different instances of the object will not occur with the same instance values. In other words, instance one and instance two of the same object should not be the same. Consider the ball again. The ball properties are color, material, size, and shape. You need to see if any of the ball objects have the same values for these properties. If they do not, then you can conclude that your property list is sufficient to describe the characteristics of a ball.

Step 3: Describe the Methods

Now you need to make a list of the actions that can be performed on your object. The purpose of this task is to make sure that you described all of the methods that you want to perform with the ball. The ball methods are throw, hit, roll, and catch. Your next task is to describe the methods using messages.

A **message** is a way that the methods of an object communicate with other objects or are given information that controls the actions performed on the object itself. This process is known as **message passing.** For example, consider the retail catalog example. The change method name method must know what value the name property should have so it can perform its task. In this case these messages are parameters to the method. The **parameter** of a method is a list of the data items it will need to perform its work.

When defining a physical object, you must consider the methods and what information is needed by them. The first method to consider is the roll method—a ball rolls a given distance based on certain conditions, such as the amount of force that is placed behind the ball and the shape of the ball. Your current definition of the ball object already includes information about the shape of the ball. However, there was no information about force so you will need to make force a part of the parameter list of the roll method. For the throw method, you will need to know the force and direction of the throw so these actions become part of the parameter list of the throw method. There are no parameters for the catch method—there is only one way to catch a ball. For the hit method, you must know the force and direction to perform the action of hit.

The message communication is not just to the method; sometimes the method will return information back to the object that caused the action to be performed. This concept is known as the **return value.** The return value might be nothing or something. When the return value is nothing, then you use the term **void** to describe the situation. When the method needs to communicate back to the method, then you need to specify what it needs to communicate. For the ball object, the throw, hit, and roll methods might communicate the distance back to the object that caused the action to be performed. The catch method should communicate whether the catch was successful or not. You create your list of object methods with the method name first, the list of information passed to the method placed in parentheses, followed by the return value. Your list of methods is:

throw (force, direction) distance
hit (force, direction) distance
roll (force) distance
catch () success?

Step 4: Combine the Information in an Object Structure Chart

The last step is to define the object in an object structure chart by drawing a box at the top of the page and then placing the name of the object in the box. Then connect this box on the next line to two boxes that have the titles properties and methods. Under the property box you make a list of the characteristics of the object. Under the methods box you list the methods you defined in Step 3. Figure 2-5 shows the object structure chart for the ball object.

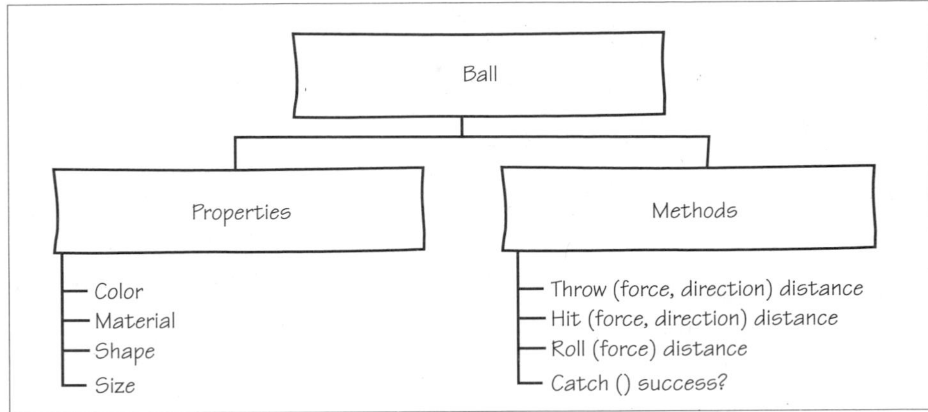

Figure 2-5: Object structure chart for the ball object

After completing these four steps, you can develop your object into Java code. Sometimes you have to consider what happens if your object is not used alone. For instance, a baseball usually is used with a bat and glove, and a tennis ball is used with a racket. For the purpose of this discussion, you will call a baseball, bat, and glove a baseball set, and a tennis ball and tennis racket a tennis set. You can name these groups of objects so there must be a way of defining them as objects, as well. Groups of objects are known as super objects.

Designing Super Objects

As you know, some objects are really combinations of multiple objects. There are additional things that you can do with a group of objects that you cannot do with just one of the objects in the group. A **super object** is an object that has other objects as part of its property list. When objects are combined in super objects, the super object has use of all of the properties and methods of the objects it contains. This concept is called inheritance. **Inheritance** is the capability of a super object to inherit, or use, all of the methods and properties of the objects it contains. When super objects are created, they often have more methods and properties than just the combination of the methods and properties of their objects. The super object can contain objects as some of its properties as well as the properties unique to the super object. In addition, unique methods can be included in the methods definition of a super object.

Consider your checking account again. A banking system processes more than just accounts. The bank has employees and other interests such as investments. The banking system has two major objects—accounts and personnel. Figure 2-6 shows the object structure chart of the bank super object.

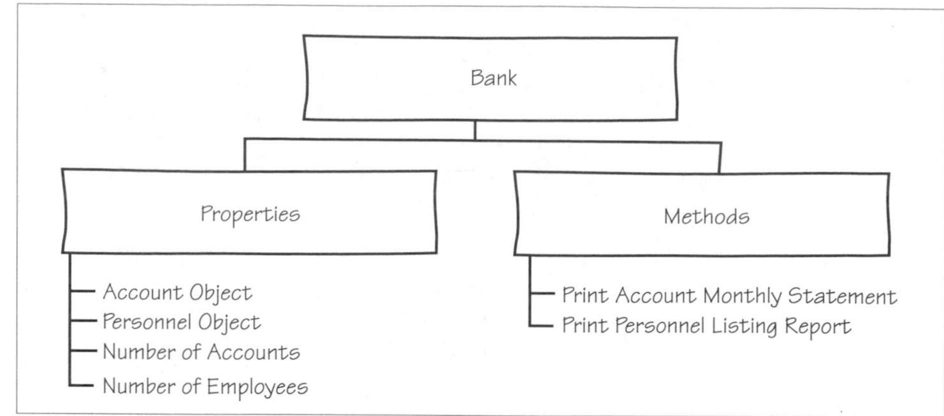

Figure 2-6: Object structure chart for the bank super object

You will notice from this example that the bank object is the super object and it contains two objects in its property list—account and personnel. Each object is defined in a separate object structure chart so the programmer refers to the structure charts of these two objects for information about them.

Also, there are some additional properties that are not part of any of the objects in the property list. The unique properties are number of accounts and number of employees. In the methods section, there are also some unique methods listed that are not part of the account or personnel objects. These methods are defined as account monthly statement and personnel listing report. The personnel and account objects define only the form and not the instance of the respective objects, so when these objects are contained in a super object, you might have a list of account objects and a list of personnel objects. If you have a list of objects, you can generate reports about multiple instances of the object in the program. The most important thing to remember about a super object is that it has properties that are themselves objects. Anything that you can do with an object can be done with a super object.

The tennis set consists of two simple objects—a ball and a racket. To characterize the tennis set, you need to know the number of rackets and the number of balls. The tennis super object has methods for serve and return. Figure 2-7 shows the object structure chart for the tennis super object.

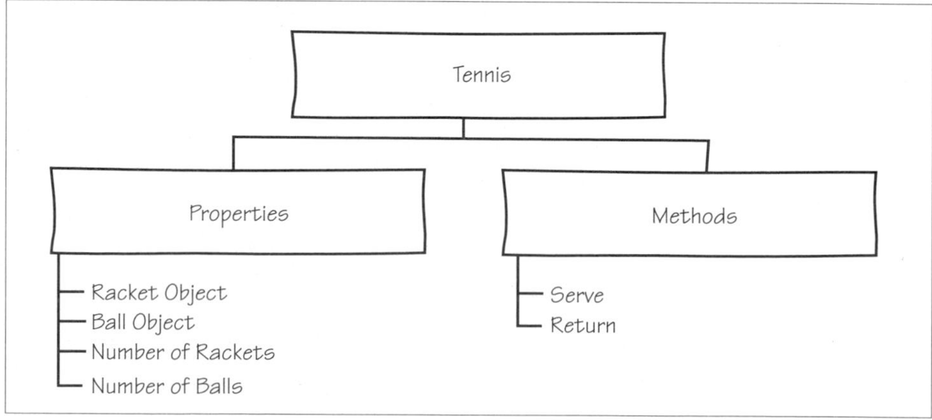

Figure 2-7: Object structure chart for the tennis super object

One of the powerful aspects of inheritance is that the methods of the super object can use methods of the simple objects to perform their tasks. For example, the serve method for the tennis super object could use the throw and hit methods of the ball object. You will use this information in Lessons B and C to work on the order entry program for Koffee Koncoctions.

Now you can take a break or complete the end-of-lesson questions and exercises.

SUMMARY

- The two types of design methods used in designing computer programs are structured analysis and object-oriented design. Structured analysis breaks down the problem into programmable pieces by focusing on the tasks of the program to be developed. Object-oriented design breaks down the problem by considering the data objects that are needed to solve the problem.
- An object is anything that can be described in terms of its characteristics (or properties) and actions (or methods).
- An object can describe a class of objects or a specific instance in that class. For example, a ball and a baseball are both objects where ball is the class definition and baseball is an instance of the ball object.
- Objects are defined by naming the object, defining the object's properties, and then defining the object's methods. An object structure chart is a way of specifying the design of the object in a graphical format.
- Methods of objects might communicate with other objects or programs. This communication is achieved through message passing. Messages that are passed to an object's methods are called parameters, while messages that the object's method sends back to the object are called return values.
- Super objects are objects that contain other objects as part of their property lists.
- Super objects can use all of the properties and methods of the objects that they contain. In object-oriented programming, this concept is called inheritance.

QUESTIONS

1. Which design method breaks down a problem based on the tasks the program must complete to solve it?
   a. debugging
   b. object-oriented design
   c. structured analysis
   d. coding
2. Which method defines a program in terms of the data objects that the program needs?
   a. debugging
   b. object-oriented design
   c. structured analysis
   d. coding
3. The characteristics of an object are called its __________.
   a. methods
   b. properties
   c. parameters
   d. return value

4. The actions of an object are called its __________.
a. methods
b. properties
c. parameters
d. return value

5. The messages that are passed to an object's methods are called __________.
a. properties
b. inheritance
c. parameters
d. return value

6. The messages that are passed back from an object's method to the requesting program are called __________.
a. properties
b. inheritance
c. parameters
d. return values

7. A(n) __________ is an object that contains other objects as part of its property list.
a. class
b. super object
c. object method
d. instance

8. When an object's properties are given specific values then it becomes a(n) __________ of an object.
a. instance
b. method
c. parameter
d. class

9. The ability of a super object to use the methods and properties of the objects it contains is called __________.
a. communication
b. structured analysis
c. inheritance
d. message passing

10. A super object __________ have properties and methods that are unique to the super object and not defined in the objects it contains.
a. can
b. cannot

EXERCISES

1. List the steps that are needed to define an object.
2. Create an object structure chart of a baseball bat object. Assume that the object has the properties of length, material, and weight and the method of swing.
3. Assume that a baseball set object consists only of a ball and bat object. Create an object structure chart for this super object. Consider what additional properties and methods the baseball set has.
4. What are the properties for the geometric objects of a square, rectangle, and circle object?
5. Define an object named bicycle that has the properties number of wheels, number of speeds, type of brakes, type of frame, and manufacturer. The methods include speed of cycle, brake distance of cycle, and distance traveled. Show your design of this object by creating an object structure chart.
6. Define an object named dog, and complete an object structure chart of your definition.
7. You are helping a local car dealership create a program to keep track of its inventory. Design an object named car, and create an object structure chart of the definition.
8. You work for a retail catalog company that sells shoes, and you are creating an inventory system. Define an object named shoe, and specify its definition in an object structure chart. Assume that the characteristics of shoe are type, gender, material, size, and color. The methods of the shoe are methods to change each property value in the object.
9. You work at a financial investment firm. This firm defines a portfolio as a list of stocks and a list of bonds. A stock object consists of the stock's company name, the current price per share, and the type of stock. A bond object consists of the term of the bond, the interest rate of the bond, and the bond's maturity date. Create a super object named portfolio that contains the stocks and bonds objects. Write down your design, but do not create an object structure chart.

LESSON B

objectives

In this lesson you will learn how to:

- **Describe and create the parts of a class object statement in Java**
- **Set the values of an instance of a class object with the assignment statement**
- **Set the value of an instance of a class object with the methods of the object**
- **Understand the standard Java library**
- **Use the import command to access functions in the Java packages**

Understanding Classes and Instances

Creating an Object with the Class Statement

A Java object is defined by a set of specific commands. A Java **command** is a sequence of keywords and user-supplied information that performs certain actions. The commands used in creating Java class objects specify the properties and methods of that object. A Java object consists of two parts—the object heading and the object body. The **object heading** is the portion of Java code that identifies the object to Java. The **object body** is the section of code that defines the properties and methods of the object. The **class statement** is the statement that allows you to define an object in Java. A Java program consists of parts to identify the environment, the object heading, the object body, and how to close the object body. You should define only one object, either simple or super, in a given file. Consequently, each file in a Java environment can be thought of as an object definition. Now, you are ready to find out what parts this file contains.

Part 1: Environment Information

The first piece of information in a Java program file is the **environment information**, which defines the object. Figure 2-8 shows the environment information for the ball object.

Line Number	Java Program Code
1	//Ball.java
2	import java.applet.*;
3	import java.awt.*;
4	import java.io.*;
5	<blank line>

Figure 2-8: Environment information for the ball object

Note: The lines in Figure 2-8 are numbered to make it easier to reference certain parts, but they are not included in a Java program file. Only the information in the Java program code column is included in the file. Also, blank lines in the program are indicated by the notation "<blank line>", but these notations are not typed in the program file.

The first line is a comment line that identifies the program. You learned in Tutorial 1 that comment lines can occur anywhere in a Java program. The comment markers (//) can occur anywhere in the program, even in the middle or at the end of a line. The comments contained in the environment section of the Java program might identify the contents of the file, its author, the date when the program was changed last, or information required by your instructor. In Figure 2-8, the comment identifies the filename of the object.

After the opening comments, the environment information section contains statements that are used to make some of the standard features of the Java language available to your object. These commands are called import commands, and they are shown in lines 2 through 4 in Figure 2-8. The **import command** is the reserved word *import* followed by the specification of the files you want to include. There is a separate import command for each group of functions that is imported.

Part 2: Object Heading

After the environment information section is the actual definition of the object in Java syntax. An object is made up of a heading and a body. Figure 2-9 shows the heading of the ball object.

Line Number	Java Program Code
1	//Ball.java
2	import java.applet.*;
3	import java.awt.*;
4	import java.io.*;
5	<blank line>
6	public class Ball extends Applet

Figure 2-9: Ball class object heading section

In line 6 you notice three keywords: *public*, *class*, and *extends*. The **public** keyword informs Java that the object and its contents should be made available to anyone who has access to where this file is stored. The **class** keyword is used to let Java know that you are defining an object. Objects in Java are called classes, rather than objects. The final keyword **extends** is used to tell Java that this object will be an extension of the applet object that is predefined in the Java language. In this book you will use the applet object because you are writing Java applets. You also need to supply some information for this class heading. The most important piece of information is the name of the class you are defining. Visual J++ requires that the first letter of the class name be capitalized.

Part 3: Object Body

The object body consists of the definition of the properties, constructors, and methods of the class object. The properties of the class object are the memory variable names that are used to hold the characteristics of the object. The **constructor section** is a special method that initializes the class property variables when a programmer creates a new instance of the object. The **methods section** of the body includes the definition of the methods that will be used on the class object. Figure 2-10 shows the property section for the Ball class object.

Line Number	Java Program Code
6	public class Ball extends Applet
7	{
8	//Properties section
9	String color = " ";
10	String material = " ";
11	String shape = " ";
12	String size = " ";
13	<blank line>

Figure 2-10: Ball class object property section

The body of the object starts with an opening brace ({) as shown in line 7 of Figure 2-10, followed by the definition of the property variables (color, material, shape, and size). The section starts with a comment line so that future programmers know that this is the property section. Following this comment on lines 9 through 12 of Figure 2-10 is the definition of the property variables. Each of these lines defines a characteristic that is designed into the object and a definition of the type of data it contains. The general format is to state the data type followed by a name for the property.

The next section of the body is the constructor method section that contains the constructor method. The **constructor method** always executes when a new instance of this class object is created by another program. Figure 2-11 shows the constructor section of the Ball class object.

Line Number	Java Program Code
9	String color = " ";
10	String material = " ";
11	String shape = " ";
12	String size = " ";
13	<blank line>
14	//Constructor method
15	Ball ()
16	{
17	color = " ";
18	material = " ";
19	shape = " ";
20	size = " ";
21	}
22	<blank line>

Figure 2-11: Ball class object constructor section

The constructor method consists of a heading and a body enclosed in an open and closing brace as shown in lines 16 through 21 in Figure 2-11. The commands shown in lines 17 through 20 of Figure 2-11 specify the initial value for the property.

The final section of the body of the Ball class object is the methods section shown in Figure 2-12.

Line Number	Java Program Code
14	//Constructor method
15	Ball ()
16	{
17	color = " ";
18	material = " ";
19	shape = " ";
20	size = " ";
21	}
22	<blank line>
23	//Methods section
24	public void setColorValue (String iValue)
25	{
26	color = iValue;
27	}
28	<blank line>
29	public void setMaterialValue (String iValue)
30	{
31	material = iValue;
32	}

Figure 2-12: Ball class object methods section

Many methods can be included in a Java object. The section begins with a comment designating that this is the methods section. Following this comment is the definition of the color methods of the class object, as shown in lines 24 through 27 in Figure 2-12. Each of the methods has a heading and a body. The heading of the first method is shown on line 24 of Figure 2-12. This line contains the public keyword, which has the same meaning as in the class statement. The public keyword is followed by the type of the return value; if the method does not return a value, then the word "void" appears, as shown in line 24. Following the return type is the name of the method and the parameter list enclosed in parentheses. The method name is specified by the programmer, and the parameter list inside the parentheses is the list of data items that is communicated to the method when it is used by another program. Lines 25 through 27 of Figure 2-12 show the body of this first method. This method also is enclosed in braces and contains Java commands that perform some action on the object. There is only one command (color) in the first method, and it is shown on line 26 of Figure 2-12. Lines 33 through 42 are not shown; they would define the other methods for the Ball class object.

Part 4: Closing the Class Object Body

The final part of the program file closes the class object body. Figure 2-13 shows the end of the Ball object file.

Line Number	Java Program Code
43	<blank line>
44	public String toString()
45	{
46	return "Color : " + color +
47	"\n" + "Material : " + material
48	"\n" + "Shape : " + shape +
49	"\n" + "Size : " + size + "\n");
50	}
51	}

Figure 2-13: Closing the ball class object

Notice that the body of the class statement ends with a closing brace (}). The instance of an object is different from the definition of the object. The instance of the object is an occurrence of the object with the values of the specified properties.

Specifying Property Values with the Assignment Statement

The class statement only defines the form and format of the object. In programming, you can use these forms to create actual data items that have the properties and methods defined in the class statement. This is a two-step process. The first step is to declare a memory location that has the form of the class you want to use. The second step is to specify the values of the properties in the instance of the object that you created. Figure 2-14 shows a portion of a program that completes this task.

Line Number	Java Program Code
1	//BallTest.java
2	import java.applet.*;
3	import java.awt.*;
4	import java.io.*;
5	<blank line>
6	public class BallTest extends Applet
7	{
8	//Instance of Ball object
9	Ball football = new Ball();
10	//Text area variable for browser display
11	TextArea ta = new TextArea(10,40);
12	<blank line>
13	public void init()
14	{
15	<blank line>
16	//Set property values
17	<blank line>
18	football.color = "brown";
19	football.material = "pigskin";
20	football.shape = "oval";
21	football.size = "medium";
22	<blank line>
23	//Display results on browser window
24	ta.setText("Football object... " + "\n" +
25	football + "\n");
26	add(ta);
27	<blank line>
28	}
29	}

Figure 2-14: Code to specify instance values

Line 9 of Figure 2-14 shows how to define a memory location with the form of the class object. Notice that the command consists of the following syntax:

<class name> <memory location name> = <initial value>;

The object that is declared in this program is a football. The football object has the class ball and is given an initial value that is a command. The command *new <class object> ()* creates a new memory location with the name football, and it executes the constructor method to assign empty values to the properties.

Lines 18 through 21 of Figure 2-14 are Java commands that specify the values of the properties so the object becomes a football instance of the Ball class object. In this example, the football's property values are set using the assignment statement. The syntax of the assignment statement is:

<receiving memory location> = <value or expression>;

Click the first Tutorial 2 link of the Online Companion for this book (http://www.course.com) to see a live Java program that illustrates this topic.

The receiving memory location in Figure 2-14 is named by using the instance of the object football, followed by a period, followed by the property that the program would assign a value. The equals sign (=) is called the **assignment operator** in Java, and it takes the value from the right side of the assignment statement and stores it in the memory location named on the left side. The value this program is storing is called a literal. A **literal** is where you specify exactly what you want to be stored in a type that is equal to the type of the memory location. This example uses words enclosed in quotation marks that are called **string literals**, and the actual sequence of characters will be stored in the named memory location.

On line 13 these commands are included in the init () method of this program file. The **init () method** is a special method in Java for use with applets. All commands that are contained in the init () method will execute automatically when the program file executes.

Now you are ready to program objects in Java. The definition of the Ball object already is saved in a file named Ball.java on your Student Disk.

To start Visual J++ and execute a Java program that uses a class object:

1. Start Visual J++ and close any open workspaces, if necessary.
2. Open the **BT.java** file from the Ball folder in the Tutorial2 folder on your Student Disk. The BT.java file opens in the Editor window.

   HELP? Close the Workspace window if necessary by right-clicking anywhere in the Workspace window, and then clicking Hide.

Remember to type the filename with the .java extension when saving files.

3. Click **File** on the menu bar, and then click **Save As** to save the file as **BallTest.java**.
4. Click in the location shown in Figure 2-15, press the **Enter** key, and then type the object instance code shown in Figure 2-15. This line of code will declare your football object as a named memory location and make it available for the rest of the program.

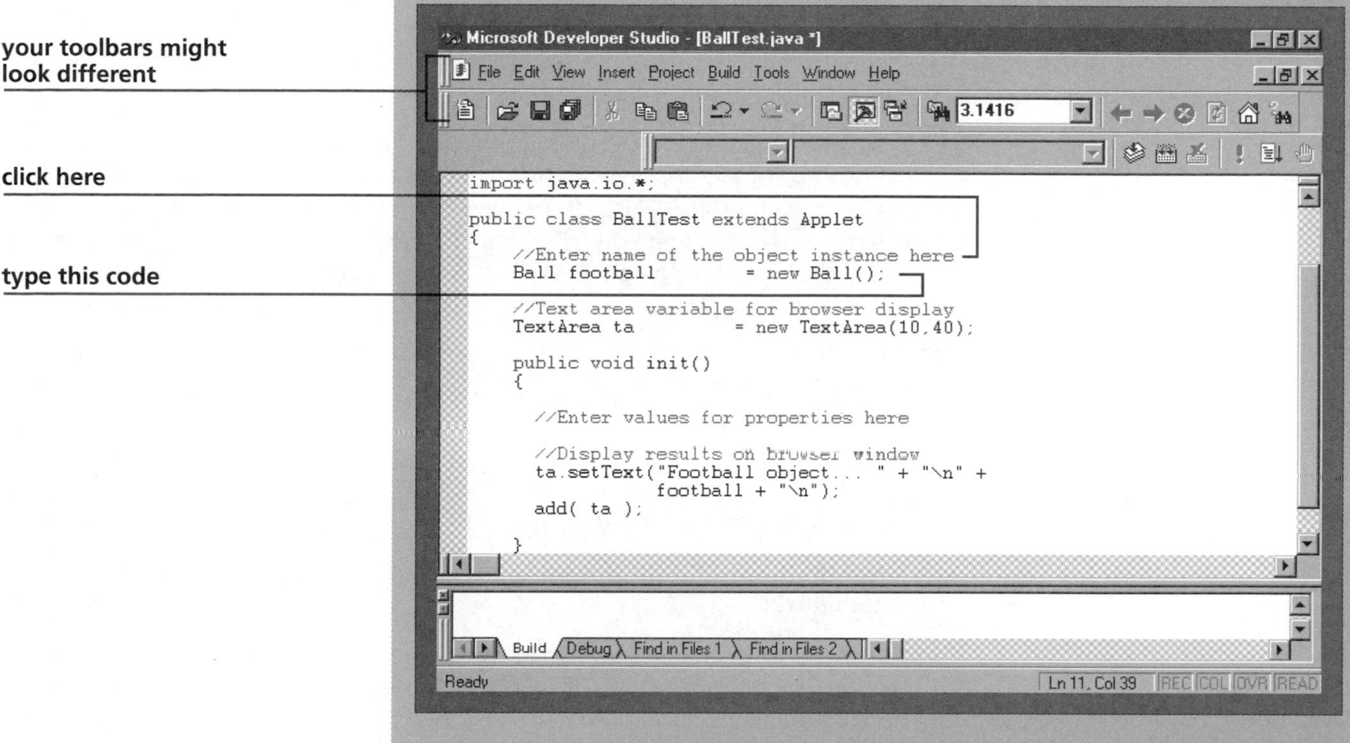

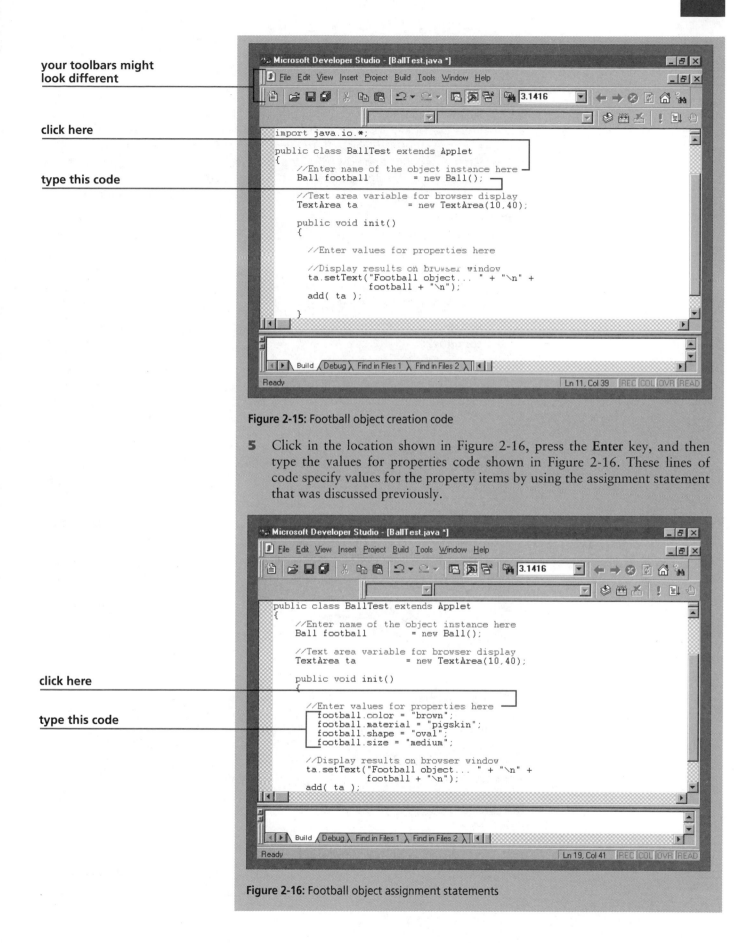

Figure 2-15: Football object creation code

5 Click in the location shown in Figure 2-16, press the **Enter** key, and then type the values for properties code shown in Figure 2-16. These lines of code specify values for the property items by using the assignment statement that was discussed previously.

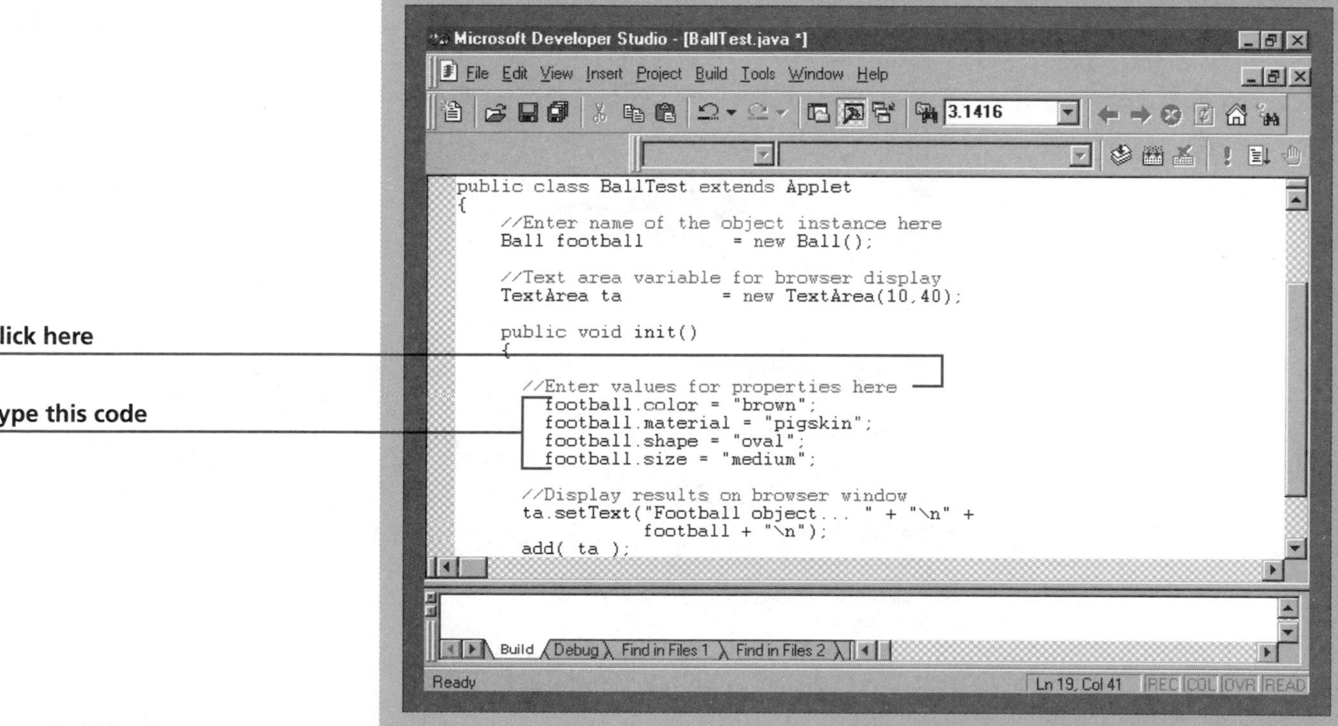

Figure 2-16: Football object assignment statements

6 Click the **Save** button on the Standard toolbar to save your changes.

7 Click the **Build** button on the Build toolbar to build the file. Click the **Yes** button to build the program in a default project workspace.

HELP? If your Output window indicates that the program contains errors, press the F4 key to move to the error location, and then check your typing against Figures 2-15 and 2-16 to make sure that you have not transposed any letters, used the wrong case, omitted the semicolons at the ends of the lines, or omitted any parentheses. Then click the Build button. If the Output window still indicates errors, ask your instructor or technical support person for help.

8 To use the HTML file on your Student Disk (instead of letting the compiler generate one), click **Project** on the menu bar, and then click **Settings.** The Project Settings dialog box opens.

9 Click the **Debug** tab, click the **Category** list arrow, and then click **Browser.** Click the **Use parameters from HTML page** option button, and then type **BallTest.html** in the HTML page text box. Click the **OK** button.

HELP? The HTML page might be set already. If it is, click the OK button to continue.

10 Click the **Execute Program** button on the Build toolbar to execute the program. The Information For Running Class dialog box opens. Type **BallTest** in the Class File name text box, and then click the **OK** button. Internet Explorer opens and executes the applet, as shown in Figure 2-17.

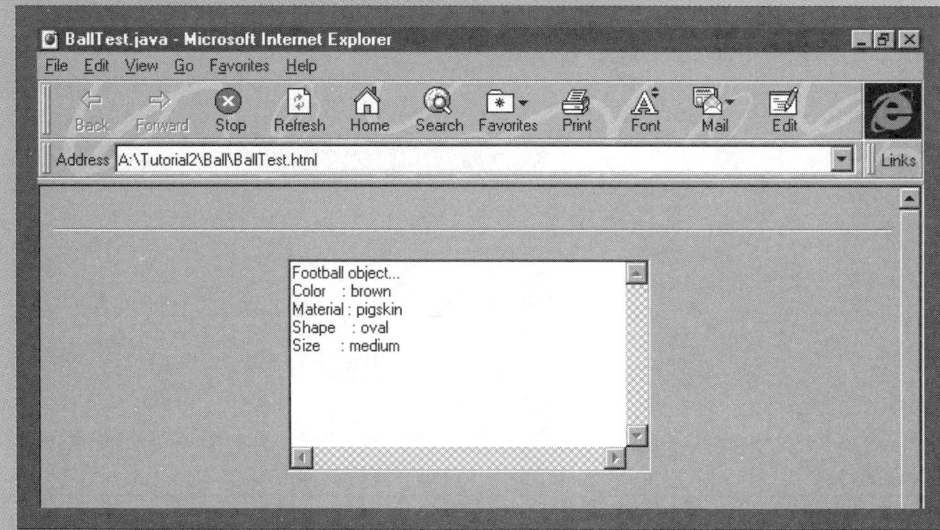

Figure 2-17: BallTest.java running in Internet Explorer

11 Close Internet Explorer.

12 Click **File** on the menu bar, click **Close Workspace**, and then click the **Yes** button to close the workspace and all document windows.

You successfully executed a Java program that uses a class object. The assignment statement is only one of two ways to specify the values of the properties of an object. This method violates the concept of encapsulation. **Encapsulation** is the idea that an object's properties should be altered only with the use of the methods of the object.

Specifying Values of an Object Instance Using Methods

The preferred way to change the values of items in a property list is to have a method that performs that task. Then other programs that use the Java class object can use the method to change values rather than setting the values of the properties directly. This method promotes the ideas that computer professionals have outlined in the concept of encapsulation. The beginning of the methods section of the Ball.java program file is shown in Figure 2-18.

Line Number	Java Program Code
23	//Methods section
24	public void setColorValue (String iValue)
25	{
26	color = iValue;
27	}
28	<blank line>
29	public void setMaterialValue (String iValue)
30	{
31	material = iValue;
32	}
33	<blank line>
34	public void setShapeValue (String iValue)
35	{
36	shape = iValue;
37	}

Figure 2-18: Ball set value methods

Click the second Tutorial 2 link of the Online Companion for this book (http://www.course.com) to see a live Java program that illustrates this topic.

Lines 24 through 27 show the first method, setColorValue, that is declared in the class object. This method is used to set the value of the property named color. Line 24 is the method heading. It starts with the reserved word "public" so the method will be available to all programs that have access to the file. Following the public keyword is the keyword void. The use of the void keyword means that this method will not return any values to the program that uses it. After the void keyword is the name of the method. A parameter list that is enclosed in parentheses follows the method name. The memory location type and name is shown in the parameter list. The setColorValue method has only one parameter; however, you could have many parameters. Lines 25 through 27 indicate the program code for the body of the setColorValue method. This body begins with an opening brace, contains the Java code for setting the value of the color property, and ends with a closing brace. You might notice that the command in this example is similar to what you used in the BallTest.java file; this is because it is an assignment statement just like the BallTest.java commands were assignment statements. The name of the object instance is not included in this command because you are working in the file that defines the Ball class object, so you do not use the instance form of the memory location name. Only the name of the property is needed on the left side of the assignment operator. Notice also that there is a method for setting each of the property variables. These methods are used to set the values of each of the properties.

You can practice setting the value of a property with a method using the BallTest2.java file on your Student Disk.

To set the value of a property with a method:

1. Open the **BT2.java** file from the Ball folder on your Student Disk.
2. Use the Save As command to save the file as **BallTest2.java.**
3. Click in the location shown in Figure 2-19, press the **Enter** key, and then type the property values shown in Figure 2-19. These lines of code set the values of the football instance of the class object by calling the methods of the Ball class.

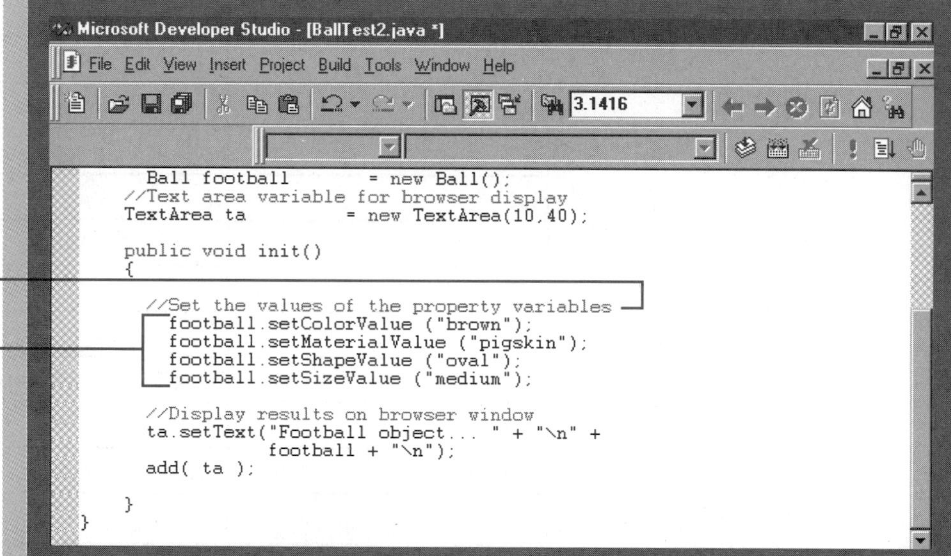

Figure 2-19: Setting the values of the football

The form of the command was the instance memory location name followed by a period, the name of the method you want to use, and the value you wanted to set the property as enclosed in parentheses and quotation marks. The quotation marks indicate that this value is a string literal, and the parentheses note the beginning and end of the parameter list. These method call lines end with a semicolon to indicate the end of a single command.

4. Save your changes.
5. Build the program in a default project workspace and correct any typing errors.
6. To use the HTML file on your Student Disk (instead of letting the compiler generate one), click **Project** on the menu bar, and then click **Settings.** Click the **Debug** tab, click the **Category** list arrow, and then click **Browser.** Click the **Use parameters from HTML page** option button, and then type **BallTest2.html** in the HTML page text box. Click the **OK** button.

7 Execute the program. The class filename is BallTest2. The program runs in Internet Explorer, as shown in Figure 2-20.

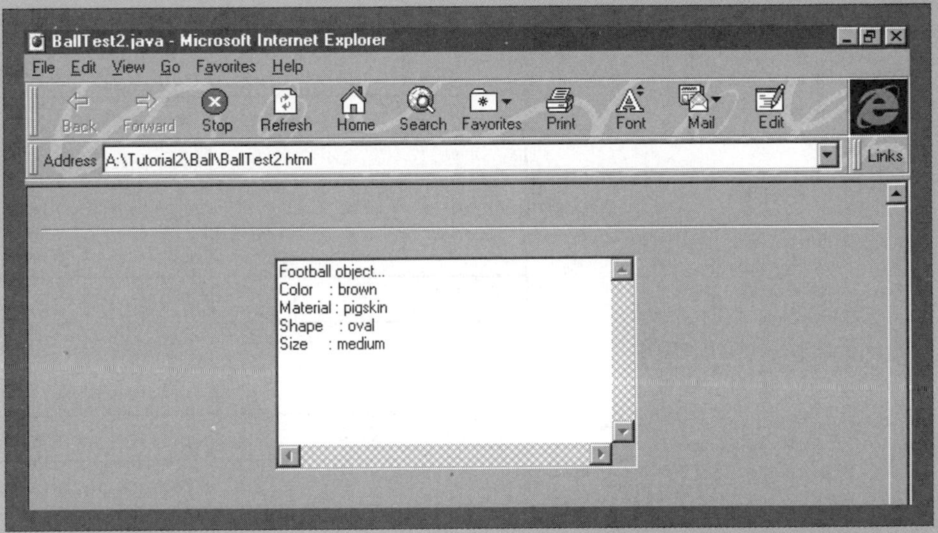

Figure 2-20: BallTest2.java running in Internet Explorer

8 Close Internet Explorer and then close the workspace.

You successfully set the property values of your football object with the methods of the Ball object. The previous set of steps is the preferred method of setting property values. You can force users of your objects to use this method for setting values by using the private command. Figure 2-21 shows the property section of the Ball.java file that uses the private capabilities of Java.

Line Number	Java Program Code
1	//Ball.java
2	import java.applet.*;
3	import java.awt.*;
4	import java.io.*;
5	<blank line>
6	public class Ball extends Applet
7	{
8	//Properties section
9	private String color = " ";
10	private String material = " ";
11	private String shape = " ";
12	private String size = " ";
13	<blank line>
14	//Constructor method
15	Ball ()
16	<blank line>

Figure 2-21: Ball object file with public and private commands

Notice that the properties in lines 9 through 12 use the private keyword. The **private** keyword tells Java that this property should be accessible only by the methods in the class object. This does not prevent a programmer from using these properties when they use the object; it only requires them to use the class object's methods to access the properties.

To understand all of the elements in your Java program, you need to know more about the import commands that contain built-in Java functions.

Using the Standard Java Libraries

The built-in Java functions are included in a number of files that are called packages. A **package** is a collection of objects and methods that is included as part of the Java language. These units are called packages because they contain more than one object. Figure 2-22 shows the standard library of Java packages.

Line Number	Java Program Code
applet	Animation and sound
awt	Abstract windows toolkit
awt.image	Image manipulation
awt.peer	Native implementation classes
io	Input/output
lang	Major language classes for primitives
net	Networked classes
util	Data structure utilities

Figure 2-22: Built-in Java packages

When you use the import command, you identify the set of functions to import into a program you are writing with the name of the package, followed by a period, and then an asterisk (*). This command tells Java to import all the functions of this package for use in your program.

Now you can take a break or complete the end-of-lesson questions and exercises.

SUMMARY

- A program file in Java consists of environment information and the definition of the class object.
- An object is coded in Java with the class command. This command is broken into a class heading and a class body.
- The body of a Java class consists of properties and methods. The methods can be either constructors or standard methods.
- A constructor method is a function that is called when a new instance of a class object is created. The purpose of the constructor is to initialize the properties.
- A class method consists of a heading and a body. The heading declares the name, parameters, and return value of the method and the body contains the actions to be performed.
- Instances of class objects can have their properties set by the assignment statement or by using the methods of the class object that have been programmed to complete this task. The use of methods is the preferred way of assigning values to properties.
- The init() method in a Java applet is a special method that executes automatically when the program file is run.
- The public and private keywords control access to items in the class object. The public keyword makes the item available to any program that uses the file. The private keyword limits access to the only class object. These keywords can be applied to properties as well as methods.
- The Java built-in functions are contained in several different sets called packages.
- The import command allows the program to access the functions of the Java package that is imported.

QUESTIONS

1. The __________ statement is used to create an object in Java.
   a. import
   b. assignment
   c. class
   d. constructor
2. In Visual J++, the first character of a Java class name must be a(n) __________.
   a. asterisk (*)
   b. uppercase character
   c. lowercase character
   d. ampersand (&)
3. The class statement consists of a(n) __________ and a __________.
   a. heading, body
   b. constructor, method
   c. import statement, property type
   d. parameter, return value
4. The __________ keyword limits access to the class object.
   a. init
   b. assignment
   c. public
   d. private
5. The __________ symbol is called the assignment operator.
   a. :=
   b. =
   c. ==
   d. ->
6. The preferred method for setting the values of properties is to use the __________.
   a. class method
   b. assignment statement
   c. public keyword
   d. private keyword
7. The __________ command is used to access functions that come with the Java compiler.
   a. public
   b. import
   c. private
   d. void
8. Sets of objects that are provided in a single library are called __________.
   a. properties
   b. packages
   c. methods
   d. constructors

9. The __________ symbol indicates the end of a single Java command.
   a. @
   b. *
   c. ;
   d. :
10. A __________ is a line or portion of a line that is included to give future users of the object more information than what is contained in the commands.
   a. comment
   b. constructor
   c. method
   d. property

EXERCISES

For each exercise, change the HTML page to the page with the same filename as the program, which is stored in the same file as the program on your Student Disk.

1. Use the BallTest.java program to create an instance of a basketball that has the characteristics of color: brown; shape: round; size: medium; and material: rubber. Save the file as BallTestEx1.java in the Tutorial2\Exercises\Exercise1B folder on your Student Disk.
2. Use the methods shown in the BallTest2.java program to create a basketball instance in the BallTest.java program with the property values stated in Exercise 1. Save the file as BallTestEx2.java in the Tutorial2\Exercises\Exercise2B folder on your Student Disk.
3. Add the private keyword to the properties of the Ball object. What happens if you try to execute BallTest2.java?
4. List the parts of a class object file.
5. Create the code for the class heading, property list, and constructor method section for the object you designed in Exercise 7 in Lesson A. Use the Ball.java program as a guide to performing this task. Save the file as BallEx5.java in the Tutorial2\Exercises\Exercise5B folder on your Student Disk.
6. Create the code for the class heading, property list, and constructor method for the object you designed in Exercise 8 in Lesson A. Use the Ball.java program as a guide to performing this task. Save the file as BallEx6.java in the Tutorial2\Exercises\Exercise6B folder on your Student Disk.
7. Explain the use of the import command.
8. Describe the function of the public and private keywords.

LESSON C

objectives

In this lesson you will learn how to:

- Design a simple class object
- Program a simple class object in Java
- Design a super class object
- Program a super class object in Java

Designing and Programming Class Objects

Designing a Simple Class Object

Maria gave you a copy of a customer order shown in Figure 2-23. This information is the start of the code that you need to develop for the online order entry program for Koffee Koncoctions.

Customer Order		
Name:	Lenny Franz	
Address:	222 First St.	
City:	Denver	
State:	CO	
Zip Code:	44555	
Item	Cost	Qty
Kona	4.50	1
Kona Decaf	5.50	2
Ship Method:	UPS	
Payment Terms:	Cash	

Figure 2-23: Customer order

Maria explained that customers usually complete a paper copy of a form with this information and mail it to Koffee Koncoctions for processing. A data entry clerk calculates the total cost for the order; then the order is copied and sent to the shipping department for processing. Maria wants you to put this form on the Web site to encourage customers to use it to order directly. Then the system will generate the necessary information to bill and ship the order. Right now you need to develop an applet to take this information and to create a customer order. Maria also wants you to add some other pieces of information about the coffee products on the customer order, such as the color and flavor of the coffee item.

The design process consists of four steps: define the application you want to program, break the desired application into data objects, specify the objects using an object structure chart, and program the object.

Step 1: Define the Application You Want to Program

You will use Java to design the application because it is a program for the Web.

Step 2: Break the Desired Application into Data Objects

In this step, you want to view the program you are developing from a data perspective. You should classify sets of data items that will be used in the program and then combine these data items into objects. You reviewed the customer order that Maria gave you and the two additional pieces of information that Maria wanted to include for the coffee items. You need two simple objects in the customer order: a customer object and a coffee object. The order form is really a super object that contains the customer and coffee objects. For your first attempt at program design, you will consider only the simple objects.

Step 3: Specify the Objects Using an Object Structure Chart

In Lesson A you learned that an object structure chart is a helpful tool when you are designing and programming an object. You will name the customer object "Customer" and the coffee object "Coffees." The object structure chart you developed for the Customer object is shown in Figure 2-24, and the chart for the Coffees object is shown in Figure 2-25.

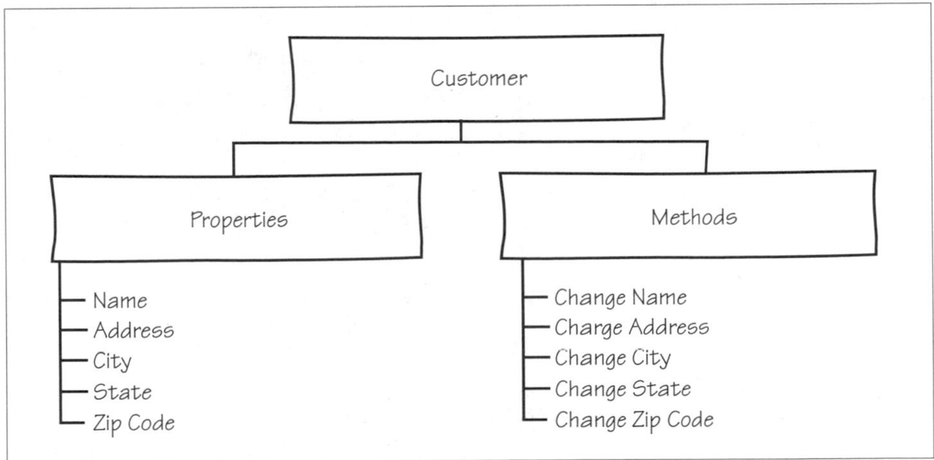

Figure 2-24: Object structure chart for the Customer object

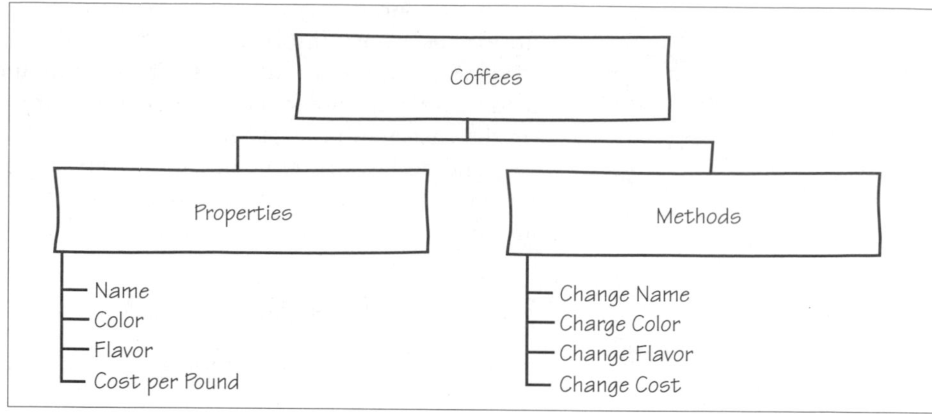

Figure 2-25: Object structure chart for the Coffees object

Step 4: Program the Object in the Desired Language

You will program the object using Java. Now you are finished with the steps for designing the object so you can begin the programming process.

Programming a Simple Class Object

You can use the information from the previous section to program the Customer class object in Java.

To program the Customer class object in Java:

1. Start Visual J++ and close any open project workspaces.
2. Click **File** on the menu bar, and then click **New** to open the New dialog box.
3. Click the **Files** tab, and then double-click **Java Source File** to start a new Java file.
4. Save the file as **Customer.java** in the Koffee folder on your Student Disk.
5. Enter the environment code for your new Customer class by typing the code shown in Figure 2-26.

tip

Type any information requested by your instructor in the comment line.

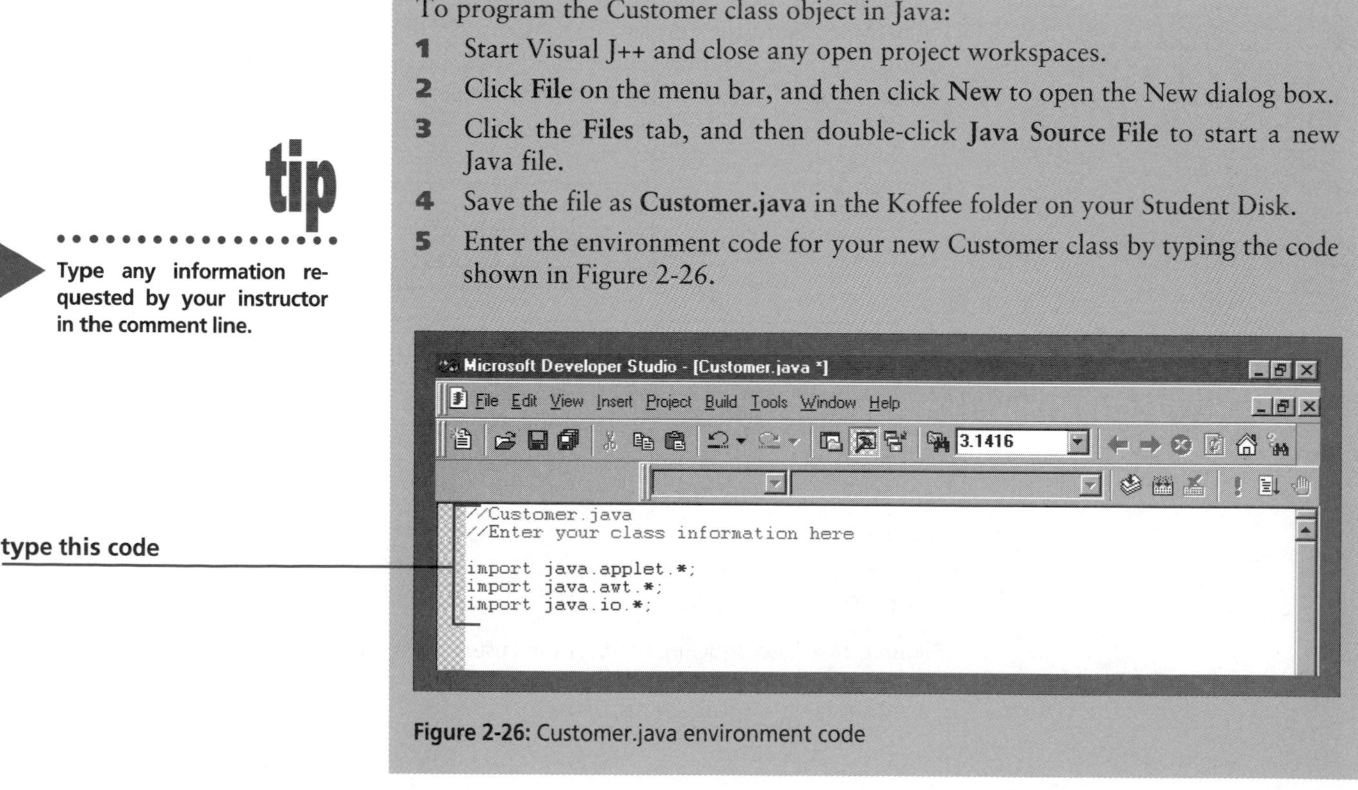

Figure 2-26: Customer.java environment code

The variable name "addressLn" is just a shorthand notation for the address variable.

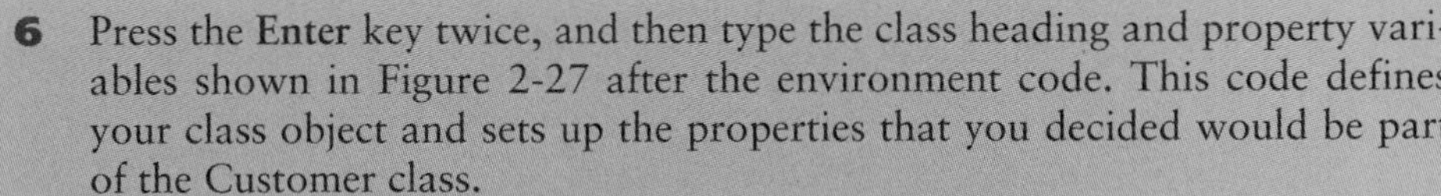

6 Press the **Enter** key twice, and then type the class heading and property variables shown in Figure 2-27 after the environment code. This code defines your class object and sets up the properties that you decided would be part of the Customer class.

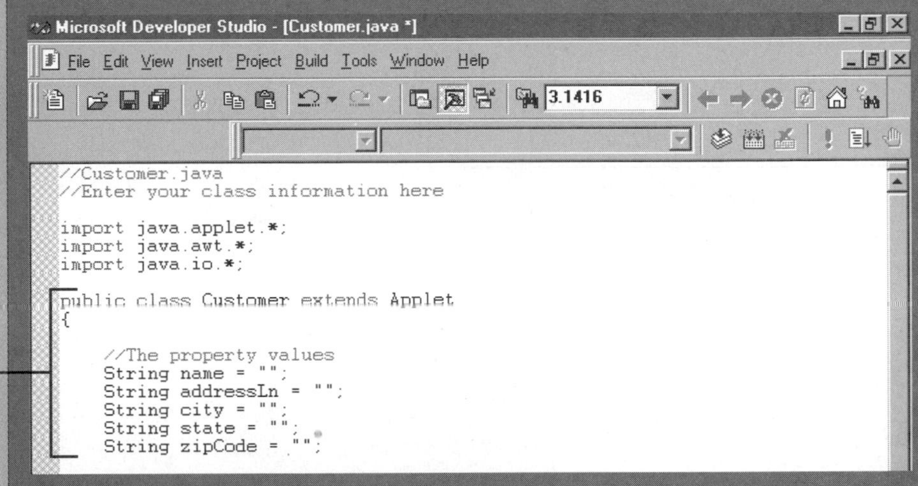

Figure 2-27: Customer.java class heading and properties

7 Press the **Enter** key twice, and then type the code shown in Figure 2-28 for the constructor method. The constructor method is used to initialize the properties by Java when a new instance of the class object is declared.

Be careful to type the code exactly as it is shown in the figures. In Java uppercase and lowercase letters are considered as different letters. At times, spaces are important.

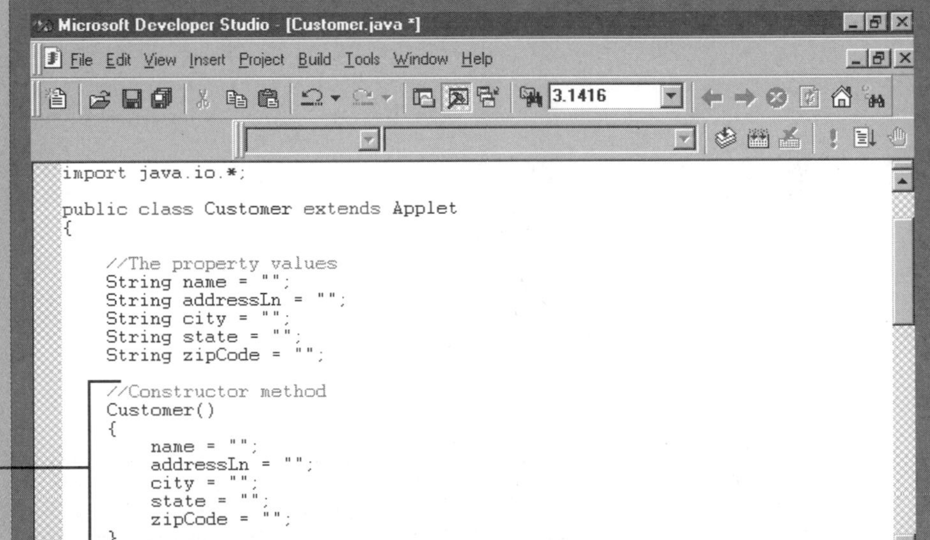

Figure 2-28: Customer object constructor method

8 Press the **Enter** key twice, and then type the code shown in Figure 2-29 for the methods that set the values of the individual properties.

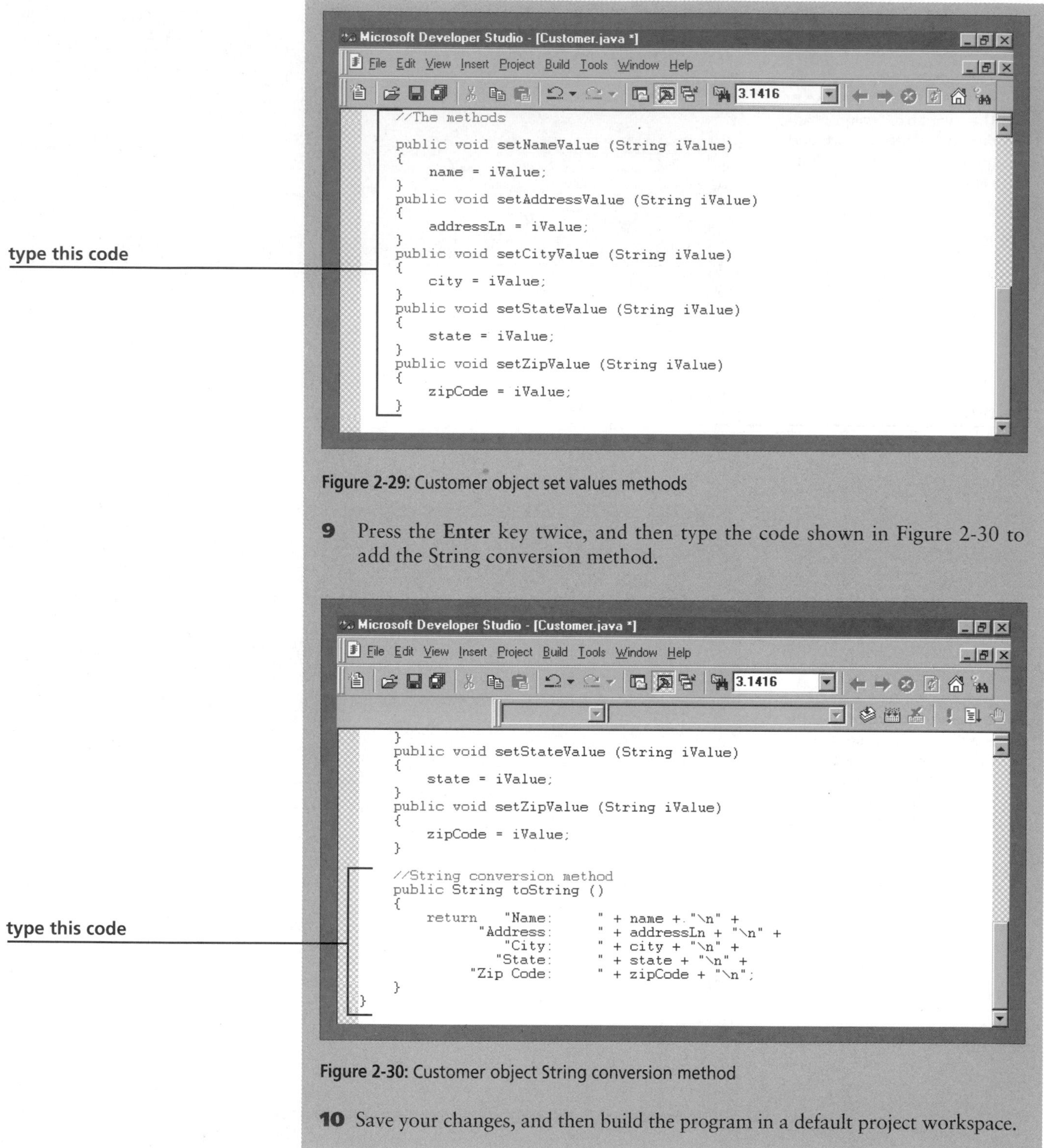

Figure 2-29: Customer object set values methods

9 Press the **Enter** key twice, and then type the code shown in Figure 2-30 to add the String conversion method.

Figure 2-30: Customer object String conversion method

10 Save your changes, and then build the program in a default project workspace.

You created a Java class object named Customer. You will notice that you did not execute this program. The Customer.java file is the code for defining the class object Customer, but by itself it does not do anything if you try to execute it. The Customer.java file is designed to be used by other programs as the Customer definition. To make sure that your object works like you designed it, you can create a test program like the one you saw in the BallTest.java file. You will do this next.

To create a test program for the Customer.java file:

1. Close the workspace.
2. Click **File** on the menu bar, click **New**, and then use the New dialog box to create a new Java source file.
3. Save the file as **CustomerTest.java** in the Koffee folder on your Student Disk.
4. Enter the environment code shown in Figure 2-31 for your CustomerTest.java program to import functions from the built-in packages.

type this code

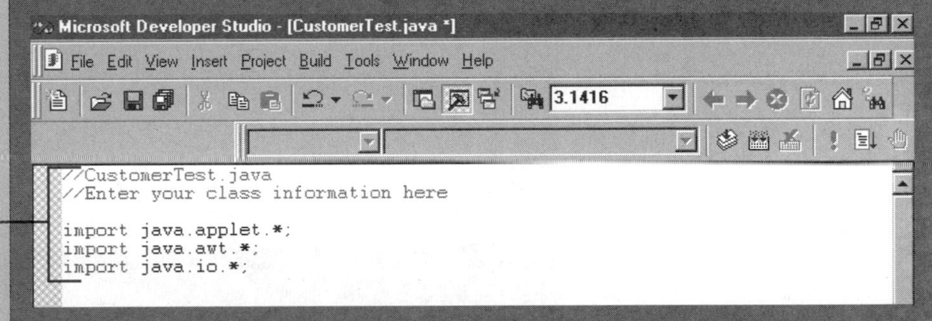


```
//CustomerTest.java
//Enter your class information here

import java.applet.*;
import java.awt.*;
import java.io.*;
```

Figure 2-31: CustomerTest.java environment section

5. Press the **Enter** key twice, and then type the code shown in Figure 2-32 to add the class heading and property variables. This code defines a class named CustomerTest. All programs in Java are class objects, so even your test program will be a class object.

type this code

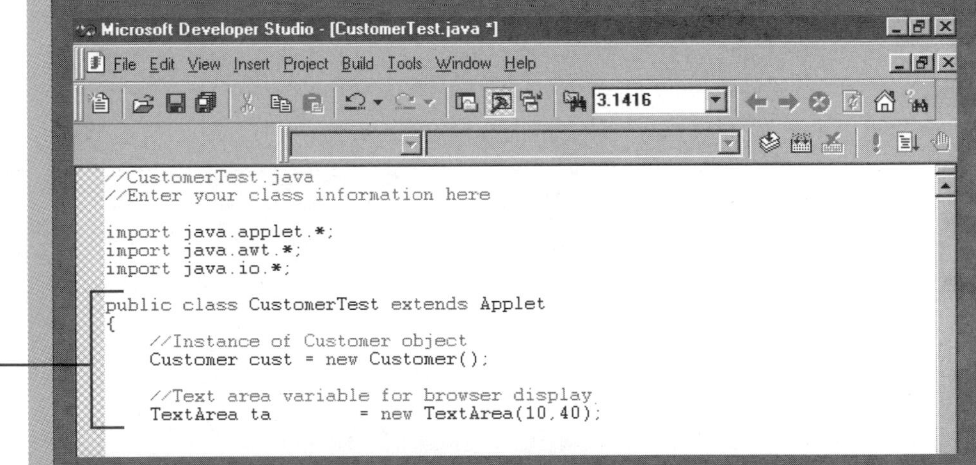


```
//CustomerTest.java
//Enter your class information here

import java.applet.*;
import java.awt.*;
import java.io.*;

public class CustomerTest extends Applet
{
    //Instance of Customer object
    Customer cust = new Customer();

    //Text area variable for browser display
    TextArea ta         = new TextArea(10,40);
```

Figure 2-32: CustomerTest.java class heading and properties

6. Press the **Enter** key twice, and then type the code shown in Figure 2-33 for the init () method. This method is used by Java to start the execution of an applet when you execute this file.

type this code

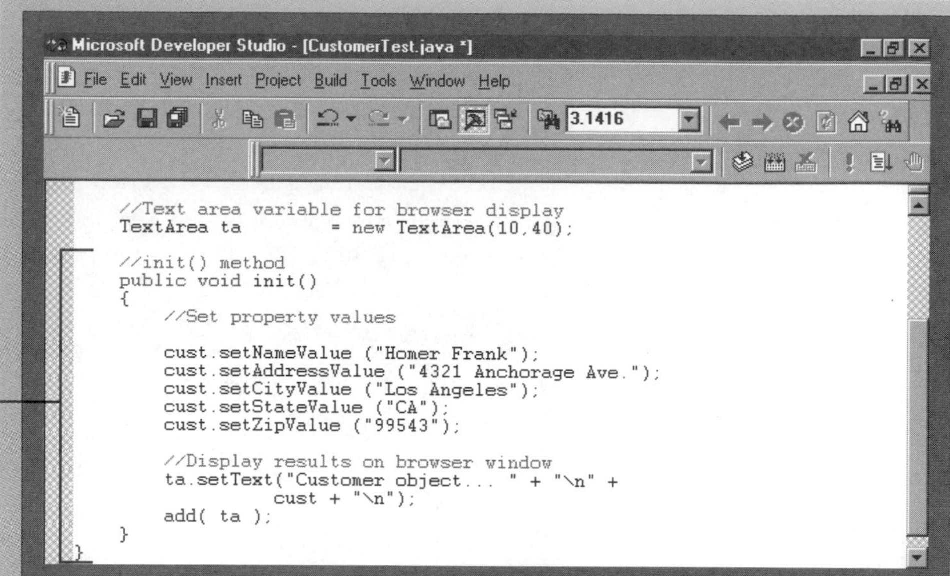

Microsoft Developer Studio - [CustomerTest.java *]
File Edit View Insert Project Build Tools Window Help
3.1416
//Text area variable for browser display
TextArea ta = new TextArea(10,40);
//init() method
public void init()
{
//Set property values
cust.setNameValue ("Homer Frank");
cust.setAddressValue ("4321 Anchorage Ave.");
cust.setCityValue ("Los Angeles");
cust.setStateValue ("CA");
cust.setZipValue ("99543");
//Display results on browser window
ta.setText("Customer object... " + "\n" +
cust + "\n");
add(ta);
}
}

Figure 2-33: CustomerTest.java init() method

7 Save your changes, and then build the file in a default project workspace.

8 To use the HTML file on your Student Disk (instead of letting the compiler generate one), click **Project** on the menu bar, and then click **Settings.** Click the **Debug** tab, click the **Category** list arrow, and then click **Browser.** Click the **Use parameters from HTML page** option button, and then type **CustomerTest.html** in the HTML page text box. Click the **OK** button.

9 Execute the program. The class filename is **CustomerTest.** See Figure 2-34.

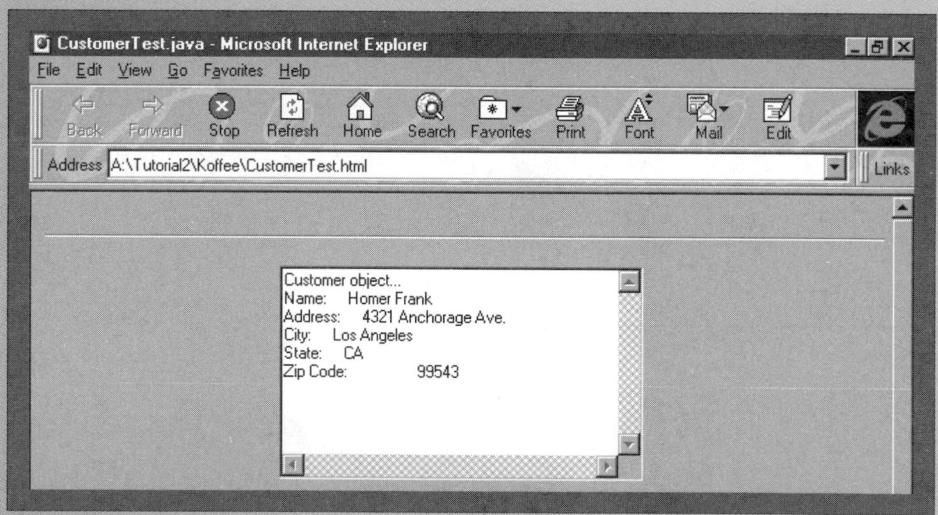

Figure 2-34: CustomerTest.java running in Internet Explorer

HELP? The alignment of the data in your CustomerTest.java file might be different—just make sure that the data is the same.

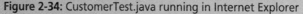

HELP? If your file builds correctly with no errors, but you cannot execute the program in Internet Explorer, close Internet Explorer, click File on the menu bar, click Close Workspace, and then click the Yes button. Then open the CustomerTest.java file again, build the file, and execute the program. If you still are having problems, consult your instructor for help.

10 Close Internet Explorer and then close the workspace.

You programmed and tested the Customer class object successfully. Now you need to complete the programming of the Coffees class object before you can work on the Order object. Now it is time to consider the design of a super object.

Designing a Super Class Object

tip

Click the third Tutorial 2 link of the Online Companion for this book (http://www.course.com) to see a live Java program that illustrates this topic.

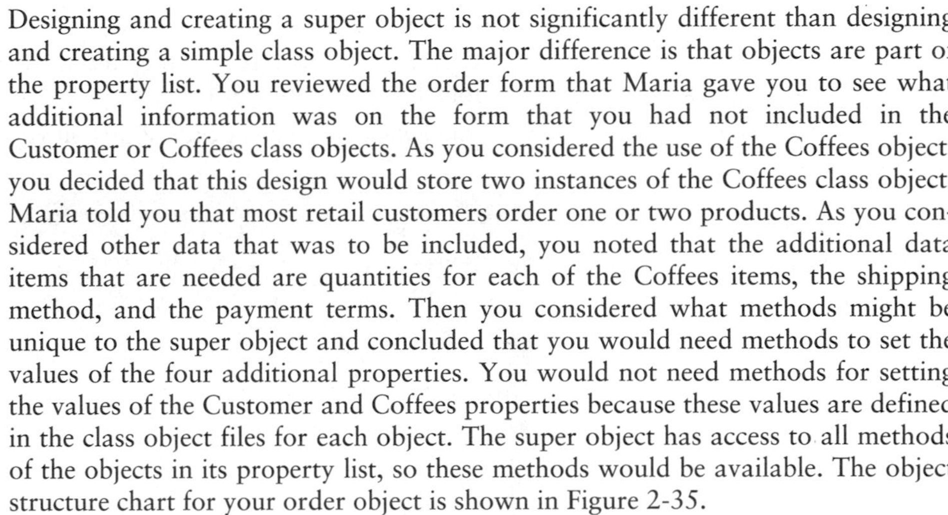

Designing and creating a super object is not significantly different than designing and creating a simple class object. The major difference is that objects are part of the property list. You reviewed the order form that Maria gave you to see what additional information was on the form that you had not included in the Customer or Coffees class objects. As you considered the use of the Coffees object, you decided that this design would store two instances of the Coffees class object. Maria told you that most retail customers order one or two products. As you considered other data that was to be included, you noted that the additional data items that are needed are quantities for each of the Coffees items, the shipping method, and the payment terms. Then you considered what methods might be unique to the super object and concluded that you would need methods to set the values of the four additional properties. You would not need methods for setting the values of the Customer and Coffees properties because these values are defined in the class object files for each object. The super object has access to all methods of the objects in its property list, so these methods would be available. The object structure chart for your order object is shown in Figure 2-35.

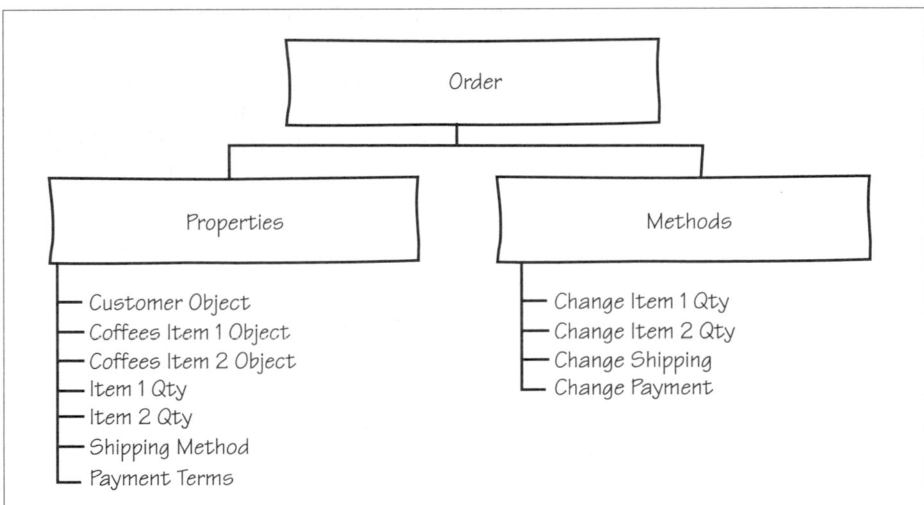

Figure 2-35: Object structure chart for the Order object

This chart indicates that two of the properties in the order object are objects themselves. Also, the additional properties and methods are defined in the chart. Now you are ready to program this object.

Programming a Super Class Object

The code for the super class object has only a few differences from the simple class object. The major difference is in declaring a property that is an object. In your design you decided that these properties would include an instance of the Customer class object and two instances of the Coffees class object. You also noted that this class object would need a quantity property for each of the Coffees objects and two other properties that hold data about the shipment method and payment terms.

To create the Order super class object:

1 Create a new Java source file, and then save it as **Order.java** in the Koffee folder on your Student Disk.

2 Enter the environment code shown in Figure 2-36.

type this code

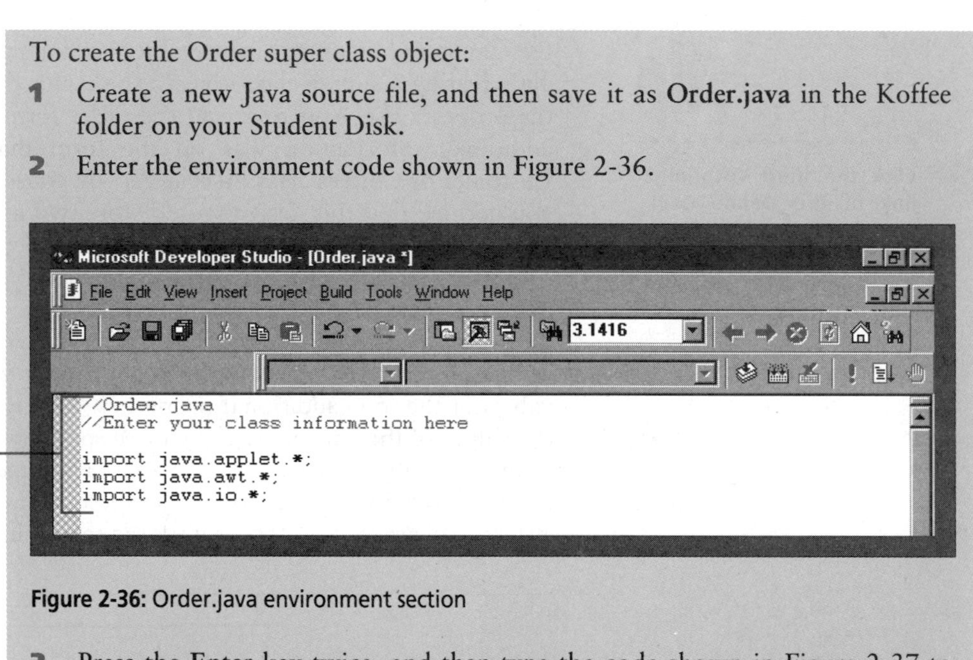

Figure 2-36: Order.java environment section

3 Press the **Enter** key twice, and then type the code shown in Figure 2-37 to add the class heading and property variables. This code defines your class object and sets up the properties for the Order object. Some of these properties are objects, and some are simple memory locations. The object properties make the Order class object a super object.

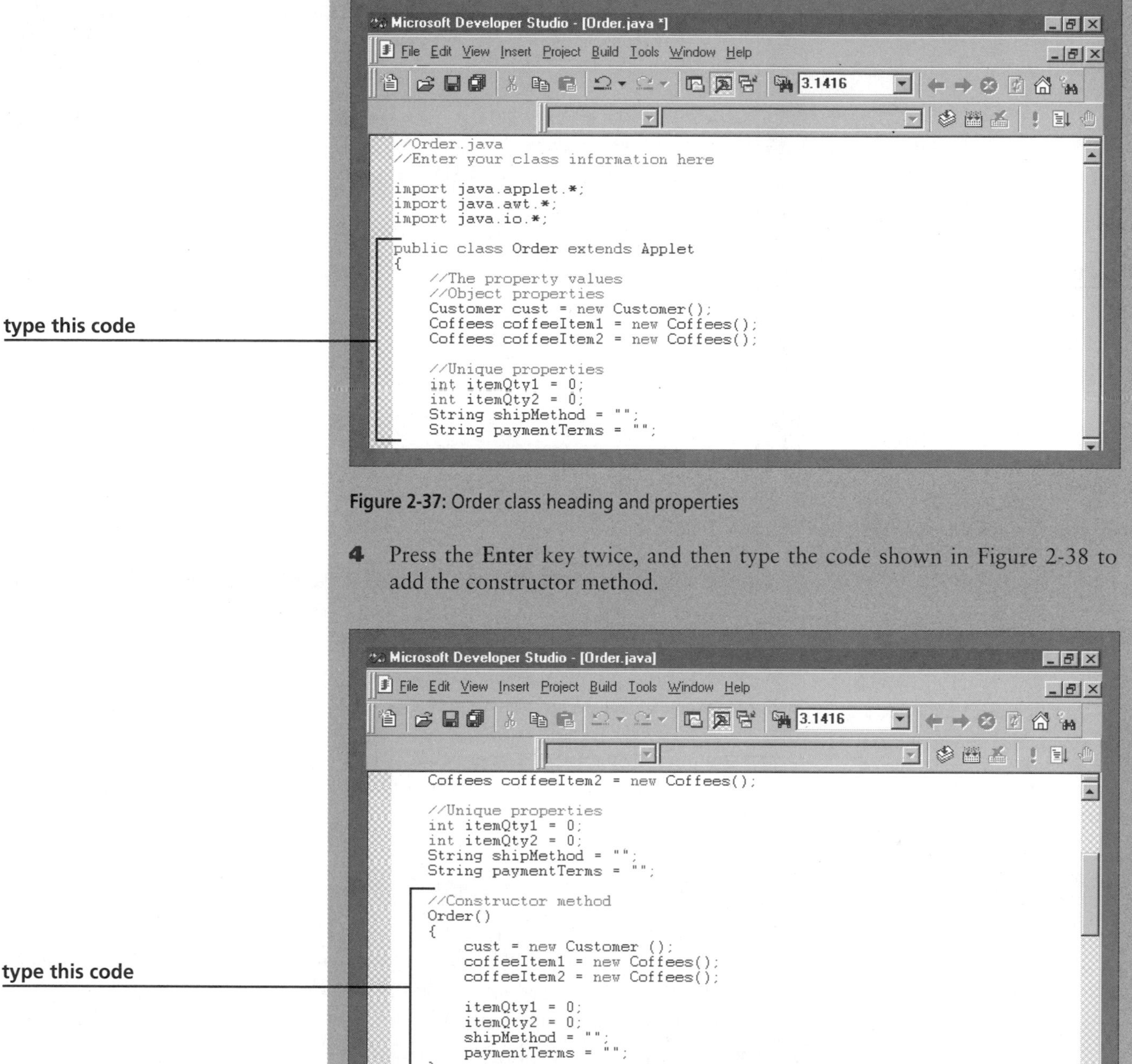

Figure 2-37: Order class heading and properties

4 Press the **Enter** key twice, and then type the code shown in Figure 2-38 to add the constructor method.

Figure 2-38: Order object constructor method

5 Press the **Enter** key twice, and then type the code shown in Figure 2-39 to add the methods that set the values of the unique properties of the Order class object.

type this code

click to return to Visual J++ program window

```
//Methods section
public void setItemQty1Value (int iValue)
{
    itemQty1 = iValue;
}
public void setItemQty2Value (int iValue)
{
    itemQty2 = iValue;
}
public void setShipValue (String iValue)
{
    shipMethod = iValue;
}
public void setPaymentValue (String iValue)
{
    paymentTerms = iValue;
}
//String conversion method
public String toString()
{
    return  "Customer Information..." + "\n" +
            cust + "\n" +
            "Coffee Item Information..." + "\n" +
            "Coffee Item 1:" + "\n" +
            coffeeItem1 + "\n" +
            "Quantity: " + itemQty1 + "\n" +
            "Coffee Item 2:" + "\n" +
            coffeeItem2 + "\n" +
            "Quantity: " + itemQty2 + "\n" +
            "Order Information..." + "\n" +
            "Ship Method: " + shipMethod + "\n" +
            "Payment Terms: " + paymentTerms + "\n";
}
}
```

Figure 2-39: Order object methods section

6 Save your changes, and then build the project in a default project workspace.

tip

Figure 2-39 shows the J++ window in Full Screen view, so that you can see all of the code required in Step 5. To change your screen to Full Screen view, click View on the menu bar, and then click Full Screen. To return to the J++ window, click the icon shown in Figure 2-39.

You have now created a super class object named Order. You will not execute the Order object but you can create another test program to make sure that it works correctly.

To create a test program for the Order.java file:

1 Close the workspace.

2 Create a new Java source file, and then save it as **OrderTest.java** in the Koffee folder on your Student Disk.

3 Enter the environment code shown in Figure 2-40.

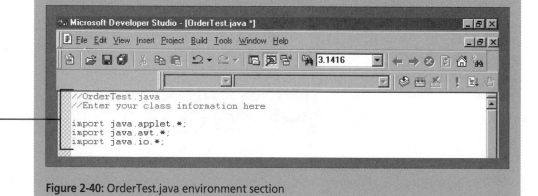

type this code

Microsoft Developer Studio - [OrderTest.java *]

File Edit View Insert Project Build Tools Window Help

```
//OrderTest.java
//Enter your class information here

import java.applet.*;
import java.awt.*;
import java.io.*;
```

Figure 2-40: OrderTest.java environment section

4. Press the **Enter** key twice, and then type the code shown in Figure 2-41 to add the class heading and property variables. This code defines a class named OrderTest.

type this code

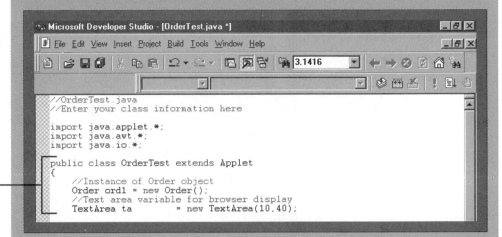

```
//OrderTest.java
//Enter your class information here

import java.applet.*;
import java.awt.*;
import java.io.*;

public class OrderTest extends Applet
{
    //Instance of Order object
    Order ord1 = new Order();
    //Text area variable for browser display
    TextArea ta        = new TextArea(10,40);
```

Figure 2-41: OrderTest class heading and properties

5. Press the **Enter** key twice, and then type the code shown in Figure 2-42 to add the init () method. The commands used in this method are somewhat different from those used in the previous test program, particularly the lines that set the values of the Customer instance of the Customer class object and the lines that do the same for the two instances, CoffeeItem1 and CoffeeItem2, of the Coffees product. The values for the properties of these instances of class objects are being set using the methods of the instance of the class object.

type this code

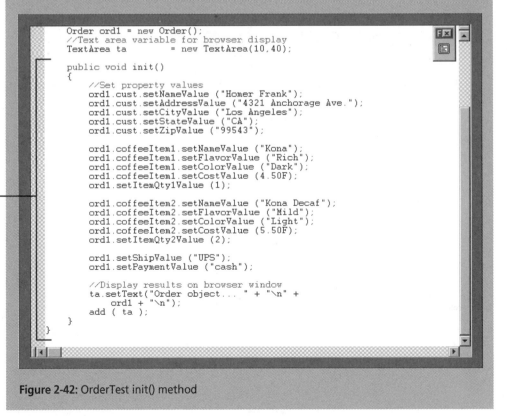

```
    Order ord1 = new Order();
    //Text area variable for browser display
    TextArea ta        = new TextArea(10,40);

    public void init()
    {
        //Set property values
        ord1.cust.setNameValue ("Homer Frank");
        ord1.cust.setAddressValue ("4321 Anchorage Ave.");
        ord1.cust.setCityValue ("Los Angeles");
        ord1.cust.setStateValue ("CA");
        ord1.cust.setZipValue ("99543");

        ord1.coffeeItem1.setNameValue ("Kona");
        ord1.coffeeItem1.setFlavorValue ("Rich");
        ord1.coffeeItem1.setColorValue ("Dark");
        ord1.coffeeItem1.setCostValue (4.50F);
        ord1.setItemQty1Value (1);

        ord1.coffeeItem2.setNameValue ("Kona Decaf");
        ord1.coffeeItem2.setFlavorValue ("Mild");
        ord1.coffeeItem2.setColorValue ("Light");
        ord1.coffeeItem2.setCostValue (5.50F);
        ord1.setItemQty2Value (2);

        ord1.setShipValue ("UPS");
        ord1.setPaymentValue ("cash");

        //Display results on browser window
        ta.setText("Order object...  " + "\n" +
           ord1 + "\n");
        add ( ta );
    }
}
```

Figure 2-42: OrderTest init() method

6 Save your changes and then build the program in a default project workspace.

7 Change the default html file to **OrderTest.html.**

8 Execute the program. The class filename is **OrderTest**. See Figure 2-43.

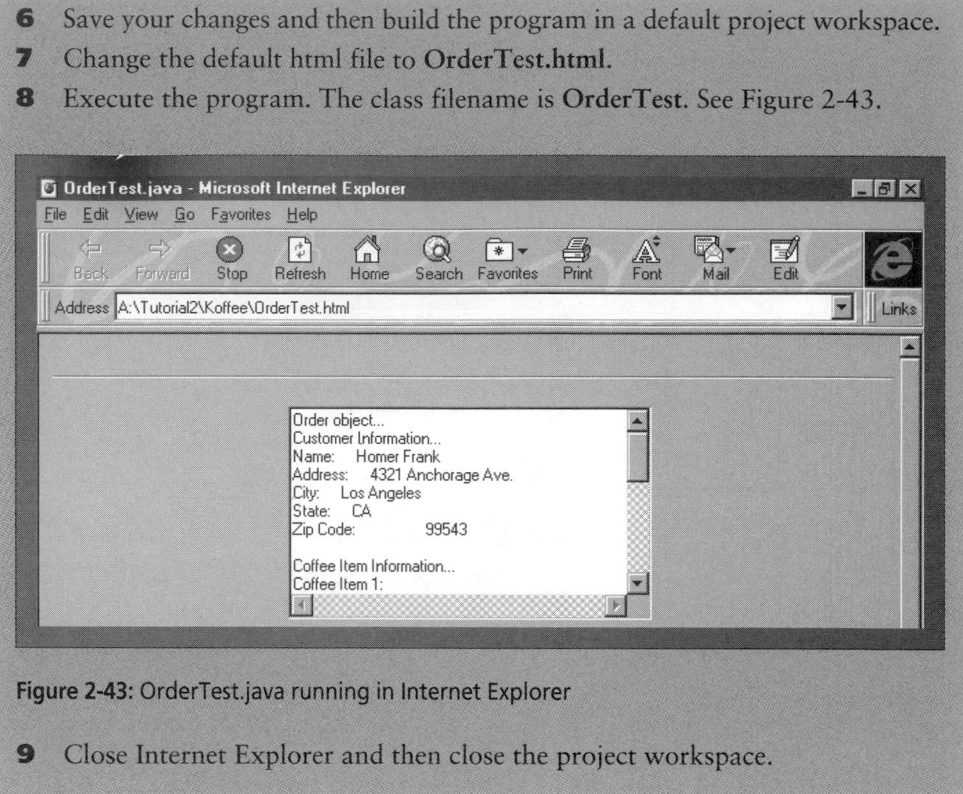

Figure 2-43: OrderTest.java running in Internet Explorer

9 Close Internet Explorer and then close the project workspace.

Now you have successfully completed designing and programming a super class object in Java. You can exit Visual J++ and take a break or complete the end-of-lesson questions and exercises.

SUMMARY

- The four steps to design an object are define the desired application, break down the application into data objects, specify the data objects using object structure charts, and program the object in a specific language.
- A class object program file in Java that does not have an init() method will not perform any tasks if executed.
- Objects like Customer, Coffees, and Order do not contain init() methods because they are used by other programs that have this method.
- Test programs are written to test the code of simple and super objects.
- A super object is coded using the same conventions and commands as the simple object.
- A super object has properties that are of the type object and this object is identified in the properties section of the code.
- When setting the property values of objects contained in the super object, the name of the instance is appended to the method name that sets the property.

QUESTIONS

1. The first step in developing a class object in Java is to __________.
   a. define the application
   b. code the object in a given language
   c. specify the object with an object structure chart
   d. break down the program into data objects

2. The second step in the program design process is to __________.
   a. define the application
   b. code the object in a given language
   c. specify the object with an object structure chart
   d. break down the program into data objects
3. The third step in the program design process is to __________.
   a. define the application
   b. code the object in a given language
   c. specify the object with an object structure chart
   d. break down the program into data objects
4. The __________ method of the class object initializes the property values when a new instance of the object is created.
   a. constructor
   b. init
   c. set value
   d. toString
5. The __________ converts the class object's properties into a single string.
   a. constructor
   b. init
   c. set value
   d. toString
6. A super object has properties that are __________.
   a. objects
   b. packages
   c. comments
   d. methods
7. To use an existing HTML file instead of letting the compiler generate one for you, you should click _________ on the Project menu.
   a. HTML
   b. Build
   c. Execute
   d. Settings
8. A(n) __________ is a function that performs some activity on an object.
   a. property
   b. method
   c. class heading
   d. instance
9. The class definition of an object designates the __________ of an object.
   a. format
   b. structure chart
   c. import functions
   d. comments
10. A class object program file will not execute unless it has a(n) __________.
    a. init() method
    b. constructor method
    c. HTML page
    d. active workspace

EXERCISES

For each exercise, change the HTML page to the page with the same filename as the program, which is stored in the same file as the program on your Student Disk.

1. Adjust the CustomerTest.java program to assign the following values to the properties. Save the program as CustomerTestEx1.java in the Tutorial2\Exercises\Exercise1C folder on your Student Disk.

   Name: Henri Fontaine
   Address: 22 First St.
   City: Atlanta
   State: GA
   Zip Code: 33213

2. Using the Coffees.java object on your Student Disk, design and program a test program for the object. Use the CustomerTest.java program as a guide. Save the test program as CustomerTestEx2.java in the Tutorial2\Exercises\Exercise2C folder on your Student Disk.
3. Design and code the class heading and properties section of a program that defines the tennis super object that you worked on in Lesson A. Assume that the objects ball and racket already exist. Save the file as Ex2 in the Tutorial2\Exercises\Exercise3C folder on your Student Disk.
4. Modify the OrderTest.java program to set the property values for the following order. Save the program as OrderTestEx4.java in the Tutorial2\Exercises\Exercise4C folder on your Student Disk.

   Customer Items
     Name: Jennifer Fields
     Address: 55 West St.
     City: Remington
     State: MD
     Zip Code: 04555
   Coffee Items Information
     CoffeeItem1 Name: Kona
     CoffeeItem2 Name: Kona Decaf
     CoffeeItem1 Color: Dark
     CoffeeItem2 Color: Light
     CoffeeItem1 Flavor: Rich
     CoffeeItem2 Flavor: Mild
     CoffeeItem1 Cost: 4.50
     CoffeeItem2 Cost: 5.50
   Order Information
     CoffeeItem1 Quantity: 3
     CoffeeItem2 Quantity: 1
     Ship Method: UPS
     Payment Terms: cash

5. Modify the Order.java object so it contains three coffee items instead of two. Modify the OrderTest.java program to make sure your changes work correctly. Save the Order.java program as OrderEx5.java and the OrderTest.java program as OrderTestEx5.java in the Tutorial2\Exercises\Exercise5C folder on your Student Disk.
6. Modify the Customer.java object by deleting the zip code property. Modify and run the CustomerTest.java program to make sure your deletion occurred. Save the Customer.java program as CustomerEx6.java and the CustomerTest.java program as CustomerTestEx6.java in the Tutorial2\Exercises\Exercise6C folder on your Student Disk. What things besides properties did you have to delete?

TUTORIAL 3

Using Variables and Expressions

Creating an Online Order Form for Koffee Koncoctions

case In this tutorial you will work with variables and expressions using the BeanJar applet, and then design programs with input and output variables and use expressions. When you are done, you will have an order entry screen that can be used for entering orders and an invoice report that generates customer orders for Koffee Koncoctions. You also will learn how to do calculations and create input and output fields in Java. First you will make some changes in the BeanJar applet. Maria then wants you to make some changes to the online ordering system.

LESSON A

objectives

In this lesson you will learn how to:

- Describe the three characteristics and the naming rules of variables
- Describe and use the two major categories of types in Java
- Define constants and literals
- Describe the difference between Strings and characters
- Convert values from one type to another
- Concatenate a String
- Access and modify an object's data fields

Naming and Creating Variables

Using Variables and Expressions to Store Information

Naming Variables

An effective computer program accepts information from users and returns the correct results. To accomplish this task, the computer must store information and use that information to formulate the results. A **variable** is used to define data to store in computer memory. You must use a variable to store information that comes from outside the program when it is used as data by the program. An **expression** is the part of a Java statement that produces a result based on the variables.

In object-oriented programming, a variable is the smallest unit of data. While it is possible for variables to stand alone, most of the time variables are part of an object. Objects contain both data (set up as variables) and methods (programming code that works with the data stored in the object variables). Java variables have three characteristics: name, type, and value.

Variable Naming Rules

Originally, when programmers wanted to store values in the computer memory, they had to know the exact location of the value being stored. Computer memory consists of a very large number of small storage locations, like boxes in a post office, and each memory location has an address (see Figure 3-1). An **address** is the number assigned to a memory location. An address might be the number 0 or the number 0110011010010011. Programming became much easier when programmers started using names to represent the values, or variables, to store and manipulate in memory.

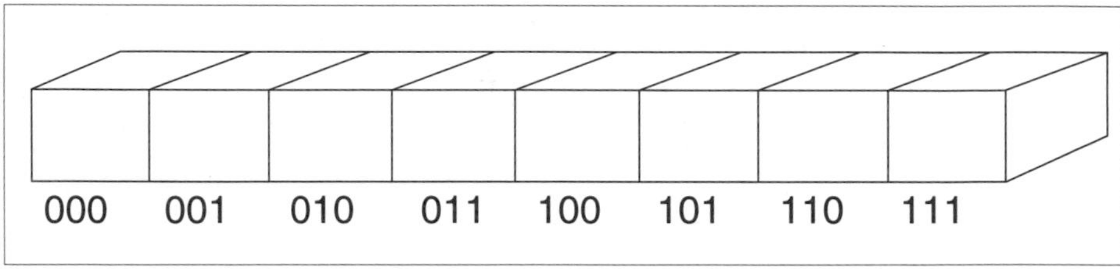

Figure 3-1: Computer memory example

According to the Java Language Specification (click the Java link on the CT Online Companion), **identifiers** (such as variable names) are an unlimited-length sequence of Java letters and Java digits, the first of which must be a Java letter. This definition means that Java variable names must start with a letter, and can have any combination and number of letters and numbers, but cannot include spaces or punctuation marks, with the exception of the underscore (_) and dollar sign ($).

Click the first Tutorial 3 link of the Online Companion for this book (http://www.course.com) to see a live Java program that illustrates this topic.

While in theory a Java identifier can have any combination of letters and numbers, there are accepted conventions for naming variables. Variable names should be a noun or noun phrase. The first letter is in lowercase, and if the variable name is more than one word, the first letter of each subsequent word is in uppercase. Using only uppercase letters in a variable name is not considered acceptable. Figure 3-2 shows samples of acceptable and unacceptable variable names.

Acceptable Variable Name	Unacceptable Variable Name	Reason Not Accepted
studentNum	student's number	Cannot contain punctuation marks
radius1	1radius	Must start with a letter
foodEaten	Food To Be Eaten	Spaces are not allowed
numberOfBeans	BEANS	Must use lowercase and uppercase letters, based on conventions

Figure 3-2: Acceptable and unacceptable Java variable names

You cannot assign variable names that are keywords in Java. **Keywords** are words that are reserved for special use, the most common of which are command names. In Java, programmers cannot use keywords as variable names. Figure 3-3 lists words that cannot be used as Java variable names.

abstract	else	interface	switch
boolean	extends	long	synchronized
break	false	native	this
byte	final	new	throw
case	finally	null	throws
catch	float	package	transient
char	for	private	true
class	goto	protected	try
const	if	public	void
continue	implements	return	volatile
default	import	short	while
do	instanceof	static	
double	int	super	

Figure 3-3: Keywords in Java

Naming Other Java Objects

You can apply the same rules for naming variables to other Java objects, such as classes, class methods, and constants. All object names must start with a letter and can have any combination of Java letters and numbers. Figure 3-4 shows the rules and examples for naming other Java objects. The convention for constants contains an underscore character. This is a legal character that can be used in naming any kind of object in Java.

Type	Example	Rule
Class	MyNewClass	Capitalize the first letter of each new word; do not use spaces
Method	myNewMethod	First word is in lowercase; capitalize only first letter of other words
Constant	MY_NEW_CONSTANT	Capitalize every letter; separate words with underscores

Figure 3-4: Naming rules for other Java objects

Variables and Types

The second property of variables is that of type. The **type** of a variable determines the kind of information the variable can store, such as numbers or letters. In Java, programmers must write explicit Java statements to reinterpret a variable as another type. For example, in the BeanJar applet, you use a formula that produces a floating point value to calculate the number of beans that will fit in the jar. But you do not want your output to show that 896.372 beans will fit in the jar—you want to show whole numbers. So you need to convert this floating point value to an integer. This conversion can be done, but you must use the programming statements included in Java to do so.

Java types are organized in a hierarchy of two categories: primitive and reference. The **primitive types** are called that because they are based on the types that are included in older, non-object oriented languages, like Basic, Pascal, FORTRAN, COBOL, etc. As shown in Figure 3-5, the primitive types are boolean and numeric. The **numeric types** consist of integral (byte, short, int, long, and char) and floating point (float and double). For now, the emphasis will be on the primitive types.

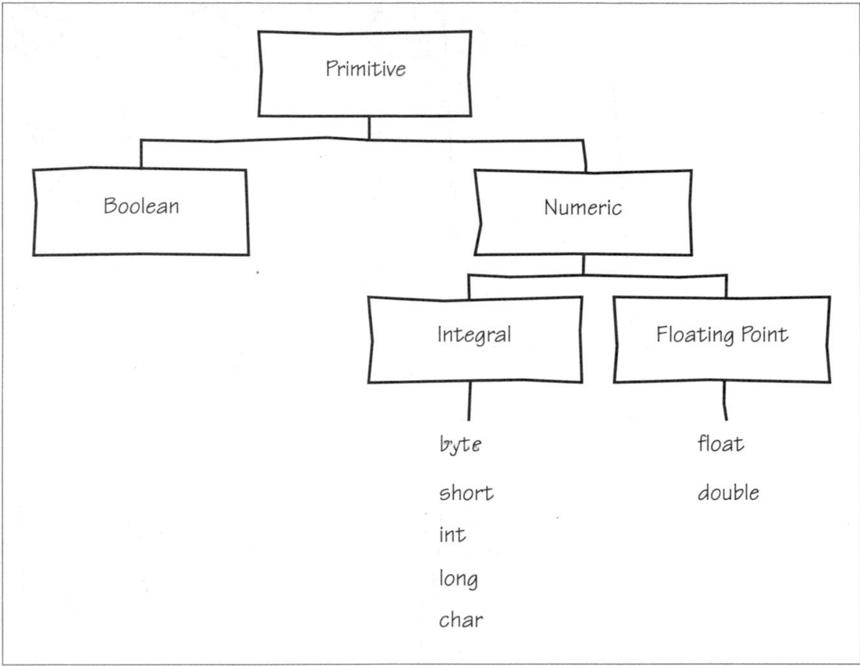

Figure 3-5: Java primitive type hierarchy

Boolean Type

The **boolean type** is named for the British mathematician, George Boole, who is the father of Boolean algebra. There are only two values in this type: true and false. You will learn more about boolean types in Tutorials 4 and 5. Even though the words "true" and "false" are not keywords in Java, it is illegal to redefine the words "true" or "false" to be variables, objects, or methods.

Integral Types

An **integral** type is either an integer (whole) number or an alphanumeric or a control character. There are five integral types: byte, short, int, long, and char. The first four types are different ways to store integer (numeric) data; the **char** type stores character data. One simple way to think of the char data type is to think of the letter and number keys on a keyboard. All of the keyboard characters are part of the char data type. The problem with restricting the char data type to just keyboard characters is the global nature of computing and the Internet. There are many languages that do not use an English-based 26-letter alphabet, so all characters are coded in 16-bit Unicode. The standard 8-bit ASCII (American Standard Code for Information Interchange) codes are associated with the standard English alphabet. The extra eight bits in Unicode allows for the addition of non-ASCII characters that are not represented on the standard English keyboard.

The four other integral types allow programmers to store integers in the smallest memory space possible for a given range of values. Another name for integers is "counting numbers" because integers are whole numbers, with no decimals. Figure 3-6 shows the integral types and their legal value ranges.

Type	Memory Used	Legal Values
byte	1 byte	-128 to 127
short	2 bytes	-32,768 to 32,767
int	4 bytes	-2,147,483,648 to 2,147,483,647
long	8 bytes	-9,223,372,036,854,775,808 to 9,223,372,036,854,775,807
char	2 bytes	'\u0000' to '\uffff', or 0 to 65,535

Figure 3-6: Integral types and legal values

What happens if you try to store the value 128 in a byte variable? If you assign the value 128 to the byte variable, the Visual J++ compiler generates an error message. However, if you try to add a value to the value currently stored in the byte variable, the compiler will miss it and you will have a logic error. For example, if a byte variable contains the value 127, and the program adds the value 1 to it, the result will be -128. Think of the byte range (and of the range of any of the other integral types) as a necklace with a certain number of beads. Each bead is connected to the one just before it and the one just after it. The bead just before -128 is 127. So by adding 1 to 127 the result becomes -128. In other words, the largest number is *next to* smallest number. This concept is true for all integral types, as well.

Floating Point Types

A **floating point** type is any number with a decimal, such as 5.56. There are only two floating point types: float and double. Like the integral types, the two floating point types allow programmers to store values in memory efficiently. The double type is 8 bytes and stores larger numbers than the float data type, which is 4 bytes—this additional storage makes the double type more precise. The more precise floating point number is more reliable because there can be more digits in the number. Figure 3-7 shows the two types and their storage sizes, precision in digits, and approximate minimum and maximum values.

Type Characteristics	float Type	double Type
Storage	4 bytes	8 bytes
Precision (in digits)	7	15
Approximate minimum absolute value	1.40239846E-45	4.94065645841246544E-324
Approximate maximum absolute value	3.40282347E+38	1.79769313486231570E+308

Figure 3-7: Characteristics of floating point types

Notice that the values shown in Figure 3-7 for the approximate minimum and maximum absolute values include the letter "E" to indicate **exponential notation**, or **scientific notation**. When you must store very large or very small numbers, such as the distance that light will travel in one year or the size of the nucleus of an atom, you can use exponential notation to simplify your calculations. For example, one light year is 9.463E17 centimeters. In standard number notation, this number is written as 946,300,000,000,000,000. The "E17" in the exponential number indicates that there are 17 places to the left of the decimal point. In a computer program, you should note that the commas are *not* stored as part of the number so the same number is 946300000000000000. For very small numbers, such as the size of the nucleus of an atom, the notation 1.0E-14 represents the number 0.00000000000001, where the number after the "E" is a negative number to indicate how many zeros appear to the right of the decimal point.

Constants and Literals

Variables are values in memory that can be changed while the program is running. The memory also can hold values that do not change during execution. A **constant** is a named memory location that holds a value that cannot be changed. A **literal value** is a value that is "literally" written in the program. A literal has only a value and no name, but because it is part of the program, it uses memory space.

Because literal values are easy to use in a program, why would a programmer need to have a variable that never changes? There are two reasons. The first reason is to eliminate the possibility of the programmer typing the literal incorrectly. If you type the name of a constant incorrectly, the Visual J++ compiler will display an error message. However, if you type the number *45* instead of *54*, there would be no error message. Also, programs written using constants instead of literals are easier to update. If the number 45 is the number of items that a Koffee Koncoctions customer has to buy to receive a discount, the program would have to be rewritten to change the discount to 40 items purchased. However, if the discount item rate is coded as a constant at the beginning of the program, the programmer would have to change only one statement to change the discount. For example, both literals and constants are in the BeanJar program, but a literal is just a value, while the constant has a name. In the BeanJar applet, the formula to compute the size of a coffee bean has literals but no constants.

Strings and Characters

The char and String data types look like they should be related, but they are not. The char data type is actually an integral type, and the String data type is an object, which is one of the reference types. The char data type stores characters, but it can store only one character at a time. The String data type also stores characters, but it can store a large number of characters at one time. Another difference between the char and String data types is the use of delimiters. A **delimiter** is the character that marks the beginning and end of something, like bookends on a bookshelf. The char delimiter for characters is the single quotation mark ('), and the delimiter for strings is the double quotation mark ("). Figure 3-8 shows the use of legal characters and strings.

Characters	Strings
'A'	"A string"
'z'	"My name is Ishmael"
'3'	"My hat it has three corners"

Figure 3-8: Legal characters and String literals

Unicode contains keyboard letters and numbers and special control characters. These control characters are specified in one of two ways. Both ways start with the backslash (\). One way to specify the control characters is by using a one character code. The other way is to use the Unicode notation. Both methods involve placing the backslash and the code inside the single quotation marks. By the way, using control characters is the only time that you can store more than one character inside the single quotation marks. Figure 3-9 shows both ways to specify the control characters and the meaning of some commonly used control characters.

Unicode	Character Codes	Meaning
'\u0008'	'\b'	Backspace
'\u0009'	'\t'	Tab
'\u000A'	'\n'	New line
'\u000C'	'\f'	Form feed
'\u000D'	'\r'	Line return
'\u00DD'	'\"'	Double quotation marks
'\u0027'	'\''	Single quotation marks
'\u005C'	'\\'	Backslash

Figure 3-9: Common control character sequences in Unicode and character codes

Type Conversions

In general, once you assign a type to a variable, you cannot change it. However, there are methods that convert values from one primitive type to another or from a primitive type to a String. Before discussing how to convert variables from one type to another, you must understand why a programmer needs to convert values. Primitive type conversions are used to convert values into a type that is acceptable in a method parameter list. A **parameter list** is one or more values that are passed to a method, as discussed in Tutorial 2. When using a class method, it is important to have the right number of parameters, and the parameters must be of the correct type. So if the program generates a float value, and the method needs a double value, you can convert it. Conversions can be grouped into three categories: widening primitive conversions, narrowing primitive conversions, and String conversions.

Widening primitive conversions are when a smaller type value is placed into a larger type variable. Most of these conversions are "free" in the sense that no data or significant digits are lost. When a byte is converted to a short, int, long, float, or a double type, no information or precision is lost. Conversion of an int or a long type to a float type, or of a long type to a double type can result in some loss of precision. In other words, the int and long types can hold more digits than the float or double types so the value will lose accuracy. When the largest long value (9,223,372,036,854,775,807) is converted to either a float or double it becomes 9.22337E+18. The 13 additional places contain zeros so the new value is actually 2,036,854,775,807 less than the original value.

Narrowing primitive conversions are when a larger type value is placed into a smaller type variable. This type of conversion has a much higher chance of losing precision or of containing a misleading value. For example, if a short type variable containing the value 128 is converted to a byte type, the byte value will be -128. The most common narrowing primitive conversion is converting a floating point number to an integer, which **truncates**, or cuts off, the decimal component.

String conversions occur when other primitive types are placed into a String, or when a String value is converted into one of the primitive types. To put other primitive types in a String, you must concatenate the String. **String concatenation** is a way of building a String out of smaller pieces, including Strings and primitive types. To concatenate a String, the pieces get "joined together" using the String concatenation operator + (the plus sign). There are methods that take the information a user types in a text box and convert the String into one of the numeric types. This conversion is useful because the data in a text object is String data.

Reference Types

There are only three kinds of Java reference types: class, interface, and array, as shown in Figure 3-10. In this book you will learn about classes and arrays—interfaces are a way of specifying how different classes can work together, but are beyond the scope of this book. This tutorial will concentrate on the class type, but many of the differences between reference types and primitive types also apply to arrays. What are the differences between primitive types and the class type? Class types are created, accessed, and modified differently from primitive types.

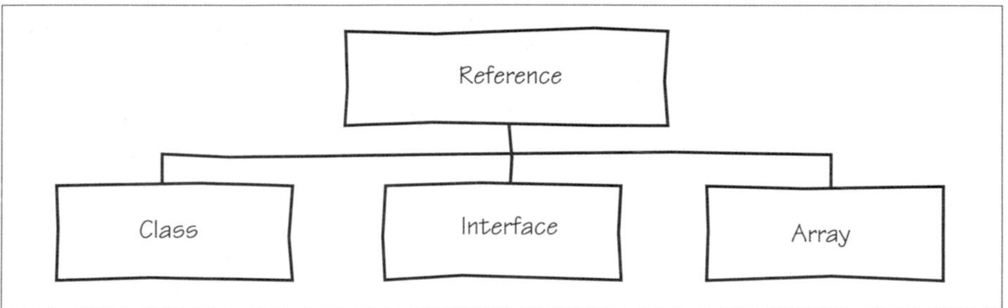

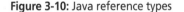

Figure 3-10: Java reference types

The biggest difference between using a primitive and a class type is that you can define a new class. So far you have declared new class types in your Java programs. You cannot add new primitive types because they are part of the Java language. In fact, all primitive type names are keywords and cannot be redefined. You learned how to write the class definition in Tutorial 2 by first writing the heading statement *public class <name> extends <name>*, and then writing the body. In the body of the class definition, you included both the properties and the methods. To use a class type, you declare an object. Variables are primitive types; objects are class types. You learned how to declare objects by using constructors.

The statement *Label myLabel = new Label("This is a label")* uses a constructor. Each class has at least one constructor; sometimes there might be more than one constructor. The constructors for the Label class are listed in Figure 3-11.

Constructor	Example	Description
public Label ()	Label myLabel = new Label ();	Creates a blank label
public Label (String label)	Label myLabel = new Label("My Label");	Creates the label "My Label"
public Label (String label, int align)	Label myLabel = new Label("My Label", Label.CENTER);	Creates the label "My Label" that is centered on the label

Figure 3-11: Label object constructors

How does the compiler know what constructor to use when there is more than one? Although all three constructors have the same name, none of the constructors have the same argument list. The **argument list** contains the items inside the parentheses. The arguments are values that the method requires to do its job. The compiler picks the constructor based on the number of arguments in the argument list. What if the programmer has too many arguments? The compiler will give an error message to the programmer and will not compile the program. By the way, having more than one method with the same name is called **overloading**.

Accessing and Modifying a Class Type

Accessing the data portion of an object should be done only by the methods that are part of the object's classes. In all the predefined classes there are methods that allow the programmer to access the information in the object. Let's use the Label class as an example. Remember from Tutorial 2 that there are four parts to the method header: level of accessibility, return value, name, and argument list. Figure 3-12 shows a list of the other methods associated with the Label class. The Label class has methods that allow you to view and/or modify the alignment of the Label text while the applet is running. You should access or modify an object's properties only through that object's methods.

Method	Description
public int getAlignment ()	Returns the integer value showing the label alignment
public String getText ()	Returns the label text as a String
protected String paramString ()	Returns a String that reports the status of the label; used in debugging
public void setAlignment (int alignment)	Sets the alignment of the label, using Label.LEFT, Label.CENTER, or Label.RIGHT as arguments
public void setText (String label)	Sets the text of the label to the String argument

Figure 3-12: Label class methods

Now you can either take a break or complete the end-of-lesson questions and exercises.

SUMMARY

- The three characteristics of variables are name, type, and value.
- A memory address is a unique binary number assigned to a location in the computer's memory.
- Identifier names must start with a letter and can have any combinations of letters and numbers. An identifier cannot be a keyword.
- There are accepted conventions for Java identifiers. For methods and variables, the first word must start with a lowercase letter, and every other word must start with an uppercase letter; for classes, capitalize the first letter of every word; and for constants, use all capital letters and separate words with an underscore.
- The two major categories of types in Java are primitive and reference. The primitive types are boolean, integral (char, byte, short, int, long), float, and double.
- Constants have all the properties of variables except their contents cannot be changed.
- Literals are values that are part of the program code. They are not input or calculated values.
- Strings can contain multiple characters but the char data type can contain only one character.
- Control characters use Unicode to display characters that are not keyboard characters or that are difficult to input.
- The three categories of type conversion are widening primitive conversion, narrowing primitive conversion, and String conversion.
- String concatenation allows the programmer to build a larger String from smaller pieces by using the + operator to concatenate the pieces.
- The three reference types are arrays, classes, and interfaces.
- A constructor function builds an object of a given class.
- To access and modify an object's data fields legally, use the methods provided by the class.

QUESTIONS

1. Where does a program store data in a variable?
   a. on the hard drive
   b. on a floppy disk
   c. on a CD-ROM
   d. on the computer's memory
2. Which of the following items is not a property of a variable?
   a. method
   b. type
   c. value
   d. name
3. Which of the following items is an acceptable first character in a Java identifier?
   a. number
   b. letter
   c. period
   d. semicolon

4. Which of the following items is an acceptable Java identifier?
 a. 2Be
 b. Be2
 c. .2Be
 d. ;2Be
5. The accepted rule for naming Java identifiers states that __________ must include all capital letters with underscores between words.
 a. fields
 b. methods
 c. classes
 d. constants
6. The two categories of primitive types are __________.
 a. boolean and numeric
 b. floating point and integers
 c. object and class
 d. short and long
7. The order of integral types, from smallest to largest is __________.
 a. short, byte, int, long, and char
 b. int, byte, short, char, and long
 c. byte, short, char, int, and long
 d. byte, short, char, long, and int
8. Which of the following items is a legal char literal?
 a. "A"
 b. 'aba'
 c. '/n'
 d. 'A'
9. Which of the following items is a widening primitive conversion, given the following declarations:
 int intA;
 byte byteA;
 short shortA;
 float floatA;
 a. intA = byteA
 b. byteA = intA
 c. byteA = shortA
 d. floatA = doubleA
10. Describe the following method. What is its name, what does it return, and what are its arguments?
 public String myString (int num, String Word)

EXERCISES

1. Write legal Java identifiers for each of the following values.
 a. cost of an item
 b. water temperature
 c. number of children
 d. person's age
 e. years in school
 f. number of siblings

2. Explain why each of the following assignment statements is invalid.
   a. int 2Age = 45;
   b. char myLetter = "C";
   c. byte numFingers = 237;
   d. float weight = "43.9";
   e. int Joe'sKids = 4;
   f. short price = 243.67;
3. Write statements to concatenate each of the following short Strings.
   a. "I" "love" "you"
   b. "I need " 5 " items at the store"
   c. "I see" 11 "students"
   d. "I have" 6 "cookies to share"
   e. "Where are" "you" "going?"
   f. "There are" 101 "Dalmatians on the lawn"
4. Create labels to store the following text.
   a. first name
   b. student identification number
   c. marital status
   d. [blank]
   e. teacher's name
   f. overall units

LESSON B

objectives

In this lesson you will learn how to:

- Determine the variables and their types to use and to include in an applet
- Declare a variable and assign values to simple variables
- Assign values using expressions
- Assign values using interactive input
- Declare a constant
- Convert types using Java statements
- Use output commands

Using Variables and Expressions in the BeanJar Applet

Designing and Defining a Type

In Tutorial 1, the TOE chart in Figure 1-25 described the different objects that are part of the BeanJar applet: a text field, a text area, labels, and the button. You did not determine the numeric primitive types that are used. The program needs numeric variables to hold the number of beans in the jar (the result), the height of the jar (the input), the volume of the jar, and the volume of one coffee bean. How does a programmer decide what type of numeric variables to use? There are two factors to keep in mind: the possible range of values and the way the output should be shown.

You might think that the number of beans should be an integer because the program is designed to calculate the number of whole beans that fit in the jar. To make your program simpler, the input for the jar height is in whole inches, so the input is an integer. Bean volume and jar volume are floating point numbers because the formula for computing both values needs to use the mathematical constant Pi (3.1416). To decide the actual types of the variables, you need to consider the range of values. Because there are only two floating point numbers, and the size of the coffee beans is so small, these types will be double. Now, just to keep things simple, the types for jar height and number of beans are int. The number of beans cannot be an integer because the formula for computing the number of beans needs to use the jar volume and bean volume values, and they are both floating point numbers.

Declaring and Assigning Values to Simple Variables

Now you are ready to change the object types in the BeanJar.java applet. You will use the saved version of the applet on your Student Disk instead of the one you used in Tutorial 1.

To open the BeanJar.java applet:

1. Start Visual J++ and close any open workspaces, if necessary.
2. Open the **BJ.java** file from the BeanJar3 folder of the Tutorial3 folder on your Student Disk, and then use the Save As command to save it as **BeanJar3.java.**

The easiest way to declare a variable is to use the *typeName variableName* format.

To declare the variables using the *typeName variableName* format:

1. Click in the location shown in Figure 3-13, press the **Enter** key, and then type the lines shown in Figure 3-13.

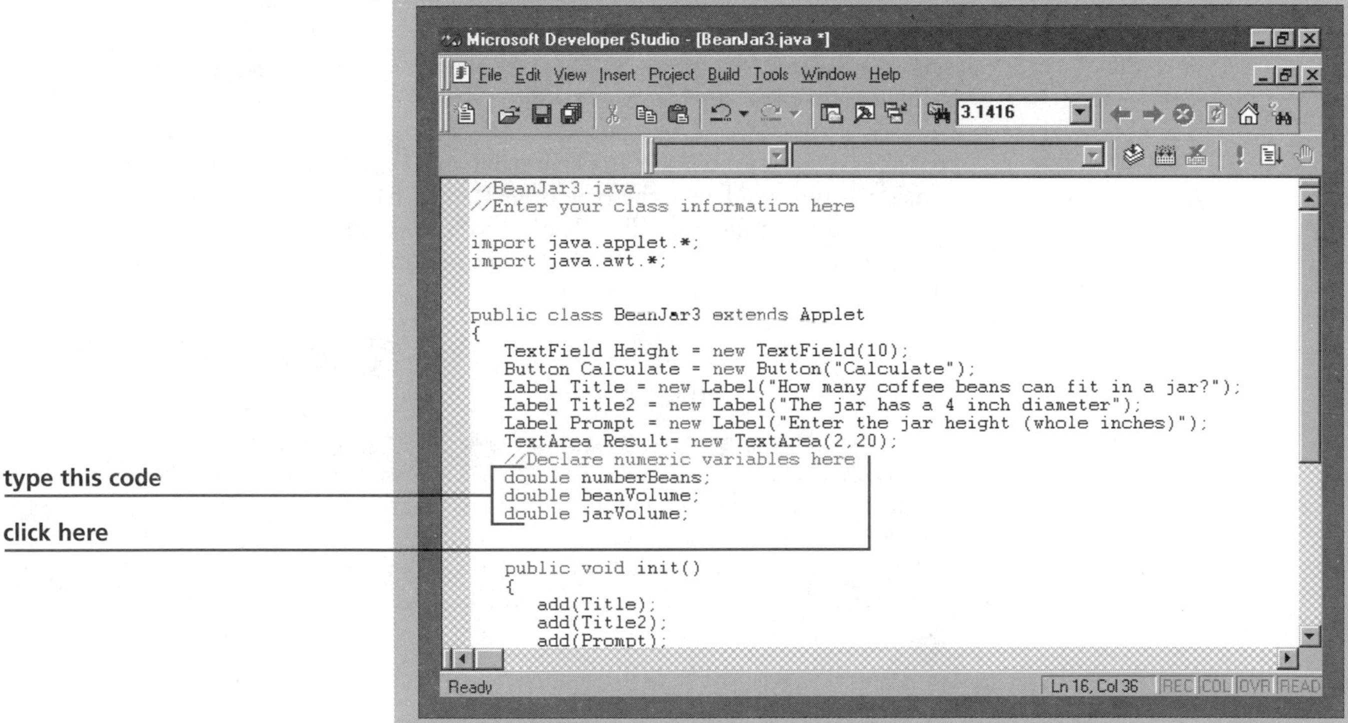

Figure 3-13: Declaring a variable

Before a variable can be used, it must have a value. There are three ways to store a value in a variable: use a default value, assign a value, and accept input. In the previous set of steps, default values were assigned to the variables. A **default value** is a value that a variable should hold if the program user does not specify another value. The default value for numeric types is zero—for integral types that is 0 and for floating point types that is 0.0. For the char type, the default value is the null character (Unicode '\u0000'), and for the boolean type the default is "false." Now the three variables that you just declared have default values. Next you will declare and assign a value to the jarRadius variable.

To declare the default value:

1 Press the **Enter** key, and then type **double jarRadius = 2.0;**.

The statement *double jarRadius = 2.0;* accomplishes two things at once. Not only is the double variable jarRadius being created, but an initial value of 2.0 is being stored in the variable. Now the statement as it stands works, but what if you change the type from double to float? Is 2.0 a float value? An interesting thing happens when you convert literals such as 2.0 to float—they are assigned a default type. All floating point types are assumed to be doubles. Take a look at what happens when jarRadius is changed from double to float.

To change jarRadius from double to float:

1 Select the word **double** in the double jarRadius = 2.0; line, and then type **float**.
2 Click the **Save** button on the Standard toolbar to save your changes.
3 Click the **Build** button on the Standard toolbar, and then click the **Yes** button to build the program in a default project workspace. The Output window reports one error.
4 Press the **F4** key to see the error message. The error message is "error J0068: Cannot implicitly convert 'double' to 'float'."

There are two ways to fix the problem of 2.0 being treated as a double. The easiest way is to change the type of jarRadius back to double. But to demonstrate that not all floating point literals need to be doubles, another method will be used to indicate that 2.0 is a float value, and not a double value. This is done by typing the letter "F" (or "f") after the number.

To correct the error:

1 Click in the location shown in Figure 3-14, and then type **F**.

click here

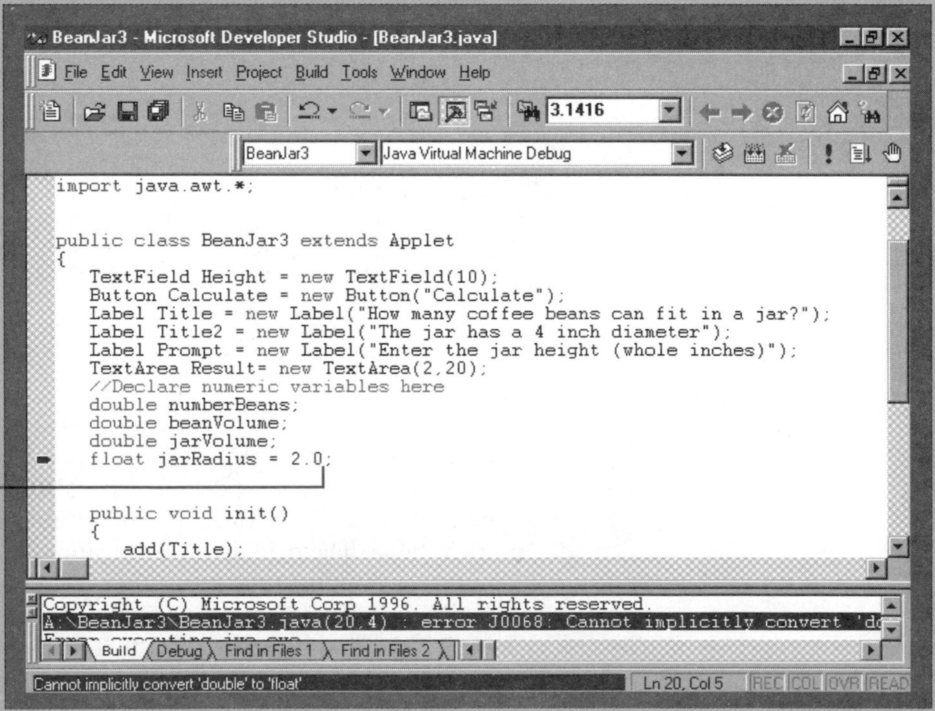
BeanJar3 - Microsoft Developer Studio - [BeanJar3.java]
File Edit View Insert Project Build Tools Window Help
3.1416
BeanJar3
Java Virtual Machine Debug
import java.awt.*;
public class BeanJar3 extends Applet
{
TextField Height = new TextField(10);
Button Calculate = new Button("Calculate");
Label Title = new Label("How many coffee beans can fit in a jar?");
Label Title2 = new Label("The jar has a 4 inch diameter");
Label Prompt = new Label("Enter the jar height (whole inches)");
TextArea Result= new TextArea(2,20);
//Declare numeric variables here
double numberBeans;
double beanVolume;
double jarVolume;
float jarRadius = 2.0;
public void init()
{
add(Title);
Copyright (C) Microsoft Corp 1996. All rights reserved.
A:\BeanJar3\BeanJar3.java(20,4) : error J0068: Cannot implicitly convert
Build Debug Find in Files 1 Find in Files 2
Cannot implicitly convert 'double' to 'float'
Ln 20, Col 5
REC COL OVR READ

Figure 3-14: Double into float error

2 Save your changes.

3 Build the program again. There should be no errors now.

Just as with floating point literals, an integer literal is assumed to be a certain type—the int type. When you need to store an integer literal in a long variable, type an "L" (or "l") after the value using the same steps.

Assigning Values Using Expressions

Take a closer look at the statement *float jarRadius = 2.0F;*. The syntax for the elements to the left of the equals sign (=) is familiar, but what about the right side? In an assignment statement, the part of the statement to the right of the equals sign is called an expression. An expression, as defined earlier, is a part of a Java statement that produces a result. A literal value is a very simple expression. If an expression produces a result, what kind of result does 2.0 produce? The result that 2.0 produces is its own value.

The syntax for the assignment statement is *variableName = expression*. This tutorial uses mathematical expressions. (Other types of expressions are covered later in the book.) In a mathematical expression, separate values (either literals or numeric variables) are "stuck together" using mathematical operators as a kind of glue. Most of the operators work with both floating point and integer values, but there is one that works only with integers, as shown in Figure 3-15.

Operator	Function	Types
+	Adds	Floating point and integer
-	Subtracts	Floating point and integer
*	Multiplies	Floating point and integer
/	Divides	Floating point and integer
%	Remainder	Integer only

Figure 3-15: Java operators

After using just one value, the next level up in terms of mathematical expressions is two values, called operands, and one operator. An **operand** is a value that is used by an operator. Figure 3-16 shows some sample assignment statements using two operands and one operator. Most of the results in Figure 3-16 are as expected. There are three unexpected outcomes, and all of them are in the integer assignments. The *intA* = 7 / 2 result of 3 demonstrates that integer division truncates the result. For example, if the floating point result is 3.999999, the truncated integer result is 3. The last remainder operation, *intA* = 2 % 7 is actually very logical.

int Assignment	Result	Double Assignment	Result
intA = 5 + 10;	15	doubleA = 5.0 + 10.0	15.0
intA = intA - 8	7	doubleA = doubleA - 8.0	7.0
intA = 8 / 2	4	doubleA = 8.0 / 2.0	4.0
intA = 7 / 2	3	doubleA = 7.0 / 2.0	3.5
intA = 8 % 2	0		
intA = 7 % 2	1		
intA = 2 % 7	2		

Figure 3-16: Sample two-operand assignments

The remainder operator % (the percent sign) is what remains after you divide the first operand by the second operand. As you can see in Figure 3-17, when you divide 2 by 7, that 7 goes into 2 zero times with a remainder of 2. The expression 7 % 2 has a result of 2.

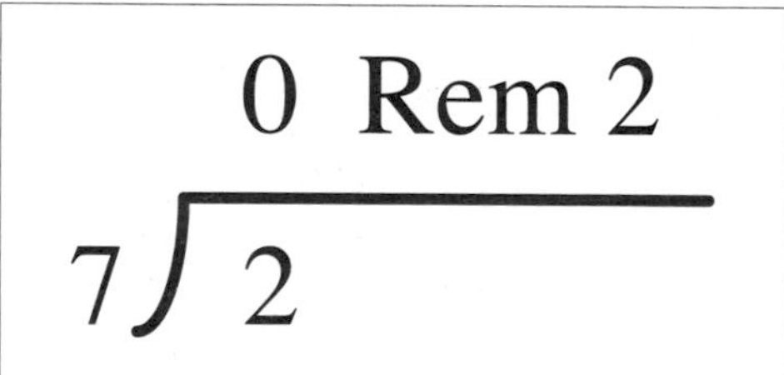

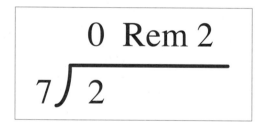

Figure 3-17: Long division

Shortcut Operators

A common thing to do in programming is to take some variable, change it by some operation, and then store the new results back in the same variable. Figure 3-18 shows the special operators to do just that. The advantage of using these operators is that they save typing time. Assume that intA is 7 and doubleA is 7.0 and then consider the first operator, +=. To write an assignment statement without using the shortcut operator, you would type *intA = intA + 5* instead of what is in Figure 3-18.

Operator	Sample Assignments	Result
+=	intA += 5; doubleA += 5.0;	12 12.0
-=	intA -= 5 doubleA -= 5.0	2 2.0
*=	intA *= 5 doubleA *= 5.0	35 35.0
/=	intA /= 2 doubleA /= 2.0	3 3.5
%=	intA %= 5	2

Figure 3-18: Shortcut operators

There is another class of shortcut operators to consider: the increment (++) and decrement (--) operators. These operators can be applied only to variables, and not to literals. The operators take the value in the variable and either add one (++) or subtract one (--). So if intA contains 5, intA++ changes intA to contain 6, intA -- changes intA to contain 4. These operators can be used with the floating point types as well.

Order of Operations

What happens in Java when there is more than one operator in an expression? Assignment statements like *intA = 5 + 2 * 3 / 4* are legal statements. But what value gets stored in intA? It all depends on the order of operation. The precedence rule for mathematics is parentheses, multiplication, division, addition, and subtraction to determine the calculation order when there is more than one operator in a single expression. In Java, operations are performed in the order shown in Figure 3-19. What happens when there is more than one operator from a given level in the expression? In this case the operations are performed from left to right. For example, in the expression *4 + 5 - 2*, the addition is done first.

Type	Operators
Increment/decrement/unary	++, --, and + -
Division/multiplication	/, %, and *
Addition/subtraction	+ and -
Assignment	=

Figure 3-19: Order of Java operators

Now you need to add some expressions to the BeanJar3 applet. The calculations needed are for calculating the volume of a coffee bean, the volume of the jar, and the number of beans. First you have to figure out how to calculate the volume of a coffee bean. You can treat the coffee bean as being like a flat biscuit, with two half-cylinders separated by a box. So to calculate the volume of the coffee bean, you need to calculate the volume of a cylinder and of a box. The formula for calculating the volume of a coffee bean is $(Pi * 0.125^2 * 0.15) + (0.25 * 0.25 * 0.15)$. Next you will update the BeanJar3 applet.

To add the formula to calculate the volume of a bean:

1 Click between the "e" and ";" as shown in Figure 3-20, and then type = **(3.1416 * (0.125 * 0.125) * 0.15) + (0.25 * 0.25 * 0.15).**

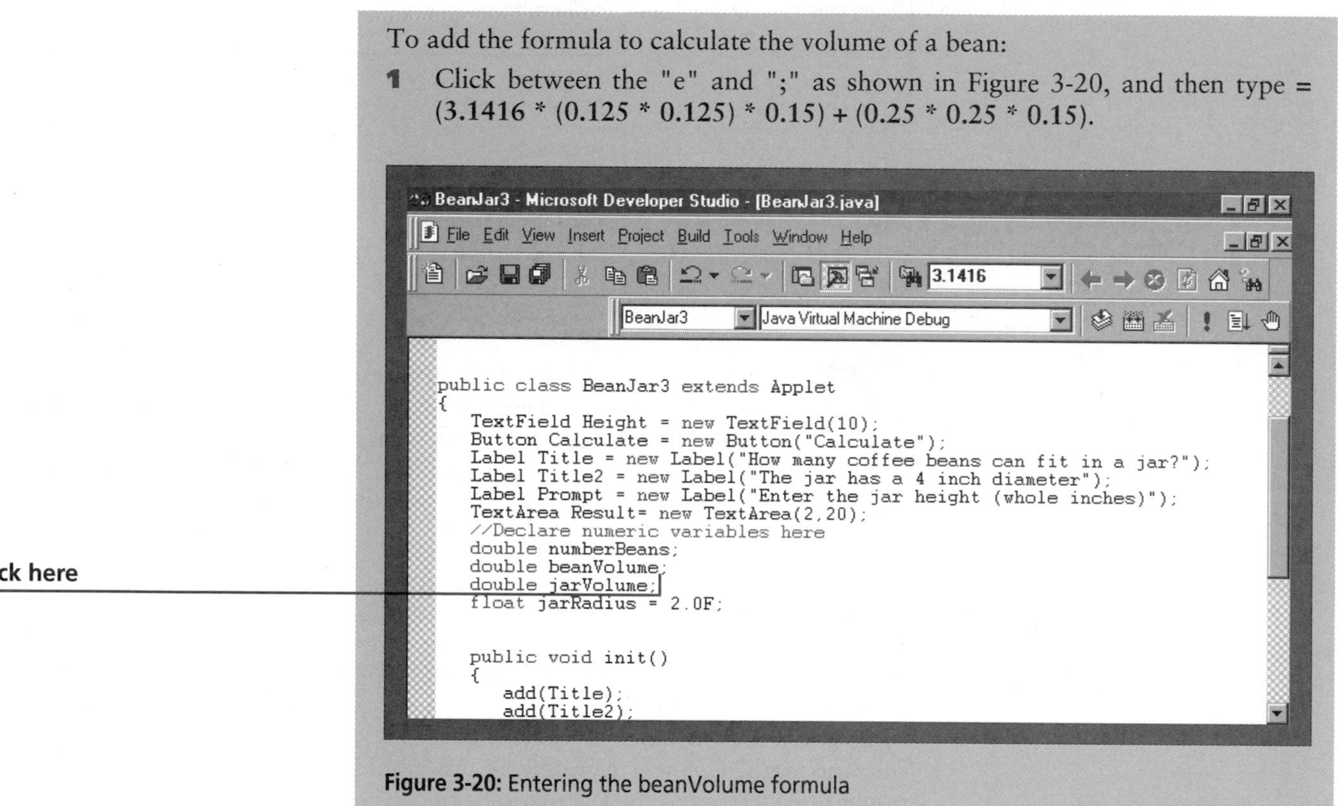


```
public class BeanJar3 extends Applet
{
   TextField Height = new TextField(10);
   Button Calculate = new Button("Calculate");
   Label Title = new Label("How many coffee beans can fit in a jar?");
   Label Title2 = new Label("The jar has a 4 inch diameter");
   Label Prompt = new Label("Enter the jar height (whole inches)");
   TextArea Result= new TextArea(2,20);
   //Declare numeric variables here
   double numberBeans;
   double beanVolume;
   double jarVolume;
   float jarRadius = 2.0F;

   public void init()
   {
      add(Title);
      add(Title2);
```

Figure 3-20: Entering the beanVolume formula

Next you will add two formulas in the action method because they depend on information input while the applet is running. The jarVolume formula is the formula for computing the volume of a cylinder ($Pi * radius^2 * height$) and the numberBeans formula is the jarVolume divided by the beanVolume, multiplied by the packing density, or a "fudge factor" of 60%. The fudge factor allows for the fact that there is still some air space in the jar. The beans do not fill all the space in the jar completely, even when the jar is full.

To add the jarVolume formula and the fudge factor:

1 Click in the location shown in Figure 3-21, press the **Enter** key, and then type the line shown in Figure 3-21.

BeanJar3 - Microsoft Developer Studio - [BeanJar3.java *]

File Edit View Insert Project Build Tools Window Help

3.1416

BeanJar3 | Java Virtual Machine Debug

```
float jarRadius = 2.0F;

public void init()
{
   add(Title);
   add(Title2);
   add(Prompt);
   add(Height);
   add(Calculate);
   add(Result);

}
public boolean action(Event thisEvent, Object thisObject)
{
    //Get numeric input here
    //Calculate values here
    jarVolume = 3.1416 * (2 * 2) * jarHeight;
    //Put output statements here
    return true;
```

click here

type this code

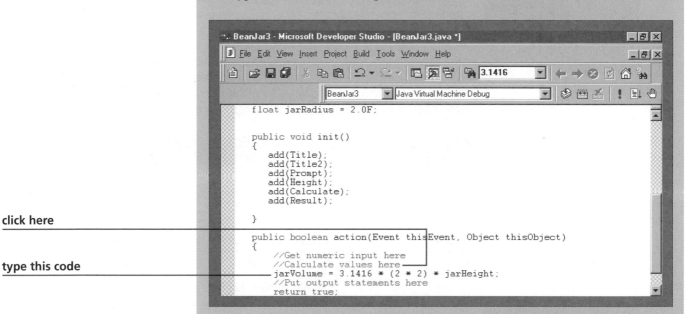

Figure 3-21: Adding the jarVolume formula and the fudge factor

2 Press the **Enter** key to go to the next line, and then type **numberBeans = (jarVolume / beanVolume) * 0.6; //60% fudge factor**, as shown in Figure 3-22.

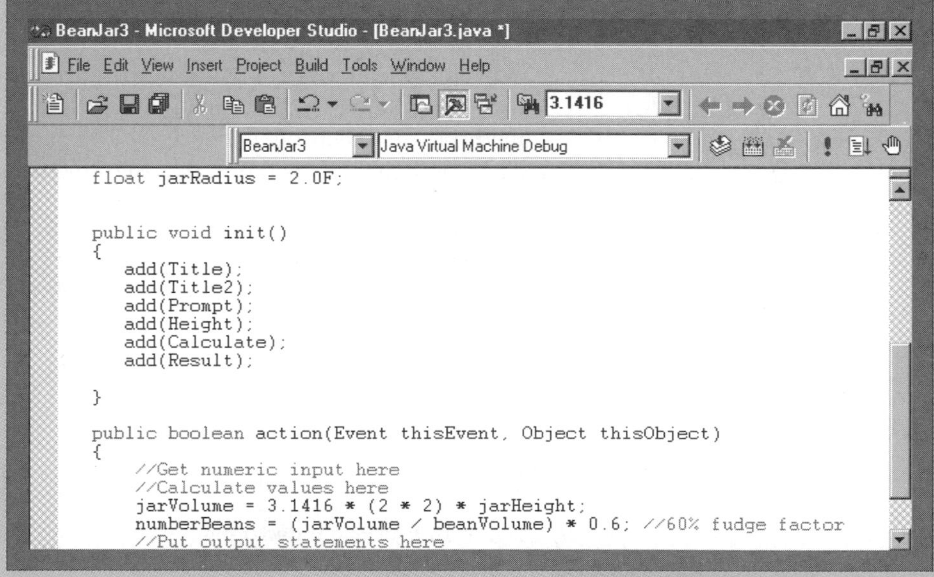

Figure 3-22: Adding action method formulas

Assigning Values Using Interactive Input

The program is designed so a user can type a number in the Height text field. Unfortunately, Java text components (text field and text area) return a String to the applet. Because you cannot use a String in a mathematical formula, you need to convert the inputted value from a String into an integer. You can do this by using a wrapper class. A **wrapper class** is a class that contains a primitive type. The purpose of wrapper classes is to allow programmers to manipulate primitive type variables in the same way that they can manipulate objects. For most of the primitive types there is a method associated with the corresponding wrapper class that translates a String into a variable of that primitive type, as shown in Figure 3-23.

Primitive Type	Method Name	Example
boolean	ValueOf (String s)	Boolean.valueOf("false")
double	ValueOf (String s)	Double.valueOf("1234.67")
float	ValueOf (String s)	Float.valueOf("1234.67F")
integer	ParseInt (String s)	Integer.parseInt("45")
long	ParseLong (String s)	Long.parseLong("1278900")

Figure 3-23: String translation methods

You can use a feature of Java that allows you to use one statement to get the input from the text field, convert it to an integer, and then assign the value to the variable. You can do this because of the order in which expressions are evaluated. Figure 3-24 shows the result of each part of the statement. Because the overall statement is an assignment statement, the expression to the right of the equals sign is evaluated first. Next, because the parseInt method needs a String, its argument list is evaluated. Finally, the argument list is evaluated, and because it is an object method, that method is executed and it returns the String that parseInt needs. Then the parseInt method gives that int to the assignment statement, and that int is stored in jarHeight.

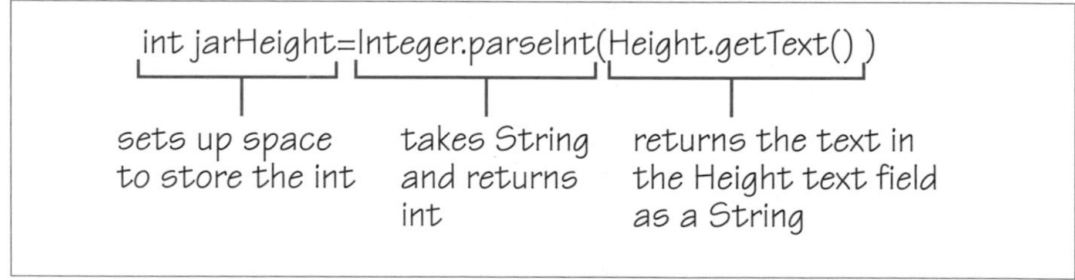

Figure 3-24: jarHeight declaration

To add the parseInt method:

1 Click in the location shown in Figure 3-25, press the **Enter** key, and then type the line shown in Figure 3-25.

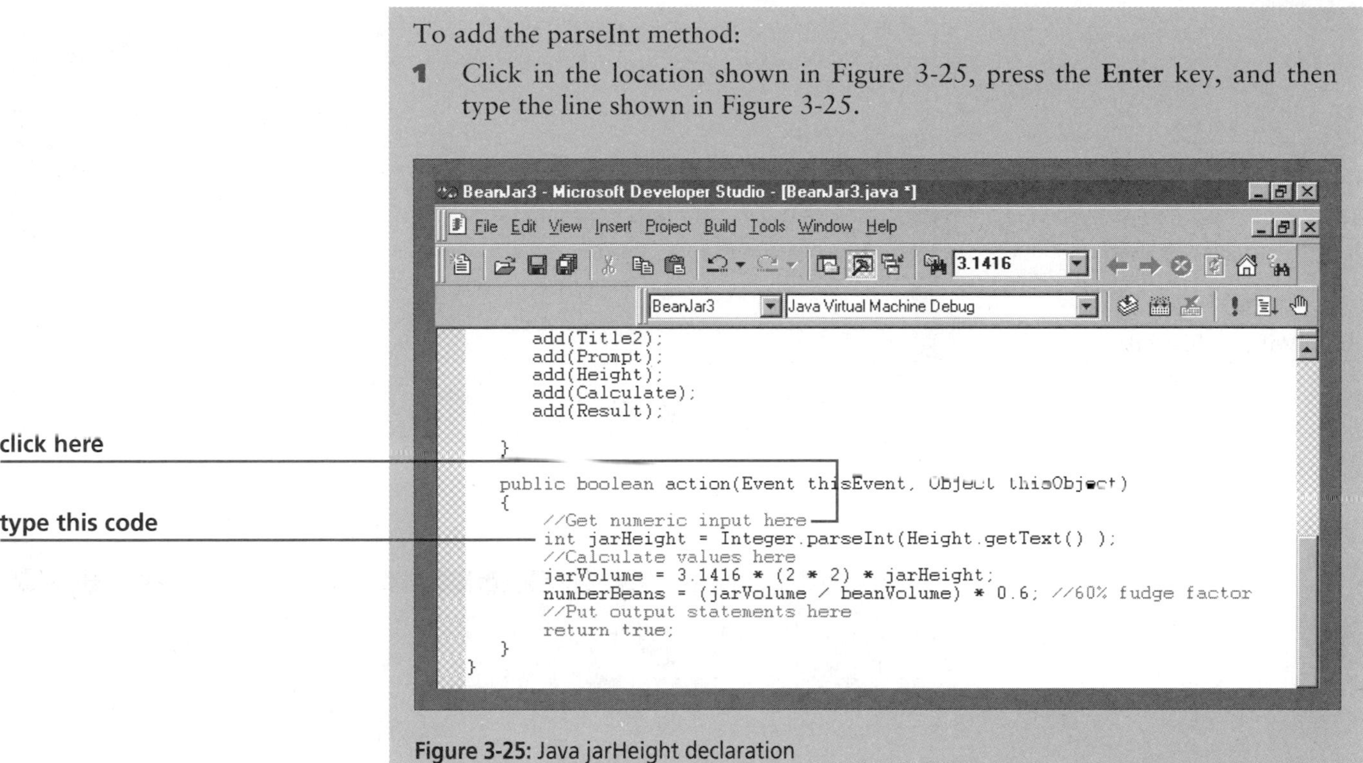

Figure 3-25: Java jarHeight declaration

Declaring a Constant

You might notice that you typed the value for Pi several times in your applet. Because this is a constant value, you can declare this value as a constant. In Java, any declaration with "final" as a qualifier will make that variable impossible to change using statements inside the applet. In the math class that is included in Java, one of the constants is defined is the **PI constant**. You can use math.PI instead of the literal value, 3.1416. Visual J++ defines math.PI as 3.14159265358979323846, which is much closer to the true value of PI than what you are using. Now while the BeanJar applet is not rocket science, this is a painless way to be more accurate in your calculations.

In this next group of steps, you will define two constants, MY_PI, and you will change the beanVolume variable to a constant as well. The convention for constants is to define them at the beginning of an applet, so you will move the beanVolume declaration before the GUI elements.

To move the beanVolume declaration and set the constant:

1 Press **Ctrl + Home** to go to the top of the applet.

2 Select the **double beanVolume** line, and then click the **Cut** button on the Standard toolbar.

3 Position the pointer to the left of the "T" in the TextField line.

4 Click the **Paste** button on the Standard toolbar, and then either press the **Enter** key or the **Spacebar** as needed to realign the TextField line with the surrounding lines of code, as shown in Figure 3-26.

new location of beanVolume formula

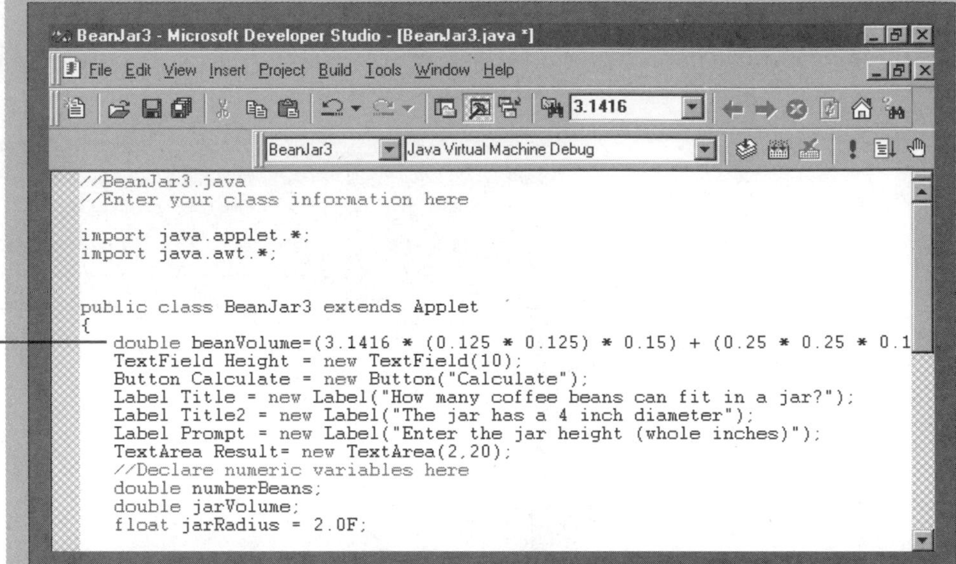

Figure 3-26: Moving beanVolume

5 Click in front of the word "double" in the beanVolume line, type **final**, and then press the **spacebar**.

6 Click at the beginning of the beanVolume line, and then press the **Enter** key to insert a blank line. Press ↑ to move the insertion point to the blank line, and then type **final double MY_PI = Math.PI;**.

7 Click **Edit** on the menu bar, and then click **Replace** to open the Replace dialog box, as shown in Figure 3-27.

tip

You also can press Ctrl + H to open the Replace dialog box.

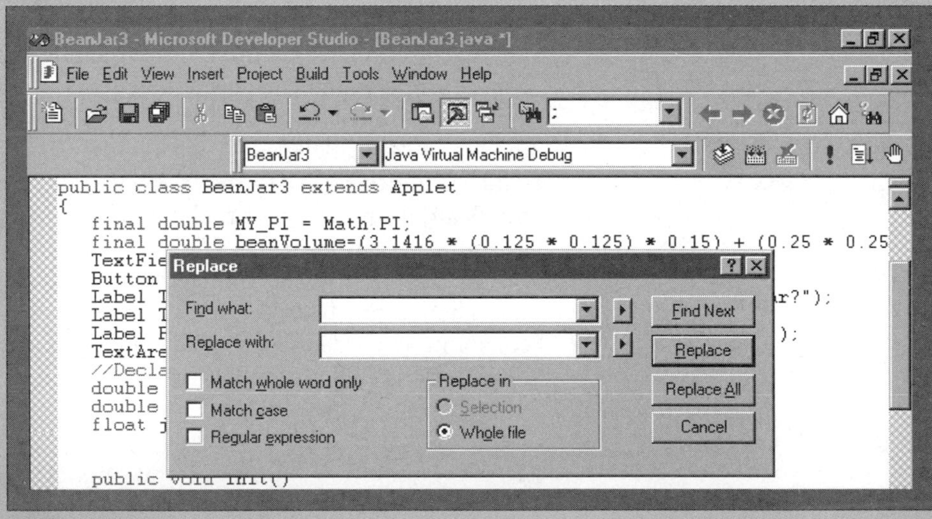

Figure 3-27: Replace dialog box

8 Type **3.1416** in the Find what text box, press the **Tab** key, type **MY_PI** in the Replace with text box, and then click the **Replace All** button.

9 Click the **Close** button to close the Replace dialog box.

10 Save your changes.

Now you have replaced the Pi values with a constant. Next you will use Java commands to convert types.

Click the second Tutorial 3 link of the Online Companion for this book (http://www.course.com) to see a live Java program that illustrates this topic.

Converting Types with Java Commands

To make sure that the numberBeans variable produces a result that is an integer, you must convert the floating point numbers to integers by using a method from the math class. The round method takes a double argument, and returns a long.

To convert from double to long:

1 Scroll down to the action method.

2 Click in the location shown in Figure 3-28, press the **Enter** key to insert a blank line, and then type the line shown in Figure 3-28.

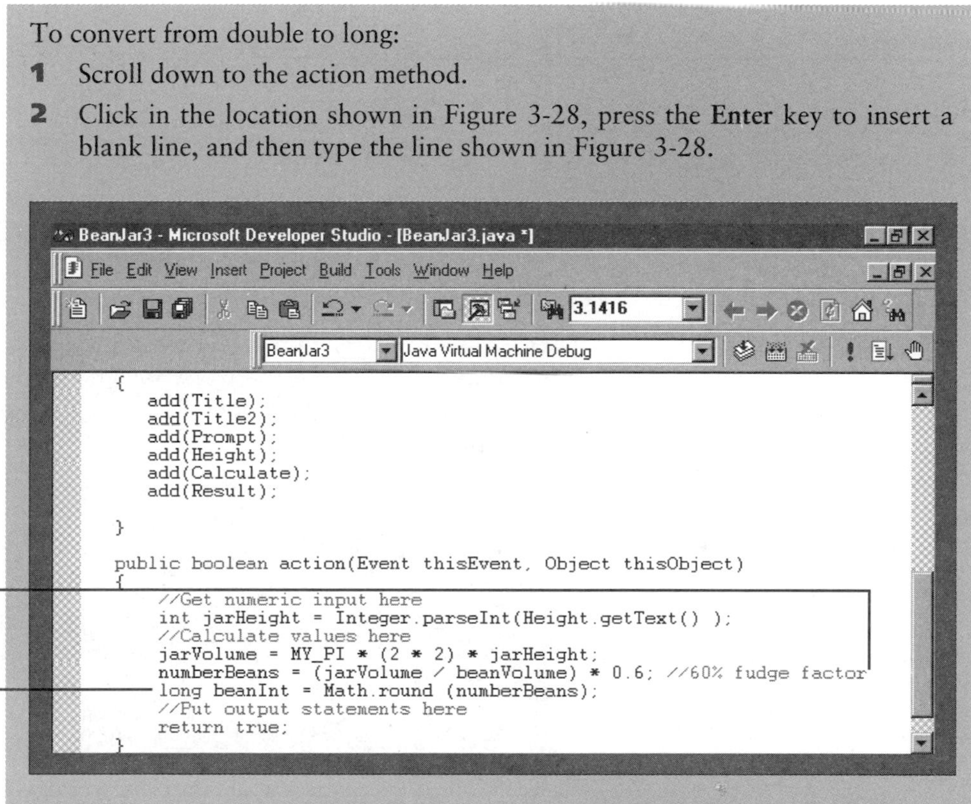


```
{
    add(Title);
    add(Title2);
    add(Prompt);
    add(Height);
    add(Calculate);
    add(Result);

}

public boolean action(Event thisEvent, Object thisObject)
{
    //Get numeric input here
    int jarHeight = Integer.parseInt(Height.getText() );
    //Calculate values here
    jarVolume = MY_PI * (2 * 2) * jarHeight;
    numberBeans = (jarVolume / beanVolume) * 0.6; //60% fudge factor
    long beanInt = Math.round (numberBeans);
    //Put output statements here
    return true;
}
```

Figure 3-28: Converting a double type to a long type

Pressing the Enter key might move the comment out of line; press the spacebar and the Delete key as needed to reposition the comment line.

Displaying and Using Output Commands

After adding the output statement, your applet will be done. You can use the appendText method of the text area object to add the output statement. The appendText method works only with Strings, and you have Strings and other primitives to work with. In the String class, concatenating a String automatically converts primitives to Strings. String concatenation is a way of making a long String out of short Strings and other values. To concatenate a String, tie the entire expression together using the + operator.

To concatenate the String:

1 Click in the location shown in Figure 3-29, press the **Enter** key, and then type the lines shown in Figure 3-29.

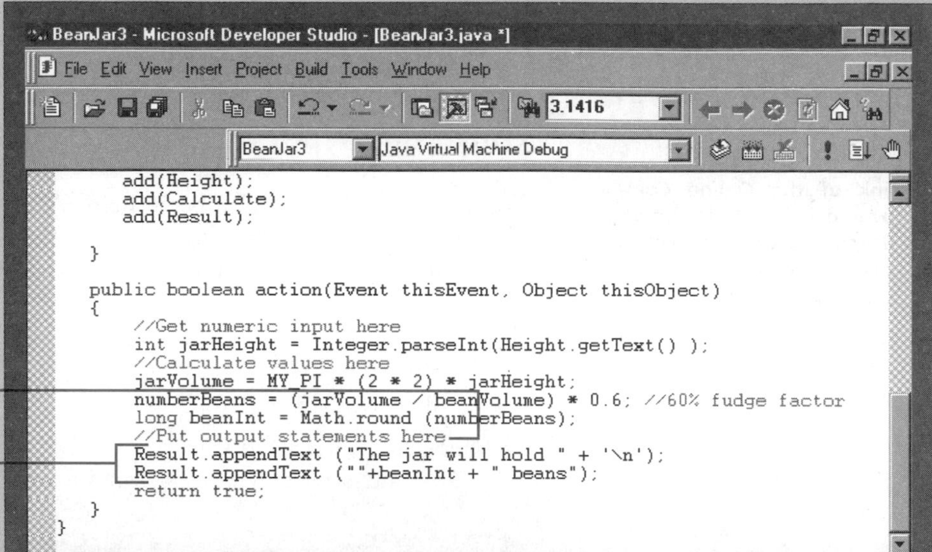

Figure 3-29: Output statements

HELP? Make sure that you press the spacebar after typing + in the first statement, and before the word "beans" in the second statement so that both your applet and your applet code will be more readable.

2 Save your changes.

3 Build the program and correct any errors.

4 Execute the program. The class filename is **BeanJar3**. The applet runs in Internet Explorer, as shown in Figure 3-30.

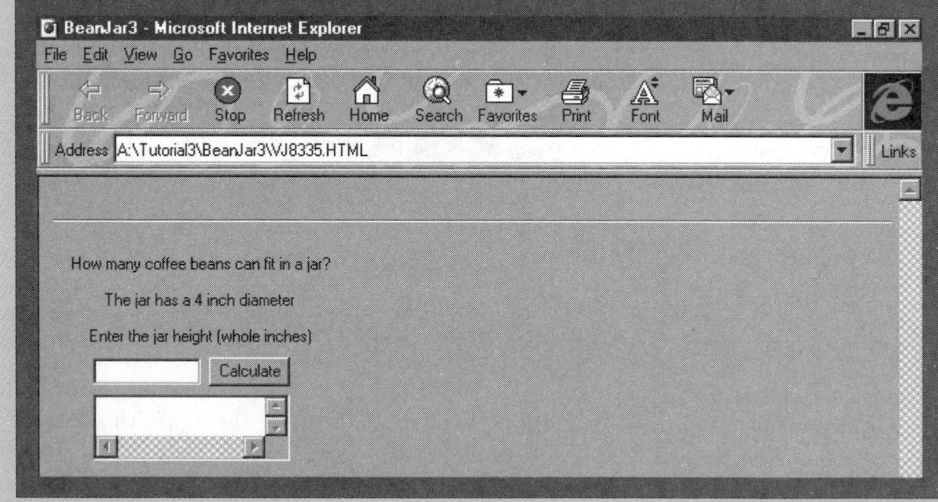

Figure 3-30: BeanJar3 running in Internet Explorer

5 Type 5 in the text box, and then click the **Calculate** button to test the applet. The jar can hold 2,252 beans.

6 Close Internet Explorer, close the project workspace and all document windows, and then close Visual J++.

Now you can either take a break or complete the end-of-lesson questions and exercises.

SUMMARY

- Programmers decide what types of variables to use by looking at the possible range of output values, and then selecting a type that can contain that range of values.
- To declare a primitive variable, the syntax is *TypeName VariableName*; to create a reference variable, the syntax is *ClassName ObjectName* = new *ClassName* (*Arguments*);.
- To assign values to simple variables, the syntax is *TypeName VariableName* = *Value*;.
- To force a floating point literal into a double variable, type an "F" (or "f") at the end of the literal.
- To force an integer literal into a long variable, type an "L" (or "l") at the end of the literal.
- To assign values using expressions, the syntax is *VariableName* = *Expression.*
- A mathematical expression can be a sequence of any number of operands and operators.
- The order of precedence in Java is increment/decrement/unary, division/multiplication, addition/subtraction, and then assignment.
- To assign values using interactive input from text fields or text areas, use the getText () method, which returns a String.
- To declare a constant, place the final keyword in front of the type, and then assign a value to the constant.
- To convert types using Java statements, use the wrapper classes.
- To output to a text area, use either the *textarea.setText* or *textarea.appendText* commands.

QUESTIONS

1. If a value is in the range 1 to 10, what is the smallest type that can store it?
a. byte
b. char
c. short
d. long

2. Which of the following declarations is illegal?
a. int = 5;
b. long drive;
c. long drive = 45690;
d. char ltr = 'a';

3. The literal 2.5 is stored as a __________.
   a. float
   b. double
   c. String
   d. long
4. The literal 546 is stored as a(n) __________.
   a. byte
   b. int
   c. short
   d. long
5. Which operator can be used only with integers?
   a. +
   b. *
   c. /
   d. %
6. Which of the following statements is invalid?
   a. intA += 8;
   b. intA -= 2;
   c. intA %= 3;
   d. intA += intA + 4;
7. What is the correct order of operations for the Java expression *5 + 2 * 3 / 4 - 2*?
   a. * / + -
   b. + * / -
   c. - / * +
   d. + - * /
8. Which of the following statements creates a valid constant?
   a. const days = 5;
   b. final days = 5;
   c. int days = 5;
   d. final int days = 5;
9. What does typing an "F" or an "L" do when assigning literal values to the appropriately typed variables?
10. What do the ++ and -- operators do?

EXERCISES

1. Use Visual J++ to write an applet to determine the number of hours from the present time until Saturday. Use labels and text fields to accept the number of days until Saturday and the number of hours that remain in the current day. Then multiply the number of days minus one times the constant 24 and add the number of hours that remain in the current day, triggered by a calculate button. The output should be in a text field. Use the T.java file from the Exercise1B folder in the Tutorial3 folder on your Student Disk as a model. Save the applet as Time.java in the Exercise1B folder in the Tutorial3 folder on your Student Disk. Test the applet with the following data:

Number of days	Number of hours
1	10
5	6
6	12

2. Use Visual J++ to write an applet to convert a time interval in hours, minutes, and seconds into total seconds. Use labels and text fields to accept the input, convert the value into seconds, and then use a text field to show the results. A Convert button should trigger the conversion. Use the C.java file from the Exercise2B folder in the Tutorial3 folder on your Student Disk as a model. Save the applet as Convert.java in the Exercise2B folder in the Tutorial3 folder on your Student Disk. Test the applet with the following data:

Hours	Minutes	Seconds
1	1	0
2	59	34
9	45	12

3. Use Visual J++ to write an applet to calculate your GPA. The input is number of units taken and total number of grade points (both numbers are integers). Use labels and text fields to accept the input, calculate the GPA (float value), and then display the result in a text field. A GPA button should trigger the calculation. Use the G.java file from the Exercise3B folder in the Tutorial3 folder on your Student Disk as a model. Save the applet as GPA.java in the Exercise3B folder in the Tutorial 3 folder on your Student Disk. Test the applet with the following data:

Units	Grade points
12	48
48	100
68	2454

4. Use Visual J++ to write an applet to calculate the number of gallons of paint that are needed to paint a house. Use a constant of 200 square feet covered per gallon of paint. Enter the square feet to be painted as a whole number, calculate the number of whole gallons needed (when the Gallons button is clicked), and then show the result in a text field. The applet should use labels and text fields as necessary. Use the P.java file from the Exercise4B folder in the Tutorial3 folder on your Student Disk as a model. Save the applet as Paint.java in the Exercise4B folder in the Tutorial3 folder on your Student Disk. Test the applet using 200, 500, and 1,000 square feet.

LESSON C

objectives

In this lesson you will learn how to:

- Update and modify a class design
- Write constructor functions
- Add new methods
- Add new fields
- Write an action method

Designing and Using Classes

Designing and Implementing a User Interface

Updating the Class Designs

The BeanJar3 applet works well, and now it is time to review and update the classes for the order entry program. One change to make for all classes is to add a version of the constructor method that uses a parameter list to place data in the data fields. Constructors are the conventional way to create objects. You will begin working with the Coffees class, and then work on the Customer class. You will change the Order class later in this tutorial. First you need to determine what additional elements—both data and methods—each class needs to create an effective order entry system.

Consider the coffee product class (Coffees). While it seems to have most of the correct data elements, or fields, there is one missing element—the caffeine field. At Koffee Koncoctions, many coffee products are available with or without caffeine. You need to add a boolean caffeine field that identifies the product as caffeinated or decaffeinated. Because you are adding a field, you need to modify the toString method and the empty parameter list constructor, and then add the change_caffeine method and the full parameter list constructor function. The updated Coffees class is shown in Figure 3-31.

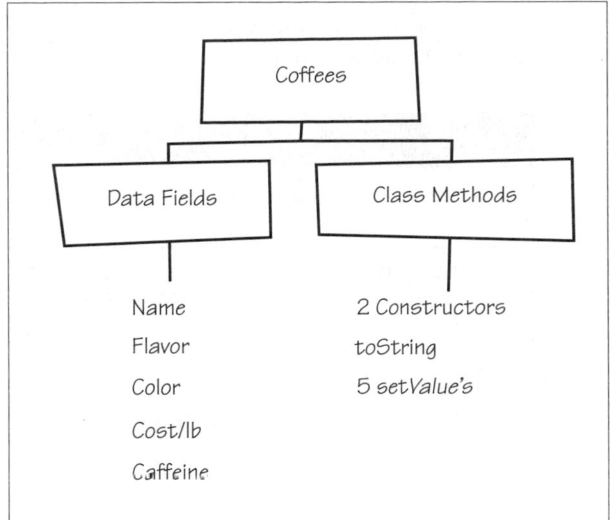

Figure 3-31: Updated Coffees class

There are several changes to make for the Customer class. First, the Name field should include separate fields for each customer's first and last names. You need to have a way for customers to use a credit card as payment. You can add two new fields to accept credit card payments, a boolean field to indicate the use of a credit card, and a String field to store the card number. To add these new methods, you will need to update the toString, and the empty parameter list constructor, and change_name methods, and then add the new methods change_charge, change_cardNum, and the full parameter list constructor method. The modified Customer class is shown in Figure 3-32.

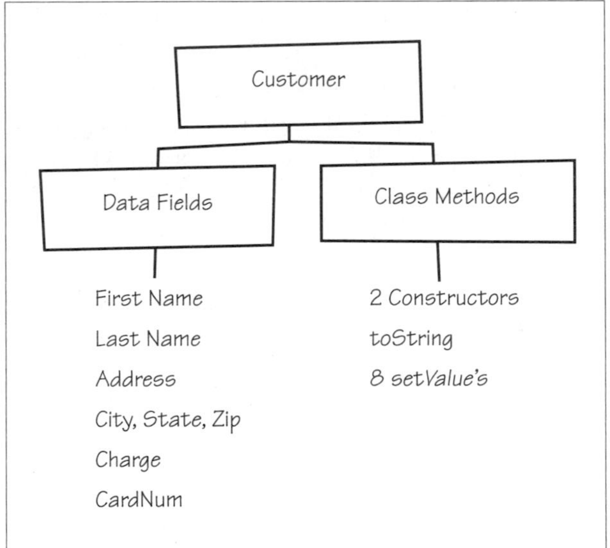

Figure 3-32: Updated Customer class

You decide to make a list of the necessary changes to keep track of what needs to be done. Your list is shown in Figure 3-33.

Task	Coffees	Customer
Add fields	Caffeine	First Name, Last Name, charge, cardNum
Add methods	setCaffeineValue full parameter list constructor	setLastNameValue, setChargeValue, setCardNumValue full parameter list constructor
Modify methods	toString, empty parameter list constructor	toString, setNameValue, empty parameter list constructor

Figure 3-33: List of tasks to complete the order entry system applet

Modifying the Coffees Class

In the Coffees class, you need to add a field, modify two methods, and add two methods. On the surface, it would seem that adding one field is a small change. But to stay within the guidelines of object-oriented programming, you need to add a method to change the contents of the new field and modify any methods that access all the fields. Adding the new field is a good place to start.

To add the new field:

1. Start Visual J++ and close any open workspaces, if necessary.
2. Open the **Cof.java** file in the Tutorial3C folder on your Student Disk, and then save it as **Coffees.java**.
3. Click in the location shown in Figure 3-34, press the **Enter** key, and then type the line shown in Figure 3-34.

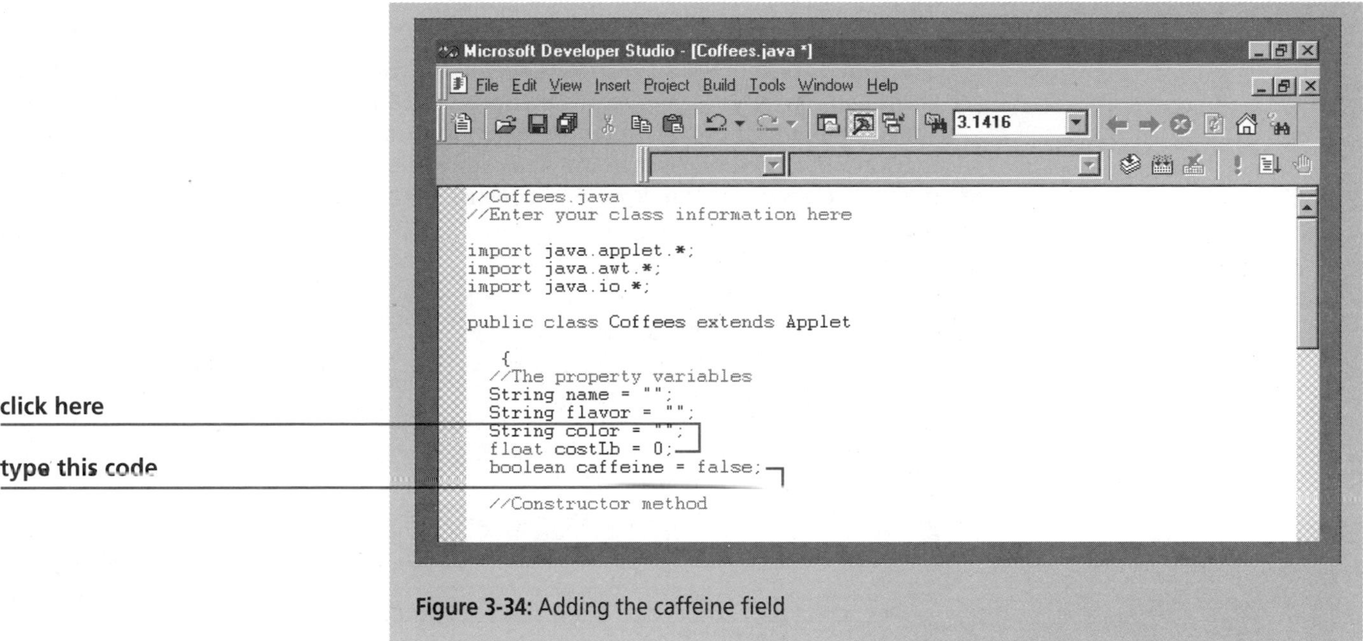

Figure 3-34: Adding the caffeine field

The toString method needs only one change—to add the Caffeine value to the String.

To change the toString method:

1. Click in the location shown in Figure 3-35, press the **Enter** key, and then type the code shown in Figure 3-35.

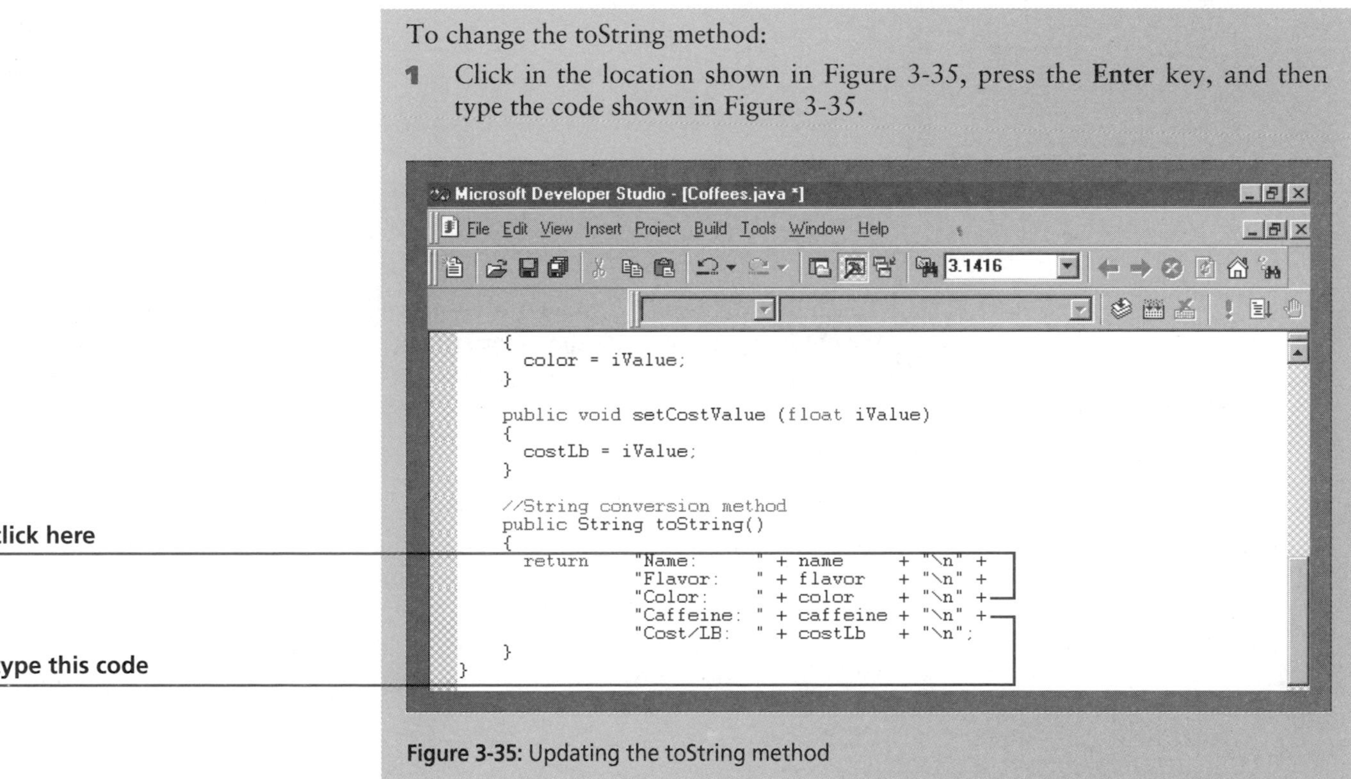

Figure 3-35: Updating the toString method

Writing and Modifying Constructor Functions

You can have more than one constructor function in Java. The Coffees.java program will have two constructor functions. The first constructor function (that you added in Tutorial 2) constructs a coffee product with null values in the fields, and the second constructor function will require all the values to be passed as parameters. All classes need at least one constructor method to "build" an instance of that class.

To add the constructor function:

1 Click in the location shown in Figure 3-36, press the **Enter** key, and type the new constructor shown in Figure 3-36.

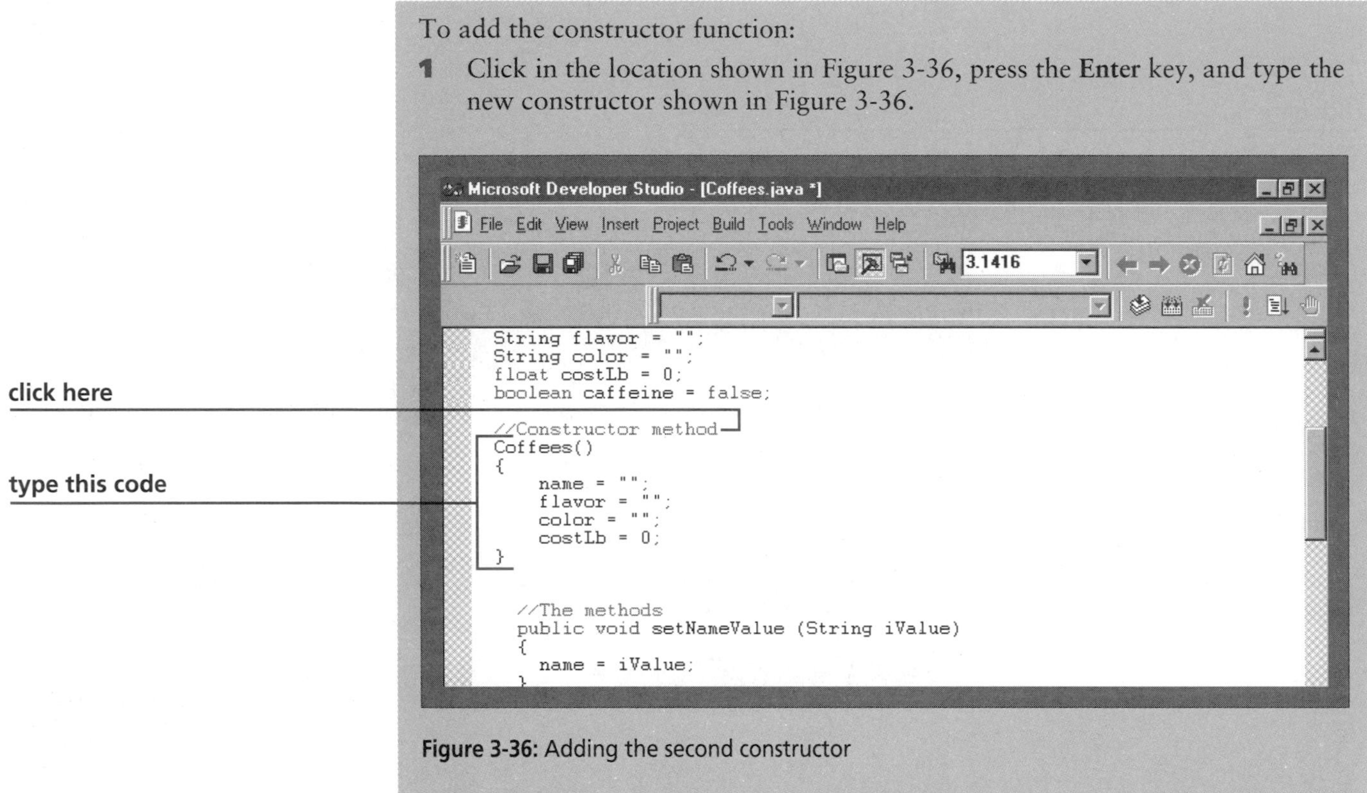

Figure 3-36: Adding the second constructor

2 To modify the empty argument list constructor method, click at the end of the color = " "; line, press the **Enter** key, and then type **caffeine = false;**.

Adding the New Method

There is only one new method, other than the full parameter constructor, to add to the Coffees class—to change the value stored in the caffeine field. In object-oriented programming, fields cannot be modified by any methods that do not belong to the class.

To add the new method:

1 Click in the location shown in Figure 3-37, press the **Enter** key twice, and type the setCaffeine method shown in Figure 3-37.

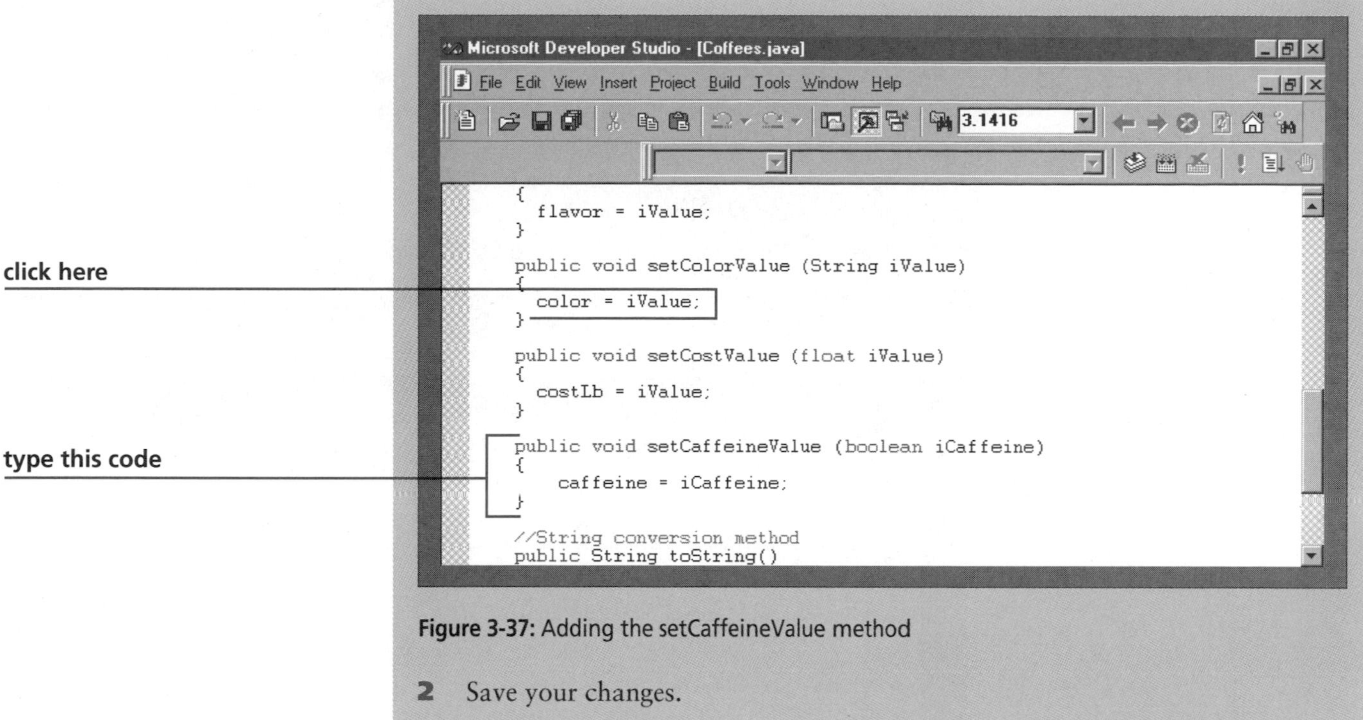

Figure 3-37: Adding the setCaffeineValue method

2 Save your changes.

At this point, it is important to test Coffees. You can compile the program, instead of building it, to test the program. If there are any syntax errors, they can be fixed now, instead of waiting until the other classes are modified.

To compile the program:

1 Click the **Compile** button on the Standard toolbar. Click the **Yes** button in the dialog box to create a default project workspace.

2 Correct any errors that appear in the Output window. Check for typing mistakes, problems with uppercase and lowercase letters, and missing semicolons, parentheses, or quotation marks.

Modifying the Customer Class

Now you can change the Customer class. You need to remove the name field and replace it with a firstName field and a lastName field. You need to add the boolean field, charge, and a String field named cardNum. For the methods, you need to add the full parameter list constructor, similar to the one you added to the Coffees class, and methods to change the name field, charge field, and the cardNum field. ToString, setNameValue, and empty parameter list constructor need to be modified.

To modify the Customer class:

1 Close the project workspace and all document windows.

2 Open the **Cust.java** file in the Tutorial3C folder on your Student Disk, and then save it as **Customer.java**.

3 Select the text **name = "";** (under the //The property values comment line), and then type **firstName = "";**.

4 Press the **Enter** key, and then type **String lastName = "";**.

5 Click at the end of the String zipCode = ""; line, press the **Enter** key, and then type the text shown in Figure 3-38.

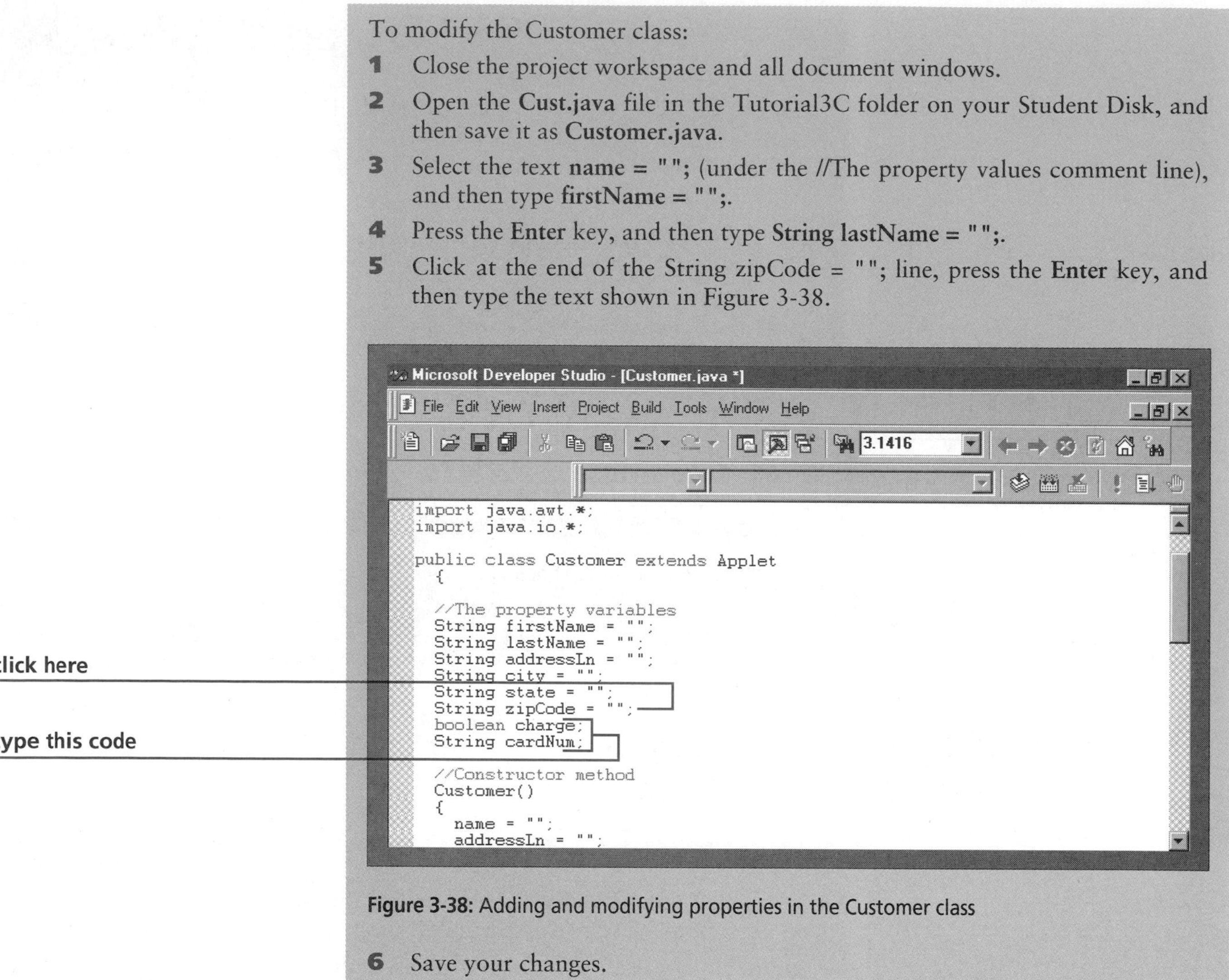

Figure 3-38: Adding and modifying properties in the Customer class

6 Save your changes.

You need to make several changes to the toString method: remove the name field, and then add firstName, lastName, charge, and cardNum to the String.

To change the toString method:

1 Scroll down and select the word **name**, as shown in Figure 3-39, and then type **firstName + " " + lastName**.

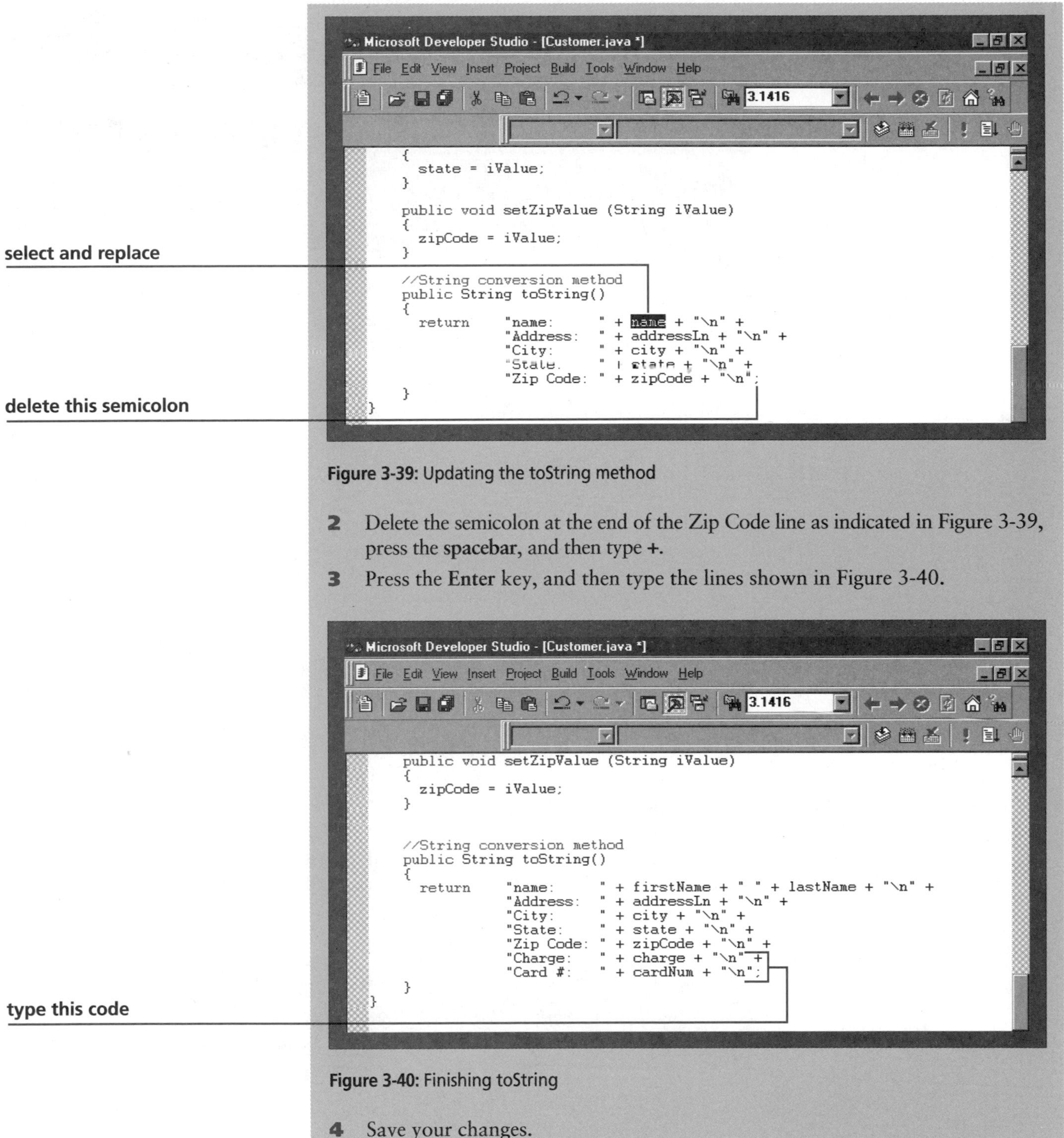

Figure 3-39: Updating the toString method

2 Delete the semicolon at the end of the Zip Code line as indicated in Figure 3-39, press the **spacebar**, and then type **+**.

3 Press the **Enter** key, and then type the lines shown in Figure 3-40.

Figure 3-40: Finishing toString

4 Save your changes.

Writing and Modifying the Constructor Functions

Just like in the Coffees class, you need to add the full parameter list constructor method to the Customer class.

To add the parameter list:

1 Click in the location shown in Figure 3-41, press the **Enter** key twice, and then type the full parameter list constructor method shown in Figure 3-41.

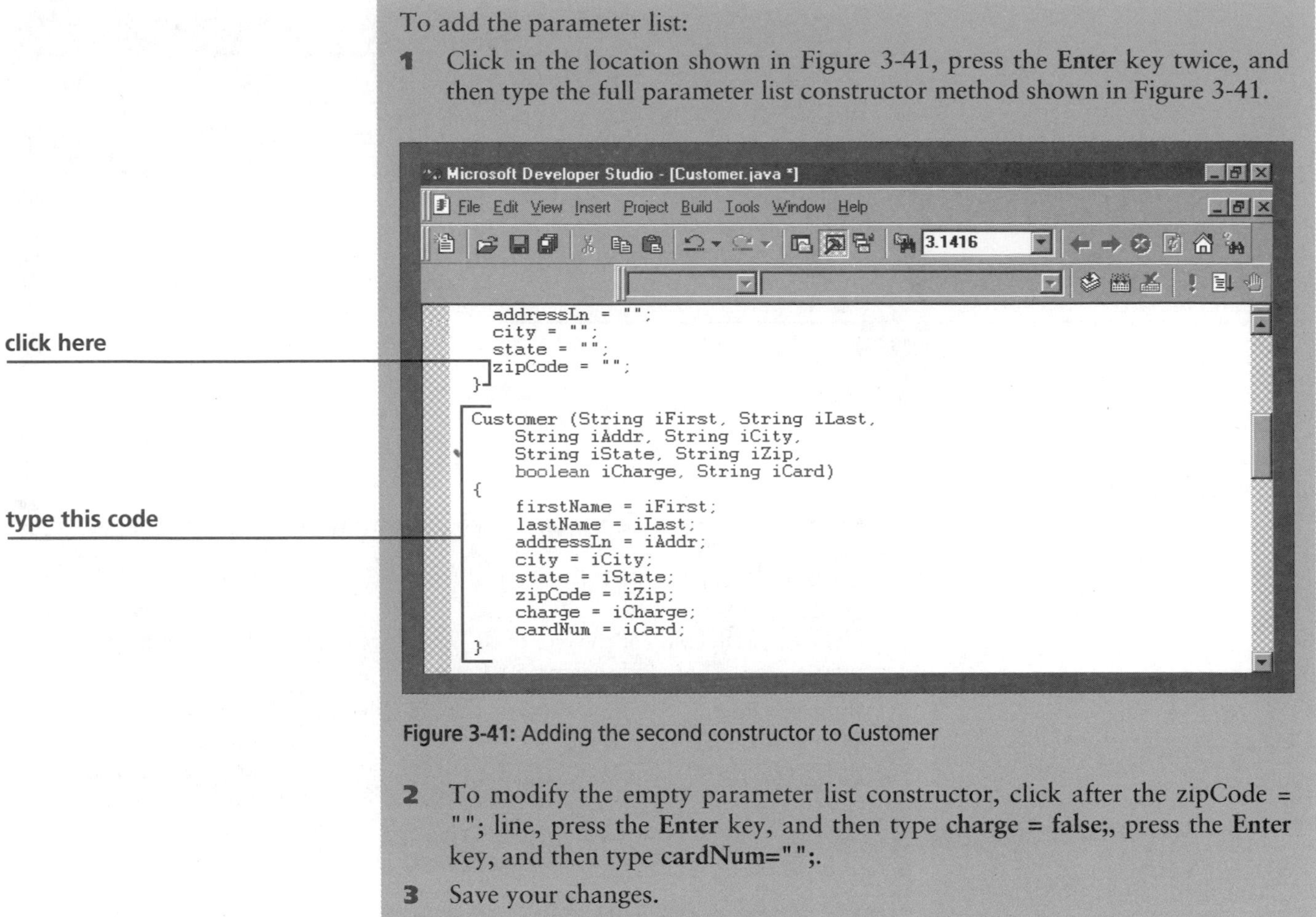

Figure 3-41: Adding the second constructor to Customer

2 To modify the empty parameter list constructor, click after the zipCode = ""; line, press the **Enter** key, and then type **charge = false;**, press the **Enter** key, and then type **cardNum="";**.

3 Save your changes.

Adding the New Methods

There are three new methods to add to the Customer class. You need to write the methods that will change the values stored in the last name, charge, and cardNum fields.

To add the new methods:

1 Click in the location shown in Figure 3-42, press the **Enter** key twice, and then type the setLastNameValue method shown in Figure 3-42.

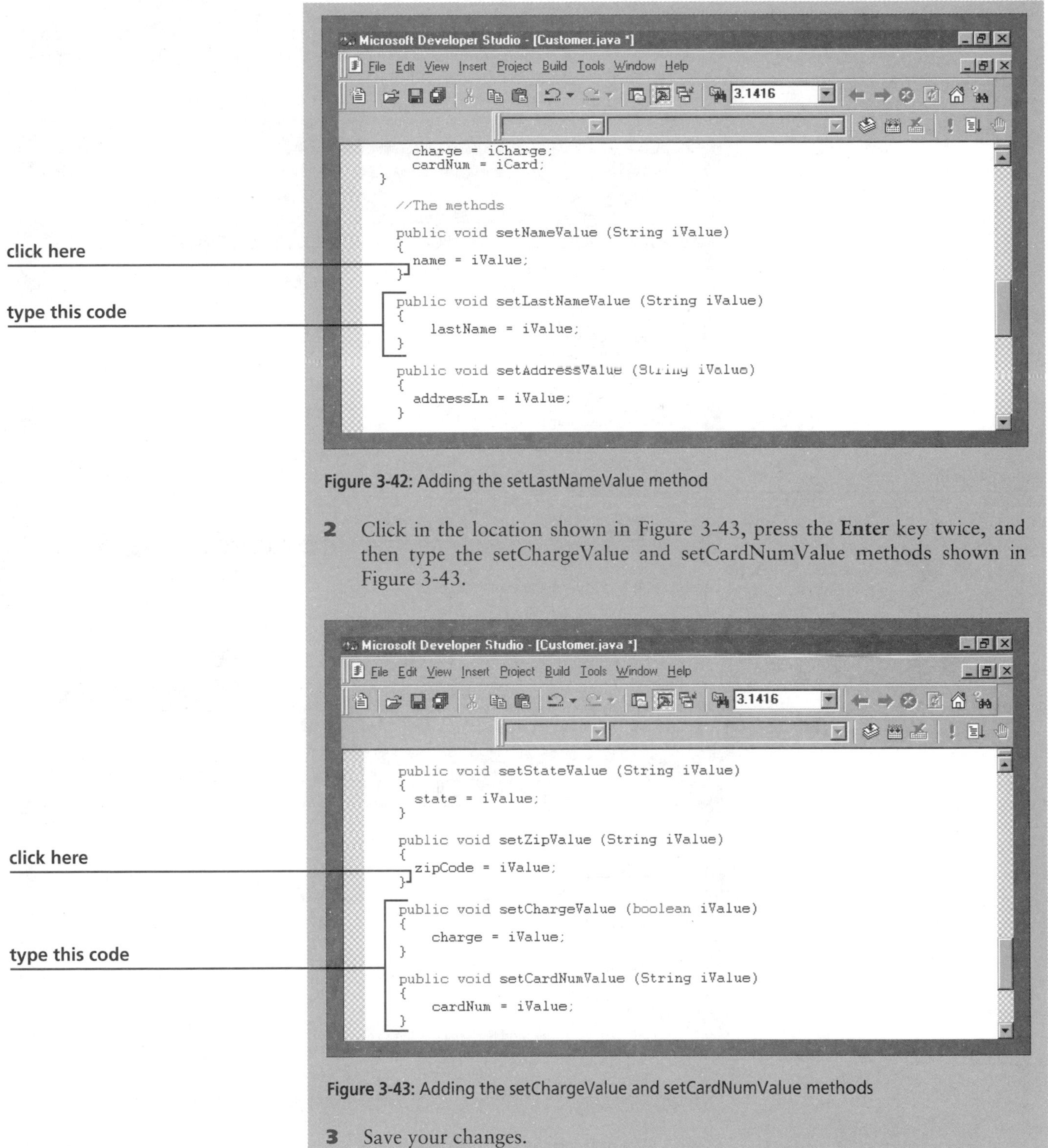

Figure 3-42: Adding the setLastNameValue method

2 Click in the location shown in Figure 3-43, press the **Enter** key twice, and then type the setChargeValue and setCardNumValue methods shown in Figure 3-43.

Figure 3-43: Adding the setChargeValue and setCardNumValue methods

3 Save your changes.

At this point, it is important to test the Customer class by compiling the program, instead of building it. If there are any syntax errors, they can be fixed now, instead of waiting until the other classes are modified. But first, you need to modify the setNameValue and the original constructor.

To modify the setNameValue method:

1 Select the line shown in Figure 3-44, and then type **firstName = "";**, press the **Enter** key, then type **lastName = "";**.

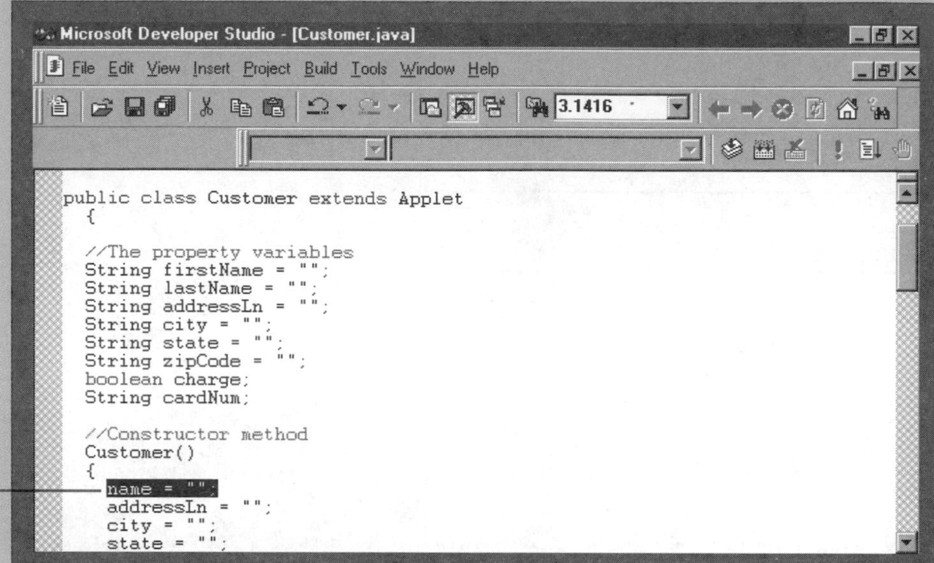

Figure 3-44: Modifying the constructor

2. Scroll down to the setNameValue method, and change it to look like Figure 3-45.

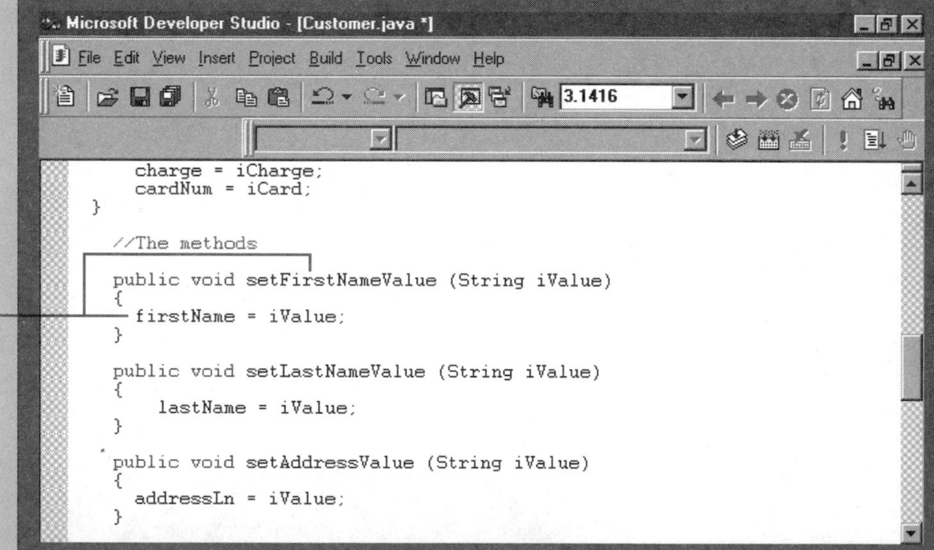

Figure 3-45: Modifying the setNameValue

3 Save your changes.

4 Click the **Compile** button on the Build toolbar. Click the **Yes** button to create a default project workspace.

5 Correct any errors that appear in the Output window.

Modifying the Order Class

For the Order class, Koffee Koncoctions wants to allow customers to order more than one product. As a first step toward allowing customers to order more than one product, you will expand the order class to include two coffee products. Then you will add calculated fields to determine netPrice, tax, shipping, and totalOrder. You also will modify two of the fields. Currently, the shipMethod and paymentTerms fields are Strings; you will change them to bytes, using a one-digit code to indicate shipping and payment methods. The Order class is shown in Figure 3-46.

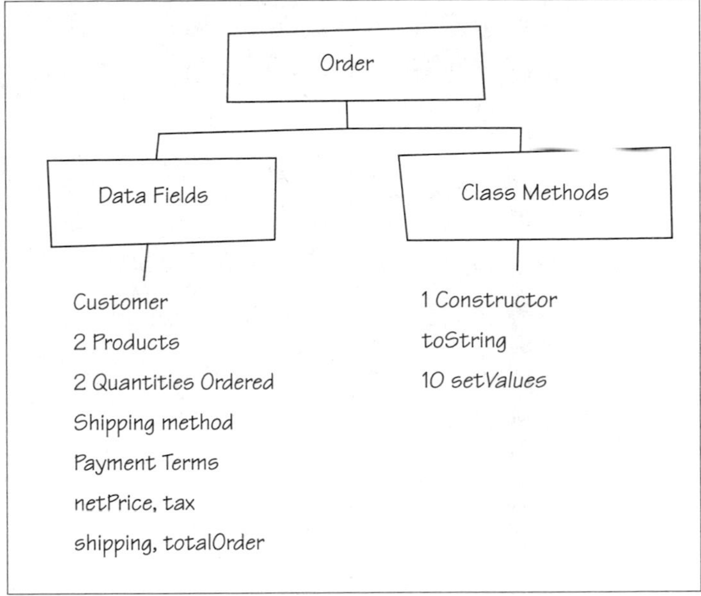

Figure 3-46: Updated Order class

Because the changes to the Order class are complex, you decide to make a checklist for the Order class. Figure 3-47 shows your checklist.

Task	Order Class
Add fields	netPrice, tax, shipping, totalOrder
Modify fields	itemQty1, itemQty2, shipMethod, paymentTerms
Add methods	setCustomerValue, setItem1Value, setItem2Value, setNetPriceValue, setTaxValue, setTotalOrderValue
Modify methods	setItemQty1Value, setItemQty2Value, setShipValue, setPaymentValue

Figure 3-47: Order class modifications

First you will add and modify fields. One of the changes that you will make is to change how you are using the objects from the Coffees and Customer classes. Currently you both declare and initialize, or set up with the empty constructor, both coffee items and the customer information. To change the Order class so that you can use the full parameter list constructors, you will declare only the objects, and not assign them to new instances.

To modify the Order class:

1 Close the project workspace and all document windows.

2 Open the **Ord.java** file from the Tutorial3C folder on your Student Disk, and then save it as **Order.java**.

3 Change the Customer cust = new Customer(); line to **Customer cust;**.

4 Delete **= new Coffees()** from the coffeeItem1 and 2 lines.

5 Click in the location shown in Figure 3-48, press the **Enter** key, and then type the code shown in Figure 3-48.

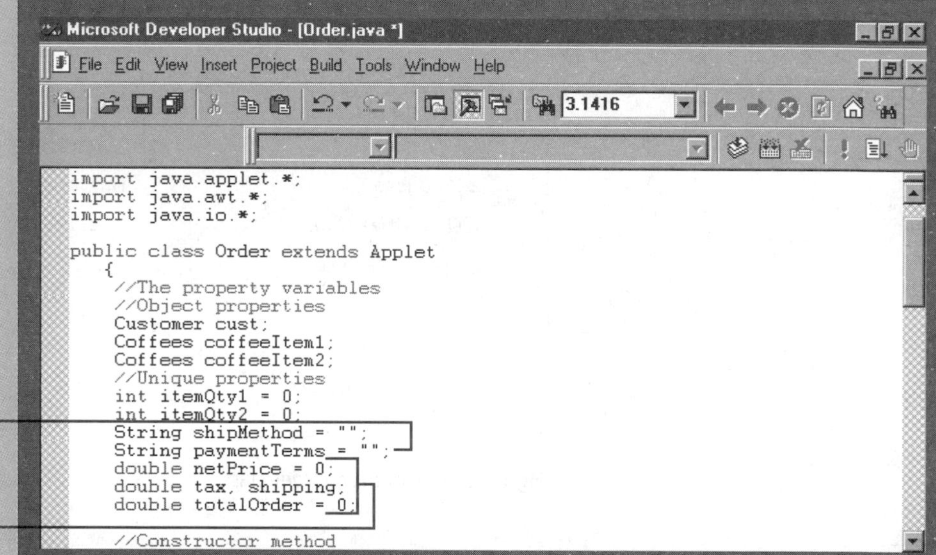

Figure 3-48: Modifying Order properties

6 Change the word "String" to **byte** for the shipMethod line and the paymentTerms line, and then change the empty quotation marks ("") to 2 for both lines. This will be the default value for both fields.

7 Change the type for both itemQty fields from int to **double**. This will allow customers to order in fractions of pounds. The properties section should now look like Figure 3-49.

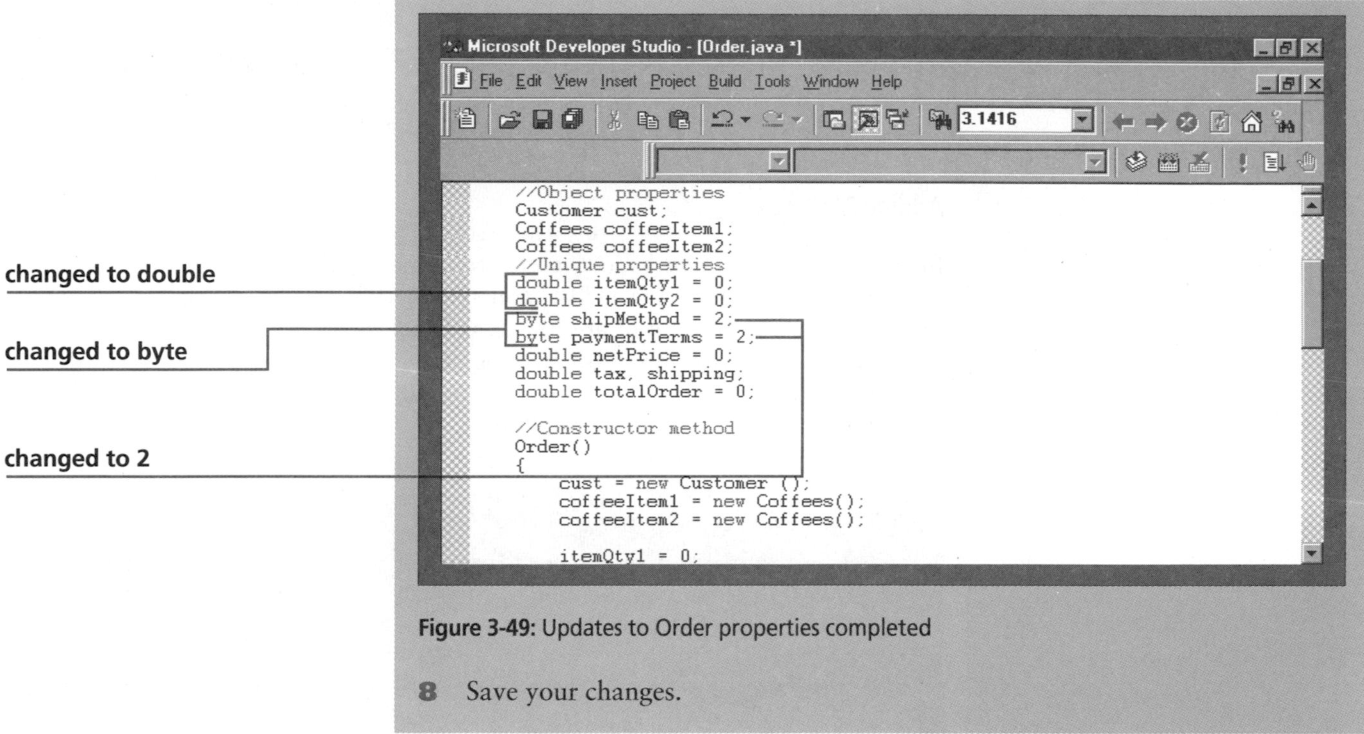

Figure 3-49: Updates to Order properties completed

8 Save your changes.

Next you need to modify the setValue methods for those properties that now have different types: itemQty1, itemQty2, shipMethod, and paymentTerms.

To modify the set value methods:

1 Change the int type to **double** and the String type to **byte** as shown in Figure 3-50.

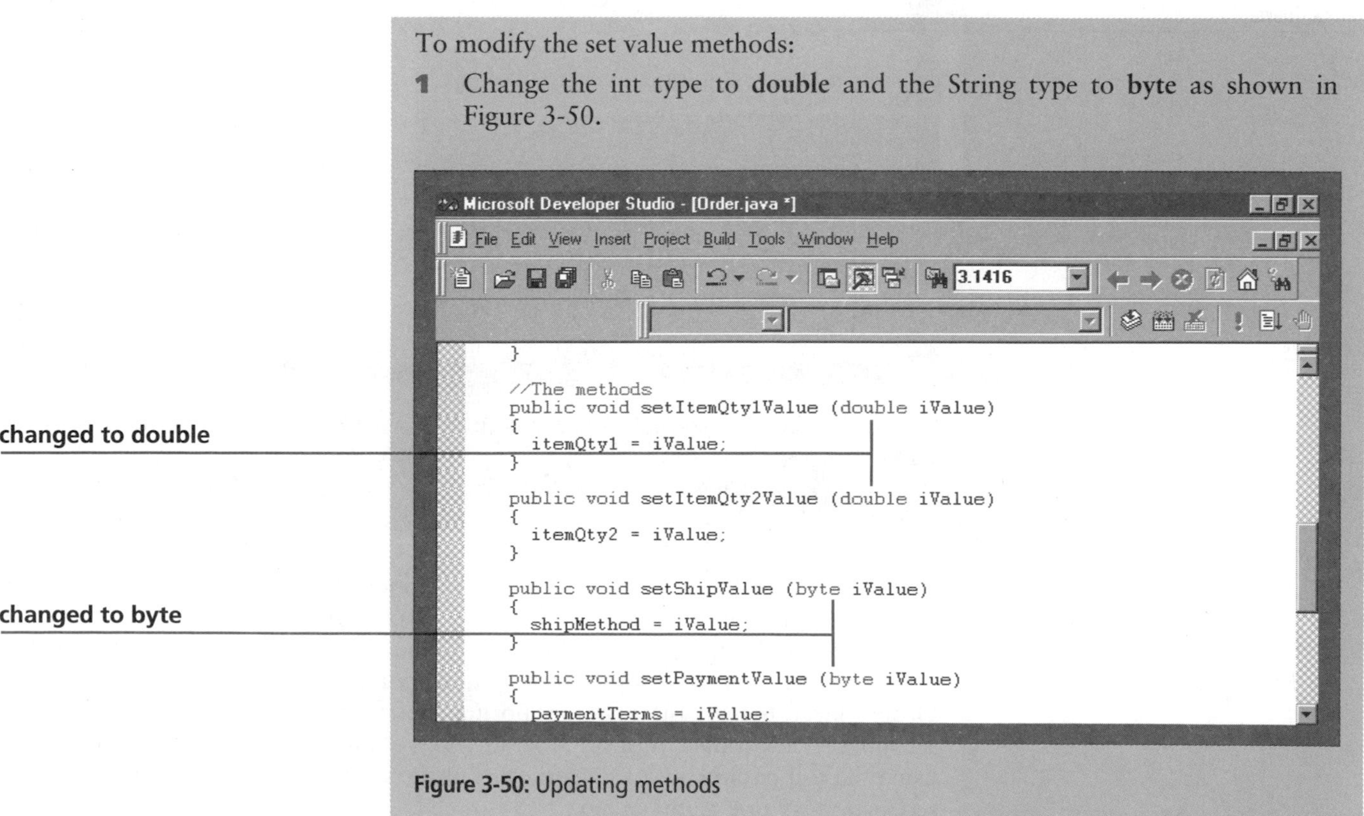

Figure 3-50: Updating methods

2 Before saving your changes, you need to modify the constructor method. Change both the shipMethod and paymentTerms assignments from "" to 2.

3 Save your changes.

Adding Methods

In the other classes, you have two constructors—one with no arguments and one with arguments for all the fields. You realize that having a constructor for the Order class with a full set of arguments will not work. All of the Order fields will come from interactive input. So for this class there will be only one constructor that you wrote in Tutorial 2. You need to add the set value methods for the new properties of netPrice, tax, and totalOrder.

To add the new methods:

1 Click in the location shown in Figure 3-51, press the **Enter** key twice, and then type the setNetPriceValue, setTaxValue, and setTotalOrderValue methods shown in Figure 3-51.

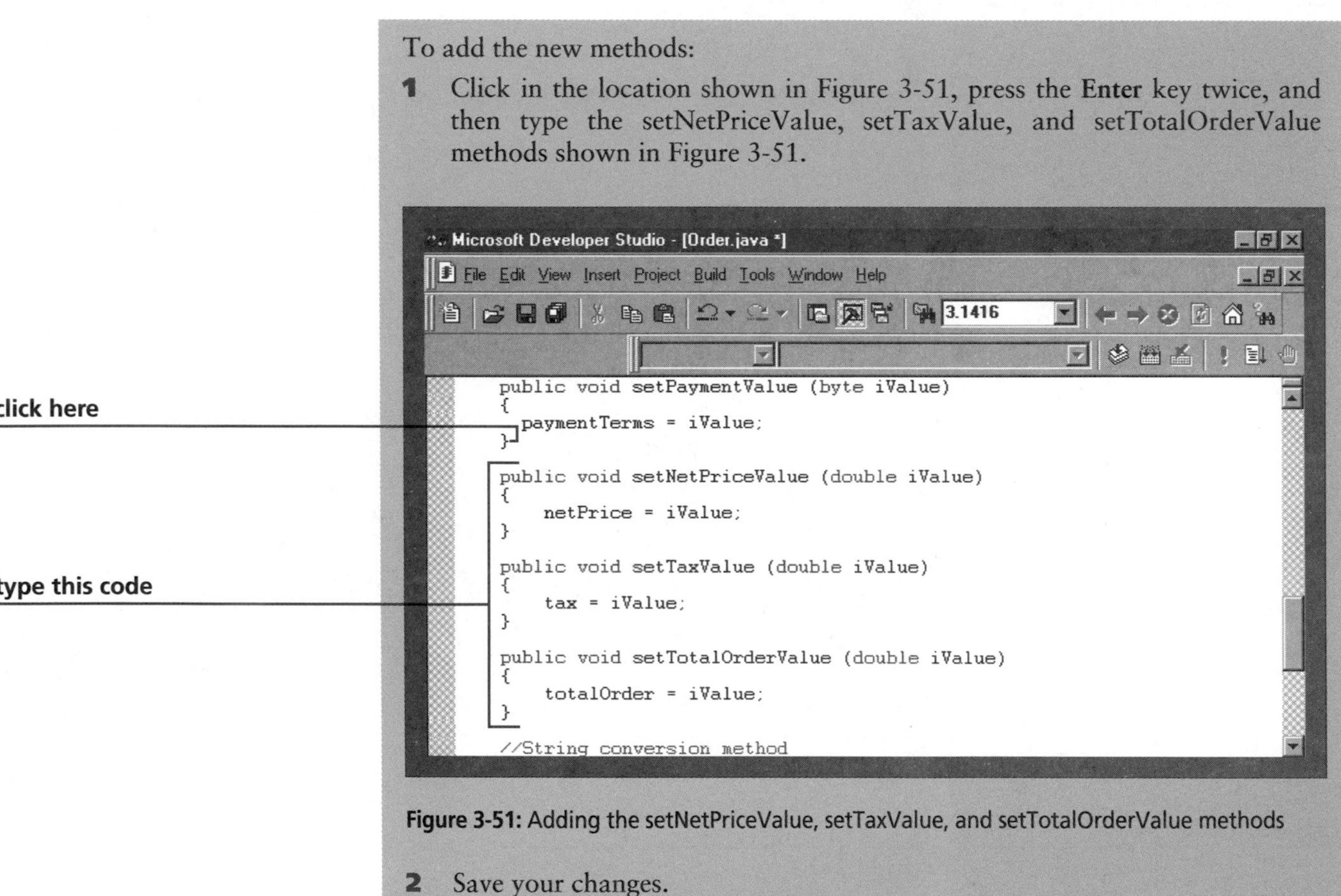

click here
type this code
Microsoft Developer Studio - [Order.java *]
File Edit View Insert Project Build Tools Window Help
3.1416
public void setPaymentValue (byte iValue)
{
paymentTerms = iValue;
}
public void setNetPriceValue (double iValue)
{
netPrice = iValue;
}
public void setTaxValue (double iValue)
{
tax = iValue;
}
public void setTotalOrderValue (double iValue)
{
totalOrder = iValue;
}
//String conversion method

Figure 3-51: Adding the setNetPriceValue, setTaxValue, and setTotalOrderValue methods

2 Save your changes.

You decide to implement the new methods that are necessary for the interactive input systems. These additional three methods are setCustomerValue, setCoffeeItem1Value, and setCoffeeItem2Value. These methods are designed to be used with the interactive input form, and allow updating of specific portions of an Order object, namely the customer portion, the first coffee product portion, or the second coffee product portion. For all three of these new methods, you will be using the full parameter list constructors of the appropriate class. You will add the setCustomerValue methods next.

To add the setCustomerValue methods:

1 Click in the location shown in Figure 3-52, press the **Enter** key twice, and then type the new method exactly as shown in Figure 3-52.

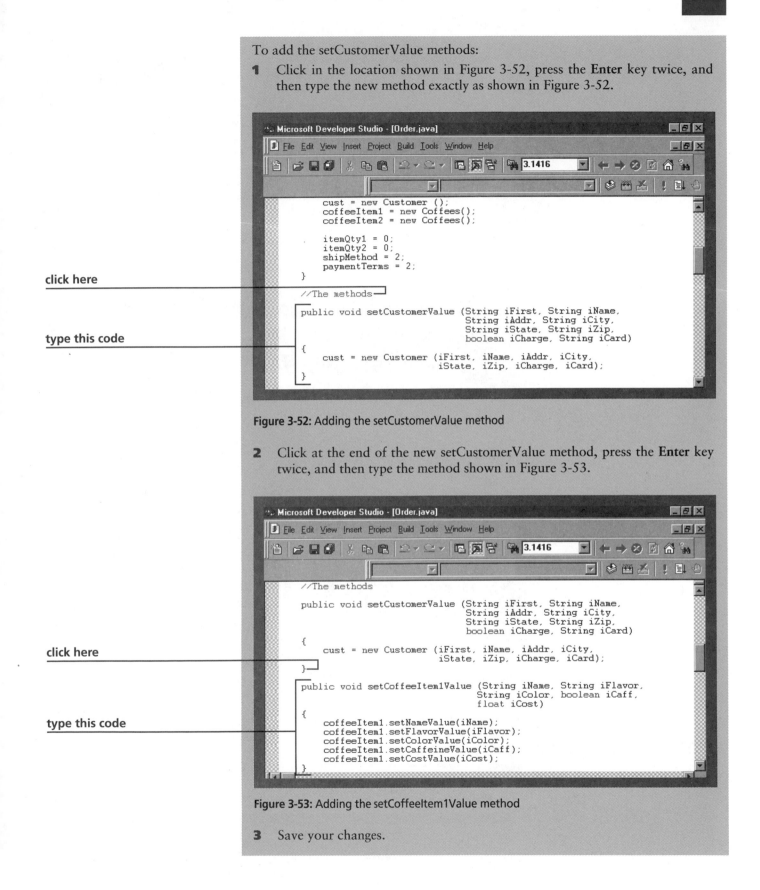

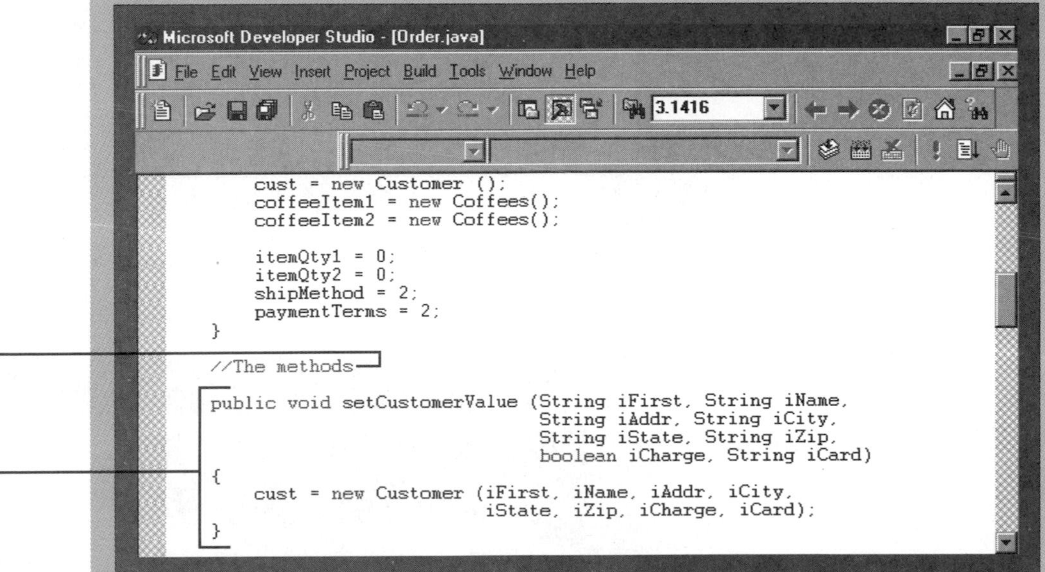

Figure 3-52: Adding the setCustomerValue method

2 Click at the end of the new setCustomerValue method, press the **Enter** key twice, and then type the method shown in Figure 3-53.

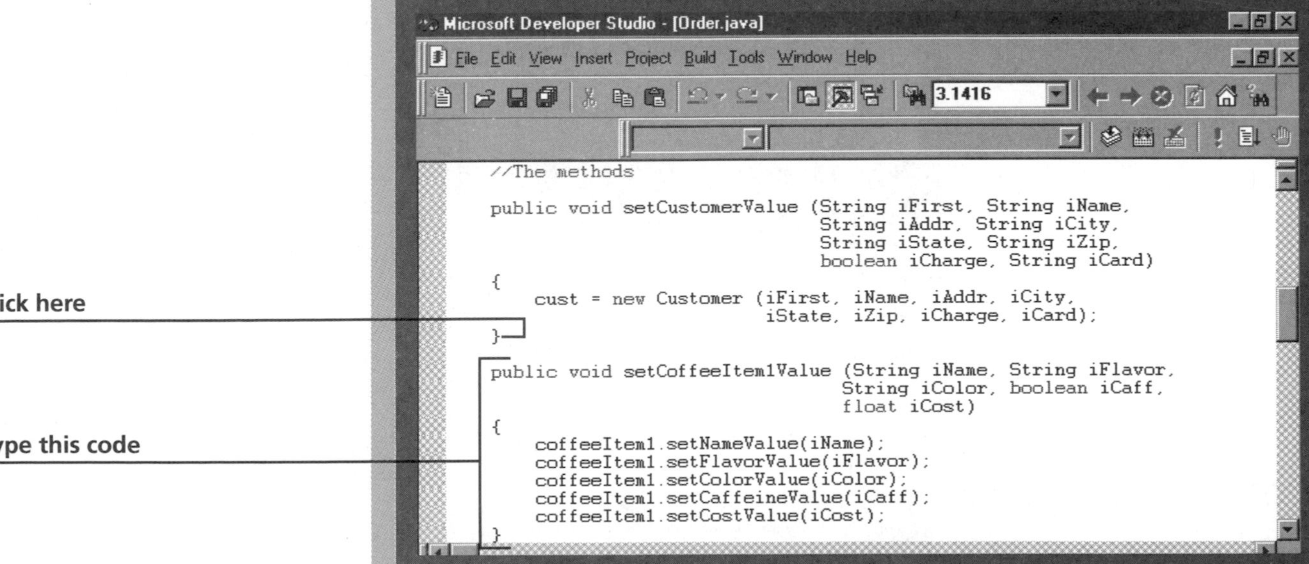

Figure 3-53: Adding the setCoffeeItem1Value method

3 Save your changes.

4 Select the **setCoffeeItem1Value** method, as shown in Figure 3-54. You can use the copy and paste method to add the setCoffeeItem2Value method to save time.

Microsoft Developer Studio - [Order.java]

```
public void setCustomerValue (String iFirst, String iName,
                              String iAddr, String iCity,
                              String iState, String iZip,
                              boolean iCharge, String iCard)
{
    cust = new Customer (iFirst, iName, iAddr, iCity,
                         iState, iZip, iCharge, iCard);
}

public void setCoffeeItem1Value (String iName, String iFlavor,
                                 String iColor, boolean iCaff,
                                 float iCost)
{
    coffeeItem1.setNameValue(iName);
    coffeeItem1.setFlavorValue(iFlavor);
    coffeeItem1.setColorValue(iColor);
    coffeeItem1.setCaffeineValue(iCaff);
    coffeeItem1.setCostValue(iCost);
}
```

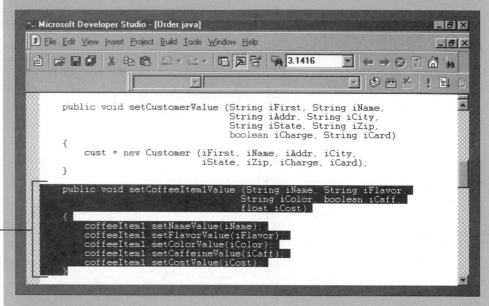

select these lines to copy

Figure 3-54: setCoffeeItem1Value method selected

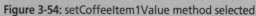

5 Click the **Copy** button on the Standard toolbar, click after the setCoffeeItem1Value method, and then press the **Enter** key twice.

6 Click the **Paste** button on the Standard toolbar.

7 Change the number 1 to **2** in the copy of setCoffeeItem, as shown in Figure 3-55.

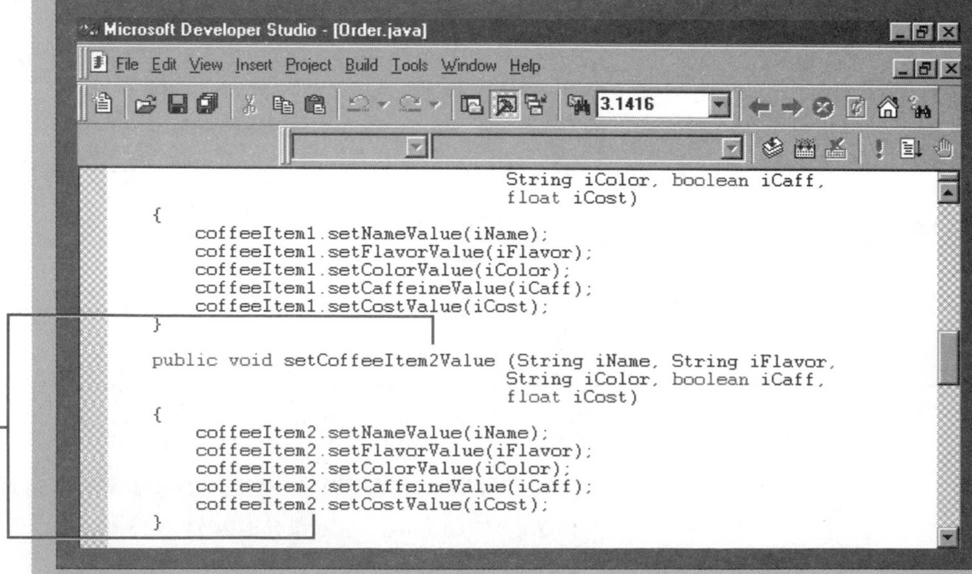

Figure 3-55: Modifying the copy of setCoffeeItem1Value method to setCoffeeItem2Value

8 Save your changes.

9 To test the Order class, click the **Compile** button on the Build toolbar, and then click the **Yes** button to create a default project workspace. Correct any output errors.

Designing an Interactive Input Form

There is something new in this code that needs to be examined. Because part of the data fields of the Object class are other objects—one customer and two coffee products—there has to be a way that a method in Order can access these values. A statement like *coffeeItem1.setNameValue(iName)* can be divided into three parts. The syntax for this statement is *objectName.method(arguments)*. You are using the coffeeItem1 Coffees object, the setNameValue method, and passing the method to the iName argument. The methods for setting properties of both coffee products use the same type of statements.

Now that you have created your classes, you can write the applet that pulls all the classes together into one applet. You need programs to create an interactive interface so an order clerk can use the applet to input customer data and order data, to calculate an order total, and to display the order information on the screen. Figure 3-56 shows a TOE chart for a limited implementation. You decide to concentrate on the customer mailing information, two coffee products, calculating totals, and displaying an invoice.

Task	Object	Event
Ask for first name	Label	Start
Ask for last name	Label	Start
Ask for address	Label	Start
Ask for city	Label	Start
Ask for state	Label	Start
Ask for Zip code	Label	Start
Ask for coffee name	Label	Start
Ask for flavor	Label	Start
Ask for color	Label	Start
Ask for caffeine	Label	Start
Ask for cost per lb.	Label	Start
Ask for pounds	Label	Start
Accept first name	TextField	Type
Accept last name	TextField	Type
Accept address	TextField	Type
Accept city	TextField	Type
Accept state	TextField	Type
Accept Zip code	TextField	Type
Accept coffee name	TextField	Type
Accept flavor	TextField	Type
Accept color	TextField	Type
Accept caffeine	TextField	Type
Accept cost per lb.	TextField	Type
Accept pounds	TextField	Type
Calculate net price	Button	Click
Calculate tax	Button	Click
Calculate shipping	Button	Click
Calculate total order	Button	Click
Display customer	TextArea	Button click
Display net price	TextArea	Button click
Display tax	TextArea	Button click
Display shipping	TextArea	Button click
Display total order	TextArea	Button click

Figure 3-56: TOE chart

Now that you know the elements to include in your applet, you can use the Tut3C class design shown in Figure 3-57 to organize your work. Because of its interactive nature, the Tut3C class has two types of data components—data fields and graphical user interface (GUI) elements. The GUI elements—labels, text fields, buttons, and text areas—are similar to the elements in the BeanJar applet. The best way to write the applet is to start by adding the fields, data, and the GUI elements, and then adding the methods. But in order to reduce debugging time, you can add the methods one at a time, and then test each new method as you add it. This incremental testing method is an effective software design tool.

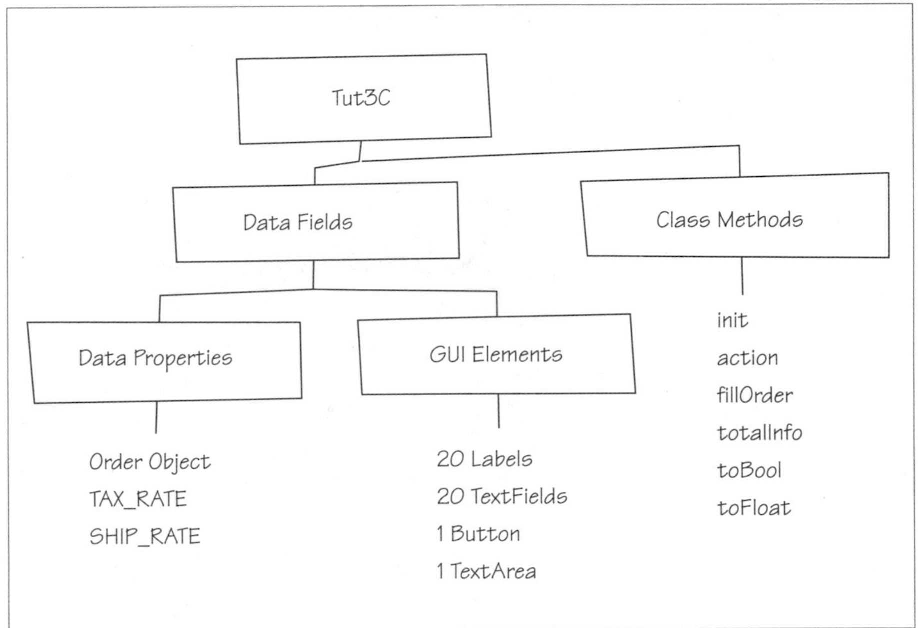

Figure 3-57: Tut3C class diagram

Adding Fields

The Tut3C.java file already has been started. Some of the GUI elements are entered into the Tut3C.java file. First you will add the data fields, and then you will add the GUI elements.

To add the data fields:

1. Close the project workspace and all document windows.
2. Open the **T3C.java** file from the Tutorial3C folder on your Student Disk, and then save it as **Tut3C.java.**
3. Click in the location shown in Figure 3-58, press the **Enter** key, and then type the property variables shown in Figure 3-58.

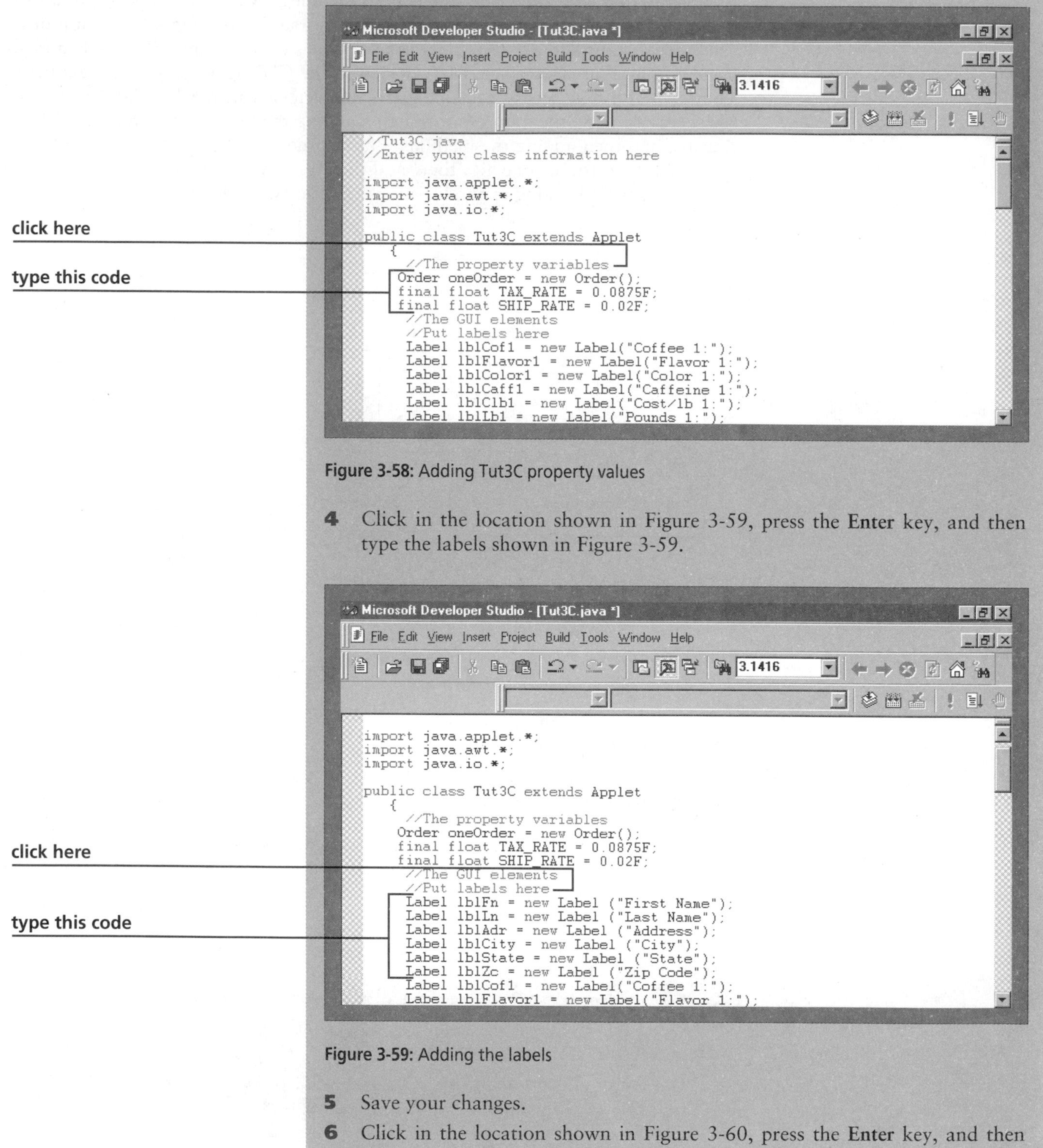

Figure 3-58: Adding Tut3C property values

4 Click in the location shown in Figure 3-59, press the **Enter** key, and then type the labels shown in Figure 3-59.

Figure 3-59: Adding the labels

5 Save your changes.

6 Click in the location shown in Figure 3-60, press the **Enter** key, and then type the code shown in Figure 3-60.

Figure 3-60: Adding the text fields

7 Click at the end of the //Put button here line, press the **Enter** key, and then type **Button calculate = new Button ("Calculate");**.

8 Click at the end of the //Put textarea here line, press the **Enter** key, and then type **TextArea invoice = new TextArea (20,70);**, as shown in Figure 3-61.

Figure 3-61: After adding the button and text area

9 Save your changes.

Adding Methods

Because your plan calls for incremental testing, the order in which you write the methods is important. Because an applet requires an init() method to run, you will develop the init() method first. When init() runs correctly, the applet will display each GUI element, and the text fields will be able to accept typed input. The action method will be next because this is the method that responds to the button click. The fillOrder method will be next as it is the method that transfers the data from the text fields into the Order object, followed by the conversion methods, toBool, and toFloat. The last method will be the totalInfo method.

Writing the init() Method

This method is long because it has to "add" all the GUI elements to the applet. Some of the statements appear already in the file. You will add the rest of the statements.

To complete the init() method:

1 Click at the end of the //Start init here line, press the **Enter** key, and then type the code shown in Figure 3-62.

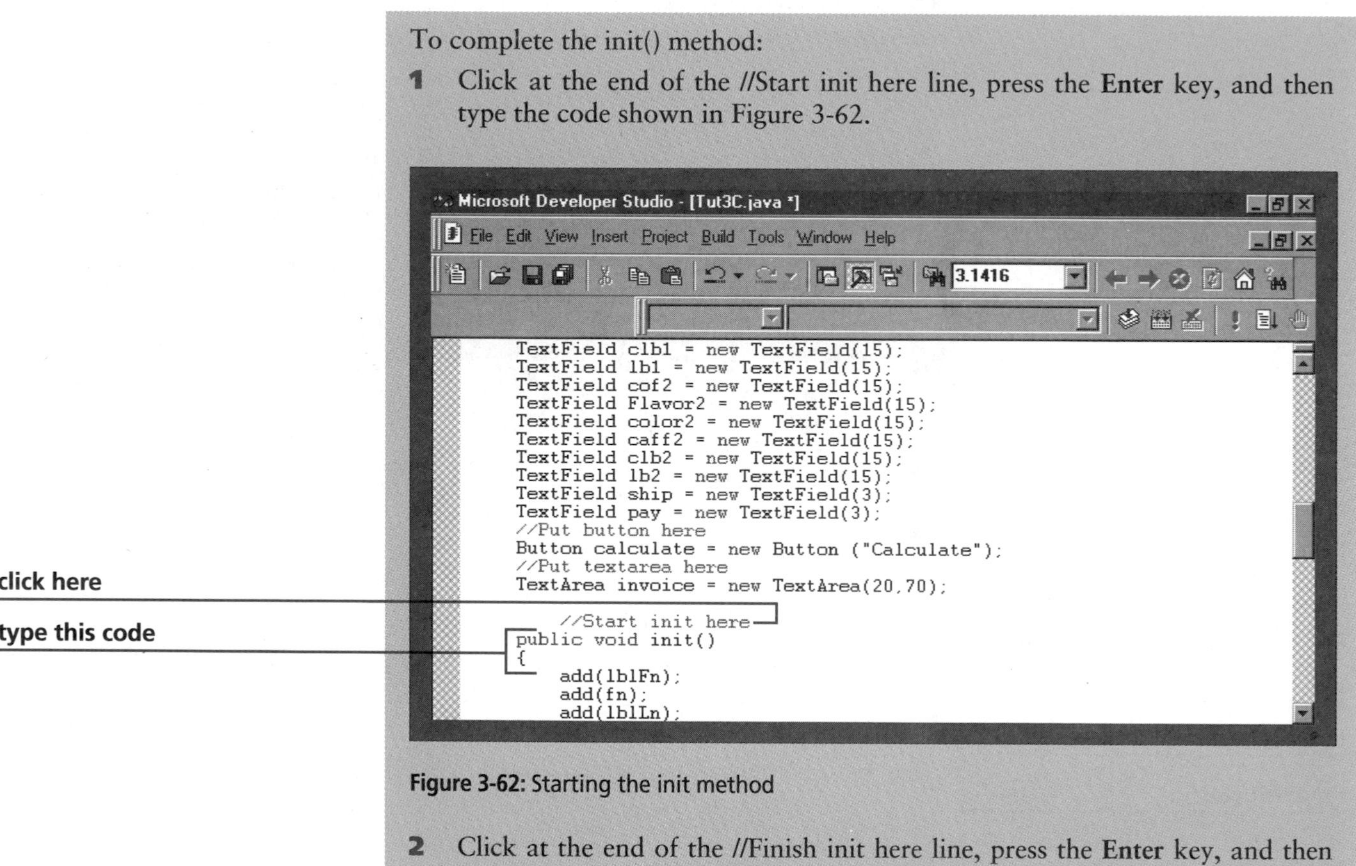

Figure 3-62: Starting the init method

2 Click at the end of the //Finish init here line, press the **Enter** key, and then type the code shown in Figure 3-63.

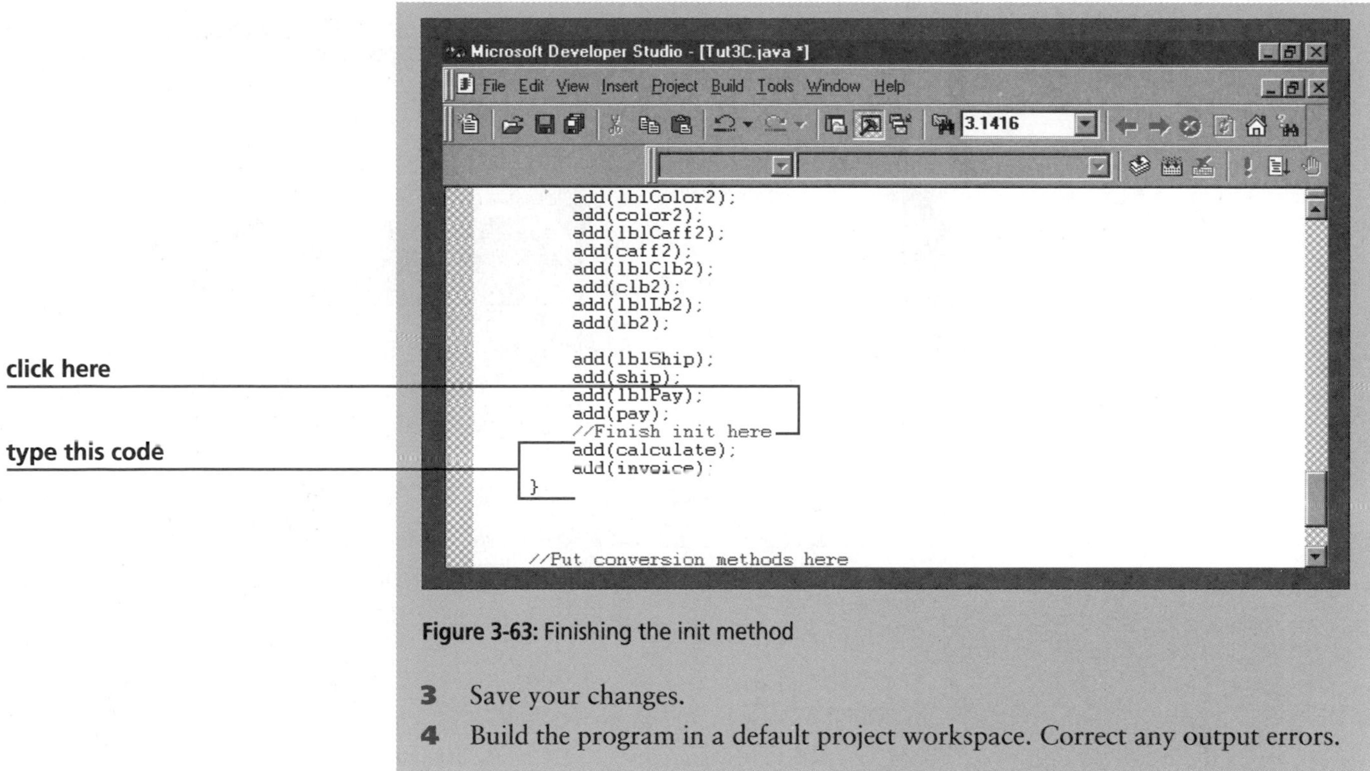

Figure 3-63: Finishing the init method

3 Save your changes.

4 Build the program in a default project workspace. Correct any output errors.

Before executing the Tut3C program, you need to specify the HTML page. The default width and height that Visual J++ uses will not be big enough for this applet, so you will use the HTML file on your Student Disk.

To use the HTML file on your Student Disk:

1 Click **Project** on the menu bar, and then click **Settings**. Click the **Debug** tab, click the **Category** list arrow, and then click **Browser**. Click the **Use parameters from HTML page** option button, and then type **Tut3C.html** in the HTML page text box. See Figure 3-64.

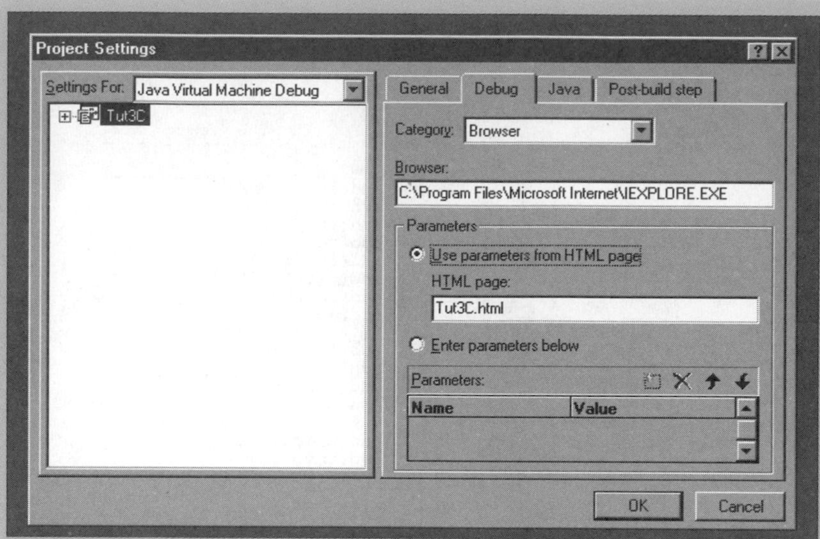

Figure 3-64: Specifying an HTML file in the Project Settings dialog box

2. Click the **OK** button.
3. To add all the files into this project, click **Project** on the menu bar, click **Add To Project**, and then click **Files**.
4. Click the **Coffees.java** file, and then click the **OK** button.
5. Repeat Steps 3 and 4 to add the **Customer.java** and **Order.java** files.
6. Click the **Execute Program** button on the Build toolbar.
7. Type **Tut3C** in the Class file name text box, and then click the **OK** button. Internet Explorer starts and loads the applet, as shown in Figure 3-65.

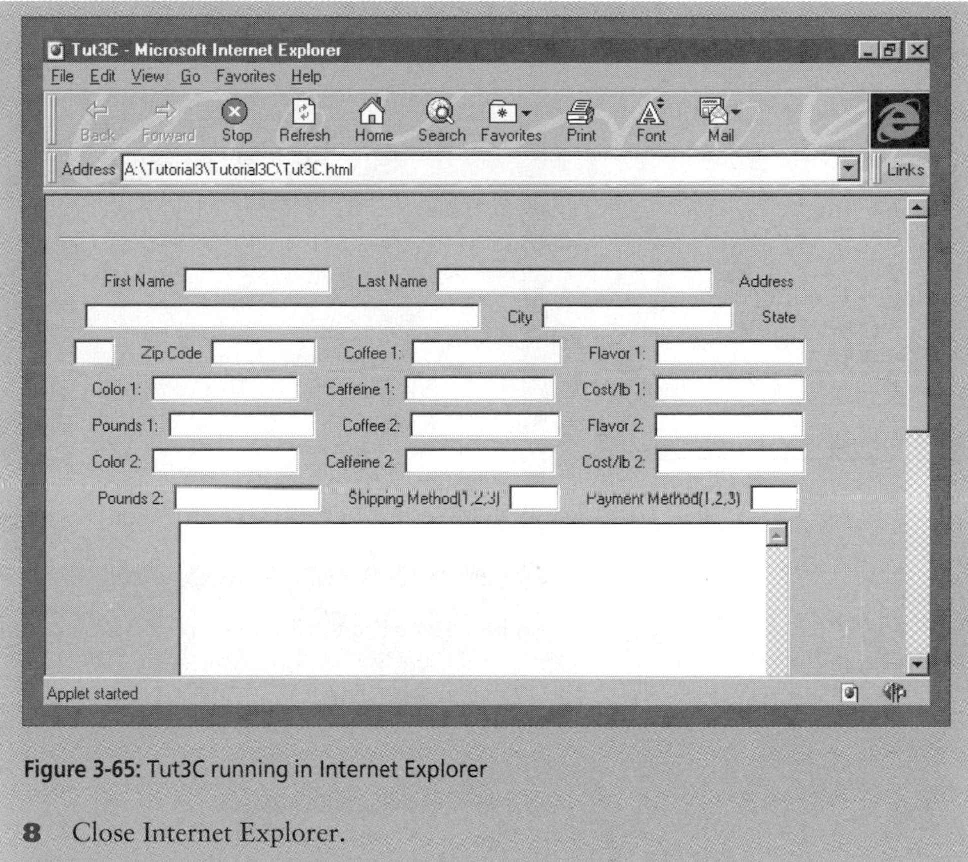

Figure 3-65: Tut3C running in Internet Explorer

8 Close Internet Explorer.

Writing the Action Method

You successfully placed all the GUI elements on the screen, but the applet does nothing. For the applet to respond to the button click, you need the action method. The **action method** in Java is the method that handles all the events, like button clicks. The format of the action method is predefined in Java. The action method is required to return a boolean value, and to have two arguments in the parameter list—an Event and an Object. While Tut3C only has one possible object and event combination—clicking the Calculate button—this will not always be the case. Later in this book you will learn how to handle multiple events.

You will add all of the code now, but one part will be left out so that incremental testing can continue.

To add the action method:

1 Click at the end of the //Put action here line, press the **Enter** key, and then type the lines shown in Figure 3-66.

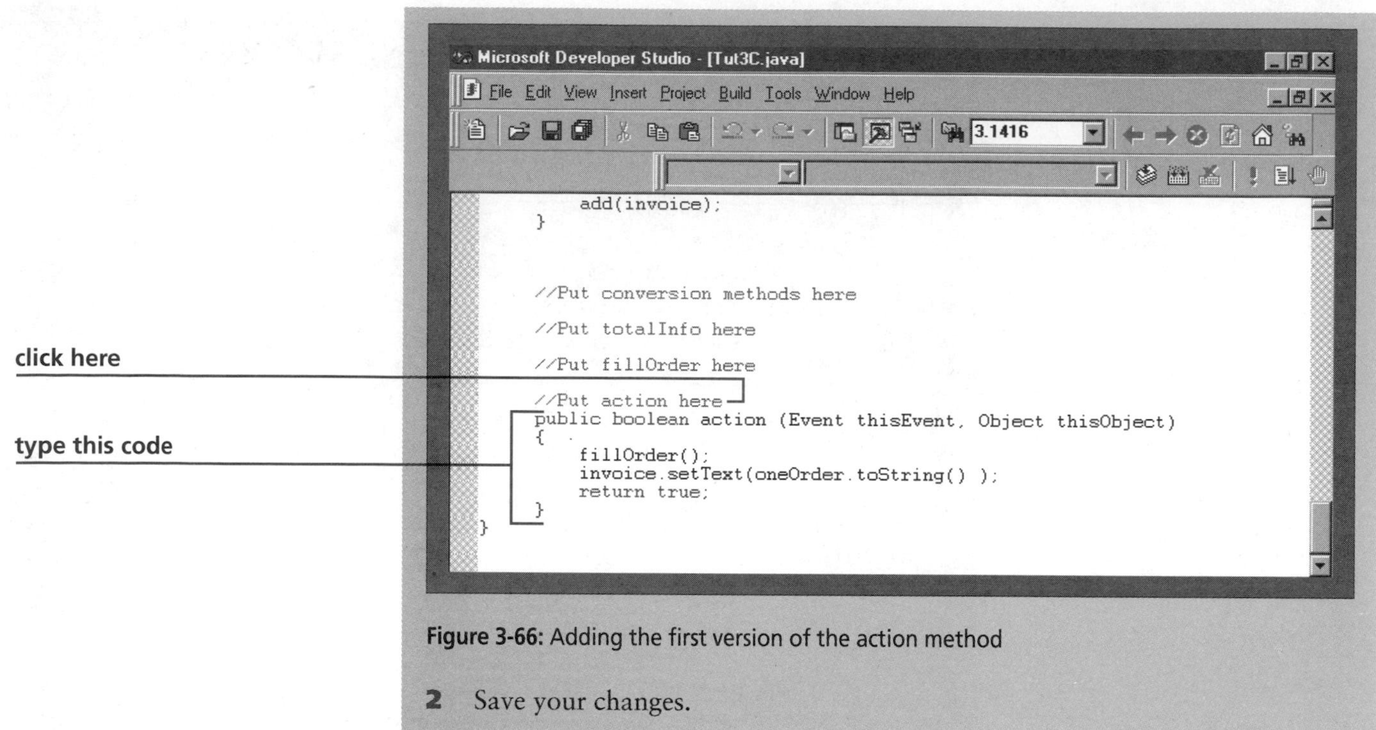

Figure 3-66: Adding the first version of the action method

2 Save your changes.

Writing the fillOrder Method

The fillOrder method uses three of the new methods added to the Object class: setCustomerValue, setCoffeeItem1Value, and setCoffeeItem2Value. If all the arguments passed to these methods were Strings, there would be no problems. But because some of the arguments are floats and booleans, there is a slight problem. The problem is that it is more difficult than it appears on the surface to convert from Strings to floating point and boolean values. The BeanJar applet converted from a String to an integer, and this is a straightforward conversion. Floating point numbers and booleans are a different matter. You need to write two conversion methods for the Tut3C applet, but for now, you will write and test fillOrder by passing literals to the Object class methods. In the first statement in this method, methods are used inside the argument list, as you saw in Lesson B.

After this method is added and builds successfully, it can be executed. This version of the applet will accept input and display most of it in the invoice text area. This version of this applet is a "rough draft" because it will not be possible to tab from input field to input field—you must click each field before typing its input.

To add the fillOrder method:

1 Click at the end of the //Put fillOrder here line, press the **Enter** key, and then type the code shown in Figure 3-67.

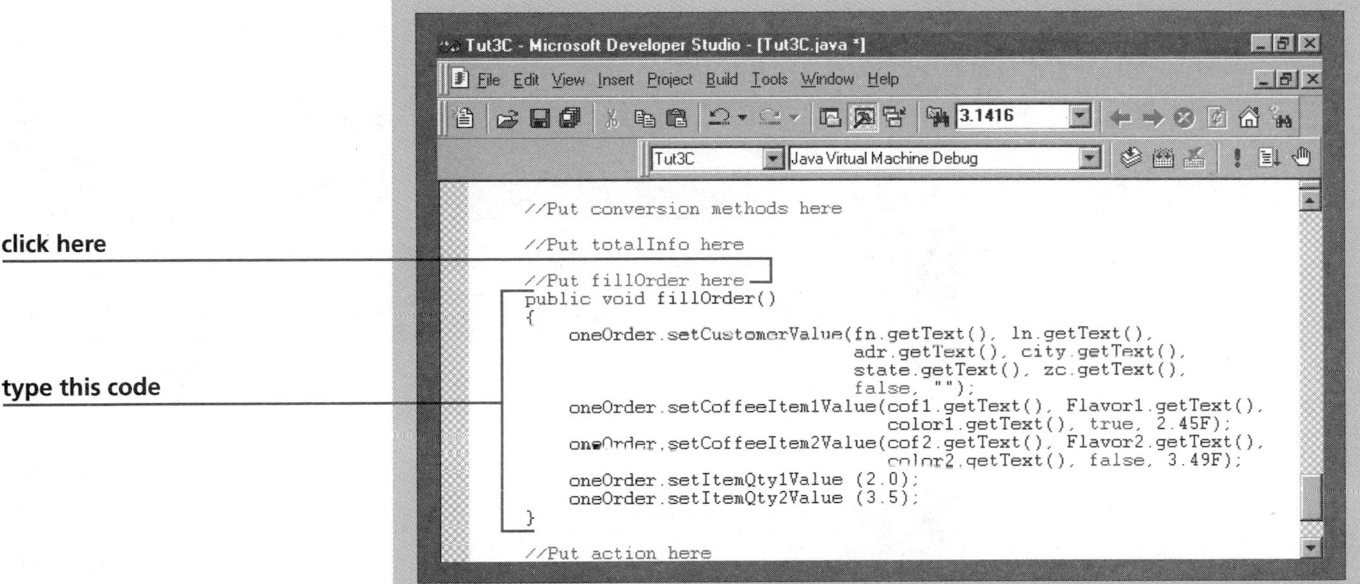

Figure 3-67: Adding the fillOrder method

2 Save your changes.

3 Build the program. Correct any output errors.

4 Execute the program.

5 Input the record shown in Figure 3-68. Click in each text box to enter the data.

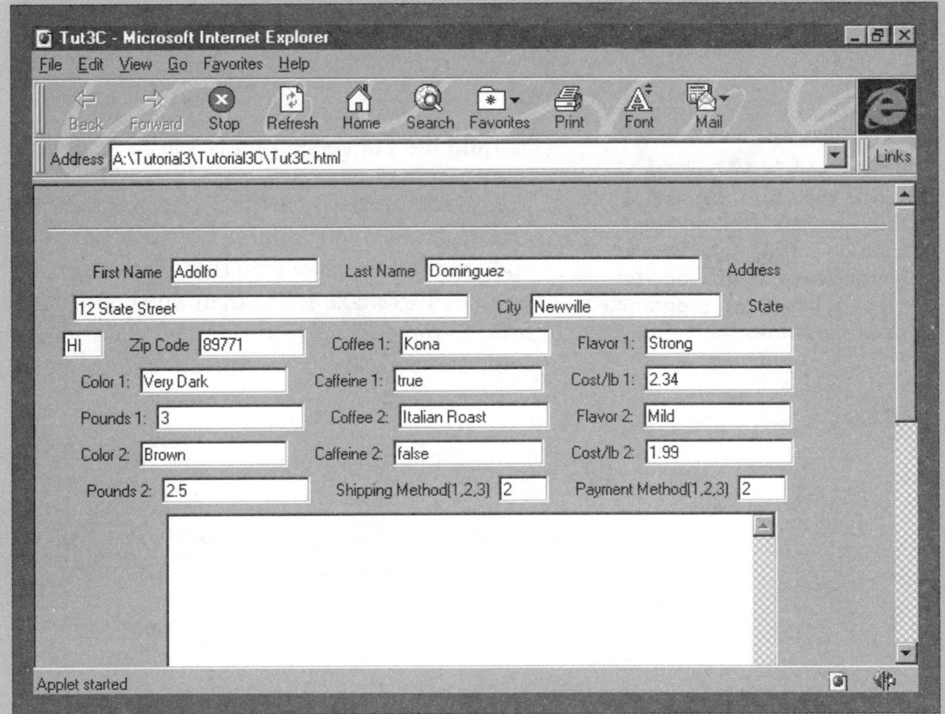

Figure 3-68: Input data for Tut3C

6 Click the **Calculate** button. The invoice text area looks like Figure 3-69.

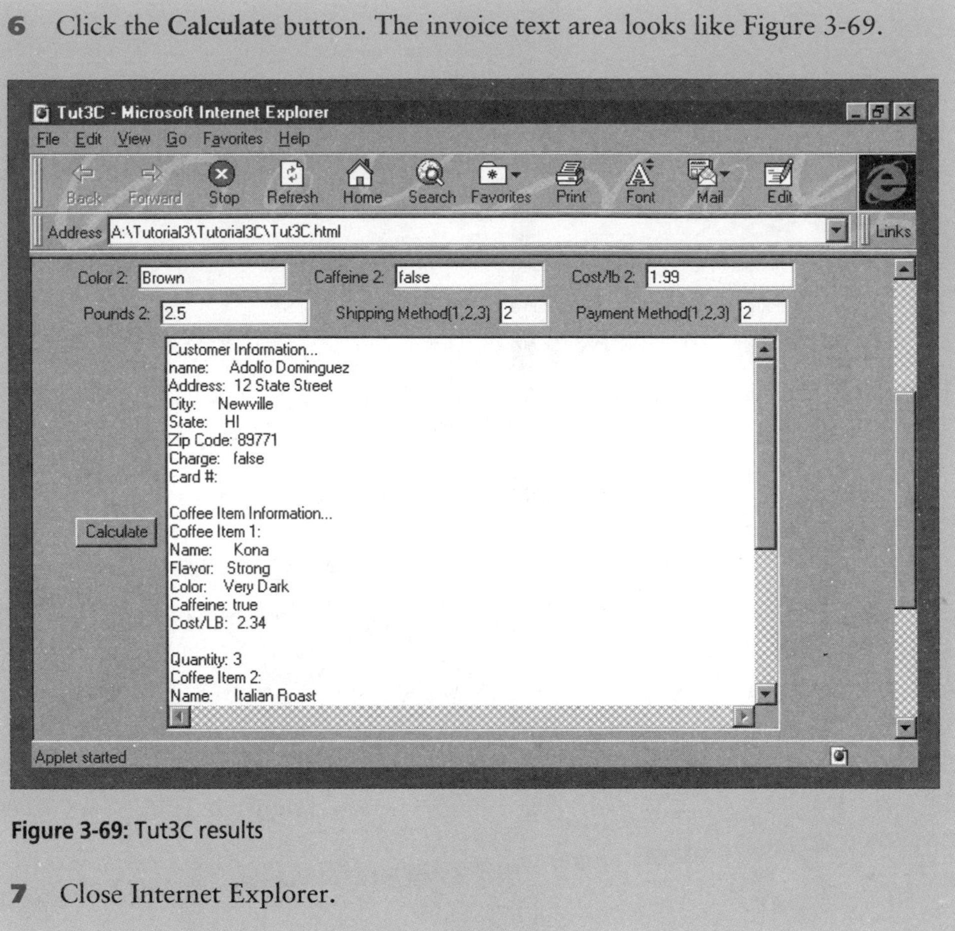

Figure 3-69: Tut3C results

7 Close Internet Explorer.

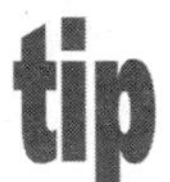

tip

Click the third Tutorial 3 link of the Online Companion for this book (http://www.course.com) to see a live Java program that illustrates this topic.

Writing the Conversion Tools

There are methods in Java that you can use to convert from Strings to boolean and floating point values. If you need to make only one conversion, the messy code needed to make sure that the conversion will work is acceptable. But because you need to make more than one conversion, you will add the utility methods of toBool and toFloat to the Tut3C class. A **utility method** is one that you use like a tool to accomplish a routine job and to reuse when needed.

To add the conversion methods:

1 Click at the end of the //Put conversion methods here line, press the **Enter** key, and then type the code shown in Figure 3-70.

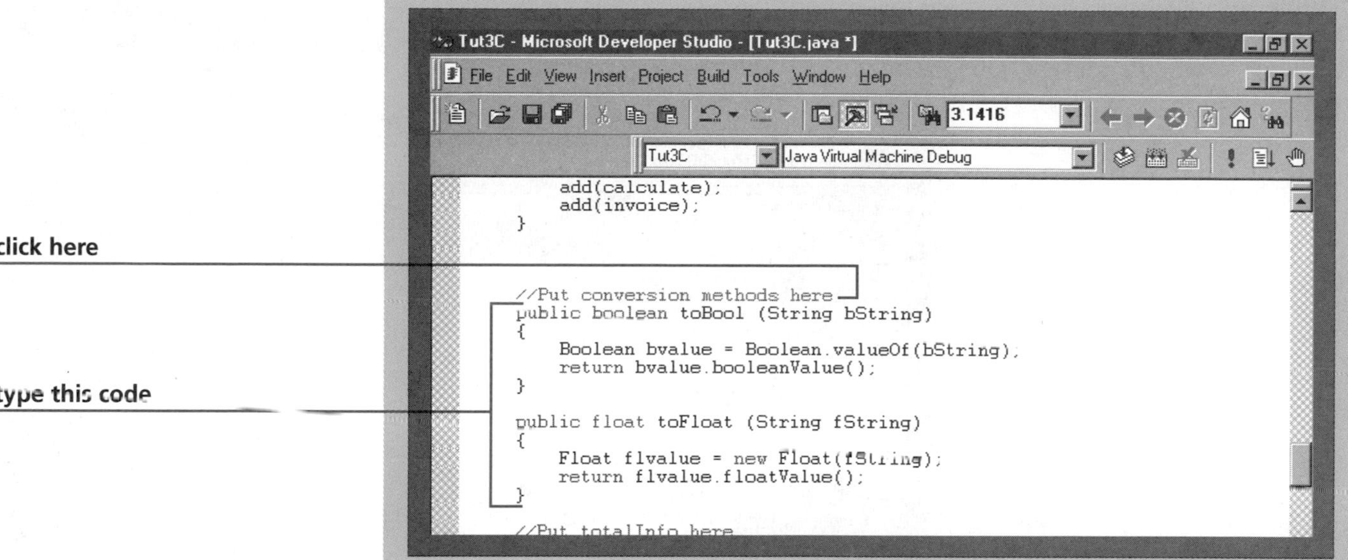
click here
type this code
Tut3C - Microsoft Developer Studio - [Tut3C.java *]
File Edit View Insert Project Build Tools Window Help
3.1416
Tut3C
Java Virtual Machine Debug
add(calculate);
add(invoice);
}
//Put conversion methods here
public boolean toBool (String bString)
{
Boolean bvalue = Boolean.valueOf(bString);
return bvalue.booleanValue();
}
public float toFloat (String fString)
{
Float flvalue = new Float(fString);
return flvalue.floatValue();
}
//Put totalInfo here

Figure 3-70: Adding the utility methods

2 Click at the beginning of the line that begins "oneOrder.setCoffeeItem1Value." To use these methods, some changes need to be made to the fillOrder method.

3 Press the Enter key, press ↑ to move to the blank line, and then type **boolean caff = toBool (caff1.getText());**, press the **Enter** key, and then type **float cost = toFloat (clb1.getText());**.

4 Click at the beginning of the line that begins "oneOrder.setCoffeeItem2Value," press the **Enter** key, press ↑ to move to the blank line, and then type **caff = toBool (caff2.getText());**, press the **Enter** key, and then type **cost = toFloat (clb2.getText());**.

5 Change the word "true" to **caff** and the number 2.45F to **cost** in the oneOrder.setCoffeeItem1Value statement, and then change the word "false" to **caff** and the number 3.49F to **cost** in the oneOrder.setCoffeeItem2Value statement.

6 Change the two lines assigning values to the coffee product pound fields (itemQty1 and itemQty2), by selecting the lines and then typing the following lines exactly as shown:

oneOrder.setItemQty1Value (toFloat (lb1.getText()));
oneOrder.setItemQty2Value (toFloat (lb2.getText()));

7 Save your changes, and then build Tut3C.java. Make any necessary changes.

8 Execute Tut3C.java.

9 Type the information shown in Figure 3-68, and then click the **Calculate** button. The invoice text area should look like Figure 3-71.

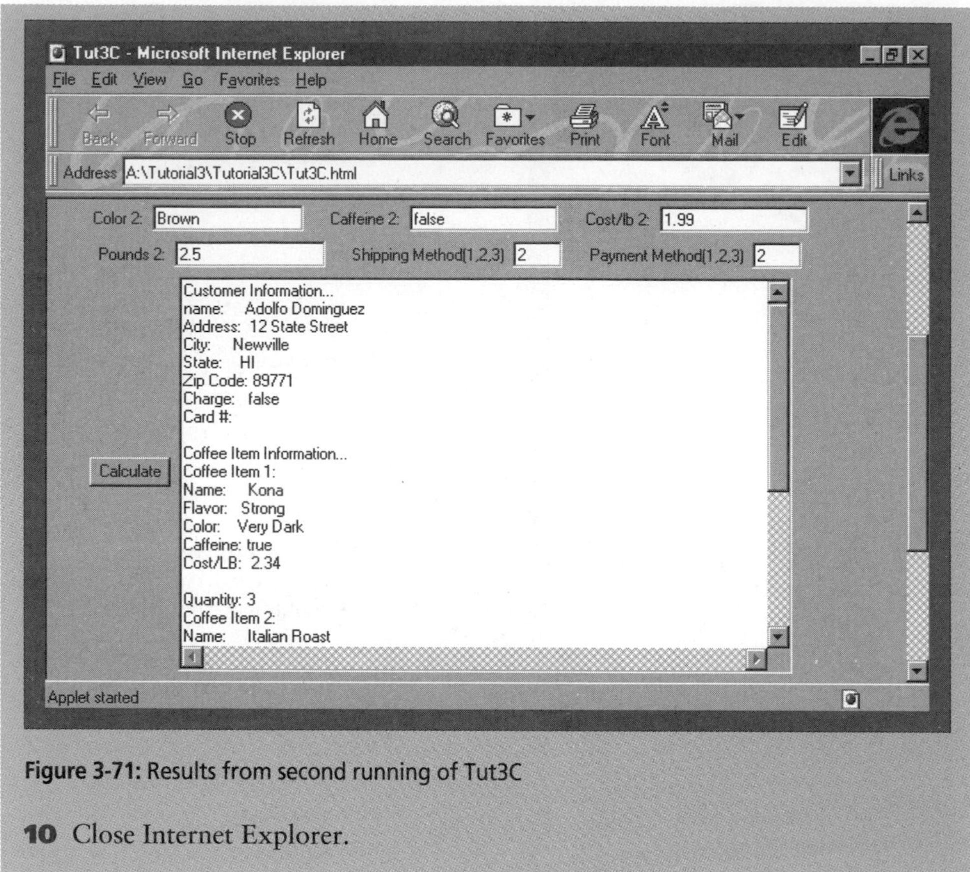

Figure 3-71: Results from second running of Tut3C

10 Close Internet Explorer.

Writing the totalInfo Method

The purpose of the totalInfo method is to calculate the invoice values from the input values. This method uses the constants TAX_RATE and SHIP_RATE. This method calculates the invoice total and subtotals, and constructs a String that is used in the action method. You should note that the results of this method are formatted poorly. Values that are supposed to represent dollars and cents will display more than two decimal places.

To add the values:

1 Click at the end of the //Put totalInfo here line, press the **Enter** key, and then type the lines indicated in Figure 3-72.

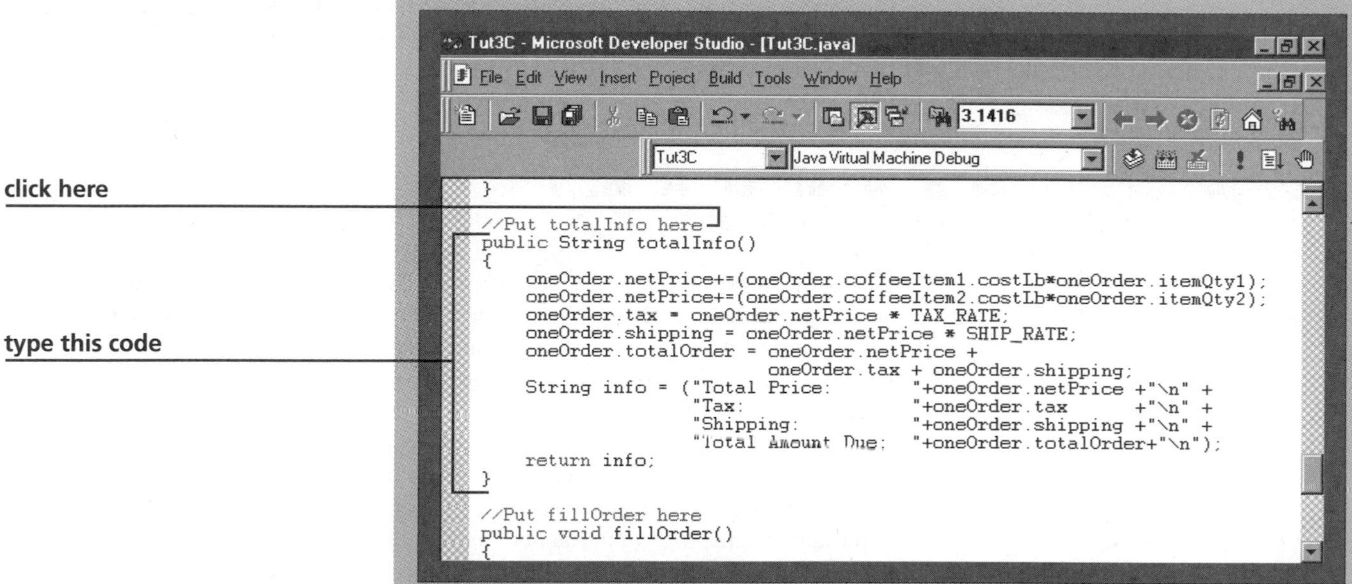

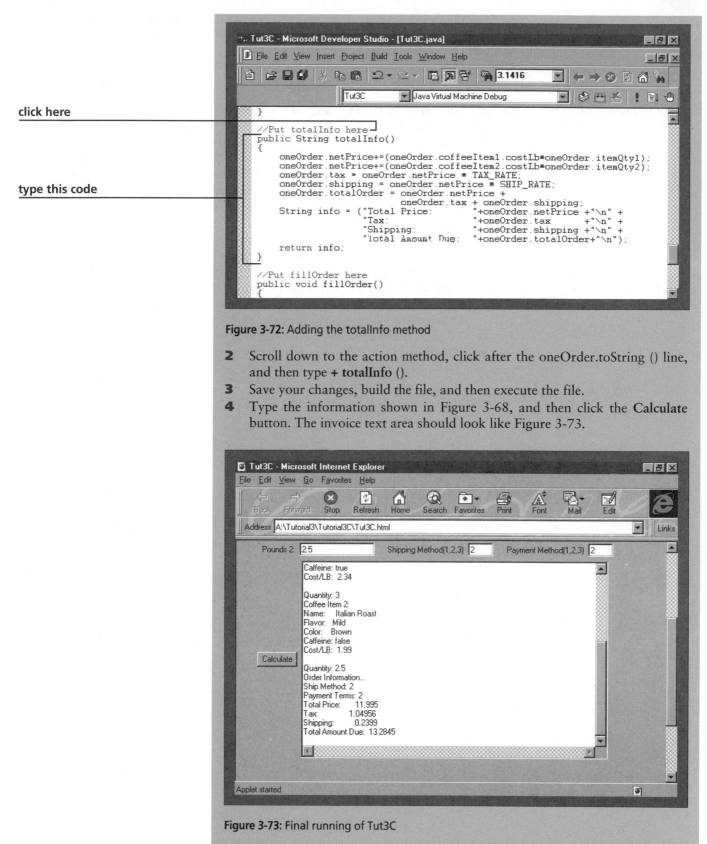

Figure 3-72: Adding the totalInfo method

2 Scroll down to the action method, click after the oneOrder.toString () line, and then type **+ totalInfo** ().

3 Save your changes, build the file, and then execute the file.

4 Type the information shown in Figure 3-68, and then click the **Calculate** button. The invoice text area should look like Figure 3-73.

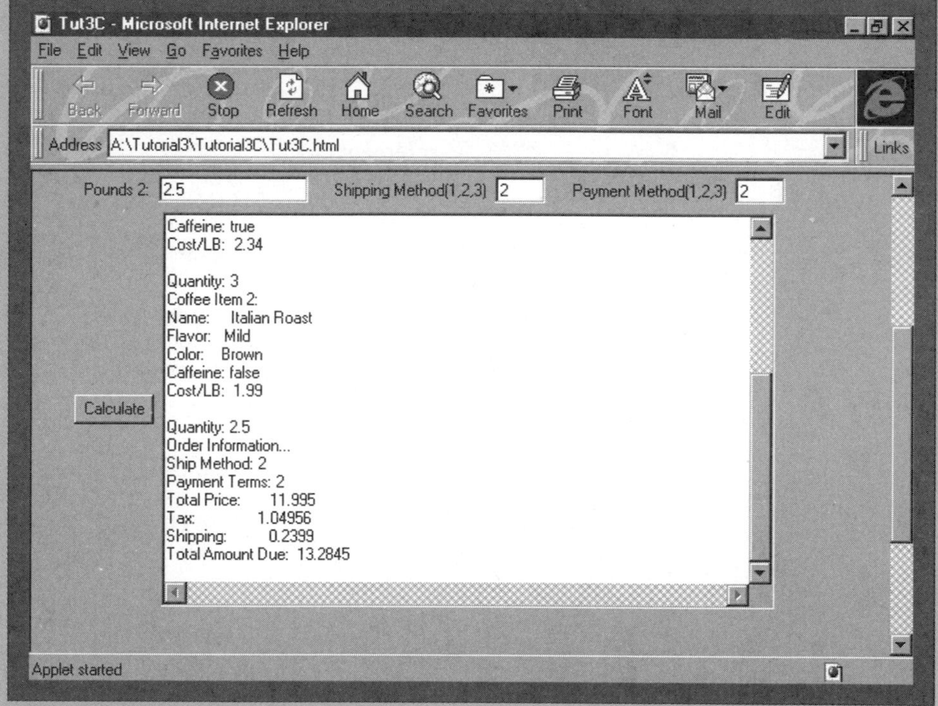

Figure 3-73: Final running of Tut3C

5 Close Internet Explorer, close the project workspace, and then close Visual J++.

One modification that you will leave for later in the book is handling the credit issue in the user interface. Now you can either take a break or complete the end-of-lesson questions and exercises.

SUMMARY

- You can write two types of Java constructors. The first type has a blank argument list, and assigns default values or empty Strings to the data fields. The second type has a full argument list, and assigns values from the argument list to the data fields.
- It is important to plan complex changes to a class. Even a minor change can cause a ripple effect in having to change the data properties and class methods.
- To add data fields, type the new fields with the other data fields. Make sure that any needed changes to methods or new methods are added.
- To add class methods, position them in the methods area of the file. Order is not important for the program to run but might be important for readability.
- Compiling a single Java file is a good way to test for syntax errors. Click the Compile button on the Build toolbar to compile a single file.
- To access a field in an embedded object, use the *ObjectName.fieldName* statement.
- Use a TOE chart to design an applet with interactive input.
- Incremental testing is a process of writing a small portion of the applet at a time and testing to see if the newest portion works.
- The syntax for the init method is:
  public void init ()
  {
    <statements>;
  }
- The syntax for an action method is:
  public boolean action (*Event thisEvent*, *Object thisObject*)
  {
    <statements>;
    return true;
  }
- Conversion methods can be written by the programmer to allow conversion from one type to another.
- To write a method that returns a value, the type of the method must be the type of the value to return, and the method must have at least one return statement that returns a value of the stated type.

QUESTIONS

1. Which of the following items is a valid full constructor header for the class circle with data members *int color* and *float radius*?
   a. circle();
   b. circle (int c, float r);
   c. circle(double c, char r);
   d. circle(String c);
2. __________ testing is the process of testing small parts of the program one at a time.
   a. Incremental
   b. Additive
   c. Series
   d. Boolean
3. In what method are the GUI elements placed into an applet?
   a. action
   b. convert
   c. init
   d. select
4. Which method can respond to an event in an applet?
   a. action
   b. convert
   c. init
   d. select
5. If a method does not return a value, what should the method type be?
   a. null
   b. [no type]
   c. nil
   d. void
6. What type of value does a text field return?
   a. String
   b. char
   c. boolean
   d. numeric
7. Which of the following items accesses the color data field of the myCircle object?
   a. Circle.color
   b. myCircle.color()
   c. myCircle.color
   d. myCircle!color
8. What is the return type of the following method *public int myHours (int intDays)*?
   a. public
   b. int
   c. myHours
   d. intDays
9. Write a Java statement that assigns the value 4.5 to the radius field of the myCircle object.
10. Write a statement that assigns the value from the text field inField to the String myInput.

EXERCISES

For all the exercises in this lesson, prepare the following:

- TOE chart for the GUI elements
- Class diagram showing the data fields and class methods
- A Java file with just the class in it
- A Java file that uses the class and contains the interactive elements

1. Write an applet that calculates commissions. The data fields for the SalesPerson class are name, weekly sales, commission rate, and commission due. The methods are empty constructor, full constructor, change data in each field, and calculate commission due. The interactive input should use the appropriate GUI methods. Include a Calculate button to start calculations. Save the Java class file as Commission1.java and save the applet as Commission.java in the Exercise1C folder in the Exercises folder in the Tutorial3 folder on your Student Disk.
2. Write an applet that calculates costs of laying underground cabling. The data fields for the Cabling class are digging cost per foot (constant $85.00), String for type of cable, cable cost per foot, and total cost for the job. The methods are empty constructor, full constructor, change data in each field, and calculate total cost due. The interactive input should use the appropriate GUI methods. Include a Calculate button to start calculations. Save the Java class file as Cable1.java and save the applet as Cable.java in the Exercise2C folder in the Exercises folder in the Tutorial3 folder on your Student Disk.
3. Write an applet that writes invoices for a repair shop. The data fields for the Repair class are worker's name, number of hours, hourly rate, cost of parts, and total job cost. The methods are empty constructor, full constructor, change data in each field, and calculate total job cost. The interactive input should use the appropriate GUI methods. Include a Calculate button to start calculations. Save the Java class file as Repair1.java and save the applet as Repair.java in the Exercise3C folder in the Exercises folder in the Tutorial3 folder on your Student Disk.

TUTORIAL

4

Using Control Structures

Improving the Order Entry Program for Koffee Koncoctions

case The customer order program that you developed needs some work, but it is starting to take shape. After reviewing the program, you decide to work further on the change field methods as well as trying to incorporate input checking. All of Koffee Koncoctions' products are predefined relative to color, flavor, and cost. This information can be used to check the processed orders.

Control structures in Java, such as the if and switch statements, can be used to code the change field methods as a single method to reduce the number of methods in the program; to code programs to check for invalid user input and determine the action to be taken in each situation; and to code programs that are able to process both simple and complex decisions.

In this tutorial you will incorporate decision control structures into parts of the customer order program. When you finish the lessons, you will have an updated order entry program that includes objects to make better use of the Java commands available and to reduce the size of your object code.

LESSON A

objectives

In this lesson you will learn how to:

- **Define boolean logic and describe two types of operators in Boolean algebra**
- **Define the relational operators and logical operators, and describe how they work**
- **Use relational operators to express simple conditions in a precise way**
- **Use nested structures to design complex decisions with more than one condition**
- **Use logical operators to combine relational expressions into more complex structures**
- **Use decision tables to define the logic of a narrative decision process**
- **Convert decision tables into relational and logical expressions using pseudocode**

Using Boolean Logic

Creating and Using Decision Tables

Understanding Boolean Logic

Decision making in computer programming provides the basis for a significant amount of power and intelligence in computer software. This decision mechanism is based on the concepts and techniques of Boolean algebra. **Boolean algebra** is the branch of mathematics that deals with logic. In this lesson you will learn about boolean logic and the ways that it is used to incorporate decision making in software.

Computers are really simple objects. At the highest level of understanding, they only know "on" or "off." Technically, they know positive or negative voltage at the hardware level, but this usually is referred to as "on" and "off." The developers of the computer realized that they needed a form of logic. Programmers used boolean logic to describe these two computer states. **Boolean logic** is based on the base-2 number system and has only two states—true and false. The **true state** corresponds to the on condition of the computer and the **false state** corresponds to the off condition. Programmers still needed a method for describing these states. They developed a charting technique called truth tables for this task.

A **truth table** is a table that defines the inputs into and outputs from a given portion of logic. For example, a bank might have a policy that if you are over 21 years of age and have a monthly income greater than $1,000, then they will consider your application for a credit card. The logic that is contained in a computer program about this decision can be shown in a truth table. Figure 4-1 shows the truth table for this example.

Age (years)	Salary (dollars)	Consider for Credit?
0-21	0-1000	false
0-21	1001+	false
22+	0-1000	false
22+	1001+	true

Figure 4-1: Truth table for bank credit policy

Notice that the inputs into and output from the policy process are columns in the table. Each row in the table indicates a particular situation. When a situation exists where the input columns (Age and Salary) of a given row match that circumstance, the output column (Consider for Credit?) should be the decision the logic returns. If a person who is 19 with a monthly income of $1,500 comes into the bank, he or she will not be considered for a credit card. This situation matches row two of the table where the age is 0-21 and the monthly income is 1001+. Notice that the output column is an action to be taken and the values it can receive are true and false as is required by boolean logic.

Two functions in the logic just described require the computer to perform two basic types of functions. These functions are relational comparisons and logical combinations of relationships. A **relational function** is a function that takes two values (operands) and uses a relational operator to generate a result of true or false. **Logical functions** are a way of combining relational functions, boolean variables, literals, and constants in a more complex way to generate the same kinds of results as relational functions: true and false. These functions often are called expressions, and they are basic to computer programming.

Understanding Relational Operators

Relational operators are the method that Java uses to compare two items and determine the boolean value that should be returned. The items of the relational expression are called operands and the specific relationship that is programmed is called the operator. Figure 4-2 lists the Java relational operators and a brief description.

Relational Operator	Description
==	Operand 1 and operand 2 are exactly equal
<	Operand 1 is less than operand 2
>	Operand 1 is greater than operand 2
!=	Operand 1 is not equal to operand 2
<=	Operand 1 is less than or equal to operand 2
>=	Operand 1 is greater than or equal to operand 2

Figure 4-2: Java relational operators

When boolean operators and operands are joined together to form a statement, the statement is called a **boolean** or **relational expression**. The syntax is: *<operand 1> <operator> <operand 2>*.

The operands of the expression can be a literal value, variable, mathematical expression, or a method call. In the Java programming language, any type of operand can be used in a relational expression. The only restriction is that the operands must be of compatible types. In Tutorial 3 you learned that there are functions in Java that will convert operands from one type to another. These functions can be very useful when you are trying to code a relational expression and need to make the operands compatible. As an example of relational expressions, suppose that a financial organization wants the borrower's age to be greater than or equal to 18. The organization could code this relationship as: *borrowerAge >= 18*.

If Greg, who is 25 years old, and Diane, who is 16 years old, want to borrow money, this relational expression can be used to check their eligibility. Greg would pass this test because he is older than 18, but Diane would not pass because she is only 16. Figure 4-3 illustrates how the relational operators work, using different values for operand1 and operand2.

Operand1	Operand2	<	>	==	<=	>=	!=
55	10	false	true	false	false	true	true
15	25	true	false	false	true	false	true
33	33	false	false	true	true	true	false

Figure 4-3: Relational operator truth table

In this table, operand1 and operand2 are integer variables. The rows of the table show some possible values that these operands might have. In each row, the column headed by the relational operator specifies the value that is returned if an expression *operand1 <operator> operand2* is used. Thus, row one shows that operand1 is equal to 55 and operand2 is equal to 10. The < column has the value false because 55 is not less than 10 (operand1 < operand2). The entire table can be read in this manner to show the actions of the relational operators in any given situation.

In most programming tasks, you will not be given the actual relational expression that is to be used in the logic of the program you are writing, so you need to know how to design relational expressions.

Designing Relational Expressions

Click the first Tutorial 4 link of the Online Companion for this book (http://www.course.com) to see a live Java program that illustrates this topic.

You can use boolean logic and relational operators to convert simple problems into relational expressions by creating a decision table. A **decision table** is like a truth table except the decision column is not limited to boolean values. The **decision column** or **action column** in a decision table usually indicates the actions to be performed if a situation matches a given row. The rest of the columns in a decision table indicate the inputs that will be checked in the decision process. You can use the decision table to define the logic of an imprecise narrative. For example, suppose ABC Oil Corporation determines the cost of its oil based on the type of customer. ABC Oil has defined three types of customers: refinery, government, and public, which are coded using the integer values of 1, 2, and 3, respectively. Different formulas determine the price that each customer is charged per barrel of oil based on the customer's type. Figure 4-4 shows the logic of this narrative in greater detail.

customerType	Cost Calculation
1	costBarrel = worldMarketPrice * 0.6
2	costBarrel = worldMarketPrice * 0.4
3	costBarrel = worldMarketPrice * 1.3

Figure 4-4: ABC Oil decision table

The table consists of an input column named customerType and an action column for this logic that is named Cost Calculation. If the customer is type 1 (refinery), the calculation that is used for determining the cost for each barrel of oil is *worldMarketPrice * 0.6*. This calculation states that another variable is available to the program named worldMarketPrice, which is a constant that determines the cost that ABC Oil charges each type of customer. The rows for type 2 (government) and type 3 (public) customers can be read in the same way.

Each row in Figure 4-4 defines an exclusive condition in this problem. An **exclusive condition** is a situation that should not occur when two rows of the table match the input values. The rows in this table are exclusive because a customerType variable cannot equal more than one value, and the values are not duplicated in the input column. The table also should be exhaustive. An **exhaustive table** is one where all of the possible values of the inputs have been considered. ABC Oil only designates three types of customers, so this table is exhaustive. The issues of exclusivity and exhaustiveness are key to defining a narrative problem in a precise table. You can create a table like the one shown in Figure 4-4 by completing the following steps:

1. Construct a table with one column for each input and one column for the action. In this example the table has two columns: one for the input customerType and one for the action that uses a calculation.
2. Complete a separate row for each of the possible inputs stated in the narrative. There are three rows because there are three customer types. Check the rows to make sure that they are exclusive.
3. Complete the table by entering the calculation that is used if the input matches the value of that row. This calculation is entered in the Cost Calculation column.
4. Check the table to make sure that all situations described in the narrative are coded in the table. This step ensures that you have an exhaustive definition of the logic of the narrative.

After completing the decision table, you can translate the information in the decision table into pseudocode. The syntax of the expression is:

```
if      <relational expression>
then    <action list>
```

This decision table, therefore, contains the following expressions:

```
if      (customerType == 1)
then costBarrel = worldMarketPrice * 0.6
if      (customerType == 2)
then costBarrel = worldMarketPrice * 0.4
if      (customerType == 3)
then costBarrel = worldMarketPrice * 1.3
```

The steps to complete the pseudocode are as follows:

1. Develop a relational expression for each row in the table. The expression used to see if the customerType is equal to the value listed in the row of the customerType column uses the == relational operator. Thus, the relational expression for row one becomes *customerType == 1*. When ranges of numbers or values make up the information in the input column, other relational operators like < or > are equally useful.
2. Write the pseudocode keyword *if* followed by an opening parenthesis. Then write the relational expression that you developed for each row, followed by a closing parenthesis.

3. On the next line, write the pseudocode keyword *then* followed by the information from the decision column of the row that you are coding. In the ABC Oil example, this was a calculation but it also could be any valid Java command.
4. Complete these steps until all of the rows have been coded in the pseudocode. Note that these expressions are completed in pseudocode and not in Java syntax, although they are somewhat similar. Using pseudocode allows you to focus on the design of the program, rather than on the syntax of the Java language.

The decision table shown in Figure 4-4 contains only one action column. Notice that the definition of the pseudocode states that you could have an action list. When the table has more than one action column, you list the actions for each column, separated by commas. It is not necessary, however, to rewrite the condition or the if portion because the pseudocode lets you have more than one action for a given relational expression. For example, ABC Oil computes not only the base cost as shown in Figure 4-4, but also the total cost that includes any government taxes. Currently, ABC Oil must charge refineries a tax of five percent and public customers a tax of eight percent. Government customers are not taxed. The revised decision table for this problem is shown in Figure 4-5.

customerType	costBarrel	finalCost
1	costBarrel = worldMarketPrice *0.6	finalCost = costBarrel + (costBarrel * 0.05)
2	costBarrel = worldMarketPrice *0.4	finalCost = costBarrel
3	costBarrel = worldMarketPrice *1.3	finalCost = costBarrel + (costBarrel * 0.08)

Figure 4-5: ABC Oil cost calculation with taxes

Notice that you now have two decision columns. One of the decision columns calculates the base cost and the other decision column calculates the final cost. The new pseudocode for the first row of the table is:

if (customerType == 1)
*then costBarrel = worldMarketPrice * 0.6,*
*finalCost = costBarrel + (costBarrel * 0.05)*

Notice that the actions of the action list are shown on separate lines to make the pseudocode easier to read.

Many computer programs include much more complex logic than what is available with the simple relational operators. For example, how could you define a problem that has more than one input to the decision process? To address this situation in Java you can use two methods: nested if commands and logical expressions. **Nested if commands** are commands that have if commands in their action list to represent the more complex logic. **Logical expressions** are boolean expressions that combine relational expressions using logical operators to represent a complex decision process. You will learn about nested statements and logical expressions and operators next.

Understanding and Using Nested if Constructs

ABC Oil has just become an international company. The decision process shown in Figure 4-5, consequently, is no longer accurate. ABC Oil taxes U.S. customers only; international customers are not taxed. ABC Oil has decided to add an input column named countryType that will be coded with the value 1 for U.S. customers and 2 for international customers. ABC Oil determined that these codes are the only codes needed to represent its customers. Figure 4-6 shows a decision table for this added input variable.

countryType	customerType	costBarrel	finalCost
1	1	costBarrel = worldMarketPrice * 0.6	finalCost = costBarrel + (costBarrel * 0.05)
1	2	costBarrel = worldMarketPrice * 0.4	finalCost = costBarrel
1	3	costBarrel = worldMarketPrice * 1.3	finalCost = costBarrel + (costBarrel * 0.08)
2	1	costBarrel = worldMarketPrice * 0.6	finalCost = costBarrel
2	2	costBarrel = worldMarketPrice * 0.4	finalCost = costBarrel
2	3	costBarrel = worldMarketPrice * 1.3	finalCost = costBarrel

Figure 4-6: ABC Oil international decision table

Notice that there are now two input columns—one for countryType and one for customerType—and none of the international customers are taxed. The pseudocode for Figure 4-6 is:

```
if      countryType == 1
then    if customerType == 1
        then   costBarrel = worldMarketPrice * 0.6,
               finalCost = costBarrel + (costBarrel * 0.05)
if      countryType == 1
then    if customerType == 2
        then   costBarrel = worldMarketPrice * 0.4,
               finalCost = costBarrel
if      countryType == 1
then    if customerType == 3
        then   costBarrel = worldMarketPrice * 1.3,
               finalCost = costBarrel + (costBarrel * 0.08)
if      countryType == 2
then    if customerType == 1
        then   costBarrel = worldMarketPrice * 0.6,
               finalCost = costBarrel
if      countryType == 2
then    if customerType == 2
        then   costBarrel = worldMarketPrice * 0.4,
```

```
                finalCost = costBarrel
if      countryType == 2
then    if customerType == 3
        then    costBarrel = worldMarketPrice * 1.3,
                finalCost = costBarrel
```

The steps to develop this pseudocode are:

1. Write the word *if* followed by the condition for the first input variable.
2. Write the words *then if* followed by the condition for the second variable.
3. Write the word *then* followed by the action block for the current row.
4. Repeat Steps 1 through 3 until all of the rows are converted into pseudocode.

The process of developing the decision table really is divided into sections. The first relational expression is the first input column and the rest of the columns make up the decision or action. This action contains a conditional input so the action is coded as a relational expression with the last two columns being the action list of the nested relational expression. The key process to remember is that you code the first input column in a relational expression and code subsequent input columns in the action list of the previous relational expression until you have only output actions to perform. This process produces a nested construct of two levels in the ABC Oil problem.

Nested if constructs can become very difficult to read and understand when they contain five or more input columns. In this case, using logical operators and expressions are one way to simplify the code of such problems.

Understanding Logical Operators

Click the second Tutorial 4 link of the Online Companion for this book (http://www.course.com) to see a live Java program that illustrates this topic.

Logical operators combine two relational expressions and return a single truth value for the total expression. The three common logical operators are **and**, **or**, and **not**. The *not* operator does not take two relational expressions; the *not* operator has only one operand. Figure 4-7 shows the logical operators, the symbols that are used to indicate them in Java, and a description of how they work.

Logical Operator	Operator Symbol	Description
and	&&	Both operands of the expression must be true
or	||	One operand must be true
not	!	The opposite truth value of the operand (only one operand)

Figure 4-7: Java logical operators

The purpose of logical operators is to combine relational operators in more complex structures. The syntax for a logical expression is:

<boolean expression> <logical operator> <boolean expression>

or

<not operator> <boolean expression>

The boolean expression can be any relational or logical expression that returns the values of true or false. Logical operators, unlike relational operators, must have operands that evaluate to true or false. An error occurs if you try to use illegal operands with relational and logical operators.

Logical operators are expressed in truth tables just like the relational operators. Figure 4-8 shows the truth table for logical operators. Columns one and two of this table specify the values of operand1 and operand2 respectively. The following two columns list the return value of a relational expression that has operand1 and operand2 joined by the relational operator for the column. The final column shows the value of the logical not (!) operator applied to operand1. For example, the column labeled ! returns the value of false in row one of the table. This means that the logical expression operand1 ! operand2 results in the value false.

Operand1	Operand2	&&	||	!
true	true	true	true	false
true	false	false	true	false
false	true	false	true	true
false	false	false	false	true

Figure 4-8: Logical operator truth table

Operands in a logical expression usually are relational expressions or methods that return a boolean value. The decision table that was developed when ABC Oil became an international company was shown in Figure 4-6. You can use the information shown in Figure 4-6 and logical operators to create the following pseudocode:

```
if      (countryType == 1) && (customerType == 1)
then    costBarrel = worldMarketPrice * 0.6,
        finalCost = costBarrel + (costBarrel * 0.05)
if      (countryType == 1) && (customerType == 2)
then    costBarrel = worldMarketPrice * 0.4,
        finalCost = costBarrel
if      (countryType == 1) && (customerType == 3)
then    costBarrel = worldMarketPrice * 1.3,
        finalCost = costBarrel + (costBarrel * 0.08)
if      (countryType == 2) && (customerType == 1)
then    costBarrel = worldMarketPrice * 0.6,
        finalCost = costBarrel
if      (countryType == 2) && (customerType == 2)
then    costBarrel = worldMarketPrice * 0.4,
        finalCost = costBarrel
if      (countryType == 2) && (customerType == 3)
then    costBarrel = worldMarketPrice * 1.3,
        finalCost = costBarrel
```

You can perform this task by completing the following steps:

1. Develop relational expressions for each of the input variable columns.
2. Write the word *if* followed by the relational expressions joined with the && operator.
3. Write the word *then* followed by the action block for the given row.
4. Repeat Steps 1 through 3 until all rows are coded.

Your pseudocode creates a logical expression that uses the && (and) operator and two operands. You use the && operator because you are coding a problem that has multiple input columns. Sometimes a decision table will have multiple rows with exactly the same action columns. When this occurs you can code the decision table by developing the logical expression for each row and joining the logical expressions with the || (or) operator. When you mix the use of logical operators, you will need to remember the order that Java uses in evaluating logical operators, which is described next.

Operator Precedence

The operators used in boolean expressions must follow an order of operation, or **precedence.** In Java, the relational and logical operators are combined when considering precedence so you know which operation is performed first. Figure 4-9 shows the logical and relational operators with their precedence order in Java. Operators of the same precedence are evaluated in an expression from left to right. This precedence order can be altered only by enclosing expressions in parentheses because the expressions enclosed in parentheses always are evaluated first.

Operator	Evaluation Order
parentheses ( )	First
not (!)	Second
relational operators (==, <, >, !=, <=, >=)	Third
and (&&)	Fourth
or (||)	Fifth

Figure 4-9: Precedence of relational and logical operators

For example, the order of evaluation for the expression (55 < 10) || (10 < 55) && (31 == 31) is as follows:

1. Evaluate the parenthetical expressions from left to right. Thus, (55 < 10) evaluates to false, (10 < 55) evaluates to true, and (31 == 31) evaluates to true.
2. Evaluate the *and* expression using the result of the two relational expressions on the right and left as operand one and two. Thus, operand1 is true because (10 < 55) evaluated to true, and operand2 is true because (31 == 31) evaluated to true. The logical expression operand1 && operand2 evaluates to true because true && true evaluates to true. The result of this evaluation is named operand3.

3. Evaluate the *or* operator using operand3 as the right operand and the result of the evaluation of (55 < 10), or false as the left one. This evaluation returns true because false || true evaluates to true.

Precedence order is the basis for determining that the logic coded in a program produces the desired results.

Now you can take a break or complete the end-of-lesson questions and exercises.

SUMMARY

- Computers are electronic devices that process information using two states: *true* for on and *false* for off.
- Boolean operators consist of two types—relational and logical.
- Relational operators are used to evaluate the relationship between two operands. Logical operators are used to combine two or more relational expressions into a single boolean expression.
- The relational operators are equal (==), less than (<), greater than (>), less than or equal (<=), greater than or equal (>=) and not equal (!=). The logical operators are *and* (&&), *or* (||), and *not* (!).
- Truth tables are used to describe the performance of relational and logical operators in specific situations. A truth table usually consists of a column for each operand in the boolean expression and a decision column that contains the values "true" or "false." The rows in a truth table indicate the situations that are being considered.
- Decision tables are modifications of truth tables and are used to describe the logic contained in a narrative that can be converted into boolean expressions.
- Decision tables have rows and columns. The columns note the conditions and actions and the rows indicate specific cases of the narrative. Decision tables can be expressed as simple relational expressions by coding each row in the table carefully. Decision tables can be used to develop logical expressions of two major types—*and* and *or*.
- *Or* logical expressions are noted in decision tables by rows with the same action statements. *And* logical expressions are noted in decision tables by the presence of more than one condition column.

QUESTIONS

1. The two states of a computer are __________ and __________.
a. on, off
b. active, inactive
c. waiting, executing
d. greater than, less than

2. The __________ relational operator is used in a situation when a programmer wants to check if operand1 is not less than operand2.
a. <=
b. >=
c. !=
d. ==

3. A(n) __________ is a tool that is used to translate a narrative about a decision and define it in precise terms.
   a. object chart
   b. relational operator
   c. decision table
   d. logical operator
4. Which of the following is not a logical operator?
   a. less than
   b. and
   c. or
   d. not
5. Which relational operator means *exactly equal*?
   a. <
   b. >
   c. ==
   d. !=
6. A decision table that has rows that result in the same action is expressed using the logical operator __________.
   a. and
   b. or
   c. not
   d. equal
7. Decision tables that have more than one condition column are expressed using the logical operator __________.
   a. and
   b. or
   c. not
   d. equal
8. A __________ table defines the performance of the relational or logical operators in given situations. These tables usually have a column for each operand and then a column which specifies the boolean result of the operation.
   a. truth
   b. decision
   c. relational operator
   d. logical operator
9. A relational expression will evaluate to the value __________ or __________.
   a. true, false
   b. open, closed
   c. equal, not equal
   d. and, or
10. The operands of a logical expression must be of type __________.
   a. string
   b. relational
   c. boolean
   d. integer

EXERCISES

1. Assume that the variable op1 is equal to 55 and op2 is equal to 22. Evaluate the following relational expressions as true or false.
   a. op1 != op2
   b. op1 <= op2
   c. op1 == op2
   d. op1 >= op2
   e. op1 > op2
2. Assume that the variable exp1 is equal to true, exp2 is equal to false, and exp3 is equal to true. Evaluate the following logical expressions to true or false. Write down the order in which you performed the evaluations.
   a. exp1 || exp2 && exp3
   b. exp1 && exp2
   c. exp1 && exp2 || exp3
   d. exp1 || exp3
   e. (exp1 || exp2) && exp3
3. The area of a circle is computed using the equation _2*pi*r_, the area of a rectangle is computed using the equation _length*width_, and the area of a square is computed using the equation _length*length_. Develop a decision table that has as its condition column the geometric figure desired and in its action column the formula to use for computing the area of the figure.
4. You are teaching your friend Maria Lopez the English language. Recently she learned that singular nouns have verbs that end in an *s* and plural nouns have verbs that do not end in an *s*. If a word begins with a vowel and the article *a* or *an* is desired before it, she should use the *an* article and in all other cases she should use the *a* article. Create a decision table that illustrates these two grammar rules.
5. Tawni Retail charges its customers for shipping costs based on the amount of the order. If the order total is between $1 and $100, then the shipping cost is three percent. If the order total is between $101 and $500, then the shipping cost is two percent. Order totals over $500 are charged a shipping cost of one and one-half percent. Develop the decision table and pseudocode to illustrate this policy.
6. Genieva currently is employed by an electronics parts company. She has been asked to reorganize the stocking of inventory in the warehouse. She determined that there are three major sections in the warehouse. Parts that begin with the prefix 01 through 05 are stored in section one, parts with the prefix 06 through 10 are stored in section two, and parts with the prefix 11 through 20 are stored in section three. Develop a decision table for stocking the electronic parts according to this structure, and then develop the pseudocode for the decision table.
7. Winter Financial decides the amount of credit that an individual will receive from its credit card division based on the customer credit rating and the current salary of the customer. Winter Financial codes credit ratings as 1 for excellent, 2 for average, and 3 for poor. Customers with excellent credit ratings and a monthly salary of $1,500 or more are given a credit limit of $10,000. Customers with an excellent credit rating but a monthly salary of less than $1,500 receive a credit limit of $5,000. Customers with an average credit rating and a monthly salary of $1,500 or more are given a credit limit of $5,000. Customers with an average credit rating and a monthly salary of less than $1,500 are given a credit limit of $0. All customers with a poor credit rating are given a credit limit of $0. Develop the decision table and pseudocode for this problem.

8. A local police organization assigns the cost of a speeding ticket based on the number of miles an hour the driver exceeds the speed limit. Drivers who exceed the speed limit by five to ten miles per hour are charged $50. Drivers who exceed the speed limit by 11 to 15 miles per hour are charged $100. Drivers who exceed the speed limit by more than 15 miles per hour are charged $250. Develop the decision table and pseudocode for deciding how much to charge a given driver.

9. GymBody Works determines the membership rate for its customers based on the length of the membership purchased. Customers who purchase a six-month membership are charged $100, customers who purchase a one-year membership are charged $150, and customers who purchase a two-year membership are charged $175. Develop the decision table and pseudocode for this problem.

10. Confections Candy discounts the price of its merchandise based on the length of time the candy has been in the store and the type of candy product. Confections Candy codes its merchandise as 1 for chocolate and 2 for non-chocolate. Chocolate candy that has been in the store more than two weeks is discounted 15 percent and chocolate candy that has been in the store more than one month is discounted 50 percent. Non-chocolate candy that has been in the store more than one month is discounted 10 percent and non-chocolate candy that is older than two months is discounted 30 percent. Develop a decision table and pseudocode for Confections Candy. You can assume that you will have an input variable for the candy type and the number of weeks that the candy has been in the store.

LESSON B

objectives

In this lesson you will learn how to:

- **Design simple relational conditions using boolean expressions**
- **Translate boolean expressions into simple Java if statements**
- **Design relational expressions in the Java language format**
- **Design boolean expressions for nested if statements**
- **Translate nested boolean expressions into Java code**
- **Take a narrative problem and design a solution using the Java if else statement with its variations**

Using Boolean Logic and if Statements

Incorporating Exception Handling into the Order Entry Applet

Programming with the if Command

You can combine all of the change methods in your objects using if statements. In addition, you can use exception checking when information is entered on the customer order for Koffee Koncoctions. Using the power of decision structures in Java, you can incorporate some exception handling into the order applet. In this lesson you will apply these concepts while learning how to use the if statement.

The primary command for decision control in Java is the **if command**. The syntax of a simple Java if statement is:

if (<conditional expression>)
{
<if action block>
};

This statement is read as follows. First, the condition evaluates to either true or false based on the operators used and order of precedence, and second, if the condition evaluates to true, the if action block is executed. The condition of the if statement can either be a relational or logical expression, and the action block can contain from zero to many statements. When relational expressions are used in the condition, these expressions must be enclosed in parentheses. The only constraint for using multiple statements in the action block is that you must separate them with a semicolon. All valid Java statements, including another if command, can be used. For example, consider the following Java if statement:

```
if ( borrowerAge >= 21 )
 {
  meetsAgeCriteria = true;
  needsParentSignature = false;
 };
```

This Java if statement is evaluated as follows:

1. The conditional expression (borrowerAge >= 21) is evaluated. If you apply for credit and you are 25 years of age, this expression evaluates to true because 25 is greater than 21.
2. Because the condition evaluated to true, the *meetsAgeCriteria = true* and *needsParentSignature = false* statements are executed. The assignment statement stores the value on the right side of the equal sign in the variable on the left side.

Suppose you want to borrow money and you are 16 years old. The evaluation of the Java statement is as follows:

1. The expression *16 >= 21* is evaluated to the value false.
2. Because the condition evaluates to false, the action block is not executed and the values for *meetsAgeCriteria* and *needsParentSignature* are not changed.

The next step in designing an if statement is to take problems with decisions and code them in the Java language.

Programming a Simple if Statement

You can now take the ABC Oil Company problem and code it into Java if statements. Figure 4-4 shows the first decision table that was developed for ABC Oil. You will modify this table by adding a column that lists the Java commands for each row. Figure 4-10 shows the new decision table.

customerType	costBarrel Calculation	Java Program Code

1	costBarrel = worldMarketPrice * 0.6	if (customerType == 1)
		{
		costBarrel = worldMarketPrice * 0.6;
		};

2	costBarrel = worldMarketPrice * 0.4	if (customerType == 2)
		{
		costBarrel = worldMarketPrice * 0.4;
		};

3	costBarrel = worldMarketPrice * 1.3	if (customerType == 3)
		{
		costBarrel = worldMarketPrice * 1.3;
		};

Figure 4-10: ABC Oil decision table with Java code

To develop this decision table, you use the decision table shown in Figure 4-4 and the pseudocode that was developed for that decision table. The typical sequence of steps in coding a decision in Java is to develop a decision table, develop pseudocode for the decision table, and then convert the pseudocode into Java commands. Next you will develop a Java program for ABC Oil.

To develop the Java program for ABC Oil:

1. Start Visual J++ and close any open project workspace, if necessary.
2. Click **File** on the menu bar, click **New**, click the **Files** tab, and then double-click **Java Source File** to create a new Java file.
3. Click the Save button on the Standard toolbar, and then save the file as **ABCOil1.java** in the Tutorial4\ABCOil folder on your Student Disk.
4. Enter the code shown in Figure 4-11 for the environment and heading sections. This code imports the Java libraries and defines the name of the class.

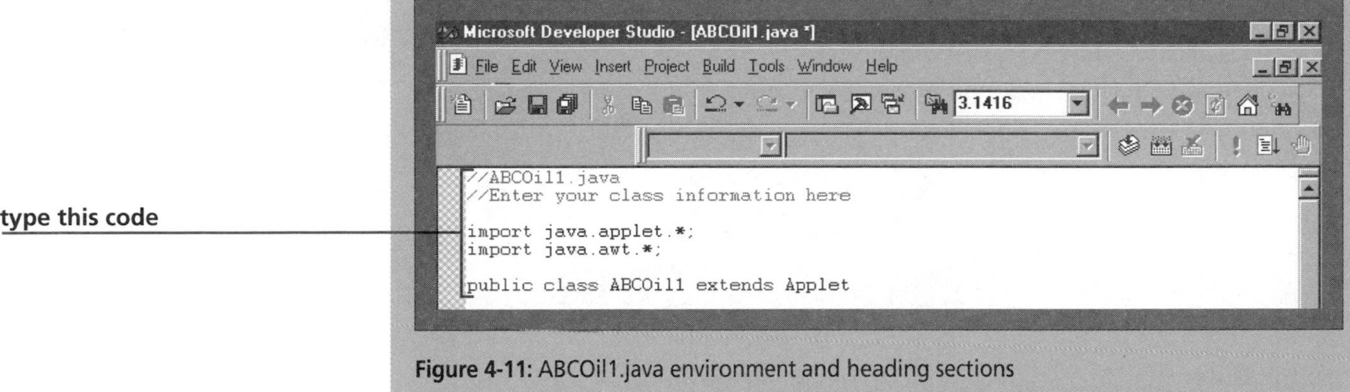

Figure 4-11: ABCOil1.java environment and heading sections

5 Press the **Enter** key, and then enter the code shown in Figure 4-12 for the property variables. This code defines the variables that are needed by Java for this program. Notice that there are variables for text input, output text areas, prompts, and calculation. This section is expanded because you are performing interactive input.

type this code

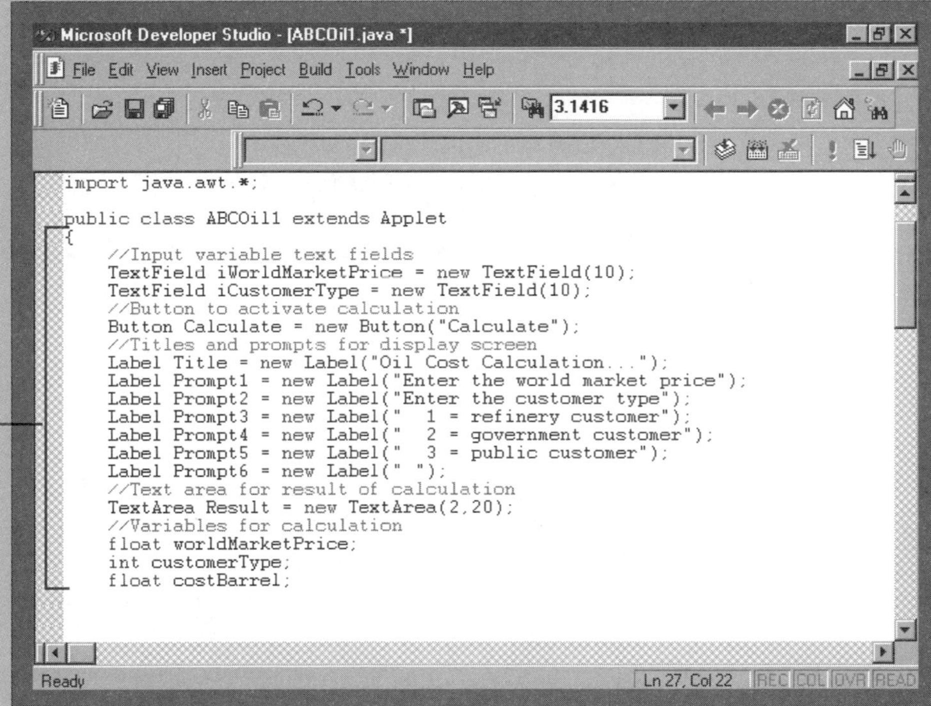

Figure 4-12: ABCOil1.java property variables

6 Press the **Enter** key twice, and then enter the code shown in Figure 4-13 for the init() method after the property variable section. This portion of code will execute automatically when the applet starts. Its basic purpose is to print information on the screen and to set a Calculate button to control the actions of the applet.

type this code

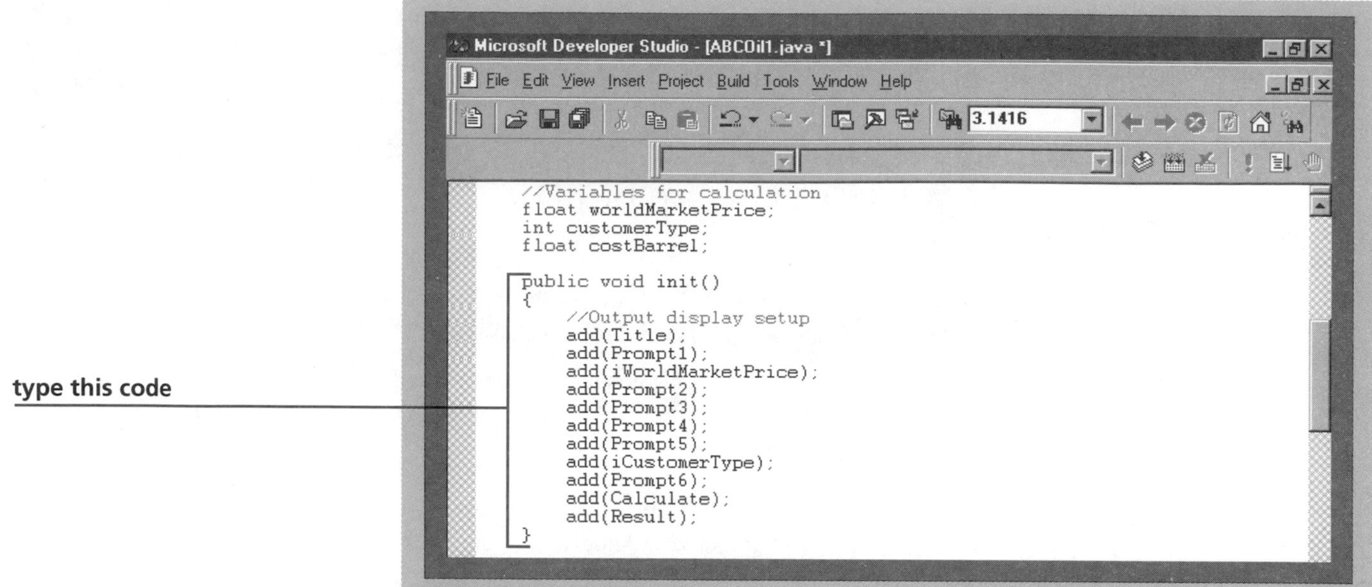

Figure 4-13: ABCOil1.java init method

7 Press the **Enter** key twice, and then enter the code shown in Figure 4-14 for the action method. This method controls the calculation of the cost of oil. It has code for retrieving user input, converting text input to numbers, calculating the cost of oil, and printing results on the screen. The figure shows the code in Full Screen view.

type this code

```
}
public boolean action(Event thisEvent, Object thisObject)
{
    //Read input and convert to numbers
    worldMarketPrice = toFloat (iWorldMarketPrice.getText() );
    customerType = toInt (iCustomerType.getText() );
    //Calculate cost of oil per barrel
    if (customerType == 1)
    {
        costBarrel = worldMarketPrice * 0.6f;
    };
    if (customerType == 2)
    {
        costBarrel = worldMarketPrice * 0.4f;
    };
    if (customerType == 3)
    {
        costBarrel = worldMarketPrice * 1.3f;
    };
    //Print calculation results
    Result.appendText ("Cost per barrel..." + "\n");
    Result.appendText ("$" + floatToString(costBarrel));
    return true;
}
//Conversion methods
public String floatToString (float value)
{
    return "" + value + "";
}
```

Figure 4-14: ABCOil1.java action method

8 Press the **Enter** key twice, and then enter the code shown in Figure 4-15 for the remaining conversion methods. These methods are incorporated in the program to provide string conversions of numbers.

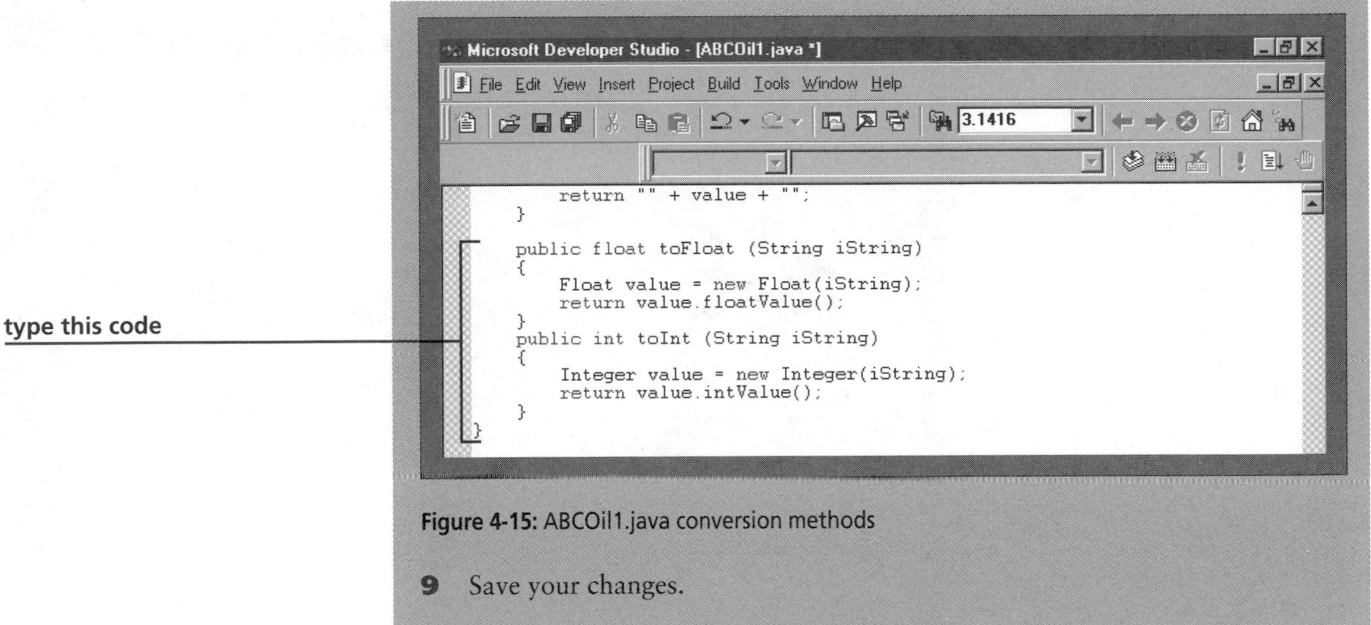

Figure 4-15: ABCOil1.java conversion methods

9 Save your changes.

Next you will build and execute the program.

To build and execute the program:

1 Click the **Build** button on the Build toolbar, and then click the **Yes** button to build the program in a default project workspace.

2 Correct any typing errors in the program.

3 If necessary, to use the HTML file on your Student Disk (instead of letting the compiler generate one), click **Project** on the menu bar, and then click **Settings**. Click the **Debug** tab, click the **Category** list arrow, and then click **Browser.** Click the **Use parameters from HTML page** option button, and then type **ABCOil1.html** in the HTML page text box. Click the **OK** button.

4 Click the **Execute Program** button on the Build toolbar to execute the program in Internet Explorer. The Information For Running Class dialog box opens. Type **ABCOil1** in the Class file name text box, and then click the **OK** button. Internet Explorer opens and runs the applet. See Figure 4-16.

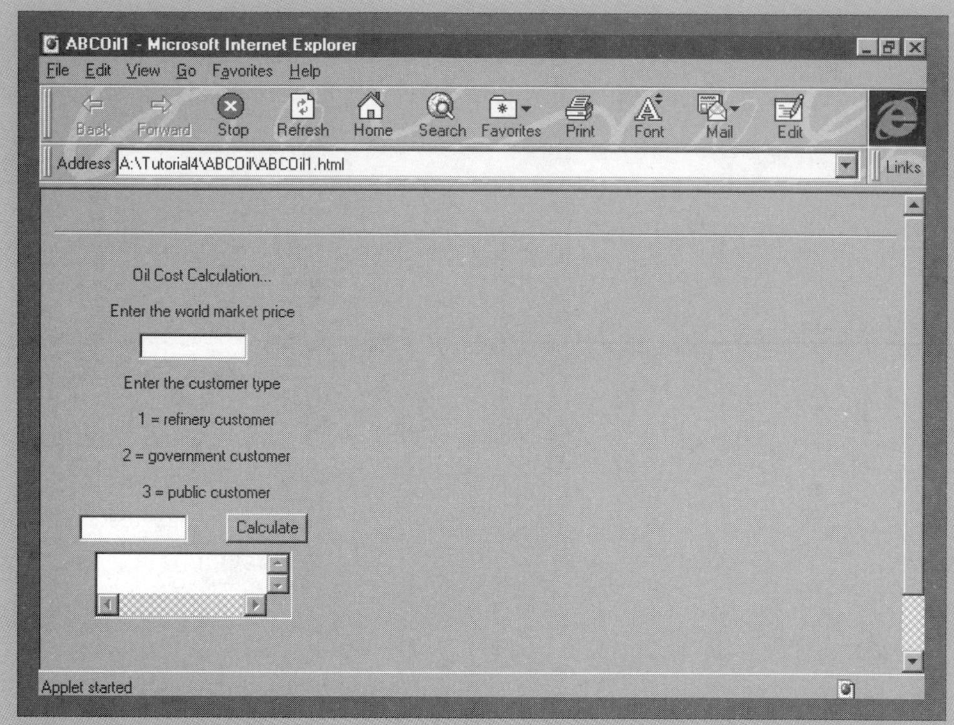

Figure 4-16: ABCOil1.java running in Internet Explorer

5 Click in the text box below the Enter the world market price prompt, and then type 100.

6 Click in the text box following the customer type prompt, and then type **1**.

7 Click the **Calculate** button. The program calculates the price of oil and displays the result in the result box as shown in Figure 4-17.

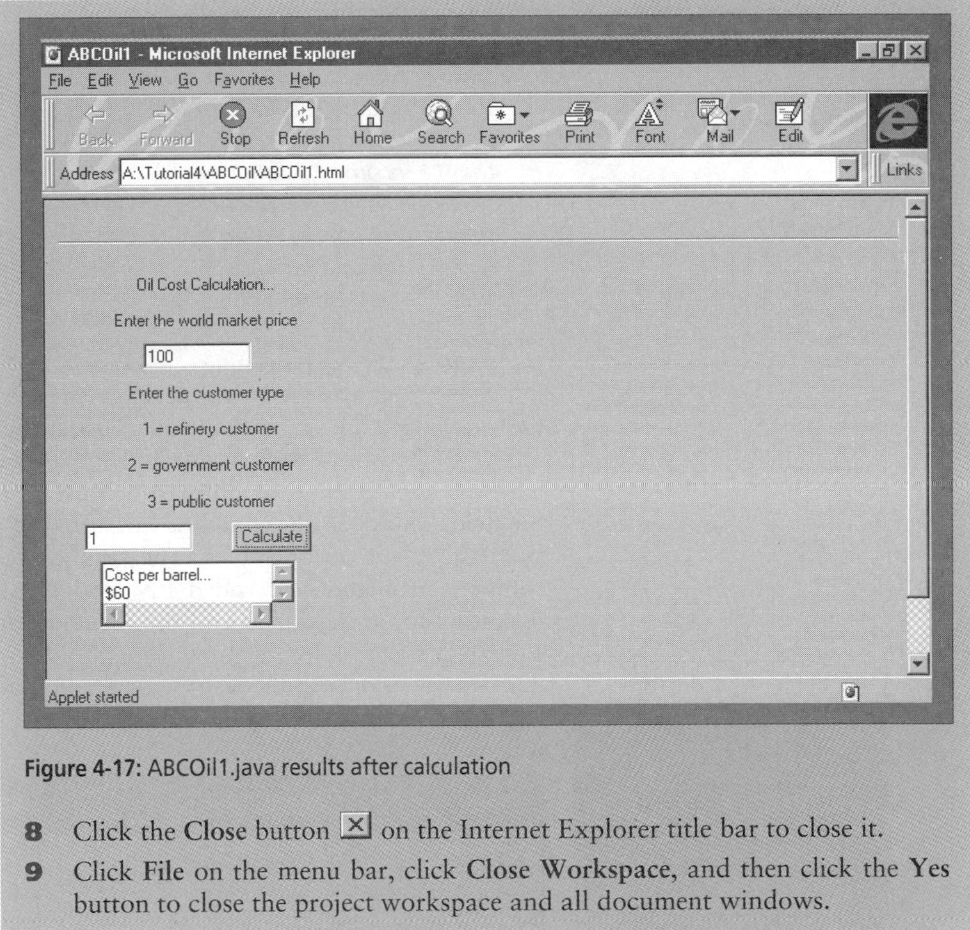

Figure 4-17: ABCOil1.java results after calculation

8 Click the **Close** button on the Internet Explorer title bar to close it.

9 Click **File** on the menu bar, click **Close Workspace**, and then click the **Yes** button to close the project workspace and all document windows.

An if statement contains the keywords for the statement, a conditional expression, and an action block that is enclosed in braces. In the ABCOil1.java program, there is only one action to perform for each if statement, so the action block contains only one statement. However, you can include any number of Java statements in the action block. When there is more than one Java statement, they are separated by semicolons.

Now you can return to your work on the order processing program for Koffee Koncoctions and work on the Coffees object. In Tutorial 2 you developed some methods that allow you to set or change the value of the fields of the objects. You can code all of the change methods in one method by using an if statement, as illustrated in the decision table shown in Figure 4-18.

iField	Variable Assignment
name	name = iValue
color	color = iValue
flavor	flavor = iValue
cost	costLb = iValue
caffeine	caffeine = iValue

Figure 4-18: Coffees object change method decision table

From this table you can develop the following pseudocode for each row in the table. Remember that pseudocode does not match Java code exactly.

if *(iField == name)*
then *name = iValue*
if *(iField == color)*
then *color = iValue*
if *(iField == flavor)*
then *flavor = iValue*
if *(iField == cost)*
then *costLb = iValue*
if *(iField = caffeine)*
then *caffeine = iValue*

Now you are ready to develop the actual Java code for this problem. However, Java does not allow you to use strings with the standard relational operators. You have two options available to solve this problem. The first method is to have the application program pass a constant that is similar to the string name of the field. This constant would be initialized to an integer value so you can use the standard relational operators. The second method is to use the group of string comparison methods provided by Java. These methods duplicate the relational operators for strings. You will use the constants method because it will give you some experience using relational operators. Figure 4-19 shows the decision table that was developed previously with a column added for the Java code that performs each row in the table.

iField	Action	Java Program Code

NAME	name = iValue	if (iField == NAME)
		{
		name = iValue;
		};

FLAVOR	flavor = iValue	if (iField == FLAVOR)
		{
		flavor = iValue;
		};

COLOR	color = iValue	if (iField == COLOR)
		{
		color = iValue;
		};

COST	costLb = iValue	if (iField == COST)
		{
		costLb = toFloat(iValue);
		};

CAFFEINE	caffeine = iValue	if (iField == CAFFEINE)
		{
		caffeine = toBoolean(iValue);
		};

Figure 4-19: Coffees object change method decision table with Java code

Notice that there are method calls in the action block to convert the string variable iValue to a float for costLb and boolean for caffeine. These methods are included because the value parameter in the method was declared as a string, and when you use this method, you need to pass the value as a string instead of a float or boolean. The conversion function changes the string into the appropriate type so that it can be stored in the variable. Now you are ready to change the Coffees.java program to use this new method.

To change the conversion function:

1. Open the **Cof.java** file in the Koffee folder on your Student Disk, and then save it as **Coffees1.java.**
2. Click in the location shown in Figure 4-20, press the **Enter** key, and then type the code shown in Figure 4-20. These variables allow the application program to specify the field to be changed.

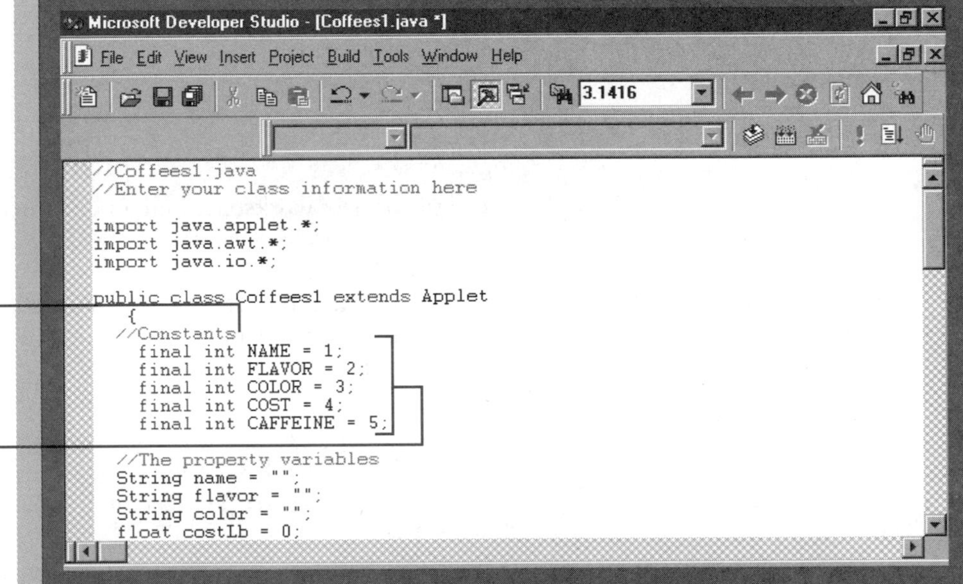

Figure 4-20: Coffees1.java constant code

3. Click in the location shown in Figure 4-21, press the **Enter** key, and then type the code shown in Figure 4-21. This is the more generic method that was designed in the decision table. This method changes the value of any of the property variables when it is called with the parameters of the field to change and the value in a string.

click here

type this code

```
//The methods
public void changeFieldValue (int iField, String iValue)
{
     if (iField == NAME)
     {
          name = iValue;
     };
     if (iField == FLAVOR)
     {
          flavor = iValue;
     };
     if (iField == COLOR)
     {
          color = iValue;
     };
     if (iField == COST)
     {
          costLb = toFloat(iValue);
     };
     if (iField == CAFFEINE)
     {
          caffeine = toBoolean(iValue);
     };
}
public void setNameValue (String iValue)
```

Figure 4-21: Coffees1.java changeFieldValue methods

4. Save your changes.
5. Build the program in a default project workspace, and then correct any typing errors.
6. Close the project workspace and all document windows.

The Coffees1.java program is not an applet; it is an object that is used by an applet. You can run a test program to check your logic. A test program is saved on your Student Disk.

To test the Coffees1.java program:

1. Open the **CoffeesTest1.java** file in the \Tutorial4\Koffee folder on your Student Disk.
2. Build the program in a default project workspace, and then correct any typing errors. Correct any compile errors in the program. You might find errors in the program, even though you did not make any changes. Check the Coffees1.java file for problems. If you are still having difficulty, ask your instructor or technical support person for help.
3. If necessary, change the default HTML file by clicking **Project** on the menu bar, and then clicking **Settings** to open the Project Settings dialog box. Click the **Debug** tab, click the **Category** list arrow, and then click **Browser**. Click the **Use parameters from HTML page** option button, press the **Tab** key, and then type **CoffeesTest1.html** in the HTML page text box. Click the **OK** button.
4. Execute the program. The class filename is **CoffeesTest1**. See Figure 4-22. Notice that the values for the Flavor field in the Coffees1 object have been set and changed by this test program.

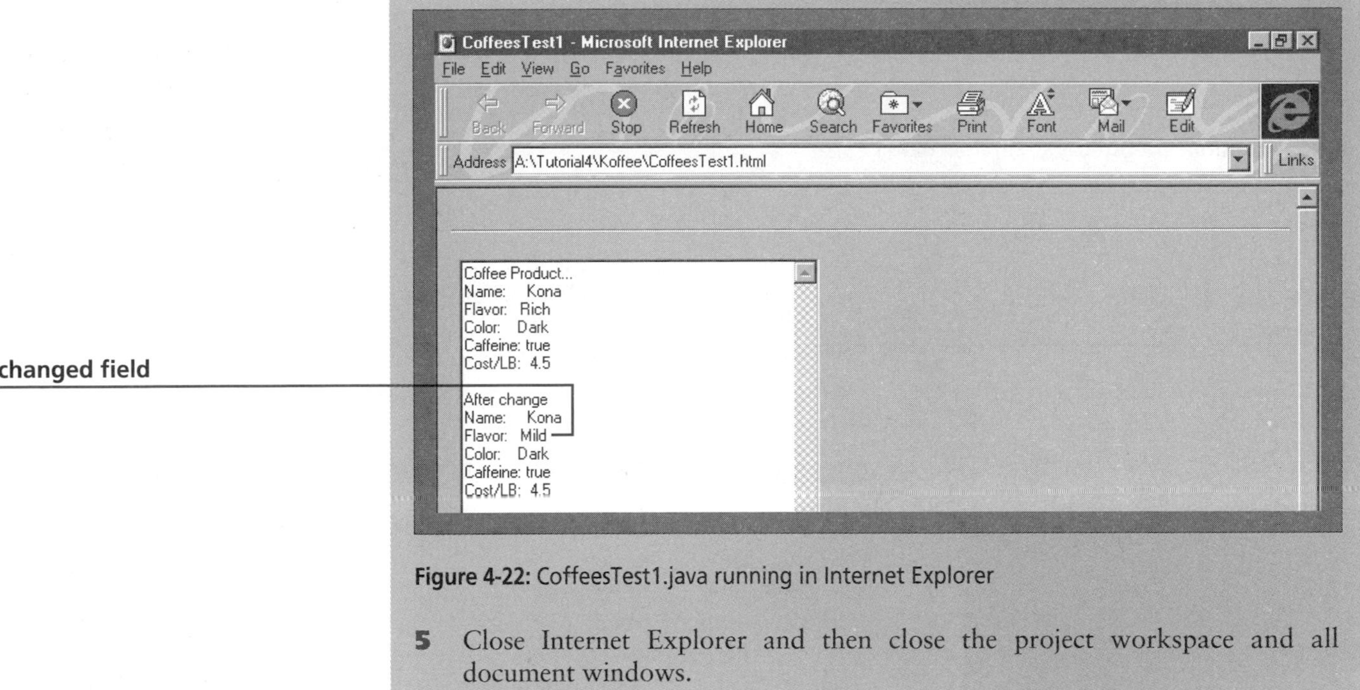

Figure 4-22: CoffeesTest1.java running in Internet Explorer

5 Close Internet Explorer and then close the project workspace and all document windows.

You can check the accuracy of your program by looking at the values that are assigned to the property variables in the CoffeesTest1.java program. If the output of the program matches the values that you entered, then your program works as designed.

In this example you used string conversion methods so that you could set the value of the boolean variable caffeine and the float variable costLb. Java also allows you to have multiple methods with the same name but different parameter lists. This process is called overloading and you were introduced to this process in Tutorial 3 when you developed multiple constructor methods. You can take the if statements that set the variables caffeine and costLb out of the original changeFieldValue method. Then you can write two other methods with the changeFieldValue name but have its parameter list be a string followed by a boolean for the caffeine field or a string followed by a float for the cost field. You will do this next.

To use multiple methods:

1 Open the **Coffees1.java** file in the Koffee folder on your Student Disk, and then save it as **Coffees2.java**.

2 Change Coffees1.java in the first comment line to **Coffees2.java**, and then change the class filename to **Coffees2**, as shown in Figure 4-23.

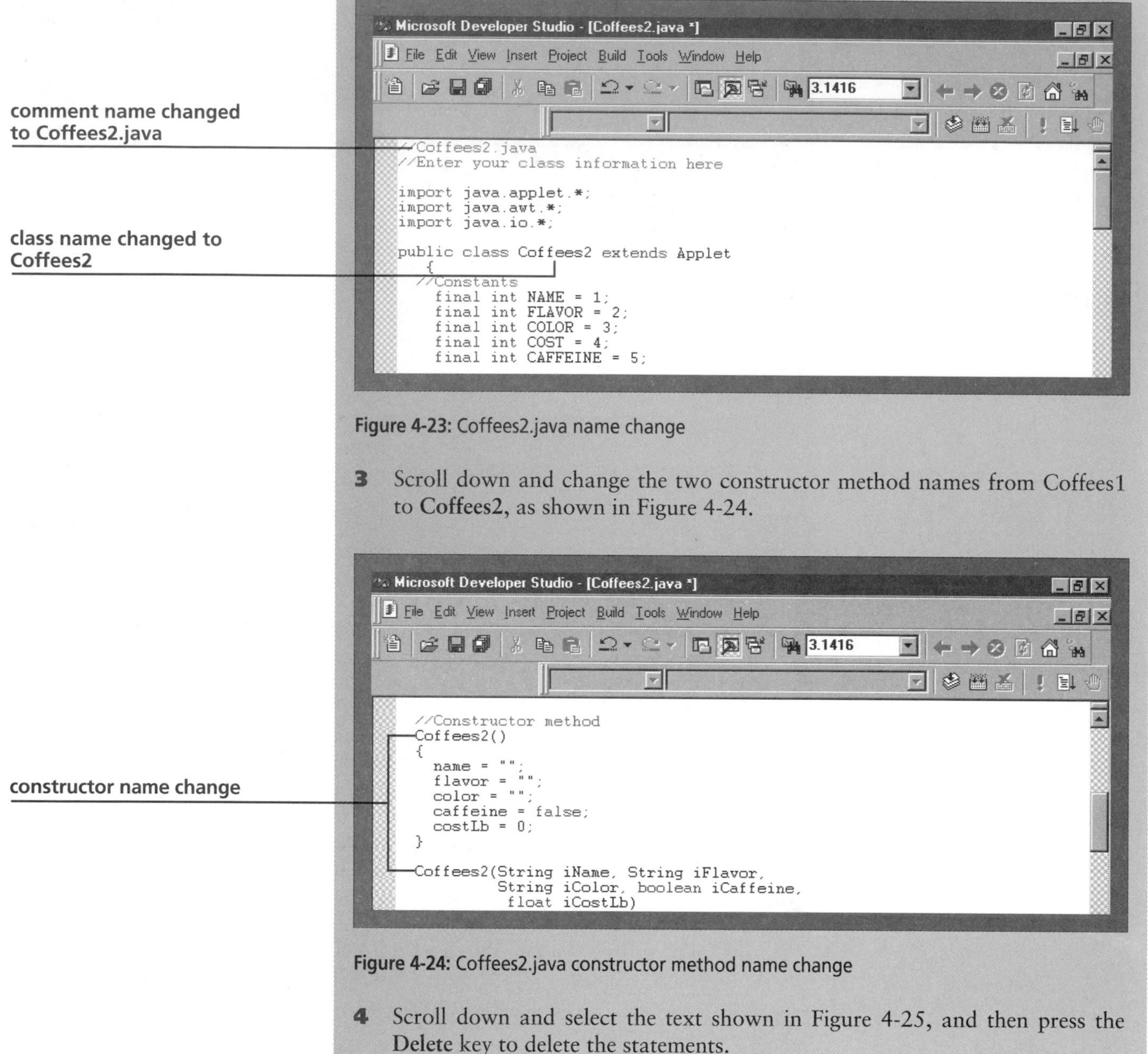

Figure 4-23: Coffees2.java name change

3 Scroll down and change the two constructor method names from Coffees1 to **Coffees2**, as shown in Figure 4-24.

Figure 4-24: Coffees2.java constructor method name change

4 Scroll down and select the text shown in Figure 4-25, and then press the Delete key to delete the statements.

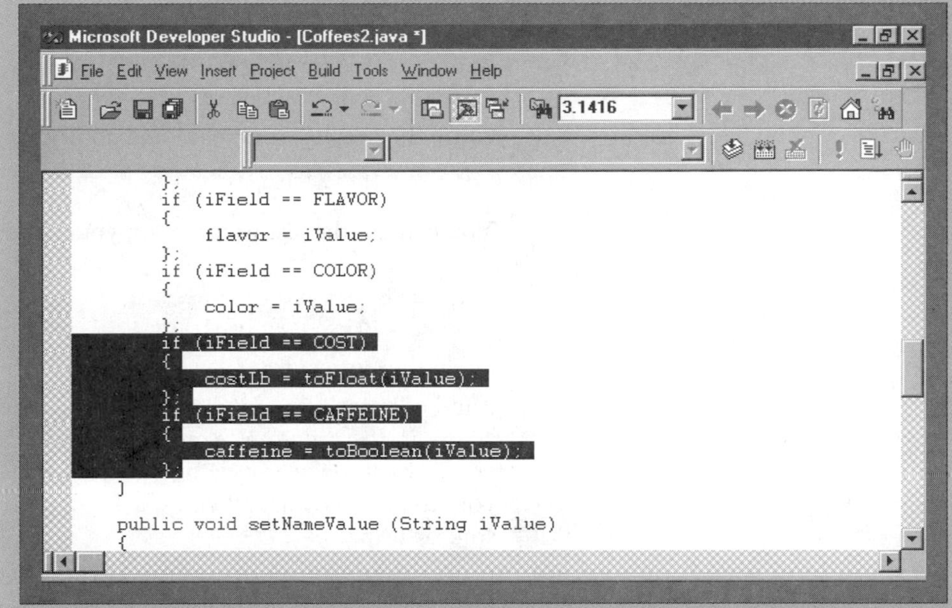

Figure 4-25: Coffees2.java if statements selected

5 Click in the location shown in Figure 4-26, press the **Enter** key twice, and then type the code shown in Figure 4-26. These two methods will perform the tasks of the two if statements you just deleted. Notice that there is a method that passes a float for the variable costLb and a method that passes a boolean for the variable caffeine. These are the overloaded methods.

Microsoft Developer Studio - [Coffees2.java *]

```
        if (iField == COLOR)
        {
            color = iValue;
        };
    }
    public void changeFieldValue (int iField, float iValue)
    {
        if (iField == COST)
        {
            costLb = iValue;
        };
    }
    public void changeFieldValue (int iField, boolean iValue)
    {
        if (iField == CAFFEINE)
        {
            caffeine = iValue;
        };
    }
    public void setNameValue (String iValue)
```

click here

type this code

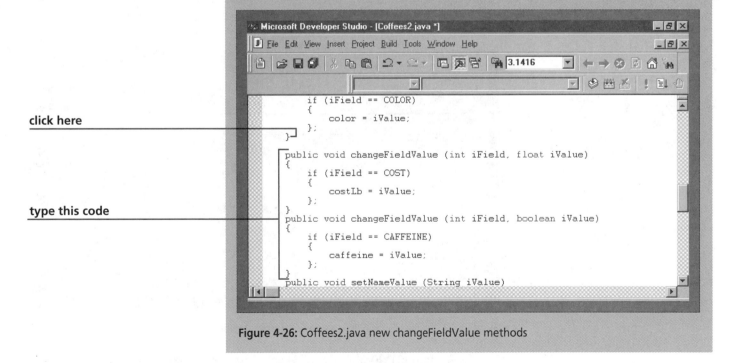

Figure 4-26: Coffees2.java new changeFieldValue methods

6 Save your changes.

7 Build the program in a default project workspace, and then correct any typing errors.

8 Close the project workspace and all document windows.

You can use the test program on your Student Disk to check your program.

To test the Coffees2.java program:

1 Open the **CoffeesTest2.java** file in the Koffee folder on your Student Disk.

2 Build the program in a default project workspace. Correct any compile errors in the program. You might find errors in the program, even though you did not make any changes. Check the Coffees2.java file for problems. If you are still having difficulty, ask your instructor or technical support person for help.

3 If necessary, change the default HTML file by clicking **Project** on the menu bar, and then clicking **Settings** to open the Project Settings dialog box. Click the **Debug** tab, click the **Category** list arrow, and then click **Browser.** Click the **Use parameters from HTML page** option button, press the **Tab** key, and then type **CoffeesTest2.html** in the HTML page text box. Click the **OK** button.

4 Execute the program. The class filename is **CoffeesTest2**. See Figure 4-27. You will notice that the values for the fields in the Coffees2 object have been set and changed by this test program. The only difference between this test program and the CoffeesTest1.java program is that you are now able to call the changeFieldValue method with a boolean and float parameter.

changed field

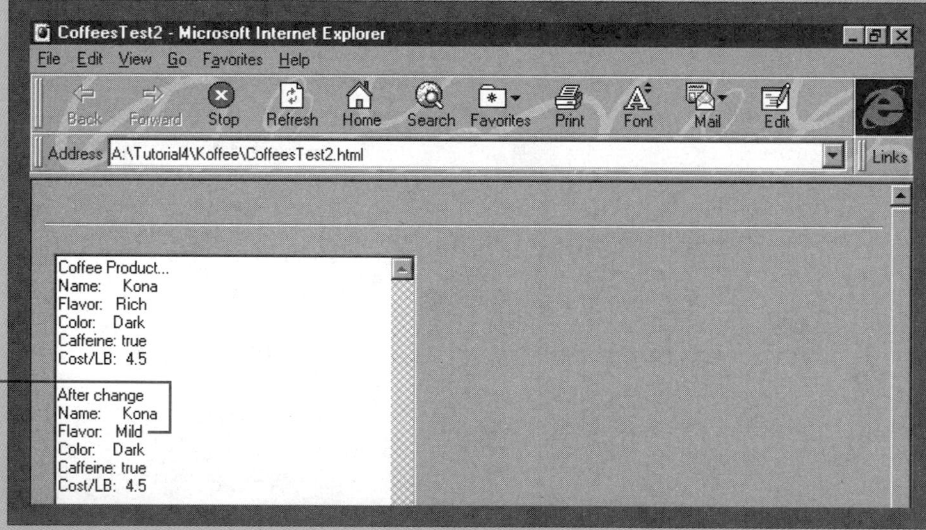

Figure 4-27: CoffeesTest2.java running in Internet Explorer

5 Close Internet Explorer and then close the project workspace and all document windows.

If you review your changeFieldValue methods in the Coffees2 object, you can see how the method executes. You took some values and walked through the code in a sequential manner. When you changed the value of the name field, the program still had to execute the remainder of the if statements. The program executed three if statements for each change of a field value. Next you will use the Java else clause to make your program more efficient.

Programming with the else Clause

The Java **else clause** is an extension of the simple if statement. When you attach an else clause to an if statement, the else clause is executed when the if statement condition evaluates to false. The syntax for using the if statement with an else clause is:

```
if ( <condition> )
{
true action block
}
else
{
false action block
};
```

You can use this structure to code your first changeFieldValue method in the Coffees2.java program. The pseudocode of the decision table is:

```
if      (iField == NAME)
then    name = iValue
else    if      (iField == FLAVOR)
        then    flavor = iValue
        else    if (iField == COLOR)
                then color = iValue
```

This pseudocode uses the else clause to improve the speed of execution of the program by reducing the number of comparisons that the program has to execute. You can develop this code from the decision table by completing the following steps:

1. Write the word *if* followed by the boolean expression for the first row in the table.
2. Write the word *then* on the next line followed by the action statements of the first row.
3. Write the words *else if* followed by the condition for the second row.
4. Write the word *then* followed by the action statements for the second row.
5. Repeat Steps 1 through 4 until you complete the final row of the table.

Now you are ready to code the revised changeFieldValue method in your Coffees2.java program. You will adjust only the first changeFieldValue method because the second method does not have multiple if statements.

To change the changeFieldValue method:

1 Open the **Coffees2.java** file in the \Tutorial4\Koffee folder on your Student Disk, and then save it as **Coffees3.java**.

2 Change the filename in the first comment line to **Coffees3.java**, and then change the class filename to **Coffees3** as shown in Figure 4-28.

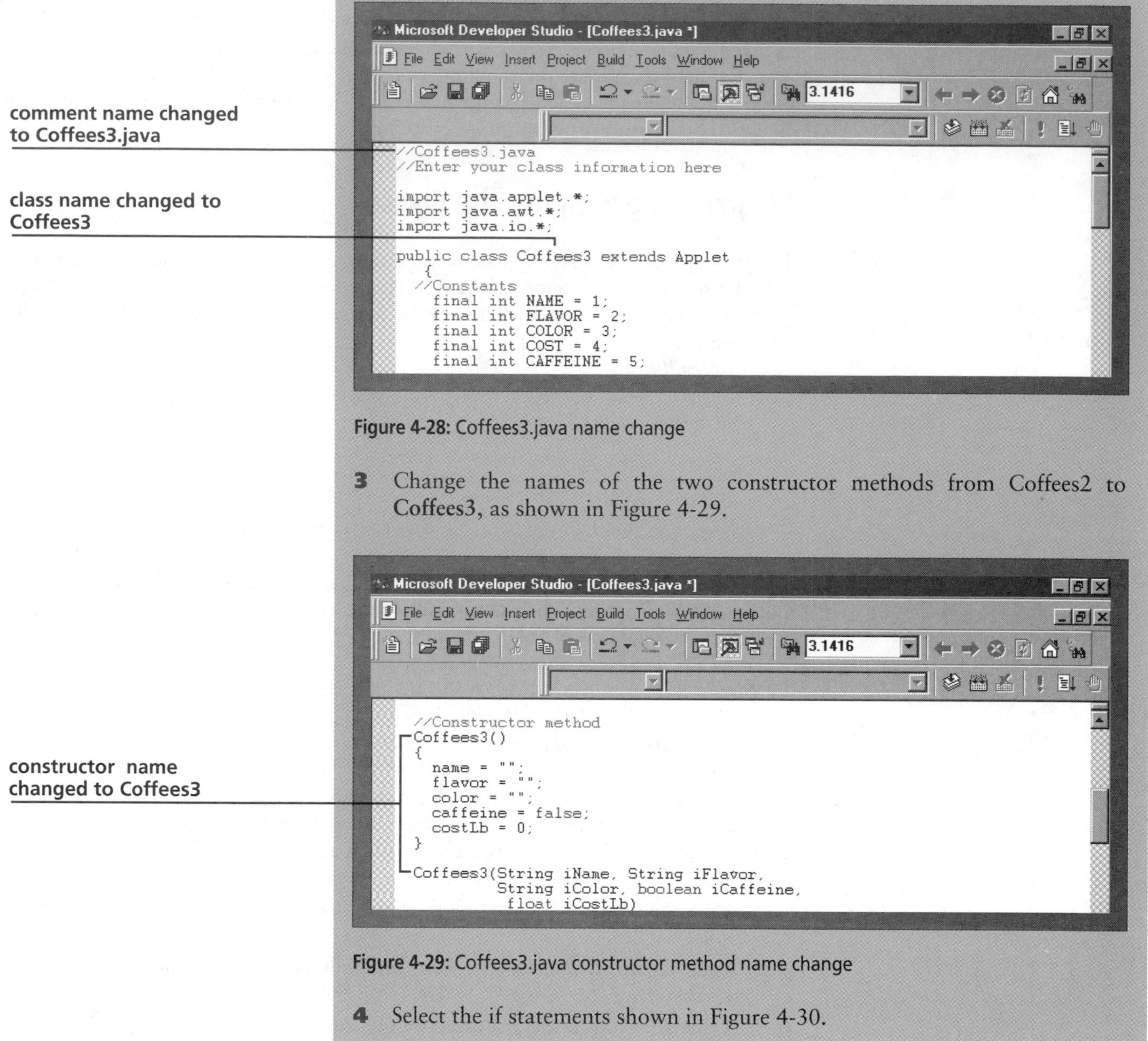

Figure 4-28: Coffees3.java name change

3 Change the names of the two constructor methods from Coffees2 to Coffees3, as shown in Figure 4-29.

Figure 4-29: Coffees3.java constructor method name change

4 Select the if statements shown in Figure 4-30.

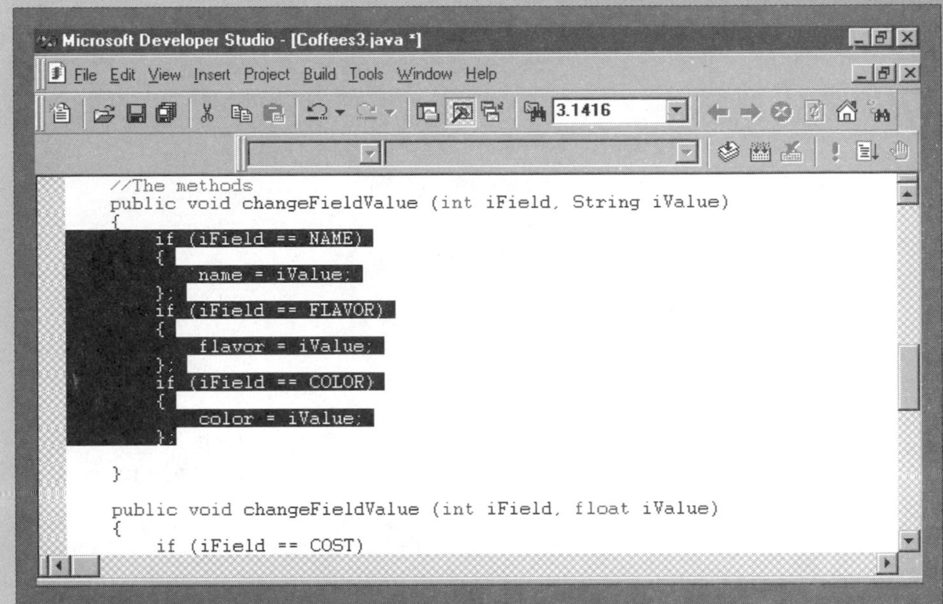

Figure 4-30: Coffees3.java if statements selected

5 Enter the new if statements shown in Figure 4-31. When you type the new code it replaces the selected code. If necessary, press the Tab key or the spacebar to align the new code to make it easier to understand.

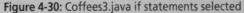

Microsoft Developer Studio - [Coffees3.java]

File Edit View Insert Project Build Tools Window Help

3.1416

type this code

```
public void changeFieldValue (int iField, String iValue)
{
        if (iField == NAME)
      {
            name = iValue;
      }
else
{
        if (iField == FLAVOR)
      {
            flavor = iValue;
      }
else
{
        if (iField == COLOR)
      {
            color = iValue;
      };
};
};
```

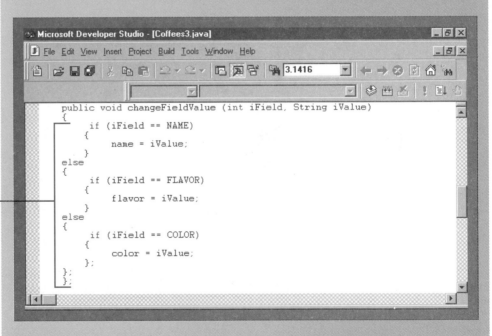

Figure 4-31: Coffees3.java if else code

6 Save your changes.

7 Build the program in a default project workspace, and then correct any typing errors.

8 Close the project workspace and all document windows.

Your Coffees3 object is now a much faster program. You might not notice the time difference in such a small program, but when there are multiple methods in an application that do not use the else clause, the application runs much slower. Next you will test your program.

To test the Coffees3.java program:

1. Open the **CoffeesTest3.java** file in the Koffee folder of your Student Disk.
2. Build the program in a default project workspace, and then correct any typing errors.
3. If necessary, change the default HTML file by clicking **Project** on the menu bar, and then clicking **Settings** to open the Project Settings dialog box. Click the **Debug** tab, click the **Category** list arrow, and then click **Browser.** Click the **Use parameters from HTML page** option button, press the **Tab** key, and then type **CoffeesTest3.html** in the HTML page text box. Click the **OK** button.
4. Execute the program. The class filename is **CoffeesTest3**. See Figure 4-32. Notice that the output from this program is exactly like the output from the CoffeesTest2.java program. You changed only the speed of execution for this program so it will run faster.

changed field

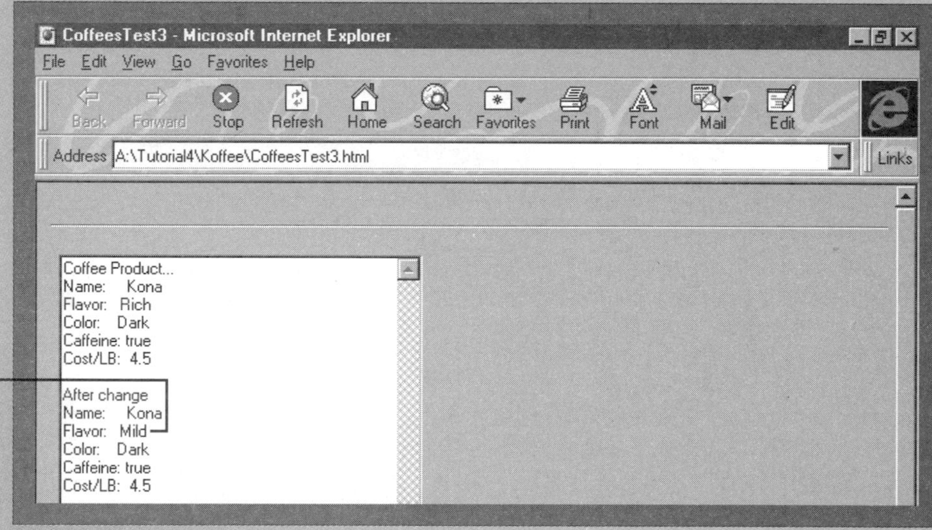

Figure 4-32: CoffeesTest3.java running in Internet Explorer

5. Close Internet Explorer and then close the project workspace and all document windows.

The else clause improved your Coffees object. You also can use the else clause when you want to check for any input that you have not included in your decision table. Remember in Lesson A that you learned that it is best if the if statements cover all possible values of the condition variables. Sometimes this is impossible, and you can use a final else to check for this error condition. The steps for using a final else clause are:

1. Write the pseudocode for the decision table that you developed using the if else format.

2. When you get to the final row of the decision table, write a final else statement with a false action block that returns some error message or code to the user. Usually in objects you will return an error code rather than printing a message directly to the screen. Then the application program can choose to use or ignore the error code.

When you use an else clause keep the following ideas in mind. First, all statements in the else action block will execute only if the condition of the if statement evaluates to false. Second, the valid statements in the true action block, which were previously referred to as the *if* action block, and the statements in the else action block can be any number of Java statements including an *if* statement. When if statements are included in either the true or false action blocks, a nested if statement is produced.

Developing Nested Constructs

Click the third Tutorial 4 link of the Online Companion for this book (http://www.course.com) to see a live Java program that illustrates this topic.

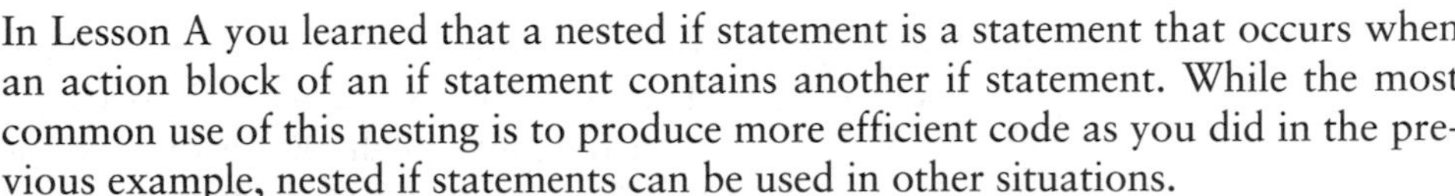

In Lesson A you learned that a nested if statement is a statement that occurs when an action block of an if statement contains another if statement. While the most common use of this nesting is to produce more efficient code as you did in the previous example, nested if statements can be used in other situations.

The decision table for the ABC Oil program you started in Lesson A is shown in Figure 4-33.

countryType	customerType	costBarrel	finalCost
1	1	costBarrel = worldMarketPrice * 0.6	finalCost = costBarrel + (costBarrel * 0.05)
1	2	costBarrel = worldMarketPrice * 0.4	finalCost = costBarrel
1	3	costBarrel = worldMarketPrice * 1.3	finalCost = costBarrel + (costBarrel * 0.08)
2	1	costBarrel = worldMarketPrice * 0.6	finalCost = costBarrel
2	2	costBarrel = worldMarketPrice * 0.4	finalCost = costBarrel
2	3	costBarrel = worldMarketPrice * 1.3	finalCost = costBarrel

Figure 4-33: ABC Oil international decision table

You can use nesting to program this decision table in a more efficient manner. The pseudocode for this decision table is:

```
if      (countryType == 1)
then    if      (customerType == 1)
        then    costBarrel = worldMarketPrice * 0.6,
                finalCost = costBarrel + (costBarrel * 0.05)
        if      (customerType == 2)
        then    costBarrel = worldMarketPrice * 0.4,
                finalCost = costBarrel
        if      (customerType == 3)
        then    costBarrel = worldMarketPrice * 1.3,
```

```
                finalCost = costBarrel + (costBarrel * 0.08)
else    if (countryType == 1)
        then    if (customerType == 1)
                then    costBarrel = worldMarketPrice * 0.6,
                        finalCost = costBarrel
                if      (customerType == 2)
                then    costBarrel = worldMarketPrice * 0.4,
                        finalCost = costBarrel
                if      (customerType == 3)
                then    costBarrel = worldMarketPrice * 1.3,
                        finalCost = costBarrel
```

You can develop this code by completing the following steps:

1. Write the word *if* followed by the condition that can be developed from the first input column.
2. Write the word *then* and the if statement that corresponds to the second input variable condition.
3. Write the word *then* followed by the action statements of the first row of the decision table. Notice that the second, third, and fourth rows of the table have the same condition for the first input variable column. This means that you can write the if statements for rows two, three, and four under the action block of the if condition that checks for U.S. customers.
4. Now you have arrived at a different value for the first input variable column. This marks where you would write the else statement.
5. Write the word *else* followed by the if statement for the condition for the second input variable on row five.
6. Write the word *then* followed by the action statements of row five. Rows five, six, and seven all have the same condition for the first input value, so you can write these in the action block as multiple if statements.

Now you can see why the use of standard indentation is extremely important in developing your pseudocode and Java programs. If you did not conform to some type of format, this small program would become unreadable quickly. Now you are ready to code this nested if statement in Java.

To code the nested if statement in Java:

1 Open the **ABCOil1.java** file from the \Tutorial4\ABCOil folder on your Student Disk, and then save it as **ABCOil2.java**.

2 Change the filename in the first comment line to **ABCOil2.java** and the class filename from ABCOil1 to **ABCOil2**, as shown in Figure 4-34.

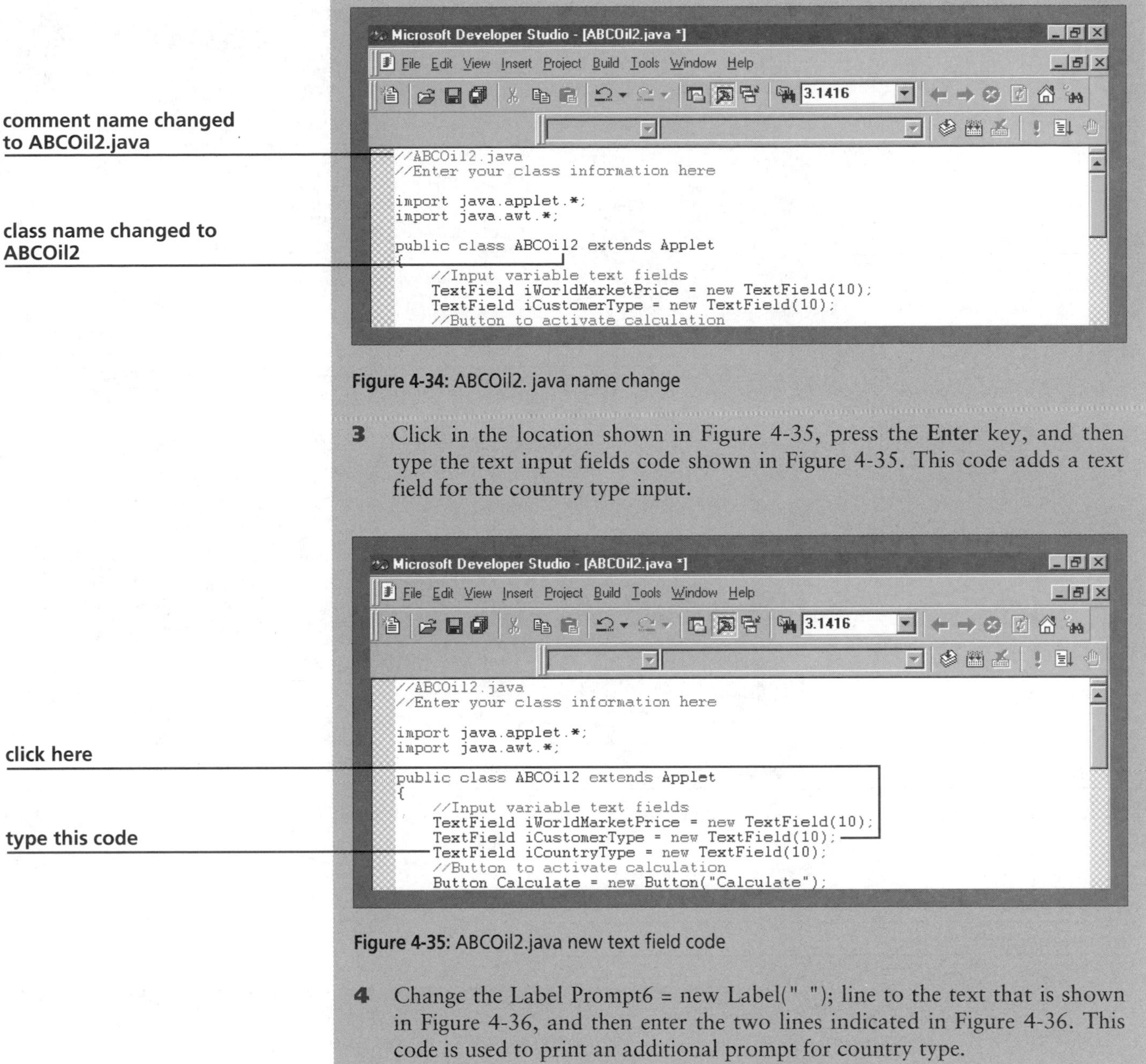

Figure 4-34: ABCOil2. java name change

3 Click in the location shown in Figure 4-35, press the **Enter** key, and then type the text input fields code shown in Figure 4-35. This code adds a text field for the country type input.

Figure 4-35: ABCOil2.java new text field code

4 Change the Label Prompt6 = new Label(" "); line to the text that is shown in Figure 4-36, and then enter the two lines indicated in Figure 4-36. This code is used to print an additional prompt for country type.

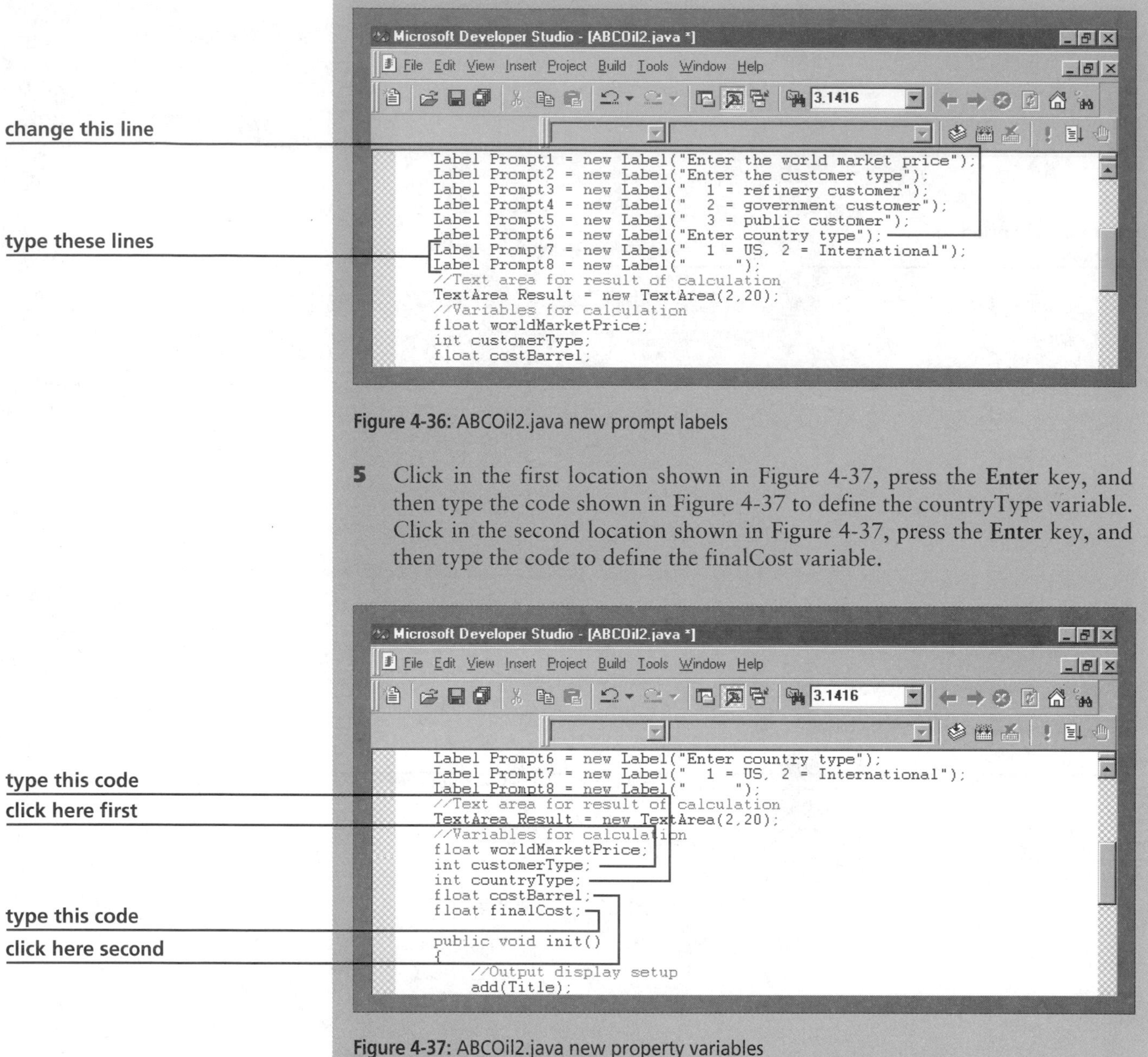
Microsoft Developer Studio - [ABCOil2.java *]
change this line
type these lines
Label Prompt1 = new Label("Enter the world market price");
Label Prompt2 = new Label("Enter the customer type");
Label Prompt3 = new Label(" 1 = refinery customer");
Label Prompt4 = new Label(" 2 = government customer");
Label Prompt5 = new Label(" 3 = public customer");
Label Prompt6 = new Label("Enter country type");
Label Prompt7 = new Label(" 1 = US, 2 = International");
Label Prompt8 = new Label("   ");
//Text area for result of calculation
TextArea Result = new TextArea(2,20);
//Variables for calculation
float worldMarketPrice;
int customerType;
float costBarrel;

Figure 4-36: ABCOil2.java new prompt labels

5 Click in the first location shown in Figure 4-37, press the **Enter** key, and then type the code shown in Figure 4-37 to define the countryType variable. Click in the second location shown in Figure 4-37, press the **Enter** key, and then type the code to define the finalCost variable.

Microsoft Developer Studio - [ABCOil2.java *]
type this code
click here first
type this code
click here second
Label Prompt6 = new Label("Enter country type");
Label Prompt7 = new Label(" 1 = US, 2 = International");
Label Prompt8 = new Label("   ");
//Text area for result of calculation
TextArea Result = new TextArea(2,20);
//Variables for calculation
float worldMarketPrice;
int customerType;
int countryType;
float costBarrel;
float finalCost;
public void init()
{
//Output display setup
add(Title);

Figure 4-37: ABCOil2.java new property variables

6 Click in the first location shown in Figure 4-38, press the **Enter** key, and then change the prompt as shown in Figure 4-38. Then click in the second location shown in Figure 4-38, press the **Enter** key, and then type the indicated code. These changes add the prompts for country type on the screen with the original prompts.

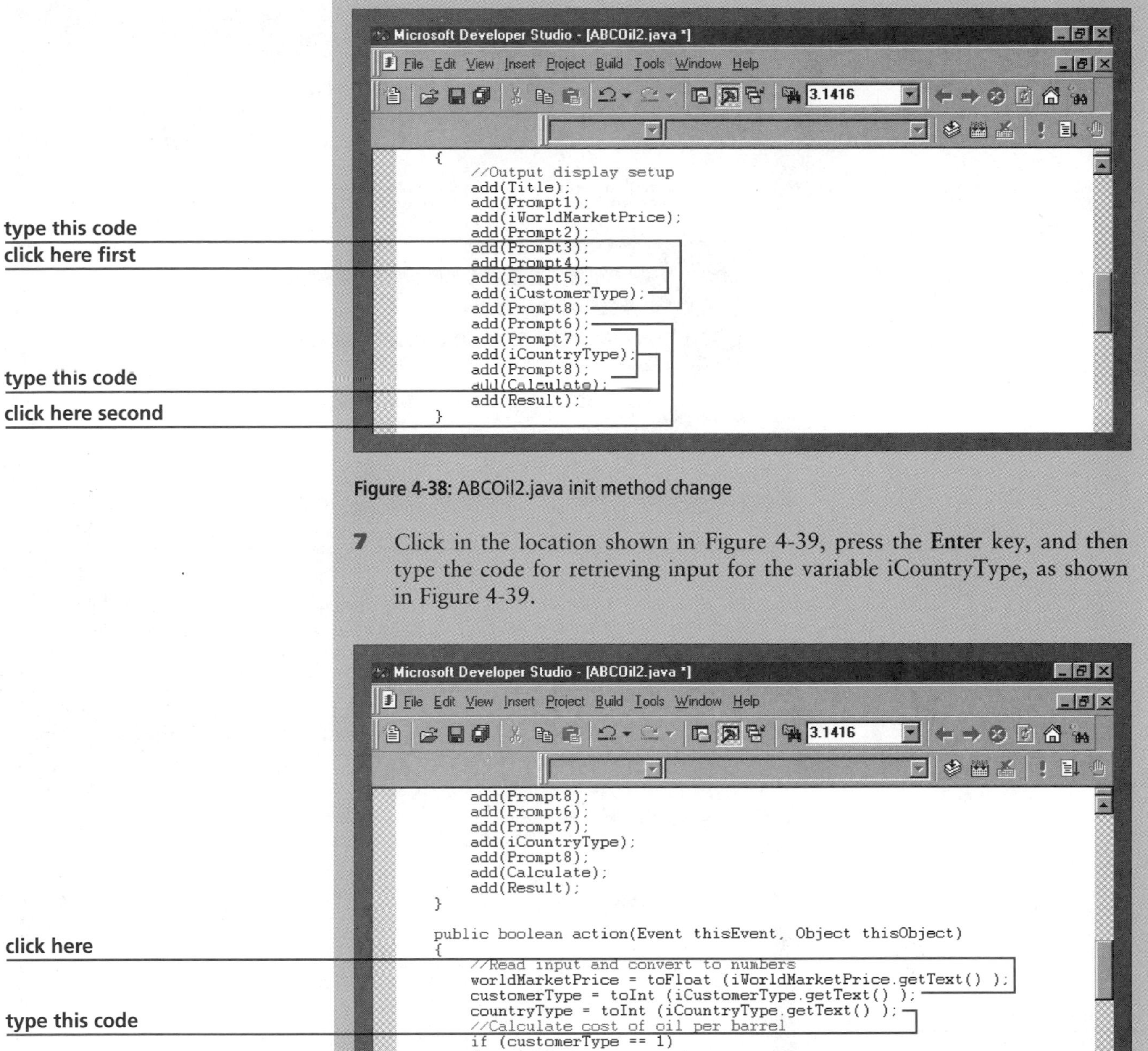

Figure 4-38: ABCOil2.java init method change

7 Click in the location shown in Figure 4-39, press the **Enter** key, and then type the code for retrieving input for the variable iCountryType, as shown in Figure 4-39.

Figure 4-39: ABCOil2.java new input statement

8 Select the if statements shown in Figure 4-40 that calculate the price of oil.

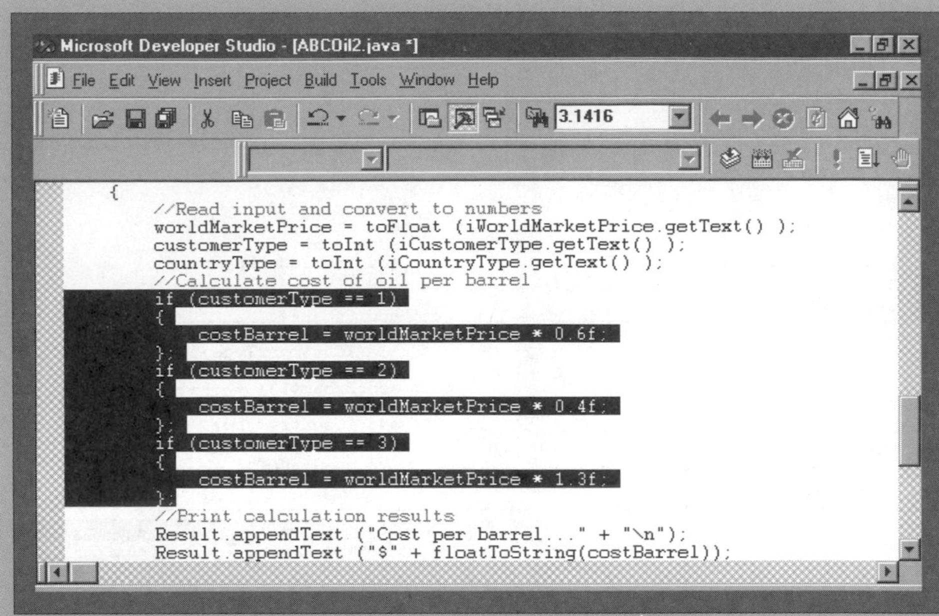

Figure 4-40: ABCOil2.java if statements selected

9 Enter the new code for the cost calculation shown in Figure 4-41. This code uses a nested if structure to compute the cost of oil based on country and customer.

Microsoft Developer Studio - [ABCOil2.java *]

File Edit View Insert Project Build Tools Window Help

3.1416

```
customerType = toInt (iCustomerType.getText() );
countryType = toInt (iCountryType.getText() );
//Calculate cost of oil per barrel
if (countryType == 1)
{
    if (customerType == 1)
    {
        costBarrel = worldMarketPrice * 0.6f;
        finalCost = costBarrel + (costBarrel * 0.05f);
    };
    if (customerType == 2)
    {
        costBarrel = worldMarketPrice * 0.4f;
        finalCost = costBarrel;
    };
    if (customerType == 3)
    {
        costBarrel = worldMarketPrice * 1.3f;
        finalCost = costBarrel + (costBarrel * 0.08f);
    };
};
```

type this code

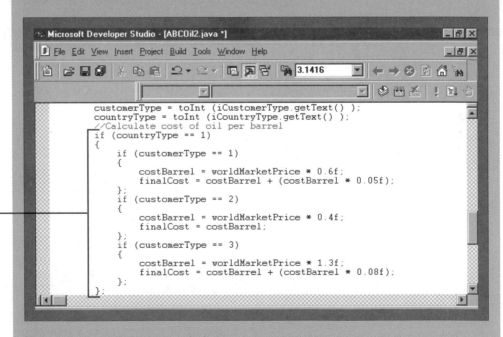

Figure 4-41: ABCOil2.java new calculation statements

10 Press the **Enter** key, and then type the code shown in Figure 4-42.

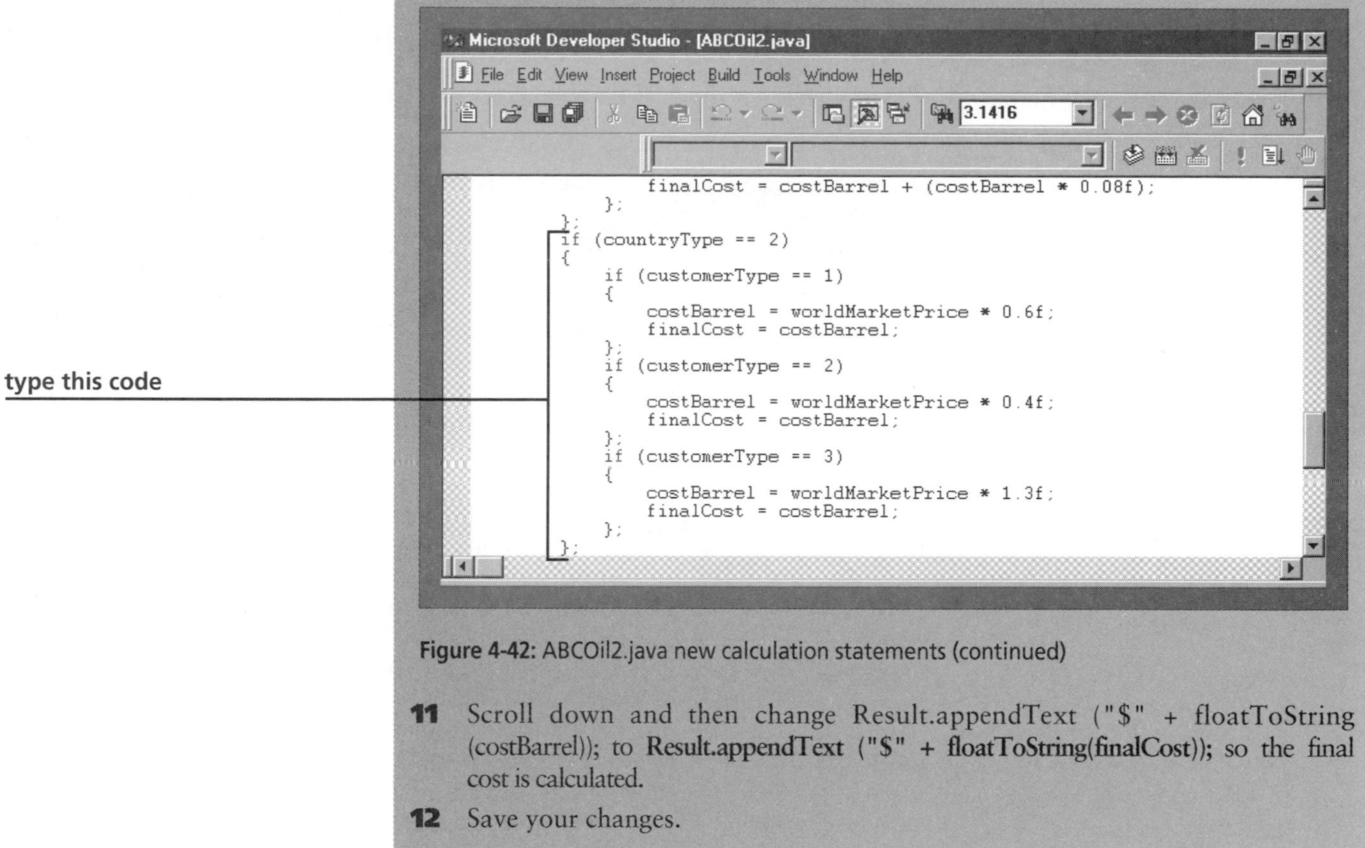

Figure 4-42: ABCOil2.java new calculation statements (continued)

11 Scroll down and then change Result.appendText ("$" + floatToString (costBarrel)); to **Result.appendText ("$" + floatToString(finalCost));** so the final cost is calculated.

12 Save your changes.

Next you will build and execute the program.

To build and execute the program:

1 Build the program in a default project workspace, and then correct any typing errors.

2 If necessary, change the default HTML file by clicking **Project** on the menu bar, and then clicking **Settings** to open the Project Settings dialog box. Click the **Debug** tab, click the **Category** list arrow, and then click **Browser.** Click the **Use parameters from HTML page** option button, press the **Tab** key, and then type **ABCOil2.html** in the HTML page text box. Click the **OK** button.

3 Execute the program. The class filename is **ABCOil2**. See Figure 4-43.

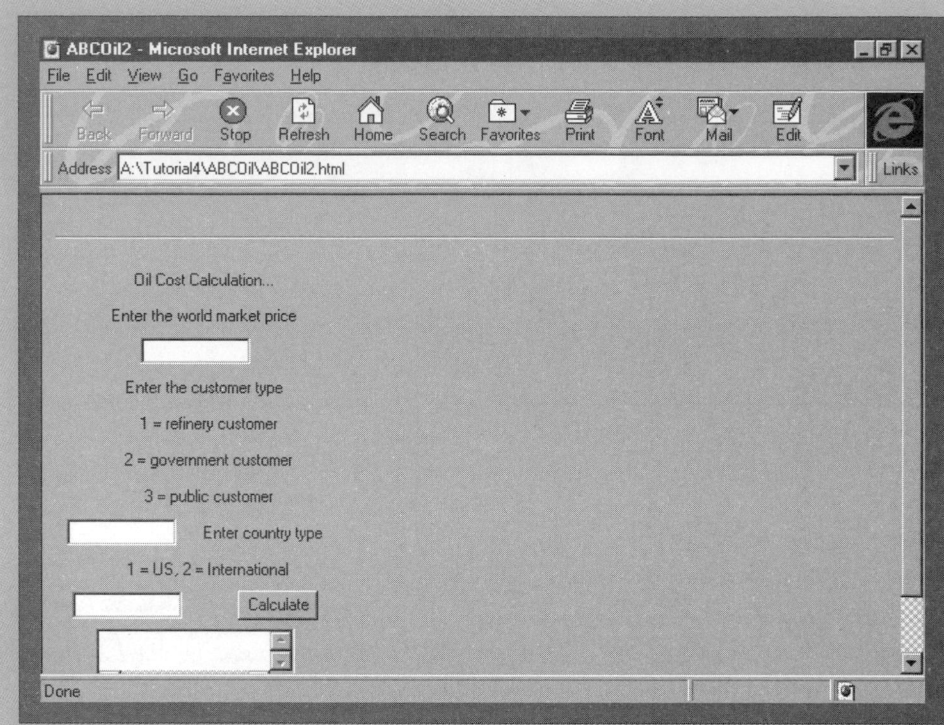

Figure 4-43: ABCOil2.java running in Internet Explorer

4. Click in the edit box below the world market price prompt, and then type **100**. Click in the edit box following the customer type prompt, and then type **1**. Click in the text field following the prompt for the country type, and then type **1**.
5. Click the **Calculate** button. The program calculates the price of oil and displays the result in the result box as shown in Figure 4-44.

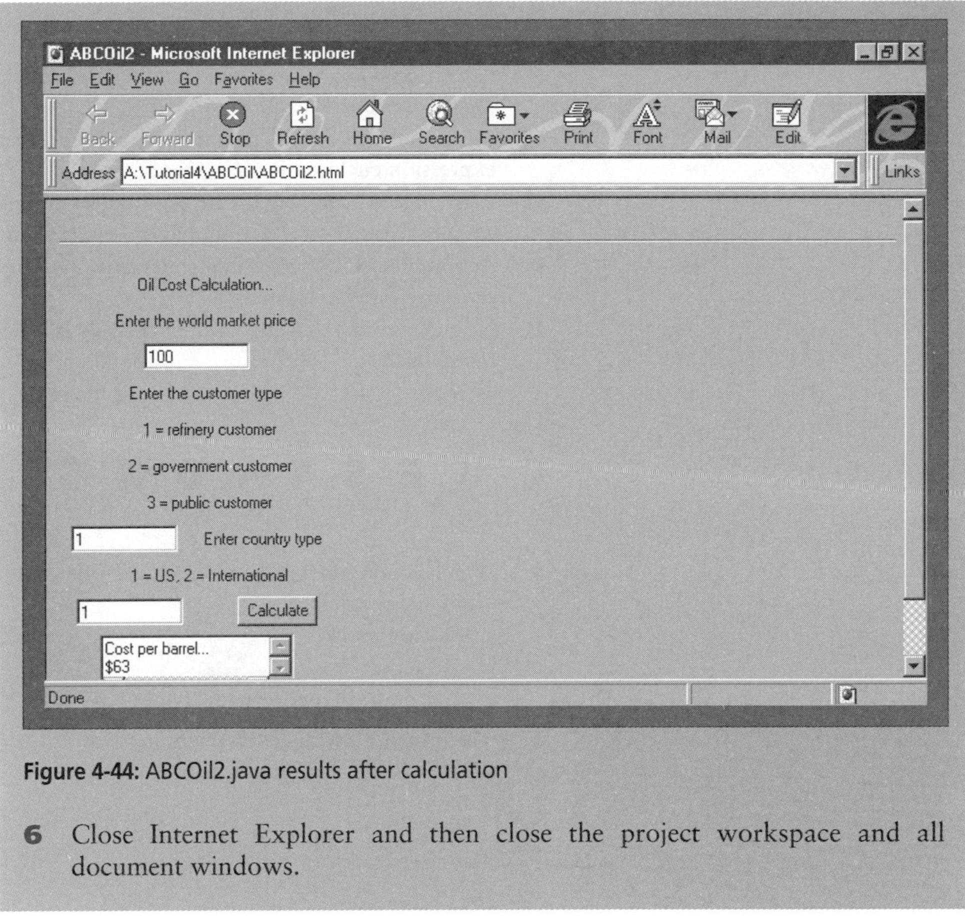

Figure 4-44: ABCOil2.java results after calculation

6 Close Internet Explorer and then close the project workspace and all document windows.

Now you have coded a nested if program successfully. You will find this method of programming very helpful when creating programs that run faster and your programs will be much easier to read.

Now you can take a break or complete the end-of-lesson questions and exercises.

S U M M A R Y

- The primary Java language command for decision making is the if else command.
- The if command is formed using the syntax:
  if <conditional expression>
  {
  <true action block>
  }
  else
  {
  <false action block>
  };
- When the if statement is executed, the conditional expression is evaluated, and if it evaluates to true, then the true action block is performed, otherwise, the false action block is performed.

- Java if statements do not require the use of the else clause. When the else clause is not used, this is called a simple if statement.
- Conditional expressions can be either simple relational expressions or more complex logical expressions.
- Relational expressions contained in a conditional expression must have each relational expression enclosed in parentheses.
- Action blocks can contain any valid Java command, and if more than one command comprises the block, they are put on separate lines with each completed by a semicolon.
- Action blocks that contain if statements in their list of commands form a structure called a nested if command.
- Nested if commands are used extensively by programmers to increase the efficiency of their code.

QUESTIONS

1. Which action block is performed when the conditional expression of an if statement is evaluated to true?
a. if action block
b. else action block
c. no actions are performed

2. Given the following if statement in Java:

```
if (A == B)
{
 x = 10;
}
else
{
 x = 20;
};
```

and the fact that A is equal to 50 and B is equal to 50, what will be the value of x after the evaluation of the if statement?
a. 10
b. 20
c. the original value of x
d. 0

3. Assuming that the variables are integers, which of the following expressions are not valid?
a. (a <= B)
b. (A == B) <= C
c. (a != B)
d. A == B

4. A conditional expression can be comprised of a(n) _______ or __________ expression.
a. logical, relational
b. simple, complex
c. if, else
d. <, >

5. When an action block contains an if statement, the structure is referred to as a __________ if statement.
a. logical
b. relational
c. nested
d. simple

6. Given the following if command:

```
if (a == b)
{
 if c == d)
 {
 y = 10;
 };
};
```

when would *y* be set to 10?

a. a = b and c != d
b. a = b and c > d
c. a = b and c = d
d. a < b and c < d

7. The nested if statement changes the __________ but not the logic of the if command.

a. format
b. condition
c. decision table
d. relational expression

8. The relational expression must be enclosed in __________.

a. { and }
b. [and]
c. < and >
d. (and)

9. When the else action block is performed, the conditional expression must have evaluated to __________.

a. true
b. false

10. When both the if and else action blocks are performed, which of the following is true?

a. The condition is evaluated to null.
b. The conditional expression is evaluated to true.
c. The conditional expression is evaluated to false.
d. There is either a syntax or logic error in the code.

EXERCISES

1. Given the following Java if command:

```
if (a <= b)
{
 x = 5;
};
```

state the value of *x* under the following conditions:

a. a = 55, b = 55
b. a = 100, b = 0
c. a = 0, b = 50
d. a = "apple," b = "orange"
e. a = 0, b = 100

2. Given the following nested Java if statement:

```
if (a == b)
    {
    x = 10;
    }
    else
    {
    if (c == d)
    {
    x = 55;
    }
    else
    {
    x = 100;
    };
    };
```

what is the value of *x* under the following conditions?
a. a = 5, b =1, c = 100, d = 50
b. a = 5, b = 10, c = 0, d = 4
c. a = 0, b = 100, c = 5, d = 0

3. Given the following decision table, write the Java code which would implement this decision table using multiple simple if statements.

Condition	**Action**
temp < 99	drug = aspirin
temp = 99 to 100	drug = acetaminophen
temp = 101 to 102	drug = ibuprofen
temp > 102	drug = none

4. Use the decision table in Exercise 3 to write the Java code using the nested if form.

5. You are working on a computer program for your class. Your instructor told you that the program should set the value of *x* to 100 if the value of iField was greater than 1,000 and set the value of *x* to 0 if the value of iField is not greater than 1,000. Design the decision table and write the Java code for this problem.

6. Write the Java if statements for the decision table and pseudocode you developed for Exercise 6 in Lesson A.

7. Write the Java code for the decision table and pseudocode you developed for Exercise 7 in Lesson A.

8. Write the Java code for the decision table and pseudocode you developed for Exercise 8 in Lesson A. Use a nested if structure for this exercise.

9. Assume that ABC Oil has decided to expand its country types. ABC Oil has decided that 1 will now be the code for U.S. customers, 2 will be the code for preferred nations, and 3 will be used for all other countries. The calculations for preferred nations will be the same as the original international calculations. Cost calculation for other nations will be two times the cost for preferred nations. Design the decision table and pseudocode for this change. Use the ABCOil2.java program you created in this lesson to alter the program and save your changes as ABCOil2a.java on your Student Disk.

10. Using the nested if techniques covered in this lesson, alter the Customer.java program that you created in Tutorial 3 to use as few change methods as possible. Review the steps covered in this tutorial for the Coffees.java program before making your changes.

LESSON C

objectives

In this lesson you will learn how to:

- Use the logical *or* operator and *and* operator to design logical expression
- Determine from a decision table if a logical *or* or *and* could be used
- Translate logical boolean expressions into Java language code
- Determine from a decision table if a boolean case structure could be expressed
- Describe the syntax of the Java switch command
- Translate a boolean case structure into the Java switch command

Using Logical Operators and Complex Decisions

Creating Data Checks for the Order Entry Applet

Java if Statements with Logical Operators

Now you know how to use nested if statements to reduce the size and increase the efficiency of your programs. Your next task is to tackle the **exception handling** of data input. In this lesson you will make data checking changes to the Coffees object and modify the Coffees program using the switch statement.

Complex decision structures are common occurrences in the programming world. In Java, you can develop and code complex decisions using logical expressions and the switch statement. The **switch statement** transforms nested if structures into a form that is much more readable and parallels the decision table more closely.

Logical operators are those boolean operators that allow you to combine a number of relational expressions into a single boolean expression, or, in the case of the logical *not* operator, to negate the value of a conditional expression. The three logical operators are *and*, *or*, and *not*. You learned in Lesson A that a programmer can determine if a logical operator (*and*, *or*) can be used by studying the decision table. A table with multiple rows that result in the same action can be coded using the *or* operator. On the other hand, decision tables that have more than one condition column can be coded with the *and* operator. The syntax for a logical conditional expression is:

<conditional expression> <logical and/or> <conditional expression>

and

<not operator> <conditional expression>

You learned about the design of logical expressions in Lesson A. The Java syntax is the only additional information. This syntax indicates only the format of the conditional expression because logical expressions are used as part of an if statement.

The list of coffee products and their accompanying characteristics is shown in Figure 4-45.

Name	Flavor	Color	Caffeine	Cost
Kona	rich	dark	yes	4.50
Kona decaf	mild	light	no	5.50
Italian Espresso	bold	medium	yes	5.00
Espresso Light	mild	light	no	5.50

Figure 4-45: Coffee products and their characteristics

You can review the table to determine that if a given coffee product matches one of the rows, then the values are correct. In addition, if the field values actually make up the conditions of your problem, the action to take is the return of an error code. You can develop the decision table shown in Figure 4-46 to illustrate the conditions.

Name	Flavor	Color	Cost	Caffeine	Return Code
Kona	rich	dark	4.50	true	true
Kona decaf	mild	light	5.50	false	true
Italian Espresso	bold	medium	5.00	true	true
Espresso Light	mild	light	5.50	false	true
Otherwise					false

Figure 4-46: Data checking decision table for Coffee products

After reviewing the decision table, you might notice two things. First, there are multiple condition columns and all of the rows except for the last row set the return code to true. Second, the last row, which references the use of an else clause, returns the value of false. The multiple condition situation suggests the use of an *and* statement. Also, the duplicate rows of action statements suggested using a logical *or*. Both could be incorporated and translated in the decision table into the following boolean expressions:

```
if     ((name == "Kona") && (flavor == "rich") &&
       (color == "dark") && (cost == 4.50) && (caffeine == true) ) ||
       ((name == "Kona decaf") && (flavor == "mild") &&
       (color == "light") && (cost == 5.50) && (caffeine == false) ) ||
       ((name == "Italian Espresso") && (flavor == "bold") &&
       (color == "medium") && (cost == 5.00) && (caffeine == true) ) ||
       ((name == "Espresso Light") && (flavor == "mild") &&
       (color == "light") && (cost == 5.50) && (caffeine == false) )
then   returnCode = true
else   returnCode = false
```

The steps you can use to accomplish this task are:

1. Determine the logical *and* expressions for each row.
2. Combine the logical *and* expressions with a logical *or*.
3. Write the word *if* followed by the conditional expression resulting from Steps 1 and 2.
4. Write the word *then* followed by the true action block.
5. Write the word *else* followed by the false action block.

Now you can translate your boolean expressions into Java code. After reviewing the syntax of the logical expression shown previously, you develop the following Java if statement.

```
if      (( name.equals("Kona")) && (flavor.equals("rich")) &&
        (color.equals("dark")) && (cost == 4.50) && (caffeine == true) ) ||
        ((name.equals("Kona decaf")) && (flavor.equals("mild")) &&
        (color.equals("light")) && (cost == 5.50) && (caffeine == false) ) ||
        ((name.equals("Italian Espresso")) && (flavor.equals("bold")) &&
        (color.equals("medium")) && (cost == 5.00) && (caffeine == true) ) ||
        ((name.equals("Espresso Light")) && (flavor.equals("mild")) &&
        (color.equals("light")) && (cost == 5.50) && (caffeine == false) )
{
        return true;
}
else
{
        return false;
};
```

Notice that with this implementation you increase the program efficiency by using both the logical *and* and *or* operators. Only one conditional expression needs to be evaluated for the program to determine the return code that should be set. You also might notice that you used the string comparison methods instead of relational operators. In Lesson B you learned that this was one option for dealing with strings. Next you will change the Coffees object. The new method will be named checkValues, and it will return a true or false depending on whether the values matched one of Koffee Koncoctions' products.

1 Start Visual J++ and close any open project workspaces, if necessary.

2 Open the **Coffees3.java** file in the \Tutorial4\Koffee folder on your Student Disk, and then save the file as **Coffees4.java**.

3 Change the filename in the first comment line to **Coffees4.java**, and then change the class filename to **Coffees4**, as shown in Figure 4-47.

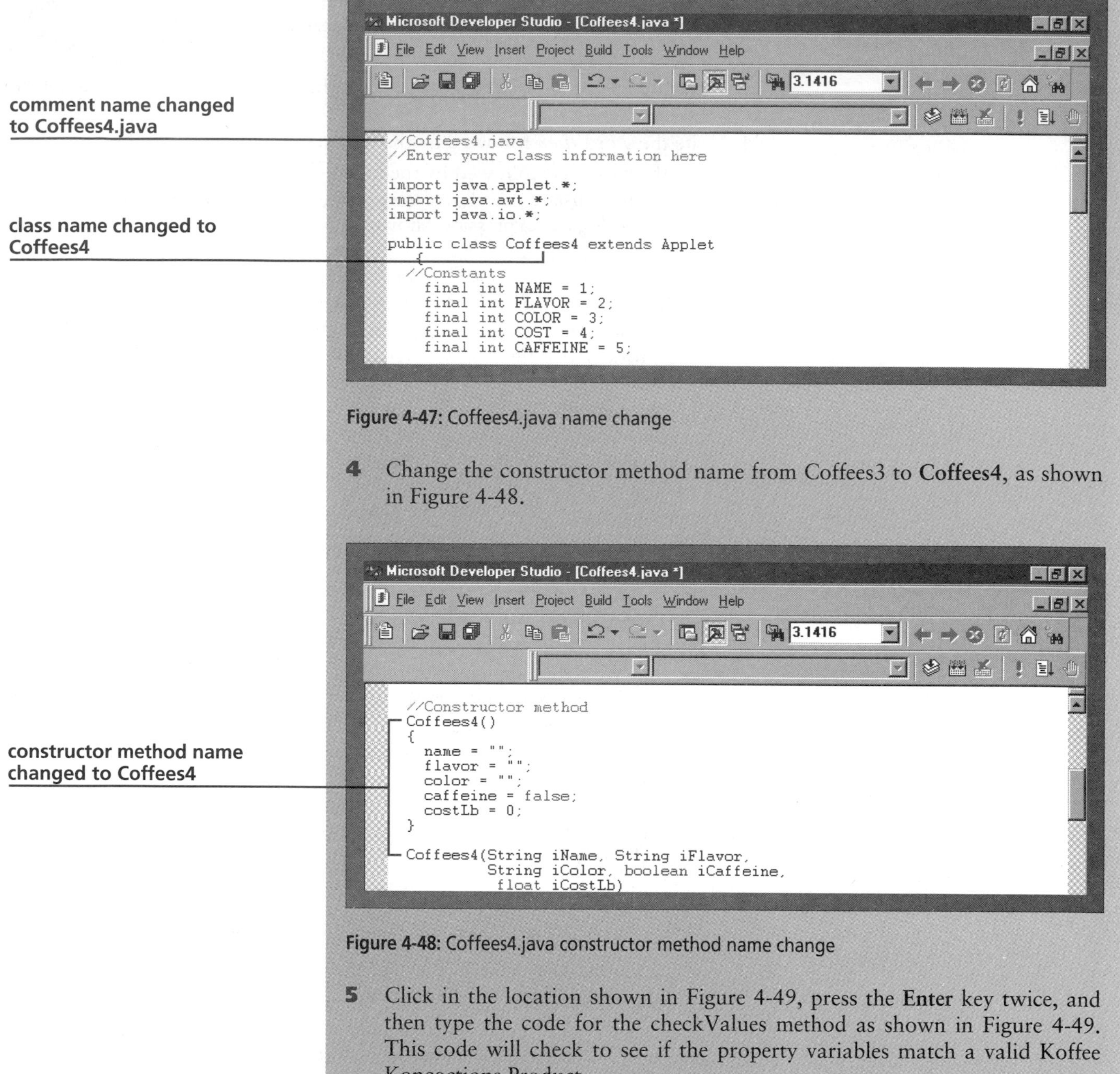

Figure 4-47: Coffees4.java name change

4 Change the constructor method name from Coffees3 to **Coffees4**, as shown in Figure 4-48.

Figure 4-48: Coffees4.java constructor method name change

5 Click in the location shown in Figure 4-49, press the **Enter** key twice, and then type the code for the checkValues method as shown in Figure 4-49. This code will check to see if the property variables match a valid Koffee Koncoctions Product.

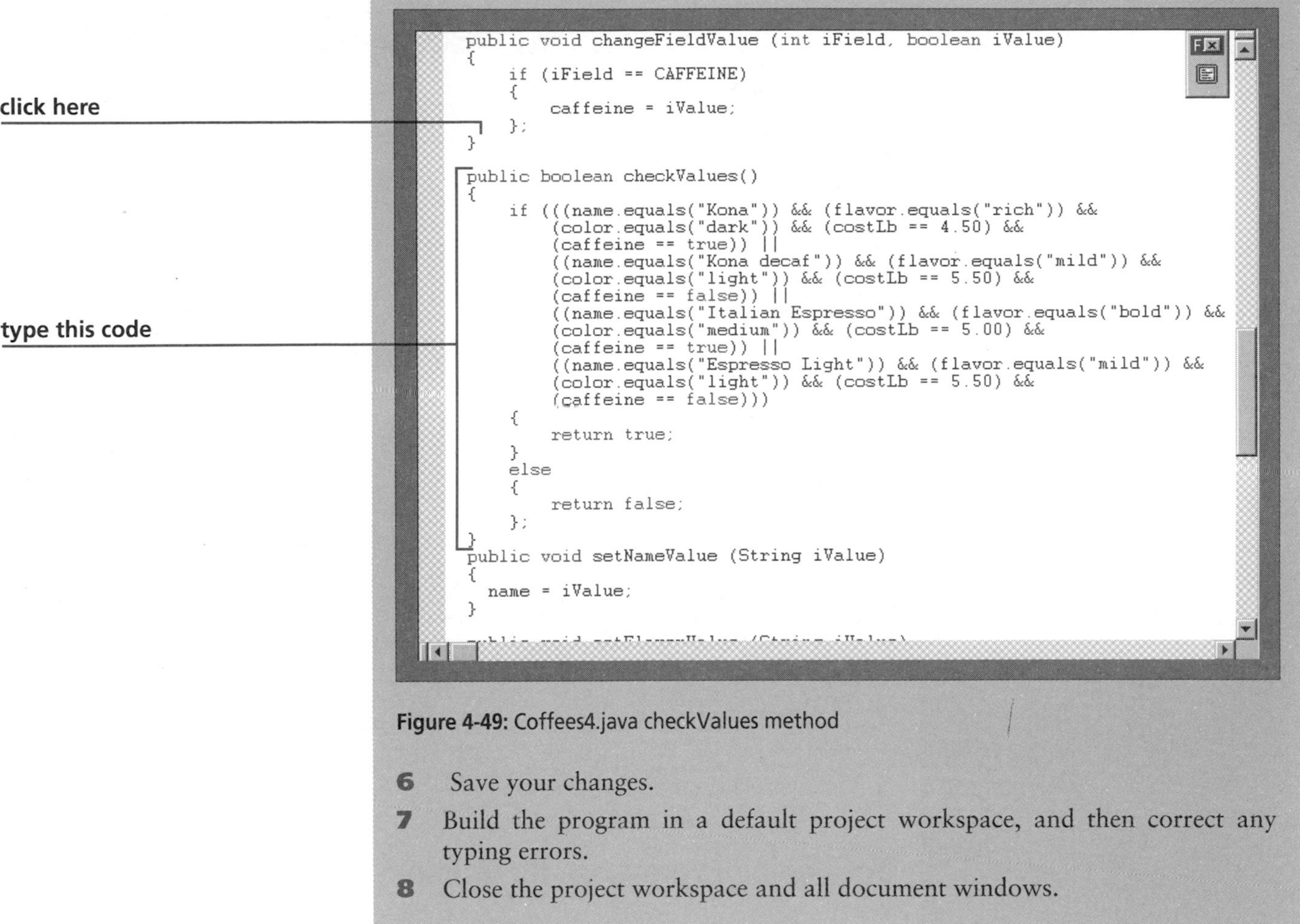
click here
type this code
```
public void changeFieldValue (int iField, boolean iValue)
{
    if (iField == CAFFEINE)
    {
        caffeine = iValue;
    };
}

public boolean checkValues()
{
    if (((name.equals("Kona")) && (flavor.equals("rich")) &&
        (color.equals("dark")) && (costLb == 4.50) &&
        (caffeine == true)) ||
        ((name.equals("Kona decaf")) && (flavor.equals("mild")) &&
        (color.equals("light")) && (costLb == 5.50) &&
        (caffeine == false)) ||
        ((name.equals("Italian Espresso")) && (flavor.equals("bold")) &&
        (color.equals("medium")) && (costLb == 5.00) &&
        (caffeine == true)) ||
        ((name.equals("Espresso Light")) && (flavor.equals("mild")) &&
        (color.equals("light")) && (costLb == 5.50) &&
        (caffeine == false)))
    {
        return true;
    }
    else
    {
        return false;
    };
}
public void setNameValue (String iValue)
{
  name = iValue;
}
```

Figure 4-49: Coffees4.java checkValues method

6 Save your changes.

7 Build the program in a default project workspace, and then correct any typing errors.

8 Close the project workspace and all document windows.

You will not execute the applet because it is an object file used by another applet. You will test the program next using a file on your Student Disk.

To test the Coffees4.java program:

1 Open the **CoffeesTest4.java** file on your Student Disk.

2 Build the program in a default project workspace. If the Output window identifies any errors, check your Coffees4.java program or consult your instructor for assistance.

3 If necessary, change the default HTML file by clicking **Project** on the menu bar, and then clicking **Settings** to open the Project Settings dialog box. Click the **Debug** tab, click the **Category** list arrow, and then click **Browser**. Click the **Use parameters from HTML page** option button, press the **Tab** key, and then type **CoffeesTest4.html** in the HTML page text box. Click the **OK** button.

4 Execute the program. The class filename is **CoffeesTest4**. See Figure 4-50. Notice that the output of this program shows the return value from the checkValues method. A return of true means that the values matched one of the Koffee Koncoctions products.

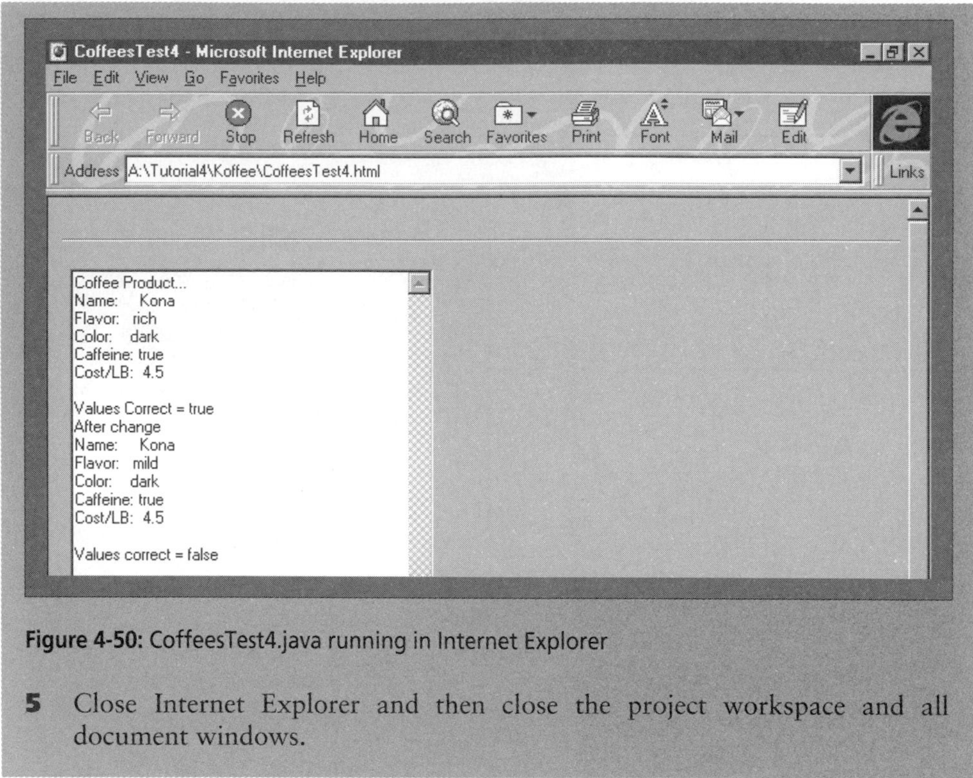

Figure 4-50: CoffeesTest4.java running in Internet Explorer

5 Close Internet Explorer and then close the project workspace and all document windows.

Your program works as designed. Next you will learn about switch statements.

Developing Expressions for Multiple Decision Paths

Most of the decision tables used in this tutorial are based on a single condition or set of conditions. While the syntax of the nested if and the logical expression can implement this type of logic correctly, it does not always reflect the underlying table. You can use a **case conditional** to specify the rows of the decision table more clearly in the actual code. A case conditional can be used when all of the rows of a decision table are based on a single condition with the same variable checked in each row. The process of developing a case structure from a decision table is:

1. Write the word case and the variable to be checked on the first line.
2. Write the value of the first row followed by a colon and the actions for that row.
3. Repeat Step 2 until all rows of the decision table are translated.

For example, suppose you need to develop a program for your employer that determines the mixture of different chemicals in different brands of shampoos. Each shampoo is a combination of two different chemicals but in different combinations of amounts. Figure 4-51 shows the decision table for this problem.

Shampoo	Mixture
100	chem1 = 2, chem2 = 1
200	chem1 = 1, chem2 = 2
300	chem1 = 2, chem2 = 2

Figure 4-51: Shampoo mixture decision table

You can translate this decision table into a case expression using the previously defined steps to create the following pseudocode:

case shampoo
100 : chem1 = 2, chem2 = 1
200 : chem1 = 1, chem2 = 2
300 : chem1 = 2, chem2 = 2

The method of execution by the language for such structures is:

1. Check the variable that follows the word case with each of the rows of values in the case structure.
2. For each match, perform the actions that are associated with that value.

The command that implements the case expression in Java is the switch command. The **switch command** has the following format:

switch <integral expression>
case <value expression> : <statement list>;
...
default : <statement list>;
};

Notice that the variable to be checked is put on the first line, and the values to check against this variable are included on subsequent lines. There can be any number of lines in the Java switch statement. One constraint of the Java command is that the values listed for each case must be an integral type (int, long, char, and boolean). Only integral types can be used, and the variable next to the switch statement must match the integral type of the values that follow. In the next section you will implement non-integral types in an integral manner so the switch statement can be used.

Designing a Decision Using the Switch Statement

Many of the methods coded in this tutorial could have used the switch command. You can modify the changeFieldValue of the Coffees object using the switch statement. First you must review the decision table for the change method in the Coffees object (see Figure 4-18). The condition of the decision table uses a variable that is not an integral type. You can use constants in Java to declare the strings that you used as integer constants and then you can implement this table using the switch command. You used this method to code the Coffees object in Lesson B. Now you will use these constants in the switch statement.

You can change your decision table to check the input field that is declared as an integer. Figure 4-52 shows the decision table with the use of the integer constants.

iField	Value Assignment
NAME	name = iValue
FLAVOR	flavor = iValue
COLOR	color = iValue

Figure 4 52: changeValue method decision table

You can translate this decision table and develop the following boolean expressions in pseudocode:

case field
NAME : name = value
FLAVOR : flavor = value
COLOR : color = value
default : ;
};

Each case includes a break statement that causes Java to jump to the end of the switch statement. If you did not include the break statement, all of the statements after a case is matched would be executed. The default case takes care of the situation where the integral expression, or field, does not match any of the value expressions, in which case you can code it as a null statement. Next you will change the Coffees.java file to reflect this design change.

To change the Coffees.java file:

1. Open the **Coffees4.java** file on your Student Disk, and then save it as **Coffees5.java.**
2. Change the filename in the first comment line to **Coffees5.java**, and then change the class heading to **Coffees5**, as shown in Figure 4-53.

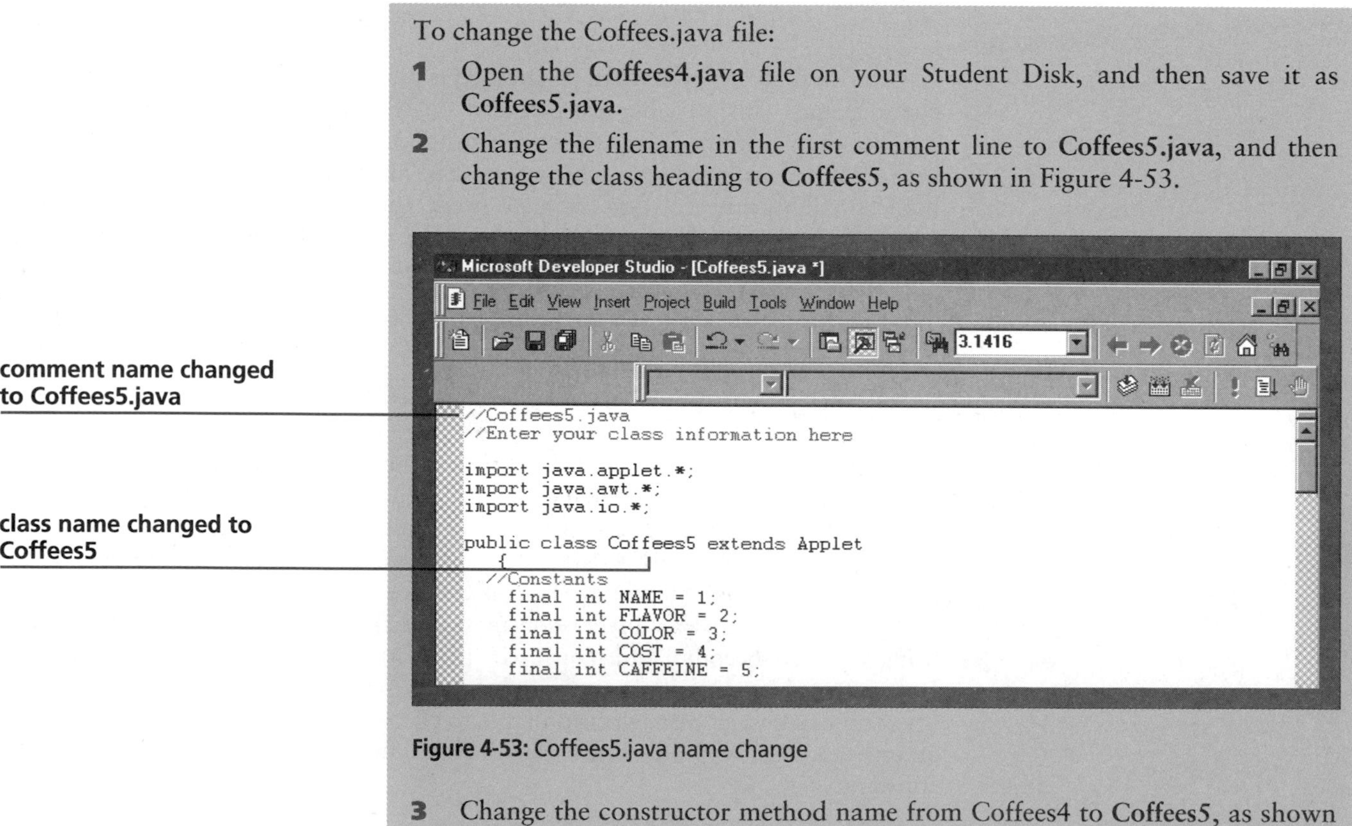

Figure 4-53: Coffees5.java name change

3. Change the constructor method name from Coffees4 to **Coffees5**, as shown in Figure 4-54.

constructor method name changed to Coffees5

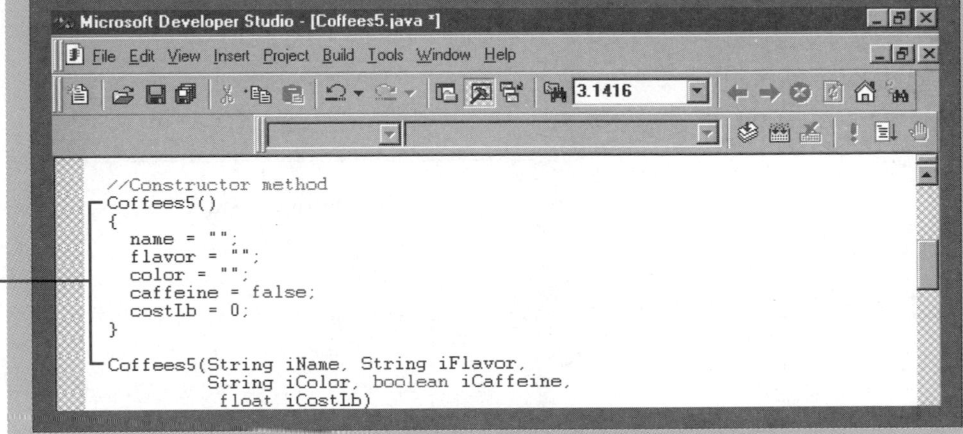

Figure 4-54: Coffees5.java constructor method name change

4 Select the if statements shown in Figure 4-55.

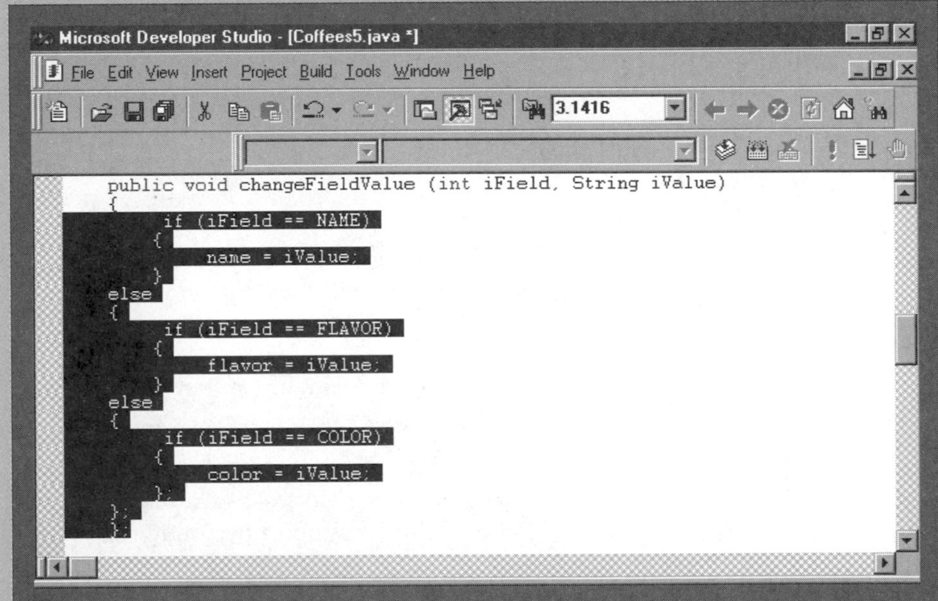

Figure 4-55: Coffees5.java if statements selected

5 Enter the code for the switch statement shown in Figure 4-56. The code you entered replaces the selected text. This code changes the nested if statement to a switch statement.

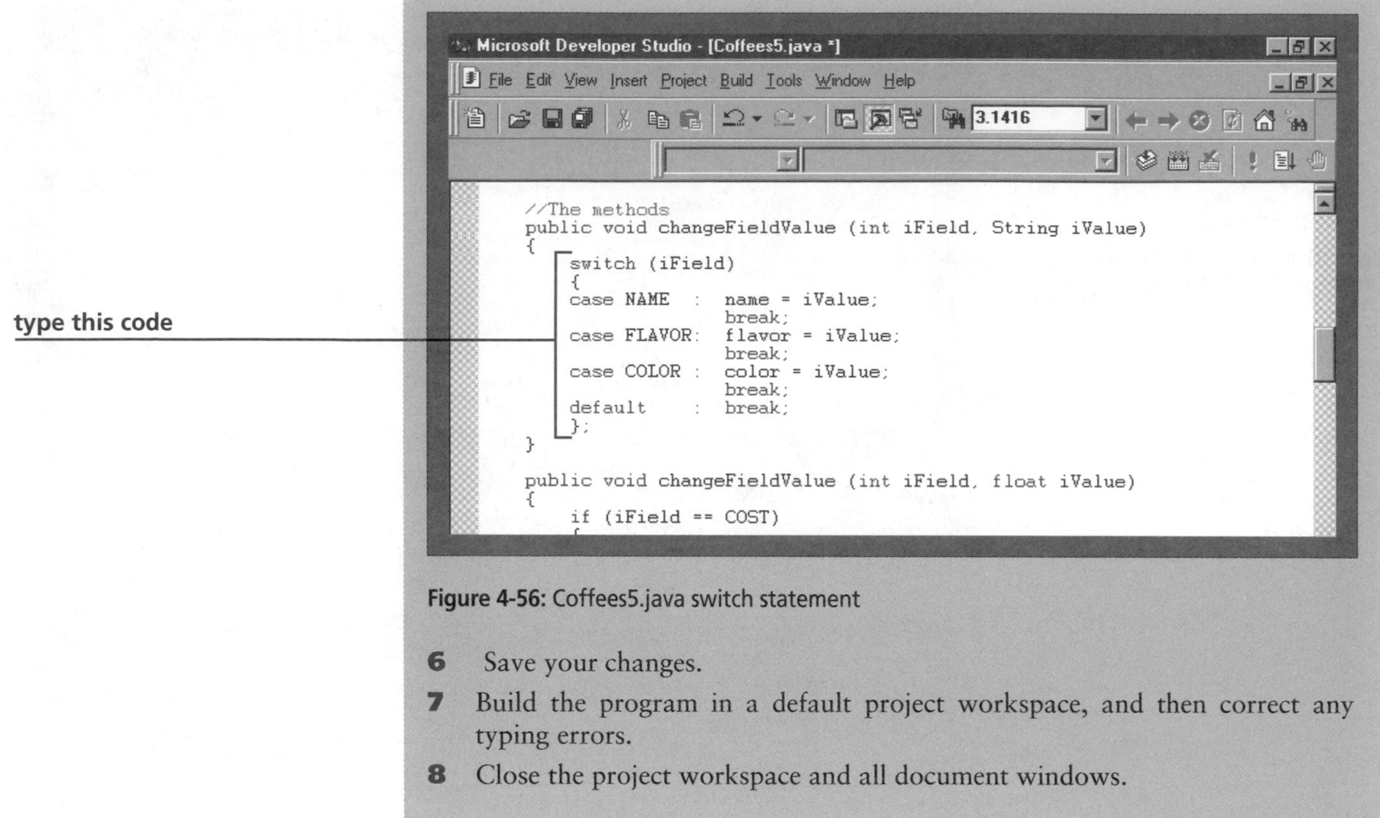

Figure 4-56: Coffees5.java switch statement

6 Save your changes.

7 Build the program in a default project workspace, and then correct any typing errors.

8 Close the project workspace and all document windows.

This program is an object for another applet so you will not execute the program. You will use a file on your Student Disk to test the program.

To test the Coffees5.java program:

1 Open the **CoffeesTest5.java** file in the Koffee folder on your Student Disk.

2 Build the program in a default project workspace, and then correct any errors in the Coffees5.java file on your Student Disk, or ask your instructor or technical support person for help.

3 If necessary, change the default HTML file by clicking **Project** on the menu bar, and then clicking **Settings** to open the Project Settings dialog box. Click the **Debug** tab, click the **Category** list arrow, and then click **Browser**. Click the **Use parameters from HTML page** option button, press the **Tab** key, and then type **CoffeesTest5.html** in the HTML page text box. Click the **OK** button.

4 Execute the program. The class filename is **CoffeesTest5**. See Figure 4-57.

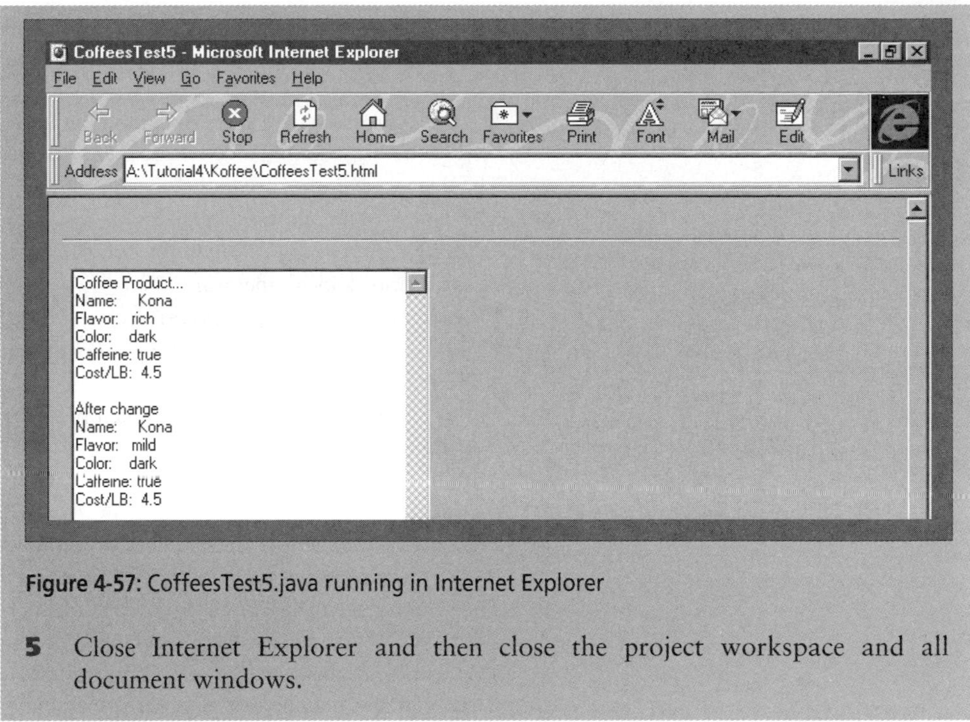

Figure 4-57: CoffeesTest5.java running in Internet Explorer

5 Close Internet Explorer and then close the project workspace and all document windows.

Now you know that your program works as designed. The break statement was used in this example and is very important in the switch statement.

Exploring the Break Statement

When the switch statement is executed in Java, all of the cases are checked to see if they match the integral expression. If the first statement matches, then the action statement is performed. Without a break statement as the last statement in each of these blocks, Java continues executing the rest of the statements. Thus, Java will execute the action blocks until it finds a break statement or comes to the end of the switch statement. To avoid this situation you can use the break statement. When the **break statement** is encountered in Java, the program skips to the end of the structure it is performing currently. The break statements in the switch command cause the program to exit the switch once a case is found that matches the integral expression. Consequently, care should be taken in the coding process that the break statement is the last statement of each case because it causes an immediate exit. This small feature of the Java language allows for faster execution of switch statements and ensures that the action statements are not executed in error.

This concludes the discussion of logical expressions and complex decision structures in Java. It should be recognized that Lesson C did not add any possible logic to the programmer's tools but gave them alternative ways to implement the logic described in Lessons A and B.

Now you can exit Visual J++ and take a break or complete the end-of-lesson questions and exercises.

SUMMARY

- Logical expressions are ways of combining multiple relational expressions into a single conditional or negating a conditional expression.
- The logical operators are and (&&), or (||) and not (!).
- The syntax of a conditional expression which uses a logical operator is:

  <expression> <logical operator> <expression>

  or for the not logical operator

  <not operator> <expression>
- The expressions used to create a logical expression must be of type boolean and evaluate to true or false.
- Multiple rows in a decision table which perform the same action is an indication of an or condition.
- Multiple condition columns in a decision table indicate the possible use of the and logical operator.
- The switch statement is a convenient way to code the logic of a nested if else statement if the variable used in the condition is an integral variable.
- The switch statement lists cases for each of the rows on the decision table and possibly a default case for all situations not considered in the rows.
- The break statement is used to exit the switch statement after the action block that is pared with the matched value is performed.
- The break statement prevents the incorrect execution of the action statements in a switch statement.

QUESTIONS

1. The logical __________ operator can be used when there are multiple rows with the same resulting action.
a. and
b. or
c. not

2. The logical __________ operator can be used when there exists more than one condition column in the decision table.
a. and
b. or
c. not

3. The logical __________ operator is used to reverse the evaluation of a boolean expression from true to false or from false to true.
a. and
b. or
c. not

4. The switch statement takes an expression and values that are of the __________ type.
a. relational
b. logical
c. boolean
d. integral

5. When a group of several relational expressions are joined with the *or* operator, __________ relational expression(s) must evaluate(s) to true for the logical expression to evaluate to true.

a. one
b. two
c. all
d. none of the relational expressions evaluate to true

6. When three relational expressions are joined by the *and* operator, there must be at least __________ of the relational expressions that evaluate to true for the logical expression to evaluate to true.
a. one
b. two
c. three
d. none of the relational expressions evaluate to true

7. The __________ command allows exiting from a switch statement when a match has occurred.
a. else
b. break
c. if
d. logical not

8. The __________ case is performed by the switch statement if a match is not found.
a. default
b. first
c. second
d. otherwise

9. When the *not* logical operator is applied to an expression that has evaluated to true, then the evaluation of the logical *not* will result in __________.
a. true
b. false
c. null

10. The use of __________ can assist the programmer in designing code with the switch statement where the original condition is not integral.
a. logical operators
b. relational operators
c. constants
d. literals

EXERCISES

1. Given the following logical condition:
(a < b) || (a > c)
what would the expression evaluate to in the following situations?
a. a = 0, b = 5, c = 0
b. a = 100, b = 500, c = 0

2. Given the following logical expression:
(a == b) && (a != c)
evaluate the expression under the following conditions
a. a = 0, b = 0, c = 5
b. a = 1, b = 50, c = 100

3. Winfred Retail basic customer discounts appear on the following table. Code the Java switch statement for this table.

customerCode	discount
0	0%
1	5%
2	10%

4. Color Coordinated determines which type of makeup should be used based on a person's complexion type. Write the Java nested if statement for this table. You will need to use the string equals method instead of the relational operators.

Skin Type	Complexion	Product Line
oily	dark	KC200
oily	light	KC100
average	dark	KC500
average	light	KC900
dry	dark	KC800
dry	light	KC400

5. Ageless Scientific computes the age of rock samples. Based on the following decision table, write the nested if statement to code this table. You will need to use both the relational operators and the string equals method.

depthFt	rockType	ageCalculation
1-1000	lime	depthFt * 400
1001+	lime	depthFt * 475
1-1000	granite	depthFt * 500
1001+	granite	depthFt * 600

6. Given the following switch statement:

```
switch (x)
{
 case 1      :      y = 10;
                    break;
 case 2      :      y = 30;
                    break;
 case 3      :      y = 50;
                    break;
 default     :      y = 100;
                    break;
};
```

What would be the value of *y* in the following situations:

a. x = 4 / 2

b. x = 5

c. x = 15 / 5

7. Modify the checkValues method of the Coffees4.java file in the Koffee folder on your Student Disk so that the following new products can be added to Koffee Koncoctions product line.

Name	Flavor	Color	Cost	Caffeine
Hawaiian Delight	rich	light	5.00	false
Hawaiian Roast	bold	dark	5.50	true

Using Repetition

TUTORIAL

5

Simplifying the User Interface for Koffee Koncoctions

case Now that you have implemented many of the decision-making techniques available in Java in your project, you show Maria the work that you have completed. She is pleased with how the project is progressing and that you addressed many of the issues of order processing. Your next tasks are to:

1. Convert the BeanJar applet so users can guess the number of beans in the jar
2. Change the order entry program so operators can complete the order by typing only the product's name
3. Allow customers to order any number of products

Many of these tasks can be accomplished using loops. In this tutorial you will learn how loops are designed and coded in Java. You will use loops to implement these changes to your programs.

LESSON A

objectives

In this lesson you will learn how to:

- Use a counting loop
- Use a pre-test loop
- Use a post-test loop
- Construct a loop

Designing Code That Repeats

Planning a Counting Loop for the Koffee Koncoctions Order Form

Using a Counting Loop

Most Java programs will need to use repetition. In programming, **repetition**, or **looping**, is a way to "repeat" a sequence of program instructions more than once. There are three types of repetition structures in Java. The first type, a **counting loop**, repeats instructions a certain number of times. The other two types of repetition are based on testing conditions at run time, but they differ based on when the condition in the loop is tested. A **pre-test loop** tests the condition before the statements inside the loop are executed. A **post-test loop** tests the condition at the end of the loop.

There are four major components to a loop: the looping statement, the loop body, the pre-loop statements, and post-loop statements. The **looping statement** controls how many times the loop will execute. The **loop body** consists of the statements inside the loop that execute while the loop is active. The **pre-loop statements** set up the information needed for the loop to execute correctly. The **post-loop statements** might be needed to report the loop result or to ensure the accuracy of the program.

When you want to repeat some steps a certain number of times, you are using a counting loop. For example, if you return the calls from people who left messages on your answering machine while you were out, you follow a list of steps a certain number of times to dial the number, talk with the other person, and hang up. Figure 5-1 shows the pseudocode algorithm for the process you use for each call. By using a loop construct, the list of instructions looks short. Without the loop construct, you would have a list of 15 instructions, or three instructions per call. If you make 100 calls, there would be 300 instructions—saving steps is why loops are important in programming.

```
Do 5 times
   Get Phone Number
   Call Phone Number
   Record Results
   End Do
```

Figure 5-1: Loop to return calls

Loops also can be used with calculations, such as when your instructor determines your final grade at the end of the term. If your instructor has 10 students and each student has 10 grades, she needs to add each student's grades and then divide each total by 10. If she does this using a calculator, Figure 5-2 shows the pseudocode for the process.

```
Total = 0
Do 10 Times
  Get Grade
  Total = Total + Grade
End Do
Average = Total / 10
```

Figure 5-2: Pseudocode for calculating grades

You can simplify this task in Java by using a for statement. The **for statement** is designed to repeat a statement, or a number of statements, a certain number of times. Figure 5-3 shows the pseudocode for the grading example translated into Java.

```
total = 0;
for (int num = 1; num <=10; num ++)
{
  lblInput.setText("Enter Grade #"+numGrade);
  grade = Integer.parseInt(Input.getText());
  total += grade;
}
average = total / 10;
```

Figure 5-3: Java code for grading example

The for Statement

The Java for statement is really three statements compacted into one. Figure 5-4 shows the syntax of the for statement. Three statements appear inside the parentheses: one statement to declare the counter, a second statement to set the ending condition, and a final statement to show the progression towards the termination of the loop.

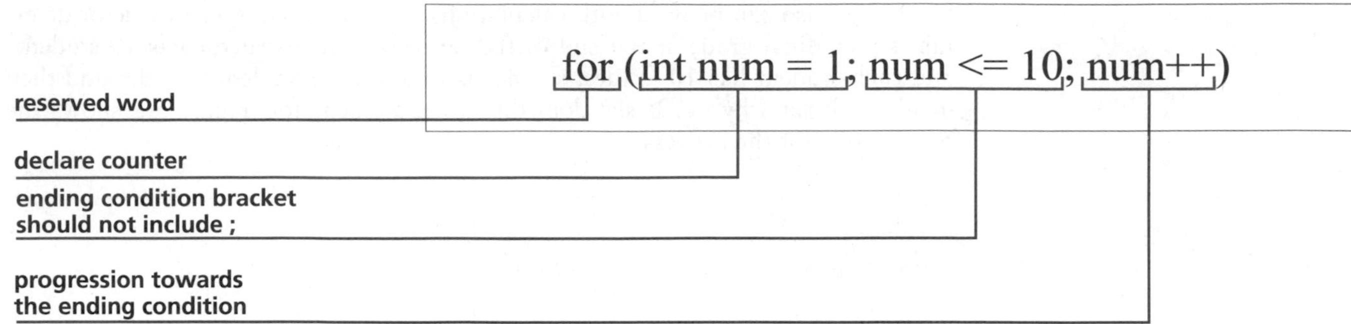

Figure 5-4: For statement syntax

The **counter** is a variable that counts events. In the statement shown in Figure 5-4, the counter is declared and set equal to 1. The *declaration of the counter* is done only the first time through the loop. In Figure 5-4 the counter is declared as an integer equal to 1. The *ending condition* is a relational statement that compares the counter to some value in such a way so that when the condition is false, the loop ends. In other words, the loop continues until the ending condition is equal to false. In Figure 5-4, the loop ends when the value is greater than 10. The *progression towards the ending condition* is the last part of the statement; this is how the counter gets changed to make the ending condition false. In Figure 5-4, the ending condition occurs when num is greater than 10, so you need to add to num so it eventually will be greater than 10. The statement in Figure 5-4 uses the increment operator (++) to add 1 to num each time through the loop. All loops must make progress towards terminating or ending. The Java for statement is the loop construct to use if you are using a count-controlled loop. A **count-controlled loop** uses a counter variable to determine when the loop will stop executing, such as when you need a loop to repeat 10 times.

Figure 5-4 shows the simplest form of a loop. You also can tell the program how many grades to average, instead of always having to use 10 grades, as shown in Figure 5-5. You need to make only two changes to calculate an average for any number of grades. The first change is to use a text field so the user can enter the number of grades to average. Then you need to change the ending condition so it compares the counter to the input value, instead of comparing the counter to a fixed number of 10.

```
total = 0;
int numGrades = Integer.parseIntƒ(Input.getText());
forƒ(int num = 1; num <=numGrades; num ++)
{
  lblInput.setText("Enter Grade #"+numGrades);
  grade = Integer.parseInt(Input.getText());
  total += grade;
}
average = total / 10;
```

Figure 5-5: For loop with user input

The counter variable does not have to be an int type; it can be any of the primitive types (char, byte, short, int, long, double, or float), except boolean. If you think about it, using a boolean counter is useless because the boolean type has only two values (true and false). Of the two examples presented, it would be possible for the counter type to be byte, short, long, or int.

Suppose that you want to write a program that records the current temperature every 15 minutes (quarter of an hour) for 24 hours. You might use a for loop that uses a double type (or a float type also would work) like the one shown in Figure 5-6. As you look at the code in Figure 5-6, you might notice that the loop will record all the temperatures, but it keeps only the last recording in memory. In Tutorial 3, you learned that a variable can hold only one value at a time. When you put a new value in an existing variable, the new value replaces the old value. You will solve this problem in Tutorial 6.

```
float temp;
for (double hour = 0.25; hour <= 24.00; hour += 0.25)
{
  lblInput.setText("Temperature @ "+hour);
  float value = new float(Input.getText());
  temp = value.floatValue();
}
```

Figure 5-6: For loop with double type counter

Using a Pre-Test Loop

The loop shown in Figure 5-6 is a pre-test loop that uses a for statement. Another kind of pre-test loop is the **while loop**. The syntax for the while statement is shown in Figure 5-7. The while loop will execute as long as the expression is tested and evaluates to true. A while loop might not execute if the controlling expression was false the first time. One important thing to remember about while loops is that no matter how many statements are in the loop, the expression gets tested only when all the steps inside the loop have executed, and it has "looped" back to the top.

while (*expression*)

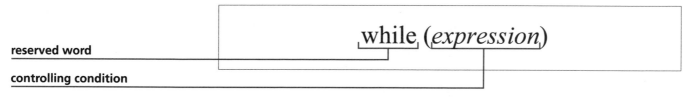

reserved word

controlling condition

Figure 5-7: While statement syntax

All of the previous for loops also can be written using while loops. The while loop can be used as a count-controlled loop. For example, the Java code from Figure 5-3 appears in Figure 5-8 as a while loop. Along with the change in the loop statement, there are two other changes in the code in Figure 5-8. First, the NumGrades variable must be declared and assigned a value before the loop in a pre-loop statement. The other change is that because the while loop does not take care of incrementing (or adding to) the counter variable, you need a statement inside the loop to do this. Remember that every loop must be designed so it will end eventually. If the statement *numGrades++;* is removed from the code, you would create an infinite loop. An **infinite loop** is a loop that never ends without the user intervening and stopping the program.

```
int total = 0;
int numGrades = 0;
while (numGrades < 10)
{
  lblInput.setText("Enter Grade #"+numGrade);
  grade = Integer.parseInt(Input.getText());
  total += grade;
  numGrades++;
}
average = total / 10;
```

Figure 5-8: While loop to average 10 grades

The while statement can do more than just count-controlled loops. There will be many times when you need to perform a loop while a certain condition exists; in which case, it is appropriate to use a while loop. After all, there are fewer statements in a count-controlled for loop than in a count-controlled while loop.

Suppose that you are a corporate account manager at an office supply retailer and you need to make sure that your account holders' balances do not exceed their credit limits. You could write a loop like the one shown in Figure 5-9 where the code will loop "while" the currentAmount is less than the creditLimit. When the currentAmount is either equal to or greater than the creditLimit amount, the loop will stop.

```
float price;
while (currentAmount < creditLimit)
{
 lblInput.setText("Enter new amount");
 float value = new float(Input.getText());
 price = value.floatValue();
 currentAmount += price;
}
```

Figure 5-9: Credit limit while loop

There is a problem with the code shown in Figure 5-9. What if a customer wants to order only a few items and the total does not exceed their credit limit? In this case, the loop cannot handle the processing so you need to use a more complex expression. One solution is to ask the customer how many items he or she wants to purchase, but that can be a problem because the customer might change his or her mind. A better way to solve this problem is to use a sentinel value. A **sentinel value** is a value that the user inputs as a signal to end the loop. You could use -1 as a sentinel in the price variable because there are no items that have a negative price. A sentinel value always should be a value that does not occur *normally* in the input. For example, if 5 could be an input, it should not be a sentinel value. Figure 5-10 shows the corrected code.

```
float price;
lblInput.setText("Enter new amount");
float value = new float(Input.getText());
price = value.floatValue();
while ((currentAmount < creditLimit) && (price != -1))
{
 currentAmount += price;
 lblInput.setText("Enter new amount");
 float value = new float(Input.getText());
 price = value.floatValue();
}
```

Figure 5-10: Correct while loop

You need to change more than the controlling expression. When any part of a controlling expression depends on input, you must do a priming read. A **priming read** is input that is accepted before the loop starts. The main reason why you need a priming read is that the price variable needs a value in it before it is compared to the sentinel value. It is possible to assign a value to price, like zero, but there is another reason as well. Notice that by using the priming read the order of instructions inside the loop changes so price is added to the currentAmount before the new price is input. This change means that the sentinel value will not be added to currentAmount, thus avoiding the need to adjust the currentAmount by adding one to undo the action of adding the sentinel.

Using a Post-Test Loop

There are two types of Java pre-test loops, but there is only one type of post-test loop—the **do while loop.** Figure 5-11 shows the syntax for the do while loop. The do while loop is like a sandwich with the keyword *do* on the top, the action statement (or compound statement) in the middle, and the while (expression) on the bottom.

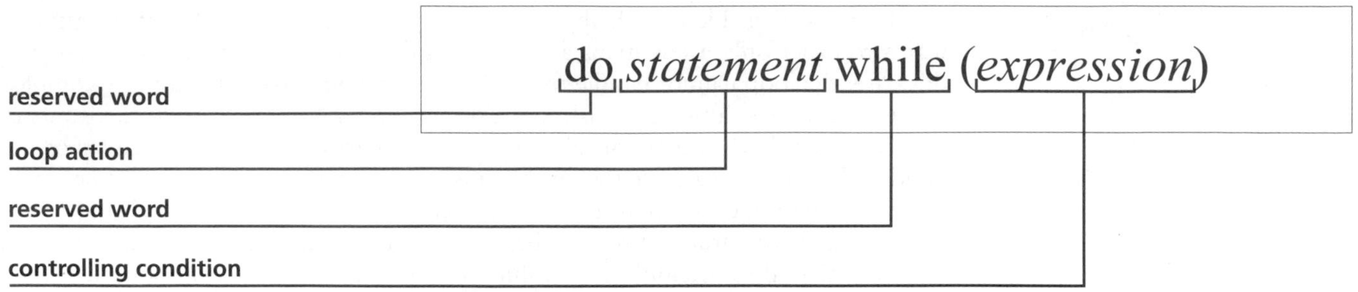

do *statement* while (*expression*)

reserved word
loop action
reserved word
controlling condition

Figure 5-11: Do while statement syntax

The biggest difference between the do while loop and the while loop is that the do while loop always executes at least once because the controlling condition is not tested until the end of the loop, after the action statements execute. You can rewrite the loop from Figure 5-10 using the do while loop shown in Figure 5-12.

```
float price;
do
{
  lblInput.setText("Enter new amount");
  float value = new float(Input.getText());
  price = value.floatValue();
  currentAmount += price;
}
while ((currentAmount < creditLimit) && (price != -1))
if (price == -1)
  currentAmount ++;
```

Figure 5-12: Using a do while loop

There are two types of situations in which you should use the do while loop. The first situation is when you use a sentinel-controlled input loop, as shown in Figure 5-12. Notice how the priming read is no longer required so all the input occurs inside the loop, even though you have to add one back to the currentAmount if the sentinel value stops the loop. The second situation in which you use a do while loop is when you want to make sure that the user enters a correct value. For example, suppose you write an applet where the user must enter a correct project code using a boolean method that tests the code. Figure 5-13 shows the code for a loop that prevents the user from inputting an incorrect code. This loop continues until the user enters a valid code. If the code is not valid, the text field is cleared, and the insertion point returns to the text field.

```
lblInput.setText("Enter Project Code");
do
{
  Input.setText("");
  Input.requestFocus();
  Code = Input.getText();
}
while (! (Valid (Code))
```

Figure 5-13: Preventing invalid input

Constructing a Loop

Click the first Tutorial 5 link of the Online Companion for this book (http://www.course.com) to see a live Java program that illustrates this topic.

After you determine that a loop is needed, there are five steps in constructing a loop. The first two steps deal with what kind of loop is necessary and how the loop will end, and the last three steps deal with writing the statements that appear before, inside, and after the loop. For example, suppose you are a very generous manager and you are going to loan to one of your employees $1,000 at an annual interest rate of 12 percent. Your employee will repay the loan at a rate of $25 a month. You can create a program to calculate how many months it will take the employee to pay you back by following these steps:

1. Determine the controlling condition.
2. Decide on the loop type.
3. Write any pre-loop statements.
4. Write the loop action statements.
5. Write any post-loop statements.

Step 1: Determine the Controlling Condition

Planning the controlling condition is critical because if a user has to stop an infinite loop, all the program information is lost. The controlling condition that you need to use is based on subtracting payments from the balance until the balance is zero or less. Therefore, your controlling condition is to loop while the balance is greater than zero. In this case, the controlling condition is *(curLoan > 0)*.

Step 2: Decide on the Loop Type

You must answer two questions before deciding on the loop type to use. The first question is to determine if the loop is a count-controlled loop. If it is a count-controlled loop, use the for loop. In our example, the loop is not a count-controlled loop because there is no way to determine in advance the number of times the loop will need to execute.

The second question is when the condition needs to be tested. Do you need to test the condition first so that, if conditions are not right, the loop never executes? Or do you always want the loop to execute at least once, necessitating the need for a post-test loop? In this situation, either a pre-test or post-test loop will work well, so you can use either one. The while statement is *while (curLoan > 0)*.

Step 3: Write Any Pre-Loop Statements

Now you can write any statements that are needed before the loop. Pre-loop statements are used to initialize variables used inside the loop, print headings, perform priming reads, etc. When you **initialize** variables you assign an initial value to variables used inside the loop. In your program, the amountBorrowed, monPayment, intRate, monIntRate, thisMonth (counter), and curLoan objects must be assigned values. Also, the heading for the text area must be printed. Figure 5-14 shows your pre-loop statements.

```
intRate = 0.12;
amountBorrowed = 1000.00;
monPayment = 25.00;
curLoan = amountBorrowed;
thisMonth = 1;
monIntRate = intRate / 12;
ta.setText("Loan Amount over Time" + "\n" +
    "Amount Borrowed: " + amountBorrowed + "\n" +
    "Annual Interest Rate: " + intRate + "\n" +
    "Monthly Payment: " + monPayment + "\n" +
    "\n");
```

Figure 5-14: Pre-loop statements

Step 4: Write the Loop Action Statements

After writing the pre-loop statements, you can write the action statements that go inside the loop. There are only three action statements needed inside the loop. The first step is to reduce the current amount by the payment, keeping in mind that part of the payment goes to interest, and not to principle. The second step is to display the result of this calculation in the text area. The third step is to increment the month number. Figure 5-15 shows the code to accomplish these tasks.

```
curLoan = curLoan - (monPayment -(curLoan * monIntRate));
ta.appendText ("After Month: " + thisMonth + '\n' +
    "Current Loan: " + curLoan + "\n\n");
thisMonth++;
```

Figure 5-15: Loop action statements

Step 5: Write Any Post-Loop Statements

In many traditional loop programs, post-loop statements are needed to print results or to correct any changes made by sentinel values. You do not need any post-loop statements in your program because all the output is done either in the pre-loop statements or inside the loop, and you did not use a sentinel value. Figure 5-16 shows the loop portion of your program.

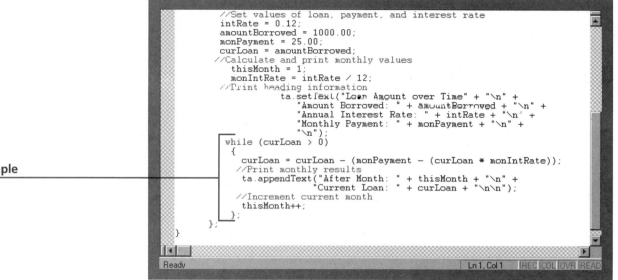

```
        //Set values of loan, payment, and interest rate
        intRate = 0.12;
        amountBorrowed = 1000.00;
        monPayment = 25.00;
        curLoan = amountBorrowed;
       //Calculate and print monthly values
          thisMonth = 1;
          monIntRate = intRate / 12;
        //Print heading information
                     ta.setText("Loan Amount over Time" + "\n" +
                        "Amount Borrowed: " + amountBorrowed + "\n" +
                        "Annual Interest Rate: " + intRate + "\n" +
                        "Monthly Payment: " + monPayment + "\n" +
                        "\n");
        while (curLoan > 0)
          {
            curLoan = curLoan - (monPayment - (curLoan * monIntRate));
           //Print monthly results
            ta.appendText("After Month: " + thisMonth + "\n" +
                          "Current Loan: " + curLoan + "\n\n");
           //Increment current month
            thisMonth++;
          };
      };
}
```

Ready | Ln 1, Col 1 | REC | COL | OVR | READ

loop example

Figure 5-16: Loop program

You can either take a break or complete the end-of-lesson questions and exercises.

S U M M A R Y

- Repetition, or looping, is the process of doing something more than once.
- Two types of repetition exist in Java: counting and conditional. Counting means doing something a set number of times; conditional means doing something until a condition is true or while a condition is true.
- The two types of repetitive loops are pre-test and post-test conditional loops.
- Pre-test loops check the value of the condition before any statements are executed. Pre-test loops are implemented in Java using the for and while statements.
- Post-test loops perform the loop at least once before checking the controlling condition. Post-test loops are implemented in Java using the do while statement.
- The three parts of a for statement conditional include portions that set up the counter, define the termination condition, and increment the counter. An example is *for (int count = 1; count <=10, count++)*.

- The while statement is more flexible than other statements because of the types of conditions that can be used with it, but it does not auto-increment the loop toward termination. An example is *while (count <=10)*.
- The do while statement is a post-test statement that will execute the statements of the loop at least once. An example is:

```
do
{
   <statements>
}
while (count <=10)
```

QUESTIONS

1. The __________ loop checks the condition before executing any statements in the loop.
   a. post-test
   b. pre-test
   c. counting
   d. forward check
2. The loop heading defines the __________ of the loop.
   a. precondition
   b. postcondition
   c. condition
   d. action statements
3. Doing a number of steps a given number of times is called __________.
   a. condition checking
   b. counting
   c. post-loop processing
   d. pre-loop processing
4. What are the three pieces of information that are contained in the parentheses of a Java for statement?
5. The for statement uses a(n) __________ to determine when the loop is done.
   a. counter
   b. while statement
   c. switch statement
   d. if statement
6. The counter can be any of the __________ types.
   a. floating point number
   b. numeric
   c. primitive
   d. String
7. The for and while loops are __________ condition loops.
   a. pre-test
   b. post-test

8. A __________ loop will execute the statements inside the body of the loop at least once.
   a. pre-test
   b. post-test
   c. for
   d. while
9. The condition of a loop statement is checked __________ time(s) during a single repetition through the loop.
   a. one
   b. two
   c. three
   d. zero
10. The __________ loop does not take care of auto-incrementing a counter.
   a. for
   b. while
   c. counting
   d. post-test
11. The __________ loop gives you more versatility than all of the loop structures in Java.
   a. for
   b. while
12. A __________ value is used to signal when a loop should end.
   a. sentinel
   b. pre-test
   c. post-test
   d. repetition
13. The do while loop is a __________ loop.
   a. pre-test
   b. post-test
14. The do while loop always executes at least __________ time(s).
   a. zero
   b. one
   c. two
   d. three
15. What are the five steps for constructing a loop?

E X E R C I S E S

1. Joann Lowrey works for a finance company that calculates the interest charged to customers based on the average daily balance. Write on paper a loop that takes a series of daily balances and computes the average of these balances. To calculate the average daily balance, you sum all the daily balances and divide by the number of days.
2. Josiah Hall works for a retail company that processes its transactions with a computer program. The program adds all of the items sold in a given day and returns the sum. The input file of these transactions ends with a sentinel of -9999. Write on paper a loop that computes this sum.

3. Francine Dominick works for a space exploration organization that provides unmanned space experiments. While one of the rockets is being launched, its temperature must be checked every five seconds during the last two minutes prior to the actual launch. If the temperature falls outside of the range of 50-100 degrees Fahrenheit, then the launch is aborted. Write on paper a loop that checks this value and sets a variable called launch to true or false depending on its findings. If the launch variable is ever set to false, it should not be changed back to true and the loop should be terminated.
4. Marvin Hinderman keeps his students' grades on a computer system. He likes to compute the average of each student's semester grade with a Java program. Write on paper a loop that accepts any number of grades and returns the average.
5. Jolitha White works for a scientific computing company. She needs to print a list of the first 10 prime numbers. A prime number is a number that is only evenly divisible by itself and 1. Write on paper a loop for Jolitha that prints the first 10 prime numbers.
6. Rowanda Nobari is employed by a company that does statistical computing. A frequent task for programmers is to compute the sum of all the integers from zero to a given number. Write on paper a loop for Rowanda that computes such a sum.
7. Tai-Chun Wong is employed by a computer chip company. Every day management takes a physical inventory of the number of defective chips that were produced as well as the total number of chips produced. Tai-Chun uses this information to compute the percentage of defective chips over a monthly cycle of 30 days. Write on paper a loop that calculates this number.
8. Mark Anthony is a programmer for a retail catalog company. The names and addresses of the customers are kept in a file with the last customer having the name ZZ End. Write a loop that prints a list of these customers until it reaches the sentinel value. Do not be concerned about how to do file input; you can design the loop as if interactive input is assumed.

LESSON B

objectives

In this lesson you will learn how to:

- Write a simple loop
- Write an input loop
- Change a loop type
- Write a nested loop

Writing Code That Repeats

Creating a Loop for the Order System

Writing a Simple Loop

In Lesson A, you learned about the three different Java loops and how to construct a loop. In this lesson, you will learn how to use those loops inside applets. Unfortunately, while those examples from Lesson A are perfectly good Java code, there are some complications when using loops in applets. You will be working on three different applets in this lesson. First you will modify the applet to track the value of an investment. You will change the BeanJar program into a guessing game. Then you will write an applet to graph the number of grades given for each letter grade.

You know that you can write an applet to show the return on an investment. Suppose your bank offers an 8 percent interest rate on a 12-month deposit of $10,000. You can write an applet to calculate the return (or interest earned) on your investment. To plan and write this applet, you will use the five steps presented in Lesson A.

Step 1: Determine the Controlling Condition

The controlling condition for the investment loop is when the investment reaches the end of the term, or 12 months. You could write the ending condition as *thisMonth <=12*, but you might want to use this applet to evaluate other investments in the future, so you will store the length of the investment in a variable named totalMonths. Therefore, the controlling condition is *thisMonth <= totalMonths*.

Step 2: Decide on the Loop Type

You need to determine two things before deciding on the type of loop to use in your program. The first task is to determine if the loop is a count-controlled loop. If it is a count-controlled loop, use the for loop. The investment problem is a count-controlled loop (12 months), so you can use a for loop.

Next you need to determine when the condition needs to be tested. Should you test the condition first so that if conditions are not right the loop never executes? Or should the loop always execute at least once, necessitating the need for a post-test loop? There also are situations when this is not a critical question, so you can chose any type of loop. In this case, it does not matter whether you test at the beginning or at the end of the loop, so you can use any one of the three loop types. In the next set of steps, you will use the while loop.

To write the while loop:

1. Start Visual J++ and close any open workspaces, if necessary.
2. Open the **In.java** file from the Invest folder in the Tutorial5 folder on your Student Disk, and then save the file as **Invest.java.**
3. Click in the location shown in Figure 5-17, press the **Enter** key, and then type the while statement shown in Figure 5-17.

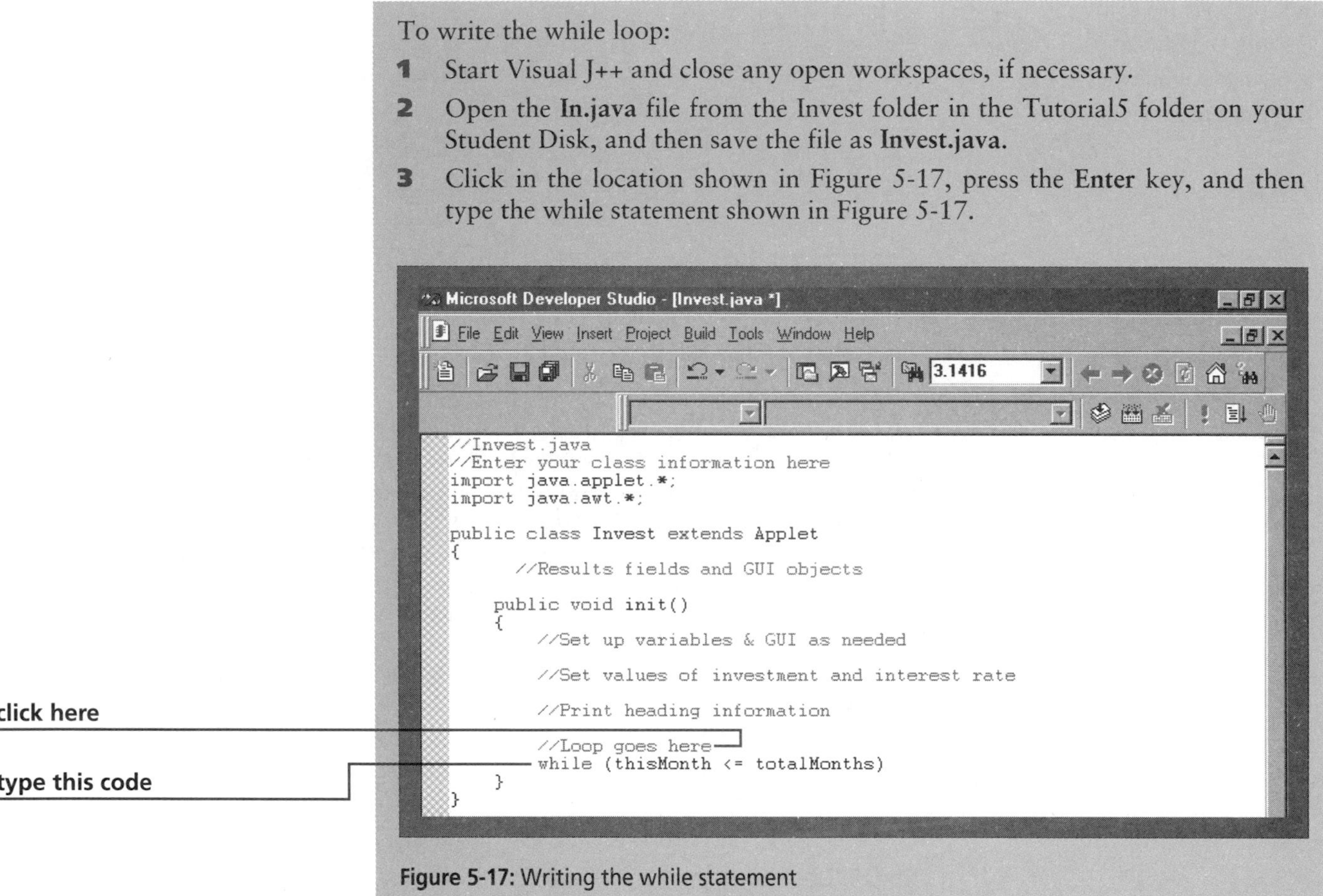

Figure 5-17: Writing the while statement

Step 3: Write Any Pre-Loop Statements

Next you will write the pre-loop statements, which can be divided into four sections: setting up the initial data fields and GUI objects, setting up the initial values and GUI objects, assigning the investment values and the interest rate, and printing the heading. You will enter almost all of this applet because the loop is the whole applet.

To write the pre-loop statements:

1. Click in the location shown in Figure 5-18, press the **Enter** key, and then type the lines shown in Figure 5-18 to declare the data fields and GUI object.

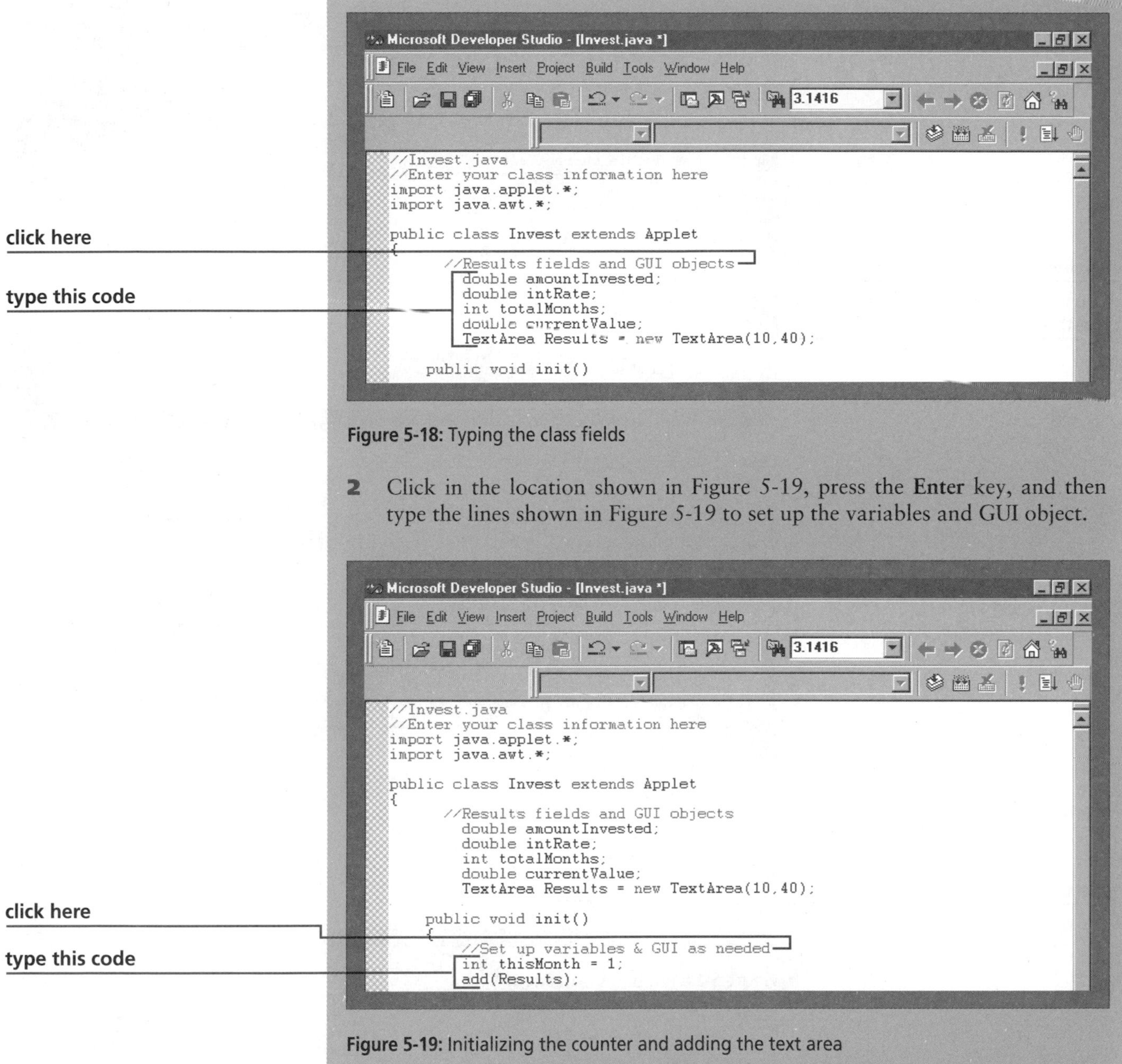

Figure 5-18: Typing the class fields

2 Click in the location shown in Figure 5-19, press the **Enter** key, and then type the lines shown in Figure 5-19 to set up the variables and GUI object.

Figure 5-19: Initializing the counter and adding the text area

3 Click in the location shown in Figure 5-20, press the **Enter** key, and then type the lines shown in Figure 5-20 to enter the investment values and interest rate.

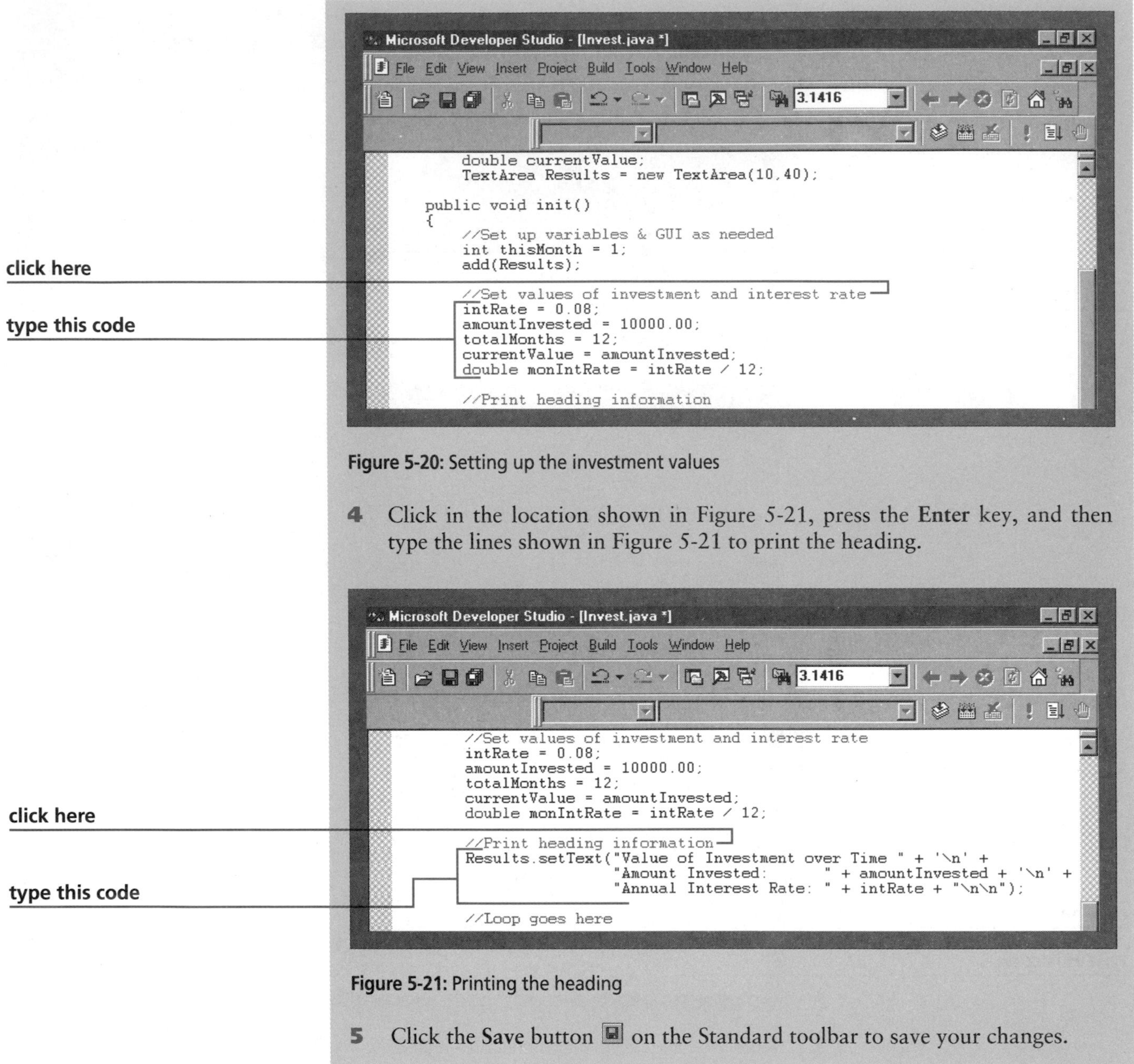

Figure 5-20: Setting up the investment values

4 Click in the location shown in Figure 5-21, press the **Enter** key, and then type the lines shown in Figure 5-21 to print the heading.

Figure 5-21: Printing the heading

5 Click the **Save** button on the Standard toolbar to save your changes.

Step 4: Write the Loop Action Statements

There will be more statements inside the while loop than if you were using a for loop. A for loop is more compact only in the sense that it is a slightly shorter program file.

To write the loop action statements:

1 Click in the location shown in Figure 5-22, press the **Enter** key, and then type the lines shown in Figure 5-22 to create the loop action statements.

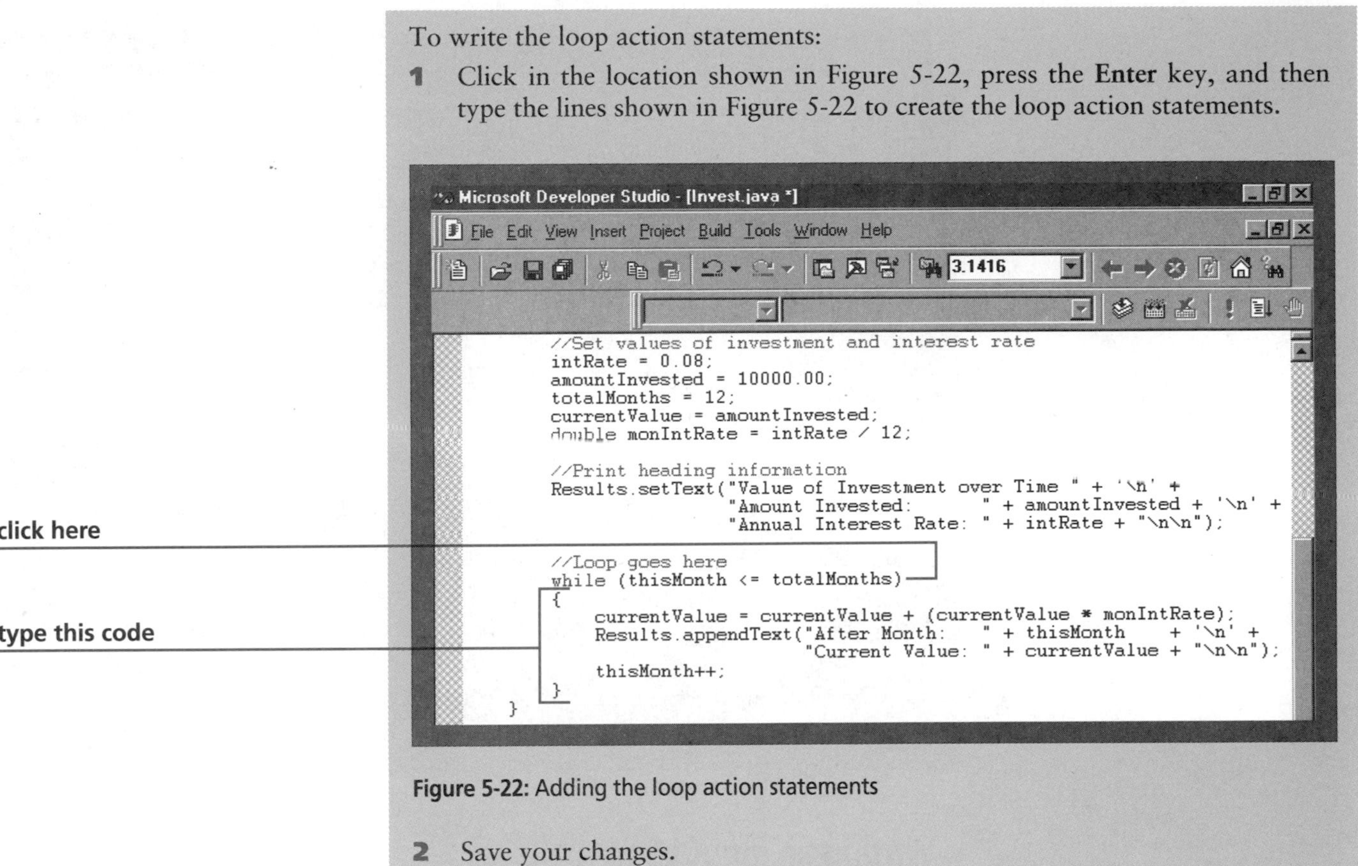

Figure 5-22: Adding the loop action statements

2 Save your changes.

Step 5: Write Any Post-Loop Statements

This applet does not need any post-loop statements because all the printing is done inside the loop. The loop is the end of the program, so there is nothing to clean up. The applet is finished so you can run it.

To run the applet:

1 Click the **Build** button on the Build toolbar, and then click the **Yes** button to build the program in a default project workspace.

HELP? If you receive syntax errors in the Output window, check your typing carefully and make sure that your punctuation and capitalization match the code shown in the figures, and then build the file again. If you still have errors, consult your instructor for help.

2 Click the **Execute Program** button on the Build toolbar to open the Information For Running Class dialog box. Type **Invest** in the Class file name text box, and then click the **OK** button. The applet executes in Internet Explorer, as shown in Figure 5-23.

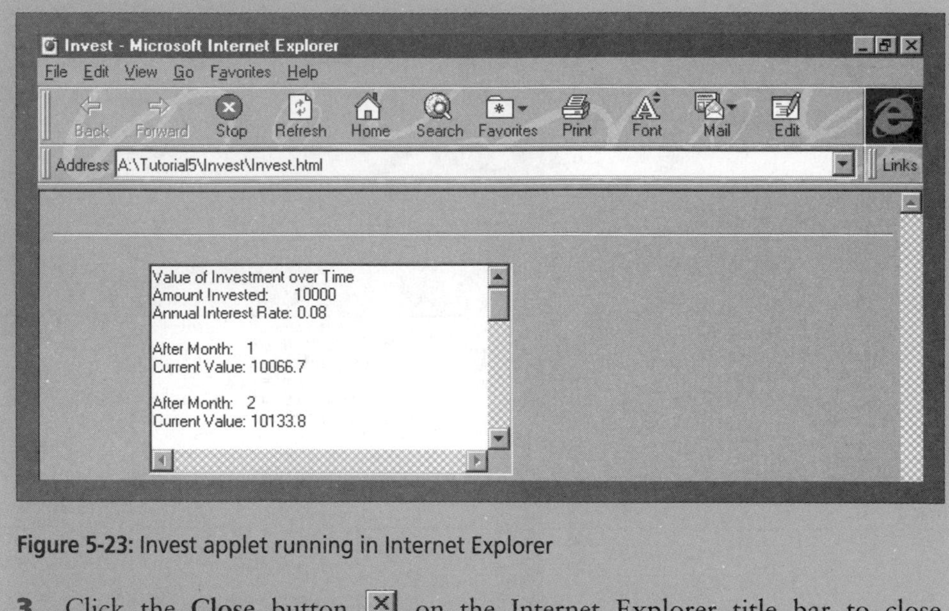

Figure 5-23: Invest applet running in Internet Explorer

3 Click the **Close** button on the Internet Explorer title bar to close Internet Explorer.

4 Click **File** on the menu bar, click **Close Workspace**, and then click the **Yes** button to close the project workspace and all document windows.

Writing an Input Loop

Maria wants you to change the BeanJar applet into a guessing game that allows visitors to the Koffee Koncoctions Web page to guess the number of beans in the jar. This new approach requires many changes. In addition to designing and writing the loop, you need to manipulate the String data that is the output of the text field. Maria wants to keep the look of the BeanJar applet simple, so she asked if there was a way to keep the applet to one text field and one text area. Java has String methods that allow you to dissect a String so you can limit the applet to the allotted space. When you **dissect** a String, you are making multiple short Strings from one long String.

Manipulating Strings

In order to change the BeanJar applet into a guessing program, you need to take one String from the input text field, cut it into three pieces, and then convert the values into integer numbers. The first task is new, but you already have done String to integer conversions. You will be able to divide this String because the program will ask the user to enter three numbers (guesses), separated by commas. The commas act as separators that define the boundary between any two of the numbers. The indexOf(char) method will give the numeric position in the String of the character you give it. Using that index, you can use the subString methods to divide the String into two pieces. If you use indexOf with a character that is not in the String, the method will return -1. Because the work of dividing the String is done inside the loop, you will see that code when you get to that step in the design process. Also, so you do not have to worry if the user types any extra blank spaces, String has a trim() method that removes any blank spaces from the beginning and end of Strings.

Step 1: Determine the Controlling Condition

You only want the user to enter three guesses, so the controlling condition is *count <=3*.

Step 2: Decide on the Loop Type

This loop is a count-controlled loop and you will use a for statement. Your code for the loop statement is *for (int count = 1; count <= 3; count++)*.

To write the loop:

1 Open the **BJ5.java** file from the BeanJar5 folder on your Student Disk, and then save it as **BeanJar5.java**.

Note: **To help you concentrate only on changes needed to implement BeanJar5 with loops, some changes have been made to the BJ5.java file that were not in the BeanJar3.java file that you used in Tutorial 3.**

2 Scroll down the file, click in the location shown in Figure 5-24, press the **Enter** key, and then type the code as shown in Figure 5-24 to write the loop statement.

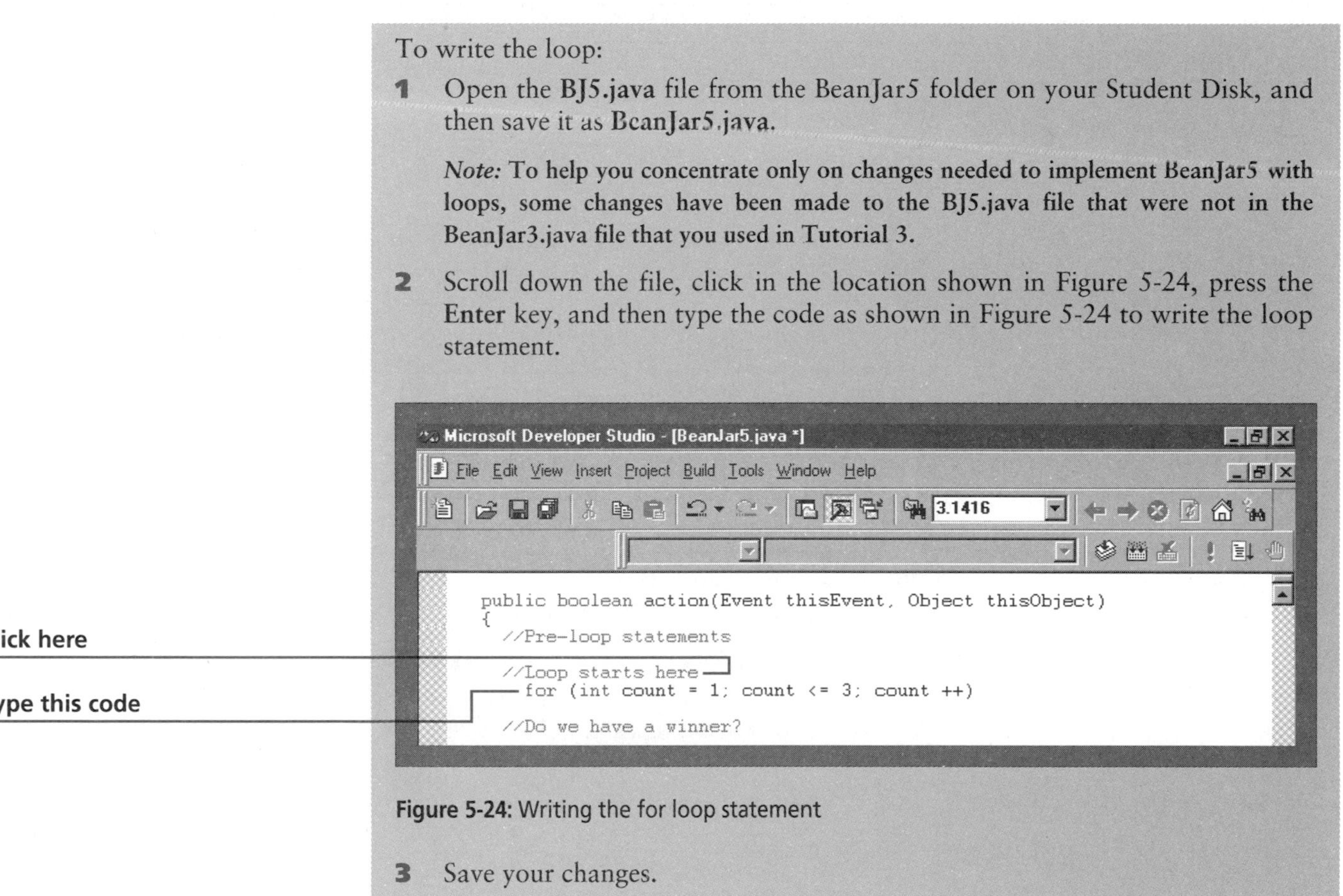

Figure 5-24: Writing the for loop statement

3 Save your changes.

Step 3: Write Any Pre-Loop Statements

You need to add statements to four areas to make this applet work correctly. Some of the work already has been done for you. You need to add high range and low range fields and a set focus statement; then you need to do some initial String manipulation and write a heading in the text area. The set focus statement allows you to place applet focus on a GUI element. When the focus is set on a text object (TextField or TextArea), that object contains the insertion point automatically. The purpose of the high range and low range fields is to give the user a margin of error when guesses are entered. The game would be impossible if your program required the user to enter the exact number, so you are going to allow a 4 percent margin of error. Therefore, a user will win if one of the guesses is plus or minus 2 percent of the exact number.

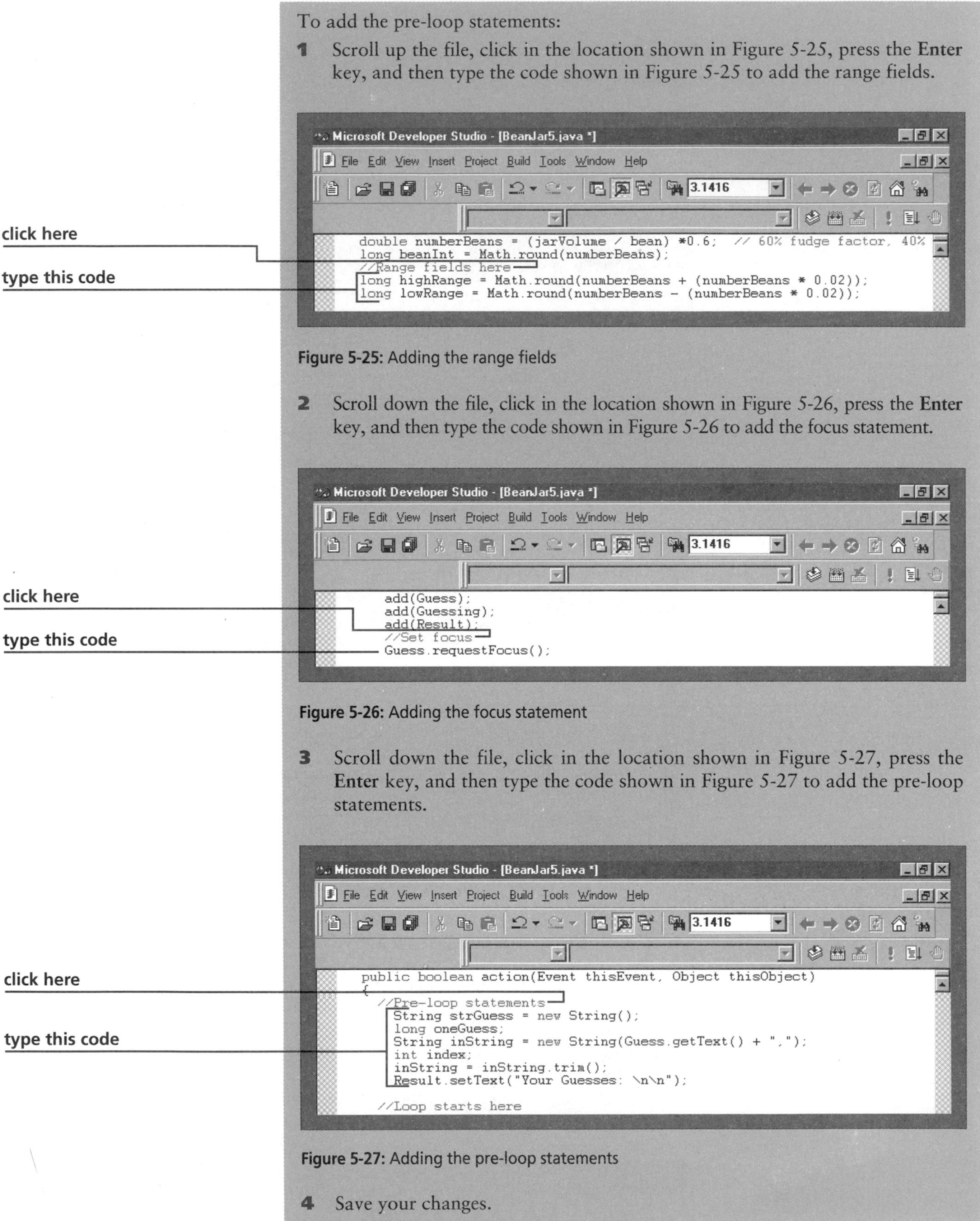

To add the pre-loop statements:

1 Scroll up the file, click in the location shown in Figure 5-25, press the **Enter** key, and then type the code shown in Figure 5-25 to add the range fields.

Microsoft Developer Studio - [BeanJar5.java *]
File Edit View Insert Project Build Tools Window Help
3.1416
click here
type this code
double numberBeans = (jarVolume / bean) *0.6; // 60% fudge factor, 40%
long beanInt = Math.round(numberBeans);
//Range fields here
long highRange = Math.round(numberBeans + (numberBeans * 0.02));
long lowRange = Math.round(numberBeans - (numberBeans * 0.02));

Figure 5-25: Adding the range fields

2 Scroll down the file, click in the location shown in Figure 5-26, press the **Enter** key, and then type the code shown in Figure 5-26 to add the focus statement.

Microsoft Developer Studio - [BeanJar5.java *]
File Edit View Insert Project Build Tools Window Help
3.1416
click here
type this code
add(Guess);
add(Guessing);
add(Result);
//Set focus
Guess.requestFocus();

Figure 5-26: Adding the focus statement

3 Scroll down the file, click in the location shown in Figure 5-27, press the **Enter** key, and then type the code shown in Figure 5-27 to add the pre-loop statements.

Microsoft Developer Studio - [BeanJar5.java *]
File Edit View Insert Project Build Tools Window Help
3.1416
click here
type this code
public boolean action(Event thisEvent, Object thisObject)
{
//Pre-loop statements
String strGuess = new String();
long oneGuess;
String inString = new String(Guess.getText() + ",");
int index;
inString = inString.trim();
Result.setText("Your Guesses: \n\n");
//Loop starts here

Figure 5-27: Adding the pre-loop statements

4 Save your changes.

You might wonder about one of the statements that you added in the pre-loop area. The *String inString = new String(Guess.getText () + ",");* statement looks different than what you have seen previously. All you are doing with this statement is taking the text typed by the user in the Guess text field, adding a comma to the end of it, and then storing the value in the inString object. Adding a comma to the end of the String means that each number in the full inString ends with a comma (instead of just the two commas entered by the user). This means that you can use the same set of instructions, three times, to get the three guesses.

Step 4: Write the Loop Action Statements

This loop is more complex than the loop in Invest.java. Figure 5-28 shows the pseudocode for the loop to help you understand it better. One thing to remember about Strings is that the character numbering starts with zero, and not with one. This is why the pseudocode pulls all the characters from location zero to the index of the comma.

```
Do these steps 3 times
  set index = location of "," in FullString
  set Guess = FullString from 0 to index
  set FullString = FullString from index to end
  Convert Guess from String to integer
Test Numeric Guess against highRange and lowRange to see if we have a winner
  If not, is the Guess too high or too low
  Print results
```

Figure 5-28: Pseudocode for the BeanJar5.java loop

To add the loop action statements:

1. Click in the location shown in Figure 5-29, press the **Enter** key, and then type the code shown in Figure 5-29 to add the String manipulation instructions.

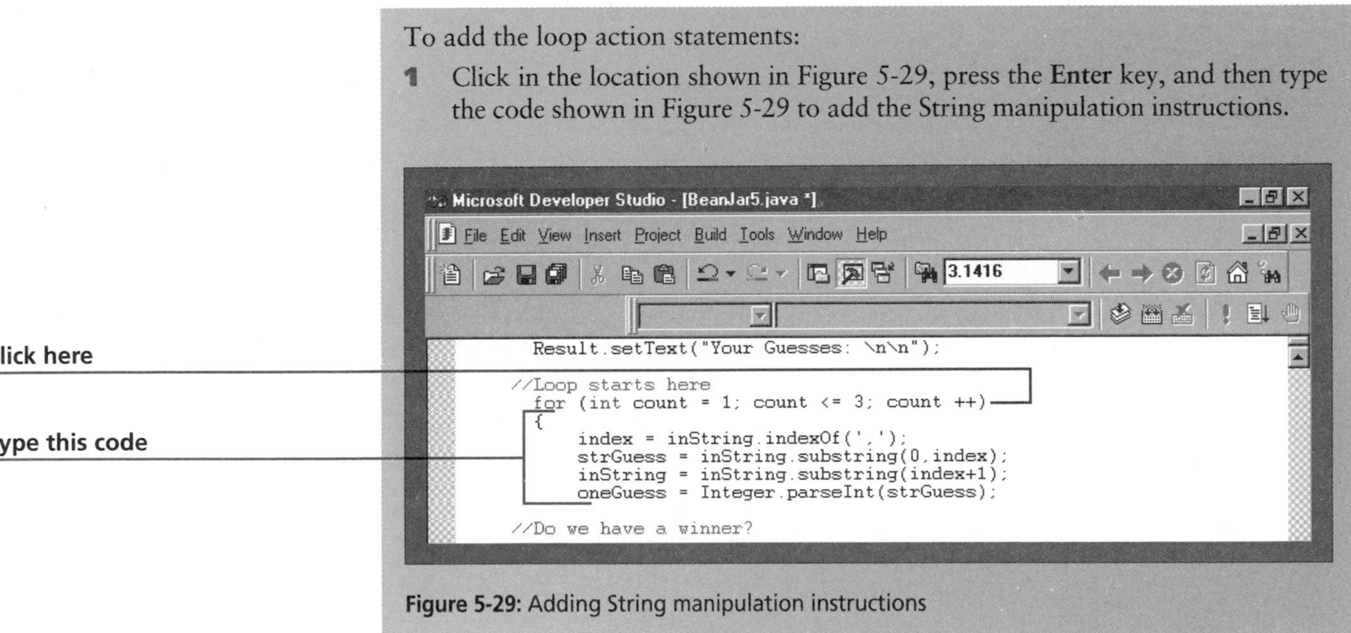

Figure 5-29: Adding String manipulation instructions

2 Click in the location shown in Figure 5-30, press the **Enter** key, and then type the code shown in Figure 5-30 to add the instructions to test the guess.

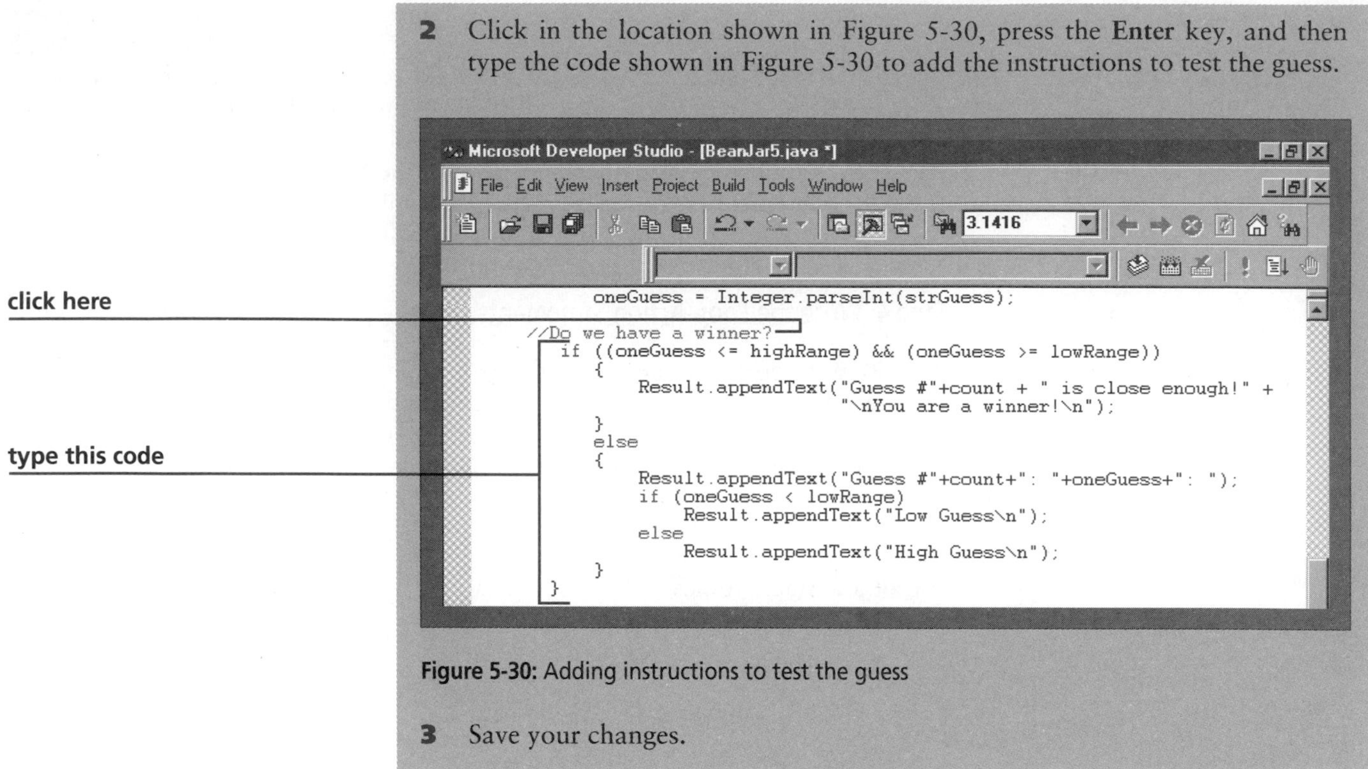

Figure 5-30: Adding instructions to test the guess

3 Save your changes.

Step 5: Write Any Post-Loop Statements

BeanJar5.java, like the Invest.java applet, does not require any post-loop statements. Now you can build and execute the applet to make sure that everything works.

To build and execute the applet:

1 Build the applet in a default project workspace.

2 Execute the applet. The class filename is **BeanJar5**. The requestFocus method moves the insertion point to the text field automatically.

3 Type **2200,2250,2300** in the text field.

4 Click the **Here are my Guesses** button. Your screen should look like Figure 5-31.

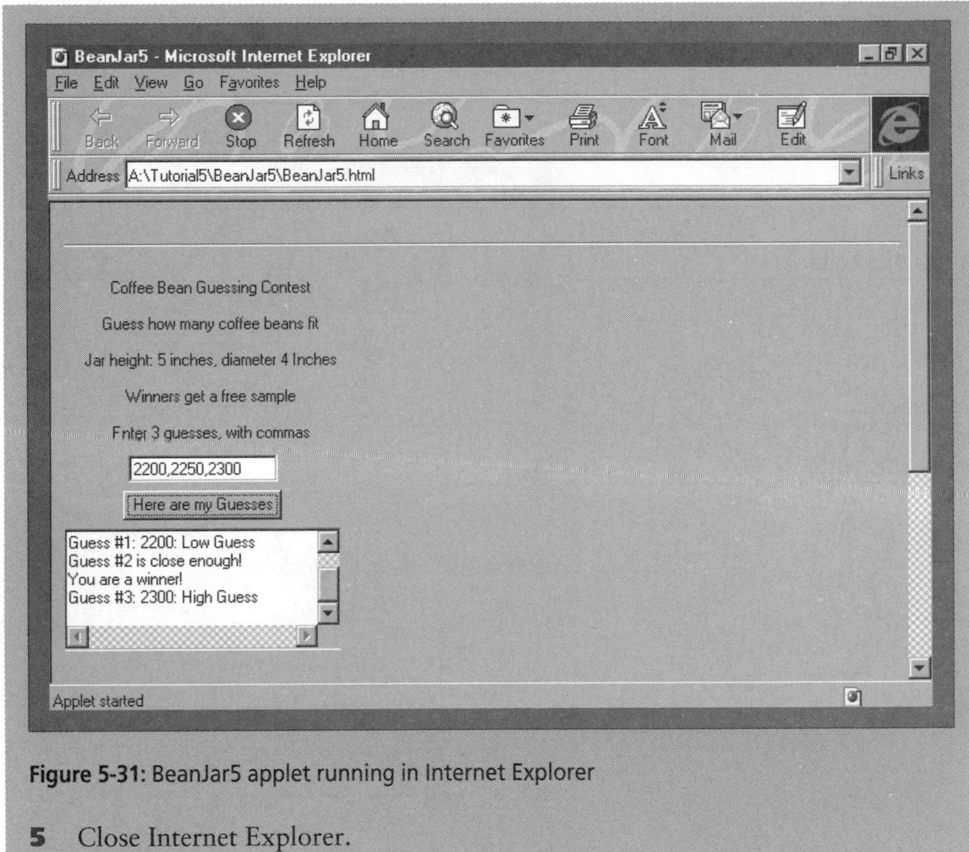

Figure 5-31: BeanJar5 applet running in Internet Explorer

5 Close Internet Explorer.

Changing Loop Types

Did you notice the problem with BeanJar5? Even though the second guess is correct, the program still evaluated the third number. You need to stop the loop if the user guesses correctly, even for the first guess. You can make this change by changing the loop to a while loop or a do while loop. It does not matter which loop you chose; for this exercise, you will use the do while loop. You will close this project workspace first because there is another version of the file in a different folder where most of the work has been done for you.

To change the loop:

1 Close the project workspace and all document windows.

2 Open the **BJ5a.java** file from the BeanJar5a folder on your Student Disk, and then save it as **BeanJar5a.java**.

3 Click in the location shown in Figure 5-32, press the **Enter** key, and then type the count initialization and do statements. Click at the end of the boolean statement here comment line, press the **Enter** key, and then type the code shown in Figure 5-32. These changes are the first part of changing the loop to a while loop.

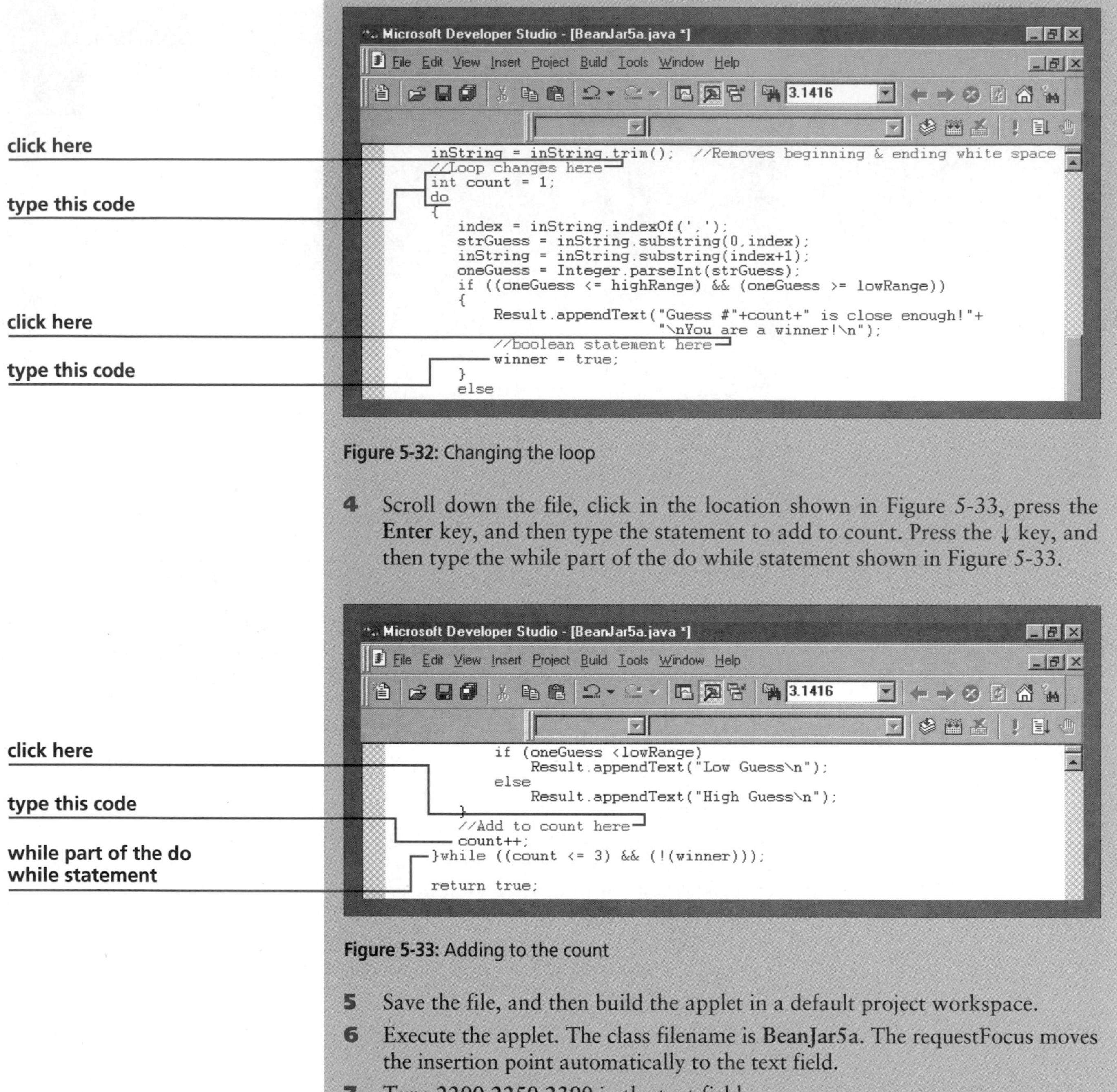

Figure 5-32: Changing the loop

4 Scroll down the file, click in the location shown in Figure 5-33, press the **Enter** key, and then type the statement to add to count. Press the ↓ key, and then type the while part of the do while statement shown in Figure 5-33.

Figure 5-33: Adding to the count

5 Save the file, and then build the applet in a default project workspace.

6 Execute the applet. The class filename is **BeanJar5a**. The requestFocus moves the insertion point automatically to the text field.

7 Type **2200,2250,2300** in the text field.

8 Click the **Here are my Guesses** button. Your screen should look like Figure 5-34.

If you want to try different guesses, click the Refresh button first, and then type some different values.

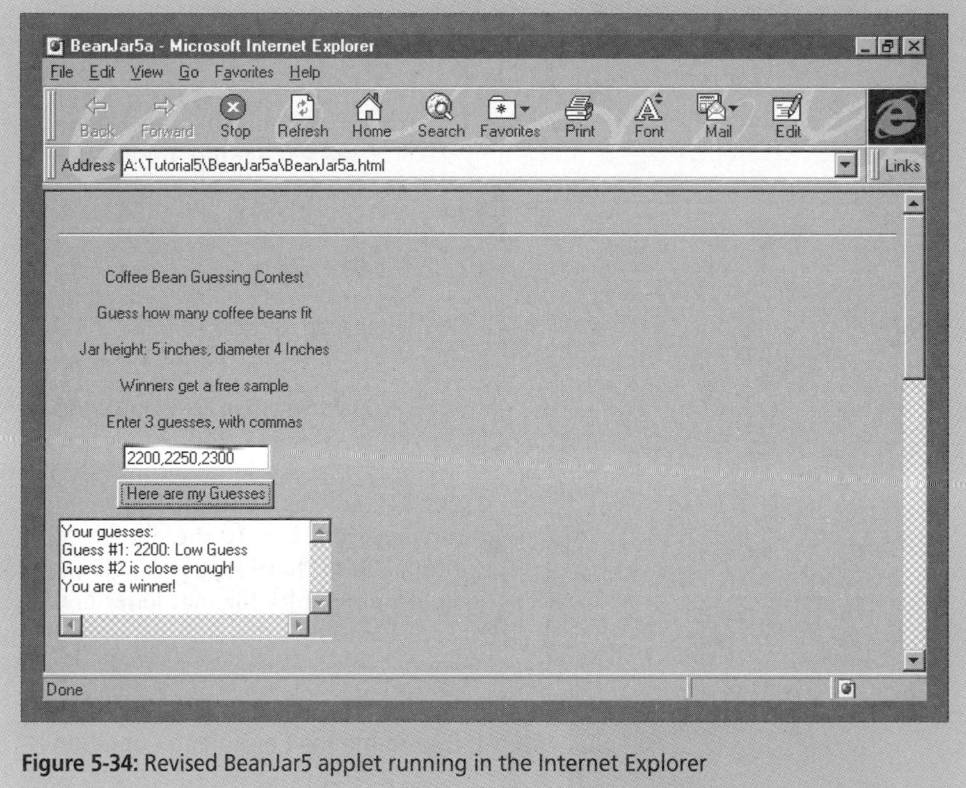

Figure 5-34: Revised BeanJar5 applet running in the Internet Explorer

If a user gets lucky on the first guess, the program will not display messages about the incorrect guesses that follow. Your applet does exactly what you intended, so you can close it.

To close the applet:

1. Close Internet Explorer.
2. Close the project workspace and all document windows.

Writing Nested Loops

Sometimes you will need to use a nested loop in your program. A **nested loop** is a construct than contains one (or more) loops inside another loop. Nested loops are like the Russian Babushka dolls, where inside the larger doll is a smaller one, then a smaller one, and so on until you get to the smallest one of all. Figure 5-35 shows the diagram of a nested loop. In all nested loops, the lines that connect the top of each loop to the bottom of the loop never cross; the inner loop is encased totally inside the outer loop.

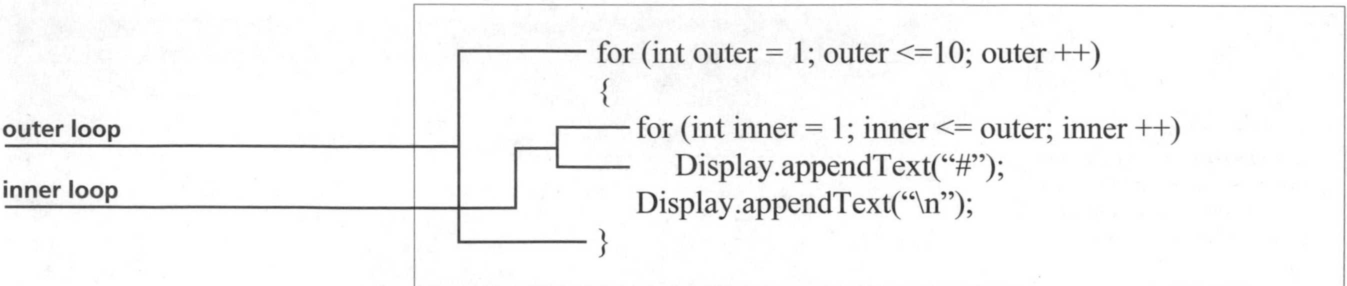

outer loop
inner loop
for (int outer = 1; outer <=10; outer ++)
{
for (int inner = 1; inner <= outer; inner ++)
Display.appendText("#");
Display.appendText("\n");
}

Figure 5-35: Nested loop diagram

Suppose your instructor asks you to build an applet that displays a graph in a text area to show how many of each letter grade she awarded in her class. This situation requires a nested loop because there are five available letter grades (A, B, C, D, and F) and there could be any number of students who received a given grade, ranging from zero to the number of students enrolled in that course. You need an outer loop that loops through each letter grade. The inner loop will run from one to numGrades for that letter grade, and print one character to represent each grade. The only difference between the planning steps for nested loops and regular loops is that you are designing more than one loop at a time.

Step 1: Determine the Controlling Condition

For the outer loop, the ltrCount variable will have the values A, B, C, D, or F. For the inner loop, the numGrades variable will have the values 1 to the number of grades entered by the user.

Step 2: Decide on the Loop Type

Both the inner and the outer loops are count-controlled, so you will write both loops as for loops. The difference between the outer and inner loops is that the counter for the outer loop is a char type, instead of an int type. The outer loop statement is *for (char ltrCount = 'A'; ltrCount <= 'F'; ltrCount++)*. The code for the inner loop is complicated and will be discussed in Step 4.

Step 3: Write Any Pre-Loop Statements

You can use this loop inside the method ShowResults() in your applet. Most of the pre-loop statements are located inside other methods. There is only one pre-loop statement inside this method, which is to print the heading inside the text area.

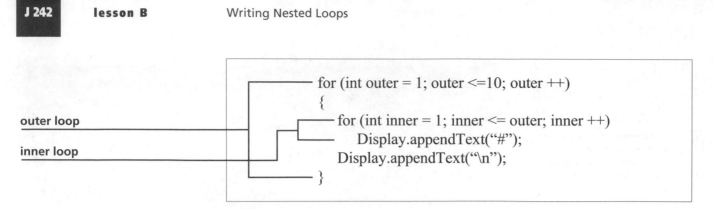

To add the pre-loop and outer loop statements:

1 Open the **GG.java** file from the GraphGrade folder on your Student Disk, and then save it as **GraphGrade.java.**

2 Scroll down the file, click in the location shown in Figure 5-36, press the **Enter** key, and then type the text shown in Figure 5-36 to add the pre-loop and outer loop statements.

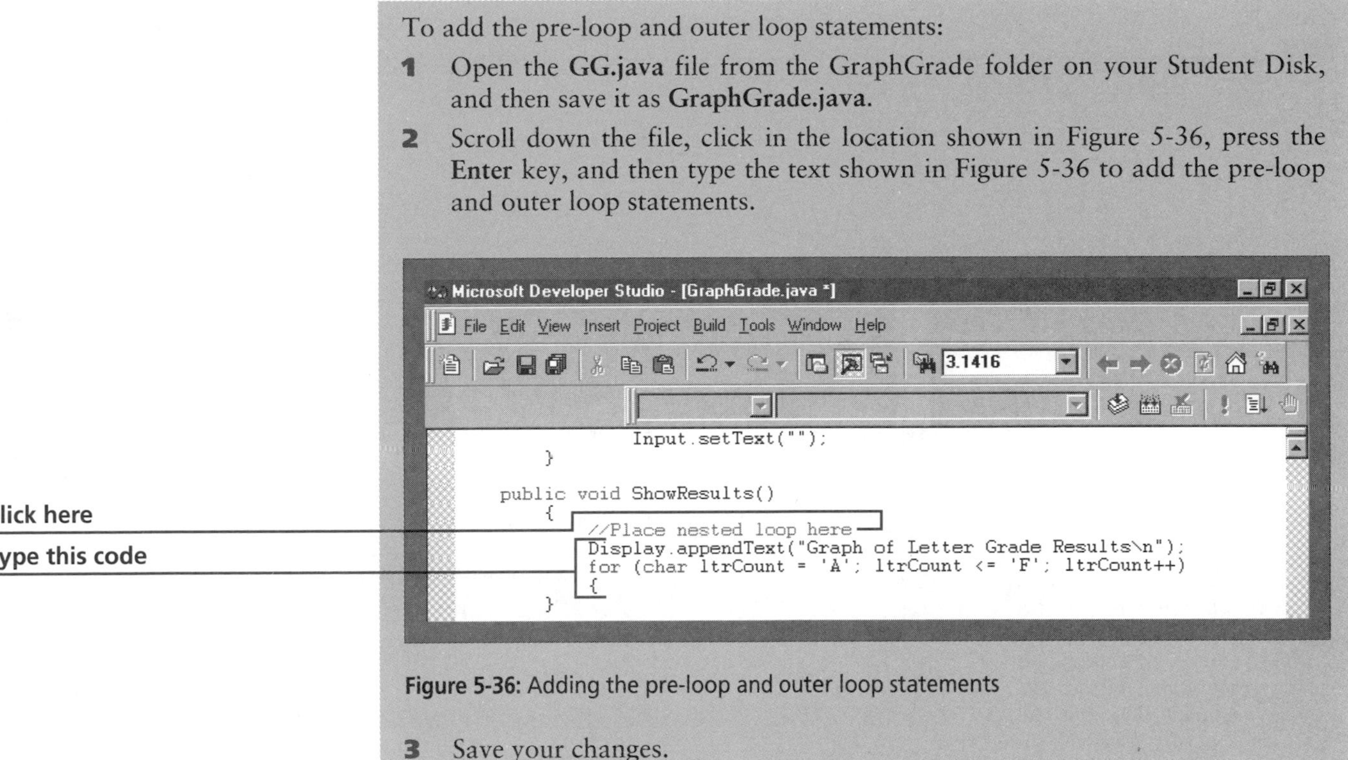
Microsoft Developer Studio - [GraphGrade.java *]
File Edit View Insert Project Build Tools Window Help
3.1416
click here
type this code
Input.setText("");
}
public void ShowResults()
{
//Place nested loop here
Display.appendText("Graph of Letter Grade Results\n");
for (char ltrCount = 'A'; ltrCount <= 'F'; ltrCount++)
{
}

Figure 5-36: Adding the pre-loop and outer loop statements

3 Save your changes.

Step 4: Write the Loop Action Statements

tip

Click the second Tutorial 5 link of the Online Companion for this book (http://www.course.com) to see a live Java program that illustrates this topic.

Your applet gets messy at this point (logically speaking). You need to use arrays to clean it up, which are covered in Tutorial 6. For now, you will use one outer loop with five little loops nested inside the big loop. Another minor complication is that the sequence of letter grades is A through F, with no E grade. The code to handle this problem also is included.There are no post-loop statements required for this applet, so after you enter the action statements, you can build and execute the applet.

To add the loop action statements:

1 Click in the location shown in Figure 5-37, press the **Enter** key, and then type the rest of the method to add the loop action statements.

Full Screen icon

click here

type this code

```
//Place nested loop here
Display.appendText("Graph of Letter Grade Results\n");
for (char ltrCount = 'A'; ltrCount <= 'F'; ltrCount++)
{
    if (ltrCount != 'E')
        Display.appendText("\n" + ltrCount + ": ");
    if (ltrCount == 'A')
    {
        for (int num = 1; num <= numA; num++)
            Display.appendText("@");
    }
    if (ltrCount == 'B')
    {
        for (int num = 1; num <= numB; num ++)
            Display.appendText("@");
    }
    if (ltrCount == 'C')
    {
        for (int num = 1; num <= numC; num ++)
            Display.appendText("@");
    }
    if (ltrCount == 'D')
    {
        for (int num = 1; num <= numD; num ++)
            Display.appendText("@");
    }
    if (ltrCount == 'F')
    {
        for (int num = 1; num <= numF; num ++)
            Display.appendText("@");
    }
}
}
```

Figure 5-37: Adding the loop action statements

tip

In order to display more lines on the screen, click View on the menu bar, and then click Full Screen. To return to the Visual J++ environment, click the Full Screen icon shown in Figure 5-37.

2 Save your changes.

3 Build the applet in a default project workspace.

4 Execute the applet. The class filename is **GraphGrade.** The requestFocus method moves the insertion point to the text field automatically, and the label asks for the number of A grades. See Figure 5-38.

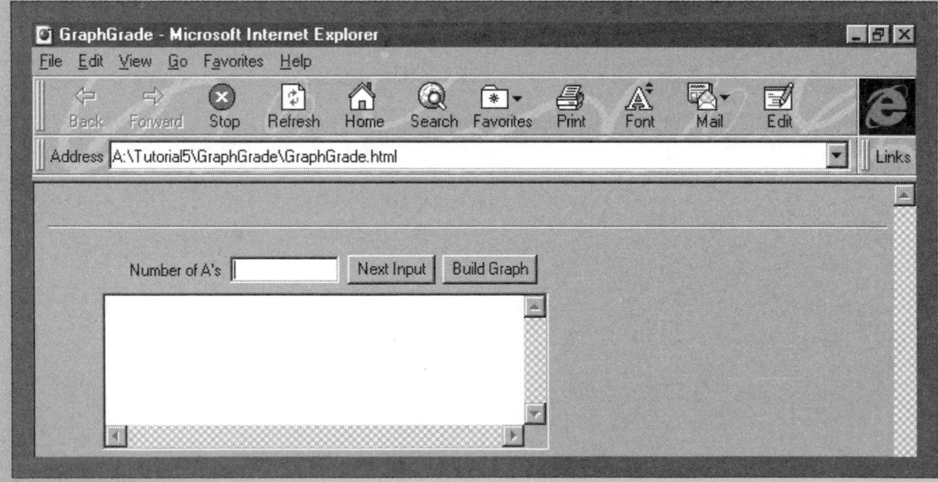

Figure 5-38: Starting the GraphGrade applet

5 Type **6** and then click the **Next Input** button. Now the label changes to ask for the number of B grades.

6 Type 8 and then click the **Next Input** button.

7 Use the same process to enter the following values for the remaining letter grades: C: **10**, D: **8**, and F: **6**.

8 Click the **Build Graph** button to display the graph in the text area, as shown in Figure 5-39.

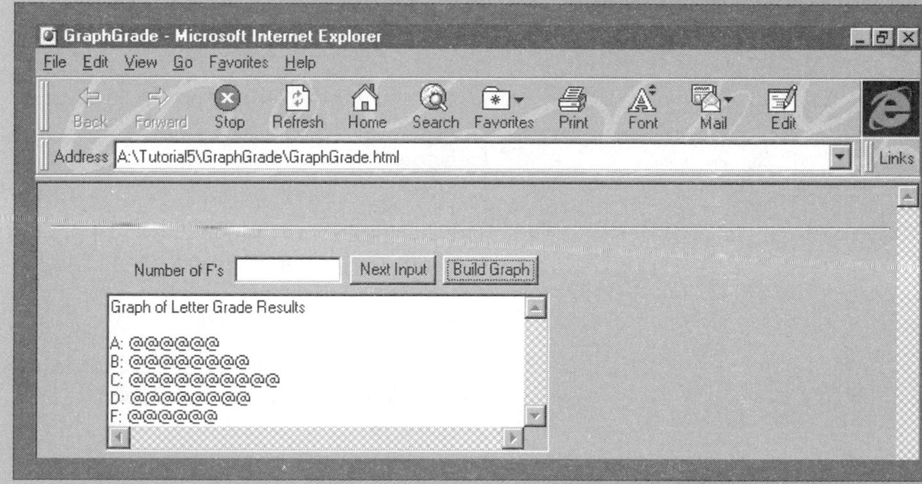

Figure 5-39: Completed GraphGrade applet

9 Close the Internet Explorer, and then close the project workspace and all document windows.

Now you can either take a break or complete the end-of-lesson questions and exercises.

SUMMARY

- The five steps used to design and write a loop statement are determining the controlling condition, deciding on the loop type, writing any required pre-loop statements, writing the loop action statements, and writing any required post-loop statements.
- The Java while statement requires the programmer to set appropriate variables for the condition that controls the loop structure. These values usually are set in the pre-loop statements.
- The while statement does not increment a controlling variable of the loop automatically, so the programmer must make sure that there are statements in the body of the loop that will move the condition toward termination.
- The post-loop statements of any of the looping structures in Java are used to perform tasks that can be done only after the loop is completed.
- The three major parts of a condition expression in the Java for statement are setting the initial value of the counter variable, defining the condition under which the loop will continue to process, and setting the increment of the counter variable. These three parts must appear in this order inside the parentheses.

- A nested loop is a construct that contains one or more loops inside another loop statement.
- The inner loop statements of a nested loop will be performed only if the controlling condition of the outer loop allows it to be performed; therefore, the nested loop is encased in the outer loop.

QUESTIONS

1. The pre-loop statements are coded __________ the loop statement.
   a. inside
   b. before
   c. after
2. The statements in the action block of a pre-test loop will be performed only if the condition of the loop evaluates to __________.
   a. true
   b. false
3. The __________ statements are used to clean up any variables or to display concluding information that results from the loop.
   a. pre-loop
   b. post-loop
   c. action block
4. The __________ loop can be used only if the controlling condition of the loop can be expressed with a counter variable.
   a. while
   b. for
   c. nested
5. A __________ loop is one that has one or more loops enclosed in the action block of another loop.
   a. pre-test
   b. post-test
   c. nested
6. In Step 2 of the loop design process, you __________.
   a. determine the controlling condition
   b. determine the type of loop
   c. code the steps to print summary information
   d. code the steps that are executed when the controlling condition is true
7. In Step 1 of the loop design process, you __________.
   a. determine the controlling condition
   b. determine the type of loop
   c. code the steps to print summary information
   d. code the steps that are executed when the controlling condition is true
8. In Step 5 of the loop design process, you __________.
   a. determine the controlling condition
   b. determine the type of loop
   c. code the steps to print summary information
   d. code the steps that are executed when the controlling condition is true

9. The code of an inner loop in a nested loop __________ cross the boundary of the outer controlling loop statement.
   a. can
   b. cannot

10. In Step 4 of the loop design process, you __________.
   a. determine the controlling condition
   b. determine the type of loop
   c. code the steps to print summary information
   d. code the steps that are executed when the controlling condition is true

EXERCISES

1. Given the following Java code for a loop, what is the value of *y* when the loop completes its execution? How many times did the loop perform the action statements?

```
y = 1;
i = 1;
endNum = 10;
while (i < endNum)
{
 y = y * 2;
 i = i + y;
};
```

2. Given the following Java code for a loop, what is the value of *j* when the loop terminates? How many times will the loop perform the action statements?

```
endNum = 12;
j = 1;
for (i=1; i <= endNum; i++)
{
 j = j * i;
};
```

3. Given the following Java code for a loop, what is the value of *x* when the nested loop terminates? How many times will the loop perform the action block of the inner loop? How many times will the loop perform the action block of the outer loop?

```
x = 1;
i = 1;
while (i < 25)
{
 j = 100;
 while (j > 50)
 {
 x = x + (i * j);
 j = j - 10;
 };
 i = i + 5;
};
```

4. Thomas Hargraves is a statistician for a research company. Some of the procedures the company uses involve number sequences that are different than simply counting. A routine Thomas currently is working on requires the use of the Fibinocci number series. This series is defined as the following:
fib(0) = 0
fib(1) = 1
*fib(n) = (n-1) *(n-2) when n > 1*

Write the code for a loop that calculates the fib(10) for Thomas.

5. Lucia Lopez works for an engineering firm that specializes in new metals. The metal she currently is investigating decreases in weight as it is heated. The relationship between the temperature of the metal and its weight is *weight = weight - (temp / 3)*. Write a program for Lucia that prints the weight of the metal between the temperatures of 50 and 100 degrees at five degree intervals (i.e. 50, 55, 60, etc.). Assume that the weight of the metal is 500 units at 50 degrees.

6. Jason Sherman needs to write an exponent calculator. The calculator should take the base number and the power (the number to which the base should be raised). Write a count-controlled loop to multiply the base by itself the correct number of times.

7. Sharon Williamson is employed by a retail company with its headquarters in Taiwan. She currently is working on a program that prints the amount of profit generated by orders of a certain size. The company provides a discount to customers according to the following: less than 50 units, full price; 50-100 units, 5 percent discount; 101-500 units, 10 percent discount; and over 500 units, 12 percent discount. Write the code for a program that prints the sales and profit for a given product for unit of sales between 1 and 1,000. Assume that the full price of the product is 5.50 and that each unit costs the company 2.50. The output of this program should list the number of units sold, the total cost to the customer for those units, and the amount of profit generated for that size order with the given discount.

LESSON C

objectives

In this lesson you will learn how to:

- Simplify the order entry screen
- Write a multiple item order loop
- Write an automatic field update method

Using Code That Repeats

Finishing the Order System Applet

Simplifying the Order Entry Screen

tip

Click the third Tutorial 5 link of the Online Companion for this book (http://www.course.com) to see a live Java program that illustrates this topic.

In this lesson, you will use loops to improve the order system for Koffee Koncoctions. You can improve the user interface by using String manipulation so there is only one input field and no input field for each piece of data. Then you will add a changeValues method to the Coffees.java file so the user has to enter only the coffee name and all the other coffee fields will be assigned the correct values. The last change that you will make is to allow multiple coffee products per order.

The last time you saw an order entry screen for Koffee Koncoctions, it had too many text fields. Now that you know how to do String manipulation, you can simplify the screen. With this many changes in the user interface, you will be working with a completely redesigned form, as shown in Figure 5-40, rather than the one you used in Tutorial 3. Instead of using multiple text fields and one text area, you will have only one text area for both the input and the output. Also, instead of just one button, you will have three buttons. The algorithm for the order entry system can be simplified into three steps: 1) get the customer data, 2) get the coffee items data, and 3) print the invoice.

text area contains the insertion point (focus)

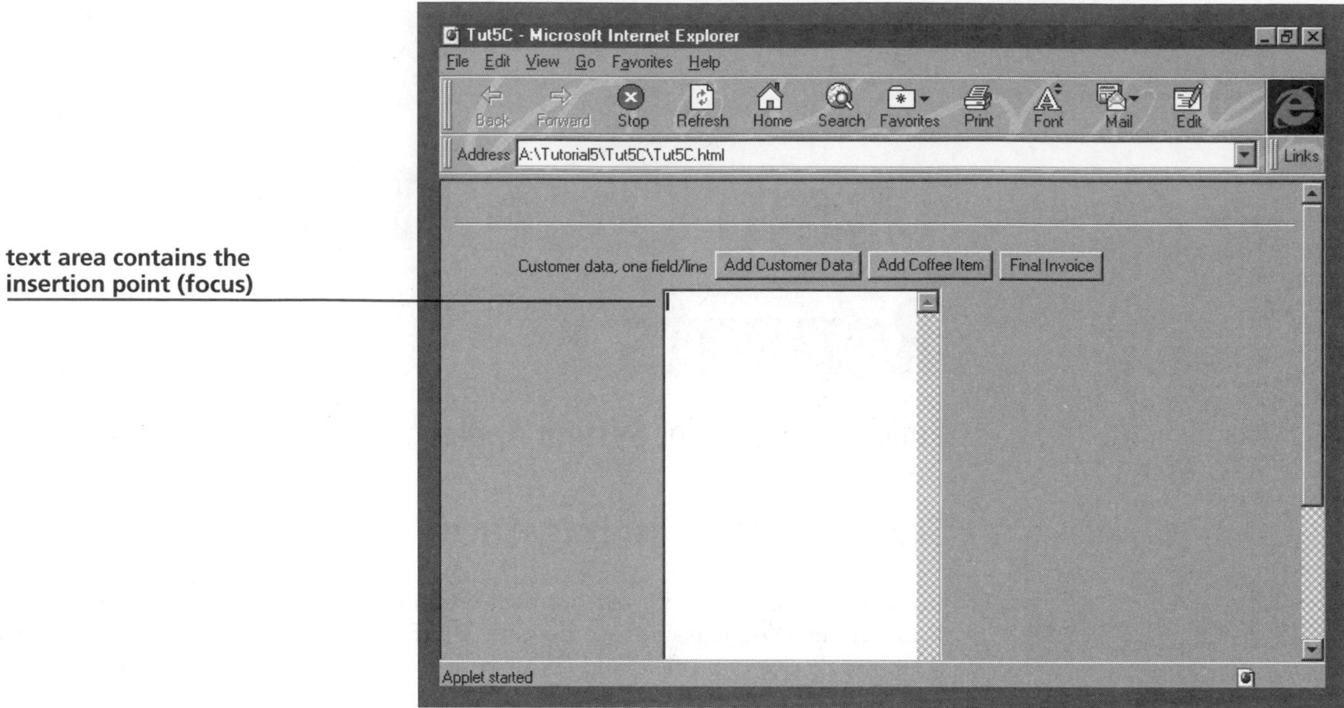

Figure 5-40: Redesigned order entry screen

Another improvement is to change the appearance of the order entry screen as the program runs. The label shown in Figure 5-40 asks the user to input the customer information. After the operator enters the information and clicks the Add Customer Data button, two screen changes occur. The label text changes to ask the user to input the coffee products information, and then the Add Customer Data button disappears from the screen. You will use the requestFocus method to place the insertion point in the text area, so the insertion point is in the correct field when the applet starts. This part of the order entry program is completely new, so you will start with a new file.

To start the new user interface:

1. Start Visual J++ and close any project workspaces, if necessary.
2. Click **File** on the menu bar, and then click **New** to open the New dialog box. Click the **Files** tab, and then double-click **Java Source File** to open a new Java file.
3. Save the file as **Tut5C.java** in the Tut5C folder in the Tutorial5 folder on your Student Disk.
4. Type the code shown in Figure 5-41, and change the comment about your class information as requested by your instructor.

type this code

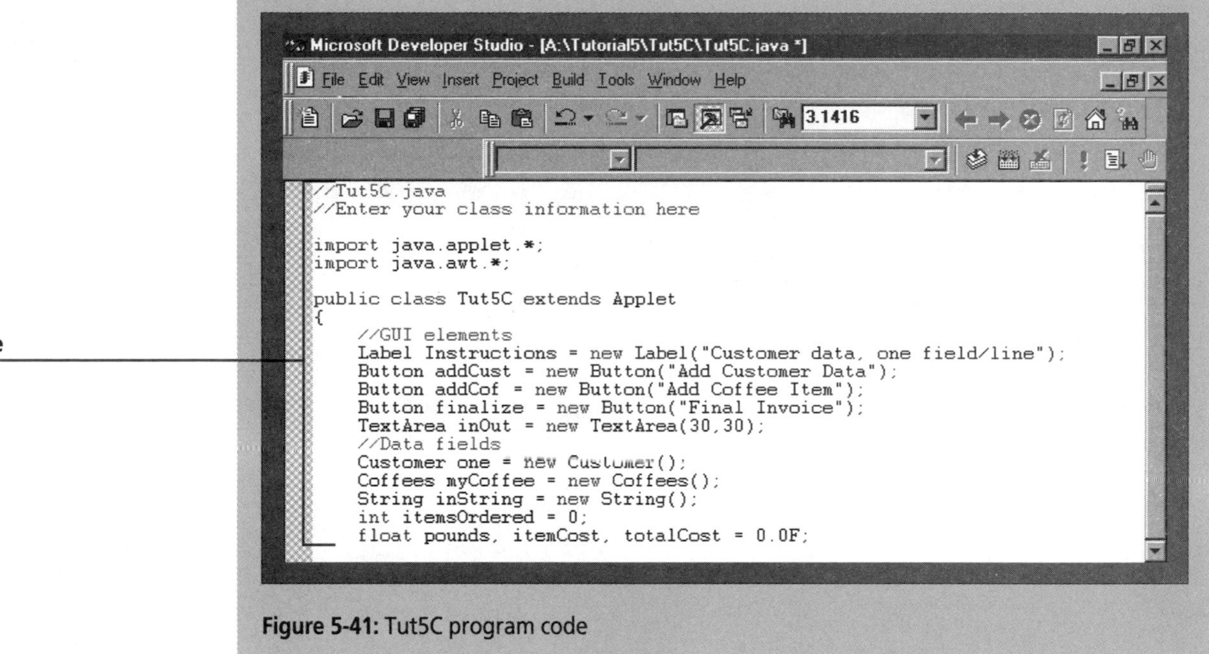

Microsoft Developer Studio - [A:\Tutorial5\Tut5C\Tut5C.java *]
File Edit View Insert Project Build Tools Window Help
3.1416
//Tut5C.java
//Enter your class information here
import java.applet.*;
import java.awt.*;
public class Tut5C extends Applet
{
//GUI elements
Label Instructions = new Label("Customer data, one field/line");
Button addCust = new Button("Add Customer Data");
Button addCof = new Button("Add Coffee Item");
Button finalize = new Button("Final Invoice");
TextArea inOut = new TextArea(30,30);
//Data fields
Customer one = new Customer();
Coffees myCoffee = new Coffees();
String inString = new String();
int itemsOrdered = 0;
float pounds, itemCost, totalCost = 0.0F;

Figure 5-41: Tut5C program code

Take a look at the code you just entered. The import statements in Java allow you to use all the GUI elements and Strings that you have been working with. Importing gives you access to predefined objects that are part of the core Java language. Any Java applet must import java.applet.*, and any Java program that uses any GUI elements must import java.awt.*.

You might notice that you are using a Customer object and a Coffees object, but no Order object. You will make some changes to the Order object in Tutorial 6 to make it easier to use. For now, because the Order object allocates space for only two coffee items, it is better not to use it. The other data fields, a String and some numeric values, are the ones that you need to hold working data.

After the declaration of the GUI and data elements for the class, the first method is the init method. In this applet you will use the init method to place the GUI elements in the applet and to set the focus to the first input field.

To add the init method:

1 Press the **Enter** key twice, and then type the init method as shown in Figure 5-42.

2 Save your changes.

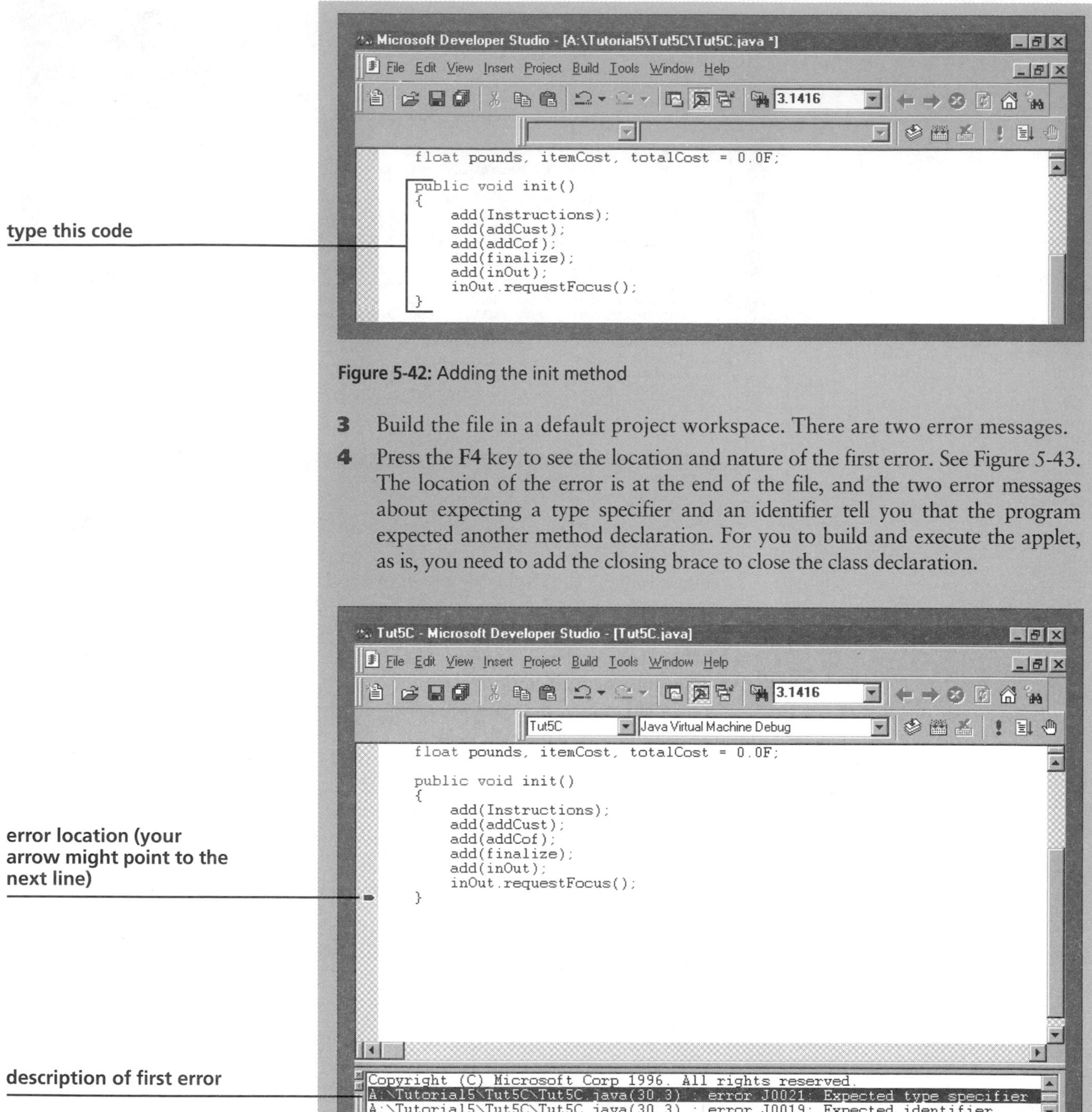

Figure 5-42: Adding the init method

3 Build the file in a default project workspace. There are two error messages.

4 Press the F4 key to see the location and nature of the first error. See Figure 5-43. The location of the error is at the end of the file, and the two error messages about expecting a type specifier and an identifier tell you that the program expected another method declaration. For you to build and execute the applet, as is, you need to add the closing brace to close the class declaration.

Figure 5-43: Errors reported in Tut5C.java

5 Press the **Enter** key and then type }, as shown in Figure 5-44.

} added here

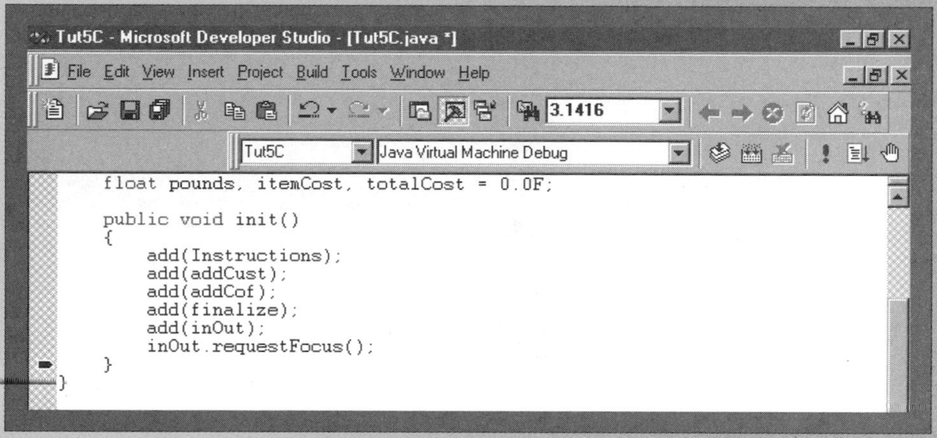
Tut5C - Microsoft Developer Studio - [Tut5C.java *]
File Edit View Insert Project Build Tools Window Help
3.1416
Tut5C
Java Virtual Machine Debug
float pounds, itemCost, totalCost = 0.0F;
public void init()
{
add(Instructions);
add(addCust);
add(addCof);
add(finalize);
add(inOut);
inOut.requestFocus();
}
}

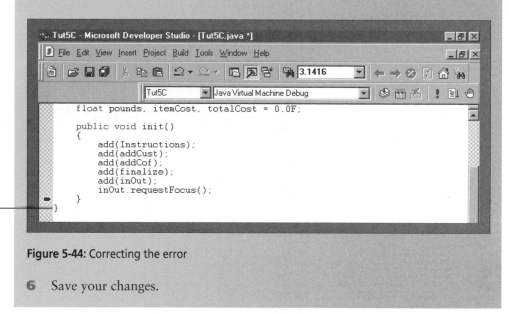

Figure 5-44: Correcting the error

6 Save your changes.

Before building the Tut5C.java program, you need to add the Coffees.java file to your project workspace because Coffees is an object in the Tut5C.java project. You will open the Cof.java file, save it as Coffees.java, and then add it to the workspace. You are adding the Coffees.java program to the project workspace, so you will *not* close the project workspace before opening the file.

To add the Coffees.java file to your project workspace:

1 Open the **Cof.java** file from the Tut5C folder on your Student Disk, and then save it as **Coffees.java.**

2 Click **Window** on the menu bar, and then click **Tut5C.java** to return to the Tut5C.java window.

3 Click **Project** on the menu bar, point to **Add To Project**, and then click **Files.** Click the **Coffees.java** file to select it, and then click the **OK** button. Now you can build Tut5C.java.

4 Click the **Build** button on the Build toolbar to build the file. You should not see any errors. If your Output window reports errors, check your typing, save all of the files again, and then rebuild the files again by clicking the Build button.

5 If necessary, change the HTML file on your Student Disk by clicking **Project** on the menu bar, and then clicking **Settings**. Click the **Debug** tab, click the **Category** list arrow, and then click **Browser.** Click the **Use parameters from HTML page** option button, and then type **Tut5C.html** in the HTML page text box. Click the **OK** button.

6 Execute the program. The class filename is **Tut5C.** See Figure 5-45.

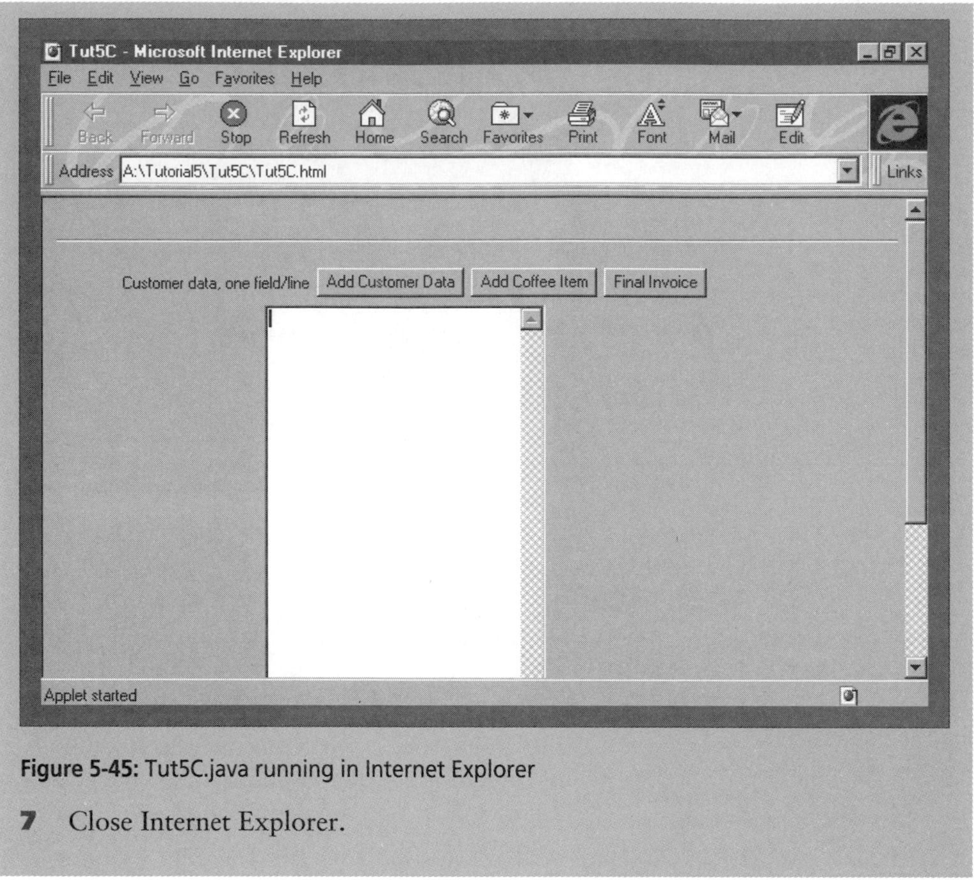

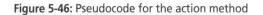

Figure 5-45: Tut5C.java running in Internet Explorer

7 Close Internet Explorer.

The next method you need to add is the action method. The action method is responsible for responding to events, such as clicking a button. This applet has three buttons, so the action method must know how to respond when each button is clicked. Figure 5-46 shows the pseudocode for the method.

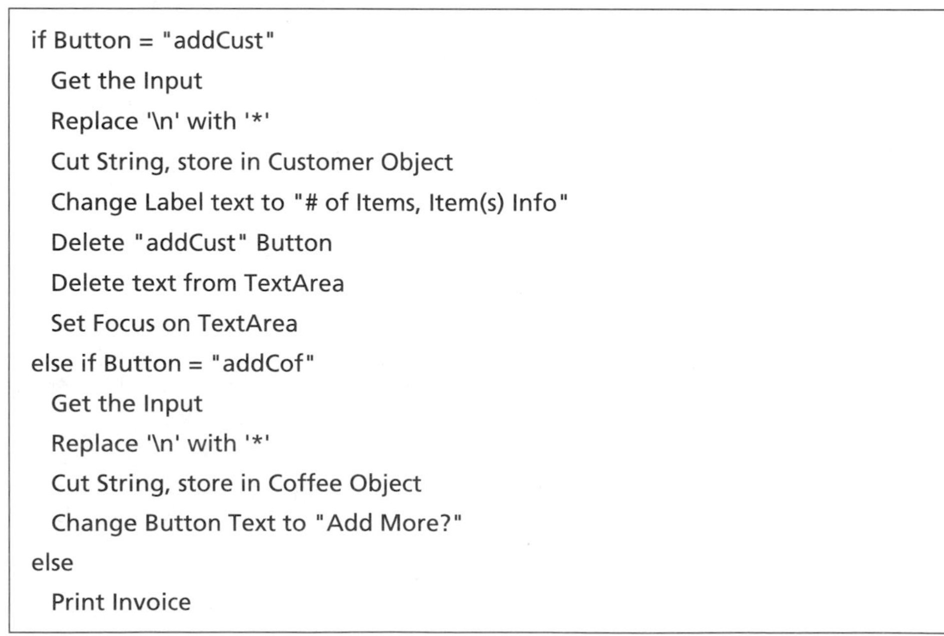

```
if Button = "addCust"
  Get the Input
  Replace '\n' with '*'
  Cut String, store in Customer Object
  Change Label text to "# of Items, Item(s) Info"
  Delete "addCust" Button
  Delete text from TextArea
  Set Focus on TextArea
else if Button = "addCof"
  Get the Input
  Replace '\n' with '*'
  Cut String, store in Coffee Object
  Change Button Text to "Add More?"
else
  Print Invoice
```

Figure 5-46: Pseudocode for the action method

You will add the code to the applet next.

To add the action method:

1 Click in the location shown in Figure 5-47, press the **Enter** key twice, and then type the action method.

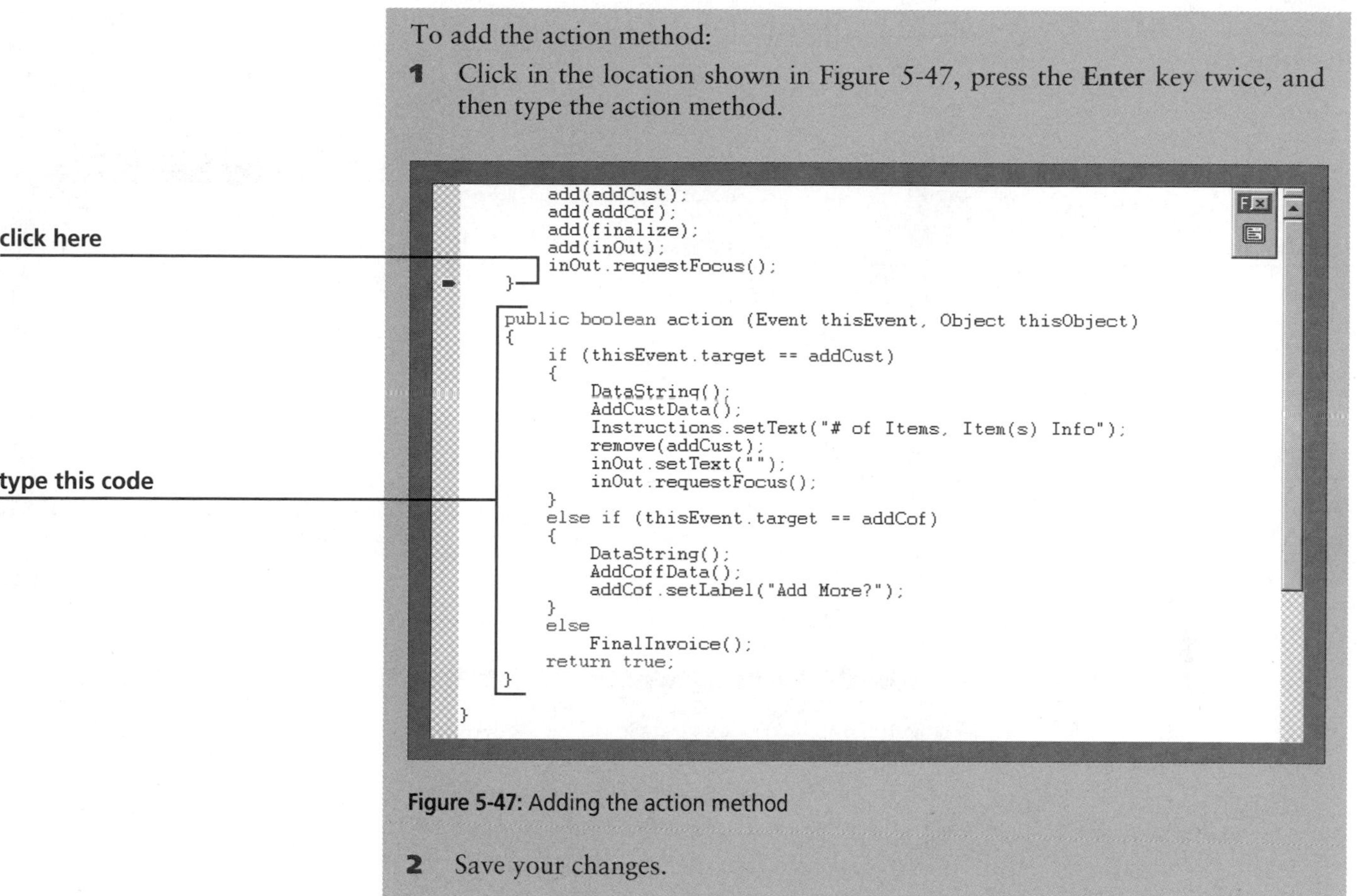


```
        add(addCust);
        add(addCof);
        add(finalize);
        add(inOut);
        inOut.requestFocus();
    }

    public boolean action (Event thisEvent, Object thisObject)
    {
        if (thisEvent.target == addCust)
        {
            DataString();
            AddCustData();
            Instructions.setText("# of Items, Item(s) Info");
            remove(addCust);
            inOut.setText("");
            inOut.requestFocus();
        }
        else if (thisEvent.target == addCof)
        {
            DataString();
            AddCoffData();
            addCof.setLabel("Add More?");
        }
        else
            FinalInvoice();
        return true;
    }
}
```

Figure 5-47: Adding the action method

2 Save your changes.

Next you need to develop the DataString and AddCustData methods. DataString takes all the data entered in the text area, puts it in a String, and then replaces all the new line characters with asterisks (*). This is an easy character to search for and makes cutting the data field values off the String manageable. The AddCustData method is more complicated and needs pseudocode to develop it properly, as illustrated in Figure 5-48. Briefly, this method takes the data String inString, and, field by field, cuts off the customer data, and uses the changeFieldValue method to place the values in the Customer product. The first five fields are done just that way: find the "mark," copy the field, store the data, and then cut the "ribbon." You cannot do the sixth field this way because there is no "mark" at the end.

```
Integer index
for count = 1 to 5 step 1
  index = position of '*' in inString
  Customer.changeFieldValue (count, (inString characters from 0 to index))
  inString = inString from index+1 to the end
Customer.changeFieldValue(6,inString)
```

Figure 5-48: Pseudocode for the AddCustData method

You will add the new methods next.

To add the DataString and AddCustData methods:

1. Click in the location shown in Figure 5-49, press the **Enter** key twice, and then type the DataString and AddCustData methods.

click here

type this code

```
            addCof.setLabel("Add More?");
        }
        else
            FinalInvoice();
        return true;
    }

    public void DataString()
    {
        inString = inOut.getText();
        inString = inString.trim();
        inString = inString.replace('\n','*');
    }
    public void AddCustData()
    {
        int index;
        for (int count = 1; count <= 5; count ++)
        {
            index = inString.indexOf('*');
            one.changeFieldValue(count,inString.substring(0,index));
            inString = inString.substring(index+1);
        }
        one.changeFieldValue(6,inString);
    }
}
```

Figure 5-49: Adding the DataString and AddCustData methods

2. Save your changes. To test the program so far, you need to comment out any methods that have not been written yet.
3. Comment out the lines shown in Figure 5-50 by clicking at the beginning of each line and then typing *//*.

comment out these three lines

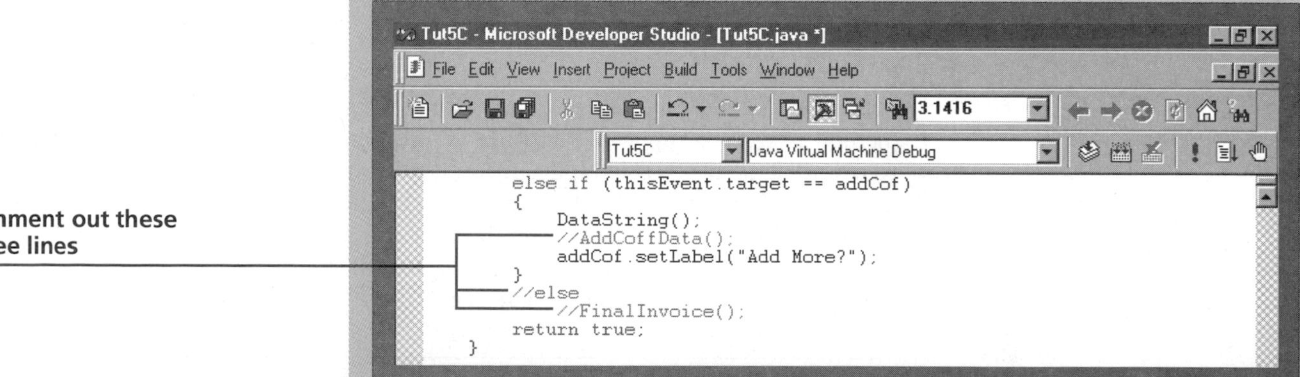
Tut5C - Microsoft Developer Studio - [Tut5C.java *]
File Edit View Insert Project Build Tools Window Help
3.1416
Tut5C
Java Virtual Machine Debug
else if (thisEvent.target == addCof)
{
DataString();
//AddCoffData();
addCof.setLabel("Add More?");
}
//else
//FinalInvoice();
return true;
}

Figure 5-50: Commenting out lines

4. Save and build the applet. Do not execute the applet yet. You can input the information, but there is no way to output it.

The next method to add is the FinalInvoice method. This method puts the customer data and the summary invoice information in the text area. You will learn how to list each coffee product ordered in Tutorial 6. There is no need to use pseudocode for this method because it is very short.

To add the FinalInvoice method:

1 Click in the location shown in Figure 5-51, press the **Enter** key twice, and then type the FinalInvoice method.

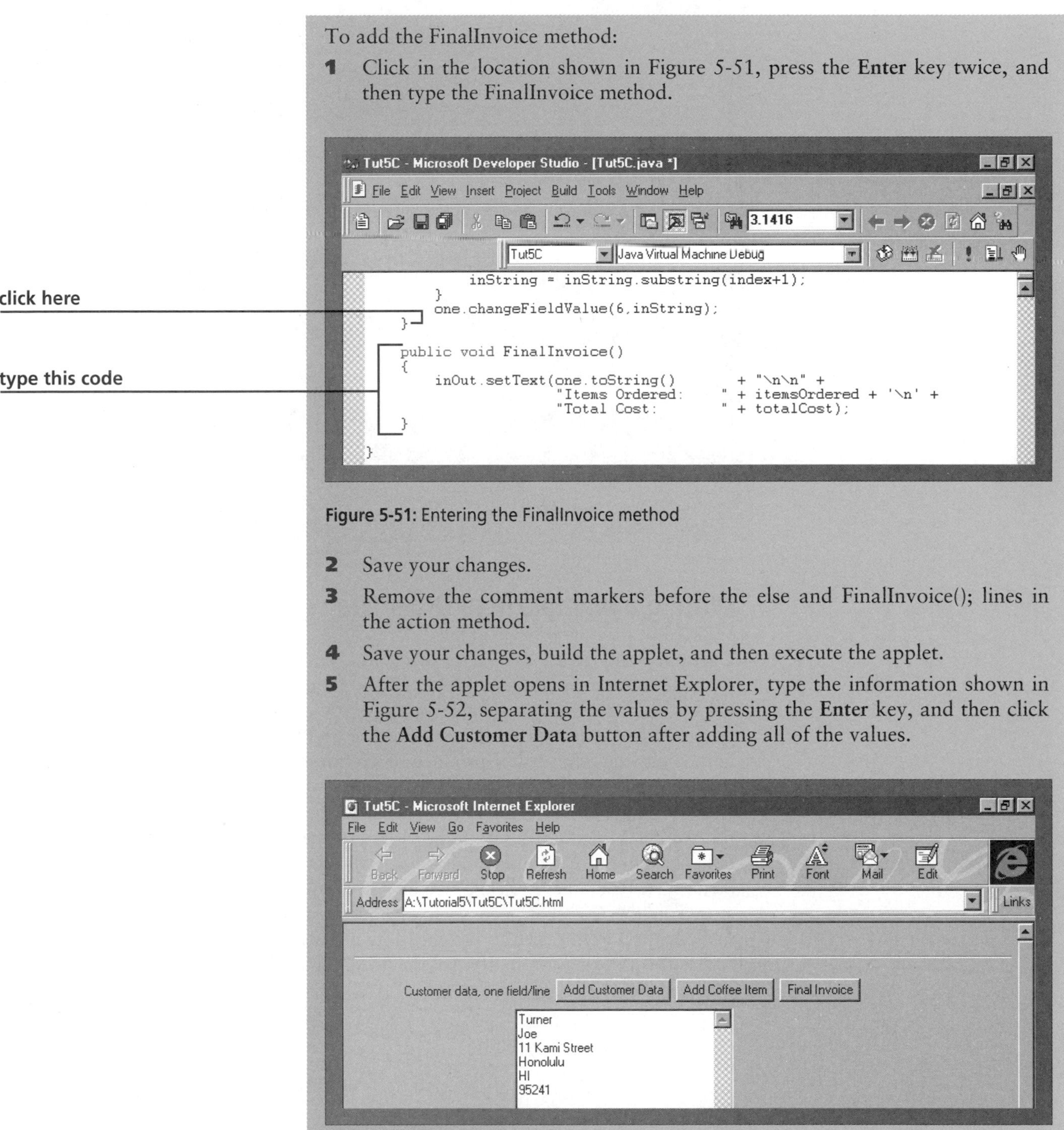

Figure 5-51: Entering the FinalInvoice method

2 Save your changes.

3 Remove the comment markers before the else and FinalInvoice(); lines in the action method.

4 Save your changes, build the applet, and then execute the applet.

5 After the applet opens in Internet Explorer, type the information shown in Figure 5-52, separating the values by pressing the **Enter** key, and then click the **Add Customer Data** button after adding all of the values.

Figure 5-52: Entering customer data

6 Click the **Final Invoice** button. The results are shown in Figure 5-53. If you want to try the applet with other data, click the Refresh button on the toolbar, and then enter any first name, last name, address, city state, and zip code. Separate the values by pressing the Enter key.

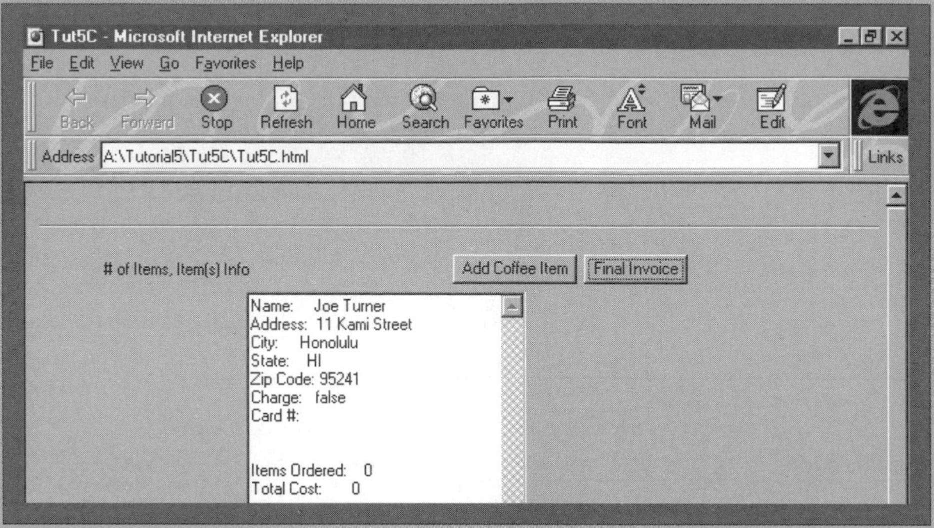

Figure 5-53: Invoice results

7 Close Internet Explorer.

Writing a Multiple Item Order Loop

There are only two more methods to add. One of Maria's goals was to make it possible to order multiple coffee products. Using a loop makes it possible for customers to order any number of products. One caution: while you can write the loop and keep track of total items ordered and total cost, there is no way to save in memory the other coffee product information. You will learn how to save information in memory in Tutorial 6.

The AddCoffData method has some complications that were not present in the AddCust method. One major difference between Customer data and Coffee data is that the Customer object has only Strings, while the Coffees object has Strings, floats, and a boolean. You also need to keep track of some data that is not stored in the Coffee object, such as pounds, item cost, and total cost. Another complication is you need to indicate how many coffee items are ordered. You need to use this information to control the loop. Figure 5-54 shows the pseudocode for this method.

```
inString = inString + "*"
String temp
int index
index = position of '*' in inString
itemsOrdered = int(inString.subString(0,index))
inString = inString from index+1 to the end
for count = 1 to itemsOrdered Step 1
  index = position of '*' in inString
  coffee.changeFieldValue (count, (inString characters from 0 to index))
  inString = inString from index+1 to end
  index = position of '*' in inString
  temp = inString characters from 0 to index
  Pounds = float(temp)
  myCoffee.changeValues
  itemCost = pounds * myCoffee.costLb
  totalCost += itemCost
```

Figure 5-54: Pseudocode for the AddCoffData method

To make the user's job easier, this method uses an automated field update method that you will add to the Coffees.java file in the next section. You can do this because all of the coffee fields can be determined by the product name. So once it has been established that the customer wants to order Kona Koffee, the values of the fields are set to the correct values automatically. When the coffee product information is entered, all the user has to type for each item is the name and the number of pounds. Unfortunately, to let the user order in fractions of a pound, the pounds has to be a float or a double. You have seen in the past that it gets tricky to convert a String to a float, but it can be done.

To add the AddCoffData, toFloat, and toBool methods:

1 Click in the location shown in Figure 5-55, press the **Enter** key twice, and then type the AddCoffData method shown in Figure 5-55.

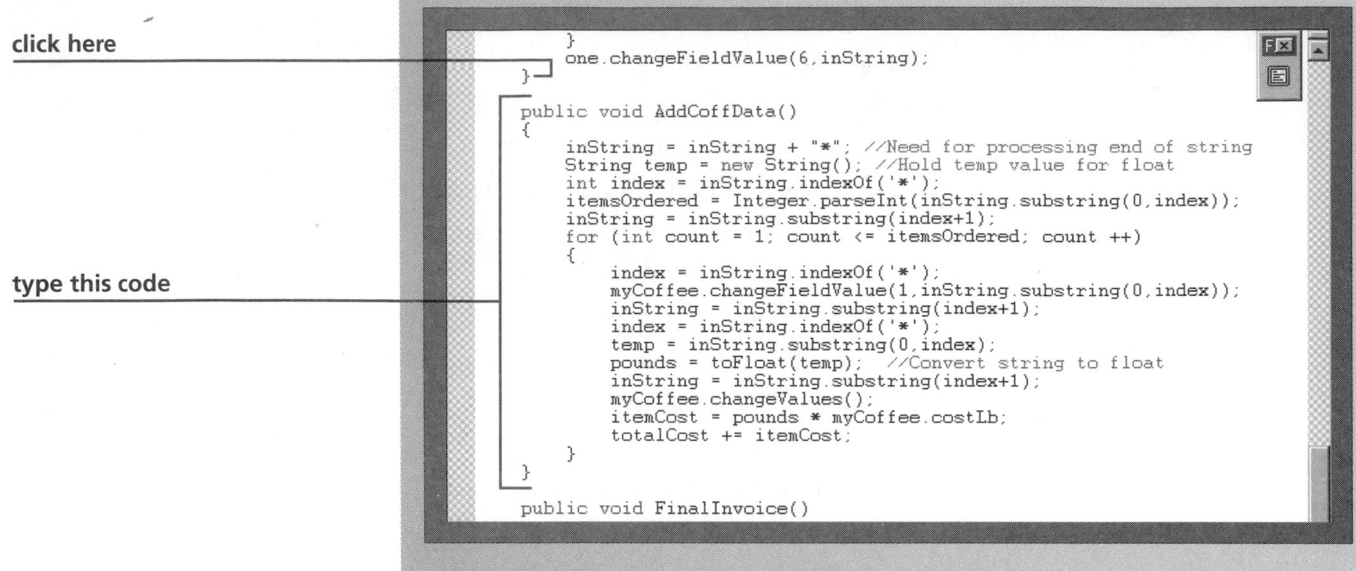

click here
type this code
}
one.changeFieldValue(6,inString);
}
public void AddCoffData()
{
inString = inString + "*"; //Need for processing end of string
String temp = new String(); //Hold temp value for float
int index = inString.indexOf('*');
itemsOrdered = Integer.parseInt(inString.substring(0,index));
inString = inString.substring(index+1);
for (int count = 1; count <= itemsOrdered; count ++)
{
index = inString.indexOf('*');
myCoffee.changeFieldValue(1,inString.substring(0,index));
inString = inString.substring(index+1);
index = inString.indexOf('*');
temp = inString.substring(0,index);
pounds = toFloat(temp); //Convert string to float
inString = inString.substring(index+1);
myCoffee.changeValues();
itemCost = pounds * myCoffee.costLb;
totalCost += itemCost;
}
}
public void FinalInvoice()

Figure 5-55: Adding the AddCoffData Method

2 Save your changes.

3 To add the last method to this file, press the **Enter** key twice, and then type the toFloat method shown in Figure 5-56.

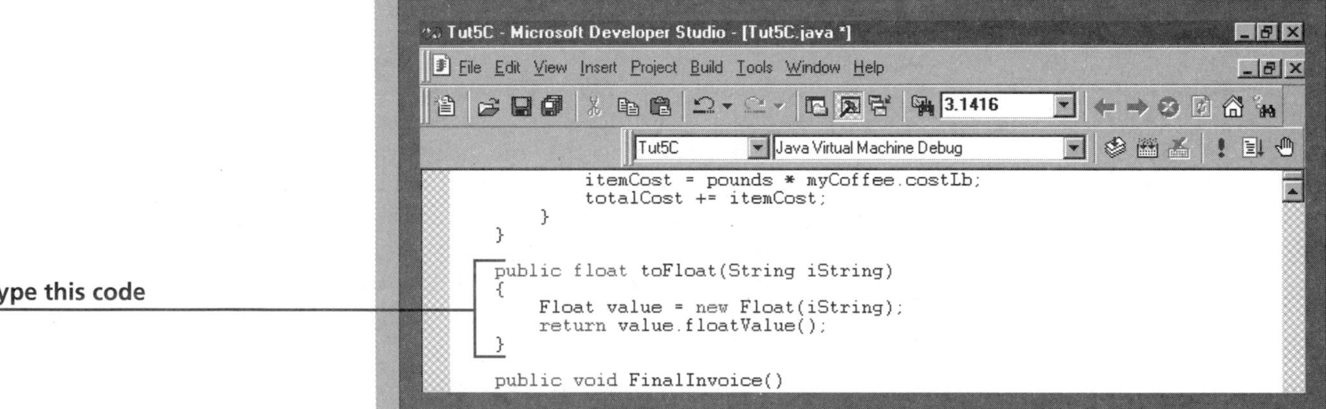

Figure 5-56: Adding the toFloat method

4 Save your changes. To build the program at this point without errors, you must comment out the use of the myCoffee.changeValues(); method.

5 Locate the myCoffee.changeValues(); line in the AddCoffData method, and then type // at the beginning of the line.

6 Save your changes and then build the applet. You should not see any errors. If you have errors check your typing and punctuation. If there are still problems, consult your instructor.

Writing an Automatic Field Update Method

There is only one more method to add to this project. Automating the order entry process helps the entry clerks work more efficiently and process more orders per day. Computers are supposed to help automate tasks, but a poorly designed program makes employees less productive. The order entry system from Tutorial 3 is a case in point. If that applet is used by the order entry personnel, with all that clicking and typing, they would not be very productive. All the fields for a coffee product are set in advance, so the order entry personnel have to enter the name and the number of pounds for each coffee product. You will change the Coffees.java file next.

To add the changeValues method and test the applet:

1 Click **Window** on the menu bar, and then click **Coffees.java** to open the Coffees.java window.

2 Click in the location shown in Figure 5-57, press the **Enter** key twice, and then type the changeValues method.

click here

type this code

```
    //The methods
public void changeValues()
{
    if (name.equalsIgnoreCase("kona"))
    {
        flavor = "rich";
        color = "dark";
        costLb = 4.50F;
        caffeine = true;
    }
    else if (name.equalsIgnoreCase("kona decaf"))
    {
        flavor = "mild";
        color = "light";
        costLb = 5.50F;
        caffeine = false;
    }
    else if (name.equalsIgnoreCase("italian espresso"))
    {
        flavor = "bold";
        color = "medium";
        costLb = 5.00F;
        caffeine = true;
    }
    else if (name.equalsIgnoreCase("espresso light"))
    {
        flavor = "mild";
        color = "light";
        costLb = 5.50F;
        caffeine = false;
    }
}
  public void changeFieldValue (int iField, String iValue)
  {
```

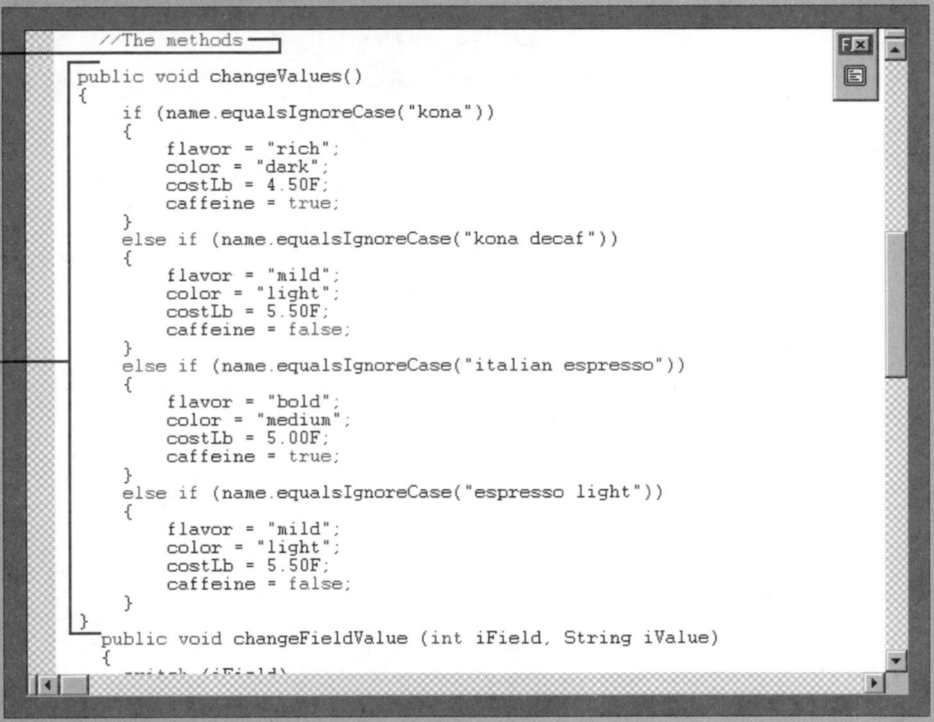

Figure 5-57: Typing the changeValues method

3 Save your changes.

4 To access the Tut5C file, click **Window** on the menu bar, then click **Tut5C.java.** Remove the comment markers from the myCoffee.changeValues(); and the AddCoffData(); lines.

5 To add the Customer.java file to the workspace, click **Project** on the menu bar, point to **Add To Project**, and then click **Files**. Click the **Customer.java** file and then click the **OK** button.

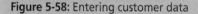

6 Click the **Save All** button on the Standard toolbar to save changes to all files in the workspace.

7 Click **Build** on the menu bar, and then click **Rebuild All**. There should be no error messages. If you receive any error messages, check for typing and punctuation mistakes. If there are still errors, consult your instructor.

8 Execute the project, enter the customer data shown in Figure 5-58, and then click the **Add Customer Data** button.

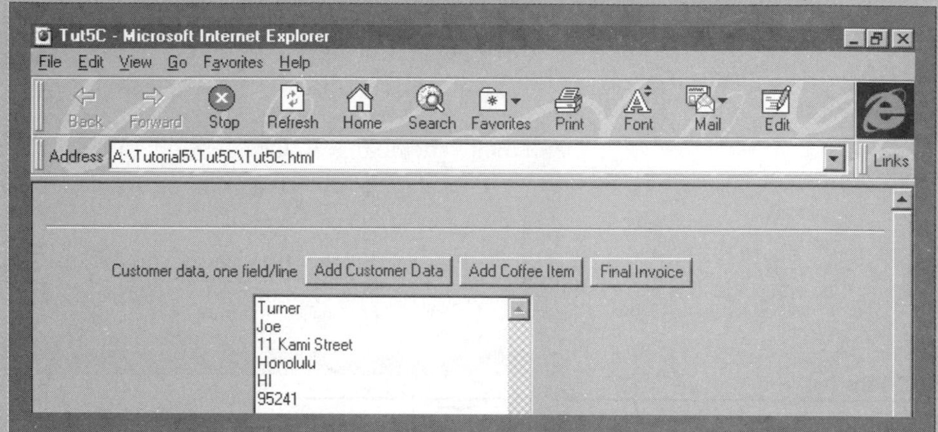

Figure 5-58: Entering customer data

9 Type the coffee data shown in Figure 5-59, pressing the **Enter** key at the end of each line, and then click the **Add Coffee Item** button after adding all of the data. The first value, 3, indicates the number of items ordered. The next six values indicate the coffee product and the number of pounds ordered.

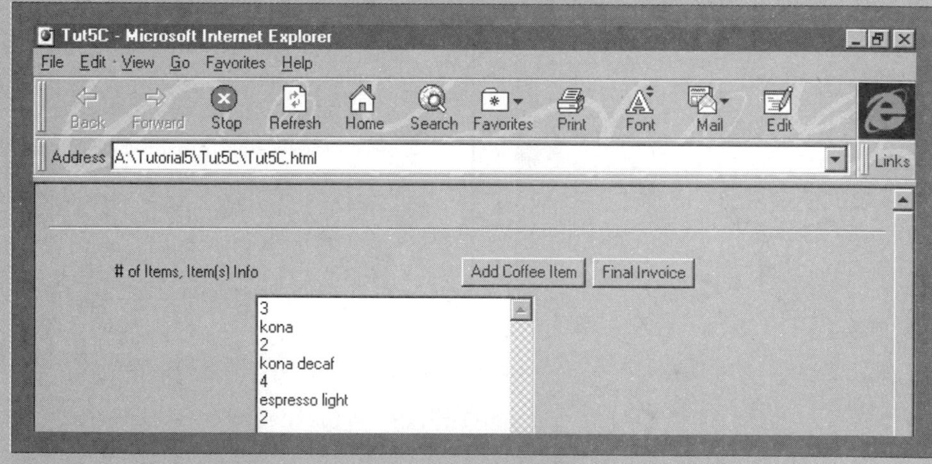

Figure 5-59: Entering coffee data

10 Click the **Final Invoice** button to see the invoice data. See Figure 5-60.

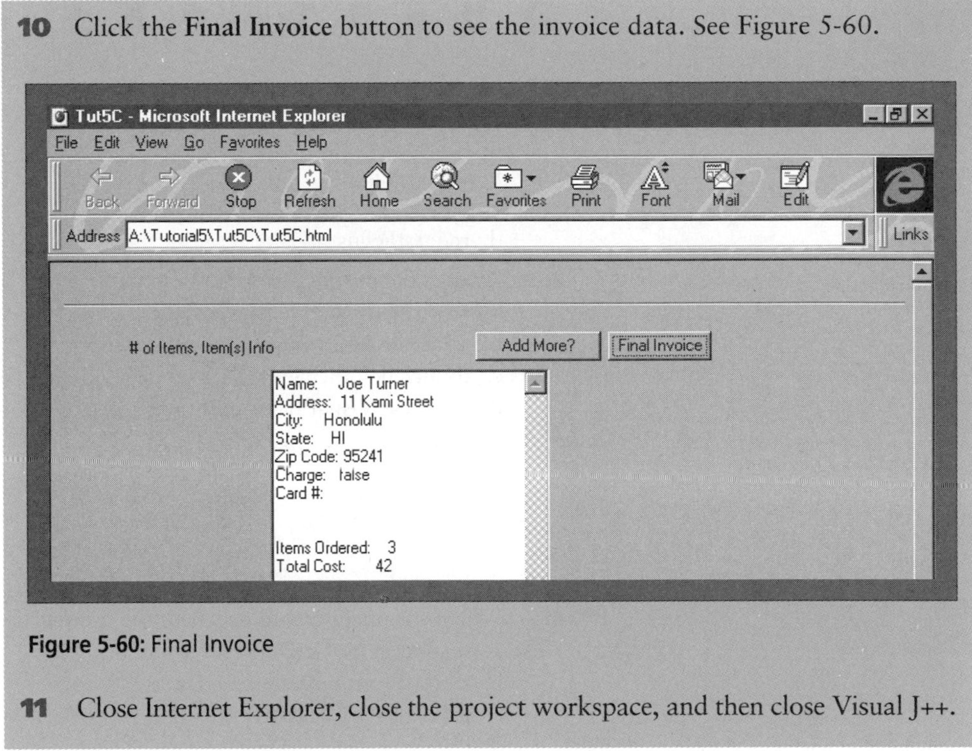

Figure 5-60: Final Invoice

11 Close Internet Explorer, close the project workspace, and then close Visual J++.

Your applet works better now. Now you can either take a break or complete the end-of-lesson questions and exercises.

SUMMARY

- The requestFocus method is used to position the insertion point in a text GUI component, such as a text field.
- Java import statements give you access to predefined objects, like Strings and GUI elements.
- When there is more than one button on a form, your action method must define what occurs when each button is clicked.
- The String method indexOf takes a character argument and returns the numeric position of the first instance it finds of that character in the String. If the character is not in the String, the method returns a value of -1.
- There are two sub methods. The first method takes only one int argument and returns a String from that int position to the end of the String. This method cuts off the front of the String. The second method uses two arguments—a beginning index and an ending index—so if you use 0 as the beginning index, you can ignore the end of the String.
- Do not make the user enter information that the program can generate automatically.

QUESTIONS

1. What method places the insertion point in a text component?
   a. indexOf
   b. subString
   c. getFocus
   d. requestFocus
2. What is the purpose of the import statement?
   a. to access predefined Java objects
   b. to access operating system functions
   c. to include other files that you developed in your project
   d. to access Visual Basic programs
3. What method is responsible for responding to an event?
   a. init
   b. getAction
   c. action
   d. respond
4. Which statement would be true if the user clicks a GetData button?
   a. if (Button == GetData)
   b. if (thisEvent.target == GetData)
   c. if (GetData.Clicked())
   d. if (Clicked == GetData)
5. What statement deletes a GUI element from the applet?
   a. delete
   b. hide
   c. invisible
   d. remove
6. Which of the following statements replaces the numeric character 1 with the capital letter A?
   a. myString.replace('1','A');
   b. myString.Replace('1','A');
   c. myString.Replace("1","A");
   d. myString.replace("A","1");
7. Which String method removes white space characters from the beginning and end of a String?
   a. deleteWhiteSpace
   b. trim
   c. cut
   d. condense
8. Rewrite the AddCustData pseudocode shown in Figure 5-48 using a do while loop.
9. Write the Java code for Question 8.
10. Rewrite the AddCoffData pseudocode shown in Figure 5-54 using a while loop.
11. Write the Java code for Question 10.

EXERCISES

1. Write on paper the code for an applet that uses the Coffees class and the Coffees.java file to allow the user to get information about the different coffee products. The user should enter only the coffee name into a text field, click an Information button, and then the text area should display the description of that product.
2. Open the Tut5C.java, Coffees.java, Customer.java, and Tut5C.html files from the Tut5C folder, and save them with the same filenames in the Exercise2C folder inside the Exercises folder in the Tutorial5 folder on your Student Disk. Change both for loops to while loops.
3. Open the Tut5C.java, Coffees.java, Customer.java, and Tut5C.html files from the Tut5C folder, and save them with the same filenames in the Exercise3C folder inside the Exercises folder in the Tutorial5 folder on your Student Disk. Change both for loops to do while loops.
4. Ronald Kim needs to produce a monthly sales report for the four sales regions of Cuddly Toys Inc. Each region sends him a total sales figure bimonthly. Write the code for a nested loop applet using one for loop and one while loop. Include the following GUI elements: one label, two buttons (Accept Data and Show Report), and one text area. The insertion point should be positioned when the applet starts, and the label should read "Enter regions, starting with one". The applet should have the user enter all 8 numbers (two values from four regions) all at one time, separated by line returns. Save the applet as Toys.java in the Exercise4C folder in the Exercises folder in the Tutorial5 folder on your Student Disk.
5. Write the code for an applet that converts dates like 6/7/99 to June 7, 1999. Include two text fields—input and output—and one button named Convert. If the user enters an invalid value, the Output area should display an error message. Do not try to keep track of leap years. Save the applet as Dates.java in the Exercise5C folder in the Exercises folder in the Tutorial5 folder on your Student Disk.
6. Write the code for an applet that converts hours, minutes, and seconds into total seconds. The input will look like: HR:MIN:SEC. There should be two text fields—input and output—and one button named Convert. If the user enters an invalid value, the output area should display an error message. Use if and if else statements to determine if the values are valid. Save the applet as Hours.java in the Exercise6C folder in the Exercises folder in the Tutorial5 folder on your Student Disk.
7. Write the code for an applet that converts yards, feet, and inches to metric values. The input will look like: YARDS:FEET:INCHES. There should be two text fields—input and output—and one button named Convert. If the user enters an invalid value, the output area should display an error message. An invalid value in inches is greater than 12, and an invalid value in feet is greater than three. Save the applet as Yards.java in the Exercise7C folder in the Exercises folder in the Tutorial5 folder on your Student Disk.
8. Write the code for an applet that takes a String with one or more words and creates a secret code by first converting all the letters to uppercase, and then assigning a number for each letter, such as A=1, B=2, ... Z=26. There should be one text area and one button named Show code. The user should enter one word per line. Save the applet as Words.java in the Exercise8C folder in the Exercises folder in the Tutorial5 folder on your Student Disk.

9. Natalie Zubinsky is the manager of a book store. She wants you to write the code for an applet that will help her give information to customers about books in her store. Write an applet that uses a Book class with the following data fields: title, author, year, and price. It should include the following methods: empty constructor, toString, and changeFieldValues. The changeFieldValues method should change the other data fields based on the title. Use any four book titles that you want. Write a user interface class that has one text area, and one button named Find Book. When a user clicks the Find Book button, all the information on that book should display in the text area. If the title is not in stock, display the message "There is no information on *BookTitle.*" Save the applet as Books.java in the Exercise9C folder in the Exercises folder in the Tutorial5 folder on your Student Disk.

10. Joey Johnson is the manager of a sporting goods store. He wants you to write the code for an applet that will help him give information to customers about equipment in his store. Write an applet that uses a SportingGoods class with the following data fields: name, sport, and price. It should include the following methods: empty constructor, toString, and changeFieldValues. The changeFieldValues method should change the other data fields based on the name. Use any four pieces of equipment that you want. Write a user interface class that has one text area, and one button named Find Item. When a user clicks the Find Item button, all the information on that item should be displayed in the text area. If the equipment is not in stock, display the message "There is no information on *name.*" Save the applet as Sports.java in the Exercise10C folder in the Exercises folder in the Tutorial5 folder on your Student Disk.

TUTORIAL

6

Understanding Arrays and Files

Planning Memory Usage for the Order System

case ▶ Maria is pleased with your progress on the Koffee Koncoctions order system. You added loops that allow the input of multiple orders and operators to change information in the orders. Maria told you today that Koffee Koncoctions will expand its product line soon so the order system must support additional products. You will change the order system to accommodate more than two items, to separate the methods from the objects, and to store the orders as text files so they can be sent to the shipping department. You can use arrays and files to solve these problems.

In this tutorial you will modify the order program to use arrays and files so future modifications of the program will be much easier. When you complete these changes, Koffee Koncoctions will have an order entry program that uses both interactive and file input and output as well as array variables to facilitate the order processing.

LESSON A

objectives

In this lesson you will learn how to:

- Use logical data structures
- Determine when and how to use arrays and lists
- Use external memory methods
- Use files

Storing Data

Understanding Data Storage

Understanding Logical Data Structures

The processing of information on computers involves massive amounts of data manipulation. **Data manipulation** is any process that moves, alters, or uses data for information processing. The typical categories of data manipulation are modification of data items, retrieval of data items, and storage of data items. Computers are electronic devices, so all of these activities involve data retrieval from an electronic storage device. There are two types of sources, or media, for data storage. **Internal storage** is the main memory of the computer, as you learned in Tutorial 3. Internal memory is **transient**, which means that the memory is lost when the computer is turned off. This type of memory is called **volatile storage**. **External storage** is media that can hold data on devices separated from the main electronics of the computer. External storage uses technologies like CD-ROM, disk drives, tape drives, and optical discs to store data permanently. External storage does not rely on an electrical current to store the data so it is called **non-volatile storage**.

For example, when you enter a Java program, that program is stored in internal memory, or volatile memory. When you save your Java programs on your Student Disk, you transfer the data from the internal memory to a non-volatile storage device.

Many methods have been developed for the manipulation of data in both internal memory and external storage. During the development of these methods, the primary concern was for accuracy and efficiency. **Accuracy** is the assurance that the data you saved is what is actually saved in internal memory or external storage. **Efficiency** deals with the speed at which the stored data can be manipulated. One other criteria—maintenance of data storage—has evolved in the last 20 years. **Maintenance** is the amount of time required to keep a program functional after its development. With this added dimension, tradeoffs between efficiency and ease of maintenance must be balanced carefully.

Data that are stored on a computer system or manipulated by its central processor can be viewed in a physical or logical manner. When the physical view of data is considered, programmers often talk about memory addresses, directory structure implementation, tracks, sectors, and bytes. While this view of data processing is important, frequently systems programmers use languages that allow them to access data items at this physical level. More important to the application programmer is the logical view of data. The logical abstract view of data sees all data as lists of objects on which certain actions can be taken. For example, an accountant keeps the records of an organization so that its administration will know its financial health. This data can be thought of as lists of financial entries; each of which might be an object of several types. The list also is an object that can be manipulated by the methods acceptable in the accounting field. These lists of financial transactions can be processed to determine the net worth of an organization, the current outstanding accounts, as well as the debts. The logical view of data gives more attention to the elements that make up the data objects and the actions that can be performed on these objects, rather than on how the computer manipulates the information electronically. This is extremely important to application programmers who are interested in the functionality of the software they design, rather than on the hardware on which it resides.

Application programmers spend most of their time dealing in program design, so at some point in time the software design must be translated into code and the issues of physical data manipulation must be considered. Although the application programmer might never need to know exactly how data are moved—byte by byte—from the internal memory to the central processor, certain general characteristics of internal and external memory devices are important for developing efficient and effective programs.

Internal Data Storage Methods

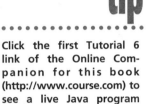

Click the first Tutorial 6 link of the Online Companion for this book (http://www.course.com) to see a live Java program that illustrates this topic.

You learned in Tutorial 3 that internal memory is that part of the computer where data are accessible immediately by the central processor. Internal memory can be thought of as the waiting room of a president's office. To get to the president—the central processor—all individuals must walk through the waiting room. The same concept is true for computers. Internal memory is wired electronically to the central processor in such a way that data travels directly from internal memory to the central processor. When you want to run a computer program, the program is loaded into internal memory and the central processor uses it directly from that location. This is the reason why you cannot run programs that use more internal memory than what is available on your system, unless you also have a system that allows external storage to act like internal memory. This type of processing is called **virtual memory**, and its concepts are beyond the scope of this book.

With internal memory, all data are stored at addressable locations. An **addressable location** is a position in the memory chips on the computer that has a coinciding binary address. In Tutorial 3 you learned that addresses are like mailboxes at a post office. The internal memory of a standard computer usually is broken into pieces called bytes. A **byte** is the amount of memory necessary to record one character of information electronically. Each byte has its own address. When data are stored in internal memory, they might need more than one byte, depending on the type of data that is stored. For example, a Java integer uses four bytes of internal memory storage. The language compilers and operating systems of most computers handle the information that determines the size of a given type so the programmer only needs to deal with the data as an integer or String, or whatever type is desired.

The primary concern in the manipulation of data in internal memory is efficiency and ease of program maintenance. In Tutorial 3 you learned how to name the memory locations of internal memory so they are easier to handle in your Java programs. Consider the following problem: You are a programmer for a medium-sized bank. You are working on a program that processes the transactions for savings accounts for every bank customer. Currently the bank has 3,000 customers and usually processes 1,000 savings transactions daily. You named all of the memory locations for each of the records separately, using the names transaction1, transaction2, etc. If you must plan for 1,000 daily transactions, then you must name 1,000 variables for these memory locations. If each transaction has three fields, then the required input code for these transactions might exceed 3,000 lines.

Maintaining this program would be extremely difficult because of its size. To solve this problem, you could consider internal memory as a series of bytes or even as a named location that uses a number of bytes based on the type of variable, which would allow the programmer to incorporate the larger object-named lists in the programming process. Then you could use a variable named savingsTransactions, which is a block of memory that holds 1,000 individual transactions. This type of storage would increase efficiency and reduce the amount of time necessary to maintain the program. The structure for accomplishing such manipulations of internal memory is called an **array**.

Understanding Arrays and Lists

An array can be logical or physical in form. Logically, an array is a list of objects that consist of the same type. For example, you can develop a list of coffee products because each coffee product is an object that consists of the same items with different values. Physically, an array is a block of internal memory that can be manipulated by using the name of the array variable and an index that indicates the item in the list you want to manipulate. The variable name of the array is called its **identifier**, and the indicator that points to the exact item in the array list is called its **index**. An array must have a name and an index. Usually the name of the array and the index are defined for a given array when it is named as a variable. The index usually must be an integer because it does not make sense to refer to a 1.5th item in a list.

For Koffee Koncoctions, the Coffees object consists of a name, flavor, color, cost per pound, and a flag to note if the coffee has caffeine. To define a list of coffee objects conceptually, you need to determine the name of the list object and the number of coffee objects that the list contains. The coffee list can be defined as *coffeeProducts : array of [10] coffees*, to represent a list object named coffeeProducts and an array that contains 10 different coffee products. This syntax is not Java code but pseudocode that is used in this lesson. The steps to follow to define an array are:

1. Determine the basic element of your list object. This element must be of the same type for all elements in the list, so, if the element is a Coffees object, then all elements in the list must be coffee products.
2. Determine how many elements to include in the list.
3. Determine a name for the list that is a variable name and is descriptive of the elements in the list.
4. Translate the list items and list name into Java code.

Figure 6-1 shows the logical view of the list of coffee products.

coffeeProducts Index	coffeeProducts Element
0	First coffee product
1	Second coffee product
2	Third coffee product
3	Fourth coffee product
4	Fifth coffee product
5	Sixth coffee product
6	Seventh coffee product
7	Eighth coffee product
8	Ninth coffee product
9	Tenth coffee product

Figure 6-1: Logical view of the coffees list

The physical view of the list looks the same as the logical view. The elements in the coffeeProducts list are stored together in memory as a block of data items with the name coffeeProducts, and the index is used by the Java compiler to determine which element to manipulate.

The index of an array is extremely important in accessing individual elements in the object. The manner in which a memory location is referenced is called **addressing**. To address a memory location does not mean that it is given a new physical binary address. The method for addressing an element in an array is the name of the array, followed by the index name. For example, you could access the fourth element in the coffeeProducts array with the identifier coffeeProducts[3]. If the element is a complex type like an object, you can specify the field you are interested in by using the standard notations for objects and then the array index. Notice that the *fourth* element in the array has an index of 3. Arrays usually are indexed beginning with the number zero so the compiler can determine the starting location of the element that is being addressed.

You might wonder how using an array helps the programmer and reduces the amount of code. In Tutorial 5 you learned about loops. If you named each of the 10 coffee products with separate variables and needed to change all of the cost values to 5.50, you would need 10 lines of code. Combining arrays and loops allows you to do the same task in the following way:

```
i = 0;
while (i <= 9)
{
  coffeeProducts.cost[i] = 5.50;
  i++;
};
```

By using an array, you reduce the amount of code from 10 lines to five lines, including the opening and closing braces. However, these five lines would work for any array size—10, 20, 3,000, or more. As the numbers get larger, the reduction of lines of code is obvious.

These examples of arrays included arrays of one dimension. A **one-dimensional array**, or a **list**, is an array in which there are rows of elements that can be addressed by a single index. Arrays also can include an object that consists of more than one dimension. For example, in the bank example, suppose you need to develop a data structure that holds savings transactions for each branch office of the bank. You could use one index to indicate the branch and the second index to indicate the element in that branch's array. This is called a **two-dimensional array** because there are two indices for locating a given element in the array—an array can have as many dimensions as needed. Arrays that have more than one index are called **multi-dimensional arrays**, or **tables**. Typically the only constraint on the array size is the amount of internal memory that is available.

The size of main memory can be a constraint in programming. Sometimes you need to develop lists that cannot fit into internal memory all at the same time. When this problem occurs, you must consider external storage devices for a solution.

Understanding External Memory Methods

External memory is any storage device that is not directly wired to the central processor. External devices usually consist of non-volatile storage facilities, although this is not absolutely required. The difference between the technology of internal memory and external storage is that internal memory uses a constant power supply to refresh the information stored on electronic chips, whereas external devices use other technologies such as magnets and lasers to encode the data on the device. While electric power is needed when the data are moved to and from these devices, the methods they incorporate ensure that the data will be retained after the power to the computer is turned off. One of the most common external memory devices is a disk drive. Disk drives come in many sizes and types—you are familiar with removable media drives such as your 3.5" floppy drive and nonremovable drives such as a hard disk. Although the size, speed, and portability of the data might be affected by your selection of a fixed over removable disk media, the manner of storing data is essentially the same.

While the electronics of the disk drive are interesting, most application programmers do not deal with data at the hardware level. Logical data organization units often are used for this purpose. The typical logical units of data storage from the smallest to largest are byte, field, record, and file. Application programmers frequently access data at each of these levels.

Remember that data stored on external devices must pass through internal memory in order to be processed by the central processor by moving data from the external storage device to a buffer and then to internal memory. A **buffer** is a holding area that is used by the computer hardware to speed up data access. Most computer systems maintain buffers for each of the physical devices that can receive output or provide input to the central processor.

When you get your Java programs to compile and execute properly, you probably do not want to turn off the computer and rewrite the program the next day. To have the program available to you at a later date, you save the program on your Student Disk, which is a standard use of an external storage device. This process, however, deals only with the file unit of logical data organization. As you will learn in this tutorial, there are many other ways of accessing and storing data in files on an external device.

Understanding File Concepts

A **file** that is contained on an external device is really a sequence of data bits and bytes for encoding the desired information. A file is the most frequently used level of logical data organization, although you usually do not work with the file all at once. The use of buffering, as described previously, allows you to use files as easily as memory locations in internal memory. For this reason, Java refers to a file as a stream. A **stream** is a sequence of characters moving from one place to another. A buffer is the temporary storage area for external data, whereas a stream is the series of data bytes that move through the buffer. In data processing, the use of a file as a supplement for internal memory requires four basic actions: open, close, get, and put. These terms are not Java language constructs but general terms used to describe the actions that are performed on a file.

You can think of a computer file as a physical file cabinet. You have lots of information stored in that cabinet that is important but you would never work on all of it at once. To use a file, you complete the following process:

1. Open the file drawer where the information is stored.
2. Scan the file folders to find the specific file you want to use.
3. Remove the file folder from the file drawer.
4. Close the file drawer.
5. Work on the information you retrieved.

When you finish using the file, you perform a similar set of steps to return the file to its proper place in the cabinet. In this example you can see the four basic actions that are performed on files. In computer programming, once a file is opened the processing of data to and from that file is not unlike other processing that you have done.

So far, you have treated files as if they are all alike. In reality, most computers store several different types of files. The two most common types of files on a personal computer are text files and binary files. A **text file** is a file that has all of its information stored as ASCII characters on the external device. **ASCII** stands for the American Standard Code for Information Interchange, and it represents characters by use of a code of eight units or bits. Your Java programs are one example of a text file. Sometimes it is more beneficial or even necessary to store data in binary format. **Binary files** are files that have taken data directly from internal memory and stored them in the exact same way as each of the corresponding bytes. Binary storage usually uses an eight-bit code because bytes in internal memory are made up of that number of bits. One example of a binary file might be a computer game that you play frequently. If the name of that file has an extension of .exe or .com, then it is a binary file that allows the computer to load the program quickly without interpreting the bytes from the file into internal memory. When you compile a program, a similar binary file is stored on the external device, which allows the user to run the program without starting the development environment software. Java is an interpreted language, which means that the files that are generated in the compile and build process are a mixture of compiled and interpreted types.

In Lesson B you will explore how Java allows the manipulation of internal data as arrays and external data as files. However, Java applets that are developed for use with browsers place significant constraints on the location of files that can be read or written. For this reason, in Lesson C you will learn about stand-alone Java programming and embedding an applet into a stand-alone program so you will have much more flexibility in the use of files.

Now you can either take a break or complete the end-of-lesson questions and exercises.

SUMMARY

- Internal storage is the memory that is accessible immediately by the central processor. Internal storage is called volatile storage because data are lost when power to the computer is turned off.
- External storage includes the various devices that do not rely on an electrical current in order to retain the data. This type of storage is called non-volatile and includes fixed drives, removable drives, CD-ROMs, and optical discs.
- The internal memory of the computer can be viewed from a physical as well as a logical perspective. The physical perspective deals with how the hardware actually maintains the data while the logical perspective addresses the functional use of the data stored.
- An array is a structure that names a block of internal memory with one variable name while it allows this block to store lists of elements that are of the same type.
- The three components of an array are its type, name, and size. All elements in an array must be of the same type, and the size of the array defines maximum the number of elements in the array.
- A specific element of an array can be accessed with a variable that includes the name of the array and the index of the element that is desired.
- Indices of arrays must be integer types and the index of a given array is in the range of one less than the array size.
- One-dimensional arrays usually are called lists. Arrays that make use of more than one index to access a given element are called multi-dimensional arrays or tables.
- A file is a structure for storing data on an external device so data are not lost when the power to the computer is turned off.
- File structures involve both a physical and logical view of the storage process. The physical view is concerned with how the hardware stores and organizes data on a specific device. The logical view of a file is the records and fields that make up the information in the file.
- The typical activities that are performed on files are open, close, get, and put.

QUESTIONS

1. The internal memory of the computer is called __________ storage.
a. volatile
b. non-volatile

2. External memory is called __________ storage.
a. volatile
b. non-volatile

3. Which of the following is not an external storage device?
a. CD-ROM
b. removable disk drives
c. random access memory (RAM)
d. optical discs

4. A(n) __________ is a block of memory that contains several data elements but only one variable name.
a. file
b. array
c. database
d. boolean expression

5. The _________ of an array specifies the element that the program accesses at a given point in time.
   a. index
   b. variable name
   c. memory address

6. Arrays that use more than one index to specify a given element are called _________.
   a. one-dimensional
   b. files
   c. external data storage
   d. multi-dimensional

7. Files are logical structures that consist of _________ and _________.
   a. names, indices
   b. records, fields
   c. names, locations

8. Which of the following are functions needed by file processing?
   a. open
   b. close
   c. get data
   d. all of the above

9. A(n) _________ file is stored exactly like it was created in internal memory.
   a. text
   b. ASCII
   c. binary
   d. internal

10. A(n) _________ is the channel or temporary holding area for data as it passes from an external device to internal memory.
   a. array
   b. variable
   c. buffer
   d. byte

EXERCISES

Use your knowledge of pseudocode from the previous tutorials to complete the following Exercises.

1. Write the pseudocode for an array that holds 50 integers in a variable named intList.
2. Write the pseudocode for the statement that could be used for setting the fifth element of the array in Exercise 1 to 222.
3. Given an array variable named Object that is defined as an array of characters, what identifier could be used to access the third character of the array?
4. James Lynch wants to develop a program that reads a list of customers from a file and stores this list in reverse order in another file. Write the pseudocode to accomplish this task. You do not need to use Java code in this exercise.
5. Kim Kahuala wants to store a list of numbers that are taken from a file in an array. These numbers are of the type int. Write the pseudocode that opens a file and reads these numbers into an array. You do not need to use Java code in this exercise.
6. Laura Lowery wants to compute the average of a list of numbers that is stored in an array named numList. There are 25 numbers in the array. Write the pseudocode that performs this calculation using a loop structure. You do not need to use Java code in this exercise.
7. List the logical steps you would perform to retrieve a file from a physical file cabinet.

LESSON B

objectives

In this lesson you will learn how to:

- **Design and code one-dimensional arrays**
- **Design a program with a one-dimensional array**
- **Design and code two-dimensional arrays**
- **Design a program with a two-dimensional array**

Using Arrays

Changing the Order System to Use Arrays

Designing and Coding One-Dimensional Arrays

Now you are ready to use arrays to increase the number of coffee products that can be ordered without increasing the complexity of the code. You also will store the orders in an array into files for the shipping department.

Arrays are the primary method for dealing with blocks of memory locations with a single variable name. The benefit of array processing is that several records can be kept in memory at the same time without a large number of variables or lines of code.

Java arrays are implemented by storing the elements of the array next to each other in memory. Using this type of memory variable allows the system software to retrieve any given element from the structure by taking the base address and adding a number to that address that is equivalent to the element's size, multiplied by the index of the desired element. Defining a Java array is not a difficult task—you name the array, determine the type of element that will be stored in the array, and then determine the size of the array. For example, a variable named numberOne could be defined in Java as an integer as *int numberOne;*. You can create an array, or list of 10 integers, named numbers, using the following code: *int numbers [ ] = new int [10];*. The general format for the Java array structure is *<Array Type> <Array Name> [ ] = new <Array Type> [<Size of Array>];*. Keep the following requirements in mind when creating an array:

- All elements in the array must be of the same type.
- The size of the array must be an integer literal or constant.
- The order of elements in the array has no significance unless you program the array as an ordered list. Each element is as significant as the other.

You can reference the previous array by using the array name with a corresponding index that determines the element that will be accessed. If you want to do something with the third integer in the array named numbers, address this element using the following identifier: *numbers[2]*. Remember, to use the third element in the array, you use the index of 2 because Java arrays begin with an index of 0 so the element with the index of 2 is really the third element in the array. The format for array identifiers is: *<array name> [<index>]*.

All of the actions that you performed on simple variables can be performed on array elements because they are simple variables as well. So, if you want to set the third element in the numbers array to 400, you would use the following command: *numbers[2] = 400;*.

When you learned to use simple variables and property variables for classes, you used a constructor method. The constructor method in Java assigns initial values to the property variables of that class. You can perform a similar task on arrays by using loops. A simple while loop that initializes the integer array to zero is:

```
arrayIndex = 0;
while (arrayIndex < 10)
{
  numbers [arrayIndex] = 0;
  arrayIndex++;
};
```

This simple loop sets all the components of numbers to the value 0, using the following steps:

1. Set the simple variable arrayIndex to 0.
2. If arrayIndex = 10, then stop.
3. Move to the element in numbers noted by arrayIndex, and set it to 0.
4. Increment arrayIndex by 1.
5. Repeat Steps 2 through 4 until the while statement causes the loop to terminate.

Now you are ready to design programs that use arrays.

Designing a Program with an Array

Before working on the order system, you will practice using arrays using the Invest.java applet on your Student Disk. The Invest.java applet perform tasks in the following manner:

1. Sets investment and interest rate amounts
2. Displays the heading information for the investment program
3. Computes the value at the end of the current month
4. Displays the computed value
5. Increments thisMonth
6. Repeats Steps 3 through 5 until the final month

In general, you should avoid mixing processing and output. However, because you have only a simple variable in this program, there is no other way to produce the information. You can use an array to store the calculated amounts for each month and then display the results after all of the calculations are done. By using element 0 as the original investment, the index of each element corresponds to the month that the investment equals the stored value. Figure 6-2 shows the pseudocode for the Invest.java applet.

```
set thisMonth to 0
set array[thisMonth] to investment
increment thisMonth
repeat until thisMonth is greater than final month
        set element in array to previous element plus interest
        increment thisMonth

display investment report heading
set thisMonth to 1
repeat until thisMonth is greater than final month
        display value of current array element
        increment thisMonth
```

Figure 6-2: Invest.java pseudocode

You will code this program all at once in a new Java file because it is a small program.

To create the Invest.java program:

1. Start Visual J++ and close the project workspace, if necessary.
2. Click **File** on the menu bar, and then click **New** to open the New dialog box. Click the **Files** tab and then double-click **Java Source File** to create a new Java source file.
3. Save the file as **Invest.java** in the Invest folder in the Tutorial6 folder on your Student Disk.
4. Type the heading information shown in Figure 6-3 to identify the file, import the necessary Java packages, and set up the class heading for Invest.java.

type this code

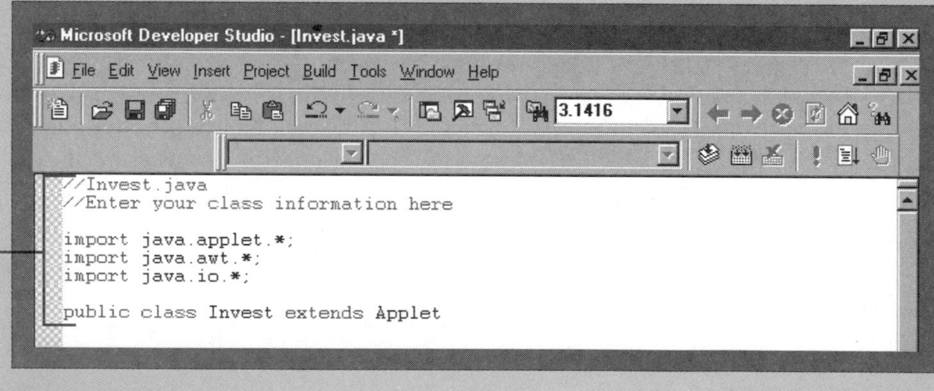

Figure 6-3: Heading code for Invest.java

5 Press the **Enter** key, and then type the property variable information shown in Figure 6-4. This code contains an array that will hold the values of the investment for each month.

type this code

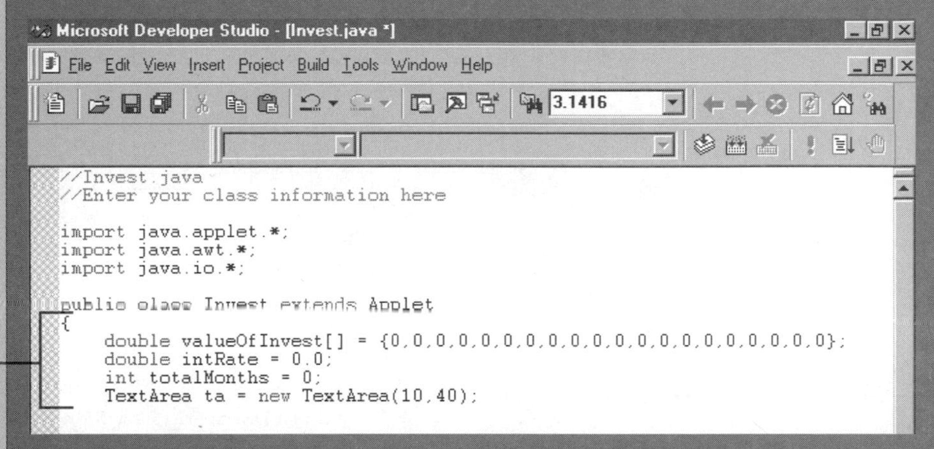

Figure 6-4: Property variable code for Invest.java

6 Press the **Enter** key twice, and then type the code shown in Figure 6-5 for initializing the variables that will be used in the program. Notice that you entered a statement to compute the value of another interest rate amount, which is the monthly interest rate. The other tasks performed by this code set up the value of the initial investment and the number of months.

type this code

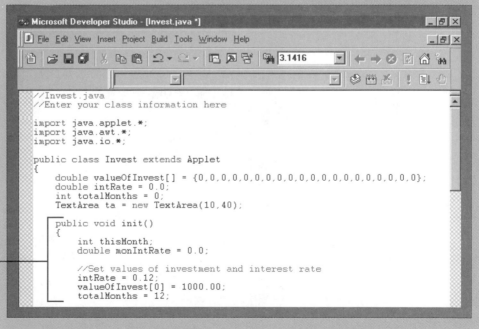

```
//Invest.java
//Enter your class information here

import java.applet.*;
import java.awt.*;
import java.io.*;

public class Invest extends Applet
{
    double valueOfInvest[] = {0,0,0,0,0,0,0,0,0,0,0,0,0,0,0,0,0,0,0,0,0,0,0};
    double intRate = 0.0;
    int totalMonths = 0;
    TextArea ta = new TextArea(10,40);

    public void init()
    {
        int thisMonth;
        double monIntRate = 0.0;

        //Set values of investment and interest rate
        intRate = 0.12;
        valueOfInvest[0] = 1000.00;
        totalMonths = 12;
```

Figure 6-5: Invest.java init method code

7 Press the **Enter** key twice, and then type the code shown in Figure 6-6 for calculating the monthly values and storing them in an array. This task uses

a while loop that implements the pseudocode shown in Figure 6-2. Notice that the array is being manipulated so that the 0th element is the initial investment and elements 1 through 12 hold the computed values for the month corresponding to the element index.

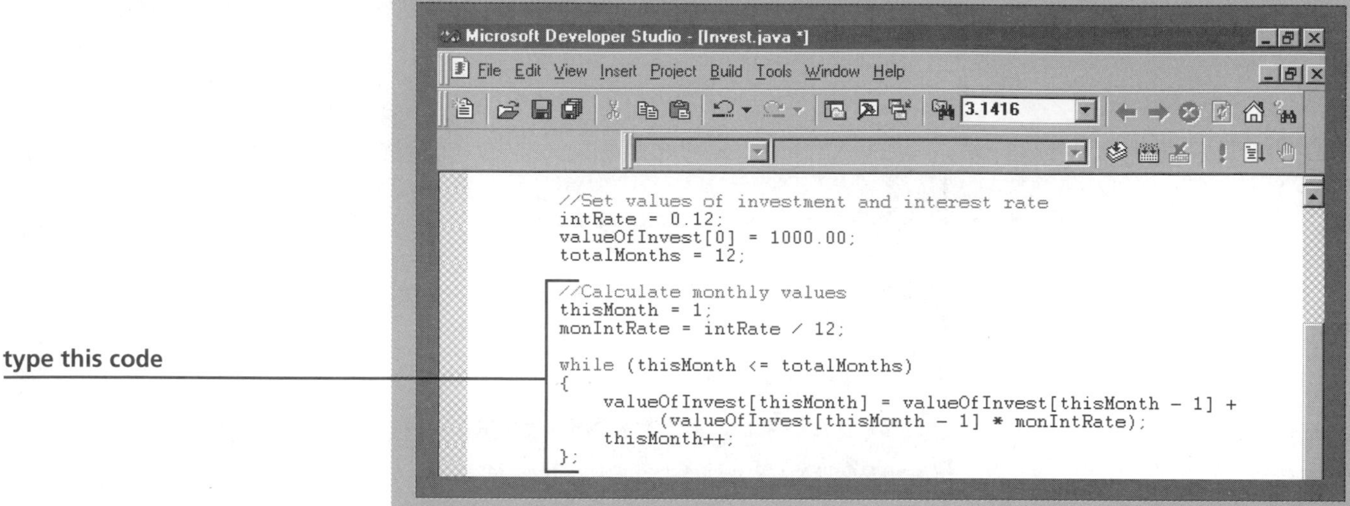

type this code

```
//Set values of investment and interest rate
intRate = 0.12;
valueOfInvest[0] = 1000.00;
totalMonths = 12;

//Calculate monthly values
thisMonth = 1;
monIntRate = intRate / 12;

while (thisMonth <= totalMonths)
{
    valueOfInvest[thisMonth] = valueOfInvest[thisMonth - 1] +
        (valueOfInvest[thisMonth - 1] * monIntRate);
    thisMonth++;
};
```

Figure 6-6: Calculation code for Invest.java

8 Press the **Enter** key twice, and then type the code shown in Figure 6-7 for displaying the results of the calculation. The heading information displays once and then uses a loop to display the values that are stored in the investment array.

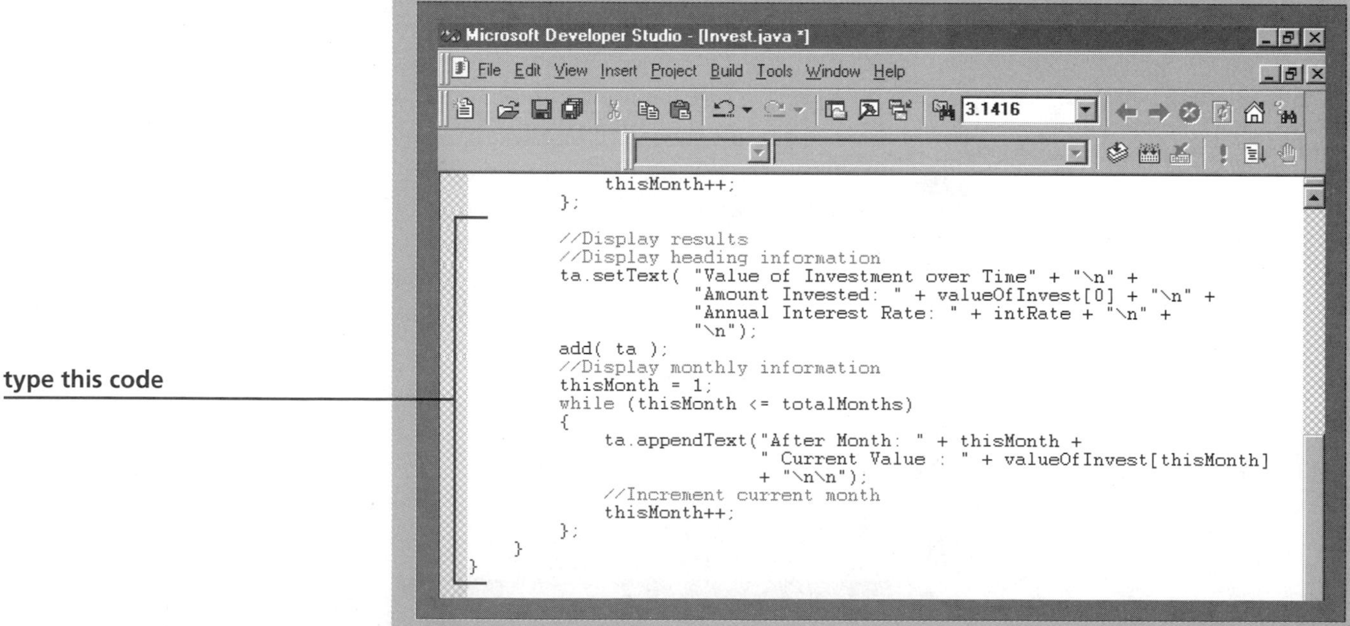

type this code

```
    thisMonth++;
};

//Display results
//Display heading information
ta.setText( "Value of Investment over Time" + "\n" +
            "Amount Invested: " + valueOfInvest[0] + "\n" +
            "Annual Interest Rate: " + intRate + "\n" +
            "\n");
add( ta );
//Display monthly information
thisMonth = 1;
while (thisMonth <= totalMonths)
{
    ta.appendText("After Month: " + thisMonth +
                  " Current Value : " + valueOfInvest[thisMonth]
                  + "\n\n");
    //Increment current month
    thisMonth++;
};
    }
}
```

Figure 6-7: Output code for Invest.java

9 Click the **Save** button on the Standard toolbar to save your changes.

Now you have entered the array investment program into a Java file. After you save the file, the file can be used at any time. Next you will build and execute the program.

To build and execute the program:

1. Click the **Build** button on the Build toolbar, and then click the **Yes** button to build the program in a default project workspace.

   HELP? Correct any syntax errors the compiler finds in your program. Refer to the previous figures to check your typing. After each set of corrections, save the file and build it again. If you still have problems, ask your instructor for help.

2. Change the HTML file on your Student Disk by clicking **Project** on the menu bar, and then clicking **Settings.** Click the **Debug** tab, click the **Category** list arrow, and then click **Browser.** Click the **Use parameters from HTML page** option button, and then type **Invest.html** in the HTML page text box. Click the **OK** button.
3. Click the **Execute Program** button on the Build toolbar, type **Invest** in the Class file name text box, and then click the **OK** button to execute the program. See Figure 6-8.

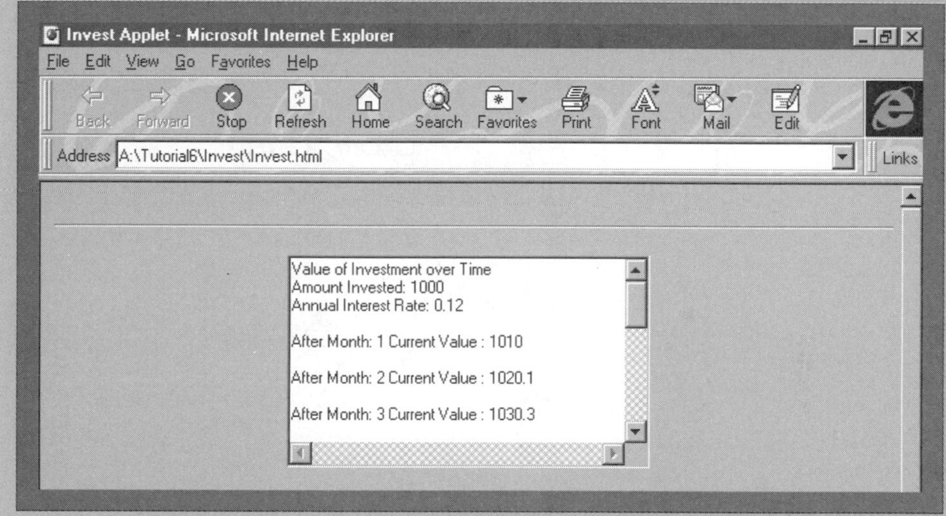

Figure 6-8: Invest.java running in Internet Explorer

4. Close Internet Explorer and then close the project workspace and all document windows.

Notice that this output looks very similar to the program you created in Tutorial 5. You did not change the logic of the program, but only how the information is stored in memory and the method of displaying that information.

Now you are ready to change the order system to use files and arrays so customers can order more than two items in a single order. The calculation and output code also needs to be changed. The requirements Maria gave you are that the Order object should contain up to five coffee products in a single order, and that the coffee pounds should be an array that coincides with the coffee products array.

You will create a new Order.java program (instead of using a file on your Student Disk) because there are a lot of changes in the program.

To create the Order.java program:

1 Create a new Java source file and then save it as **Order.java** in the Order folder in the Tutorial6 folder on your Student Disk.

2 Type the heading information shown in Figure 6-9.

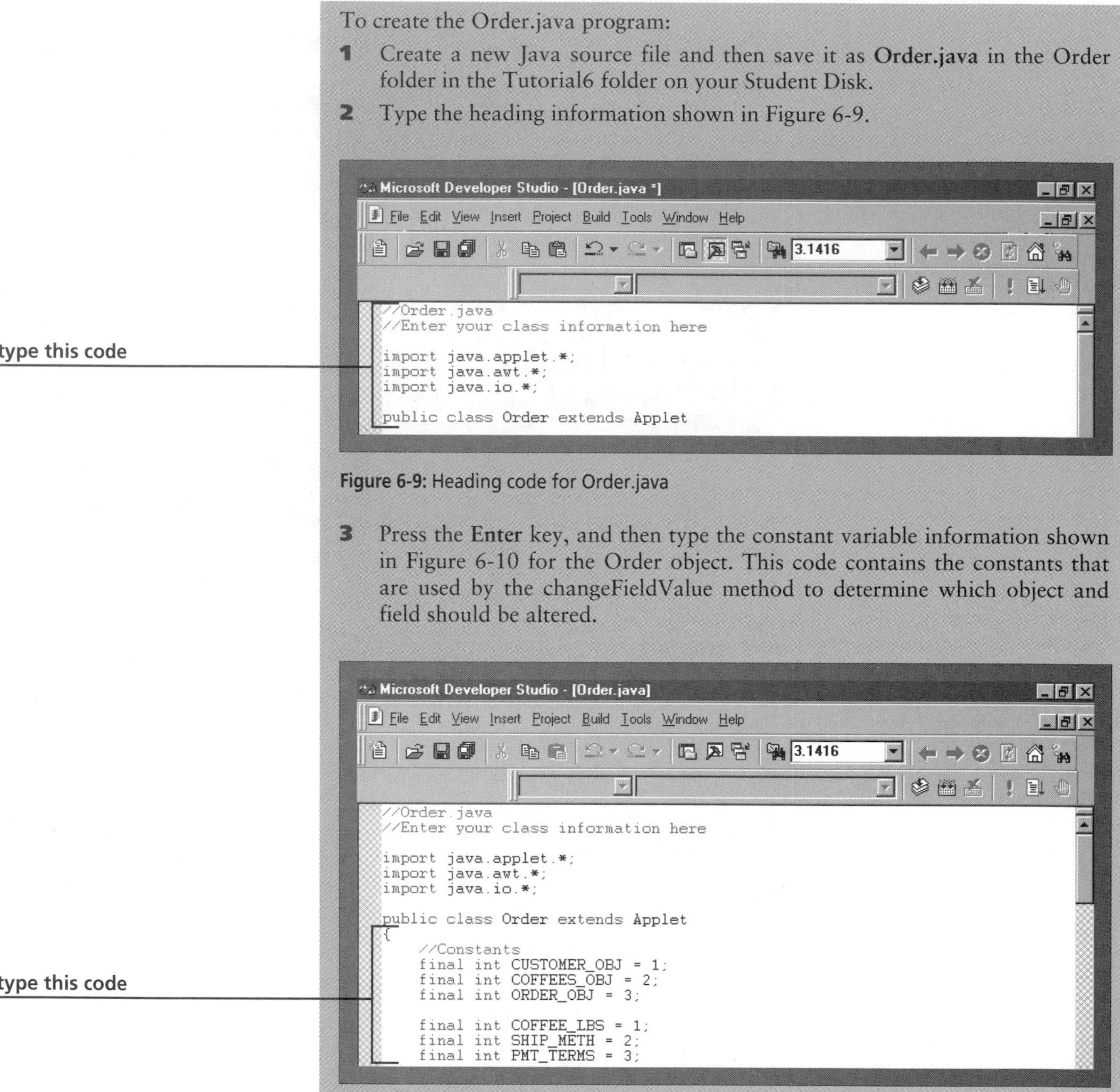

Figure 6-9: Heading code for Order.java

3 Press the **Enter** key, and then type the constant variable information shown in Figure 6-10 for the Order object. This code contains the constants that are used by the changeFieldValue method to determine which object and field should be altered.

Microsoft Developer Studio - [Order.java]

type this code

```
//Order.java
//Enter your class information here

import java.applet.*;
import java.awt.*;
import java.io.*;

public class Order extends Applet
{
    //Constants
    final int CUSTOMER_OBJ = 1;
    final int COFFEES_OBJ = 2;
    final int ORDER_OBJ = 3;

    final int COFFEE_LBS = 1;
    final int SHIP_METH = 2;
    final int PMT_TERMS = 3;
```

Figure 6-10: Object constants for Order.java

4 Press the **Enter** key twice, and then type the code shown in Figure 6-11 for the property variables for the Order object. Now the coffee products and the quantities are coded as array variables.

type this code

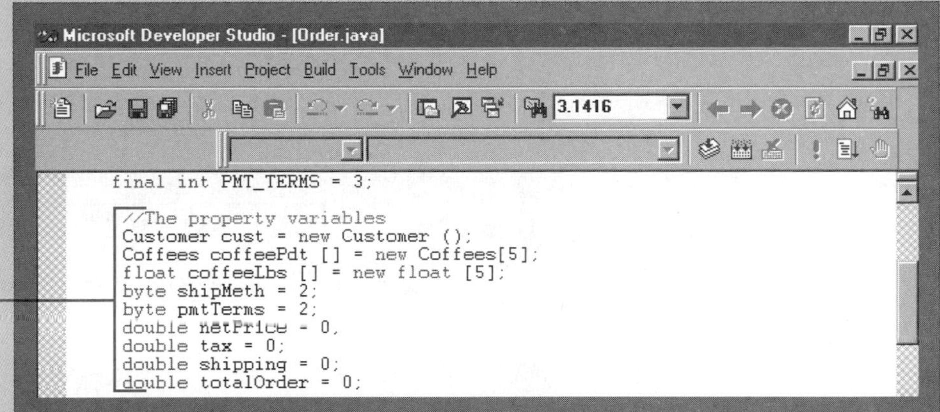

Microsoft Developer Studio - [Order.java]
File Edit View Insert Project Build Tools Window Help
3.1416
final int PMT_TERMS = 3;
//The property variables
Customer cust = new Customer ();
Coffees coffeePdt [] = new Coffees[5];
float coffeeLbs [] = new float [5];
byte shipMeth = 2;
byte pmtTerms = 2;
double netPrice = 0;
double tax = 0;
double shipping = 0;
double totalOrder = 0;

Figure 6-11: Object properties code for Order.java

5 Press the **Enter** key twice, and then type the code shown in Figure 6-12 for the constructor method for the Order object. This code contains the initialization steps that execute when the Order object is used with the new command. This constructor has a loop to initialize the values of the coffeePdt and coffeeLbs arrays.

type this code

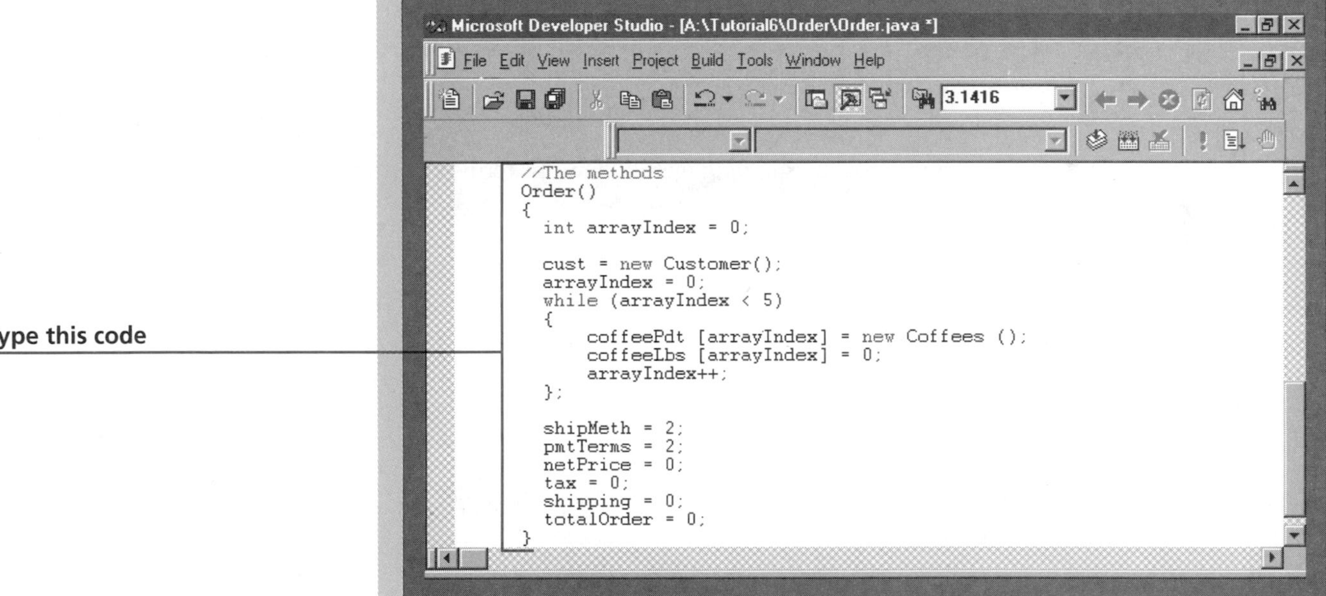

Figure 6-12: Object constant methods code for Order.java

HELP? The int arrayIndex = 0, and arrayIndex = 0; lines shown in Figure 6-12 are two different ways of initializing the array index to zero.

6 Press the **Enter** key twice, and then type the code shown in Figure 6-13 for the first two changeFieldValue methods. The first method sets the fields in the coffee product array. For this reason, an index of the coffee product that is to be changed is passed in the argument list. The second method deals with customer objects and changes the value of the customer fields.

type this code

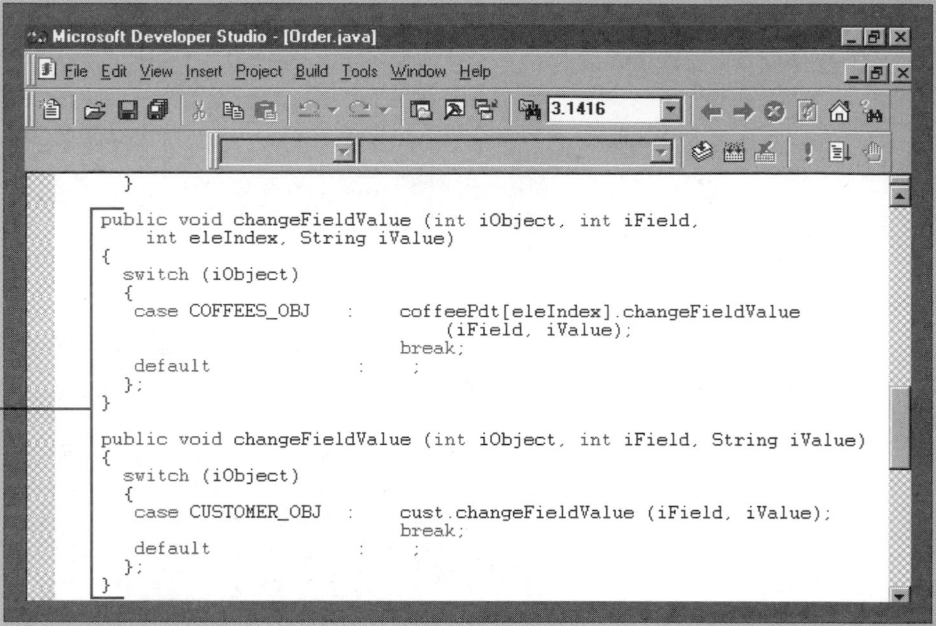

```
}

public void changeFieldValue (int iObject, int iField,
    int eleIndex, String iValue)
{
  switch (iObject)
  {
   case COFFEES_OBJ   :     coffeePdt[eleIndex].changeFieldValue
                                (iField, iValue);
                            break;
   default              :    ;
  };
}

public void changeFieldValue (int iObject, int iField, String iValue)
{
  switch (iObject)
  {
   case CUSTOMER_OBJ  :     cust.changeFieldValue (iField, iValue);
                            break;
   default              :    ;
  };
}
```

Figure 6-13: First two changeFieldValue methods code

7 Press the **Enter** key twice, and then type the code shown in Figure 6-14 for the second two changeFieldValue methods. The first method changes the quantity ordered in the appropriate array element. The second method assigns values for the shipping method and the terms of payment in the Order object.

type this code

```
    };
  }

  public void changeFieldValue (int iObject, int iField,
      int eleIndex, float iValue)
  {
    if (iObject == ORDER_OBJ)
    {
      switch (iField)
      {
        case COFFEE_LBS    :    coffeeLbs[eleIndex]=  iValue;
                                break;
        default            :    ;
      };
    };
  }

  public void changeFieldValue (int iObject, int iField, byte iValue)
  {
    if (iObject == ORDER_OBJ)
    {
      switch (iField)
      {
        case SHIP_METH     :    shipMeth = iValue;
                                break;
        case PMT_TERMS     :    pmtTerms = iValue;
                                break;
        default            :    ;
      };
    };
  }
}
```

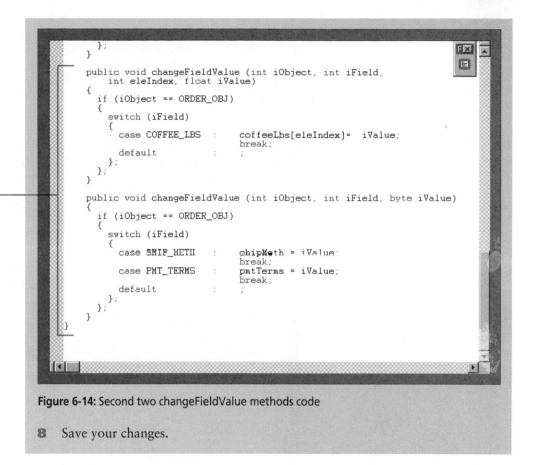

Figure 6-14: Second two changeFieldValue methods code

8 Save your changes.

You need to add the Coffees.java and Customer.java files from your Student Disk into the project workspace. You will build the program first to create a default project workspace, and then add the files. You might see errors in the Output window when you build the file because the object files are missing from the workspace.

To add the Coffees.java and Customer.java files into the project workspace:

1 Build the project in a default project workspace. You might see errors in the Output window because the object files are missing from the project workspace.

2 Click **Project** on the menu bar, point to **Add To Project**, and then click **Files**. If necessary, change to the Order folder on your Student Disk, and then double-click the **Coffees.java** file to add it to the project workspace.

3 Repeat Step 2 to add the **Customer.java** file to the project workspace.

4 Click **Build** on the menu bar, and then click **Rebuild All.**

HELP? If the Output window reports errors, check your typing in the Order.java file, and then click the Save All button on the Standard toolbar and then rebuild the files. If you still have trouble, ask your instructor for help.

5 Close the project workspace and all document windows.

You have now entered a new order object program. However, this program is not an applet so you must use another program to test it. A program called OrderTest.java is included in the Order folder in the Tutorial6 folder on your Student Disk for this purpose. You will build the program to create a default project workspace, and then add the object files to the project workspace.

To run the OrderTest.java program:

1 Open the **OrderTest.java** file from the Order folder in the Tutorial6 folder on your Student Disk.

2 Scroll down to the code shown in Figure 6-15. This section of code stores values in the Order object that use an array for holding the coffee information. You will not make any changes to the code, but you should study the code to see how it stores values in arrays.

```
//Set up values in Order object to check it
customerOrder.changeFieldValue(CUSTOMER_OBJ, LAST_NAME, "White")
customerOrder.changeFieldValue(CUSTOMER_OBJ, FIRST_NAME, "Jim");
customerOrder.changeFieldValue(CUSTOMER_OBJ, ADDRESS, "12 First St.")
customerOrder.changeFieldValue(CUSTOMER_OBJ, CITY, "Denver");
customerOrder.changeFieldValue(CUSTOMER_OBJ, STATE, "CO");
customerOrder.changeFieldValue(CUSTOMER_OBJ, ZIP_CODE, "33322");

customerOrder.coffeePdt[0].name = "kona";
customerOrder.coffeePdt[0].color = "dark";
customerOrder.coffeePdt[0].flavor = "rich";
customerOrder.coffeePdt[0].caffeine = true;
customerOrder.coffeePdt[0].costLb = 4.50F;
customerOrder.changeFieldValue(ORDER_OBJ, COFFEE_LBS, 0, 5);
customerOrder.coffeePdt[1].name = "kona decaf";
customerOrder.coffeePdt[1].color = "light";
customerOrder.coffeePdt[1].flavor = "mild";
customerOrder.coffeePdt[1].caffeine = false;
customerOrder.coffeePdt[1].costLb = 5.50F;
customerOrder.changeFieldValue(ORDER_OBJ, COFFEE_LBS, 1, 3);
customerOrder.coffeePdt[2].name = "espresso light";
customerOrder.coffeePdt[2].color = "light";
customerOrder.coffeePdt[2].flavor = "mild";
customerOrder.coffeePdt[2].caffeine = false;
customerOrder.coffeePdt[2].costLb = 5.50F;
customerOrder.changeFieldValue(ORDER_OBJ, COFFEE_LBS, 2, 1);
numOrder = 3;
```

Figure 6-15: Code to set up values in the Order object

3 Scroll down to the code shown in Figure 6-16. This code displays the coffee information that is stored in an array on the screen. You will not make any changes to the code, but you should study the code to see how information is displayed that is stored in an array.

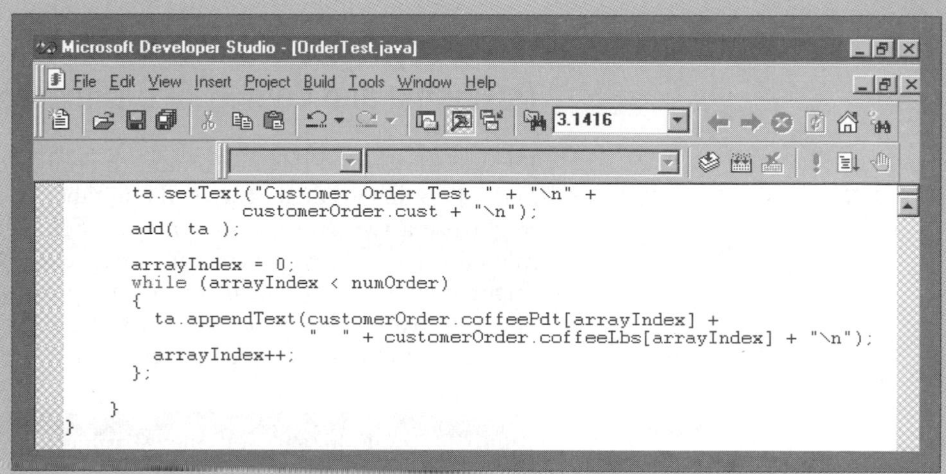

Figure 6-16: Code to display output on the screen

4 Build the program in a default project workspace. You might see errors in the Output window because the objects are missing from the workspace.

5 Add the **Coffees.java**, **Customer.java**, and **Order.java** files to the project workspace.

6 Click **Build** on the menu bar, and then click **Rebuild All** and correct any syntax errors.

7 If necessary, change the default HTML file to **OrderTest.html.**

8 Execute the program. The class filename is **OrderTest.** See Figure 6-17. The customer information displays in the text area and detail lines appear for each coffee product ordered.

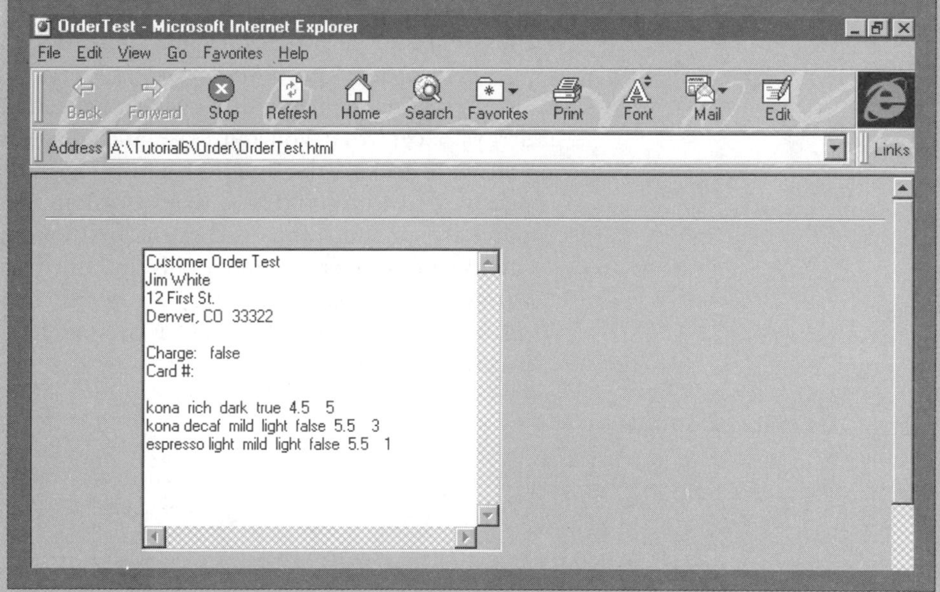

Figure 6-17: OrderTest.java running in Internet Explorer

9 Close Internet Explorer and then close the project workspace and all document windows.

Next you will learn how to code two-dimensional arrays.

Designing and Coding Two-Dimensional Arrays

For the purpose of this discussion, the only difference between a one-dimensional and a two-dimensional array is the number of indices. For example, a programmer might use a two-dimensional array to hold information about discounts that certain customers receive when their orders exceed a certain amount. The programmer might start the design of this problem by creating a table to indicate the appropriate information. Figure 6-18 shows the discounts that Koffee Koncoctions' customers receive based on their purchases.

Purchase Amount	Wholesale Customer Discount	Retail Customer Discount
$1-500	7%	5%
$501-1,000	10%	7%
$1,001+	12%	10%

Figure 6-18: Discounts based on customer type and purchases

You can use a two-dimensional array to program this table in Java, so if the discount or purchase amounts change, it will be easier to make the changes in the program. You will use a two-dimensional array because there are two criteria for determining the percentage of discount—the purchase amount and the type of customer. The syntax for the discount table is *double discountRate [ ] = new double [3] [2];*.

The discountRate array has two indices—one for each row and column. The first index corresponds to the rows in the table and the second index corresponds to the columns. The syntax for multi-dimensioned arrays is *<array type> <array name> [ ] = new <array type> [<index1>] ... [<indexn>];*.

Accessing elements in a two-dimensional array is similar to one-dimensional arrays except that you must use an index for each dimension of the array. So if you want to find the discount percentage for a wholesale customer who makes a purchase of $1,500.00, you would look in the third row, which corresponds to the purchase amount range and in the first column, which corresponds to the wholesale type customer. To move this amount from the array that holds the table to a variable called discountPercent, you use the following code: *discountPercent = discountRate [2] [0];*. The indices are one less than the row or column in the table because the index begins at zero.

Suppose you decide to set the initial values in the table to zero. There are two indices, so you need to use two loops to perform the task, as shown in Figure 6-19.

```
rowIndex = 0;
while (rowIndex < 3)
{
        colIndex = 0;

while (colIndex < 2)
        {
        discountRate [rowIndex] [colIndex] = 0;
        colIndex++;
        };
rowIndex++;
};
```

Figure 6-19: Initializing a two-dimensional array

The outer loop of the program code in Figure 6-19 processes each row, and then for each row, the inner loop processes each column. Usually you include a set of nested loops with a loop statement for each index in the array. This example shows how to initialize the array to a given amount, but the same logic could be used for displaying the values of the array or using the values in expressions.

Keep the following points in mind when creating multi-dimensional arrays:

- All elements must be of the same type.
- There must be an index for each criterion that determines a given element.
- When programming the array with loops, use a series of nested loops with a loop statement for each index.

While the concepts for designing and coding multi-dimensional arrays are greatly simplified in this discussion, it does give you the basics for designing and coding multi-dimensional arrays. More specific information about processing multi-dimensional arrays is beyond the scope of this text. However, with these basic concepts you are now ready to design and code a program with a two-dimensional array.

Designing a Program with a Two-Dimensional Array

The investment program could use a two-dimensional array. The current investment program calculates the value of an investment based on a single interest rate. Sometimes it is important to have a table of such calculated values based on several different interest rates in order to make a decision about an investment. Because higher interest rates usually require longer commitments of money or greater risk, the user could use the table to see if the increased value of the investment at a greater interest rate was worth the additional time or risk. You can modify the investment program so the second index of the array still corresponds to the month of the value that was listed in the table. The columns of the table correspond to interest rates of 10 percent, 12 percent, and 15 percent, and are referenced in the array by the first index. To convert the investment program to use a two-dimensional array, consider the following:

- The first row contains the initial investment so all of the columns are equal.
- Implement an array to hold the three interest rate amounts. This rate will be one-dimensional stored as the monthly rate.
- Each row in the table will contain the calculated value of the investment for the month corresponding to the row index.

The initialization is for a table that has three columns so you can code it as if the array variables are simple variables. Then you need an algorithm to calculate and display the values of the array. The calculation pseudocode is shown in Figure 6-20 and the display pseudocode is shown in Figure 6-21.

```
set this month to 1
while (this month <= ending month)
        set this rate to 0
        while (this rate < 3)
        calculate investment for this month and this rate
        increment this rate
        increment this month
```

Figure 6-20: Calculation pseudocode

```
set this month to 1
while (this month <= last month)
        display detail line for all three interest rates
        increment this month
```

Figure 6-21: Display pseudocode

Figure 6-22 shows the pseudocode for the program.

```
Initialize the interest rates and value of investment
Calculate the monthly interest rates
Calculate the monthly investment values for each month
Display heading information
Display a detail line for each month in the array
```

Figure 6-22: Overall pseudocode

Now you can modify the Invest.java program.

To add the array to the Invest.java program:

1 Open the **Invest.java** file from the Invest folder from the Tutorial6 folder on your Student Disk, and then save it as **Invest1.java**.

2 Change the first comment line to **Invest1.java,** and then change class line so the class name is **Invest1**, as shown in Figure 6-23.

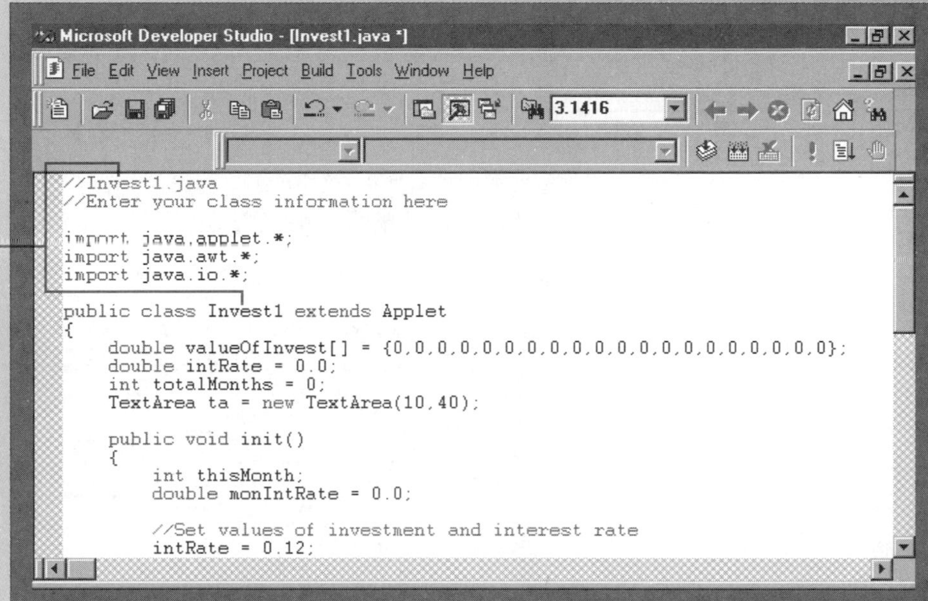

Figure 6-23: Changes to Invest1.java heading code

3 Make the changes shown in Figure 6-24. These changes make valueOfInvest a two-dimensional array with 3 as the size of the first index and 20 as the size of the second index, and make intRate a one-dimensional array of size 3.

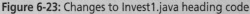

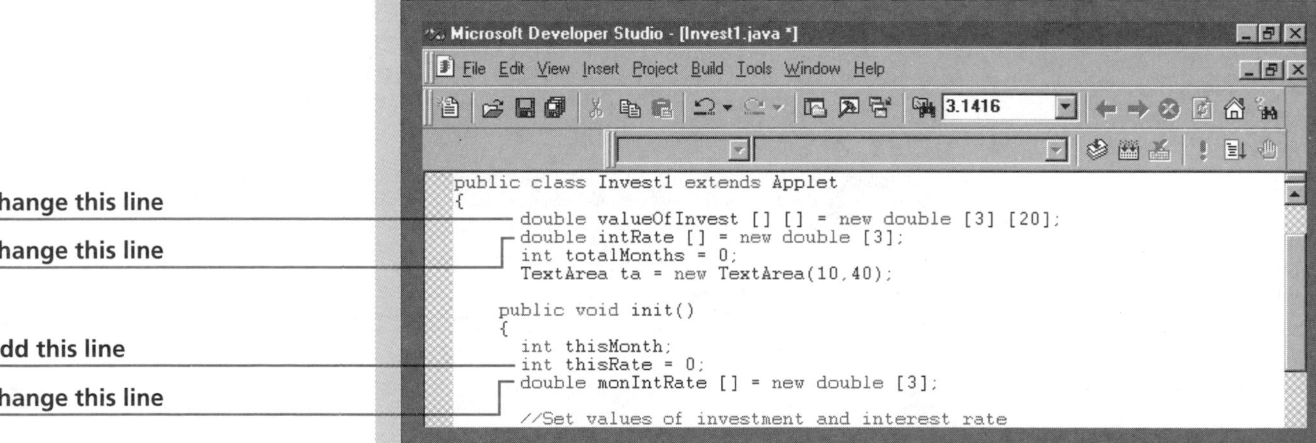

Figure 6-24: Changes to Invest1.java class variables

4 Select the code shown in Figure 6-25, and then type the code shown in Figure 6-26 to set the initial values for the interest rates and investment.

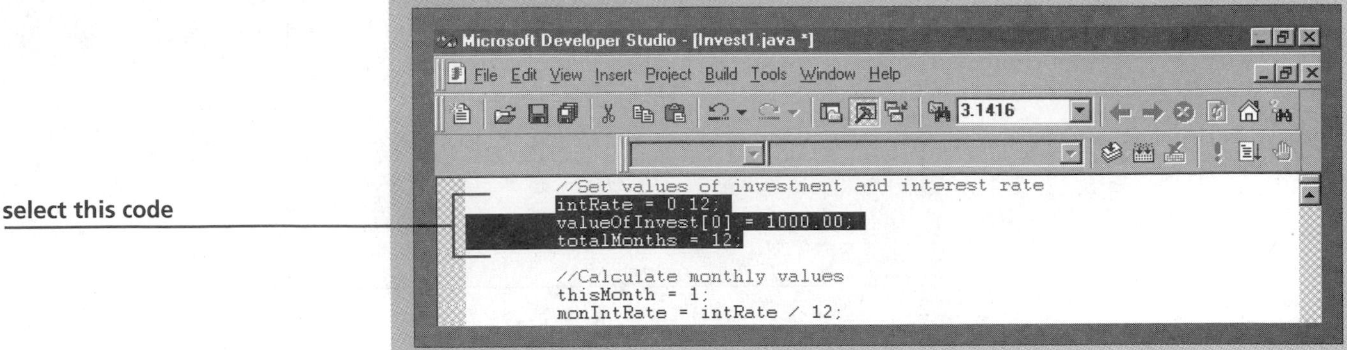

select this code

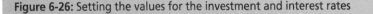

```
//Set values of investment and interest rate
intRate = 0.12;
valueOfInvest[0] = 1000.00;
totalMonths = 12;

//Calculate monthly values
thisMonth = 1;
monIntRate = intRate / 12;
```

Figure 6-25: Changing the intRate and valueOfInvest values

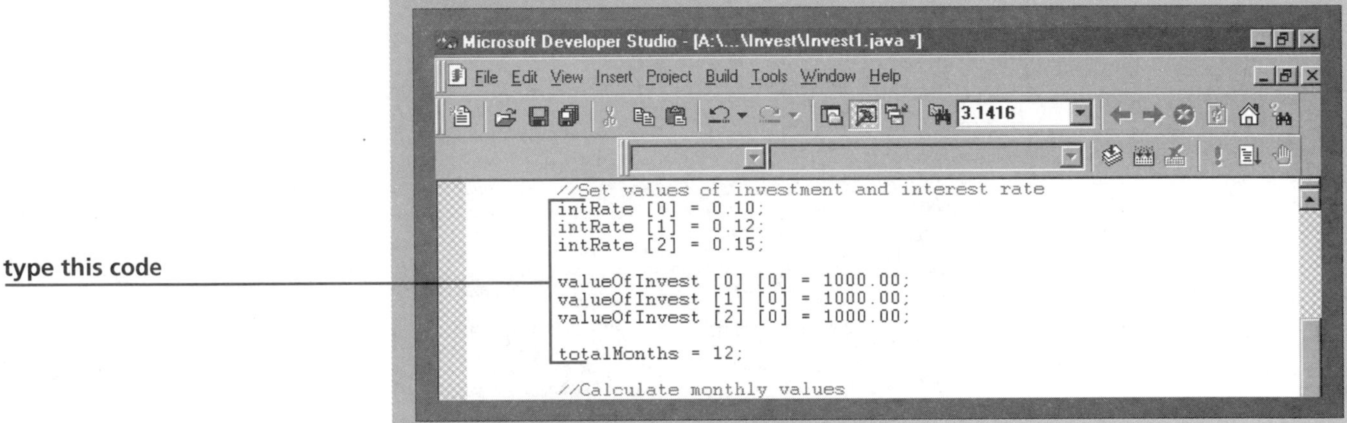

type this code

```
//Set values of investment and interest rate
intRate [0] = 0.10;
intRate [1] = 0.12;
intRate [2] = 0.15;

valueOfInvest [0] [0] = 1000.00;
valueOfInvest [1] [0] = 1000.00;
valueOfInvest [2] [0] = 1000.00;

totalMonths = 12;

//Calculate monthly values
```

Figure 6-26: Setting the values for the investment and interest rates

5 Click in the location shown in Figure 6-27, press the **Enter** key, and then type the code to use the monIntRate array variable to hold the calculation of the monthly interest rates for each of the three interest rates in the object. Then delete the old monIntRate line code shown in Figure 6-27.

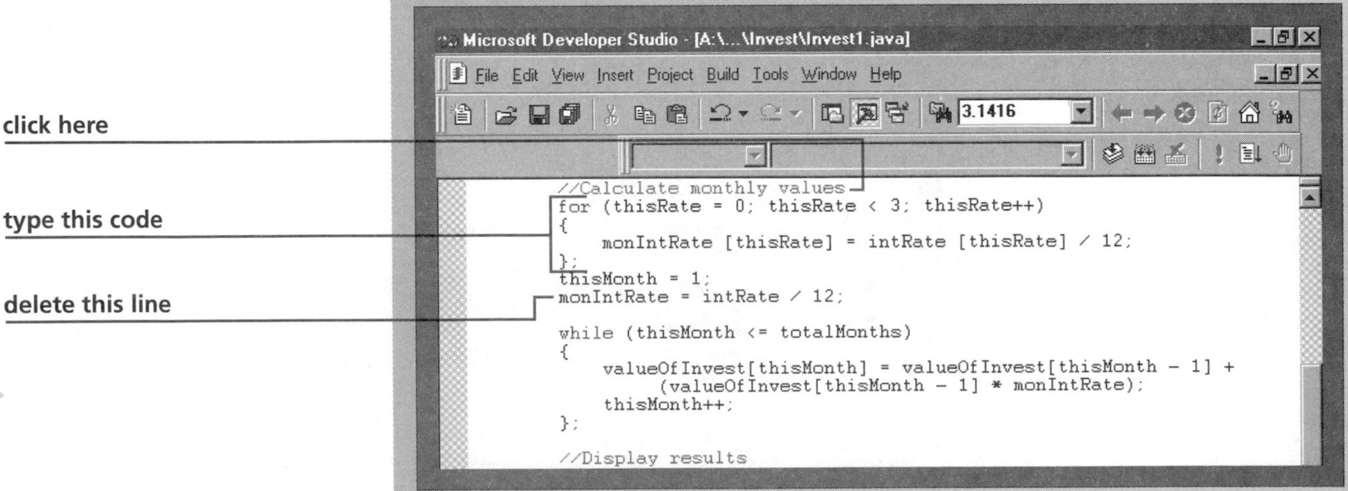

click here

type this code

delete this line

```
//Calculate monthly values
for (thisRate = 0; thisRate < 3; thisRate++)
{
    monIntRate [thisRate] = intRate [thisRate] / 12;
};
thisMonth = 1;
monIntRate = intRate / 12;

while (thisMonth <= totalMonths)
{
    valueOfInvest[thisMonth] = valueOfInvest[thisMonth - 1] +
        (valueOfInvest[thisMonth - 1] * monIntRate);
    thisMonth++;
};

//Display results
```

Figure 6-27: Changing the monIntRate variable

6 Select the valueOfInvest code shown in Figure 6-28, and then type the new code shown in Figure 6-29 to store the original investment in the 0th element of the two-dimensional array named valueOfInvest.

select this code

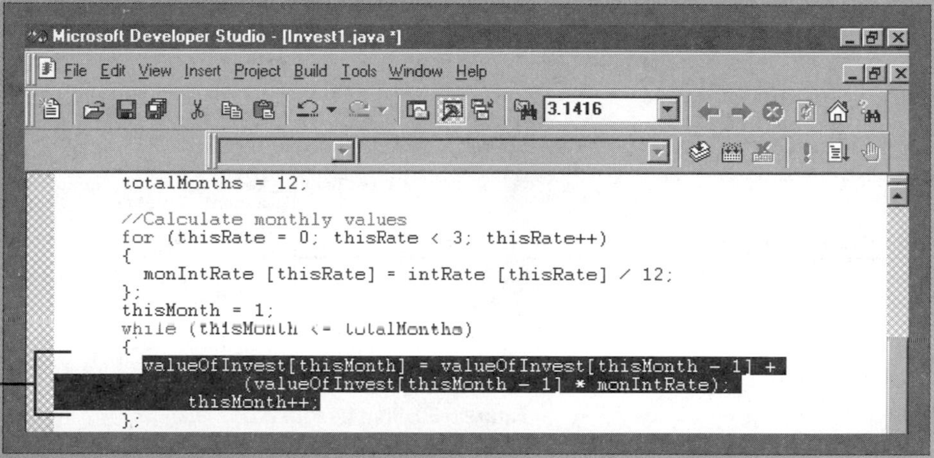

```
Microsoft Developer Studio - [Invest1.java *]
File Edit View Insert Project Build Tools Window Help
3.1416

    totalMonths = 12;

    //Calculate monthly values
    for (thisRate = 0; thisRate < 3; thisRate++)
    {
      monIntRate [thisRate] = intRate [thisRate] / 12;
    };
    thisMonth = 1;
    while (thisMonth <= totalMonths)
    {
      valueOfInvest[thisMonth] = valueOfInvest[thisMonth - 1] +
              (valueOfInvest[thisMonth - 1] * monIntRate);
          thisMonth++;
    };
```

Figure 6-28: Selecting the valueOfInvest code

type this code

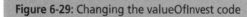

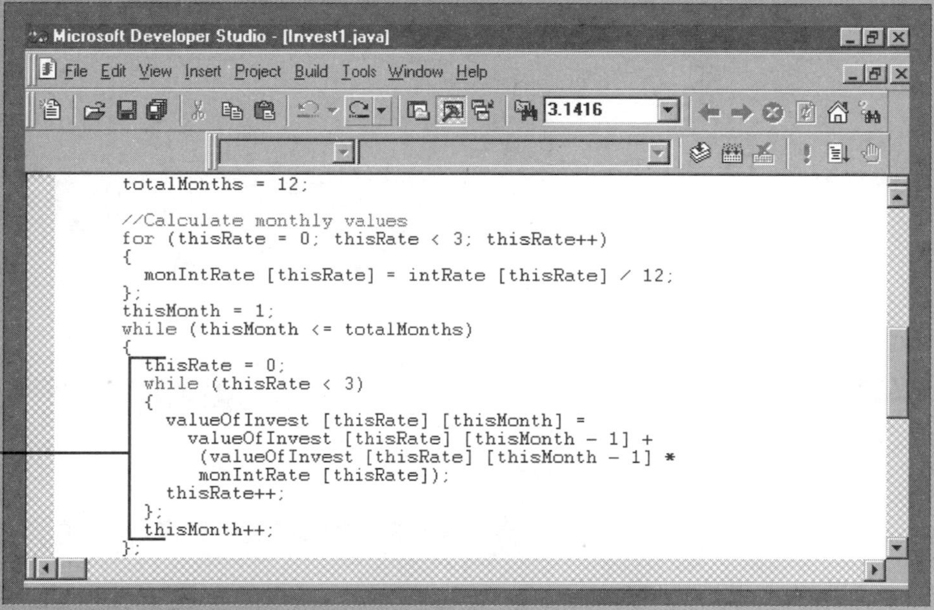

```
Microsoft Developer Studio - [Invest1.java]
File Edit View Insert Project Build Tools Window Help
3.1416

    totalMonths = 12;

    //Calculate monthly values
    for (thisRate = 0; thisRate < 3; thisRate++)
    {
      monIntRate [thisRate] = intRate [thisRate] / 12;
    };
    thisMonth = 1;
    while (thisMonth <= totalMonths)
    {
      thisRate = 0;
      while (thisRate < 3)
      {
        valueOfInvest [thisRate] [thisMonth] =
          valueOfInvest [thisRate] [thisMonth - 1] +
           (valueOfInvest [thisRate] [thisMonth - 1] *
           monIntRate [thisRate]);
        thisRate++;
      };
      thisMonth++;
    };
```

Figure 6-29: Changing the valueOfInvest code

7 Change your program as shown in Figure 6-30 to change the display information.

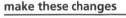

make these changes

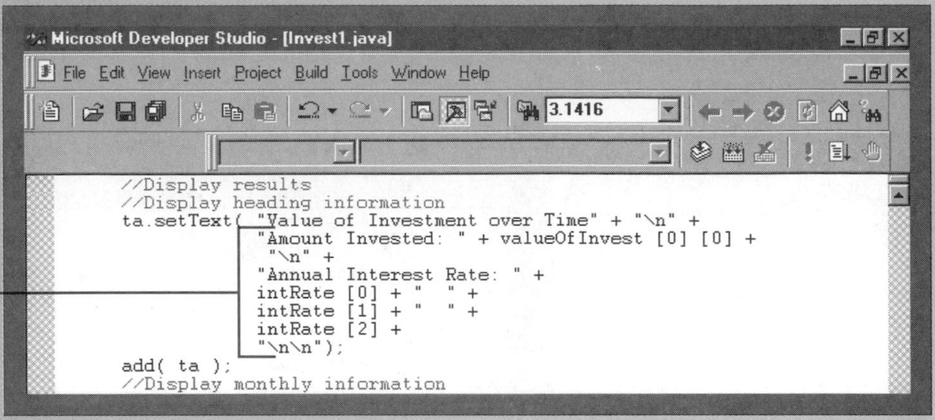

```
//Display results
//Display heading information
ta.setText( "Value of Investment over Time" + "\n" +
    "Amount Invested: " + valueOfInvest [0] [0] +
    "\n" +
    "Annual Interest Rate: " +
    intRate [0] + "    " +
    intRate [1] + "    " +
    intRate [2] +
    "\n\n");
add( ta );
//Display monthly information
```

Figure 6-30: Print heading code change

8 Select the lines of code shown in Figure 6-31 that display the investment values for each month, and then enter the code shown in Figure 6-32 so the program displays the investment values for each interest rate and each month. Because there are only three investment rates, this change was not implemented using a nested loop.

select this code

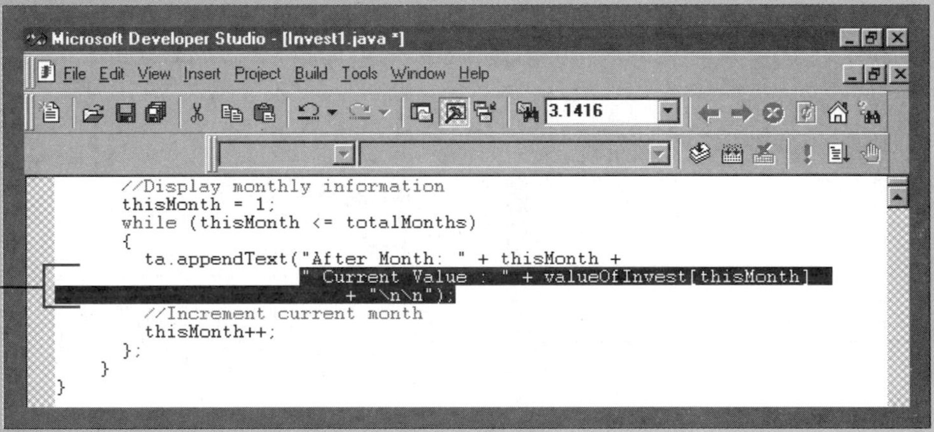

```
//Display monthly information
thisMonth = 1;
while (thisMonth <= totalMonths)
{
  ta.appendText("After Month: " + thisMonth +
        " Current Value : " + valueOfInvest[thisMonth]
            + "\n\n");
  //Increment current month
  thisMonth++;
};
}
}
```

Figure 6-31: Selecting the display information

type this code

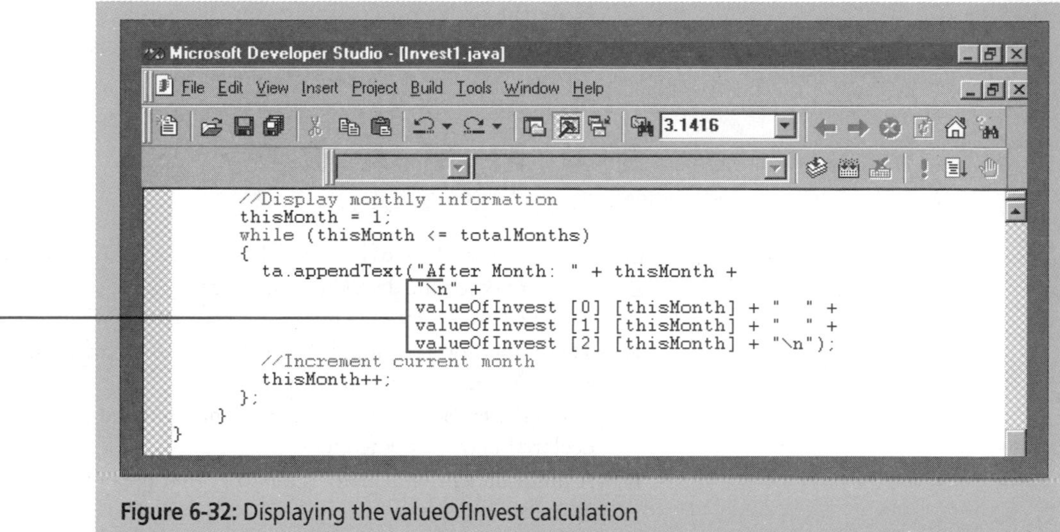

Figure 6-32: Displaying the valueOfInvest calculation

Now you have implemented the coding of your new investment program. You need to save, build, and test the program.

To save, build, and test the program:

1. Save your changes.
2. Build the program in a default project workspace, and then correct any syntax errors.
3. Change the default HTML file to **Invest1.html.**
4. Execute the program. The class filename is **Invest1**. See Figure 6-33.

tip

Select the second Tutorial 6 link of the Online Companion for this book (http://www.course.com) to see a live Java program that illustrates this topic.

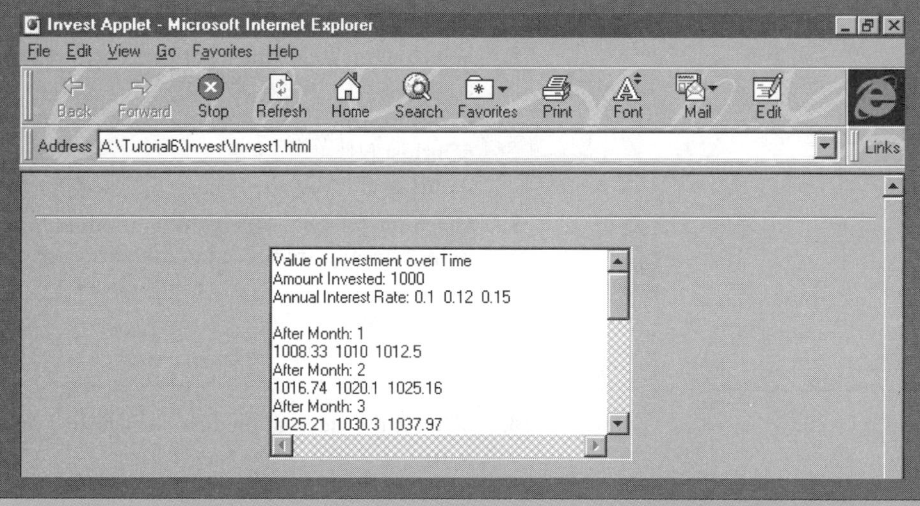

Figure 6-33: Invest1.java running in Internet Explorer

5. Close Internet Explorer, the project workspace, and all document windows, and then close Visual J++.

Now the order processing program uses arrays. You can either take a break or complete the end-of-lesson questions and exercises.

SUMMARY

- An array is a block of memory that holds a list of elements that are of the same type.
- The syntax for the declaration of an array is:
  <Array Type> <Array Name> [ ] = new <Array Type> [<Size of Array>];
- The syntax for accessing a given element of an array is:
  <arrayName> [<indexOfElement>]
- A single element of an array can be manipulated as if it is a simple variable of the type declared in the array name.
- A multi-dimensional array is an array that uses more than one index to access a single element of the array.
- The syntax for declaring and accessing multi-dimensional arrays is identical to the one-dimensional syntax except that each index is specified separately in the declaration and accessing variable.
- The processing of multi-dimensional arrays usually requires the use of nested loops. The number of levels in the nesting usually is equivalent to the number of indices of the array.

QUESTIONS

1. Which of the following is a valid declaration for an array?
a. int numList (25);
b. int numList [ ] = new int [25];
c. int numList [25];
d. all of the above

2. Which of the following identifiers accesses the third element in the array named intList?
a. intList [3]
b. intList (3)
c. intList [2]
d. intList {2}

3. Given the following array declaration: *int intList [ ] [ ] = new int [10] [10];*, how many loops typically are needed to initialize each element of the array to zero?
a. 1
b. 2
c. 3
d. 4

4. What is the index of the first element in a one-dimensional array?
a. 0
b. 1
c. 2
d. 3

5. The index of an array must be a(n) __________ type.
   a. boolean
   b. char
   c. double
   d. int
6. Multi-dimensional arrays also are called __________.
   a. files
   b. streams
   c. tables
   d. indices
7. Which of the following identifiers points to the element in the third column in the second row of a table that is declared with the row index first and the column index second?
   a. arrayName [1] [2]
   b. arrayName [2] [1]
   c. arrayName [3] [2]
   d. arrayName [2] [3]
8. What is the index of the value 50 in the following array: - 55 12 50 10 11?
   a. 3
   b. 9
   c. 2
   d. 5
9. If a two-dimensional array is declared as: *int intList [ ] [ ] = new int [colSize] [rowSize]*, which index must be the first following the identifier name?
   a. the row index
   b. the Col index
   c. either index can be first
10. An array that has two or more indices is called a(n) __________ array.
    a. simple
    b. complex
    c. multi-dimensional
    d. one-dimensional

EXERCISES

1. Given the following declaration of an array: *int nameList [ ] = new int [10]*, write on paper the code that initializes the array elements to " ".
2. Write on paper the code that declares a variable named floatList that is a two-dimensional array of type float. The array size is ten rows and five columns.
3. Given the following Java code, what is the value of each element in the array after the loop finishes?

```
int Values [ ] = new int [10];
for (Count = 0; Count < 10; Count++)
    Values[Count] = Count * 2;
```

4. Misty Marquette is helping her professor with a grading program. Her professor wants to keep a list of the name and five test grades for each student in the class. Write on paper a program that stores 10 names in a nameList array and the test grades in a gradeTable array that is two-dimensional with 5 columns and 10 rows.

5. Nicholas Wirkven is working on a program that prints the values of a two-dimensional array in a table format. The array is named numTable and holds elements of type double. He has determined that the table should be 10 columns wide and 15 rows long. Write a program for Nicholas that declares this array, puts initial values in the array, and displays it as a table in an applet. Use Visual J++ to create this program, and then save it as NumberTable.java in the Exercise5B folder in the Exercises folder in the Tutorial6 folder on your Student Disk.

6. Wendal Hargraves is a statistician for a research company. Some of the procedures at his company use number sequences that are different than simply counting. A routine Wendal currently is working on requires the use of the Fibinocci number series. This series is defined as the following:

   fib(0) = 0;
   fib(1) = 1;
   *fib(n) = (n-1) * (n-2) when n > 1*

   Design and write on paper a program that stores the first 15 Fibinocci numbers in an array and then displays their values on the display screen.

7. Lucia Lopez works for an engineering firm that specializes in new metals. The metal she currently is investigating decreases in weight as it is heated. The relationship between the temperature of the metal and its weight is *weight = weight - (temp / 3)*. Design a program for Lucia that stores the value of the weight of the metal between the temperatures of 50 and 100 degrees at 5 degree intervals (e.g. 50, 55, 60, etc.) in a one-dimensional array. Display the values that you stored in this array. Assume the initial weight of the metal is 500 units at 50 degrees. (*Hint:* The equation is written in the loop statement.) Use Visual J++ to write this program, and then save it as Metals.java in the Exercise7B folder in the Exercises folder in the Tutorial6 folder on your Student Disk.

LESSON C

objectives

In this lesson you will learn how to:

- Create stand-alone Java programs
- Use data files and streams
- Design a Java program that uses a data output file

Using Streams and Files

Creating a Stand-Alone Program for Koffee Koncoctions

Creating Stand-Alone Java Programs

Now that the order system uses arrays, you need to answer an important question before continuing. How do you expect the orders to come to Koffee Koncoctions? It is difficult to create files with an applet over the Internet; therefore the program that prints the invoice for a customer order probably needs to be stored on the client machine. Then the program could write a text file of the order after the clerk enters the information. To do this, you need to incorporate the use of output text files with the Order object. You can modify the OrderTest.java program to test whether you can output text to a given file.

A Java applet can be enclosed in a stand-alone program to store information in a disk file. External storage is the common method for long-term archiving of information on computers. The data processing technique that makes external storage possible is called **file processing**. The Java language does not easily support the reading and writing of files in an applet, so you will learn a method for writing a stand-alone Java program that contains an applet to perform disk file access. When you finish this lesson, the OrderTest program will write its information to a text file.

In this textbook you have created applets for Java programming. This method is extremely useful and shows the power of the Java programming language. However, Java programs can run as stand-alone programs as well. A stand-alone program is one that does not necessarily depend on the browser for its output. The major problem is that these programs cannot run over the Internet without downloading the program to the user's machine. They do, however, provide a reasonable programming environment when you need to use Java on a single machine.

Your Java applets use an init method. The init method is the default method for applets, and it executes automatically when the applet executes. With stand-alone programs, the default method is the main method. The **main method** is similar to the init method in that it starts automatically when a stand-alone program executes. A stand-alone program can contain a main method and an init method. In this case, the init method does not execute unless it is called by the main method or one of the methods it calls.

When you need to run a Java stand-alone program, you should remember the following issues. First, a main method must exist in the program file. Second, when executing the program in the Visual J++ environment, you must identify that you are running a stand-alone program. You can do this prior to executing the program by changing the settings in the Information For Running Class dialog box.

In this lesson, you will run a stand-alone program, but its output will appear in the browser. To output to the browser, the main method of the program needs to use an object that opens a frame in the browser and displays information that normally displays in the stand-alone program. The program AppletFrame.java on your Student Disk performs this task. When the program runs in the browser window, it will look different than what you have seen.

Using Data Files and Streams

Select the third Tutorial 6 link of the Online Companion for this book (http://www.course.com) to see a live Java program that illustrates this topic.

The early development of computers required that the input and output of data be designed according to some logical as well as physical architecture. The metaphor that was used for the transfer of data was a stream. A physical stream is a continuous flow of substances, usually in one direction, that can be manipulated at various points in time or allowed to continue flowing. Most of the early computer systems did not differentiate significantly what was being given to the programs as input. The logical view of the process was that when a program needed data it would go to the reservoir, or buffer, and take what it needed. This reservoir would be linked to a flow of data that could continue to replenish the buffer so the program would have data as necessary. When applied to output, the stream was viewed as a channel, or bus, to pass information to another place. A common example of this type of processing is in water purification systems. Large water treatment plants take water from reservoirs that has been collected from a number of locations and stored in the central storage facility. The water is filtered through the treatment system at a rate that is consistent with the equipment in use. After the water is processed, it is released through a channel to move on to the next stage. Streams in data processing act in this same manner, whether they are processing interactive input/output to the console or reading and writing to a data file. In fact, once the user knows how to manipulate input and output in a computer program, the only additional knowledge needed for file processing is the commands and constraints of the file system.

Java supports 22 types of file streams to allow file processing. In this textbook you will focus on text files and the use of print streams. Text files are those files that are stored in ASCII format, as you learned in Lesson B. Text files provide flexibility for the software that accesses them. For example, most word processing programs can read a text file that is created using another program, and many spreadsheet programs permit the use of text files for data entry to the worksheet. This adaptability makes the text file the most versatile type of file on the computer system.

The major tasks for file processing in Java are: open the file, get some data, write some data, and close the file. These four activities are used in various sequences depending on the task the programmer needs to accomplish. You will explore these four tasks relative to file processing in Java and consider the most common commands available for supporting these functions.

You learned in Lesson A that to use something from a file you first need to open that file. In Java this process informs the program of the name and location of the file to open as well as some information as to what types of access to the file are desired. Typically, there are three modes of file processing in computer programming: read-only, write-only, and read/write. When files are opened for input, they typically are opened as read-only files but might be opened as read/write files. When output of data is the desired task, then the write only mode usually is chosen, but read/write also supports the output of data. The general Java commands that support the opening of input and output files are shown next. For input files, the syntax is:

FileInputStream <stream name> =
new FileInputStream("<disk file name>");

and, for output files,

FileOutputStream <stream name> =
new FileOutputStream("<disk file name>");

When a user is finished writing to or reading from a file, the file needs to be closed. In most computer operating systems, this will be done for the program regardless of whether it specifically requests it. However, in many programming environments, when a file is an output file and data is written to the file, the data initially are transferred to the output buffer. If the program is not careful to close the file, data are sometimes left in the buffer and not written to the file when the operating system has to do the closing by default. The use of specific commands to close input and output files ensures that the output buffer is emptied or flushed of its contents and that this information has been appropriately transferred to the storage device. The Java command for closing a file, whether it is an input or an output file, is *<file stream name>.close;*.

Remember that the major purpose of opening a file is to store or retrieve data from it. The file input and output commands perform these tasks. The common input and output commands in Java will be shown by example in the remainder of this tutorial.

One final note—when files are accessed in the Java language, the methods that are used will return error messages if the user's system was not able to perform the stated task. In Java this is called **throwing an exception**. It is extremely important to at least catch these exceptions whether the program does anything with them or not. The methods used for this process are try and catch. The **try method** uses the following syntax *try { <action block> }*. The **action block** typically is made up of the commands that might cause an exception to be thrown. The try command informs the program to perform the statements in the action block and to give back an exception if one is found. Asking the program to return an exception means that you have to use at least the method that catches the exception. This method is appropriately called **catch**. The syntax for the catch method is *catch (Exception e) { }*. This line of code catches the errors thrown by the try method. You will see some examples of the use of this code in this lesson.

Designing a Program That Uses a Data File

You can use the OrderTest.java program to manipulate output files. This task requires you to store output in a text file so you are performing file output. Figure 6-34 shows the pseudocode that describes the tasks of the order system.

```
set up values of variables in order
display heading of order
set index to 0
while (index <= number of orders)
        display detail line of product element
        increment index
```

Figure 6-34: Pseudocode for order system

Now you must consider what changes must occur in order to process the output to a file. You can modify the pseudocode shown in Figure 6-34 to include file output. Figure 6-35 shows the pseudocode for the order system with file output.

```
open output file
set up values of variables in order
display heading of order
write heading to file
set index to 0
while (index <= number of orders)
        display detail line of product element
        write detail line to file
        increment index
close output file
```

Figure 6-35: Order system pseudocode with file output

Now you are ready to modify the order processing program.

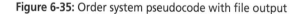

To modify the order processing program:

1. Start Visual J++ and close any project workspaces, if necessary.
2. Open the **OrderTest.java** file from the Order folder in the Tutorial6 folder on your Student Disk, and then save it as **OrderTest1.java**.
3. Change the first comment line to **OrderTest1.java**, and then change the class filename to **OrderTest1**.

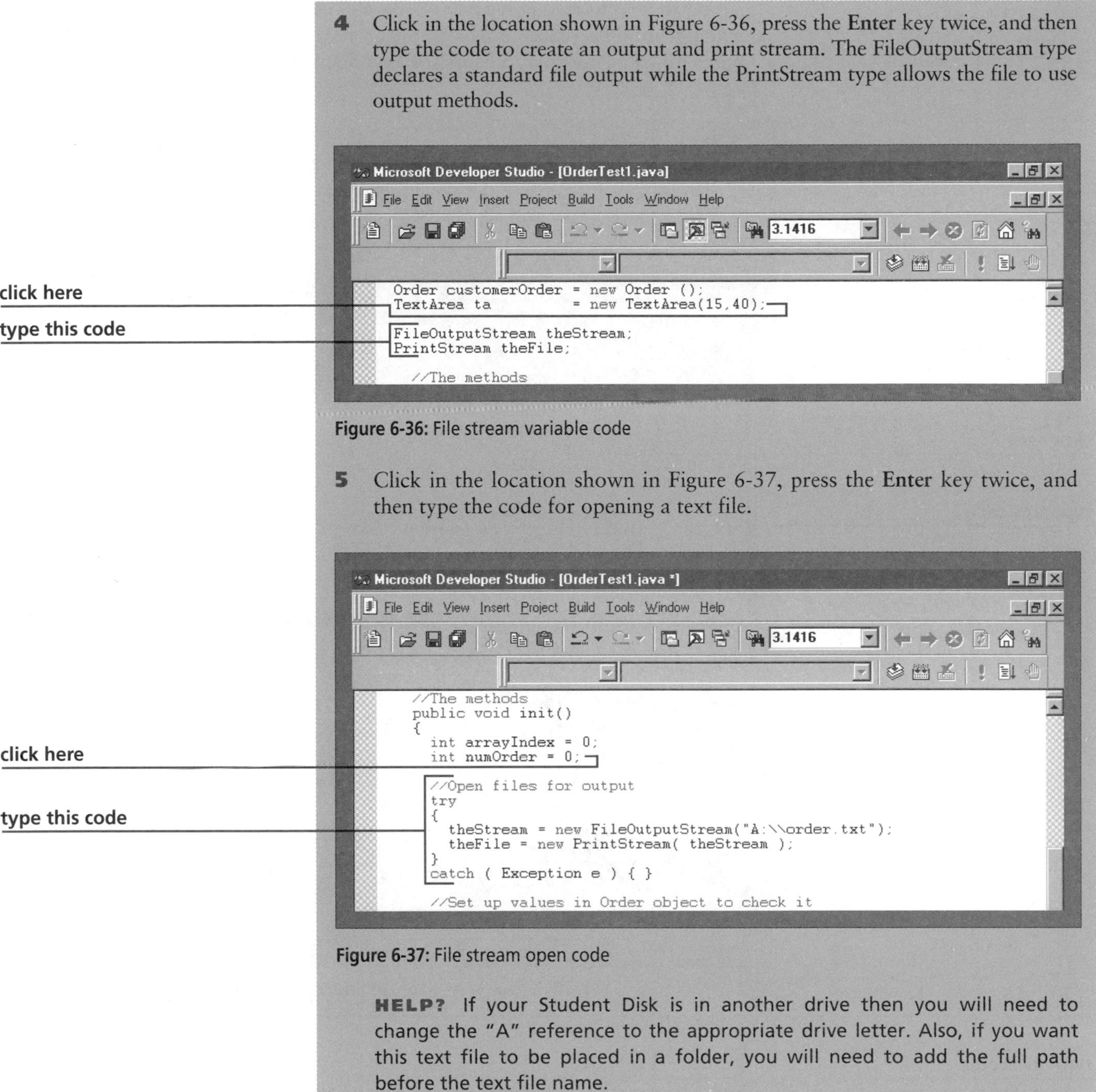

click here
type this code
Microsoft Developer Studio - [OrderTest1.java]
File Edit View Insert Project Build Tools Window Help
3.1416
Order customerOrder = new Order ();
TextArea ta = new TextArea(15,40);
FileOutputStream theStream;
PrintStream theFile;
//The methods
click here
type this code
Microsoft Developer Studio - [OrderTest1.java *]
File Edit View Insert Project Build Tools Window Help
3.1416
//The methods
public void init()
{
int arrayIndex = 0;
int numOrder = 0;
//Open files for output
try
{
theStream = new FileOutputStream("A:\\order.txt");
theFile = new PrintStream(theStream);
}
catch (Exception e) { }
//Set up values in Order object to check it

4 Click in the location shown in Figure 6-36, press the **Enter** key twice, and then type the code to create an output and print stream. The FileOutputStream type declares a standard file output while the PrintStream type allows the file to use output methods.

Figure 6-36: File stream variable code

5 Click in the location shown in Figure 6-37, press the **Enter** key twice, and then type the code for opening a text file.

Figure 6-37: File stream open code

HELP? If your Student Disk is in another drive then you will need to change the "A" reference to the appropriate drive letter. Also, if you want this text file to be placed in a folder, you will need to add the full path before the text file name.

6 Save your changes.

The code shown in Figure 6-37 is surrounded by a try and followed by a catch. These two special methods allow Java to check for any run-time errors that might occur when a file is being accessed. The try method with the code following it in braces is the code to be tested. If this code throws an exception, the catch method that follows this block of code will catch the result. You are not doing anything with the exception that might be returned. You can consult Books Online for more information about the catch method.

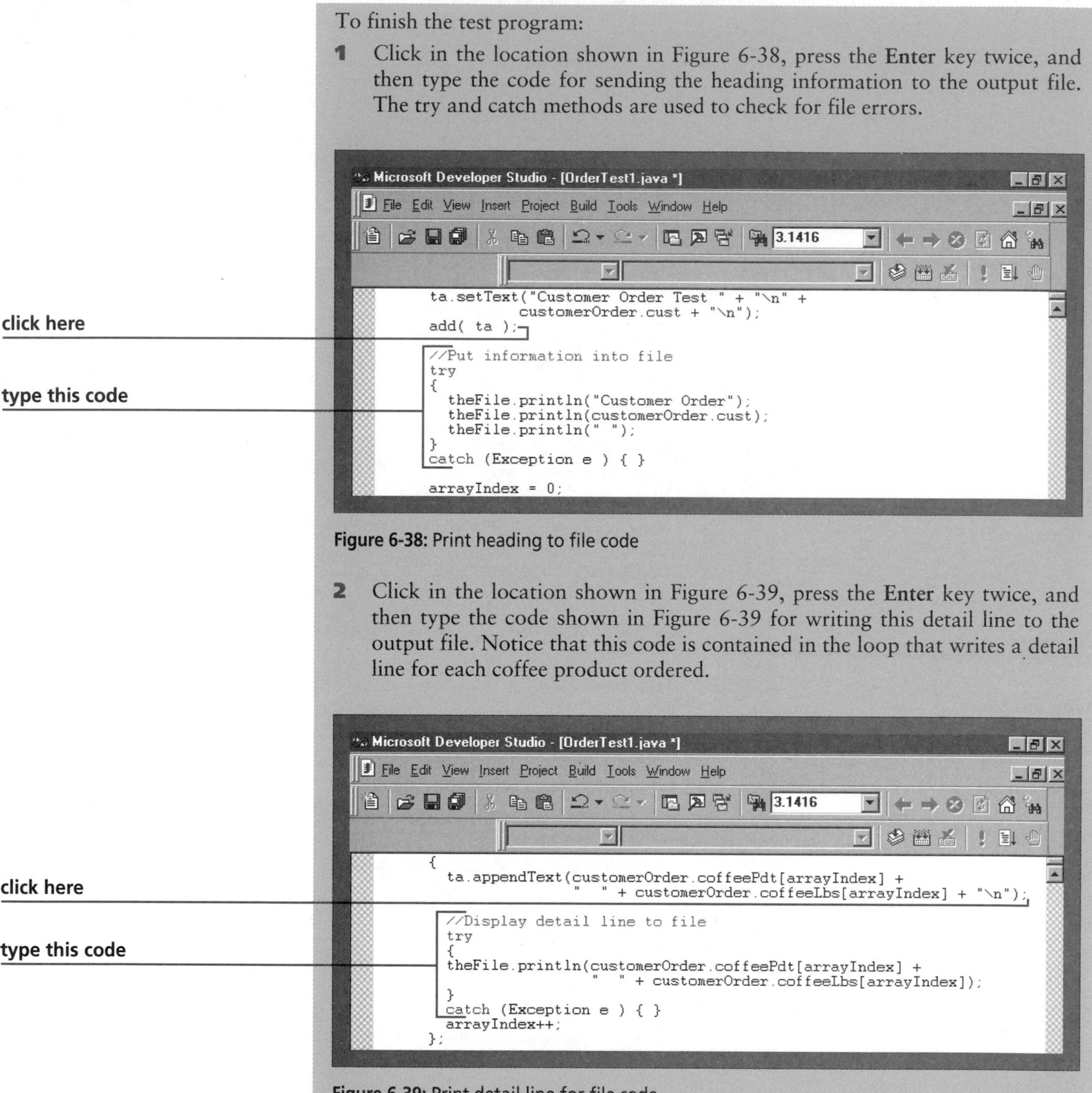

To finish the test program:

1. Click in the location shown in Figure 6-38, press the **Enter** key twice, and then type the code for sending the heading information to the output file. The try and catch methods are used to check for file errors.

Microsoft Developer Studio - [OrderTest1.java *]
File Edit View Insert Project Build Tools Window Help
3.1416
click here
type this code
ta.setText("Customer Order Test " + "\n" +
customerOrder.cust + "\n");
add(ta);
//Put information into file
try
{
theFile.println("Customer Order");
theFile.println(customerOrder.cust);
theFile.println(" ");
}
catch (Exception e) { }
arrayIndex = 0;

Figure 6-38: Print heading to file code

2. Click in the location shown in Figure 6-39, press the **Enter** key twice, and then type the code shown in Figure 6-39 for writing this detail line to the output file. Notice that this code is contained in the loop that writes a detail line for each coffee product ordered.

Microsoft Developer Studio - [OrderTest1.java *]
File Edit View Insert Project Build Tools Window Help
3.1416
click here
type this code
{
ta.appendText(customerOrder.coffeePdt[arrayIndex] +
" " + customerOrder.coffeeLbs[arrayIndex] + "\n");
//Display detail line to file
try
{
theFile.println(customerOrder.coffeePdt[arrayIndex] +
" " + customerOrder.coffeeLbs[arrayIndex]);
}
catch (Exception e) { }
arrayIndex++;
};

Figure 6-39: Print detail line for file code

3 Click in the location shown in Figure 6-40, press the **Enter** key twice, and then type the code for closing the output file. Even though Java will close the file for you, it is a good practice to flush the output buffer and close the disk file.

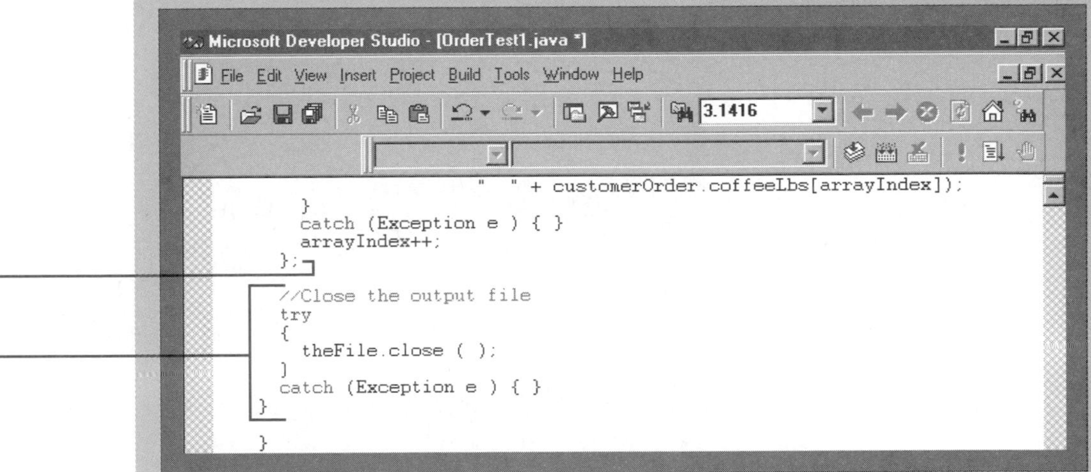

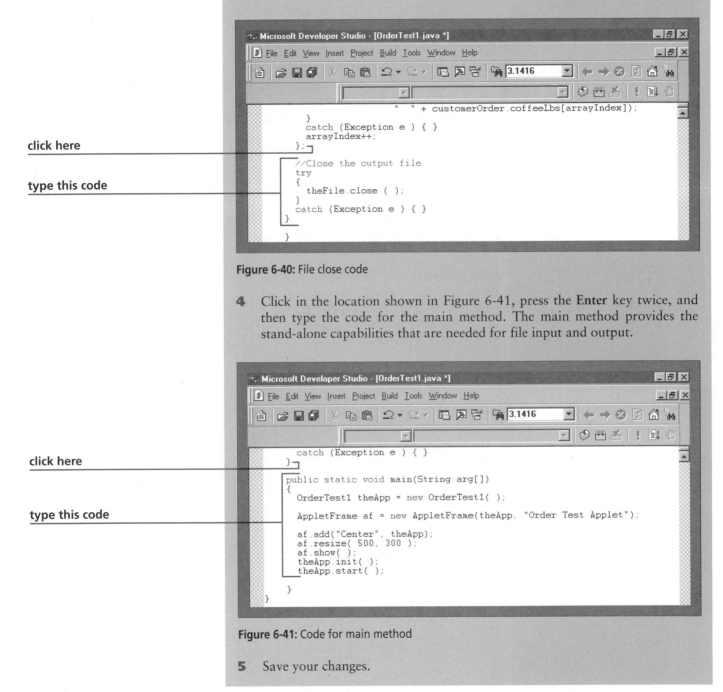

Figure 6-40: File close code

4 Click in the location shown in Figure 6-41, press the **Enter** key twice, and then type the code for the main method. The main method provides the stand-alone capabilities that are needed for file input and output.

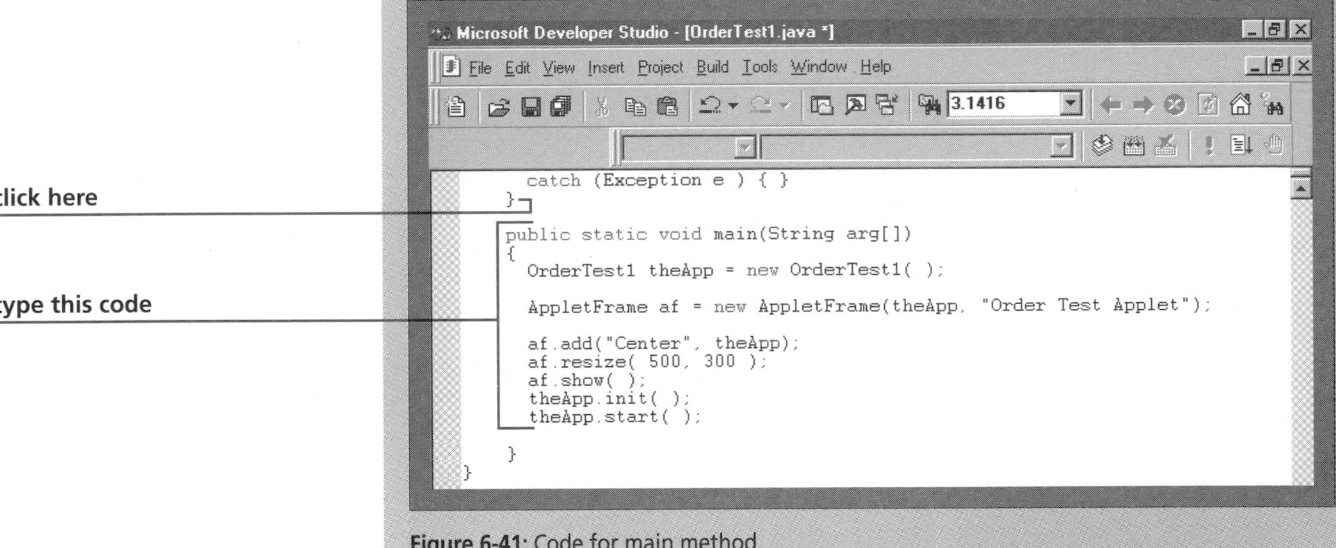

Figure 6-41: Code for main method

5 Save your changes.

Now you have completed entering and saving the new order test program that sends output to a file named order.txt on drive A. You will build and execute the program next.

To build and execute the test program:

1. Build the program in a default project workspace. The Output window might show some errors because the objects are not in the current workspace. You will add the objects next and then rebuild the program.
2. Click **Project** on the menu bar, point to **Add To Project**, and then click **Files.** Change to the Order folder on your Student Disk, and then double-click the **Coffees.java** file.
3. Repeat Step 2 to add the **Customer.java, Order.java**, and **AppletFrame.java** to the workspace.
4. Click **Build** on the menu bar, and then click **Rebuild All.** Check your typing in the OrderTest1.java file if you get any errors.
5. Execute the program. Type **OrderTest1** in the Class file name text box, and then click the **Stand-alone interpreter** option button, as shown in Figure 6-42.

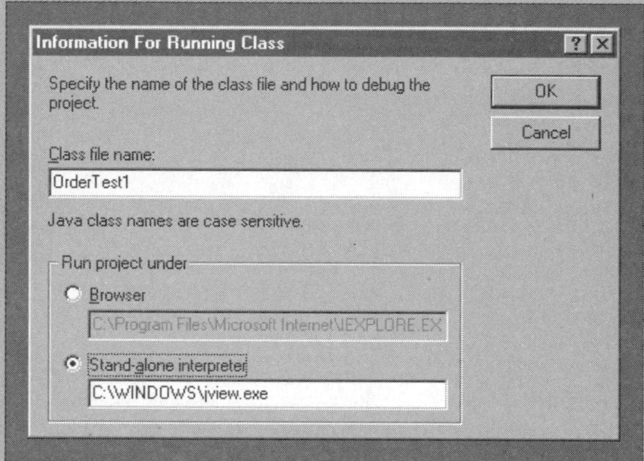

Figure 6-42: Changing to display as a stand-alone applet

6. Click the **OK** button. The frame opens, but you need to maximize the window to see the output.
7. Click the **Maximize** button on the OrderTest Applet window title bar. Figure 6-43 shows the output.

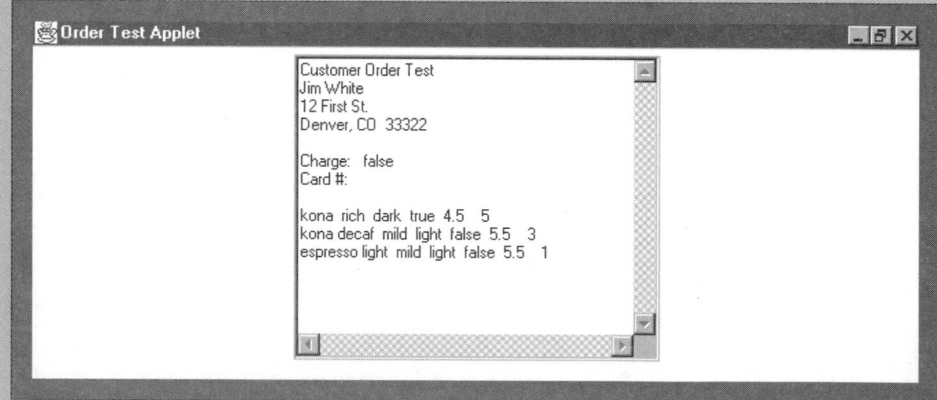

Figure 6-43: Stand-alone OrderTest1 applet

8 Click the **Close** button ☒ to close the OrderTest Applet window. The DOS window will close automatically after a few seconds.

9 Close the project workspace and all document windows.

You sent the output of this program to a file so you need to see if the file was created. You will check the output next.

To open the output file:

1 Click the **Open** button on the Standard toolbar, and then change to the root folder on your Student Disk.

2 Click the **Files of type** list arrow, scroll down and click **Text Files (.txt)**, and then double-click the **order** file. The file opens as shown in Figure 6-44.

```
Customer Order
Jim White
12 First St.
Denver, CO  33322

Charge:   false
Card #:


kona  rich  dark  true  4.5    5
kona decaf  mild  light  false  5.5    3
espresso light  mild  light  false  5.5    1
```

Figure 6-44: Contents of order.txt file

3 Close the file and then close Visual J++.

Now you have successfully manipulated an output file in Java. Files are very useful and frequently are used in programming for many types of tasks. While this example only experimented with the creation of an output file, the manipulation of an input file is not significantly different. You can consult search Books Online for FileInputStream to get more information on how this is done.

Now you can either take a break or complete the end-of-lesson questions and exercises.

SUMMARY

- A stand-alone Java program is a program that is intended to run only on the user's machine.
- The main method is the default method that is used when a stand-alone Java program executes.
- Stand-alone Java programs can be developed to work in a browser window with some special methods that open a frame.
- When programming and executing a stand-alone program in Java, you must click the Stand-alone interpreter option button in the Information For Running Class dialog box.
- A stream is a buffer, or entry area, for data to pass from external memory to internal memory.
- Streams are used in Java to permit the access of external memory data.
- Files stored on the computer typically are binary or text types.
- The four actions to remember in file processing are open, close, get, and put. All of these actions are supported for 22 different file stream types in Java.
- Reading and writing to files is not significantly different from reading and writing using interactive methods. In the Java programming language only the class methods are different.

QUESTIONS

1. A(n) __________ program is intended to run only on the user's machine.
a. applet
b. stand-alone
c. Java
d. binary

2. The default method in stand-alone Java programs is __________.
a. init
b. try
c. catch
d. main

3. A data __________ is a temporary holding area for data as it passes from external memory to internal memory.
a. byte
b. stream
c. String
d. method

4. The __________ method is used to open an output file.
a. FileInputStream
b. DataOutputStream
c. DataInputStream
d. FileOutputStream

5. Remember to __________ a file after using it to flush any remaining data from the buffer to the file.
   a. open
   b. rewrite
   c. close
   d. execute
6. The __________ type allows the program to use the more convenient methods for output like println.
   a. FileOutputStream
   b. PrintStream
   c. DataOutputStream
   d. OutputFileStream
7. A(n) __________ file is stored on an external device using ASCII code.
   a. data
   b. text
   c. binary
   d. executable
8. The __________ method writes a String line to an output device.
   a. write
   b. put
   c. println
   d. move
9. The __________ method checks to see if an error has occurred when the program uses a data file and returns that error.
   a. try
   b. find
   c. put
   d. exception
10. The __________ method is used to retrieve errors thrown by a method that manipulates a data file.
   a. try
   b. find
   c. println
   d. catch

EXERCISES

1. List the differences between a stand-alone program and an applet.
2. Chu-Te wants to write a program that prints the values of an integer array to a file. He wants the program to put each integer on a separate line. Design and code a Java program that performs this task. Use Visual J++ to code, build, debug, and execute this program. You can use the OrderTest1.java program created in this lesson as a model. Save your program as IntegerFileWrite.java in the Exercise2C folder in the Exercises folder in the Tutorial6 folder on your Student Disk. Save the text file as Integers.txt in the same folder.

3. Koffee Koncoctions wants to develop a program that takes an array of customer objects and writes the data to a text file. Design and code the program to perform this task. You do not have to incorporate interactive input in this program, but you can assign values to the customer array. Your program should have at least three customers and store the data in a file called Customer.txt. You can use the Customer.java object that was used in this lesson for the object definition. Save your program as CustomerWrite.java in the Exercise3C folder in the Exercises folder in the Tutorial6 folder on your Student Disk. Save the Customer.txt file in the same location.
4. Larry Lawrence wants to write a program that creates a gradeTable array that contains five grades for each student in the array. There also should be a column for storing the computed average of these five grades. Use Visual J++ to design and code a program that will create this array, and then write the student information to a text file named StudentGrade.txt. You do not have to use interactive input, but you can assign values to the array as was done in OrderTest1.java. Save the program as StudentGrades.java in the Exercise4C folder in the Exercises folder in the Tutorial6 folder on your Student Disk. Save the StudentGrade.txt file in the same folder.
5. Open the Invest1.java program from the Invest folder on your Student Disk, and then save it as Invest2.java in the Exercise5C folder in the Exercises folder in the Tutorial6 folder on your Student Disk. Rewrite the program so it writes its output to a text file named Investment.txt that is stored in the same folder.

TUTORIAL

7

Using Advanced Java Features

Creating the Final User Interface for Koffee Koncoctions

case ▶ With your help, Koffee Koncoctions will be ready to implement its online ordering system. Maria wants you to write an interest calculating applet that includes a small graphic of a pyramid so she can use it to plan some of the hardware upgrades that are required to implement the new ordering system. This is the perfect opportunity to learn how to use the Dialog and Graphics Editors in Visual J++ and the Resource Wizard, which generates Java code for you.

Maria is very pleased with your work so far on the ordering system. Maria wants you to develop the final version of the user interface by adding drop-down boxes and check boxes to make ordering easier. Also, she wants you to work on the appearance of the applet. Maria wonders if there is any way that you can control the placement of items in the applet. You can use layout managers to give you more control over where items are placed in your applet.

LESSON A

objectives

In this lesson you will learn how to:

- Design a dialog box
- Create a dialog box
- Use the Resource Wizard
- Create a graphic

Using Other Resources in Visual J++

Creating an Interest Calculator Dialog Box

Designing a Dialog Box

Visual J++ has several built-in resources that simplify the task of Java programming. In this lesson you will learn how to use the Dialog Editor, Graphics Editor, and the Resource Wizard. The **Dialog Editor** has features that allow you to place GUI objects, such as labels, text fields, and buttons, in a dialog box. In Java, a dialog box is really just a "container" that holds an applet's GUI elements. In your previous GUI applets, you have not controlled the exact placement of any GUI elements. You can use the Dialog Editor to place GUI elements in an exact location.

The **Resource Wizard** takes a resource file that contains a dialog box and creates the Java code to use the dialog box in your applet. A **resource file** is a file that can contain graphics images, dialog boxes, or menus generated by Visual J++ resource editors. These Java files preserve the exact layout and appearance of the dialog box when it is used with your applet. It is not recommended that you make changes to files generated by the Resource Wizard because these files are overwritten any time the Resource Wizard is used to make changes to the dialog box.

Maria wants to be able to enter the principal amount, the number of months, and the interest rate in the interest calculating applet. Then she wants the applet to calculate the total amount of principal and interest paid over the life of the loan. Maria might use the applet more than once, so there should be a way to clear the information and then input another loan. Maria also wants the company logo to appear at the bottom of the applet.

You can control the exact placement and order of the elements in the dialog box, so you need to concentrate on GUI principles that relate to placement. These principles include:

- Labels and text fields should be arranged vertically, starting in the upper-left corner of the applet.
- Buttons should be arranged along the bottom of the applet from the most used to the least used.
- Similar elements should have the same size.
- Edges of adjacent elements should align evenly.
- Labels and button captions should be concise and meaningful.
- White space, or the blank area between elements, is as important as the elements themselves.

Each of these principles is based on one basic concept—a good user interface is one that helps users accomplish their tasks without confusion or distraction. The top to bottom, left to right element placement is based on the flow of most written languages. Another way to help the user know what element to access first is by using the requestFocus method to position the insertion point. You can use the requestFocus method in the init method or at the end of any method where there is a possibility of user confusion to make an applet easier to use. A standard in most Microsoft dialog boxes is that the buttons appear on the bottom of the dialog box. In this case, the left to right principle has the buttons arranged with the most-used button on the left, followed in order from left to right to the least-used button.

Using elements with different sizes and uneven alignment is distracting to users. Users might not know what is bothering them, but small distractions can add up. A well-designed user interface, on the other hand, reduces the effort needed by the user. You might remember the user interface that you programmed in Tutorial 3 that contained numerous text fields and labels. That program was an example of a poorly designed user interface because it was difficult to input the information.

In any program, it is important to communicate to users what information is needed and what actions they need to take to use the software. Labels and button names should be concise and meaningful. When you are using applets, there is no way for a user to read the documentation if they get lost. The only instructions that users receive are what is coded into the applet. If users cannot figure out how to use the applet, they will not use it.

The last principle governs the use of white space, or blank space. If the GUI elements are too close together on the screen, it becomes hard to understand what is on the screen. The amount of space between elements is important. You should group related elements closer together than unrelated elements. For the interest calculating applet, you should group the three input fields and their labels.

The interest calculating applet needs labels, text fields, and buttons. Figure 7-1 shows a rough sketch of the dialog box that you will create. Notice that the three input fields and their labels are grouped on the left side of the dialog box and that the Amount Paid output field appears on the right. The Calculate and Clear buttons appear at the bottom of the dialog box.

Interest Calculator

Principal

Interest Rate

Months

Amount Paid

Calculate

Clear

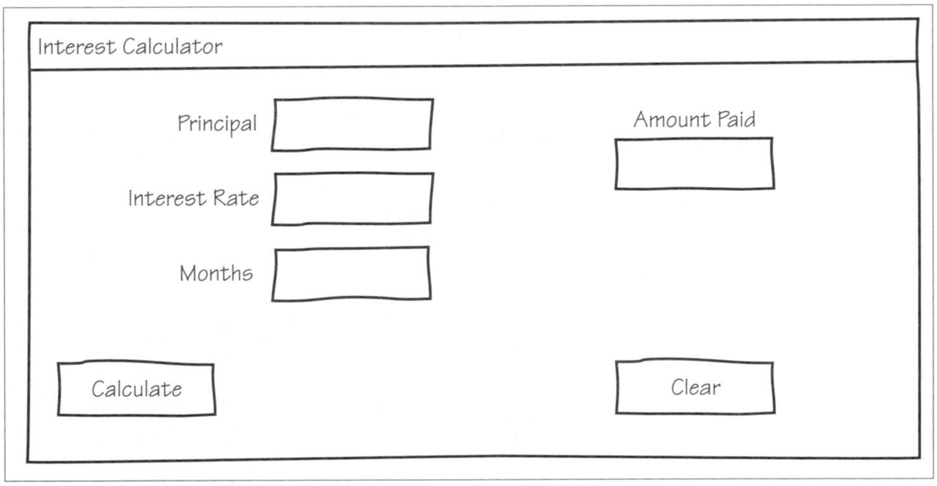

Figure 7-1: Sketch of dialog box

Creating a Dialog Box

There are two main steps to create a dialog box that can be used in an applet. The first step is to use the Dialog Editor to create the dialog box and place its GUI elements. The second step is to use the Resource Wizard to create the necessary Java files to use the dialog box. You will use the Dialog Editor to select the elements you want to place on the form, name them, and then place them exactly where you want them in the dialog box.

To start the Dialog Editor:

1. Start Visual J++ and close any open workspaces, if necessary.
2. If necessary, right-click anywhere in the Output window and then click **Hide** on the shortcut menu to hide the window.
3. Click **File** on the menu bar, and then click **New**. The New dialog box opens.
4. Click the **Files** tab and then double-click **Resource Template**. A new template file opens, as shown in Figure 7-2.

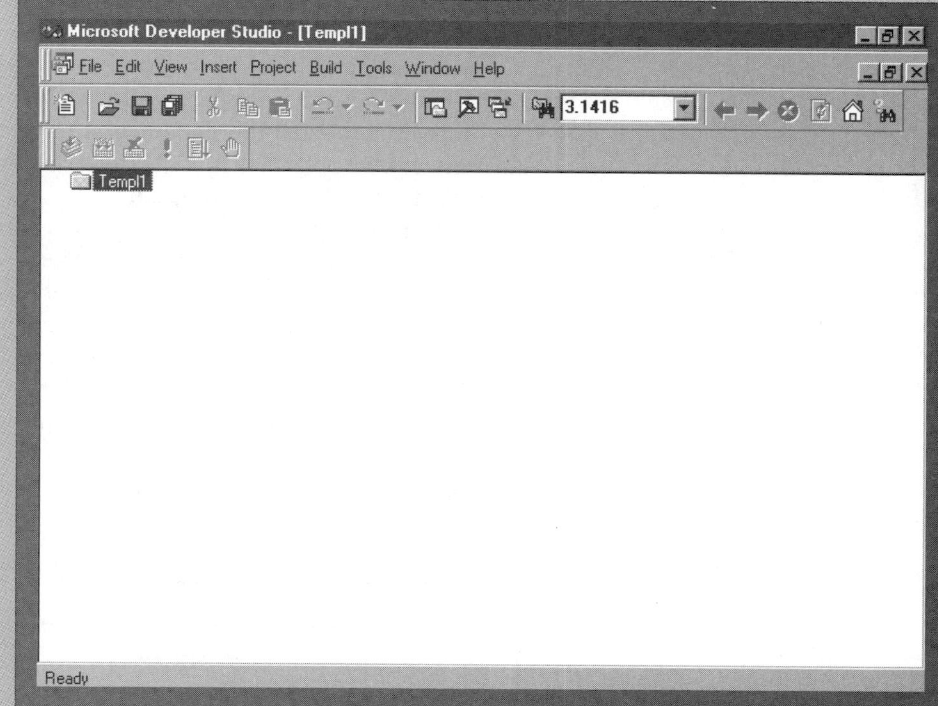

Figure 7-2: Starting a Resource Template

5. Click **Insert** on the menu bar, and then click **Resource**. The Insert Resource dialog box opens, as shown in Figure 7-3. You can use this dialog box to create new GUI elements.

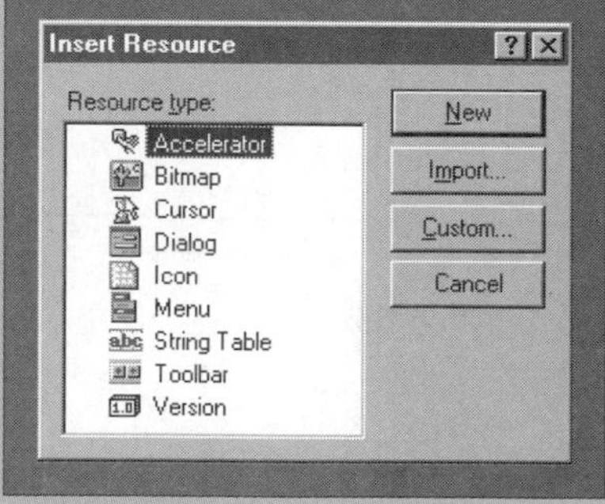

Figure 7-3: Insert Resource dialog box

6 Click **Dialog** in the Resource type list, and then click the **New** button. The Dialog Editor opens, as shown in Figure 7-4.

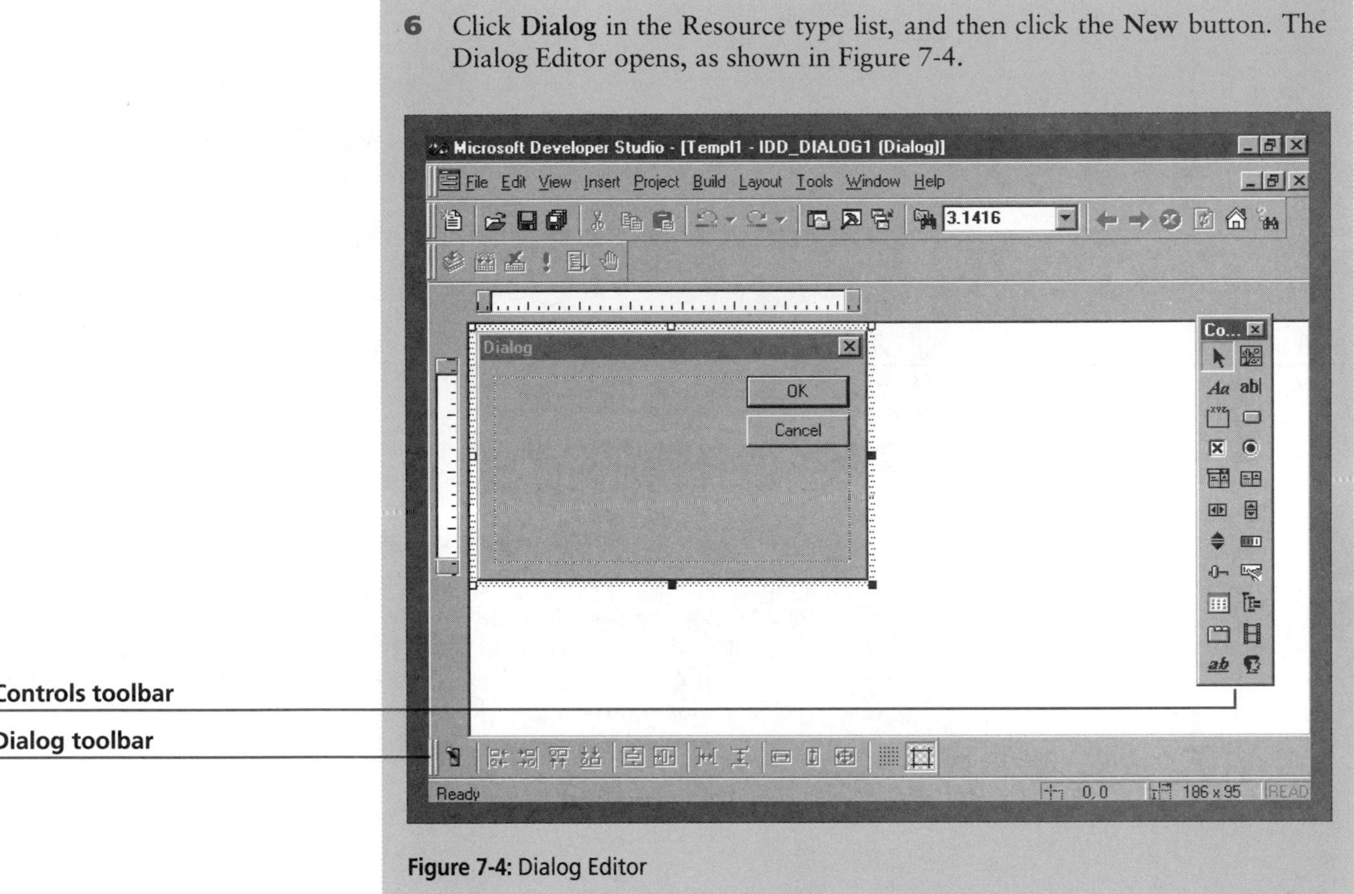

Figure 7-4: Dialog Editor

The Dialog Editor has two new toolbars. The Dialog toolbar appears across the bottom of the screen in Figure 7-4, and gives you control over the layout of the elements in the dialog box. There are tools to align, center, and size elements on your dialog box, and to switch the grid and rulers on or off. The Controls toolbar, which appears at the right in Figure 7-4, allows you to place the various controls, like labels and text fields, in your dialog box. Some of the elements in the Controls toolbar are used only in Visual C++, but because the Developer Studio is used for more than Visual J++ they are shown here. Your toolbars might appear in a different location or configuration if they have been moved or customized.

The Dialog Editor opens with a default configuration that includes an OK button and a Cancel button. This configuration does not match the sketch in Figure 7-1, so you need to change the design. Also, the Dialog Editor generates default names for the GUI elements, including the dialog box itself, that you will need to change. Another default value generated by Visual J++ is the default font for the dialog elements. To help keep your work consistent with the figures, you will check to see if your font matches those in the figures. You also will change the default name of the dialog box, increase the size of the dialog box, and then save the file.

To change the name of the dialog box and check the default font:

1 Right-click anywhere in the Dialog box (but not on a button), and then click **Properties** on the shortcut menu. The Dialog Properties dialog box opens, as shown in Figure 7-5. The text in the ID text box should be selected.

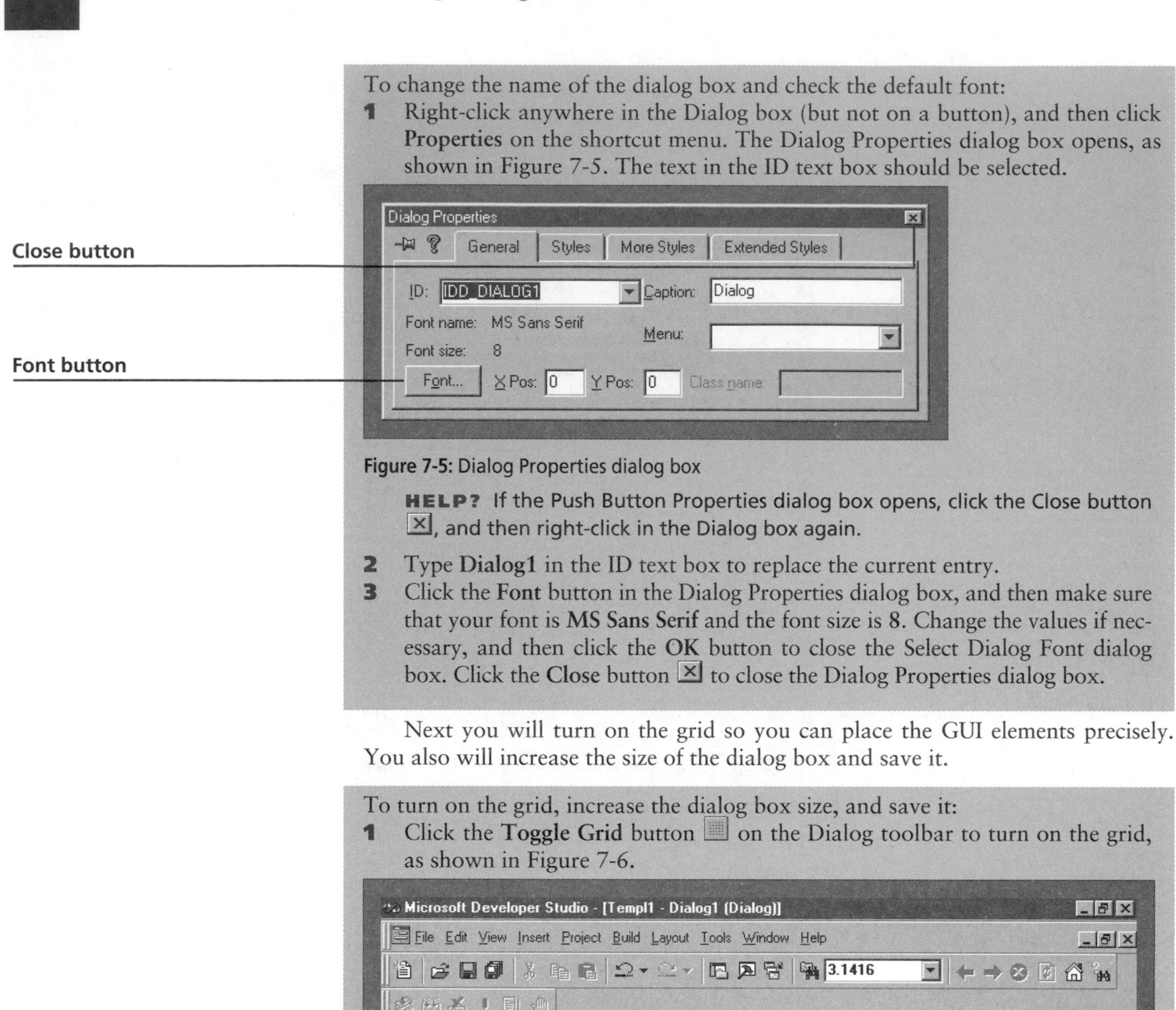

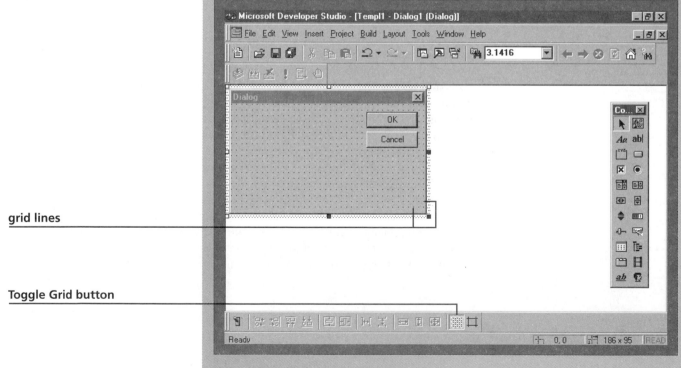

Figure 7-5: Dialog Properties dialog box

HELP? If the Push Button Properties dialog box opens, click the Close button [X], and then right-click in the Dialog box again.

2 Type **Dialog1** in the ID text box to replace the current entry.

3 Click the **Font** button in the Dialog Properties dialog box, and then make sure that your font is **MS Sans Serif** and the font size is 8. Change the values if necessary, and then click the **OK** button to close the Select Dialog Font dialog box. Click the **Close** button [X] to close the Dialog Properties dialog box.

Next you will turn on the grid so you can place the GUI elements precisely. You also will increase the size of the dialog box and save it.

To turn on the grid, increase the dialog box size, and save it:

1 Click the **Toggle Grid** button on the Dialog toolbar to turn on the grid, as shown in Figure 7-6.

grid lines

Toggle Grid button

Figure 7-6: Dialog box with grid showing

2 Position the pointer on the lower-right corner of the Dialog box so the pointer changes to ↘, click and drag the pointer until the Dialog box is 277 × 130, as shown in Figure 7-7, and then release the mouse button.

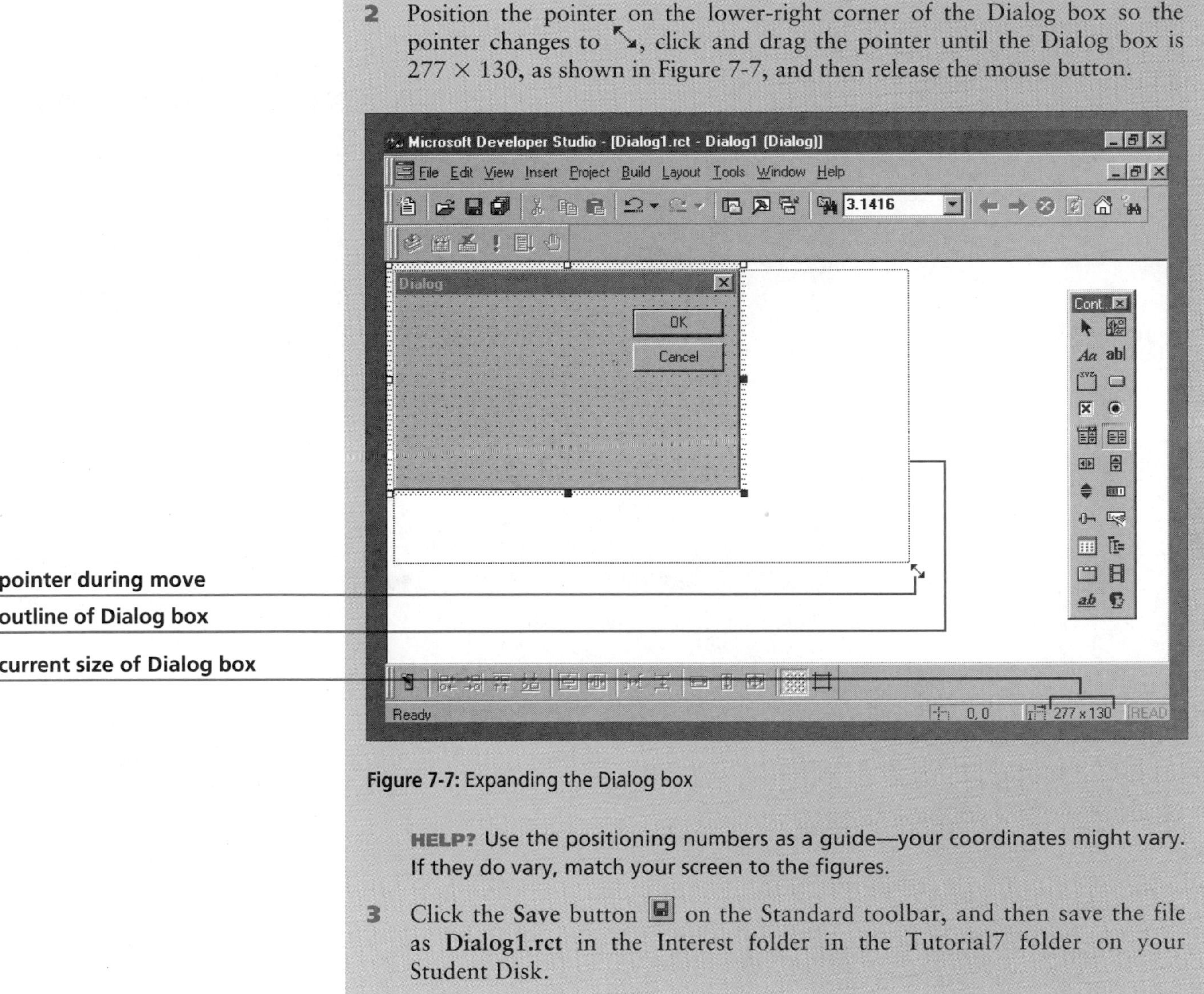

Figure 7-7: Expanding the Dialog box

HELP? Use the positioning numbers as a guide—your coordinates might vary. If they do vary, match your screen to the figures.

3 Click the **Save** button on the Standard toolbar, and then save the file as **Dialog1.rct** in the Interest folder in the Tutorial7 folder on your Student Disk.

Now that you have named the Dialog box and increased its size, it is time to position, name, and add captions to the two buttons. The default configuration includes two buttons, so you need to change them to fit the design, and you will not need to add any new buttons.

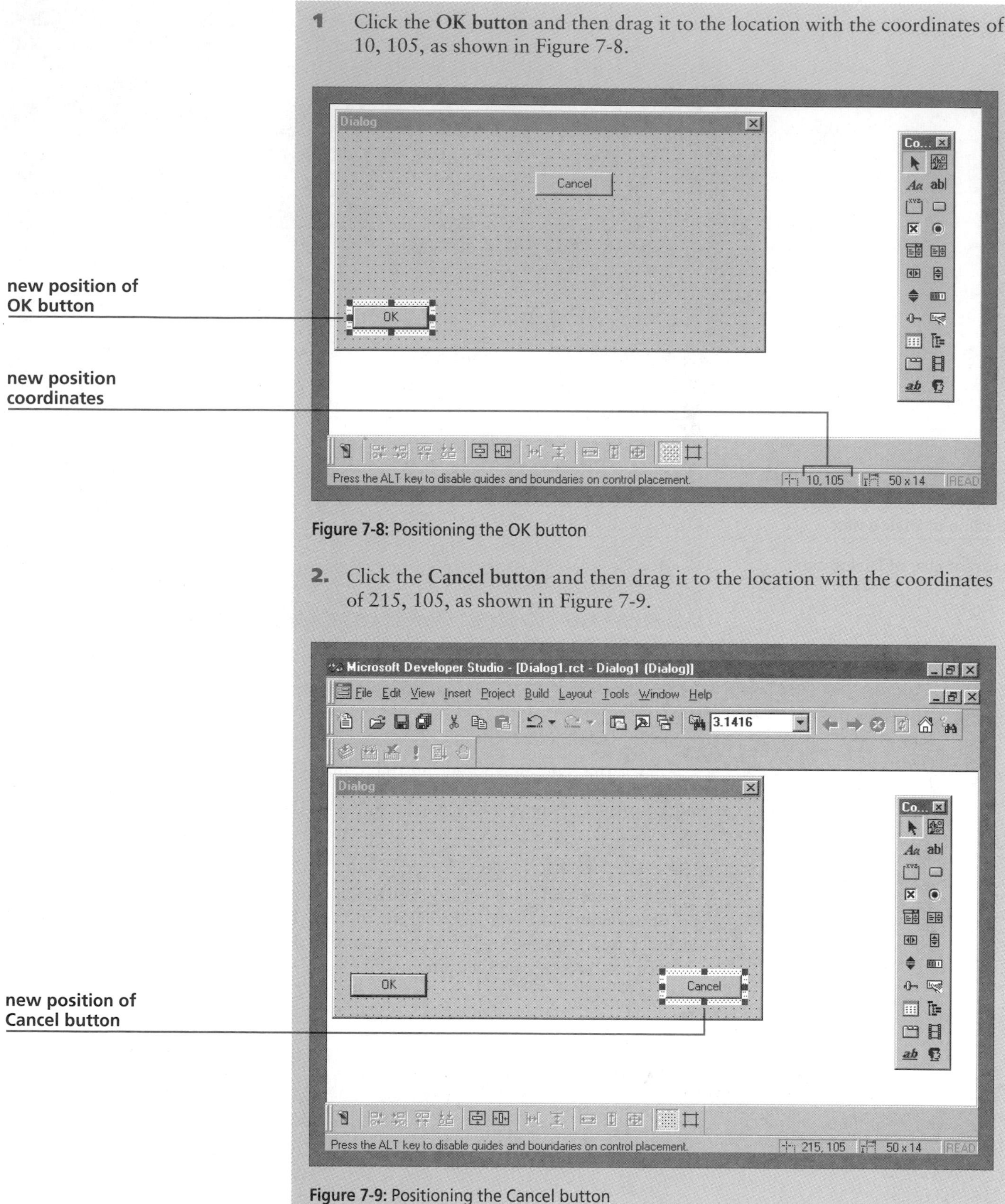

1 Click the **OK button** and then drag it to the location with the coordinates of 10, 105, as shown in Figure 7-8.

Figure 7-8: Positioning the OK button

2. Click the **Cancel button** and then drag it to the location with the coordinates of 215, 105, as shown in Figure 7-9.

Figure 7-9: Positioning the Cancel button

3 Right-click the **OK button**, and then click **Properties** on the shortcut menu to open the Push Button Properties dialog box.

4 Type **CALCULATE** in the ID text box, press the **Tab** key, type **Calculate** in the Caption text box, and then press the **Enter** key to change the button caption and name.

5 Right-click the **Cancel button**, and then click **Properties** on the shortcut menu. Type **CLEAR** in the ID text box, press the **Tab** key, type **Clear** in the Caption text box, and then press the **Enter** key to change the button caption and name. Your Dialog box should look like Figure 7-10.

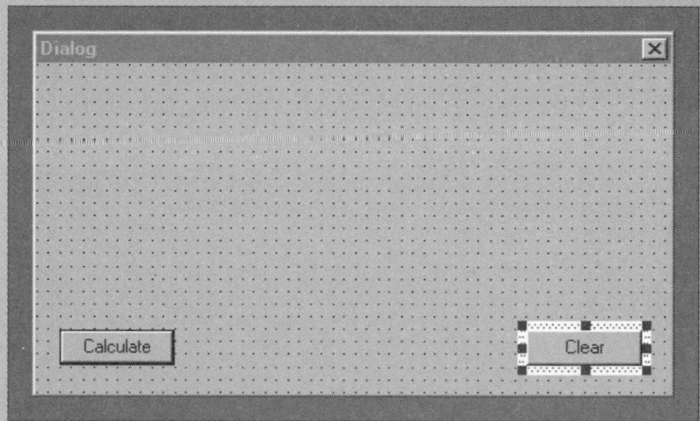

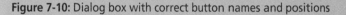

Figure 7-10: Dialog box with correct button names and positions

6 Click the **Save** button on the Standard toolbar to save your changes.

The next step is to add and position the labels for the input text fields. In the Dialog Editor, the tool that adds labels is the Static Text tool on the Controls toolbar.

To add and position the labels for the input text fields:

1 Click the **Static Text** tool on the Controls toolbar. The pointer changes to + when you move it into the Dialog box.

2 Click in the location shown in Figure 7-11 (coordinates 10, 10), drag the pointer to the position shown in Figure 7-11 (coordinates 45 × 15), and then release the mouse button. If your coordinates are different than those shown in Figure 7-11, after you release the mouse button, resize and reposition the text box as needed.

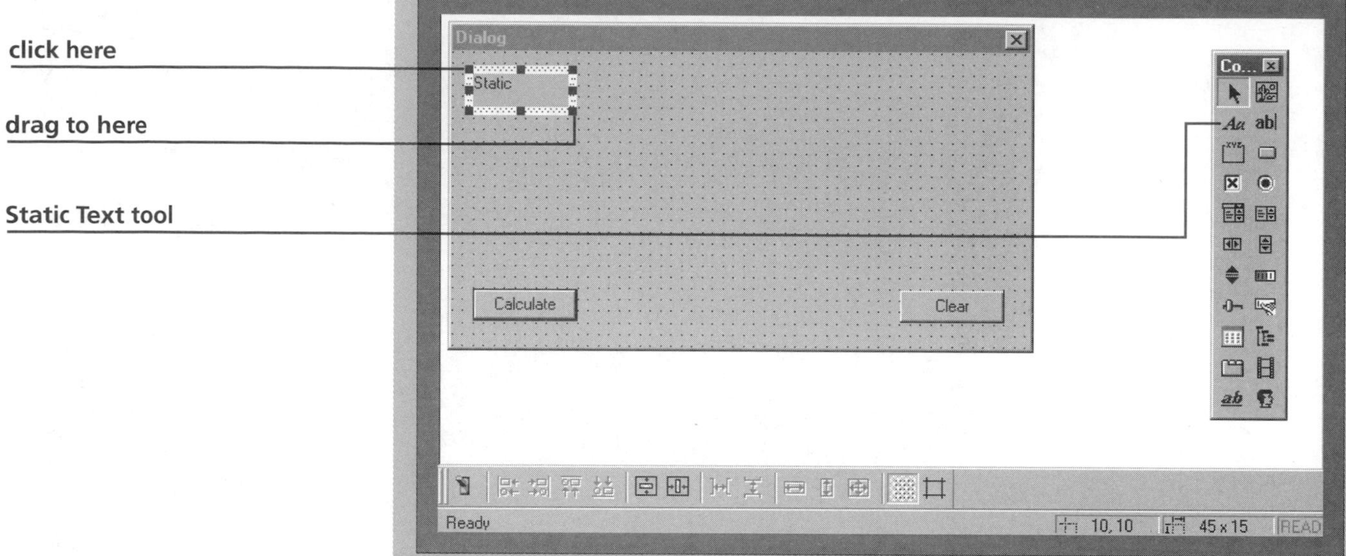

Figure 7-11: Adding and positioning the first Static Text object

3 Make sure that the Static Text object is selected, and then click the **Copy** button on the Standard toolbar to copy the Static Text object so you can paste a copy in another location.

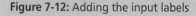

4 Click the **Paste** button on the Standard toolbar to paste a copy of the Static Text object, and then drag it to the coordinates 10, 40.

5 Click again to paste another copy of the Static Text object, and then drag it to the coordinates 10, 65. Your Dialog box should look like Figure 7-12.

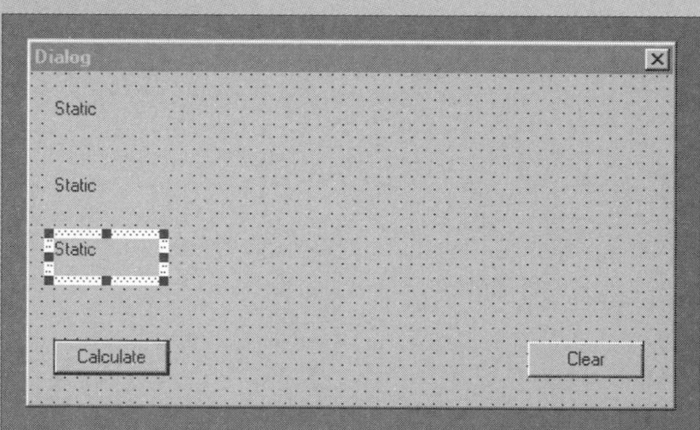

Figure 7-12: Adding the input labels

6 Right-click the top **Static Text object**, and then click **Properties** on the shortcut menu. Change the ID text to **lblPrincipal**, and change the caption to **Principal**. Click the **Styles** tab, click the **Align text** list arrow, click **Right**, and then click the **Close** button [X] to close the dialog box. The top Static Text object changes to include a new right-aligned label, as shown in Figure 7-13.

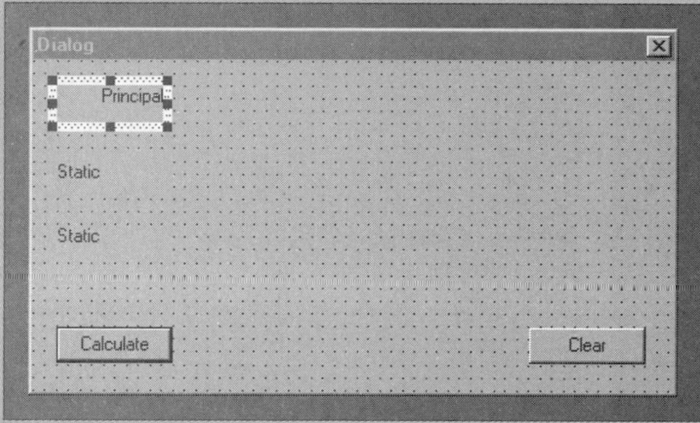

Figure 7-13: Changing the text alignment and caption

7 Right-click the middle **Static Text object**, and then click **Properties**. Click the **General** tab, and change the ID text to **lblInterest** and the caption to **Interest Rate**. Click the **Styles** tab, and then change the alignment to **Right**. You can change the properties of the last object by clicking the Keep Visible button in the dialog box.

8 Click the **Keep Visible** button in the Edit Properties dialog box, click the bottom **Static Text object**, click the **General** tab, and then change the ID to **lblMonths** and the caption to **Months**. Click the **Styles** tab, change the alignment to **Right**, and then click [X]. Click anywhere in the Dialog box to deselect the Months object. Your Dialog box should look like Figure 7-14.

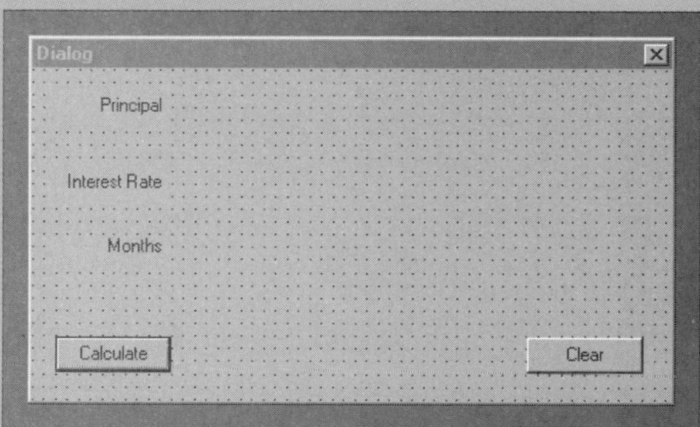

Figure 7-14: Dialog box after adding three input labels

9 Save your changes.

Now you can add and position the three input text fields. In the Dialog Editor, text fields are called Edit boxes.

To add and position the input text fields (Edit boxes):

1 Click the **Edit Box** tool on the Controls toolbar. The pointer changes to + when you move it into the Dialog box.

2 Drag to create a 45 × 15 box to the right of the Principal label, and then drag the box to position it at coordinates 70, 10, as shown in Figure 7-15.

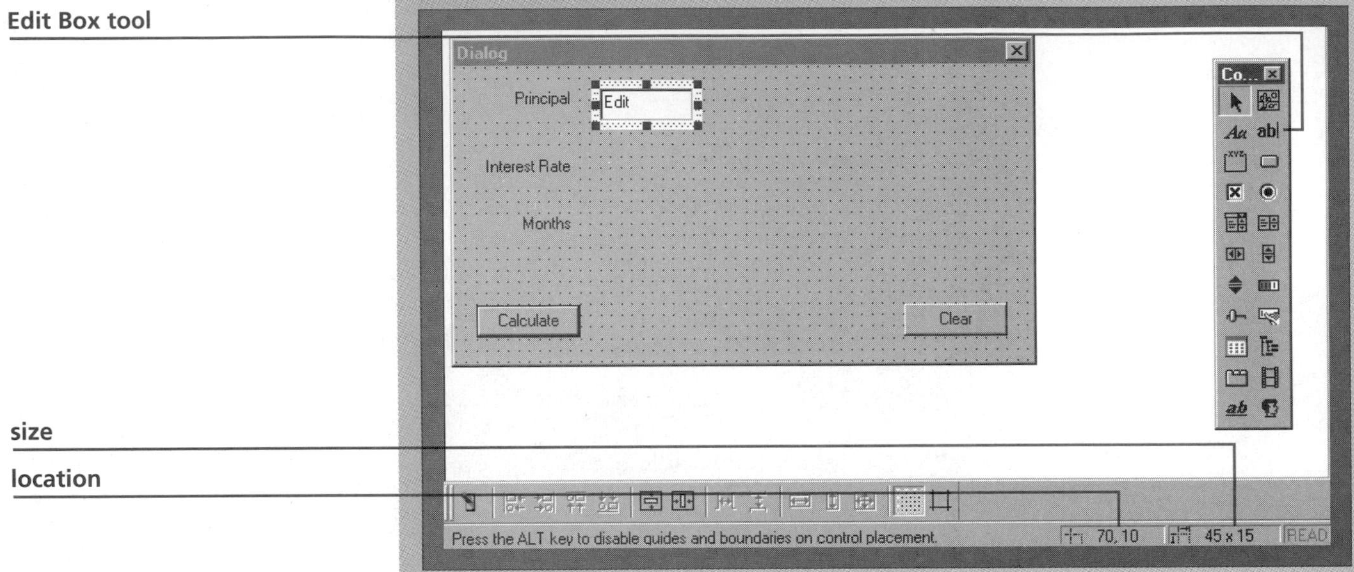

Figure 7-15: Adding and positioning the first Edit box

3 Make sure the Edit box is selected, and then click the **Copy** button on the Standard toolbar to copy the Edit box.

4 Click the **Paste** button on the Standard toolbar to paste a copy of the Edit box, and then drag the copy of the Edit box to coordinates 70, 40.

5 Click again to paste another copy of the Edit box, and then drag it to coordinates 70, 65. Your Dialog box should look like Figure 7-16.

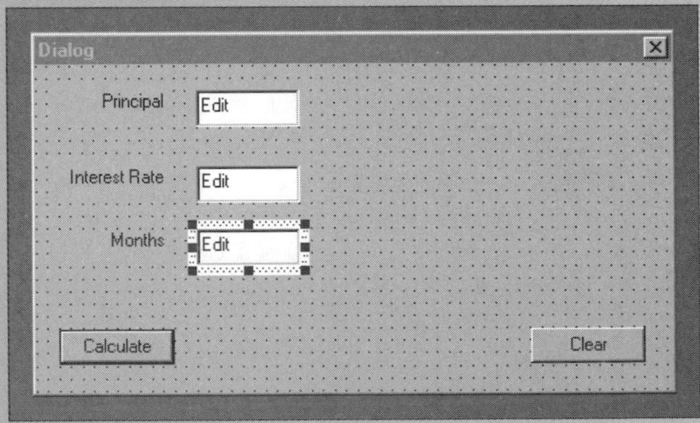

Figure 7-16: Dialog box after adding three Edit boxes

6 Right-click the top **Edit box**, click **Properties** on the shortcut menu, click the **General** tab, and then change the ID to **PRINCIPAL**.

7 Click the **Keep Visible** button in the dialog box, click the middle **Edit box**, click **Properties**, and then change the ID to **INTEREST**.

8 Click the bottom **Edit box**, click **Properties**, and then change the ID to **MONTHS**. Click the **Close** button to close the dialog box.

9 Save your changes.

The last items to add are the label and the text field for the output.

To add the output label and text field:

1 Click the **Static Text** tool on the Controls toolbar.

2 Drag to create a 45 × 15 box in the same area as shown in Figure 7-17, and then position it at coordinates 195, 30, as shown in Figure 7-17.

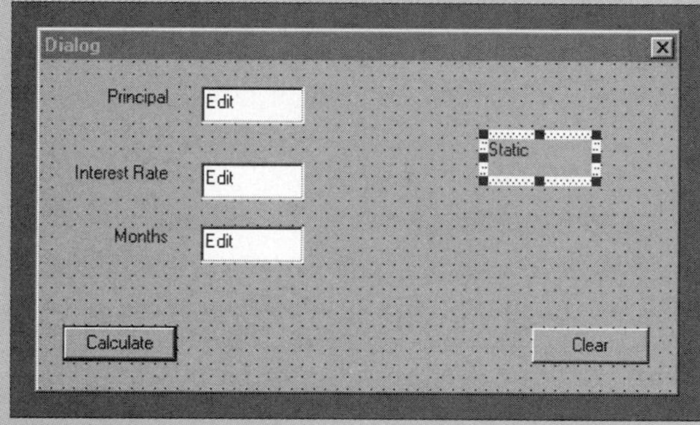

Figure 7-17: Adding and positioning the output label

3 Right-click the **Static Text object**, click **Properties** on the shortcut menu, change the ID to **lblTotal**, change the caption to **Total Amount**, and then click the **Close** button

4 Click the **Edit Box** tool on the Controls toolbar.

5 Drag to create a 45 × 15 box positioned at coordinates 195, 50, as shown in Figure 7-18.

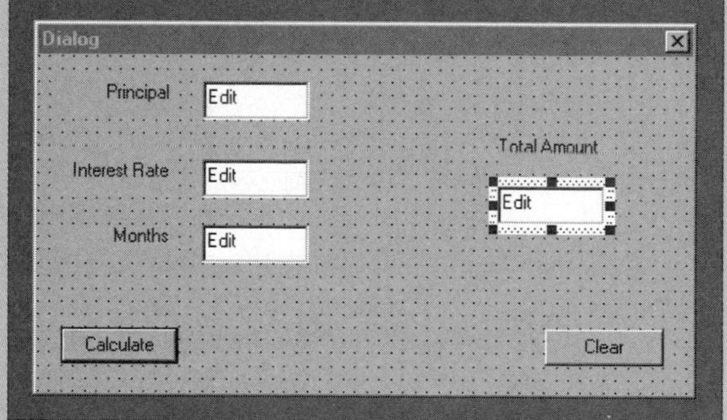

Figure 7-18: Adding and positioning the output text field

6 Right-click the **Edit box**, click **Properties**, change the ID to TOTAL, and then click ☒.

7 Save your changes.

Using the Resource Wizard

Now that you have designed and created the dialog box, how do you use it in your applet? At this point, in other versions of Java, you must write the Java code to create the dialog box. In Visual J++, you only need to write the Java code to implement the dialog box in an applet, and the Resource Wizard will generate this code for you. The Resource Wizard works with dialog boxes and menus. After you create the dialog box, the Resource Wizard will generate the Java code to use it. You should note that the wizard saves the files for you, so there are no changes to save.

To use the Resource Wizard to generate the Java code:

1 Click **Tools** on the menu bar, and then click **Java Resource Wizard.** The Java Resource Wizard dialog box opens. In the first step, you enter the filename.

2 Type **Dialog1.rct** in the File name text box, and then click the **Next** button.

3 To generate the files, click the **Finish** button. The Java Resource Wizard dialog box opens and identifies the files that were created, as shown in Figure 7-19.

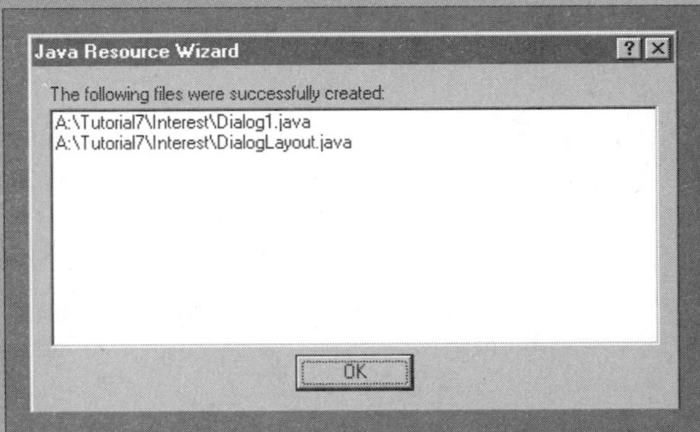

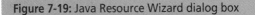

Figure 7-19: Java Resource Wizard dialog box

4 Click the **OK** button to close the Java Resource Wizard dialog box.

Now you will write the applet that uses the dialog box. The InterestCalc applet only has the dialog box as a property; the rest of the applet consists of the methods. Besides the init method, this applet will need an action method and a CalcInterest method. The values entered by users will need to be converted into float values, so you also will need a toFloat method. First you will need to start the file, write the necessary import statements, set up the dialog box, and then write the init method.

There are only two statements that you have not seen before in the code that you will enter. To use the files generated by the Java Resource Wizard, you need to include an *import Dialog1;* statement so your applet can use the code generated by the Resource Wizard in the same way that you can use the predefined classes and objects in the rest of Java. The property statement *Dialog1 One = new Dialog1(this);* is familiar—the difference is in the use of the *this* reference. To use a dialog box, it needs to be placed in something. In your applet, you will place the dialog box in the applet, so the reference refers to the applet itself, without giving the applet a name.

To place the dialog box in the applet:

1 Click **File** on the menu bar, and then click **New**. Click the **Files** tab, and double-click **Java Source File.**

2 Type the Java code shown in Figure 7-20 to import the necessary files, declare the class and GUI element, and create the init method.

type this code

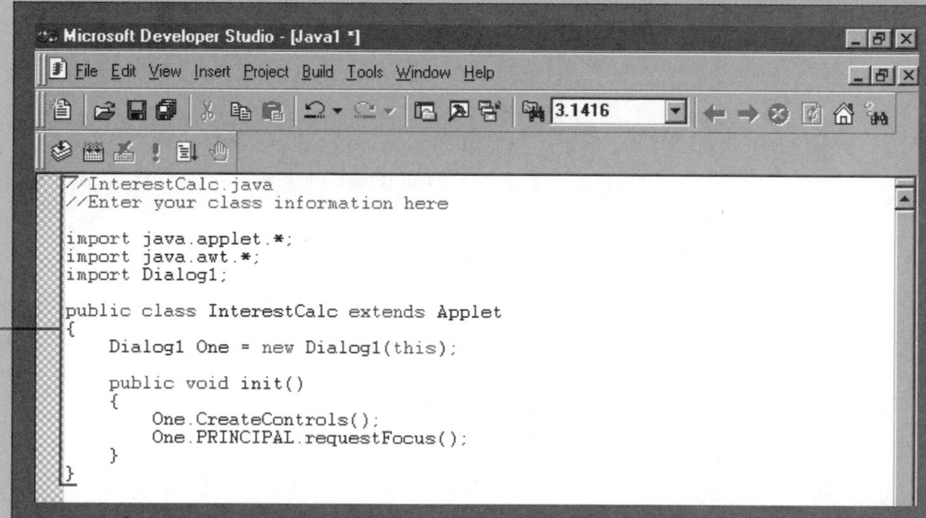


```
//InterestCalc.java
//Enter your class information here

import java.applet.*;
import java.awt.*;
import Dialog1;

public class InterestCalc extends Applet
{
    Dialog1 One = new Dialog1(this);

    public void init()
    {
        One.CreateControls();
        One.PRINCIPAL.requestFocus();
    }
}
```

Figure 7-20: InterestCalc properties and init method

3 Save the file as **InterestCalc.java** in the Interest folder in the Tutorial7 folder on your Student Disk.

4 Click the **Build** button on the Build toolbar, and then click the **Yes** button to build the program in a default project workspace. If necessary, correct any typing errors.

5 Click the **Execute Program** button on the Build toolbar to execute the program. Type **InterestCalc** in the Class file name text box, and then click the **OK** button to execute the applet in Internet Explorer. See Figure 7-21.

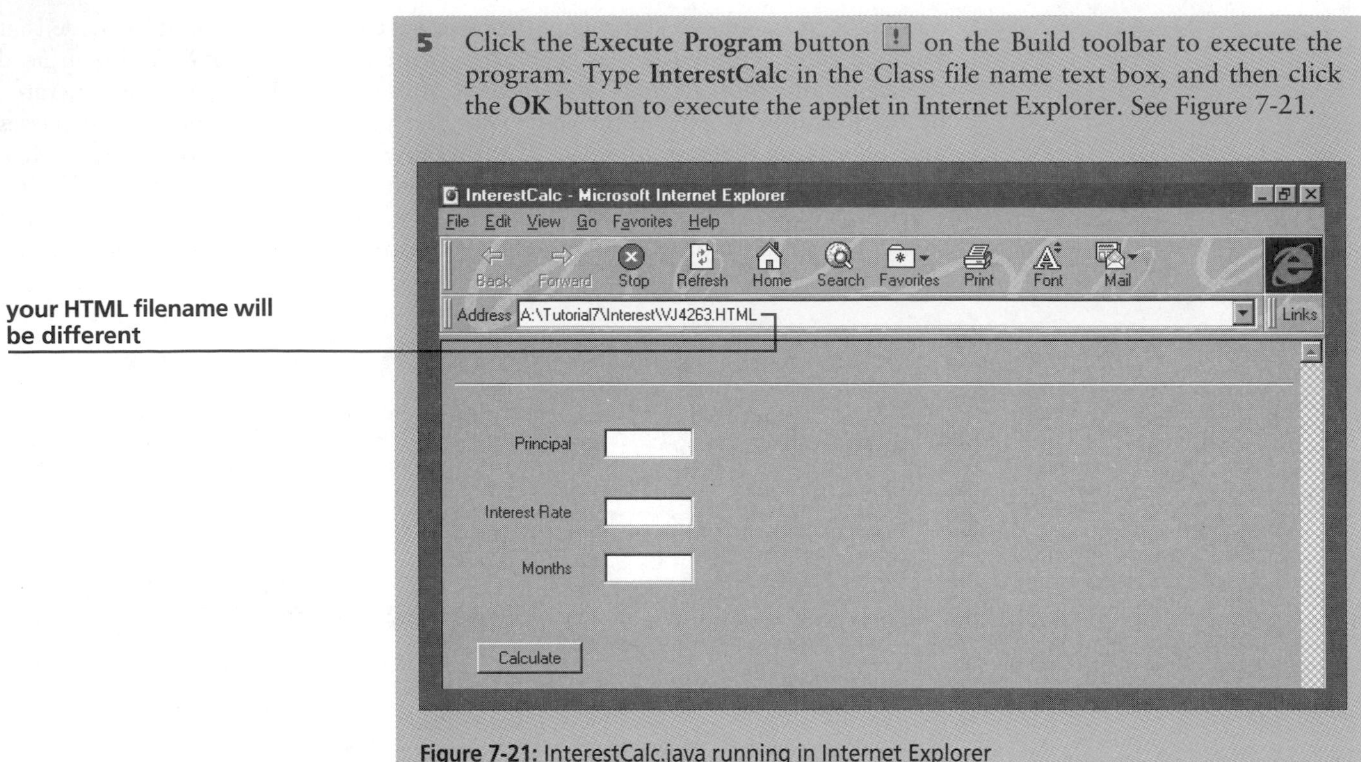

Figure 7-21: InterestCalc.java running in Internet Explorer

You might notice a problem with the applet. The entire dialog box does not display. To fix this problem, you need to change the width and height parameters in the HTML file. To do this, you need to open the HTML file that Visual J++ created. The HTML filename is generated randomly, so your filename will be different than the one shown in Figure 7-21. You will open the HTML file, change the width and height parameters, and then save the HTML file with a new name.

To change the width and height of the HTML file and save it with a new filename:

1 Close Internet Explorer.

2 Click the **Open** button on the Standard toolbar, click the **Files of type** list arrow, click **Web Files**, and then double-click the filename that appears in the list. The HTML file opens in the Editor window.

3 Scroll down and change the width value to **400** and the height value to **300**, as shown in Figure 7-22.

change these values

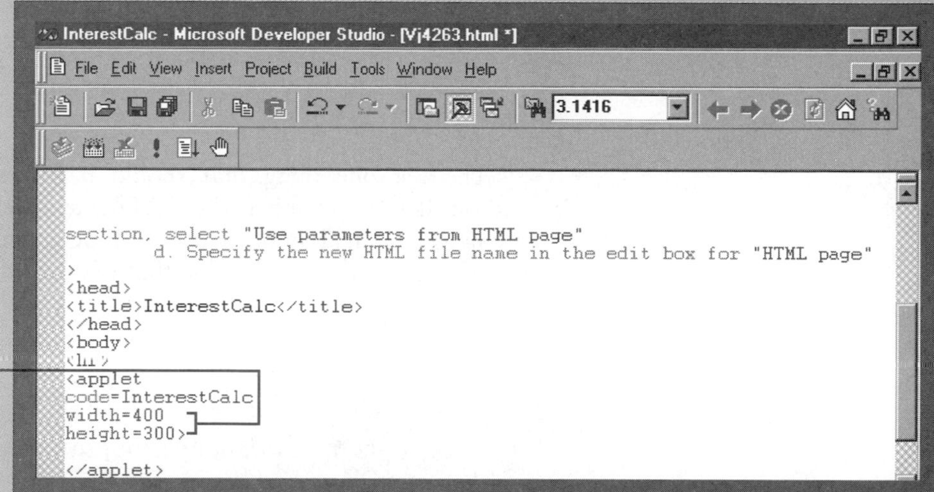

Figure 7-22: Changing the applet width

4 Click **File** on the menu bar, and then click **Save As** to save the file as **InterestCalc.html.**

5 Click **Project** on the menu bar, click **Settings,** click the **Debug** tab, click the **Category** list arrow, and then click **Browser.** Click the **Use Parameters from HTML page** option button, and then type **InterestCalc.html** in the HTML page text box. Click the **OK** button.

6 Execute the program again. Your output should look like Figure 7-23.

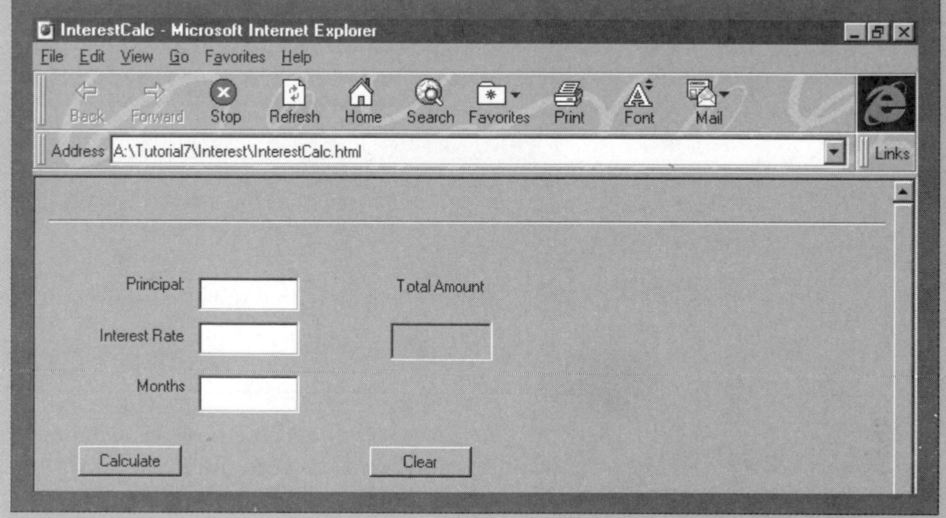

Figure 7-23: Running InterestCalc with the correct width

HELP? If your screen does not match Figure 7-23 (the Calculate and the Clear buttons should appear), open the InterestCalc.html file again, and then change the height value to 400. If only the Clear button is missing, change the width value to 500. Save the HTML file and then execute the program again. If you still have problems, ask your instructor for help.

7 Close Internet Explorer.

There is one thing that should be done before moving on to the action method. If you remember, the TOTAL text field is an output-only field. You need to change the field so users cannot type a number in the output field by making the field read-only. You will do that first and then add the action method.

To make the output field read-only and add the action method:

1 Click **Window** on the menu bar, and then click **InterestCalc.java.**

2 Click in the first location shown in Figure 7-24, press the **Enter** key, and then type the code shown in Figure 7-24.

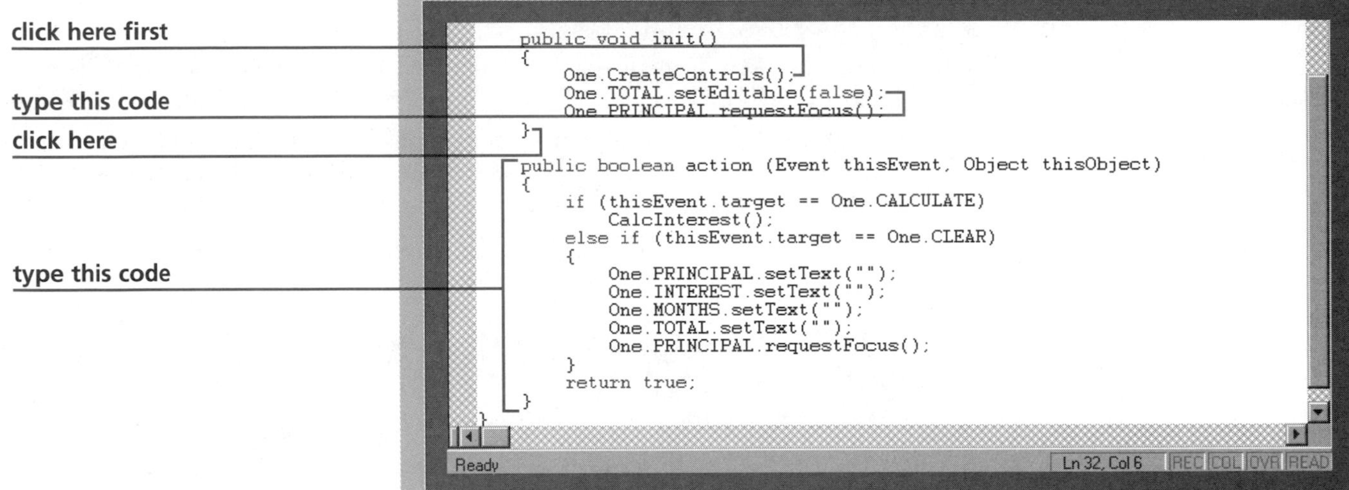

click here first
type this code
click here
type this code
public void init()
{
One.CreateControls();
One.TOTAL.setEditable(false);
One.PRINCIPAL.requestFocus();
}
public boolean action (Event thisEvent, Object thisObject)
{
if (thisEvent.target == One.CALCULATE)
CalcInterest();
else if (thisEvent.target == One.CLEAR)
{
One.PRINCIPAL.setText("");
One.INTEREST.setText("");
One.MONTHS.setText("");
One.TOTAL.setText("");
One.PRINCIPAL.requestFocus();
}
return true;
}
Ready
Ln 32, Col 6
REC COL OVR READ

Figure 7-24: Changing the Edit property and adding the action method

3 Click in the second location shown in Figure 7-24, press the **Enter** key twice, and then type the code shown in Figure 7-24.

4 Save your changes.

Next you will add methods to calculate the interest and to convert a String to a float number to be used in calculations.

To add the methods to calculate the interest and convert the number:

1 Click in the location shown in Figure 7-25, press the **Enter** key twice, and then type the CalcInterest and toFloat methods.

click here

type this code

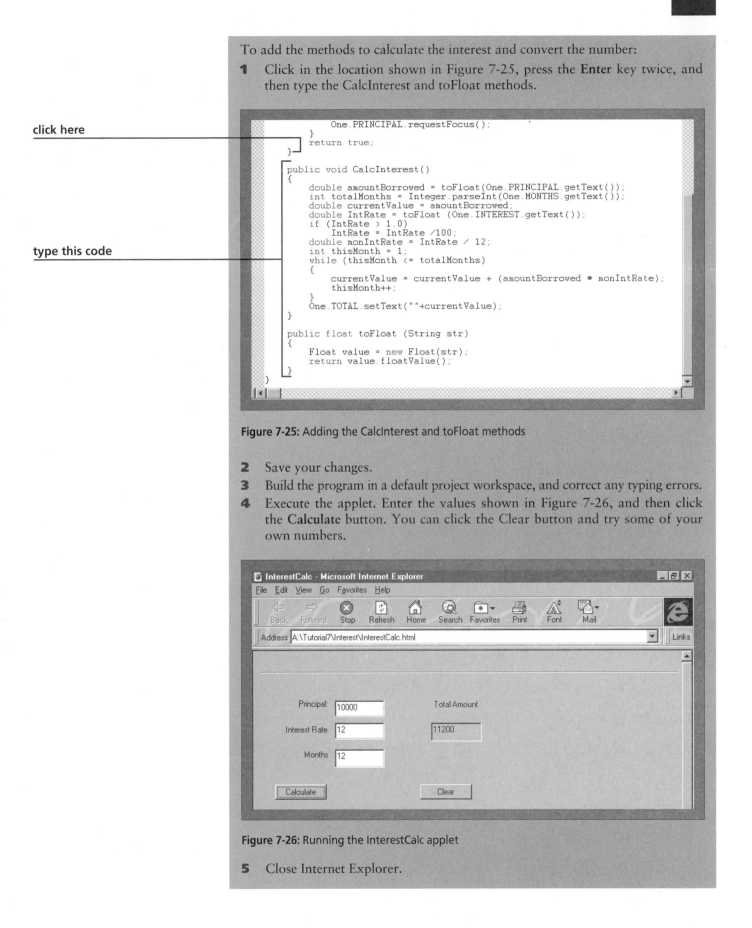

```
            One.PRINCIPAL.requestFocus();
        }
        return true;
    }
    public void CalcInterest()
    {
        double amountBorrowed = toFloat(One.PRINCIPAL.getText());
        int totalMonths = Integer.parseInt(One.MONTHS.getText());
        double currentValue = amountBorrowed;
        double IntRate = toFloat (One.INTEREST.getText());
        if (IntRate > 1.0)
            IntRate = IntRate /100;
        double monIntRate = IntRate / 12;
        int thisMonth = 1;
        while (thisMonth <= totalMonths)
        {
            currentValue = currentValue + (amountBorrowed * monIntRate);
            thisMonth++;
        }
        One.TOTAL.setText(""+currentValue);
    }

    public float toFloat (String str)
    {
        Float value = new Float(str);
        return value.floatValue();
    }
}
```

Figure 7-25: Adding the CalcInterest and toFloat methods

2 Save your changes.

3 Build the program in a default project workspace, and correct any typing errors.

4 Execute the applet. Enter the values shown in Figure 7-26, and then click the **Calculate** button. You can click the Clear button and try some of your own numbers.

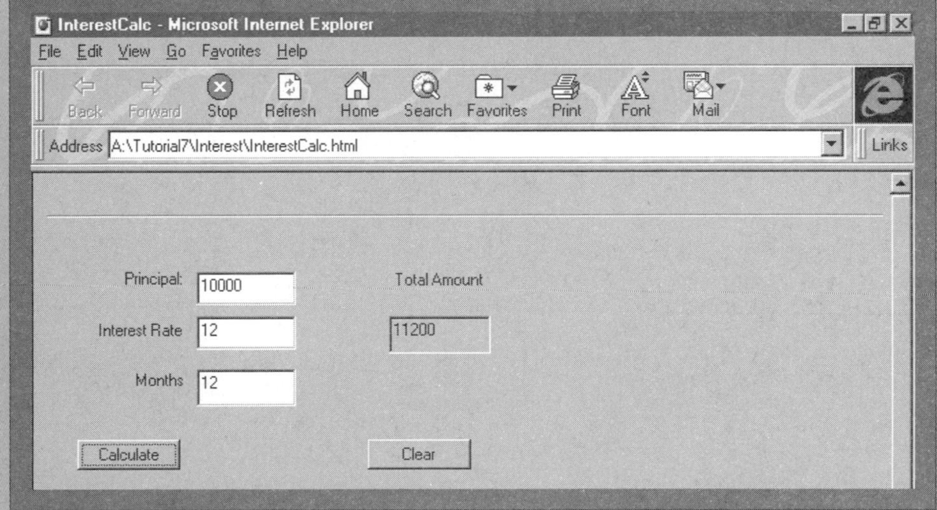

Figure 7-26: Running the InterestCalc applet

5 Close Internet Explorer.

Click the first Tutorial 7 link of the Online Companion for this book (http://www.course.com) to see a live Java program that illustrates this topic.

Creating a Graphic

Now you need to use the **Graphics Editor** to create a file that contains the company logo and then add the commands to add the graphic to the InterestCalc applet. You will use Graphics Editor to create a .gif graphics file to match the sketch shown in Figure 7-27, which Maria gave you. The graphic consists of four triangles, the company name, a gray background, and a dark blue frame. You will begin by starting a graphics file, sizing the graphics grid, coloring the background, and drawing the border.

Figure 7-27: Sketch of Koffee logo

To create the graphics file and size the graphics grid:

1. Right-click the Output window, and then click **Hide** on the shortcut menu.
2. Click **File** on the menu bar, click **New**, click the **Files** tab, and then, if necessary, click the **Add to project** check box to clear it. Double-click **Bitmap File** to open a new graphics file.
3. Scroll down the grid and position the pointer on the lower-right handle so the pointer changes to ↘, and then drag the grid to coordinates 63 × 48, as shown in Figure 7-28. Next you will change the grid color to dark gray.

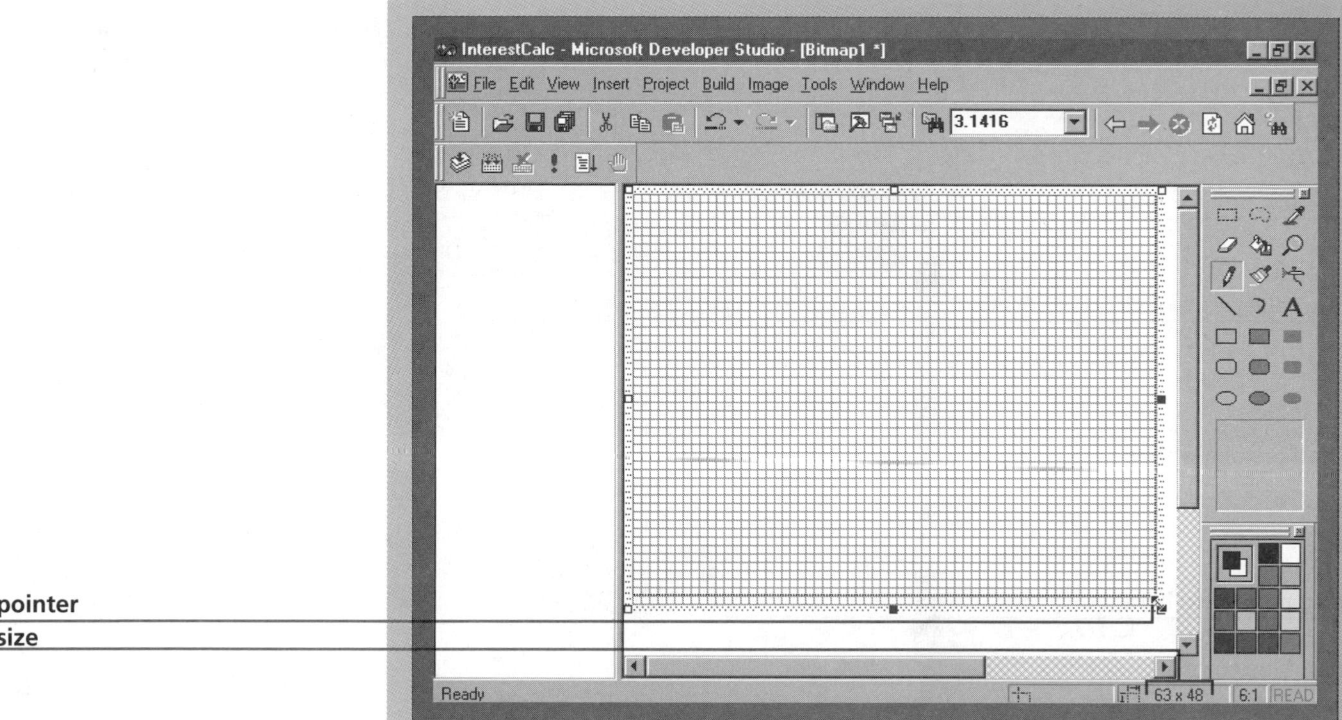

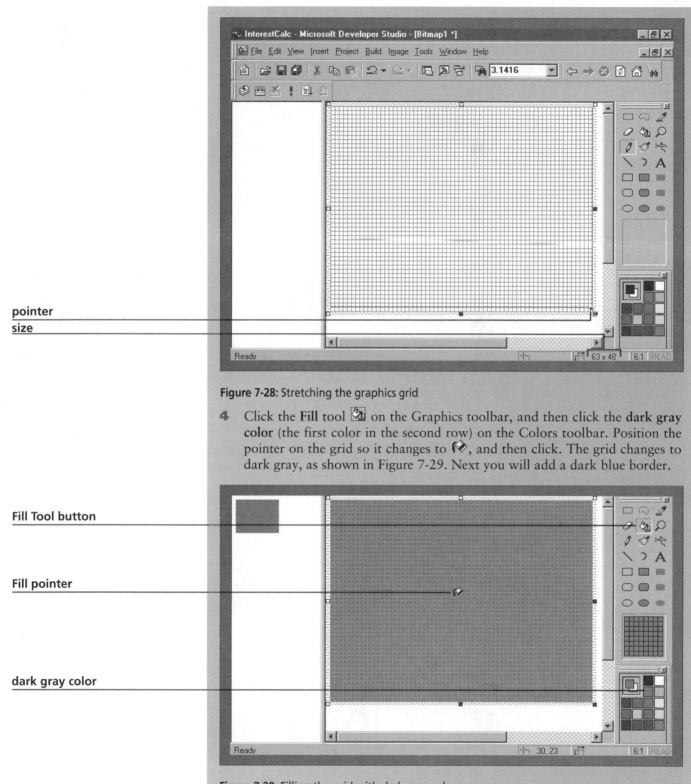

Figure 7-28: Stretching the graphics grid

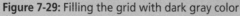

4 Click the **Fill** tool on the Graphics toolbar, and then click the **dark gray color** (the first color in the second row) on the Colors toolbar. Position the pointer on the grid so it changes to , and then click. The grid changes to dark gray, as shown in Figure 7-29. Next you will add a dark blue border.

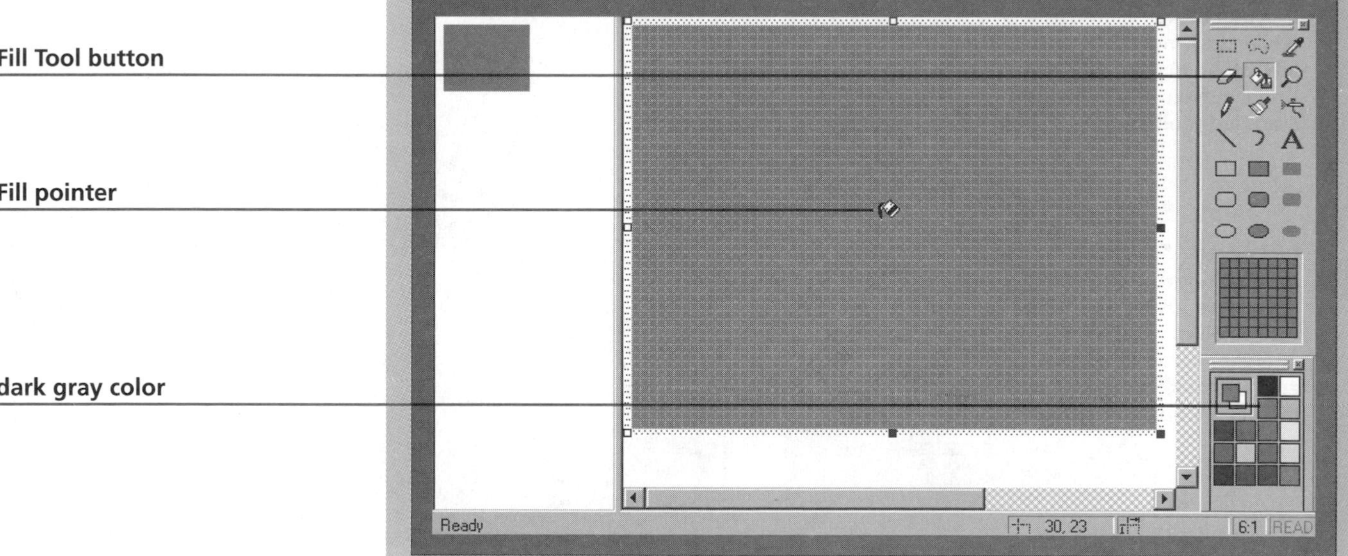

Figure 7-29: Filling the grid with dark gray color

5 Click the **Line** tool on the Graphics toolbar, and then click the **dark blue color** (the first color in the fifth row) on the Colors toolbar. To change the line width, click the **small rectangle shape** on the Graphics toolbar. See Figure 7-30.

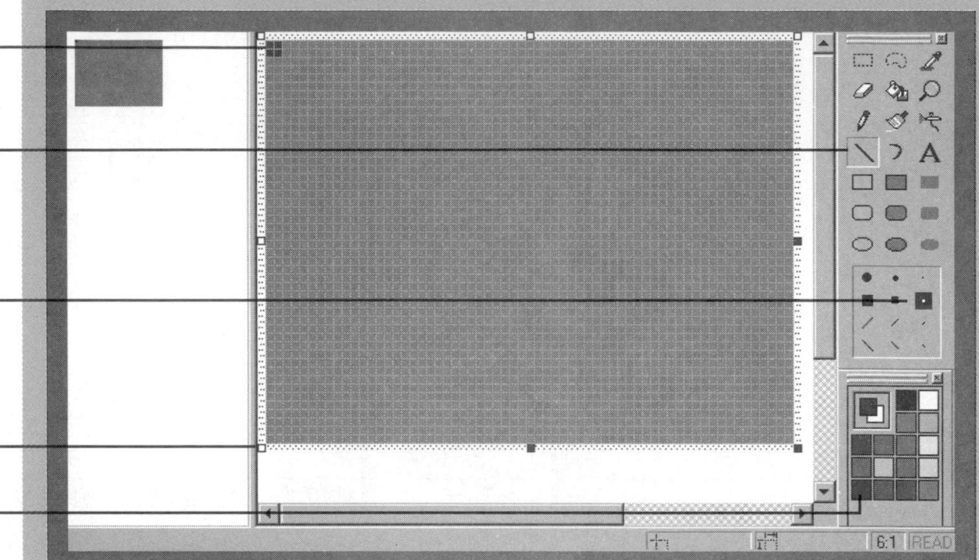

Figure 7-30: Drawing the border

If you make a mistake while drawing the line or any other object, click the Undo button on the Standard toolbar.

Holding down the Shift key while using the Line tool enables you to draw straight vertical or horizontal lines, as well as lines at a 45-degree angle.

6 Position the pointer in the upper-left corner of the grid as shown in Figure 7-30, press and hold the **Shift** key, and drag the pointer down to the lower-left corner of the grid to draw a line.

7 Repeat Steps 5 and 6 to draw each line in the rest of the border, using the Line tool and the Shift key. When you are done your border should look like Figure 7-31.

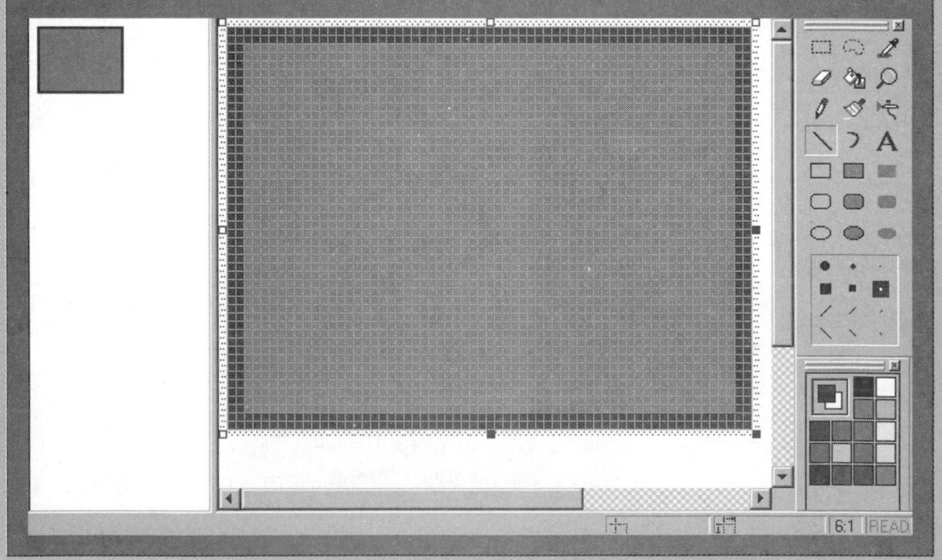

Figure 7-31: Finished border

8 Save the Bitmap file as **Koffee.gif** in the Interest folder on your Student Disk.

To center the graphic correctly, you will start by placing the two centered dark blue triangles. The gap between triangles is only one pixel wide. A **pixel** is a picture element, or one dot. Each square on the grid represents one pixel.

To add the triangles:

1 Click the **small line size** on the Graphics toolbar, and then position the pointer at coordinates 32, 4, as shown in Figure 7-32.

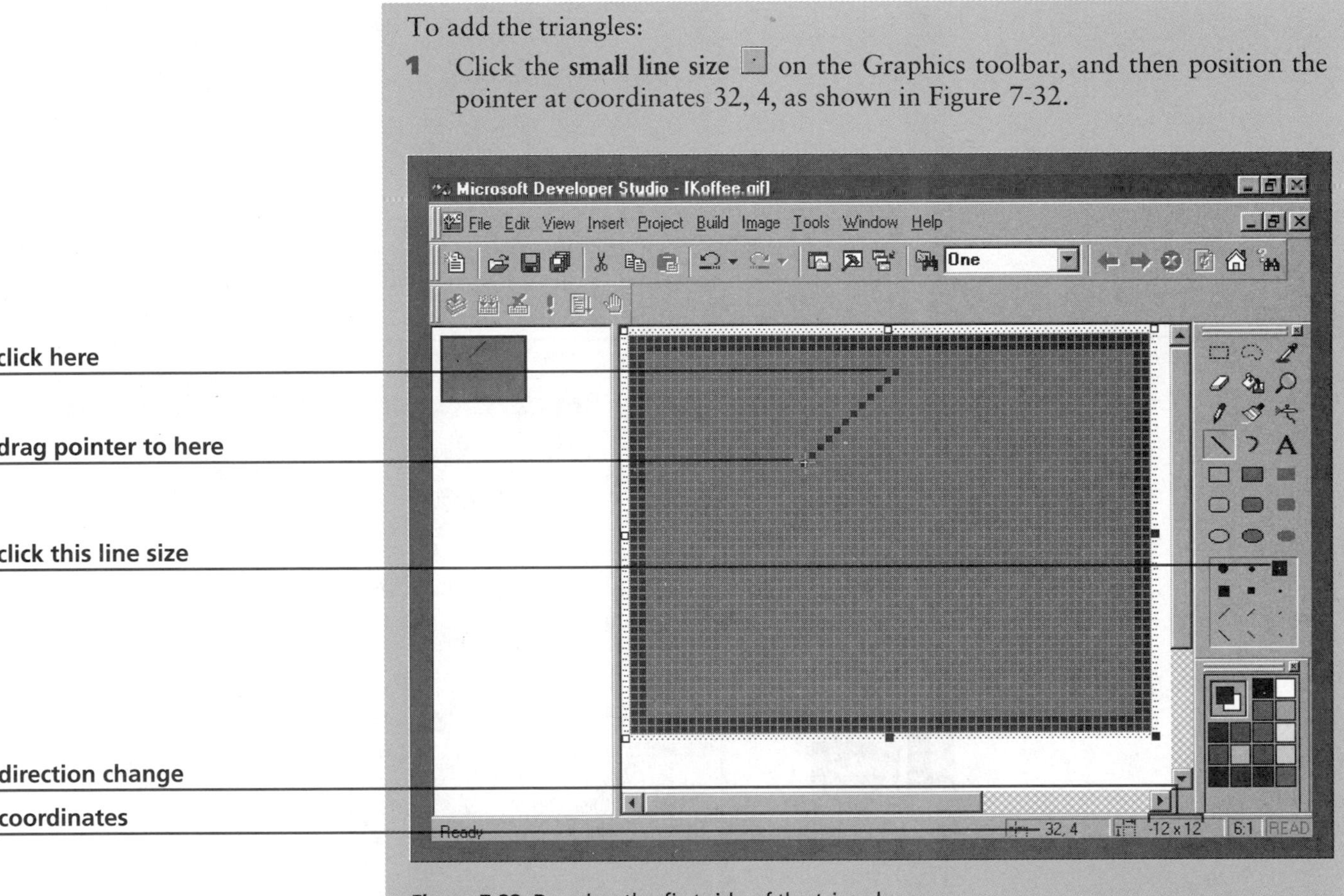

Figure 7-32: Drawing the first side of the triangle

2 Press and hold down the **Shift** key, and then drag the pointer down and to the left at a 45-degree angle and stop when the direction change is -12 × 12 as shown in Figure 7-32. Release the mouse button and then release the Shift key.

HELP? Always release the mouse button before releasing the Shift key. If you release the Shift key first, there is a chance that you will move the mouse pointer before releasing the mouse button and your line might not be straight. If this happens, click the Undo button on the Standard toolbar, and then redraw the line.

3 Position the pointer at coordinates 32, 4 again, press and hold down the **Shift** key, and then drag the pointer down and to the right until the direction change is 12 × 2, as shown in Figure 7-33.

direction change

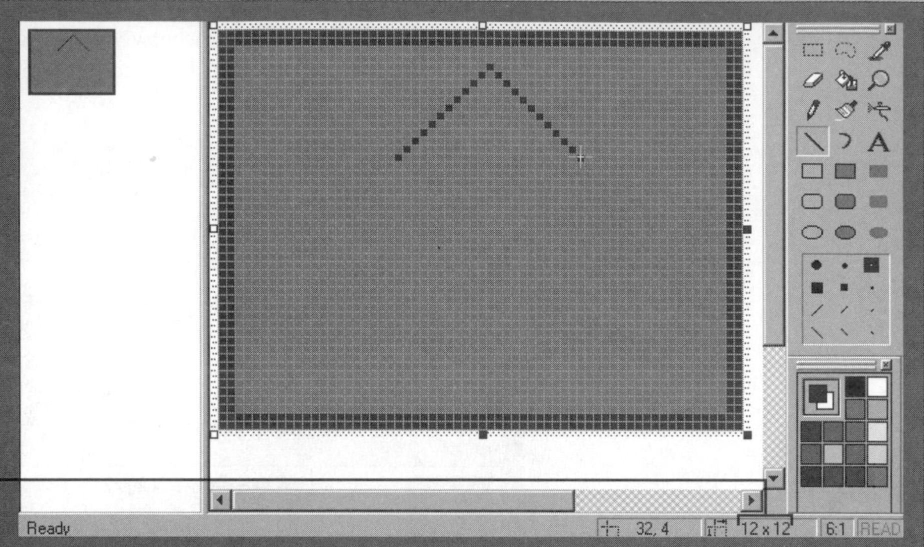

Figure 7-33: Drawing the second side of the triangle

4 Position the pointer at 21, 5, press and hold down the **Shift** key, and then drag a line to complete the triangle.

5 Position the pointer at coordinates 21, 17, and then drag the pointer to draw a line that is parallel to the line above it that starts at 21, 17 and ends at 43, 17, as shown in Figure 7-34.

end of line coordinates

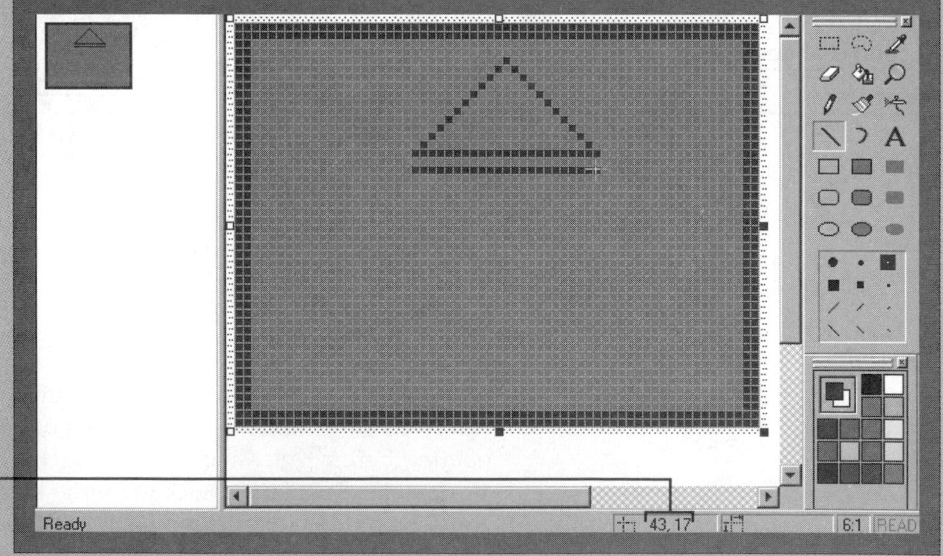

Figure 7-34: Drawing the second triangle

HELP? If the ending coordinates do not display on your screen, just make sure that the triangles are the same size.

6 Position the pointer back at coordinates 21, 17 and use the Shift key to draw a 45-degree angle down and to the right until the change is 12 × 2.

7 Use the Shift key to finish the second triangle by drawing a 45-degree angle.

8 Click the **Fill** tool on the Graphics toolbar, and then click in each triangle to fill the triangles with dark blue color, as shown in Figure 7-35.

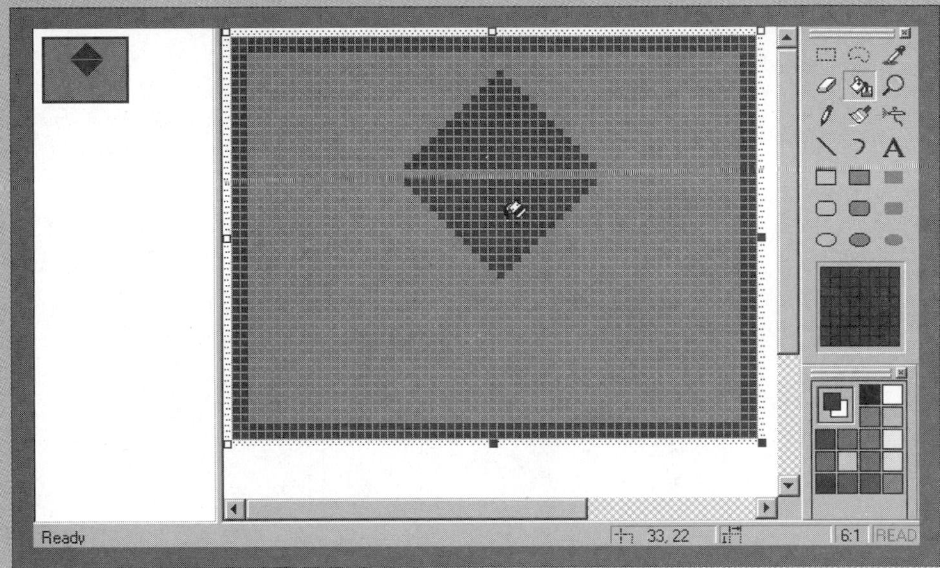

Figure 7-35: Filling the triangles with dark blue color

9 Save your changes.

Now it is time to draw the two blue triangles. Remember to hold down the Shift key so your lines will be straight. In the next set of steps, you will be told only where to start, what direction to drag in, and what the change will be.

To draw the two blue triangles:

1 Click the **blue color** (the second color in the fifth row).

2 Click the **Line** tool on the Graphics toolbar, and then click the **small line size** .

3 Position the pointer at 19, 17, and drag at a 45-degree angle down and to the right. The direction change is 12 × 12.

4 Position the pointer back at 19, 17, and drag at a 45-degree angle down and to the left. The direction change is -12 × 12.

5 Draw a line to complete the triangle.

6 Position the pointer at 45, 17, and drag at a 45-degree angle down and to the left. The direction change is -12 × 12.

7 Position the pointer back at 45, 17, and drag at a 45-degree angle down and to the right. The direction change is 12 × 12.

8 Draw a line to complete the triangle.

9 To fill the triangles with blue color, click the **Fill** tool on the Graphics toolbar, and then click each triangle. The final graphic looks like Figure 7-36.

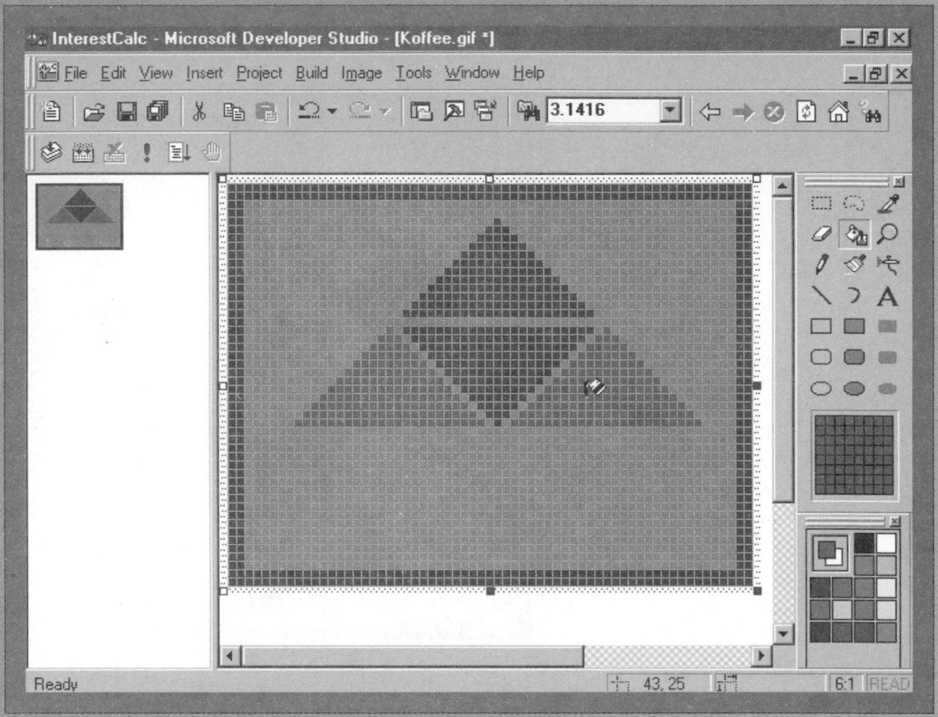

Figure 7-36: Filling the triangles with blue color

10 Save your changes.

The last change to make to the logo is to add the company name at the bottom.

1 Click the **dark blue color** (the first color in the fifth row) on the Colors toolbar, and then click the **Text** tool on the Graphics toolbar. The Text Tool dialog box opens, as shown in Figure 7-37.

Font button

Figure 7-37: Text Tool dialog box

2 Click the **Font** button in the Text Tool dialog box, make the changes shown in Figure 7-38, and then click the **OK** button.

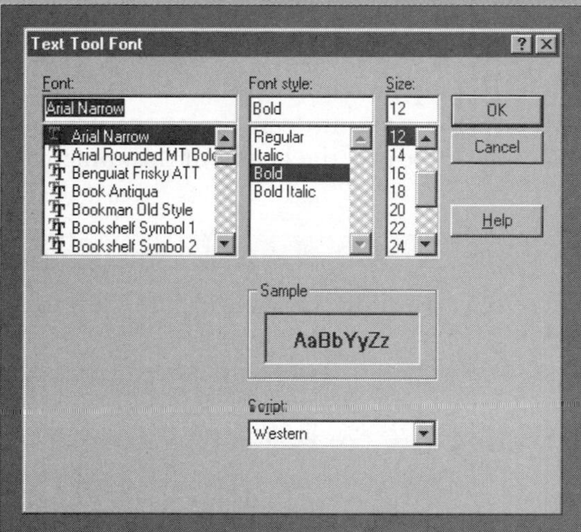

Figure 7-38: Changing the font

3 Type **Koffee**. The word "Koffee" appears in the upper-left corner of the grid and also in the Text Tool dialog box. Position the pointer on the text box in the grid so the pointer changes to ✥, and then drag the text box to the location shown in Figure 7-39.

drag text to here

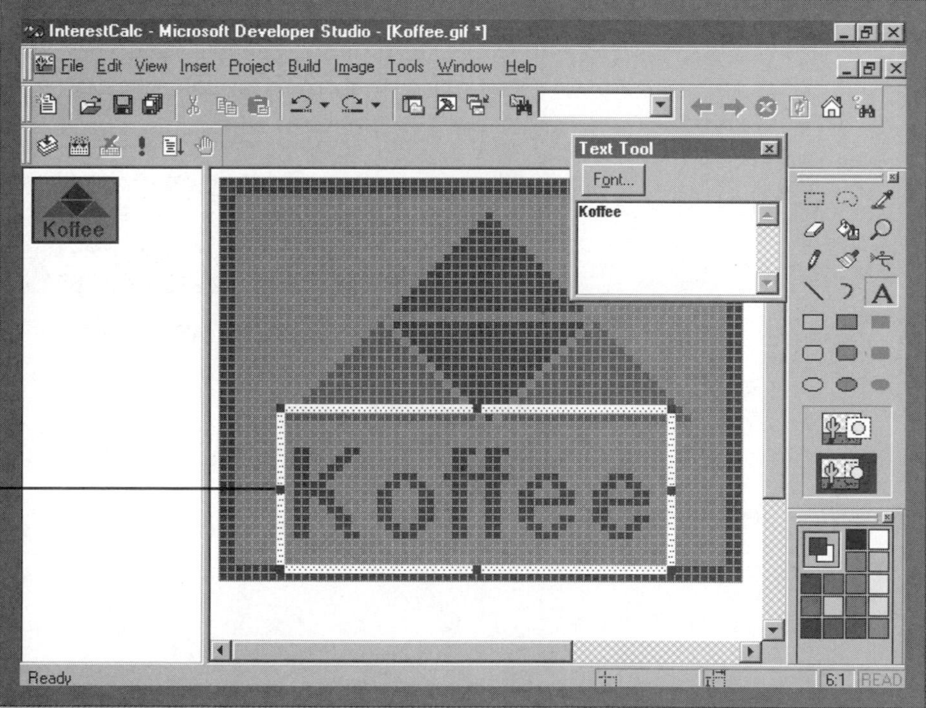

Figure 7-39: Adding the company name

4 Click the **Close** button ☒ on the Text Tool dialog box to close it.

5 Save your changes.

Click the second Tutorial 7 link of the Online Companion for this book (http://www.course.com) to see a live Java program that illustrates this topic.

Now you can add the changes to InterestCalc.java and InterestCalc.html so that the graphic will be visible in the applet. The changes to the Java file are necessary so the program can access the graphic. The changes to the HTML file are necessary because the height of the applet currently is too short.

1 Click **Window** on the menu bar, and then click **InterestCalc.java.**

2 Type the code shown in Figure 7-40 to add the image to the applet.

type this code

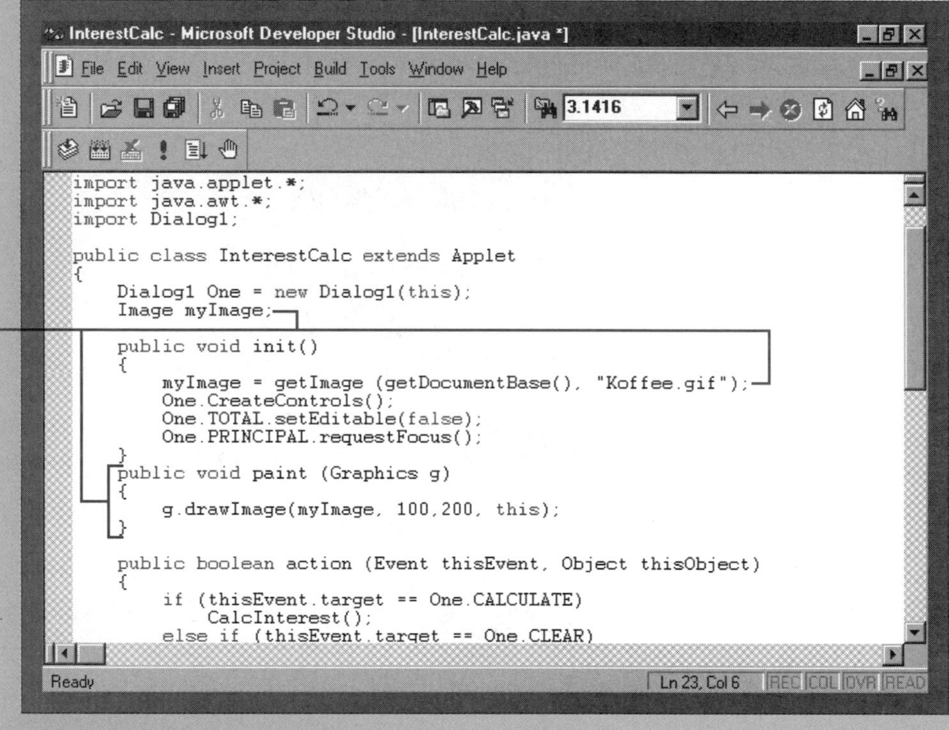

Figure 7-40: Modifying InterestCalc.java

3 Save your changes.

4 Build the applet.

5 Execute the applet, enter the information shown in Figure 7-41, and then click the **Calculate** button to get the results.

your logo might be in a slightly different position

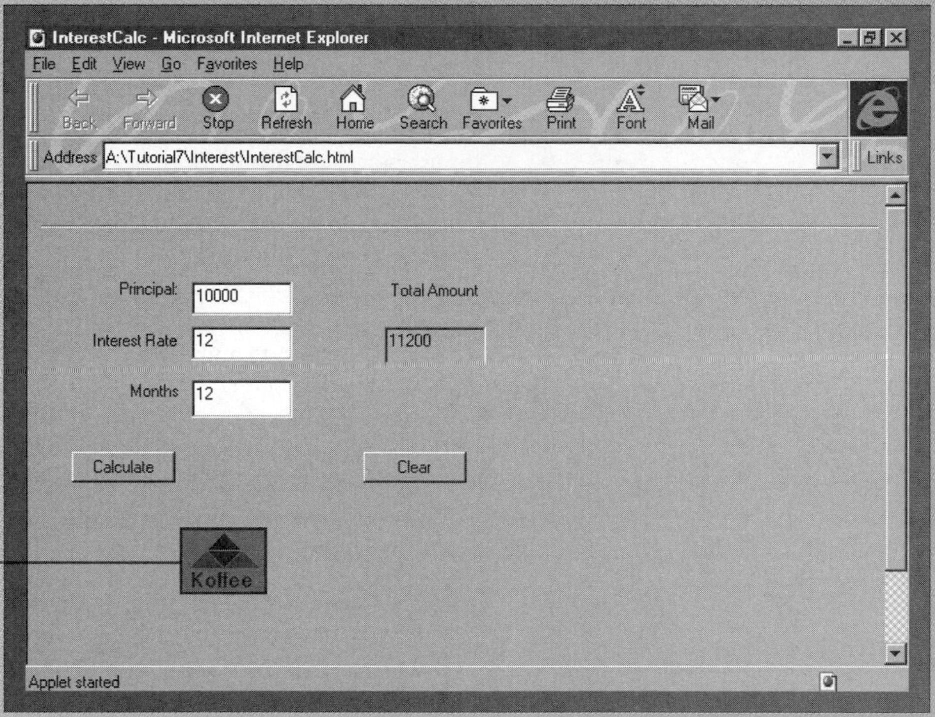

Figure 7-41: InterestCalc.java with graphic

6 Close Internet Explorer, close the project workspace and all document windows, and then close Visual J++.

Now you can either take a break or complete the end-of-lesson questions and exercises.

SUMMARY

- The Visual J++ environment includes a Dialog Editor, a Graphics Editor, and a Resource Wizard to place GUI elements in an applet.
- The graphical user interface design principles are:
  Labels and text fields should be arranged vertically, starting in the upper-left corner.
  Buttons should be in a row across the bottom, from the most-used button on the left to the least-used button on the right.
  Similar elements should have the same size.
  Edges of adjacent elements should align evenly.
  Label and button captions should be concise and meaningful.
  White space is as important as the actual elements.

- To create a dialog box:
  Click File on the menu bar, and then click New.
  Click the Files tab, and then double-click Resource Template.
  Click Insert on the menu bar, and then click Resource.
  In the Insert Resource dialog box, click Dialog, and then click the New button.
  Place your elements in the dialog box using the tools on the Graphics toolbar.
  Save the file.
- The Resource Wizard takes resources that you designed in the Dialog Editor and creates the necessary Java files to use these resources in your applet.
- To use the Resource Wizard to generate Java code for a dialog box:
  Click Tools on the menu bar, and then click Java Resource Wizard.
  Type the resource filename.
  Click the Next button, and then click the Finish button.
- The reserved word *this* allows you to refer to the current object without using a name.
- To prohibit changes to an Edit box, set the setEditable property to false using the *myText.setEditable(false);* statement.
- To create a graphics file:
  Click File on the menu bar, and then click New.
  Click the Files tab.
  Double-click Bitmap File.
- A pixel is a picture element that is equal to one dot.

QUESTIONS

1. The Visual J++ Dialog Editor allows you to design a dialog box with GUI elements such as labels and text fields.
a. true
b. false

2. Which resource in Visual J++ generates Java code to place a dialog box in an applet?
a. Dialog Editor
b. Resource Editor
c. Java Class Library Wizard
d. Resource Wizard

3. Labels and text fields in a dialog box should be arranged ______________.
a. horizontally, starting in the upper-left corner
b. vertically, starting in the upper-left corner
c. horizontally, starting in the upper-right corner
d. vertically, starting in the upper-right corner

4. Buttons in a dialog box should be arranged ______________.
a. at the top, from left to right
b. on the right side, from top to bottom
c. on the bottom, from left to right
d. on the left side, from top to bottom

5. All labels and buttons in a dialog box should be sized based only on the caption size.
a. true
b. false

6. You should place objects in a dialog box close together to minimize white space.
   a. true
   b. false
7. The Visual J++ Resource Wizard generates code for what kind of elements?
   a. dialog boxes
   b. HTML files
   c. graphics
   d. both a and b
8. You should not modify the files generated by the Resource Wizard.
   a. true
   b. false
9. You can use the reserved word *this* to refer to ______________ .
   a. an object
   b. an applet
   c. both a and b
   d. none of the above
10. Which of the following statements makes *myText textfield* read-only?
   a. myText.noEdit(true);
   b. myText.setEditable(false);
   c. myText.noEdit = true;
   d. myText.setEditable = false;

EXERCISES

Save the following exercises in the specified folder in the Exercises folder, in the Tutorial 7 folder on your Student Disk.

1. Design a dialog box using appropriate labels and text fields to solve the following problem. You need a program to calculate discounted prices. You know the original price and the discount percent. You need to calculate the price after subtracting the discount. Include a Calculate and a Clear button. The output field should be read-only. Use the Resource Wizard to generate the dialog Java files, and then use Visual J++ to write the Java applet to solve the problem. Use the Graphics Editor to generate a dollar sign ($) graphic to include at the bottom of the applet. Make sure that the HTML file has the correct width and height settings to show your dialog box and the graphic. Save the dialog box as Dialog2.rct, save the applet as Dollar.java, save the graphic as Dollar.gif, and save the HTML file as Dollar.html in the Exercise1A folder on your Student Disk.
2. Design a dialog box using appropriate labels and text fields to solve the following problem. You need to generate invoices for your childcare business. The rate per child is $45 per day. At the end of the month you bill the parents for the total number of days their child was in the program. Include a Calculate and a Clear button. The output field should be read-only. Use the Resource Wizard to generate the dialog Java files, and then use Visual J++ to write the Java applet to solve the problem. Use the Graphics Editor to generate a graphic of stacked alphabet blocks to include at the bottom of the applet. Make sure that the HTML file has the correct width and height settings to show your dialog box and the graphic. Save the dialog box as Dialog3.rct, save the applet as Childcare.java, save the graphic as Blocks.gif, and save the HTML file as Childcare.html in the Exercise2A folder on your Student Disk.

3. Design a dialog box using appropriate labels and text fields to solve the following problem. You need to generate invoices for your telephone installation company. You are given the cost of the materials, the hours worked by each employee, and the per hour charge for each employee. You also include a 5 percent surcharge on the subtotal. Include a Calculate and a Clear button. The output field should be read-only. Use the Resource Wizard to generate the dialog Java files, and then use Visual J++ to write the Java applet to solve the problem. Use the Graphics Editor to generate a telephone pole graphic to include at the bottom of the applet. Make sure that the HTML file has the correct width and height settings to show your dialog box and the graphic. Save the dialog box as Dialog4.rct, save the applet as Telephone.java, save the graphic as Pole.gif, and save the HTML file as Telephone.html in the Exercise3A folder on your Student Disk.
4. Design a dialog box using appropriate labels and text fields to solve the following problem. You need to calculate semester GPAs by finding an average of four grades and then displaying the average in a text field. Include a Calculate and a Clear button. The output field should be read-only. Use the Resource Wizard to generate the dialog Java files, and then use Visual J++ to write the Java applet to solve the problem. Use the Graphics Editor to generate a graphic based in the abbreviation of your school's name to include at the bottom of the applet. Make sure that the HTML file has the correct width and height settings to show your dialog and the graphic. Save the dialog box as Dialog4.rct, save the applet as GPA.java, save the graphic as School.gif, and save the HTML file as GPA.html in the Exercise4A folder on your Student Disk.

LESSON B

objectives

In this lesson you will learn how to:

- Use layout managers to control the appearance of your applets
- Use single and group check boxes
- Use the Choice class to create drop-down selection lists

Using Advanced GUI Elements

Finalizing the Order System for Koffee Koncoctions

Using Layout Managers

You can use the Visual J++ layout managers and the layout manager classes that are included in Java to have more control over object placement in an applet. After making the changes in this lesson, you will improve the effectiveness of the order system.

Every applet you have written so far has used a layout manager. A **layout manager** is a Java control mechanism that controls where GUI elements are placed in an applet. In the applets you wrote in previous tutorials, you used the default layout manager, which is the FlowLayout. The most commonly used layout managers are GridLayout, BorderLayout, and CardLayout. Each of the layout managers has a different method for controlling placement of the GUI elements in an applet. To understand the differences between the different managers, you will use an applet as a demonstration program that contains labels, text fields, and a button.

FlowLayout Manager

The **FlowLayout manager** places GUI elements beginning in the upper-left corner of the applet, moving across the top row until that row is filled, and then the FlowLayout manager places elements in a new row beginning again on the left side. The default layout scheme that FlowLayout uses is to center the elements, as shown in Figure 7-42.

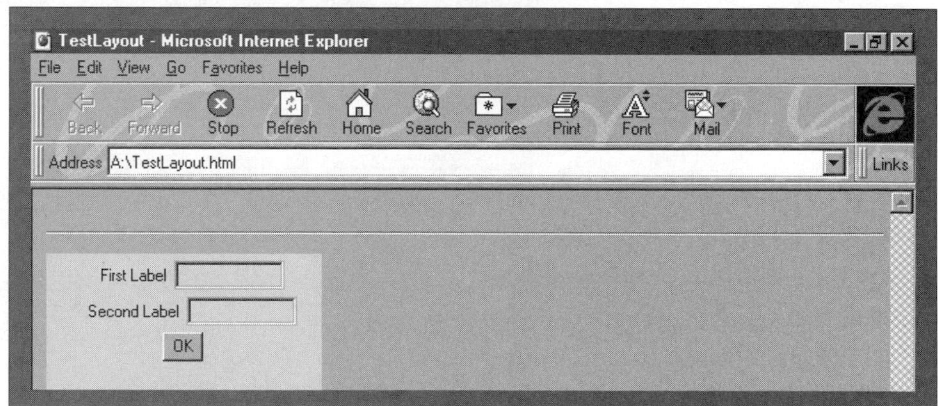

Figure 7-42: Centered FlowLayout

The only option that you can change in the FlowLayout manager is the alignment. The default alignment is centered, but you can specify either right or left alignment. Figure 7-43 shows the elements with left alignment. If you want more control over the placement of your GUI elements, you need to use one of the other layout managers. There is one more way to modify the layout of your applet that you have done in the past. You can change the size of the applet by changing the height and width parameters in the HTML file. The FlowLayout manager fits the elements inside the applet space, making it possible to move elements from one row to another by changing the width of the applet.

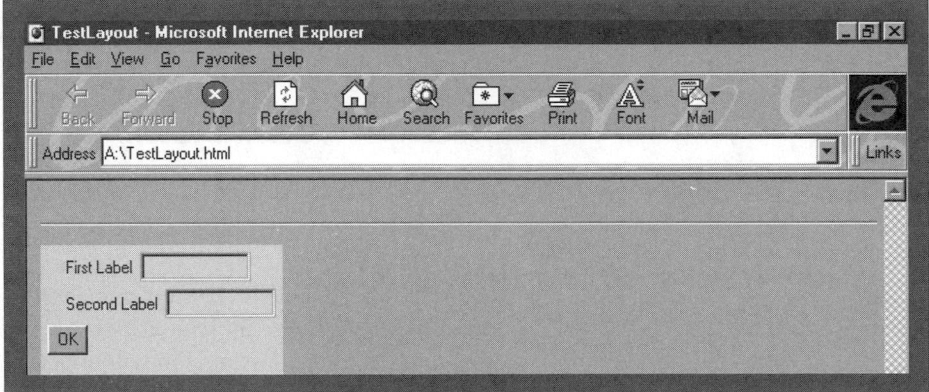

Figure 7-43: FlowLayout with left-aligned elements and changed HTML page width

GridLayout Manager

The **GridLayout manager** allows you specify a grid, or regions, where you can place your elements with one element in each region. You specify the size of the grid by indicating how many rows and columns in which to divide the applet space. One important thing to remember about GridLayout is that all the regions in the grid are the same size. This can be a problem if you are using smaller elements like labels with larger elements like text areas. Another problem is that GridLayout divides all the available space, so if your HTML file gives the applet a large space and you have only a few elements, each element will be large. Figure 7-44 shows a GridLayout with labels, text fields, and a button. The HTML page size has a width of 175 and a height of 150. As you can see, each element is the same size.

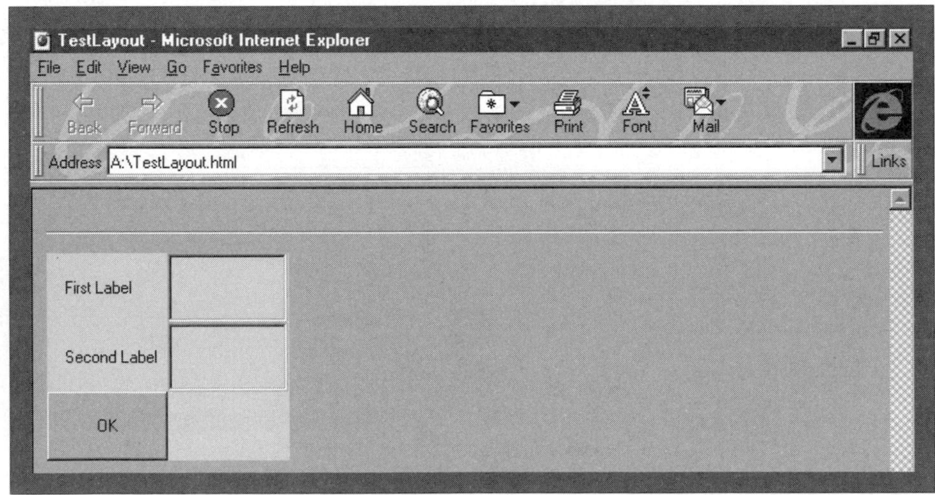

Figure 7-44: GridLayout elements

In the example shown in Figure 7-44, the grid places the elements in rows that are three rows by two columns (3 × 2). In the 3 × 2 arrangement, one region is empty because there are only five elements in this applet. Figure 7-45 shows an HTML page with a width of 400 and a height of 80 with only one row of elements (1 × 5).

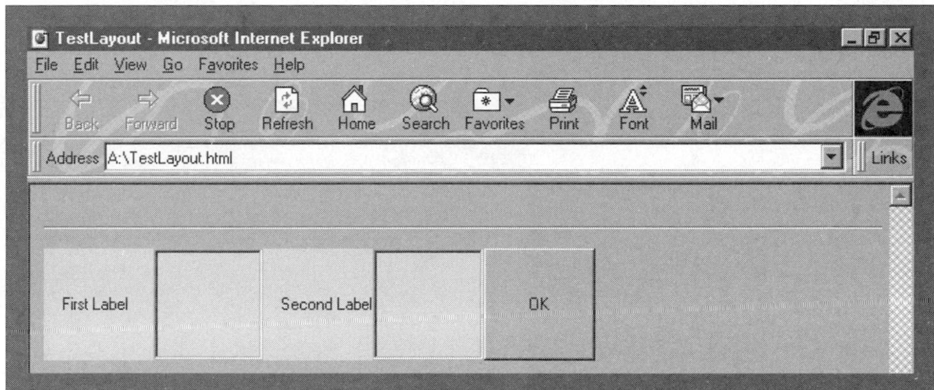

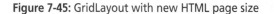

Figure 7-45: GridLayout with new HTML page size

Figure 7-46 shows another arrangement for the elements—5 × 1, width 80, and height 200.

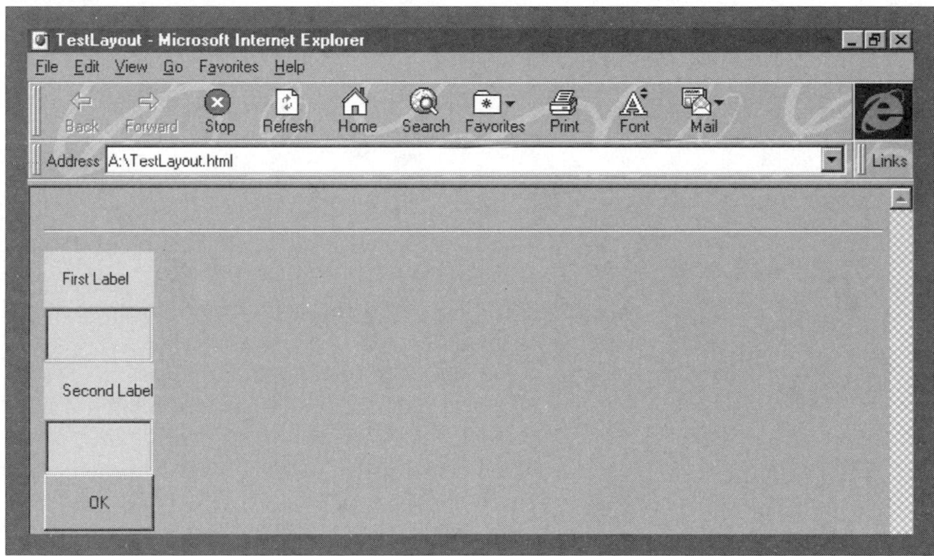

Figure 7-46: GridLayout with alternate arrangements

The GridLayout manager places all of the elements on the HTML page, even if you set the grid to hold fewer regions than elements. For example, if you specify a 1 × 1 grid for this example, your screen would look like Figure 7-47 because the GridLayout manager considers the number of rows as the critical information. Once you decide the number of rows desired, you can specify any grid as NumRows × 0. The GridLayout manager then splits the number of elements evenly over the number of rows that you requested.

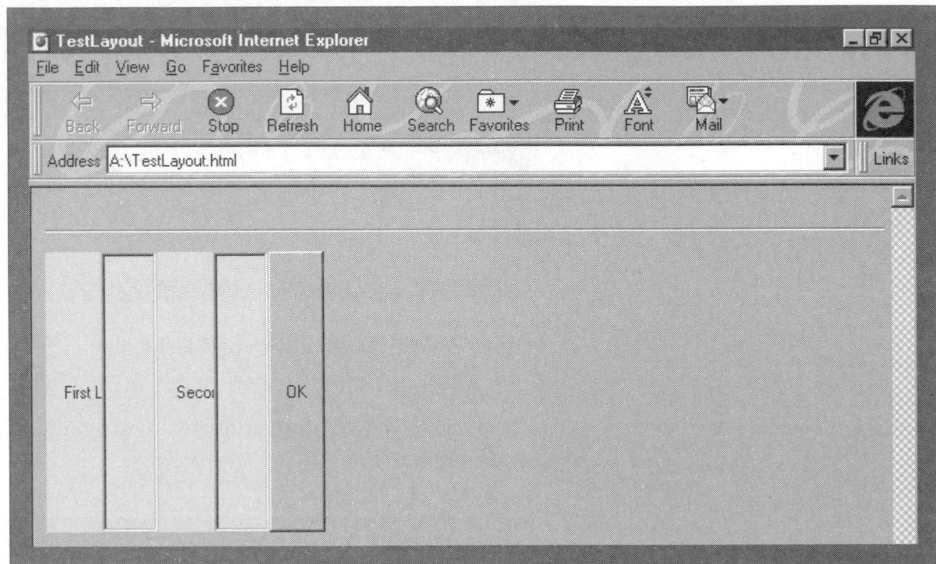

Figure 7-47: GridLayout with 1 × 1 grid

Look at Figure 7-47 again. This figure shows the applet from Figure 7-45 using the HTML default parameters of 200 3 200. There is a way to handle GridLayout without having to change the width and height parameters in the HTML file constantly. The best way to deal with the element size problem in GridLayout is to use a Panel object. A Panel object is a GUI element that holds other elements. A Panel is used as a container to hold other objects.

The code to create a Panel for the TestLayout applet is shown in Figure 7-48. To add a Panel, first you must declare a Panel object in the class properties. Next you specify that you want GridLayout in the init method, and then you add the GUI elements to the Panel and add the Panel to the applet.

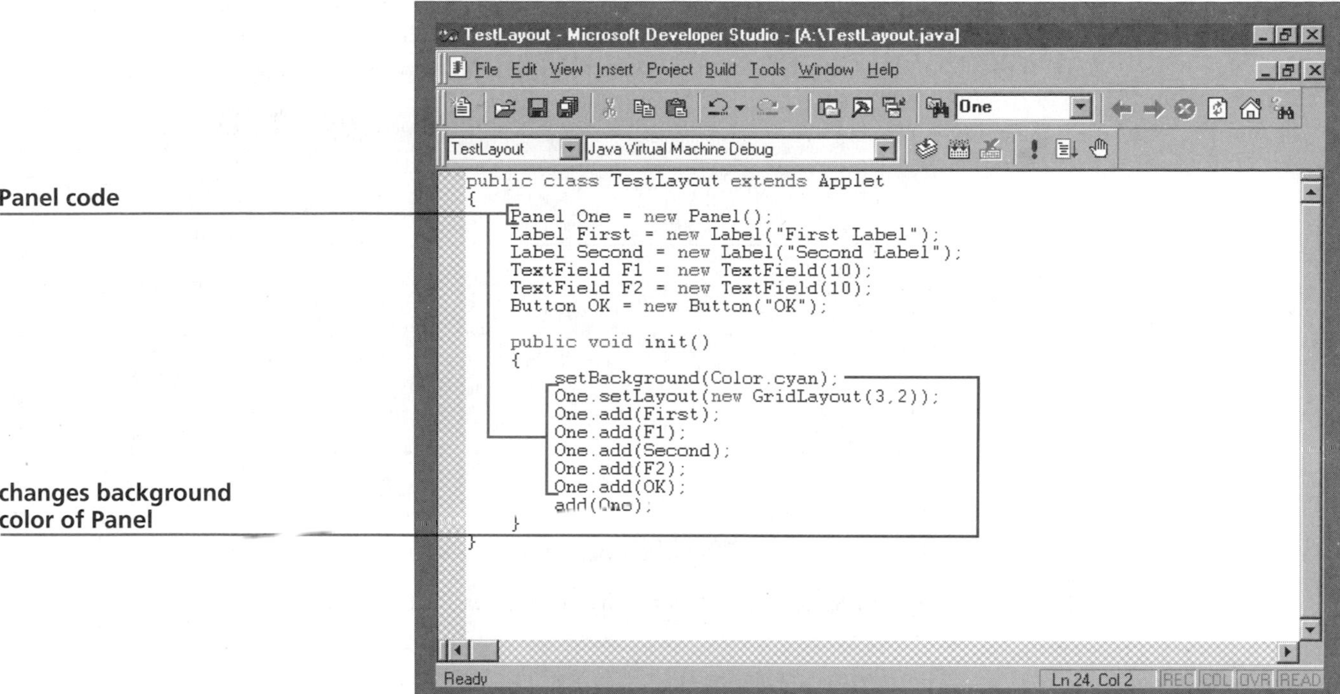

Figure 7-48: TestLayout code to create a Panel

Figure 7-49 shows the applet that contains the Panel. The user will not notice the Panel—as you can see the elements are sized and placed on the HTML page normally. You will use Panels in the rest of the examples in this lesson.

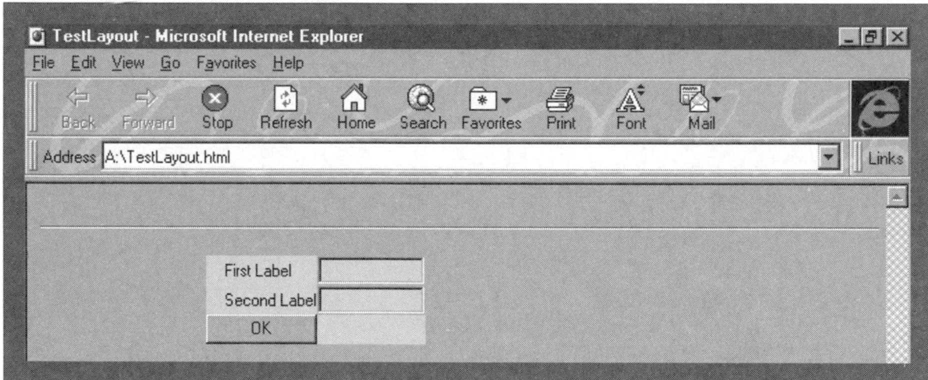

Figure 7-49: Applet with a Panel

There is a GridLayout constructor that allows you to specify the space between elements in the grid. If you do not specify a space, the spacing is set at zero, which indicates no gaps between the elements. Look at Figure 7-49 again—the elements display close together. You can change the spacing by modifying the setLayout statement to be *One.setLayout(new GridLayout(3,2,10,20));*, which changes the arrangement to a 3 × 2 column grid, with the gap between column elements set at 10 pixels (hgap), and the gap between row elements set at 20 pixels (vgap), as shown in Figure 7-50.

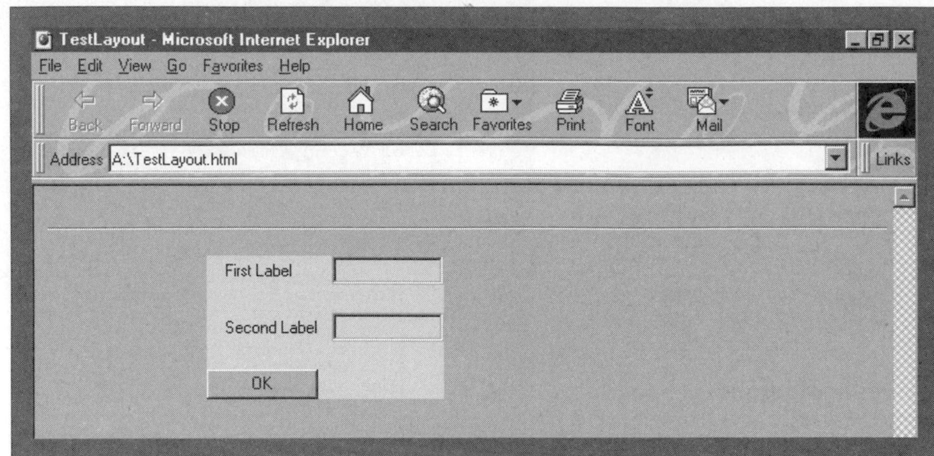

Figure 7-50: New GridLayout with increased spacing between elements

BorderLayout Manager

The GridLayout gives you more control over the placement of your elements, but its biggest drawback is the fact that all the elements are the same size. What if you want your applet to look more like a typical application with a large editing area in the middle, a scroll bar on the right, menu bars on the top, a toolbar on the right, and status boxes across the bottom? You cannot specify this arrangement in GridLayout, but you can do it using BorderLayout. The **BorderLayout manager** gives you a large Center area, with four surrounding smaller areas, called North, South, East, and West, as shown in Figure 7-51.

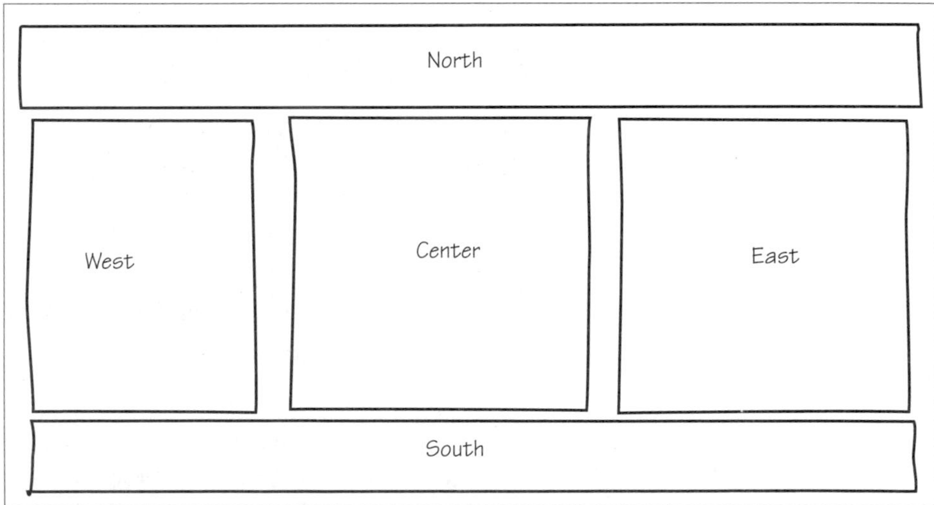

Figure 7-51: BorderLayout areas

To show how BorderLayout works with applets, Figure 7-52 shows some modifications that have been made to the TestLayout applet. One of the text fields now is a text area to show how the Center region of BorderLayout can be larger than the outside regions. The other text field and labels now are buttons (with regional captions), and the Button element has a border so you can see the true size of the element.

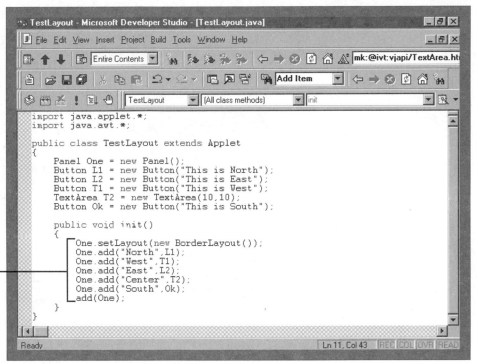

changed code

```
import java.applet.*;
import java.awt.*;

public class TestLayout extends Applet
{
    Panel One = new Panel();
    Button L1 = new Button("This is North");
    Button L2 = new Button("This is East");
    Button T1 = new Button("This is West");
    TextArea T2 = new TextArea(10,10);
    Button Ok = new Button("This is South");

    public void init()
    {
        One.setLayout(new BorderLayout());
        One.add("North",L1);
        One.add("West",T1);
        One.add("East",L2);
        One.add("Center",T2);
        One.add("South",Ok);
        add(One);
    }
}
```

Figure 7-52: TestLayout using BorderLayout

The add statement for the BorderLayout is different—it takes two parameters instead of just one. This version of the add method requires the first parameter to be a String that tells the BorderLayout manager which of the five regions you are using. You can place only one element in a component, so on the surface, you might think that you are limited to five components in BorderLayout. That is not entirely true because it is possible to have a Panel that holds several components as your one component. One drawback to BorderLayout is how it distorts the shape of some elements; you cannot change this. Figure 7-53 shows an applet that uses the BorderLayout.

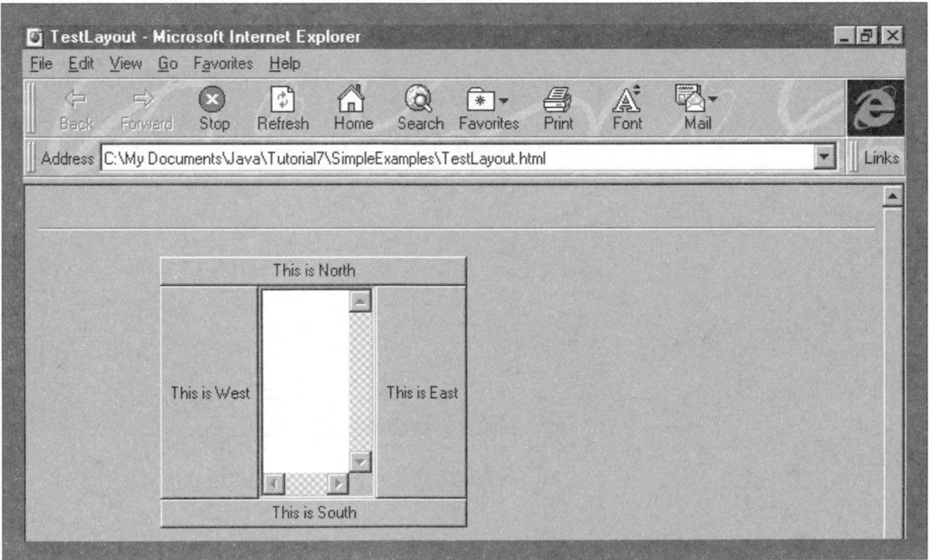

Figure 7-53: Using a BorderLayout

There are two ways to modify the use of a BorderLayout. The first way is that you do not need to use all five regions. By commenting out the line that assigns an element to the South region, the applet looks like Figure 7-54.

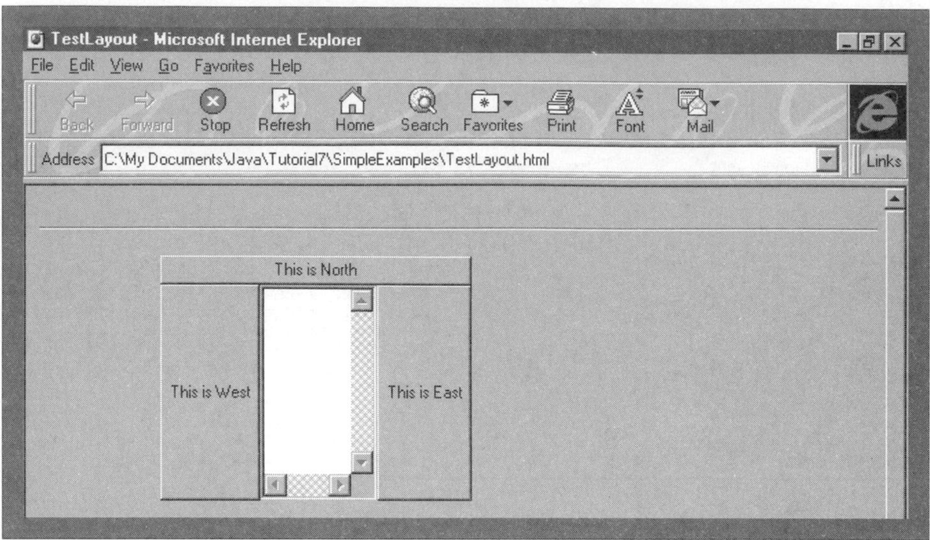

Figure 7-54: BorderLayout with no South region

You also can specify vertical and horizontal gaps, like with GridLayout. If the South region is added back in, and the setLayout statement is changed to *One.setLayout(new BorderLayout(10,10));*, the applet looks like Figure 7-55. The arguments to set the gaps in BorderLayout specify the horizontal gap first, and then the vertical gap, just like BorderLayout.

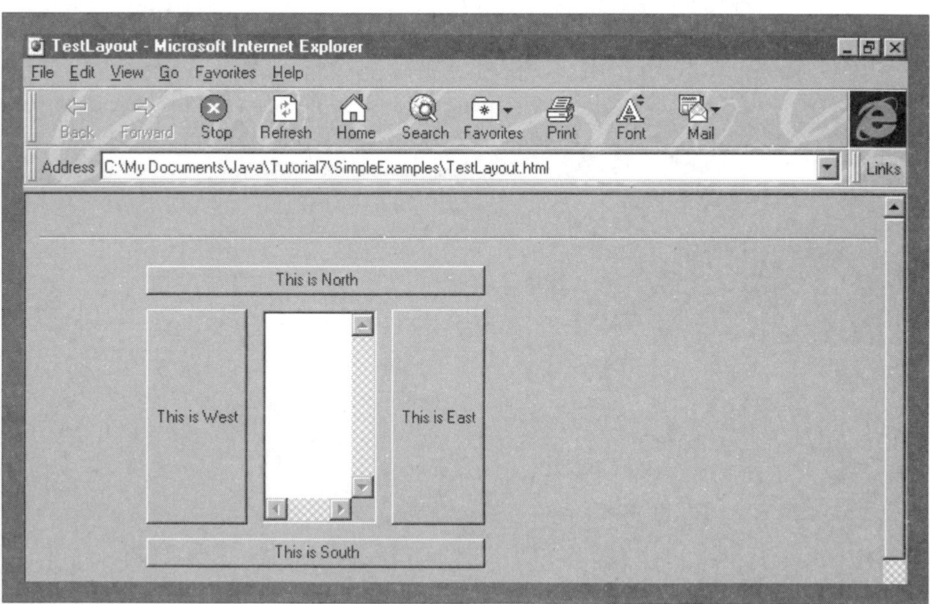

Figure 7-55: BorderLayout with gaps

CardLayout Manager

The **CardLayout manager** is different from the other managers because the other managers determine how the screen area is divided up among the GUI elements, but the CardLayout manager allows you to "stack" GUI elements on top of each other with only the top element visible. This manager got its name because it treats GUI elements like a deck of cards that you can shuffle to place different elements on the top. The CardLayout manager displays only one element at a time, which can be a Panel with multiple elements, so you can use this manager to display as many elements as you want in a Panel.

The CardLayout manager is not as easily demonstrated as the other managers, but it has some unique methods. The CardLayout add method is similar to the BorderLayout because it also can have two arguments. The name argument is optional—it is needed if you need to access the element "card" by name. The unique methods are the ones that allow you to change the top card, or the visible element. An order is established as you add cards to the layout. You can access the first card, the last card, the next card, and the previous card. You also can access a card by name. You will use these methods to develop the final version of the order system user interface.

Starting the New User Interface

You will use a two-Panel design for the large number of elements that need to appear in the user interface. The first Panel will be for user input and for displaying the invoice. By using the CardLayout manager to display one Panel at a time, the Panel does not overwhelm the user with too many elements. The other Panel will consist of buttons to access the different Panels. The next step is to decide how many cards you need and what elements will be on the cards, as shown in Figure 7-56.

Purpose	Panel Name	Elements
Get name and address	CustPanel	Label "Enter Customer Data" TextArea for input Button "Accept Data"
Get shipping and credit	Other	Check box for charge TextField card number Grouped check boxes for shipping method Button "Credit/Shipping"
Get coffee items	ItemPanel	List of items TextField for amount Button "Add Item"
Display final invoice	InvoicePanel	Label "Final Invoice" TextArea output Button "Write Invoice"
Move between cards	ButtonPanel	Button "Customer Info" Button "Other Info" Button "Items Ordered" Button "Invoice"

Figure 7-56: Assigning GUI elements

You will start by adding the GUI elements and the init method to the user interface. To keep the init method to a reasonable length, you will have the method use other methods to create the Panels and to place the GUI elements. Then you will set up the deck of cards with a temporary card for each of the four data cards and for the ButtonPanel to move between the cards. CustPanel and InvoicePanel contain only GUI elements that you are familiar with, so you will finish this section by placing the GUI elements on those Panels and writing a temporary MakeInvoice method that displays the customer information in the output text area.

To start the user interface:

1. Start Visual J++ and close any open project workspace, if necessary.
2. Open the **UI.java** file from the UserInterface folder in the Tutorial7 folder on your Student Disk, and then save it as **UserInterface.java**.
3. Click in the first location shown in Figure 7-57, press the **Enter** key, and then type the GUI elements. Click in the second location shown in Figure 7-57, press the **Enter** key, and then type the data elements.

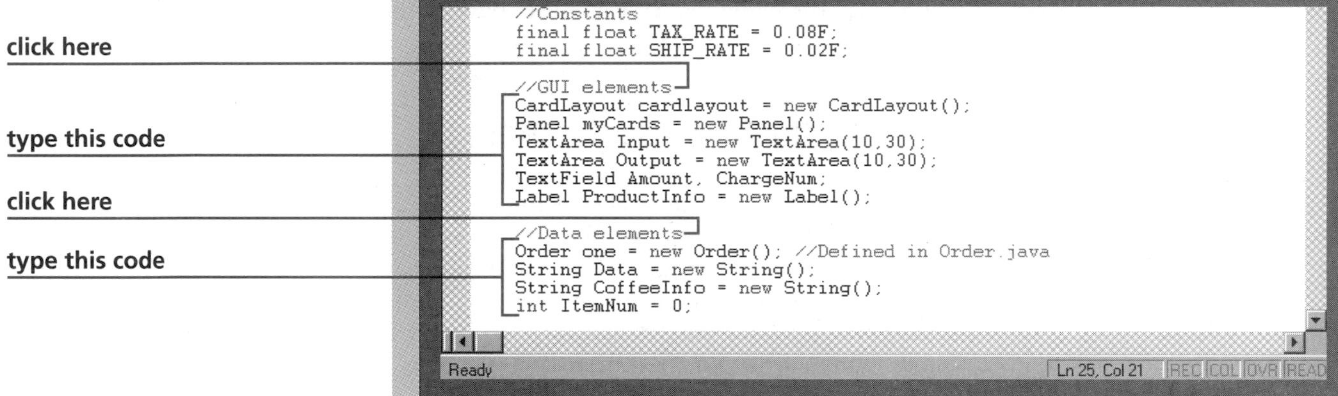


```
//Constants
final float TAX_RATE = 0.08F;
final float SHIP_RATE = 0.02F;

//GUI elements
CardLayout cardlayout = new CardLayout();
Panel myCards = new Panel();
TextArea Input = new TextArea(10,30);
TextArea Output = new TextArea(10,30);
TextField Amount, ChargeNum;
Label ProductInfo = new Label();

//Data elements
Order one = new Order(); //Defined in Order.java
String Data = new String();
String CoffeeInfo = new String();
int ItemNum = 0;
```

Figure 7-57: Adding the GUI elements

4. Click in the location shown in Figure 7-58, press the **Enter** key, and then type the init method.

click here

type this code

```
int ItemNum = 0;

//Init method
public void init()
{
    //Setting up the first card
    Panel CustPanel = new Panel();
    CustPanel = SetCustPanel(CustPanel);
    //Setting up the second card
    Panel Other = new Panel();
    Other = SetOther(Other);
    //Setting up Items Panel
    Panel ItemsPanel = new Panel();
    ItemsPanel = SetItemPanel(ItemsPanel);
    //Setting up the Invoice panel
    Panel InvoicePanel = new Panel();
    InvoicePanel = SetInvoicePanel(InvoicePanel);
    //Putting all the panels together to make the "deck"
    MakeDeck(CustPanel,Other,ItemsPanel,InvoicePanel);
    //Adding the south panel to hold the movement buttons
    Panel ButtonPanel = new Panel();
    ButtonPanel = SetButtonPanel(ButtonPanel);
    add("South",ButtonPanel);
}
```

Ready Ln 48, Col 6

Figure 7-58: Adding the init method

5 Save your changes.

In the next set of steps, you will add the Panel creation methods. For now, the Other Panel and the ItemPanel will be placeholder Panels that have a name but not the final data elements. The CustPanel gets the customer's name and address. The only elements on this Panel are a text area, a label, and a button. The elements are different sizes, and there are less than five elements. You will use the BorderLayout for this Panel. You will put the label in the North region, the button in the South region, and the text area in the Center region. The InvoicePanel also is a simple Panel with a text area, a label, and a button. The button on the InvoicePanel triggers the output and will not accept the input, so the button will be in the West region. The MakeDeck method sets up the deck of cards and places them in the Center Panel of the applet's Panel. The SetButtonPanel method sets up the card access Panel with buttons to access all the cards.

To add the Panels:

1 Click in the location shown in Figure 7-59, press the **Enter** key, and then type the SetCustPanel, SetOther, SetItemPanel, and the SetInvoicePanel methods.

click here

type this code

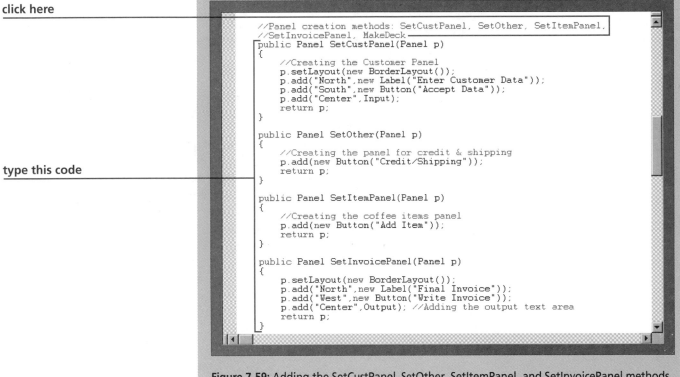

```
//Panel creation methods: SetCustPanel, SetOther, SetItemPanel,
//SetInvoicePanel, MakeDeck
public Panel SetCustPanel(Panel p)
{
    //Creating the Customer Panel
    p.setLayout(new BorderLayout());
    p.add("North",new Label("Enter Customer Data"));
    p.add("South",new Button("Accept Data"));
    p.add("Center",Input);
    return p;
}

public Panel SetOther(Panel p)
{
    //Creating the panel for credit & shipping
    p.add(new Button("Credit/Shipping"));
    return p;
}

public Panel SetItemPanel(Panel p)
{
    //Creating the coffee items panel
    p.add(new Button("Add Item"));
    return p;
}

public Panel SetInvoicePanel(Panel p)
{
    p.setLayout(new BorderLayout());
    p.add("North",new Label("Final Invoice"));
    p.add("West",new Button("Write Invoice"));
    p.add("Center",Output); //Adding the output text area
    return p;
}
```

Figure 7-59: Adding the SetCustPanel, SetOther, SetItemPanel, and SetInvoicePanel methods

2 Press the **Enter** key twice, and then add the MakeDeck and SetButtonPanel methods shown in Figure 7-60.

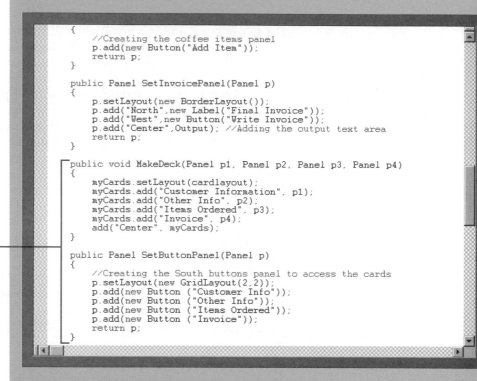

```
    {
        //Creating the coffee items panel
        p.add(new Button("Add Item"));
        return p;
    }

    public Panel SetInvoicePanel(Panel p)
    {
        p.setLayout(new BorderLayout());
        p.add("North",new Label("Final Invoice"));
        p.add("West",new Button("Write Invoice"));
        p.add("Center",Output); //Adding the output text area
        return p;
    }

    public void MakeDeck(Panel p1, Panel p2, Panel p3, Panel p4)
    {
        myCards.setLayout(cardlayout);
        myCards.add("Customer Information", p1);
        myCards.add("Other Info", p2);
        myCards.add("Items Ordered", p3);
        myCards.add("Invoice", p4);
        add("Center", myCards);
    }

    public Panel SetButtonPanel(Panel p)
    {
        //Creating the South buttons panel to access the cards
        p.setLayout(new GridLayout(2,2));
        p.add(new Button ("Customer Info"));
        p.add(new Button ("Other Info"));
        p.add(new Button ("Items Ordered"));
        p.add(new Button ("Invoice"));
        return p;
    }
```

type this code

Figure 7-60: Adding the MakeDeck and SetButtonPanel methods

3 Save your changes.

4 Build the applet in a default project workspace. Correct any typing errors.

HELP? If you still receive errors in the program, you might need to add the object files to the project workspace. Click Project on the menu bar, point to Add To Project, and then click Files. Add Coffees.java, Customer6.java, and Order.java files to the project from the UserInterface folder on your Student Disk. Then click Build on the menu bar, and then click Rebuild All to build the project again. If you still receive errors, ask your instructor for help.

5 Execute the applet. The class filename is **UserInterface**. See Figure 7-61. The applet needs more space, so you will need to change the settings in the default HTML file.

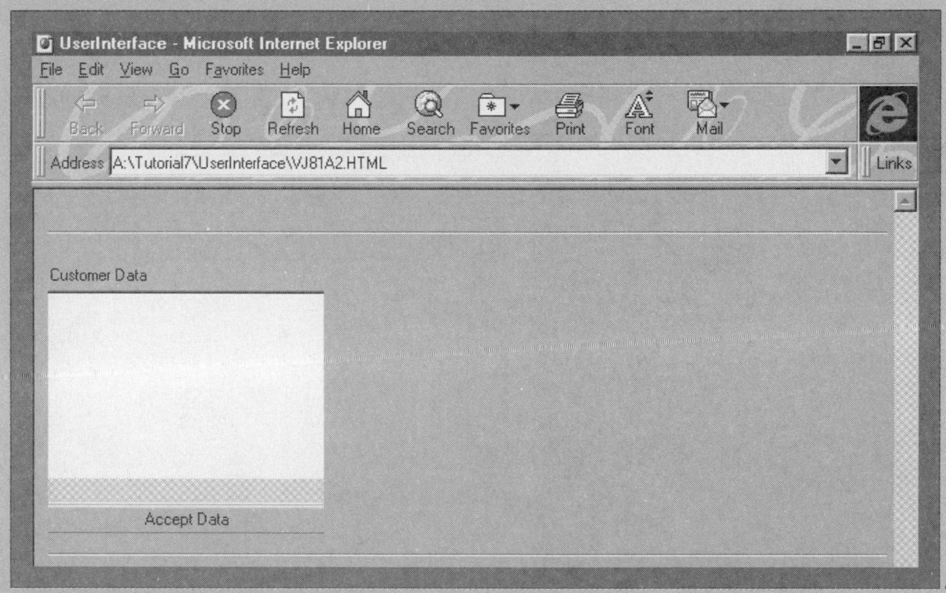

Figure 7-61: Running the UserInterface Applet the first time

6 Close Internet Explorer, open the HTML file from the UserInterface folder on your Student Disk in the Visual J++ Editor window, and then change the width value to 500 and the height value to 300.

HELP? Visual J++ generates the HTML files using random names, so your HTML file will have a different filename than what is shown in Figure 7-61.

7 Save the HTML file as **UserInterface.html** in the UserInterface folder, and then close it.

8 Click **Project** on the menu bar, and then click **Settings**. Click the **Debug** tab, click the **Category** list arrow, and then click **Browser**. Click the **Use parameters from HTML page** option button, type **UserInterface.html** in the HTML page text box, and then click the **OK** button.

9 Execute the applet again. See Figure 7-62. There is enough space now, but you cannot see the other Panels because the action method is missing.

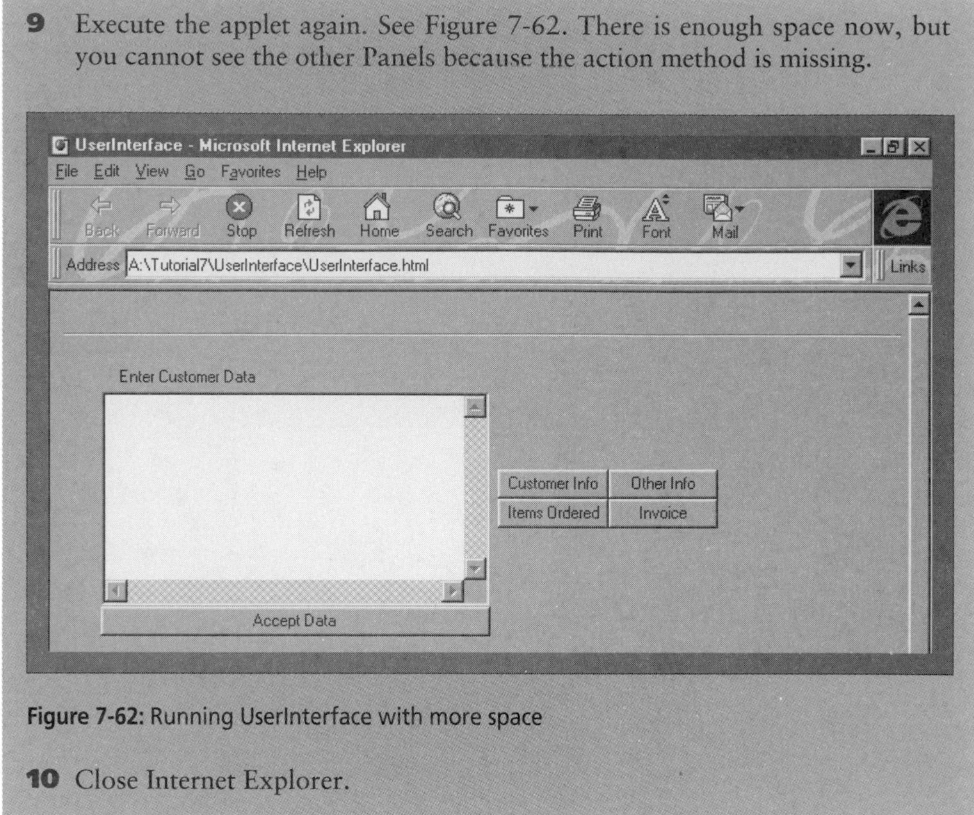

Figure 7-62: Running UserInterface with more space

10 Close Internet Explorer.

Now all the Panels have at least one item. You can add the action method with the instructions to move from one card to the next. You will use three versions of the show method. One version of the show method allows you to access the first card. You will use that method to view the CustPanel. The second method allows you to access the last card, which is the Invoice card. To access the other cards, you will use that method that accesses the card by name.

This action method will be different than ones you have done before. First, instead of using *the Event* as the test, you will use *the Object*. The other difference will be in the use of multiple returns in one method. This does two things for you. First, if one of the early conditional statements is true, the method will take up less processing time. The other advantage is that if the event is not one of the ones you are looking for, this method returns false. If you had other methods that tested for events, they would get a chance to be triggered by the return of false.

To add the action methods:

1 Click in the location shown in Figure 7-63, press the **Enter** key, and then type the action method.

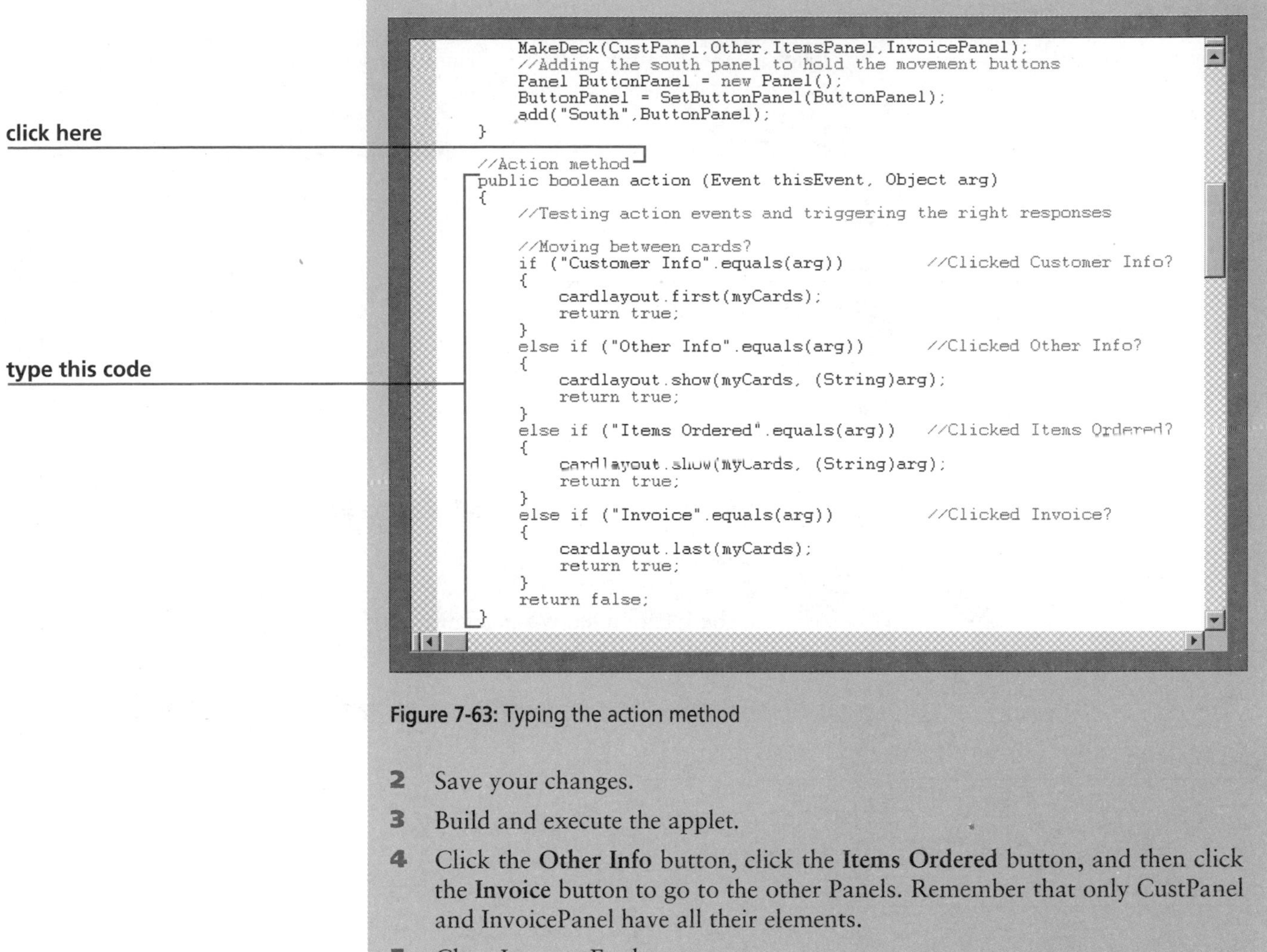

Figure 7-63: Typing the action method

2 Save your changes.

3 Build and execute the applet.

4 Click the **Other Info** button, click the **Items Ordered** button, and then click the **Invoice** button to go to the other Panels. Remember that only CustPanel and InvoicePanel have all their elements.

5 Close Internet Explorer.

Before learning about check boxes, you will test the customer processing method. To test this method, you need to write a preliminary version of MakeInvoice that will be rewritten later, and then you need to add the code to the action method that triggers the MakeInvoice and AddCustomer methods.

To test the customer processing method:

1 Click in the location shown in Figure 7-64, press the **Enter** key, and then type the MakeInvoice method.

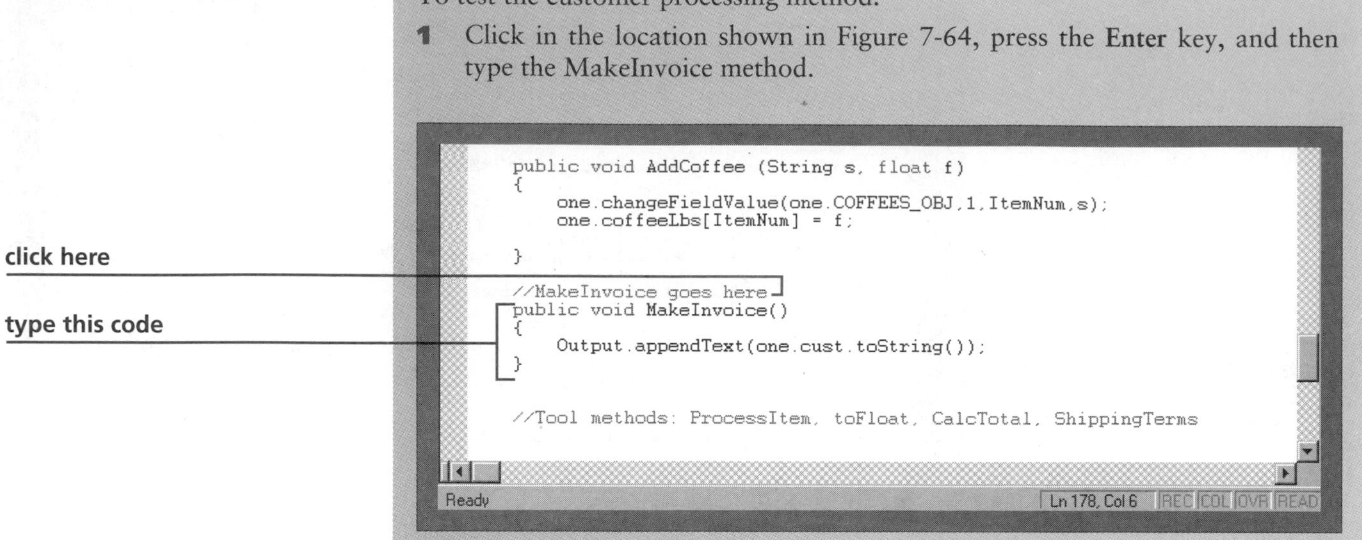
click here
type this code
public void AddCoffee (String s, float f)
{
one.changeFieldValue(one.COFFEES_OBJ,1,ItemNum,s);
one.coffeeLbs[ItemNum] = f;
}
//MakeInvoice goes here
public void MakeInvoice()
{
Output.appendText(one.cust.toString());
}
//Tool methods: ProcessItem, toFloat, CalcTotal, ShippingTerms
Ready
Ln 178, Col 6
REC COL OVR READ

Figure 7-64: Adding the MakeInvoice method

2 Click in the location shown in Figure 7-65, press the **Enter** key, and then type the conditional statements to trigger AddCustomer and MakeInvoice.

click here

type this code

```
        else if ("Invoice".equals(arg))         //Clicked Invoice?
        {
            cardlayout.last(myCards);
            return true;
        }
        //Checking for adding data buttons
        else if ("Accept Data".equals(arg))     //Clicked Accept Data?
        {
            Data = (Input.getText());
            AddCustomer(Data);
            return true;
        }
        else if ("Write Invoice".equals(arg))   //Clicked Write Invoice?
        {
            MakeInvoice();
            return true;
        }
        return false;
    }
```

Ready   Ln 87, Col 10   REC COL OVR READ

Figure 7-65: Adding the conditional statements for AddCustomer and MakeInvoice

3 Save your changes.

4 Build and execute the applet, type the information shown in Figure 7-66, and then click the **Accept Data** button.

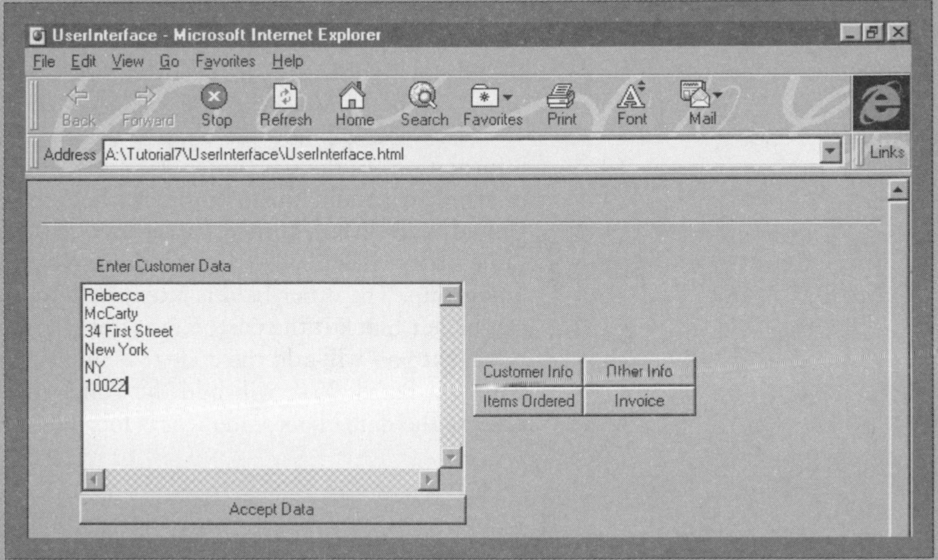

Figure 7-66: Entering the customer information

5 Click the **Invoice** button to move to the Invoice Panel. Click the **Write Invoice** button. The results appear, as shown in Figure 7-67.

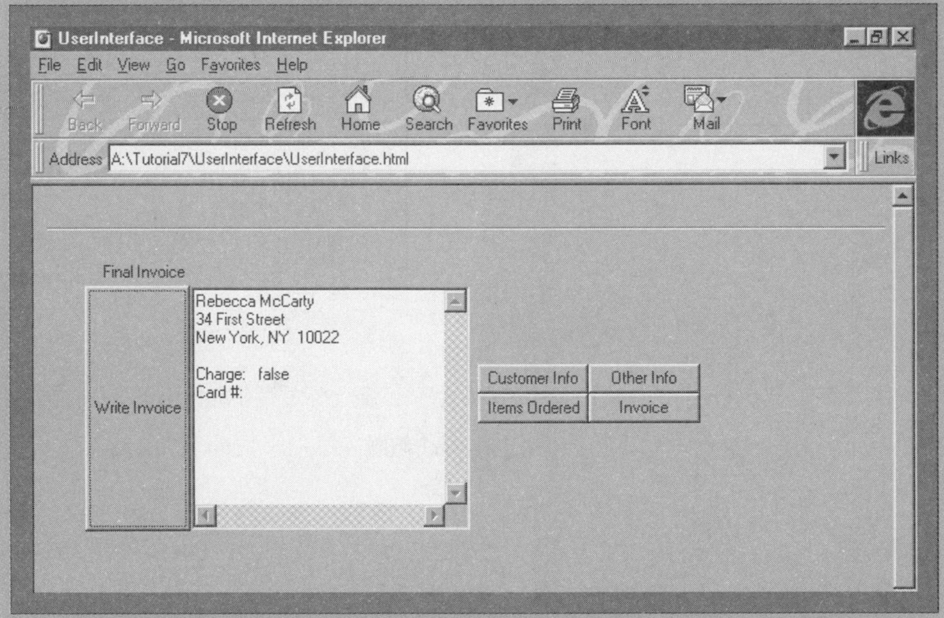

Figure 7-67: Customer results

6 Close Internet Explorer.

Using the Checkbox Class

A **check box** lets a user make a selection by checking or clearing a box. A check box also is called a **toggle switch** because it lets the user "toggle" back and forth between the item being selected and not selected. You also can group check boxes so only one check box from a series of check boxes can be selected. If you select one check box from the group, the other check boxes are cleared.

Next you will add the code to design the Panel that holds credit and shipping information. In the Customer class, the Charge field holds a boolean value, which is an ideal candidate for a single check box. There are three shipping options: United States Mail, United Parcel Service (UPS), and Federal Express (FedEx). The same order is shipped only one way, so this is an excellent candidate for a check box group. The other field is a text field to hold the credit card number. This field can be left blank if the customer is not charging the order.

Next you will add the code that implements the final version of the Credit and Shipping Panel. You will add the Panel code and the conditional statement that accepts the data. This statement is located in the init method.

To add the code for the Credit and Shipping Panel:

1. Click in the location shown in Figure 7-68, press the **Enter** key, and then type the SetOther method.

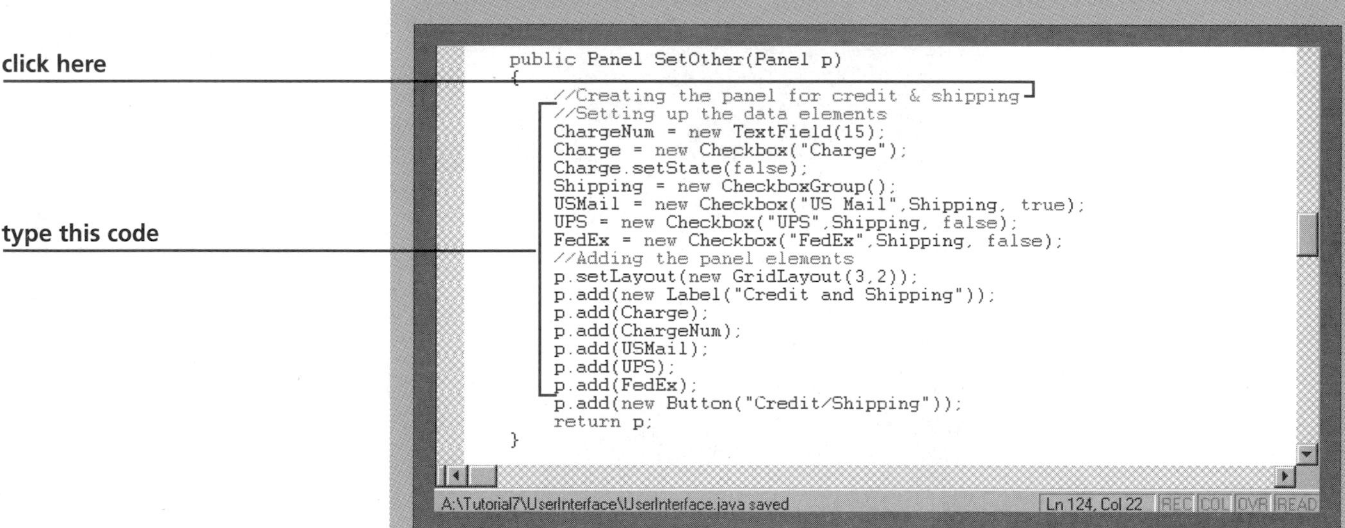

click here
type this code
public Panel SetOther(Panel p)
{
//Creating the panel for credit & shipping
//Setting up the data elements
ChargeNum = new TextField(15);
Charge = new Checkbox("Charge");
Charge.setState(false);
Shipping = new CheckboxGroup();
USMail = new Checkbox("US Mail",Shipping, true);
UPS = new Checkbox("UPS",Shipping, false);
FedEx = new Checkbox("FedEx",Shipping, false);
//Adding the panel elements
p.setLayout(new GridLayout(3,2));
p.add(new Label("Credit and Shipping"));
p.add(Charge);
p.add(ChargeNum);
p.add(USMail);
p.add(UPS);
p.add(FedEx);
p.add(new Button("Credit/Shipping"));
return p;
}
A:\Tutorial7\UserInterface\UserInterface.java saved
Ln 124, Col 22
REC COL OVR READ

Figure 7-68: Adding the SetOther method

2. To add the check box GUI elements to the class initialization section at the beginning of the applet, click in the location shown in Figure 7-69, and then type the check box declarations.

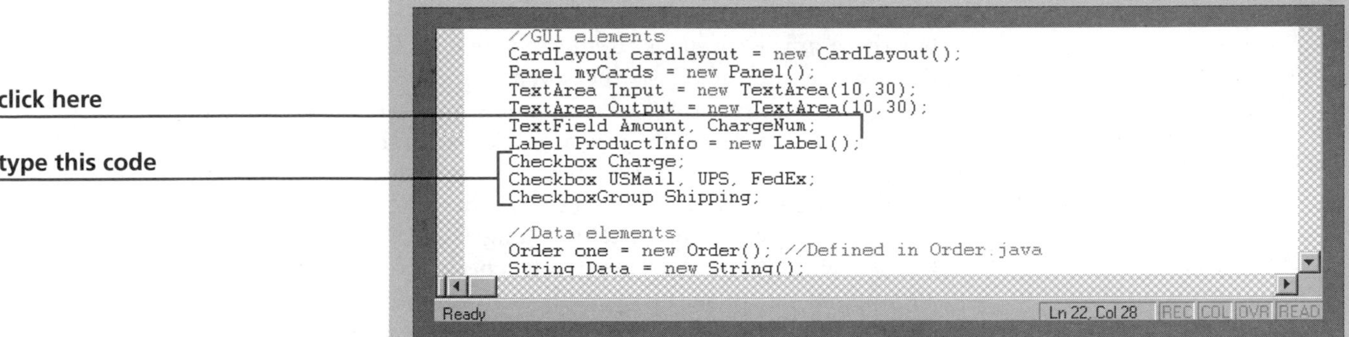

click here
type this code
//GUI elements
CardLayout cardlayout = new CardLayout();
Panel myCards = new Panel();
TextArea Input = new TextArea(10,30);
TextArea Output = new TextArea(10,30);
TextField Amount, ChargeNum;
Label ProductInfo = new Label();
Checkbox Charge;
Checkbox USMail, UPS, FedEx;
CheckboxGroup Shipping;
//Data elements
Order one = new Order(); //Defined in Order.java
String Data = new String();
Ready
Ln 22, Col 28
REC COL OVR READ

Figure 7-69: Adding the check box declaration statements

3. Save your changes.
4. Build and execute the applet. Click the **Other Info** button to see the Credit and Shipping Panel, as shown in Figure 7-70. Click the **Charge** check box two or three times. Click the three shipping options—notice that only one can have a check mark.

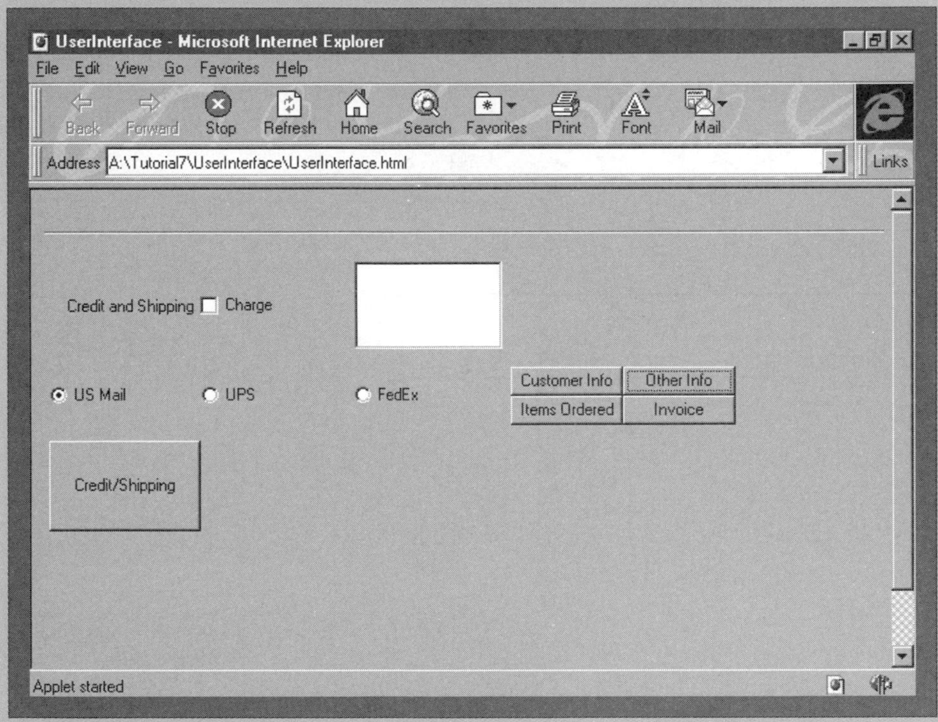

Figure 7-70: Credit and Shipping Panel

5. Close Internet Explorer.

tip

Grouped check boxes look like radio (option) buttons, as shown in Figure 7-70, to distinguish them from single check boxes (such as the Charge check box).

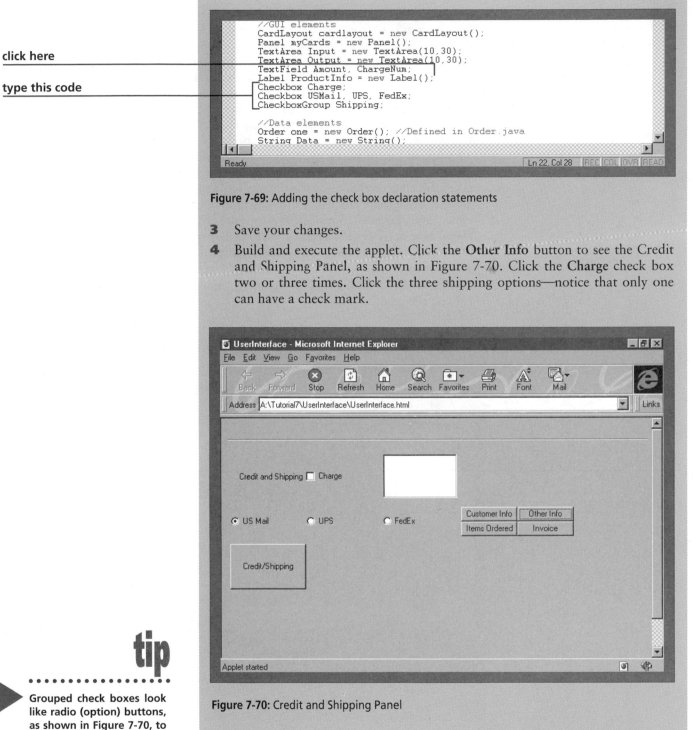

Notice that the setLayout statement is coded as three rows and two columns, but there are seven items. Remember that in GridLayout, the number of rows is the determining factor, so the seven elements get distributed among three rows, ending up with two rows of three items, and the third row contains only the button. The other interesting statements deal with the check boxes.

You added the check box declarations at the beginning of the file, but they are not used until this Panel. In the SetOther method, you use two versions of the check box constructor. For the single check box, you used *Charge = new Checkbox ("Charge");* to create one check box with the caption "Charge." After Shipping is set up as the check box group (*Shipping = new CheckboxGroup();*), the three grouped check boxes are set up. The constructor for a group check box takes three arguments: individual name, group name, and state (true or false). For a check box group, you can set up one (and only one) option to be the default true value, and the other options must be false. The other way to set the state of a check box is to use the setState method (*Charge.setState(false);*). This statement was not necessary in the code, as the default state of a check box is false.

Now it is time to add the conditional statement to the action method that detects the Credit/Shipping button, and to write the CreditandShipping method to process the input.

To write the conditional statement and the CreditandShipping method:

1 Click in the location shown in Figure 7-71, press the **Enter** key, and then type the conditional statement that responds to the Credit/Shipping button.

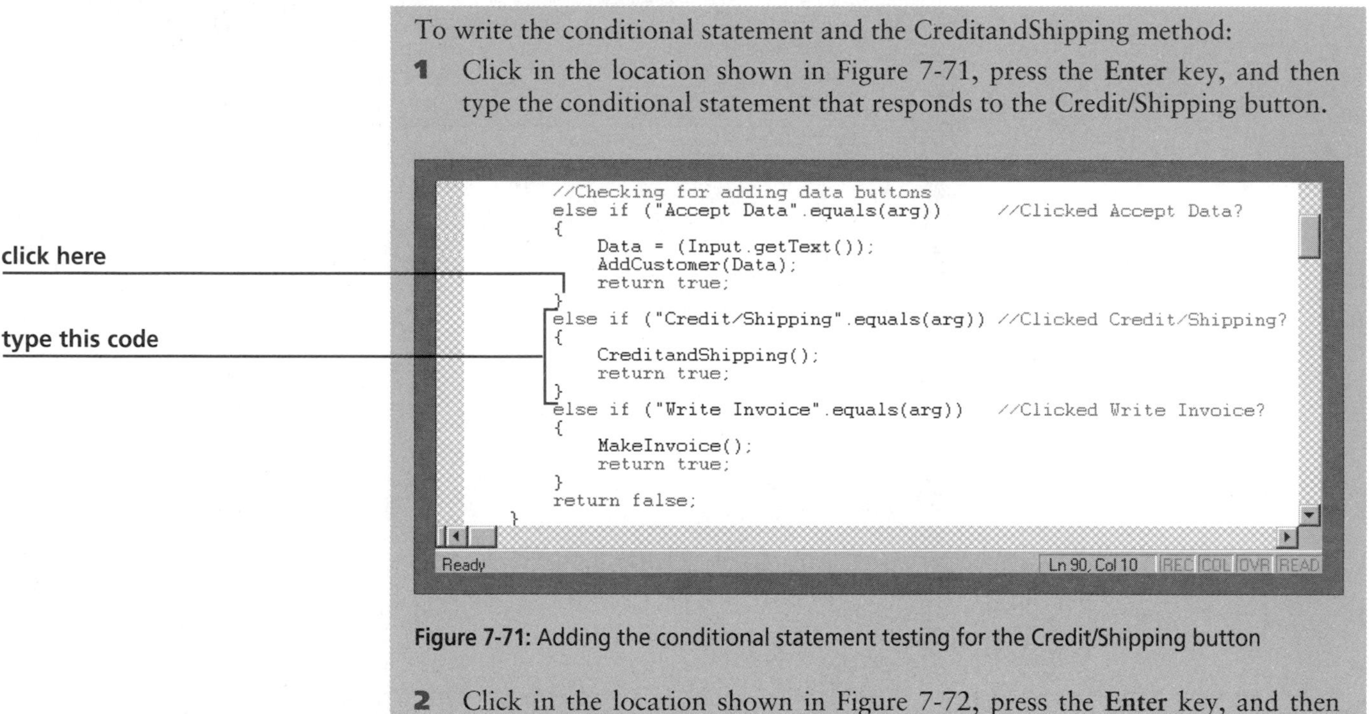


```
        //Checking for adding data buttons
        else if ("Accept Data".equals(arg))      //Clicked Accept Data?
        {
            Data = (Input.getText());
            AddCustomer(Data);
            return true;
        }
        else if ("Credit/Shipping".equals(arg)) //Clicked Credit/Shipping?
        {
            CreditandShipping();
            return true;
        }
        else if ("Write Invoice".equals(arg))   //Clicked Write Invoice?
        {
            MakeInvoice();
            return true;
        }
        return false;
    }
```

Figure 7-71: Adding the conditional statement testing for the Credit/Shipping button

2 Click in the location shown in Figure 7-72, press the **Enter** key, and then type the CreditandShipping method.

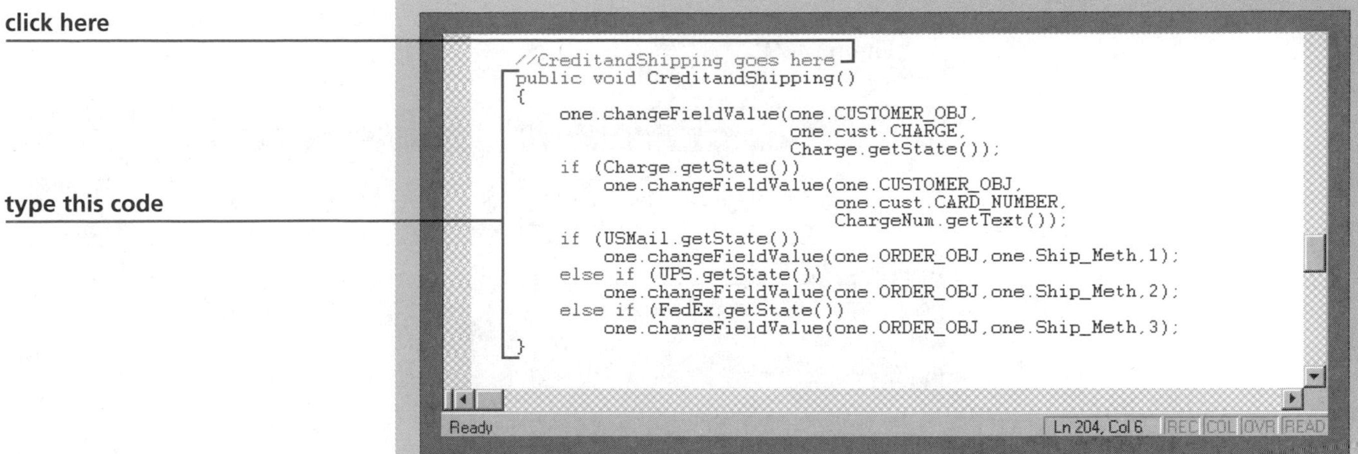
click here
type this code
//CreditandShipping goes here
public void CreditandShipping()
{
one.changeFieldValue(one.CUSTOMER_OBJ,
one.cust.CHARGE,
Charge.getState());
if (Charge.getState())
one.changeFieldValue(one.CUSTOMER_OBJ,
one.cust.CARD_NUMBER,
ChargeNum.getText());
if (USMail.getState())
one.changeFieldValue(one.ORDER_OBJ,one.Ship_Meth,1);
else if (UPS.getState())
one.changeFieldValue(one.ORDER_OBJ,one.Ship_Meth,2);
else if (FedEx.getState())
one.changeFieldValue(one.ORDER_OBJ,one.Ship_Meth,3);
}
Ready
Ln 204, Col 6
REC COL OVR READ

Figure 7-72: Adding the CreditandShipping method

3. Save your changes.
4. Build and execute the applet. Enter the customer information shown in Figure 7-66, and then click the **Accept Data** button. Click the **Other Info** button, enter the data shown in Figure 7-73, and then click the **Credit/Shipping** button.

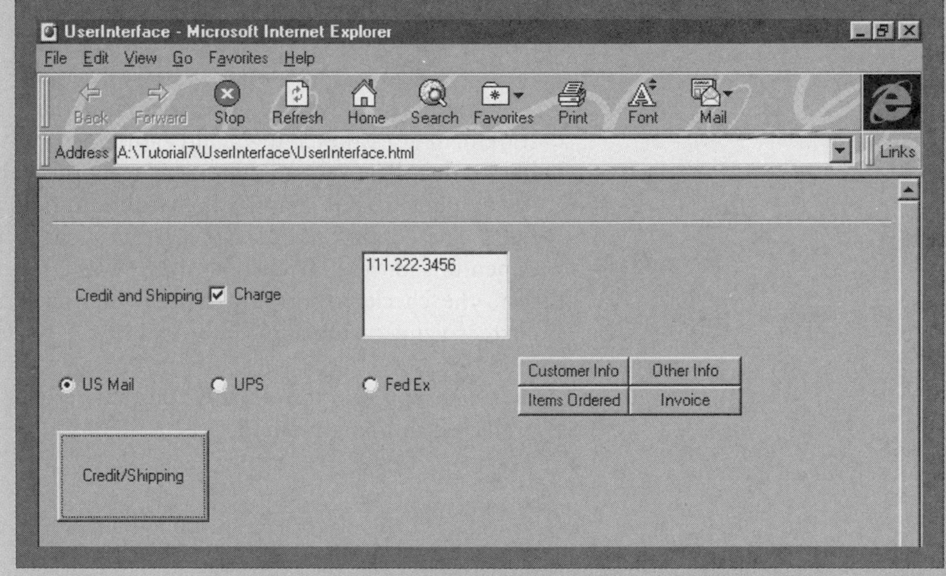
UserInterface - Microsoft Internet Explorer
File Edit View Go Favorites Help
Back Forward Stop Refresh Home Search Favorites Print Font Mail
Address A:\Tutorial7\UserInterface\UserInterface.html
Links
Credit and Shipping
Charge
111-222-3456
US Mail
UPS
Fed Ex
Customer Info
Other Info
Items Ordered
Invoice
Credit/Shipping

Figure 7-73: Credit and shipping data

5 Click the **Invoice** button, and then click the **Write Invoice** button. See Figure 7-74.

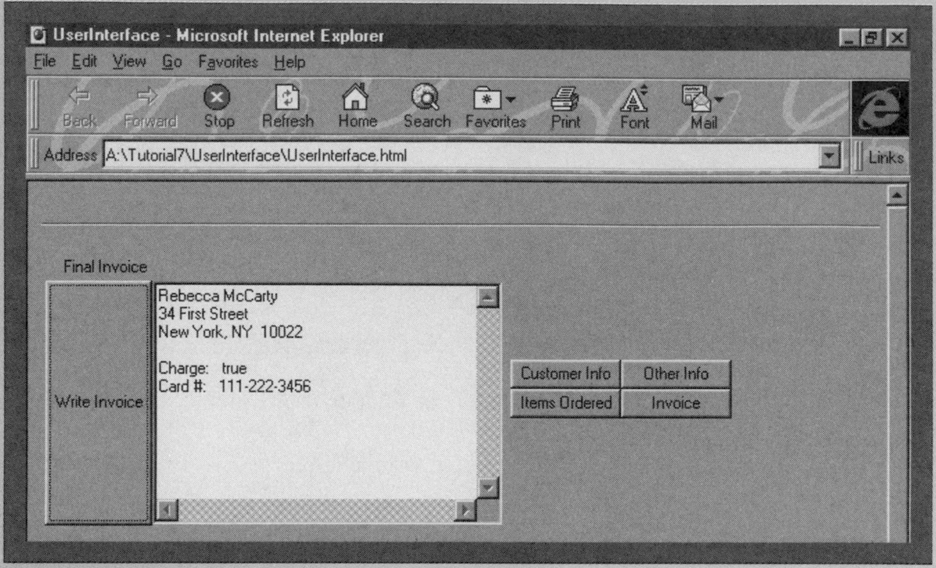

Figure 7-74: Results with credit data

6 Close Internet Explorer.

There are only three statements in the CreditandShipping method. The first statement uses the changeFieldValue method in the Order class to set the charge field value. The second statement tests the value in the Charge check box, and if the value is true, it changes the cardNum field to the value in the ChargeNum text field. The conditional uses the getState check box method to return true or false, depending on the check box state. The last statement is an if-else statement that tests the check box group to see which check box is checked, and to assign the correct value to the shipMeth field of the Order class, using the changeFieldValue method.

Now you can add the method that returns a String that reports the customer's preferred shipping method.

To return a String for the shipping method:

1 Click in the location shown in Figure 7-75, press the **Enter** key, and then type the ShippingTerms method.

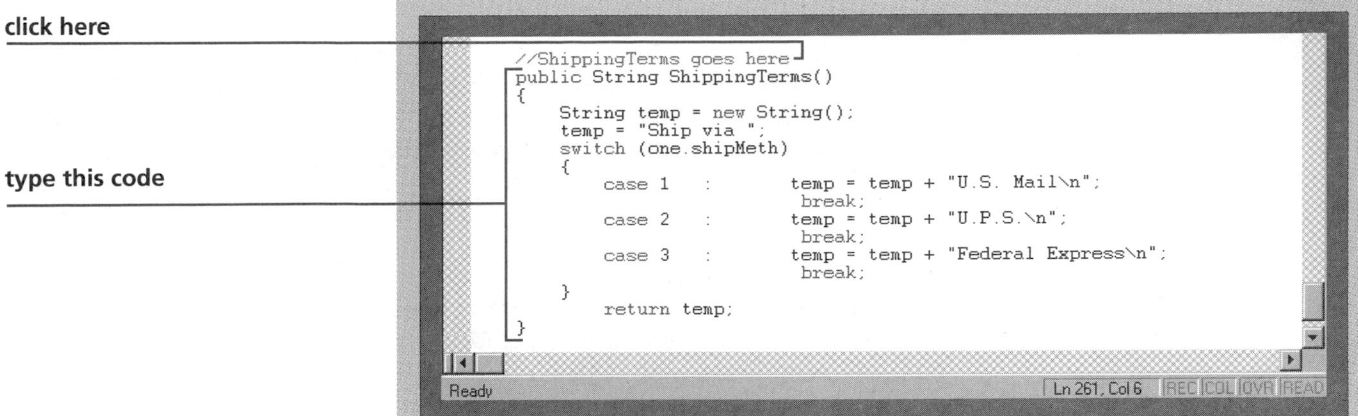

click here
type this code
//ShippingTerms goes here
public String ShippingTerms()
{
String temp = new String();
temp = "Ship via ";
switch (one.shipMeth)
{
case 1 : temp = temp + "U.S. Mail\n";
break;
case 2 : temp = temp + "U.P.S.\n";
break;
case 3 : temp = temp + "Federal Express\n";
break;
}
return temp;
}
Ready
Ln 261, Col 6
REC COL OVR READ

Figure 7-75: Adding the ShippingTerms method

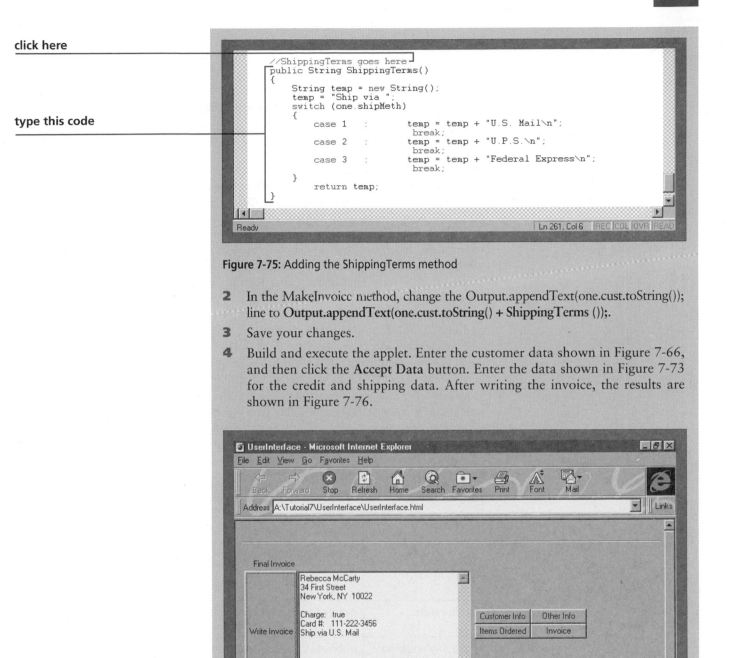

2 In the MakeInvoice method, change the Output.appendText(one.cust.toString()); line to **Output.appendText(one.cust.toString() + ShippingTerms ());**.

3 Save your changes.

4 Build and execute the applet. Enter the customer data shown in Figure 7-66, and then click the **Accept Data** button. Enter the data shown in Figure 7-73 for the credit and shipping data. After writing the invoice, the results are shown in Figure 7-76.

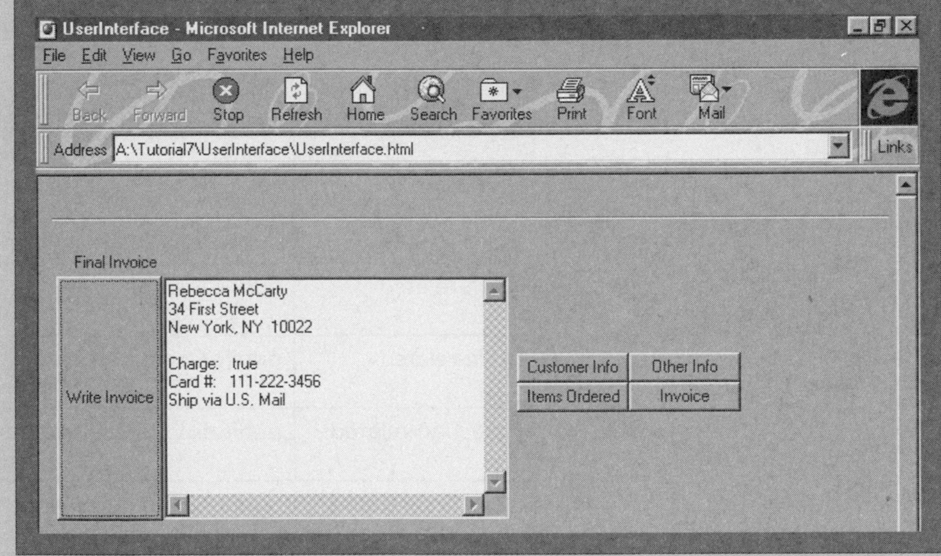

Figure 7-76: Results showing shipping information

5 Close Internet Explorer.

Using the Choice Class

The last Panel is the ItemsPanel. For this Panel, you will use a new GUI element, which is the Choice class. The **Choice class** in Java lets the user pick from a drop-down list of set items. Users cannot type in the list; they can select only what is there, which is perfect for selecting coffee products. By clicking one of the Choice elements, the user can select one item by selecting it, and then that element shows in the box.

The Choice class has only a few methods, and just one constructor with no arguments. For our purposes, there are two groups of methods—the item-related methods, and the selection-related methods. There are three item-related methods: addItem, countItems, and getItem. The addItem method has a String argument that displays in the Choice element. The countItems method has no arguments, but returns an integer that reports how many items are in the Choice. The getItem method takes an integer argument that is the numerical position on the Choice list (with the first item having the value zero), and returns the String that is at that numeric position.

There are three selection-related methods: getSelectedIndex, getSelectedItem, and select. The first two methods return a value based on what item is selected. The value that shows in the box is the selected value, even if the user has not clicked it. So, if no user interaction has taken place, the first item with an index of zero is the selected item. The getSelectedIndex returns the integer index of the selected item, and the getSelectedItem returns the String that is the text of the selected item. The select method has two versions—one that selects an item based on its integer index argument, or one that selects based on the String item name. Figure 7-77 shows the choice methods, their category, and examples.

Type	Method Syntax	Example
Constructor	public Choice()	Choice Mine = new Choice();
Item-related	public void addItem(String I)	Mine.addItem("First");
Item-related	public int countItems()	IntNum = Mine.countItems();
Item-related	public String getItem(int I)	myString = Mine.getItem(0);
Selection-related	public int getSelectedIndex()	IntNum = Mine.getSelectedIndex();
Selection-related	public String getSelectedItem()	myString = Mine.getSelectedItem();
Selection-related	public void select(int I)	Mine.select(0);
Selection-related	public void select(String I)	Mine.select("First");

Figure 7-77: Choice methods

Next you will add the GUI elements to the SetItem Panel. While on the surface this Panel seems straightforward, there is one trick that you are going to pull here. Remember from Tutorial 6 that the Order class was changed to hold five coffee items. You do not want to have one Panel for each potential item, so this one Panel will have to do. The trick will be that the label will change as the user enters more coffee items. Before the first item is accepted, the label will read "Enter Item #1." Before the second item is accepted, the label will read "Enter Item #2," and so on. After the fifth item is accepted the label will read "Cannot Add." Most of the complexity is handled on the ProcessItem method. The ItemPanel uses a GridLayout with two labels, the Choice, a text field, and a button.

To add the SetItem Panel and the Add Item conditional statement:

1 Click in the location shown in Figure 7-78, press the **Enter** key, and then type the SetItemPanel method.

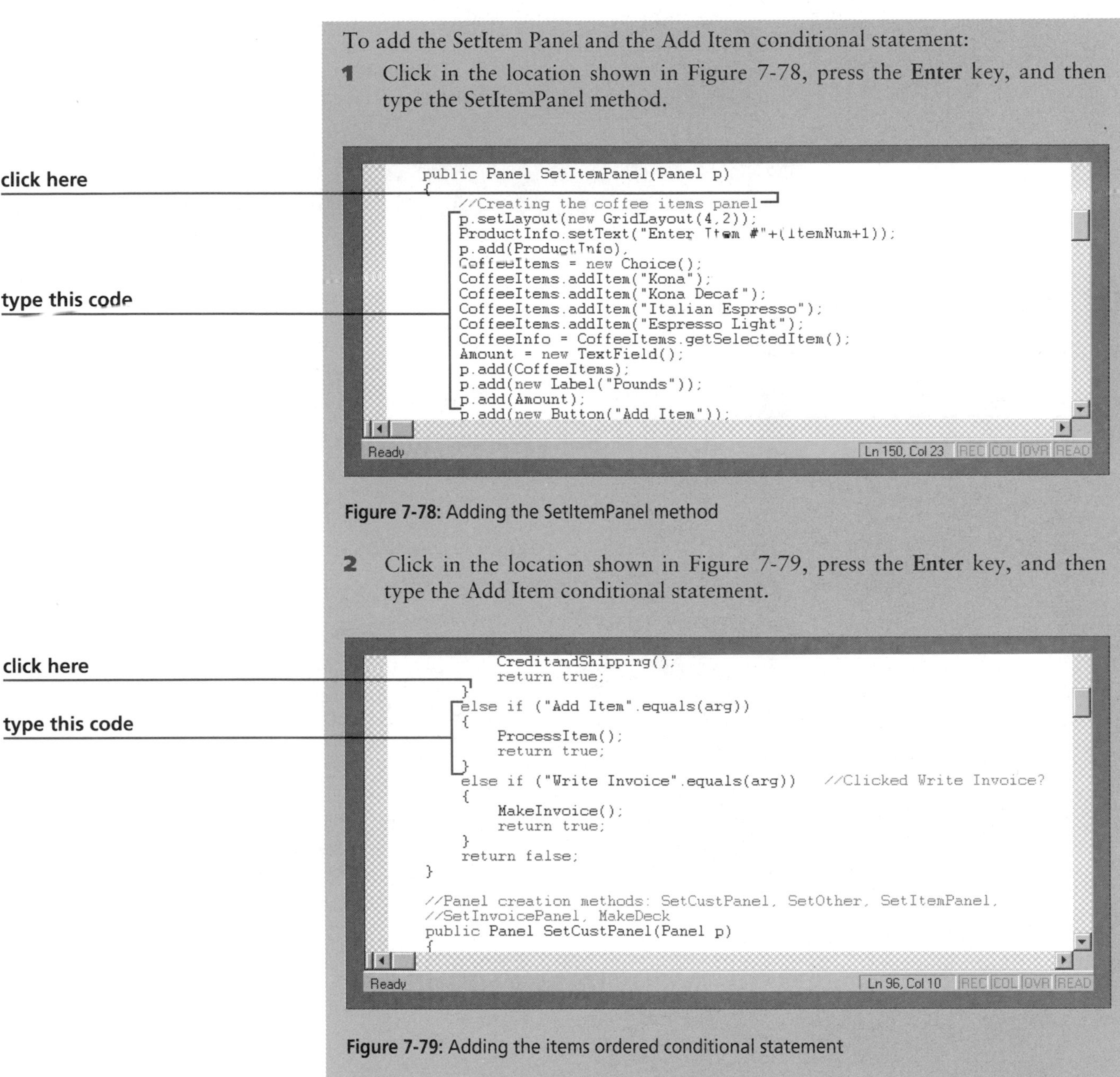
click here
type this code
public Panel SetItemPanel(Panel p)
{
//Creating the coffee items panel
p.setLayout(new GridLayout(4,2));
ProductInfo.setText("Enter Item #"+(ItemNum+1));
p.add(ProductInfo);
CoffeeItems = new Choice();
CoffeeItems.addItem("Kona");
CoffeeItems.addItem("Kona Decaf");
CoffeeItems.addItem("Italian Espresso");
CoffeeItems.addItem("Espresso Light");
CoffeeInfo = CoffeeItems.getSelectedItem();
Amount = new TextField();
p.add(CoffeeItems);
p.add(new Label("Pounds"));
p.add(Amount);
p.add(new Button("Add Item"));
Ready
Ln 150, Col 23
REC COL OVR READ
click here
type this code
CreditandShipping();
return true;
}
else if ("Add Item".equals(arg))
{
ProcessItem();
return true;
}
else if ("Write Invoice".equals(arg)) //Clicked Write Invoice?
{
MakeInvoice();
return true;
}
return false;
}
//Panel creation methods: SetCustPanel, SetOther, SetItemPanel,
//SetInvoicePanel, MakeDeck
public Panel SetCustPanel(Panel p)
{
Ready
Ln 96, Col 10
REC COL OVR READ

Figure 7-78: Adding the SetItemPanel method

2 Click in the location shown in Figure 7-79, press the **Enter** key, and then type the Add Item conditional statement.

Figure 7-79: Adding the items ordered conditional statement

3 Save your changes.

There are only two more methods to add—the ProcessItem method (which handles the coffee items), and the full version of the MakeInvoice method. As part of the processing of a coffee item, there is an ItemNum data field for the UserInterface class. In the declarations area, ItemNum was initialized to zero for the first element in the coffee products array. The ProcessItem method gets the user input, passes the input to the AddCoffees method (already in the file), adds to ItemNum, and changes the ItemPanel label.

The full version of the MakeInvoice invoice displays all the customer data, information about all the coffee products ordered, the purchase price information, shipping and tax charges, the total due, and the shipping information. This information is joined into one String and is displayed in the output text area.

To finalize the program:

1 Click in the location shown in Figure 7-80, press the **Enter** key, and then type the ProcessItem method.

click here

type this code

```
    //ProcessItem goes here
    public void ProcessItem()
    {
        CoffeeInfo = CoffeeItems.getSelectedItem();
        float Quantity = toFloat(Amount.getText());
        AddCoffee(CoffeeInfo,Quantity);
        ItemNum++;
        if (ItemNum >=5)
            ProductInfo.setText("Cannot add");
        else
            ProductInfo.setText("Enter Item #"+(ItemNum+1));
    }


        public float toFloat (String iString)
    {
        Float value = new Float(iString);
        return value.floatValue();
    }
```

Ready   Ln 264, Col 6 REC COL OVR READ

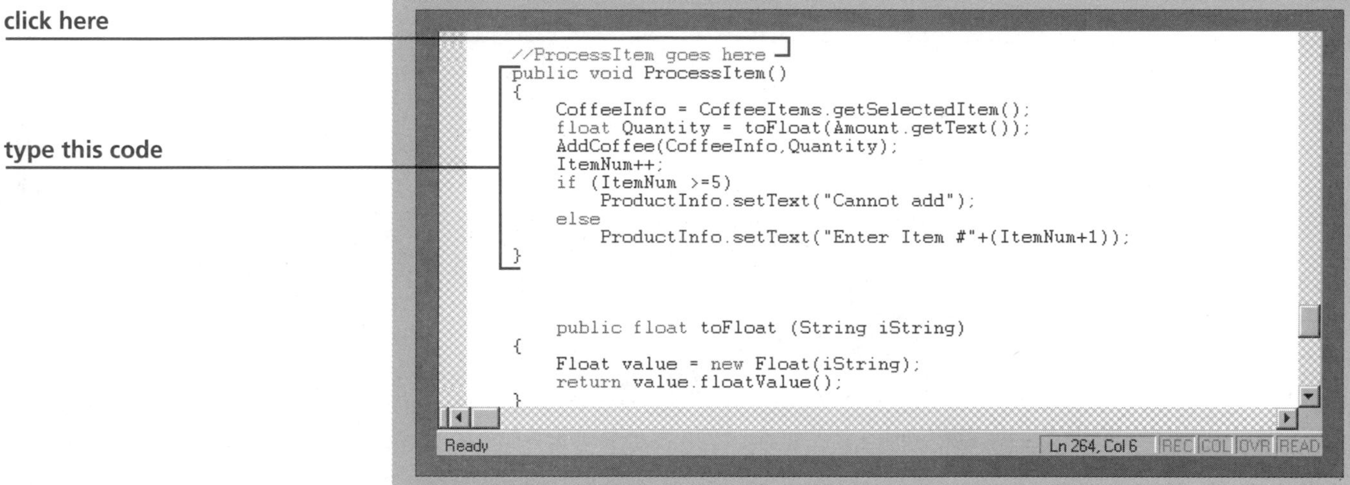

Figure 7-80: Adding the ProcessItem method

2 Move to the MakeInvoice method, and delete the **Output.appendText (one.cust.toString() + ShippingTerms());** line inside the method.

3 Click in the location shown in Figure 7-81, press the **Enter** key, and then type the new code for the MakeInvoice method.

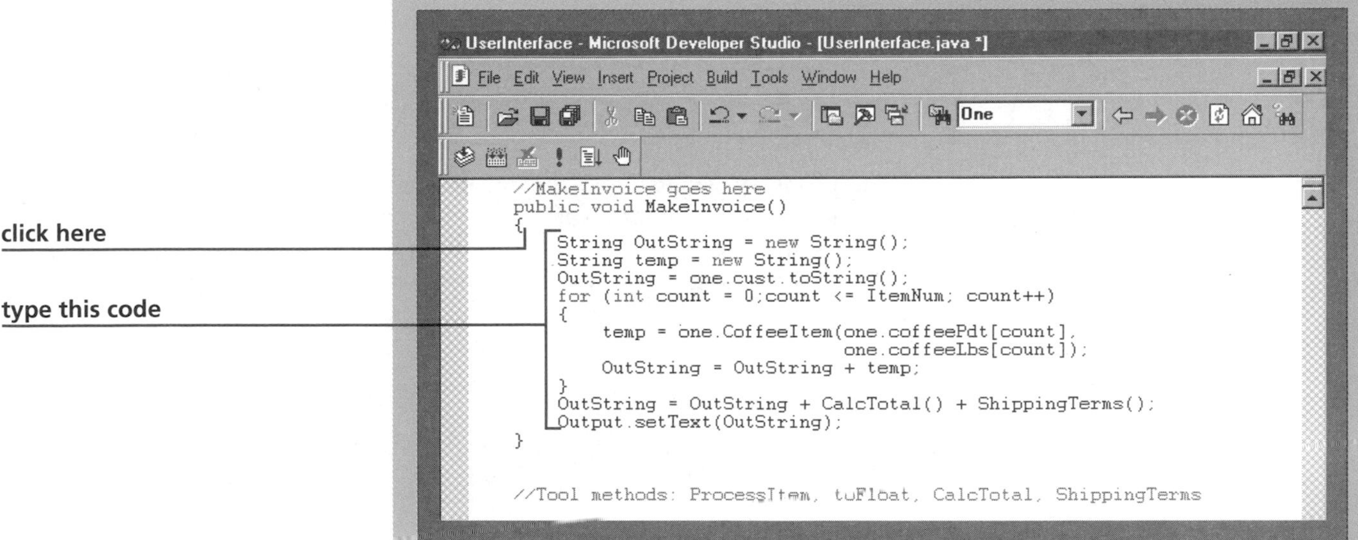
click here
type this code
UserInterface - Microsoft Developer Studio - [UserInterface.java *]
File Edit View Insert Project Build Tools Window Help
One
//MakeInvoice goes here
public void MakeInvoice()
{
String OutString = new String();
String temp = new String();
OutString = one.cust.toString();
for (int count = 0;count <= ItemNum; count++)
{
temp = one.CoffeeItem(one.coffeePdt[count],
one.coffeeLbs[count]);
OutString = OutString + temp;
}
OutString = OutString + CalcTotal() + ShippingTerms();
Output.setText(OutString);
}
//Tool methods: ProcessItem, toFloat, CalcTotal, ShippingTerms

Figure 7-81: Adding the full version of MakeInvoice

4 Scroll to the top of the file, click after the CheckboxGroup Shipping; line, press the **Enter** key, and then type **Choice CoffeeItems;**.

5 Save your changes.

6 Build and execute the applet. Enter the customer data from Figure 7-66, and then click the **Accept Data** button. Enter the data from Figure 7-73 for the credit and shipping data, but change the shipping to FedEx. For coffee items, order 5 pounds of Kona, and 6.5 pounds of Italian Espresso. Wait—there is a problem here, you cannot select Italian Espresso. See Figure 7-82.

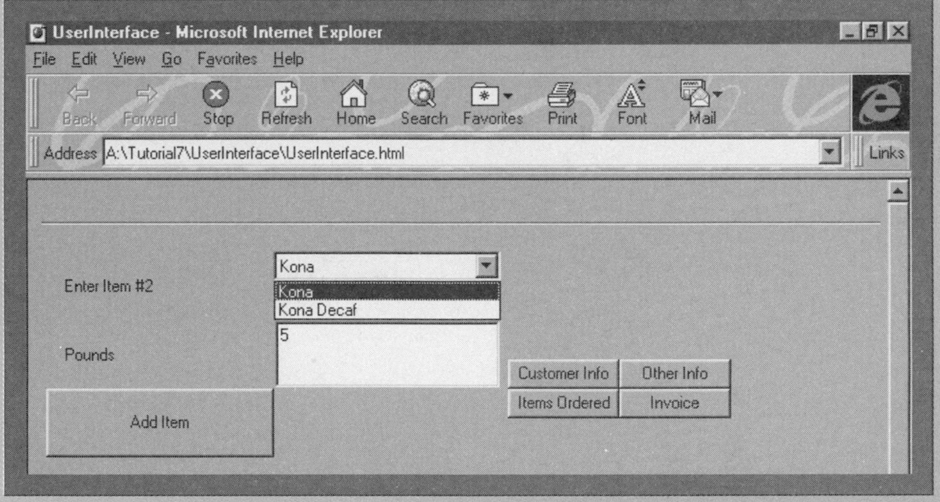
UserInterface - Microsoft Internet Explorer
File Edit View Go Favorites Help
Back Forward Stop Refresh Home Search Favorites Print Font Mail
Address A:\Tutorial7\UserInterface\UserInterface.html
Links
Enter Item #2
Kona
Kona
Kona Decaf
Pounds
5
Add Item
Customer Info
Other Info
Items Ordered
Invoice

Figure 7-82: Item order problem

HELP? Depending on your monitor resolution, you might see all of the choices. Continue with the steps.

7 Close Internet Explorer.

The problem is that the GUI elements are too close together on the screen. The Choice element cannot display over the text field below it. There is an easy way to fix it. GridLayout has a constructor that takes four arguments: rows, columns, horizontal gap, vertical gap. If you change to this form of the constructor, you can add some space between the elements.

To add space between the elements:

1 Change the GridLayout from two arguments to four arguments as shown in Figure 7-83.

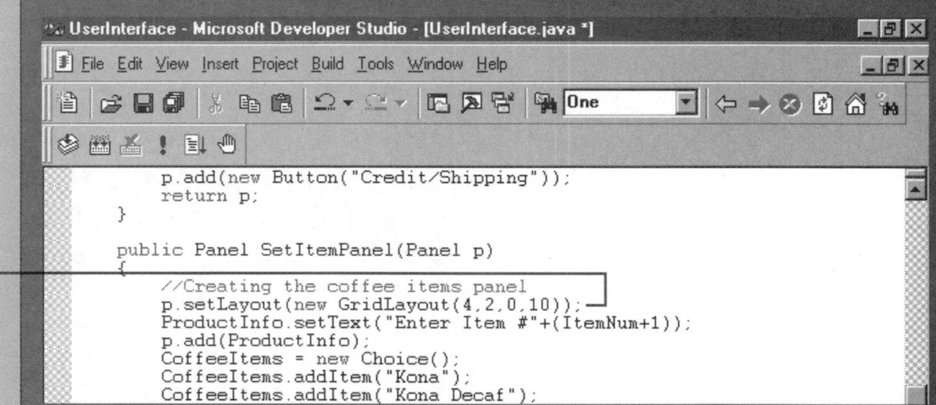
change this line
UserInterface - Microsoft Developer Studio - [UserInterface.java *]
File Edit View Insert Project Build Tools Window Help
One
p.add(new Button("Credit/Shipping"));
return p;
}
public Panel SetItemPanel(Panel p)
{
//Creating the coffee items panel
p.setLayout(new GridLayout(4,2,0,10));
ProductInfo.setText("Enter Item #"+(ItemNum+1));
p.add(ProductInfo);
CoffeeItems = new Choice();
CoffeeItems.addItem("Kona");
CoffeeItems.addItem("Kona Decaf");

Figure 7-83: Fixing the GridLayout statement

2 Build and execute the applet. Enter the customer data from Figure 7-66, and then click the **Accept Data** button. Enter the data from Figure 7-73 for the credit and shipping data, but change the shipping to FedEx. For coffee items, order 5 pounds of Kona, and 6.5 pounds of Italian Espresso. Click the **Write Invoice** button on the InvoicePanel. The results should look like those in Figure 7-84.

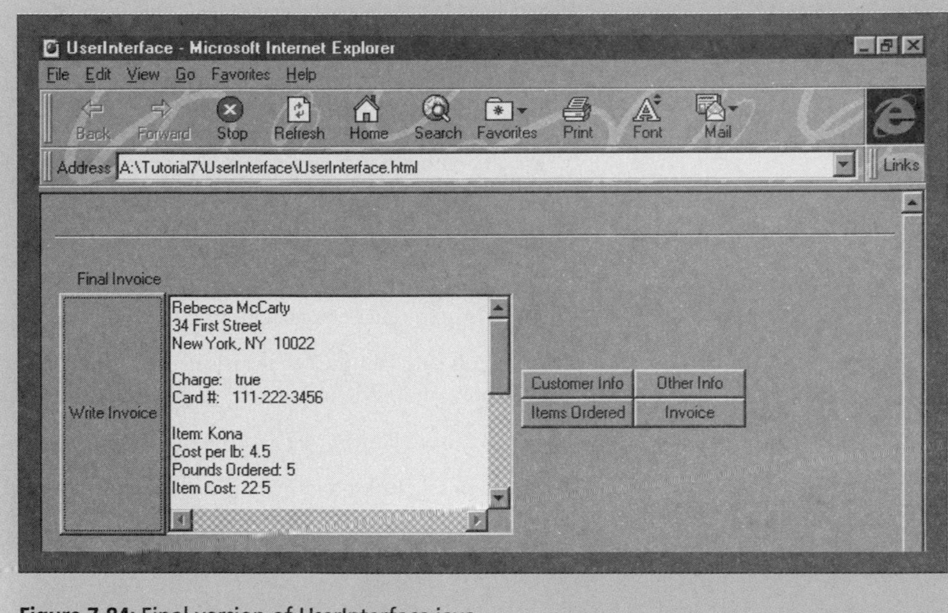

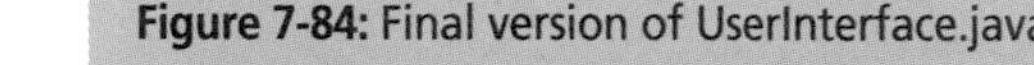
Figure 7-84: Final version of UserInterface.java

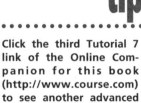

3 If you want, click the **Refresh** button on the toolbar, and try some data of your own.

4 Close Internet Explorer, close the project workspace, and then close Visual J++.

Click the third Tutorial 7 link of the Online Companion for this book (http://www.course.com) to see another advanced usage of Java programming.

Now you can either take a break or complete the end-of-lesson questions and exercises.

S U M M A R Y

- A Java layout manager controls where GUI elements are placed in an applet.
- The FlowLayout manager is the default manager that positions elements from left to right in rows.
- The FlowLayout manager default alignment is centered.
- Another way to control the appearance of your applet is to change the height and width parameters in the HTML file.
- The GridLayout manager arranges elements in a grid where each element takes up the same amount of space on the screen.

- The GridLayout manager uses the number of rows as the critical information.
- A Panel object is a Java object that holds GUI elements.
- You can specify space between the regions using the GridLayout manager.
- The BorderLayout manager separates the page into five regions—North, South, East, West, and Center—to lay out up to five objects (one in each region).
- You do not have to use all the regions in BorderLayout.
- The CardLayout manager allows you to "stack" GUI elements on top of each other. Only the element currently on the top is visible.
- You can "shuffle" the cards in a CardLayout by referring to the first, last, next, and previous card, and by referring to the card by name.
- By using Panels, you can use more than one kind of layout in an applet.
- Group check boxes will allow only one check box in a group to be checked.
- The Java Choice class is a GUI element that lets the user pick a selection from a drop-down list. The currently selected item is at the top of the list.

QUESTIONS

1. Which layout manager is the default?

a. BorderLayout

b. CardLayout

c. FlowLayout

d. GridLayout

2. Which layout manager creates a layout based on regions of equal size that are organized in rows and columns?

a. BorderLayout

b. CardLayout

c. FlowLayout

d. GridLayout

3. Which layout manager creates a layout with five regions with different sizes?

a. BorderLayout

b. CardLayout

c. FlowLayout

d. GridLayout

4. Which layout manager allows you to stack GUI elements on top of each other?

a. BorderLayout

b. CardLayout

c. FlowLayout

d. GridLayout

5. What is the default alignment in FlowLayout?

a. center

b. right

c. left

6. You can allocate different amounts of space to the elements in a GridLayout.

a. true

b. false

7. A check box can have only one of two states.

a. true

b. false

8. You can have multiple check boxes checked in a group of check boxes.

a. true

b. false

9. What statement adds to a Choice list?

a. myChoice.AddItem("Item One");

b. myChoice.Item0 = "ItemOne";

c. myChoice.addItem("Item One");

d. myChoice.Index[1] = "Item One";

10. What statement assigns the selected value from a Choice list to a String named myString?

a. myString = myChoice.getSelectedItem();

b. myChoice.getSelectedItem(myString);

c. myString = myChoice.getItem();

d. myChoice.getItem(myString);

EXERCISES

1. You need an applet that lists the names, extensions, and departments of Koffee Koncoctions' employees. Hold the data in a two-dimensional array that holds the String name, extension, and department. Your applet should use a GridLayout with the GUI elements being a Choice list of names, read-only text fields that will hold the extension and department (with the appropriate labels), and a Find button. Save the following files in the Exercise1B folder in the Exercises folder in the Tutorial7 folder on your Student Disk: Koffee.java and Koffee.html. The data you should use is:

Name	Extension	Department
Maria Jinnez	306	Marketing
Susan McGill	267	Art
Wen-Fong Wu	182	Accounting
Ilana Markovich	234	Information Services

2. Western Real Estate needs a commission calculator for its agents. There are three levels of commissions—5%, 7.5%, and 10%—based on the number of years of service agents are employed by the agency. Use grouped check boxes for the agents to select their commission rate. The applet should use a BorderLayout—North should be a title label, West should be the grouped check boxes, East should be the Calculate button, and South should be a Clear button. The Center should be a Panel using GridLayout with text fields and labels for current month sales and current month commission. The commission text field should be read-only. Save the following files in the Exercise2B folder in the Exercises folder in the Tutorial7 folder on your Student Disk: Western.java and Western.html.

3. Your history professor needs an applet that explains the grading requirements in his "History of Technology" course. Use a BorderLayout with the Center region being a Panel with a CardLayout. South should be a Panel with card movement keys for first, last, and by name. The cards will be grade requirements: Agrade, Bgrade, Cgrade, and Dgrade. All of the grade requirements will be read-only text areas. Save the following files in the Exercise3B folder in the Exercises folder in the Tutorial7 folder on your Student Disk: History.java and History.html. The grading requirements are:

Grade	Requirements
A	30 page research paper
	10 minute oral presentation
	Web page with 3 images and 10 links
	Average grade of 87% or higher on all quizzes and tests
B	20 page research paper
	5 minute oral presentation
	Web page with 2 images and 8 links
	Average grade of 77% to 86% on all quizzes and tests
C	15 page research paper
	No oral presentation
	Web page with 1 image and 5 links
	Average grade of 67% to 76% on all quizzes and tests

D	10 page research paper
	No oral presentation
	Web page with 7 links
	Average grade of 57% to 66% on all quizzes and tests

4. Joe's Food to Go needs a food ordering applet. It should have a group check box for hamburger, cheeseburger, or chicken, and single check boxes for side orders of french fries, onion rings, fried zucchini, and corn fritters. A text area shows the order after clicking the Show Order button. Use the GridLayout manager with hgap of 5, vgap of 10. Save the following files in the Exercise4B folder in the Exercises folder in the Tutorial7 folder on your Student Disk: Joes.java and Joes.html.

5. Complete Exercise 4 using a BorderLayout with the text area in the center, the group check boxes in the west, the single check boxes in the east, and the Show Order button in the south. Save the following files in the Exercise5B folder in the Exercises folder in the Tutorial7 folder on your Student Disk: Joes1.java and Joes1.html.

APPENDIX

A

HTML Basics

HTML, or **hypertext markup language**, is a group of commands, like a programming language, that informs a Web browser, such as Internet Explorer, how to display the text in a given file in the browser. HTML is used extensively in Web technology and has been the basic Web standard since 1990. The current version of HTML is version 3 although some browsers might not support all of the functions of the newest version.

Note: All of the tags in this appendix have been tested with Internet Explorer version 3.

HTML is a simple yet extensive set of commands that are included in a text document to inform browsers how to treat the document information. HTML commands also are called **tags**. HTML currently is a standardized language, making it available to any Web browser. HTML provides the following general functions:

- Displays and manipulates hypertext news, mail, and documents
- Displays and controls menus of links to hypertext documents
- Displays database information and results of queries
- Displays documents with in-line graphics and with wrap-around text
- Provides a platform for applet display with the Java language

The goal of this appendix is to provide an abbreviated reference to the HTML language as well as an example of the use of HTML to create Web pages with a single link.

HTML Syntax Definition

HTML uses specific standardized tags to inform the browser how to display text. Usually HTML tags are enclosed in angle brackets (< and >). There are two HTML tags—block and single. A **block tag** is a function that has an opening and a closing marker, such as *<tag>* and *</tag>*. The text that appears between these two tags displays based on the command in the tags. For example, the HTML block tag *<TITLE>An Introduction to HTML</TITLE>* indicates that the title for the document is "An Introduction to HTML." The tags identify where the title begins and ends. Many HTML tags are block tags.

The second type of tag in HTML is the **single tag**, which provides all information between one set of angle brackets so it does not need an opening and closing marker. For example, the tag *<IMG SRC="picture.gif">* defines a graphic object to the browser that displays on the current page. IMG indicates that this is a graphic image and the SRC= attribute tells the browser where to find the file.

Another standard that is used by HTML is the resource designator for filenames and other Web resources. The standard adopted by HTML is the **universal resource locator** (**URL**). URL is used in HTML to indicate filenames of resources, links to other Web sites, and links to specific locations in the current file.

In this appendix, the syntax will show the keywords in uppercase and user-supplied information in italics. HTML does not require that the tags be in uppercase; this format is adopted only for clarity.

The HTML Document

The HTML document is a text document made up of two parts—the heading and body. The **heading section** of the document typically contains tags that are informational to the browser for finding documents that might be linked from the current document and default settings the user wants to initiate. The heading section of the HTML document is a block tag that starts with the <HEAD> tag and ends with the </HEAD> tag.

The **body section** of the document contains the document information and images that the developer wants to display on the browser. The tags in this section might format text, place graphic images, or provide links to other documents or labeled sections in the current document or to Java applets. The body section of the document starts with the <BODY> tag and ends with the </BODY> tag. Tag elements are enclosed within the BODY tags to control the appearance of the document. The first tag in the HTML document is <HTML> and the closing tag is </HTML>, which usually is the last line of the file. The HTML block tag informs the browser that all of the information between the opening and closing tags is HTML text and commands.

This general format is used in the example at the end of this appendix. Some programmers create a sample skeleton of the most commonly used tags, which they use as a template when creating other documents. Many software programs include utilities to convert word processing files into HTML documents. You also will find many Web authoring software packages that automatically convert your documents into HTML code.

Heading Elements

Titles should be limited to 64 characters. Titles should be specific, rather than generic. For example, "An Introduction to Java" is better than "Introduction."

The **heading elements** of an HTML document provide general information to the browser that accesses its information. Many Web sites use HTML so it is important to inform users in a standardized format and location of important information such as where the text files of the HTML document are located. The heading is an identifying construct that allows other users to navigate through the information. Some commonly used heading tags are <TITLE> and </TITLE>, which inform users who open the specific HTML document of that document's name. This information often is used by client systems to display the title in the title bar of the browser, although not all browsers support this feature. This information also might be accessed by Web programs that maintain indices of resources and information available to clients.

BASE Tag

The syntax for the base tag is <BASE HREF="*URL*">.

The **base tag** informs the client system of the base address of the files that might be linked in a given document. When the client is an Internet user and the current document is stored on another machine, the user will not know the correct folders in which to find the files unless the optional base tag is included. The base tag also makes it easier for a developer to move a set of documents to another folder and update the information by changing only the base address tag.

LINK Marker Tag

The syntax for the link marker is <LINK REL=*link title* HREF="*URL*">. Usually the link marker is used to reference authorship, older versions of the document, and important indices. For general document links, the anchor marker that is included in the body section of the document is the better choice for linking to other resources.

The **link marker** is used to identify hyperlinks in the heading section. The link marker is similar to the anchor marker in that it provides links to other documents or sections in the same document. A heading can have any number of link commands.

Body Elements

The **body** of the HTML document contains the text and tags that control the display and access of information. The heading is like the Java class definition and the property variable definition, while the body is like the methods in a Java program. Some common tags used in the body of an HTML document are described next.

Object Elements

Object elements are HTML tags that describe the placement of text elements, such as headings and text. These tags usually work on a larger block of text, although the amount of text can be any length. One of the most common object tags is <H*n*>...</H*n*>, where *n* is an integer from 1 to 6 that designates headings and subheadings of the HTML document. There are six levels of headings available in HTML. The formatting and style of text used for each of the heading levels are determined by the client browser. The syntax for the heading is <H*n*> *Heading Text* </H*n*>. Levels should not be skipped when using the H1 to H6 tags. The default formatting for each heading is determined by the client browser and might vary between systems. Other tags, such as <P>, can be used in the heading text section.

The <P>...</P> tags designate paragraphs in HTML. The actual formatting of the text between the beginning and ending tags conforms to preset values. This format information can be changed by a number of tags. The syntax for the paragraph tags is <P *attributes text block*> </P>.

Attribute Formatting

Formatting and anchor tags can be used in the text block.

Indentation is controlled by the browser or previous settings that control the indentation of text.

The **ALIGN=*alignment* tag,** where *alignment* is either LEFT, CENTER, or RIGHT, determines the margin alignment of the text to be formatted. The <P> tag might have other tags included in its block of text. These tags are interpreted as HTML elements. A new <P> block is needed for separating paragraphs. ALIGN=LEFT is usually the default format.

The **<PRE> tag** defines the block of text within its markers and designates text to be displayed exactly as entered. Return characters in the text block will result in a line return when the text is displayed without having to use the <BR> tag, which indicates a manual line return. The syntax for the <PRE> tag is <PRE *attributes*> *text block* </PRE>.

The **WIDTH=number of characters** command sets the width of the displayed line to a maximum of the specified number of characters.

The **<BLOCKQUOTE>...</BLOCKQUOTE> tag** designates that the block of text is a quote from another source. The text will display as indented in the left and right margins, and might be italicized depending on the browser. The syntax for BLOCKQUOTE is <BLOCKQUOTE> *text block* </BLOCKQUOTE>.

Text Formatting

Text format tags control the appearance of text when it displays in the Web browser. These tags display text as bold, italics, or in other formats. The most common text format tags are described in Figure A-1.

Tag	Description	Syntax
<M>...</M>	Displays text as emphasized; browser controls what special formatting is applied to text	<M> *text block* </M>
<STRONG>...</STRONG>	Displays text as strongly emphasized; browser controls the format applied to text	<STRONG> *text block* </STRONG>
<B>...</B>	Displays the block of text as bold	<B> *text block* </B>
<I>...</I>	Displays the block of text in italics	<I> *text block* </I>
<U>...</U>	Displays text as underlined	<U> *text block* </U>
 	Begins a new line	
<HR>	Specifies to the browser to place a single horizontal line to break sections of text or for emphasis	<HR>

Figure A-1: Text format tags

Link Elements

The anchor command is used to link to other sections in the current file or to another file. This tag has a number of different attributes that affect linking. Figure A-2 describes some common link commands.

Command	Description	Notes
<AHREF="*URL*" *attributes*> *link text block* </A>	Specifies that the link is being made to another file or a destination in the current file; the URL specifies the destination of the link.	The text in the link text is the item that provides a link to another location. When a user clicks a link the browser goes to the link.
<APPLET *attributes*> </APPLET>	The applet tag informs the browser to run a Java applet and defines the attributes of the window that will be used for the applet.	
<APPLET> attributes The following attributes occur within the <APPLET> </APPLET> tags		
CODE=*filename*	Specifies the name of the Java code to run; the .java extension is not needed.	
WIDTH=*n*	Specifies the width (in pixels) of the window that is used to display the applet.	
HEIGHT=*n*	Specifies the height (in pixels) of the window that is used to display the applet.	
<IMG *attributes*>	The image tag displays and positions graphic images in the browser window.	Internet Explorer processes .gif files and images produced by Visual J++ wizards.
<IMG> attributes The following attributes occur within the <IMG> tag		
SRC="*URL*"	Specifies the location or source of the image file in a URL format.	
ALIGN=*alignment*	Specifies the vertical alignment relative to the text.	TOP indicates the top of the image will align with the top of the accompanying text. CENTER indicates that that the image will be centered with the text. BOTTOM indicates that the bottom of the image will align with the base-line of the first line of text.
ALT=*alternative string*	Specifies the string to accompany the image for those client browsers unable to display graphics. attribute is used.	Client browsers that are not able to display in-line graphics will ignore the image tag unless the ALT
HEIGHT=*n*	Specifies the height of the image in pixels.	
WIDTH=*n*	Specifies the width of the image in pixels.	

Figure A-2: Common link commands (continued on next page)

Command	Description	Notes
Other Elements		
<UL> *list elements* </UL>	Displays the block of text as an unordered list. The displayed text is usually bulleted and indented. The block of text can contain other block tags such as <P>.	The list tags manipulate text as lists or menus. These tags format the text in ordered or unordered lists to attract the reader's attention. The items in the list are indicated by the <LI> tag.
<OL> *list elements* </OL>	Displays the block of text as an ordered list.	The displayed text usually is numbered sequentially based on the order of the <LI> tags. Items in the list might include other tags just like the <UL> tags. The items in the list are indicated by the <LI> tag.
<MENU> *list elements* </MENU>	Displays the list of items as menu items.	The <A> tag might be used as part of the list element. The items of the menu are indicated with the <LI> tag.
<LI> *list item text*	Defines an element in an ordered or unordered list.	The block of text manipulated by the <LI> tag might contain other tags. The tag does not need an ending marker but uses the next <LI> or ending list marker to determine the end of the list element.

Figure A-2: Common link commands (continued)

An Example

Koffee Koncoctions developed a Web page to advertise its products globally. The process of designing the Web page using HTML is described next. You can apply these steps to any project.

First, develop a skeleton HTML file that contains the elements you want to include in your Web page. Koffee Koncoctions started its Web page development by creating a skeleton of the required parts of an HTML document. Figure A-3 shows the skeleton structure that Koffee Koncoctions produced.

Line Number	HTML Code
1	<HTML>
2	<HEAD>
3	</HEAD>
4	<BODY>
5	</BODY>
6	</HTML>

Figure A-3: HTML program skeleton

The skeleton includes the tags necessary for the heading, body, and the beginning and ending of the HTML file.

Next, develop the heading section. The heading section of an HTML file usually is the next item to be considered in the creation of the Web page. The only tag that Koffee Koncoctions used in this section is the <TITLE> tag. The HTML file that resulted from adding this code is shown in Figure A-4.

```
<HTML>
<HEAD>
<TITLE>
Koffee Koncoctions International
</TITLE>
</HEAD>
<BODY>
</BODY>
</HTML>
```

Figure A-4: HTML program with heading section

The third step is to determine the items in the body. Koffee Koncoctions determined that it would include four items in the body of its home page: the name and address of the company, a graphic logo for the company, a short description of Koffee Koncoctions, and a link to another page that describes the products the company sells. Figure A-5 shows the HTML code that adds the name and address to the page. The name of the company is listed as an <H1> line while the address and contact information is listed as an <H2> line.

```
<HTML>
<HEAD>
<TITLE>
Koffee Koncoctions International
</TITLE>
</HEAD>
<BODY>
<H1 ALIGN=CENTER>
Koffee Koncoctions International
</H1>
<H2 ALIGN=CENTER>
555 Koffee Trail<BR>
Honolulu, HI 99562<BR>
Telephone: (910) 555-5644<BR>
Internet: koffee@hawaiikoffee.com<BR>
</H2>
</BODY>
</HTML>
```

Figure A-5: HTML program with company name and address

Figure A-6 shows the HTML code to add the graphic logo and links to the coffee product descriptions. The <IMG> tag displays the graphic image, and the <A> tag controls the link to the second page. The <IMG> tag is nested in the <H1> tag so the company name displays to the right of the graphic image.

```
<HTML>
<HEAD>
<TITLE>
Koffee Koncoctions International
</TITLE>
</HEAD>
<BODY>
<H1 ALIGN=CENTER>
<IMG SRC="FILE:mug1.gif"
width=75
height=75
ALIGN=CENTER>
Koffee Koncoctions International
</H1>
<H2 ALIGN=CENTER>
555 Koffee Trail<BR>
Honolulu, HI 99562<BR>
Telephone: (910) 555-5644<BR>
Internet: koffee@hawaiikoffee.com<BR>
</H2>
<MENU>
<li>
<A
HREF="koffee2.html">
Coffee Product Information
</A>
</MENU>
</BODY>
</HTML>
```

Figure A-6: HTML program with graphics and links

Finally, a short marketing description of the company was developed and coded. The marketing statement appears after the company information but before the link to the second home page. The <P> tag controls the display of information. Horizontal lines are included with the <HR> tag to separate the sections. Figure A-7 shows the HTML file after coding the marketing description.

```
<HTML>
<HEAD>
<TITLE>
Koffee Koncoctions International
</TITLE>
</HEAD>
<BODY>
<H1 ALIGN=CENTER>
<IMG SRC="FILE:mug1.gif"
width=75
height=75
ALIGN=CENTER>
Koffee Koncoctions International
</H1>
<H2 ALIGN=CENTER>
555 Koffee Trail<BR>
Honolulu, HI 99562<BR>
Telephone: (910) 555-5644<BR>
Internet: koffee@hawaiikoffee.com<BR>
</H2>
<HR>
<P ALIGN=JUSTIFY>
Koffee Koncoctions is the producer of
some of the most exotic tropical coffees
in the world. For over 25 years
Koffee Koncoctions International has
supplied lovers of coffee blends around
the globe. For more information or to
place an order contact Koffee Koncoctions
at the above address or telephone number
```

Figure A-7: HTML final program (continues on next page)

```
or by e-mail.
</P>
</HR>
<MENU>
<LI>
<A
HREF="koffee2.html">
Coffee Product Information
</A>
</MENU>
</BODY>
</HTML>
```

Figure A-7: HTML final program (continued)

When users click the link to the second Web page the browser automatically displays it, as you will see next.

To see the Koffee Koncoctions Web pages:

1. Open Windows Explorer, open the Appendix folder on your Student Disk, and then double-click the **Koffee1.html** file. Internet Explorer (or your default Web browser) starts and opens the Koffee Koncoctions Web page.
2. Scroll to the bottom of the page, and then click the **Coffee Product Information** link to see the second page.
3. Close Internet Explorer.

Note: The information in this appendix is not intended to provide a comprehensive treatment of HTML, but rather, an introduction to common HTML codes and uses. Course Technology publishes a wide range of textbooks on HTML. For more information, please contact your Course Technology sales representative or visit the Course Technology Web page at http://www.course.com.

APPENDIX

B

The Visual J++ Interactive Debugger

Computer programs can be affected by two different types of errors—compile and logic. Compile errors are found when the program is compiled or built. These errors typically involve syntax problems or missing data. Logic errors can occur even if a program compiles correctly. Logic errors involve problems with the design of the code that results in output that is not what is expected. The **interactive debugger** is a tool that assists the programmer in finding and correcting logic errors. The interactive debugger provides the following features:

- Status of compile, build, and execution of the program
- Interactive modification of program variables to test results
- Controlled execution of program with display of important variables and sequence information to trace the logic

This appendix will introduce you to using the interactive debugger to correct logic errors.

The Interactive Debugging Environment

The interactive debugger is a tool that controls execution of a program so the programmer can review the status of the variables and the sequence of the execution. Visual J++ provides these debugging functions through the use of step and breakpoint execution. **Step execution** is a mode where the program code is performed one command at a time and the status windows are updated to reflect the effect of the last command. **Breakpoint debugging** involves inserting symbols called **breakpoints** in the Java program where the programmer wants the execution to pause. When the debugger is working in breakpoint mode, the debugger executes all statements up to the breakpoint symbol and then displays updated status information about the variables and program sequence. Both breakpoint and step execution cause the program to pause. The programmer can resume the execution of the program after it has stopped at a step or breakpoint. The programmer also can terminate the program if it is no longer necessary to watch the effects of the execution.

The debugger is an interactive tool that works through the use of commands that display information in windows. You can use the interactive debugger only after the program has compiled without errors. To use the debugger, click Build on the menu bar, point to Start Debug, and then click a debug command. You can debug a program only after it has been built. Figure B-1 shows the Debug menu commands.

Command	Action
Go	Executes from the current statement until a breakpoint or the end of program is reached
Run To Cursor	Executes the current program until the insertion pointer is reached
Step Into	Executes the current program one statement at a time

Figure B-1: Debug menu commands

The debugger operates in one of two basic modes, depending on the action selected. **Breakpoint mode** is used when the programmer wants to debug the program with larger steps than a single statement. You enter breakpoints in the program by clicking Edit on the menu bar, and then clicking Breakpoints after the project is built. Then you can use the Breakpoints dialog box to add or delete breakpoints. The breakpoint will be ignored when the program is executed normally.

Another form of breakpoint processing is the **Run to Cursor** execution. Run to Cursor causes the program to run until it reaches the location of the insertion point in the Editor window. You position the insertion point in the file and it acts as a breakpoint that can be moved and the execution resumed. **Step into execution** is a debugging mode that runs the program one statement at a time. After the execution of each statement, the status windows are updated. In both modes, you can resume the execution of the program.

When you are debugging a program, the Debug toolbar displays, and the menu commands change to include debugging commands. The Output window changes to show the debug status. Figure B-2 lists the debugger action commands.

Command	Action
Break Execution	Pauses the execution of the program
Go	Executes the program from the current point until a breakpoint or the end of program is reached
Restart	Reloads the program into memory and erases all variable values (breakpoints and watch expressions are remembered and the program executes until the main() or init() method is reached)
Run to Cursor	Executes the program from its current location until the insertion point in the Editor window is reached
Step Into	Executes the next statement of the program code
Step Over	Executes the program one statement at a time except for method calls that are treated as a single statement
Step Out	Executes the remainder of the current method and stops at the first statement following the method call
Stop Debugging	Terminates the execution of the program and returns to Editor window

Figure B-2: Debugger action commands

Visual J++ provides a number of windows with different types of information for debugging the logic of your programs. In addition, Visual J++ uses interactive dialog boxes to communicate important information. You can turn the windows on or off using the View menu after the debugger starts and identifies errors. The Output window opens automatically when you build the program. You can access the windows shown in Figure B-3 by clicking View on the menu bar, pointing to Debug Windows, and then clicking the desired window name.

Window	Description of Contents
Call Stack	Displays the stack of all methods that have not returned
Disassembly	Displays the machine byte code of the disassembled compiled program
Memory	Displays the current memory status
Registers	Displays information contained in the general purpose and CPU status registers
Output	Displays information about compile or build errors and exception errors returned from threads
Variables	Displays information about variables from current and previous statements and variables local to the current method
Watch	Displays names and values of variables and expressions

Figure B-3: Interactive debugging windows

An additional feature of the Visual J++ interactive debugger is the use of dialog boxes to communicate the status of the program and to allow changes during execution. Figure B-4 describes the interactive dialog boxes.

Dialog Box	Description of Contents
Breakpoint	Displays all breakpoints in program and allows the addition of breakpoints to the program
Exceptions	Displays all system and user-defined exception handling and allows changes to be made in exception handling
Quick Watch	Displays and allows variables to be displayed in the watch window or their values changed
Threads	Displays application program threads available for debugging and allows threads to be suspended or resumed

Figure B-4: Interactive dialog boxes

For additional information about the debugger, consult Books Online.

Using the Interactive Debugger

The steps for using the interactive debugger are:

1. Open the Java program file that you need to debug.
2. Build the program and correct any syntax errors.
3. Click Build on the menu bar, point to Start Debug, and then click the desired debug option to start the Debugger and enable the debug commands and Windows.
4. Add any breakpoints.
5. Select the desired windows from the View menu. You can turn these windows on and off by clicking the menu item that corresponds to the window. If a check mark appears next to the window, clicking on the option will turn it off. If a check mark does not appear next to the window it can be turned on by clicking the option.
6. Execute the program using the debug action commands.
7. When the debugging program is complete, stop the execution of the program, and close the project workspace.

APPENDIX C

Common Visual J++ Errors

You might encounter some common compile errors as you complete the examples and exercises in this book. If you receive output errors, always check your typing first by comparing your code to the code shown in the figures in the book. Even something as simple as typing a colon instead of a semicolon can be the cause of 10 or more compile errors. Always save the file after making corrections and before rebuilding it. If you still have problems, Figure C-1 lists some of these errors, the time when they are found (compile, execute, or Internet Explorer), and suggestions for some possible causes and solutions to the problem.

Error	Time of Display	Cause/Solution
Expected class or interface	Compile	Occurs when a closing brace of a method is omitted. Check the opening and closing braces for matches.
Expecting statement	Compile	Occurs when a closing brace is omitted. Check that all opening braces are matched with a closing brace.
Load class	Explorer	This error appears in the status bar not found when Internet Explorer tries to run a Java applet. It usually occurs when Java cannot find the class filename. It also can occur if the compiler is not set to the folder where the file resides. Use Windows Explorer to delete all files with the applet name except for the .java and .html files, open the .java program again, and then rebuild the program.
Missing return type	Compile	Occurs when the constructor method does not match the class name or a return type has been omitted from a method heading. Check the constructor name with the class name, and if the error occurs on a method other than a constructor, check to see that a return type has been specified.
Object should not be defined in file	Compile	Occurs when the Java filename and the class filename are different. Check spelling of filename and class name, and make sure that uppercase and lowercase letters match exactly.
One or more files are out of date	Execution	Displayed in a dialog box, this error occurs when Java finds files missing or files that have been saved after the last build of the file. Click the Yes button to continue. You can avoid this problem by saving your .java files before building or executing them.
Undefined name	Compile	Occurs when a name is not recognized as a defined variable or class by the compiler. If the name is a variable, check the spelling of the name, including the case of the characters. If this error occurs on the use of a class object that is defined in another file, check to see that the spelling, including case, matches. Also, if the file does exist as typed, try inserting the Java file of the class object into the current project workspace.

Figure C-1: Common Visual J++ errors

If you do not see the output errors in Figure C-1, press the F4 key to select the error in the Output window, and then press the F1 key to open Books Online to an appropriate topic for debugging the error. If you still have problems, consult your instructor for help.

Index

A

D

E

F

G

H

I

M

N

O

P

Q

R

S

T